The Sound Studies Reader

The Sound Studies Reader is a groundbreaking anthology blending recent work that self-consciously describes itself as "sound studies" with earlier and lesser-known scholarship on sound.

The collection begins with an introduction to welcome novice readers to the field and acquaint them with key themes and concepts in sound studies. Individual section introductions to give readers further background on the essays and an extensive up-to-date bibliography for further reading in "sound studies" make this an original and accessible guide to the field.

Jonathan Sterne teaches in the Department of Art History and Communication Studies and the History and Philosophy of Science Program at McGill University. He is author of *The Audible Past: Cultural Origins of Sound Reproduction* (2003); *MP3: The Meaning of a Format* (2012); and numerous articles on media, technologies and the politics of culture. He also makes sound. Visit his website at http://sterneworks.org.

The

Sound Studies Reader

Edited by

Jonathan Sterne

Routledge
Taylor & Francis Group

LONDON AND NEW YORK

First published 2012
by Routledge
2 Park Square, Milton Park, Abingdon, Oxon OX14 4RN

Simultaneously published in the USA and Canada
by Routledge
711 Third Avenue, New York, NY 10017

Routledge is an imprint of the Taylor & Francis Group, an informa business

British Library Cataloguing in Publication Data
A catalogue record for this book is available from the British Library

Library of Congress Cataloging in Publication Data
The sound studies reader / edited by Jonathan Sterne.
   p. cm.
Includes bibliographical references and index.
1. Sound—Recording and reproducing—History.   2. Sound—Recording
and reproducing—Social aspects.   3. Hearing.   4. Listening.   I. Sterne,
Jonathan, 1970-
TK7881.4.S684 2012
621.389—dc23
                                                        2011052981

ISBN: 978-0-415-77130-6 (hbk)
ISBN: 978-0-415-77131-3 (pbk)

Typeset in Baskerville
by RefineCatch Limited, Bungay, Suffolk

MIX
Paper from
responsible sources
FSC® C004839
www.fsc.org

Printed and bound by CPI Group (UK) Ltd, Croydon, CR0 4YY

Contents

Acknowledgements

2. Ihde, Don. 1974. The Auditory Dimension. In *Listening and Voice: A Phenomenology of Sound*. Athens: Ohio University Press. Pp. 49–55

3. Attali, Jacques. 1985. Listening. In *Noise: The Political Economy of Music*. Translated by B. Massumi. Minneapolis: University of Minnesota Press. Pp. 3–12 & 18–20

4. Berland, Jody. 1993. Contradicting Media: Toward a Political Phenomenology of Listening. In *Radiotext(e)*, edited by N. Strauss. New York: Semiotext(e). Pp. 209–17

5. Chion, Michel. 1994. The Three Listening Modes. In *Audio-Vision*. Translated by C. Gorbman. New York: Columbia University Press. Pp. 25–34

6. Hirschkind, Charles. 2006. Introduction In *The Ethical Soundscape: Cassette Sermons and Islamic Counterpublics*. New York: Columbia University Press. Pp. 1–9 & 18–25

7. Goodman, Steve. 2010. The Ontology of Vibrational Force. In *Sonic Warfare: Sound, Affect and the Ecology of Fear*. Cambridge: MIT Press. Pp. 81–84

8. Mills, Mara. 2011. Hearing Aids and the History of Electronics Miniaturization. *IEEE Journal of the History of Computing*. Pp. 24–27

9. Crawford, Kate. 2009. Following You: Disciplines of Listening in Social Media. *Continuum: Journal of Media and Cultural Studies* 23 (4): 525–35

10. Schafer, R. Murray. 1994. The Soundscape. In *The Soundscape: Our Sonic Environment and the Tuning of the World*. Rochester, Vermont: Destiny Books. Pp. 3–12

11. Hosokawa, Shuhei. 1984. The Walkman Effect. *Popular Music* 4: 165–80

12. Thompson, Emily. 2002. Sound, Modernity and History. In *The Soundscape of Modernity: Architectural Acoustics and the Culture of Listening in America 1900–1930*. Cambridge: MIT Press. Pp. 1–12

13. Rath, Richard Cullen. 2003. No Corner for the Devil to Hide. In *How Early America Sounded*. Ithaca: Cornell University Press. Pp. 97–107 & 113–19

14. Picker, John. 2003. The Soundproof Study. In *Victorian Soundscapes*. New York: Oxford University Press. Pp. 41–52

15. Bijsterveld, Karin. 2006. Listening to Machines: Industrial Noise, Hearing Loss and the Cultural Meaning of Sound. *Interdisciplinary Science Reviews* 31 (4): 323–37

16. Helmreich, Stefan. 2007. An Anthropologist Underwater: Immersive Soundscapes, Submarine Cyborgs and Transductive Ethnography. *American Ethnologist* 34 (4): 621–27

17. Blesser, Barry, and Linda-Ruth Salter. 2007. Auditory Awareness as an Extension of Religion. In *Spaces Speak, Are You Listening? Experiencing Aural Architecture*. Cambridge: MIT Press. Pp. 82–93

18. Bull, Michael. 2008. The Audio-Visual iPod. In *Sound Moves: iPod Culture and Urban Experience*. New York: Routledge. Pp. 38–49

19. Mowitt, John. 1987. The Sound of Music in the Era of Its Electronic Reproducibility. In *Music and Society: The Politics of Composition, Performance and Reception*, edited by R. Leppert and S. McClary. New York: Cambridge University Press. Pp. 184–97

20. Altman, Rick. 1992. Four and a Half Film Fallacies. In *Sound Theory/Sound Practice*, edited by R. Altman. New York: Routledge. Pp. 35–45

21. Kittler, Friedrich. 1999. Gramophone. In *Gramophone-Film-Typewriter*. Translated by G. Winthrop-Young and M. Wutz. Stanford: Stanford University Press. Pp. 21–37

22. Lastra, James. 2000. Sound Theory. "Fidelity Versus Intelligibility". In *Sound Technology and American Cinema: Perception, Representation, Modernity*. New York: Columbia University Press. Pp. 138–43

23.   Pinch, Trevor, and Frank Trocco. 2002. Shaping the Synthesizer. In *Analog Days: The Invention and Impact of the Moog Synthesizer*. Cambridge: Harvard University Press. Pp. 52–69

24.   Meintjes, Louise. 2003. The Recording Studio as Fetish. In *Sound of Africa!: Making Music Zulu in a South African Studio*. Durham: Duke University Press. Pp. 81–98

25.   Gitelman, Lisa. 2006. New Media Publics. In *Always Already New: Media, History and the Data of Culture*. Cambridge: MIT Press. Pp. 25–44

26.   Stanyek, Jason, and Benjamin Piekut. 2010. Deadness: Technologies of the Intermundane. *The Drama Review* 54 (1): Pp. 14–21 & Pp. 27–38

27.   Fanon, Frantz. 1965. This is the Voice of Algeria. In *A Dying Colonialism*. Translated by H. Chevalier. New York: Monthly Review Press. Pp. 82–88 & 93–97

28.   Martin, Michèle. 1991. The Culture of the Telephone. *"Hello, Central?": Gender, Technology and Culture in the Formation of Telephone Systems*. Montreal: McGill-Queens University Press. Pp 140–41 & 150–63

29.   Hilmes, Michelle. 1997. Radiating Culture. In *Radio Voices: America Broadcasting 1922–1952*. Minneapolis: University of Minnesota Press, pp. 11–23

30.   Peters, John Durham. 1999. Reach Out Someone: the Telephonic Uncanny. In *Speaking Into the Air: A History of the Idea of Communication*. Chicago: University of Chicago Press. Pp. 195–205

31.   Goggin, Gerard. 2006. Cellular Disability: Consumption, Design and Access. In *Cell Phone Culture*. London and New York: Routledge, pp. 89–103

32.   Ochoa Gautier, Ana María. 2006. Social Transculturation, Epistemologies of Purification and the Aural Public Sphere in Latin America. *Social Identities* 12 (6): 803–9, 813–25. Excerpt: 803–9 (to end of section " . . . on the other"); 813 beginning with "Folklore and the Aural Public Sphere in the Era of Nationalism" to end (825).

33.   Leppert, Richard. 1993. Desire, Power and the Sonorous Landscape. In *The Sight of Sound: Music, Representation and the Body*. Berkeley: University of California Press. Pp. 18–28

34.   Born, Georgina. 1995. Science, Technology and the Avant-Garde. In *Rationalizing Culture: IRCAM, Boulez and the Institutionalization of the Musical Avant-Garde*. Berkeley: University of California Press. Pp. 193–202

35.   Kahn, Douglas. 1999. Noises of the Avant-Garde. In *Noise, Water, Meat: A History of Sound in the Arts*. Cambridge: MIT Press. Pp. 45–67

36.   Eshun, Kodwo. 1999. Operating System for the Redesign of Sonic Reality. In *More Brilliant Than The Sun: Adventures in Sonic Fiction*, London. Quartet Books. Pp –7 to –1

37.   Veal, Michael. 2007. Starship Africa. In *Dub: Soundscapes and Shattered Songs in Jamaican Reggae*. Hanover: Wesleyan University Press. Pp. 196–208

38.   Labelle, Brandon. 2008. Auditory Relations. In *Background Noise: Perspectives on Sound Art*. New York: Continuum. Pp. ix-xvi.

39.   Rodgers, Tara. 2010. Introduction. *Pink Noises: Women on Electronic Music and Sound*. Durham: Duke University Press. Pp. 6–16

40.   Derrida, Jacques. 1973. The Voice that Keeps Silence. In *Speech and Phenomena and Other Essays on Husserl's Theory of Signs*. Translated by D. B. Allison. Chicago: Northwestern University Press. Pp. 74–87

41.   Barthes, Roland. 1977. The Grain of the Voice. In *Image-Music-Text*. Translated by S. Heath. London: Fontana Press. Pp. 179–89

42.   Weheliye, Alexander. 2002. "Feenin": Posthuman Voices in Contemporary Black Popular Music. *Social Text* 20 (2): 33–47

43.   Cavarero, Adriana. 2005. Introduction. In *For More Than One Voice: Toward a Philosophy of Vocal Expression*. Stanford: Stanford University Press. Pp. 1–16

44.   Smith, Jacob. 2005. The Frenzy of the Audible: Pleasure, Authenticity and Recorded Laughter. *Television and New Media* 6 (1): 40–45

45.   Dolar, Mladen. 2006. The Linguistics of the Voice. In *A Voice and Nothing More*. Cambridge: MIT Press. Pp. 13–32

Chapter 1

Jonathan Sterne

SONIC IMAGINATIONS[1]

ACCORDING TO JACQUES ATTALI, the power to reproduce sound used to belong to the gods.[2] With over 5.3 billion mobile phones now in use, that power now belongs to most of humanity. We live in a world whose sonic texture is constantly transforming, and has been for centuries. New, never-before-heard sounds like ringtones enter and leave everyday life in the course of a few years. New processes for manipulating, transforming and working with sound come and go in the space of decades. But this is not just a condition of late modernity.[3] Plato purged flautists and flute-makers from his ideal state; 17th-century Londoners complained of the new noises filling their city—"he that loves noise must buy a pig"—and people in positions of power all over 19th-century Europe were so worked up about the different standards for orchestral tuning that many countries passed laws to resolve the problem.[4] Like those auditors, we might imagine that our changing state of affairs disrupts some prior, more organic and dependable sonic world. But it may be more accurate to say that in most times and places, sonic culture is characterized by the tensions held within its configuration of difference and sameness. If you can, take a good long listen around you—for a few days. Whether or not you can listen yourself, consider what others are hearing. How many of the sounds in everyday life existed ten years ago? Twenty? Thirty? Fifty? That's just the sounds—but what of the contexts in which they happen, the ways of hearing or not-hearing attached to them, the practices, people and institutions associated with them? Now think of what the previous generation of sounds must have replaced, and what those sounds and their worlds replaced in turn. In this small exercise, you will join generations of intellectuals, who have lifted their ears toward the sonic airspace around them, taken stock of it, and reacted to the changes they heard.

As sonic worlds have changed, so too have the conceptual infrastructures writers have built to behold them. Today, there is a boom in writings on sound by authors in the humanities and social sciences, whose work is distinguished by self-consciousness of its place in a larger interdisciplinary discussion of sound. Dozens of monographs on one or another aspect of sonic culture have appeared since the early 1990s, alongside countless journal articles, book chapters, and a growing list of anthologies (one need only look over the dates in many of the authors' bibliographies to see this). Major interdisciplinary journals and leading journals in older disciplines have devoted special issues to sound.[5] Professional associations in almost every field of the human sciences have devoted panels to sound in one form or another and some now have sound-related divisions or interest groups. New thematic conferences on sound pop up each year.[6]

Sound studies is a name for the interdisciplinary ferment in the human sciences that takes sound as its analytical point of departure or arrival. By analyzing both sonic practices and the discourses and institutions that describe them, it redescribes what sound does in the human world, and what humans do in the sonic world. (I say it *redescribes* rather than *describes* because good scholarship always goes beyond the common-sense categories used in everyday descriptive language—it tells us what we don't already know). It reaches across registers, moments and spaces, and it thinks across disciplines and traditions, some that have long considered sound, and some that have not done so until more recently. Sound studies is academic, but it can also move beyond the university. It can begin from obviously sonic phenomena like speech, hearing, sound technologies, architecture, art, or music. But it does not have to. It may *think sonically* as it moves underwater, through the laboratory or into the halls of government; considers religion or nationalisms old and new; explores cities; tarries with the history of philosophy, literature or ideas; or critiques relations of power, property or intersubjectivity. It is a global phenomenon as well. Work that self-consciously defines itself as sound studies has now appeared in English, German, Dutch, French, Italian, Portuguese, Japanese, Korean, Hebrew and Spanish, among other languages.

It is tempting to call sound studies a response to our changing sonic world—and it is that. But so have been many other important intellectual movements around sound in the 20th century: when W.E.B. Du Bois wanted to rethink the role of race in American life, he turned to sound as a key modality for thinking through African American culture:

> Before each thought that I have written in this book I have set a phrase, a haunting echo of these weird old songs in which the soul of the black slave spoke to men [. . .] the rhythmic cry of the slave—stands to-day not simply as the sole American music, but as the most beautiful expression of human experience born this side of the seas. It has been neglected, it has been, and is, half despised, and above all it has been persistently mistaken and misunderstood; but not withstanding, it still remains the singular spiritual heritage of the nation and the greatest gift of the Negro people.[7]

Other canonical writers were quick to highlight new sound media as calling into question the very basis of experience and existence. For Martin Heidegger in 1927, radio effected a "de-distancing" for its listeners, "by way of expanding and destroying the everyday surrounding world." For Sigmund Freud in 1929, sound recording allowed for the retention of "fleeting" auditory memories.[8]

Avant-garde musicians, artists and writers have throughout the century turned to changes in sonic culture as the basis for broad philosophical reflections. In the 1950s, 1960s and 1970s, writers turning to sound in philosophy, aesthetics and design similarly pointed to historical change as the basis for their sonic interests. Writers during the 1980s and 1990s rethinking what it meant to study music turned to sound and technology as a way of making sense of massive changes that had happened to culture over the previous decades.[9] To think sonically is to think conjuncturally about sound and culture: each of the writers I have quoted above used sound to ask big questions about their cultural moments and the crises and problems of their time. Sound studies' challenge is to think across sounds, to consider sonic phenomena in relationship to one another—*as types of sonic phenomena rather than as things-in-themselves*—whether they be music, voices, listening, media, buildings, performances, or another other path into sonic life.

As a body of thought, sound studies today is certainly an intellectual reaction to changes in culture and technology, just as earlier modalities of sonic thought were. But it is also a product of changes in thought and the organization of the disciplines. Just as work on visual culture and material culture took off when writers in fields like art history, literature, cultural studies, history, anthropology, and many other fields realized that they were all working on related problems and would benefit from talking with another, so too has sound studies arisen from the same felt need—that no *one* field's approach to or take on sound is enough. This ambiguity extends on down to the name for the field. Is it sound studies or the study of sound culture, sonic culture, auditory culture or aural culture?[10] As Michele Hilmes puts it, the study of sound, "hailed as an 'emerging field' for the last hundred years, exhibits a strong tendency to remain that way, always emerging, never emerged."[11] Sound studies does, however, have a rich and growing scholarly literature, a large number of professors and graduate students working in the area, a growing presence in the curricula of many fields, all of which increasingly influence writers whose work may touch on sonic issues (or even use sonic figures) even though their primary concern is not sound. This reader is offered in the hope that it will make a useful contribution to all those populations.

We need a name for people who do sound studies; I propose *sound students*. Since the field as it is known today has its roots after 1945, sound students are not strictly speaking -osophers, -ologists or -ographers. In his 1997 attack on cultural studies, Todd Gitlin used the phrase "cultural students" to describe practitioners of the field. Although the coinage was probably not intended generously, calling practitioners of "studies" fields "students" is a lovely and inspiring turn of phrase, and so I adapt it here. Student has meant "a person who is engaged in or addicted to study"; students undergo courses of study, they are associated with educational institutions, they have teachers and they always have more to learn.[12] Most sound students are also something else: historians, philosophers, musicologists, anthropologists, literary critics, art historians, geographers, or residents of one of the many other postwar "studies" fields—media studies, disability studies, cinema studies, cultural studies, gender studies, science and technology studies, postcolonial studies, communication studies, queer studies, American studies and on and on.

Sound students produce and transform knowledge about sound and in the process reflexively attend to the (cultural, political, environmental, aesthetic. . .) stakes of that knowledge production. By reflexivity, I refer to arguments developed by Pierre Bourdieu and Donna Haraway. Both argued that knowers must place themselves in relation to what it is they want to know: they must account for their own positions and prejudices, lest scholars misattribute them as qualities of the object of study. This means that if we use concepts drawn from the study of human auditory perception, we must account for the historicity of that knowledge (rather than simply saying "this is how your ear works" as if the ear is the same in all times and places). But it also means we must eschew what a colleague of mine once called "the uncritical use of the critical," where the imperative to critique overtakes the critical faculty itself. Haraway famously used vision metaphors to describe perspective as a constitutive feature of epistemology, but one could use audition just as easily. Depending on the positioning of hearers, a space may sound totally different. If you hear the same sound in two different spaces, you may not even recognize it as the same sound. Hearing requires positionality.

A broad transdisciplinary curiosity and an awareness of partiality—even when it is paired with great speculative ambition—are the most important defining characteristic differences between people who think of themselves as sound students, and people who think of themselves as sound scientists, sound artists, sound engineers, sound anthropologists, sound critics, sound historians or for that matter psycho-acousticians, acousticians and linguists. The list could go on, though of course there can be traffic among all these categories and it would be impossible to draw definitive lines between them. But the difference between sound studies and these other fields is that they don't *require* engagement with alternative epistemologies, methods or approaches.

However wonderfully audacious sound students can make our work, it must also be grounded in a sense of its own partiality, its authors' and readers' knowledge that all the key terms we might use to describe and analyze sound belong to multiple traditions, and are under debate. Sound students problematize sound and the phenomena around it, including their own intellectual traditions. Sound studies is an intellectual exercise, one that for the moment is most grounded in academia, though certainly non-academics produce fascinating work about sound all the time, and sound students can and should move beyond the academy to try and effect change in the world. Sound studies work is written and spoken. Although it can also be imaged and sounded, it is fundamentally a verbal practice because it is *about* sound (though emerging practices of digital publication offer scholars opportunities to find new ways to juxtapose words and sound, the analysis and the objects of analysis). Collectively we think about sound through reading about it, listening to it, contemplating it, writing and talking about it, and working with it. Of course, some of the selections in this reader contradict what's in these aspirational paragraphs, but that is the point. Sound studies names a set of shared intellectual aspirations; not a discrete set of objects, methods or the space between them. We might condense my description of sound studies like this:[13]

- Sound studies is an academic field in the humanities and social sciences defined by combination of object and approach. Not all scholarship about or with sound is "sound studies," just as not all scholarship about society is Sociology, not all scholarship with a concept of culture is cultural studies or Anthropology, not all scholarship that works with concepts of language is Linguistics. The inside/outside description is useful for characterization, but is not useful in the first instance for the judgment of relevance or quality.

- Sound students recognize sound as a problem that cuts across academic disciplines, methods and objects, though the field's institutional existence will vary as it moves across different national university cultures (and all disciplines begin as interdisciplines).[14]
- Sound studies work reflexively attends to its core concepts and objects.
- Sound studies work is conscious of its own historicity. Sound students are aware that they are part of an ongoing conversation about sound that spans eras, traditions, places, and disciplines; they are also aware of the specific histories of inquiring about and writing about sound in their home disciplines.
- Sound studies has an essential "critical" element, in the broadest sense of critique. It may also take on characteristics of a producer, policy, technical, political, artistic or training discourse. But without critique, it is art, technical discourse, science, cultural production or training practices "about sound," and not sound studies (though such work will often be of great interest to sound students).

Today, many people have become sound students to cultivate and facilitate their *sonic imaginations*, as well as those of people in other fields as sound becomes important to their work. *Sonic imagination* is a deliberately synaesthetic neologism—it is about sound but occupies an ambiguous position between sound culture and a space of contemplation outside it. Sonic imaginations are necessarily plural, recursive, reflexive, driven to represent, refigure and redescribe.[15] They are fascinated by sound but driven to fashion some new intellectual facility to make sense of some part of the sonic world. The concept is meant to reference an intellectual history of thinking about our own creative and critical capacities: it reaches back into aesthetic propositions such as T.S. Eliot's figure of the "auditory imagination" and cultural-theoretical constructs such as C. Wright Mills's "sociological imagination" and Anne Balsamo's "technological imagination." Like its tributaries—themselves rivers of thought to which it aspires to contribute—sonic imagination places sound as a fundamentally human problem. Sound is certainly more than a human problem—we can talk of animals' hearing, of underwater sound, or sound on other planets—but for the next few pages, let us consider sound as a category defined in relation to ideas of the human before we explode that formulation.

T.S. Eliot writes: "'The auditory imagination' is the feeling for syllable and rhythm, penetrating far below the conscious levels of thought and feeling, invigorating every word; sinking to the most primitive and forgotten, returning to the origin and bringing something back, seeking the beginning and the end. It works through meanings, certainly, or not without meanings in the ordinary sense, and fuses the old and obliterated and the trite, the current, and the new and surprising, the most ancient and the most civilized mentality."[16] Eliot's notion of auditory imagination arises when he discusses the criticism of poetry, but it is possible to imagine the definition much more broadly for thinking with all manners of sounding things. We need only substitute the general "sound" for the specific "syllable" in his first sentence to achieve this broader meaning. It is an openness to sound as part of culture, a feel for it. For Eliot, the movement across registers is also a crucial quality of imagination. This resonates with C. Wright Mills's notion of sociological imagination: a "quality of mind that enables its possessor to understand the larger historical scene in terms of its meaning for the inner life and external career of a variety of individuals." The sociological imagination is based in "the capacity to shift from one perspective to another. [. . .] It is the capacity to range from the most impersonal and remote transformations to the most intimate features of the human self—and to see the relations between the two."[17] Sonic imaginations bring us to particular conjunctures[18] and problems, but they also redescribe them from unexpected standpoints. Don Ihde writes that valid description of sonic experience requires the phenomenologist's gesture of epoché, "which means 'to suspend' or 'to put out of play.' [. . .] It is a suspension of 'presuppositions.'"[19] In another register, Pierre Bourdieu and his collaborators write of the "epistemological rupture" through which scholars leave behind the force of the various prenotions that operate in the field they study, to confront their objects of study with fresh perspectives, and to construct them anew. As Paul Fauconnet and Marcel Mauss wrote over a century ago, "serious research leads one to unite what is ordinarily separated or to distinguish what is ordinarily confused."[20]

Imagination is also a creative force: Anne Balsamo conceives the technological imagination as "the wellspring of technological innovation." It is a mindset that "enables people to think with technology, to transform what is known into what is possible." To once again indulge in substituting sound for others' keywords, sonic imaginations rework culture through the development of new narratives, new histories, new technologies, and new alternatives. Sonic imaginations "reproduce cultural understandings at every turn"—there is no knowledge of sound that comes from outside culture, only knowledge that works from particular limits. These limits in turn work like affordances—baseline assumptions and massive traditions to build from, as well as conventions worth playing with or struggling against. "This imagination is performative: it improvises within constraints to produce something new."[21] As a creative capacity, a robust sonic imagination is not that different from good musicianship: both aim to satisfy and frustrate expectations in order to produce something meaningful and engaging (for themselves and for their communities and audiences). Douglas Kahn explains it best:

> "sound," rather than being a destination, has been a potent and necessary means for accessing and understanding the world; in effect, it leads away from itself. A very nebulous notion of methodology, but also something that kicks in before methodology.[22]

This is an important first principle: there is no a priori privileged group of methodologies for sound studies. Instead, sonic imaginations are guided by an orienting curiosity, a figural practice that reaches into fields of sonic knowledge and practice, and blends them with other questions, problems, fields, spaces and histories. Method matters, but it should arise from the questions asked and the knowledge fields engaged, not the other way around. We could go further to argue that sound studies should borrow a page from cultural studies and operate by way of engaging its objects or problems of study contextually, as sites rather than as totalities that can be grasped through a single method or combination of methods, or whose political or cultural significance is guaranteed ahead of time by what we think we "know" about sound, politics or culture.[23]

These abstract questions bear down on even the most basic attempts to define one of the field's central concepts, "sound," and to decide how one comes to imagine or know it. Does sound refer to a phenomenon out in the world which ears then pick up? Does it refer to a human phenomenon that only exists in relation to the physical world? Or is it something else? The answer to the question has tremendous implications for both the objects and methods of sound studies. Can we study sounds "in themselves" or as part of a field of vibration that exists in and for itself? Must we always start the cultural study of sound from the position of people? Can sound be described separately from the position of the person who describes it? In the past, my own position on this question has been somewhat human-centered:

> the boundary between vibration that is sound and vibration that is not-sound is not derived from any quality of the vibration in itself or the air that conveys the vibrations. Rather, the boundary between sound and not-sound is based on the understood possibilities of the faculty of hearing—whether we are talking about a person or a squirrel. Therefore, as people and squirrels change, so too will sound—by definition. Species have histories.[24]

But that raises more questions than it answers. If we are really talking about the stratifying power of the cultured ear, perhaps we should follow Michael Bull and Les Back in calling the field "auditory culture" to reflect the degree to which sound is a sensory problem, a sensibility echoed more recently by Trevor Pinch and Karin Bijsterveld when they situate sound studies as partly emanating from something they call "sensory studies."[25] This approach has a special appeal insofar as sound scholars aim to disrupt narratives of the so-called hegemony of the visual and the privileging of the eye. It also has the advantage of a certain terminological parallelism with "visual culture." Bull and Back call for a "democracy of the senses," and as is clear in their volume as well as this one, many classic studies of sound begin by contrasting the auditory and visual registers. When they make this move, authors more often talk about ears and eyes than sounds and light.

But this is not the only critical path into sound studies. Another path in more or less assumes the physicality of sound and then considers its cultural valence. Francis Dyson argues for an irreducible positivity to sounds as having their own "ontological" existence.[26] In this volume, Steve Goodman argues for the privileging of vibration as a primary category of analysis, taking sound as a point of orientation, but not further substantializing it. Similarly Michele Friedner and Stefan Helmreich have argued that vibration is a crucial plane on which sound studies can intersect with deaf studies, and that sound is best taken as "a vibration of a certain frequency in a material medium, rather than centering vibrations in a hearing ear." Their approach suggests that vibration, as the register of reality from which sound is carved out, "is itself in need of cultural and historical situating."[27] Yet another approach is Veit Erlmann's use of the term *aurality*, which considers both "the materiality of perception" and the "conditions that must be given for something to become recognized, labeled and valorized as audible in the first place."[28] No sound student can write anything of substance without at least implicitly taking a position in these debates, and the choice has direct consequences for what gets studied in terms of what counts as the fundamental phenomenon under investigation and the very definition of context. And in most cases, defining the object of sound studies (or whatever you call it) is inextricably bound up in negotiating fields of knowledge that pertain to sound.

Knowledge is a problem in sound studies in at least three ways. Knowledge is a problem of epistemology and method—how do sound students acquire, shape, build and disseminate knowledge about sound in their own practice? Knowledge is also a problem for the field in the sense that there are many competing knowledges of sound in the world, they have their own politics, historicity and cultural domains, and exert their effects on everything we study. Knowledge is also a problem because it is situated among vectors of power and difference. Tara Rodgers's point about histories of electronic music could be extended to all areas of sonic history: readily-circulated "origin stories tend to normalize hegemonic cultural practices that follow."[29]

Many of the most cited figures of knowing in sound studies try to deal with all these problems of knowledge at once. Composer Pauline Oliveros coined the term "deep listening" to describe a total, mindful, reflexive sonic awareness that moves between trying to hear everything at once and deep attentive focus on a single sound or set of sounds. Her listening practices were meant both as a way of assessing the sonic world and cultivating attitudes for changing it, and her career as a composer and theorist has also been bound up with the critique of a still strongly patriarchal culture in many fields of avant-garde music.[30] Steven Feld uses the term "acoustemology" to describe "one's sonic way of knowing and being in the world."[31] Feld's own work might be described as developing anthropological methods to adequately make sense of and deal with the acoustemologies of the cultures he studies, but "acoustemology" has also sometimes been used to describe academics' own sonic epistemologies. Both Feld, in his work on Kaluli sound culture, and later writers like Stefan Helmreich, in his work on underwater sound, have problematized anthropological conceptions of "immersion" that are so central to standard accounts of ethnographic method.[32]

Particular ways of knowing sound have been integral to the development of key modern sonic practices. Psychoacoustics—the quantitative study of auditory perception—has been integral to the development of almost every major sound technology in the 20th century. If another field of knowledge replaced psychoacoustics in communication engineering, everything from telephones to tape recorders to MP3s would sound, work and mean differently than they do today.[33] The same can be said for information theory and the design of digital media, physical acoustics and architecture, sound cognition and hearing aids and cochlear implants (and for that matter speech education and speech therapy), noise and vibration studies and urban zoning. As Mara Mills has demonstrated, this same arc of research has done much to define the boundaries between normal and abnormal hearing, and while many sound scholars still imagine listening subjects as possessing a certain kind of whole, undamaged hearing, the Deaf and hard-of-hearing were central both to the development of contemporary sound technologies *and* our most basic ideas of audition.[34] It is not just fields that claim the mantle of science: there are intimate connections between religious thought and devotional song and listening; rhetoric and oratory; tropics and literature; lexicons of conventionalized sound aesthetics and sound design for everything from movies to cars and games.[35] Every field of sonic practice is partially shaped by a set of knowledges of sound that it motivates, utilizes and operationalizes.

Sound studies is also bound by this condition. We have the methods and intellectual traditions we inherit from our own fields, as well as those practical or formal knowledges we encounter in the objects we study. Throughout our projects, we must therefore place these ways of knowing in tension. We must do the hard work of making a "break" with pregiven or common-sense notions, regardless of where they come from. We must not automatically take any discourse about sound in its own terms, but rather interrogate the terms upon which it is built. We must attend to the formations of power and subjectivity with which various knowledges transact.

Sonic imaginations denote a quality of mind, but not a totality of mind. In addition to carving out their own intellectual spaces within other fields, sound students facilitate the sonic imaginations of scholars who might deal with sound in their work even though it is not their primary concern. Just as concepts of the gaze and images bounce back and forth between studies of visual culture and much broader fields of social and cultural thought, so too do concepts with a sonic dimension like hearing, listening, voice, space and transduction (to name just a few)—and sound itself. Figurations of these terms already populate whole fields whether they are consciously attended to or not. Voice has long been conflated with ideas of agency in political theory and some strands of feminist- and Marxist-influenced writing. Consider the latest iteration of this tendency: as Kate Crawford points out, "not only has the metaphor of voice become the sine qua non of 'being' online, but it has been charged with all the political currents of democratic practice."[36] Despite the realities being somewhat different, seeing and hearing are still often associated with a set of presumed and somewhat clichéd attributes, a configuration I call *the audiovisual litany*:

- hearing is spherical, vision is directional;
- hearing immerses its subject, vision offers a perspective;
- sounds come to us, but vision travels to its object;
- hearing is concerned with interiors, vision is concerned with surfaces;
- hearing involves physical contact with the outside world, vision requires distance from it;
- hearing places you inside an event, seeing gives you a perspective on the event;
- hearing tends toward subjectivity, vision tends toward objectivity;
- hearing brings us into the living world, sight moves us toward atrophy and death;
- hearing is about affect, vision is about intellect;
- hearing is a primarily temporal sense, vision is a primarily spatial sense;
- hearing is a sense that immerses us in the world, while vision removes us from it.[37]

The problem with the litany is that it elevates a set of cultural prenotions about the senses (prejudices, really) to the level of theory. To figure sound in these terms is to misattribute causes and effects. As Leigh Eric Schmidt writes, "the identification of visuality as supremely modern and Western has also been sustained (most noticeably in the work of Marshall McLuhan) through the othering of the auditory as 'primitive' or even 'African.' The equation of modernity with its gaze has often upheld some of the most basic cultural oppositions of us and them."[38] Similarly, some writers have long associated hearing with intersubjectivity and deafness with its refusal in philosophical writing, thereby elevating a stigma that the hearing attach to Deaf people as a kind of philosophical principle.[39] We could find related stories for the careers of other sonic phenomena, from music to rhythm to echoes. By this measure, sound studies as a self-conscious field is late to the scene. But it can be a productive site for thinking through these keywords that populate theory and description in so many areas of study, challenging unthought prenotions and lending conceptual vigor to sonic description in many other fields. Sound studies should be a central meeting place where sonic imaginations go to be challenged, nurtured, refreshed and transformed.

One of my hopes for this reader is that it will be useful to people whose primary academic calling is not at first blush sonic. As with the best work in any field, the best sound studies echo beyond their local conversations, problems, questions, preoccupations and objects. As a field, sound studies should not close in upon itself to protect sound as an object from the encroachment of other fields or to claim it as privileged disciplinary property. Instead, it should seek out points of connection and reflection; it should be the name for a group of people who reflexively *mind sound*. Other writers have argued implicitly or explicitly for different centers to sound study and another one will no doubt emerge from the essays assembled in this collection. In a way, we have no choice: the academic study of sound needs to begin somewhere and it belongs in many homes in many disciplines, so long as it also reaches across them. But the point is not that there should be schools of sound studies that must be defended or advanced in the pages of journals and at contentious panels at conferences, but rather that novice and advanced researchers alike need to position their own thought in relation to different traditions of minding sound depending on the particular problems they confront and their own combination of biography and history, to use C. Wright Mills's terms.

Not all the selections in this collection would meet a test for sound studies by the definition I have provided. Some of the authors in the collection and cited in this introduction wouldn't describe their work as "sound studies" (and we should grant them that leeway—I included them because I believe that scholars interested in sound studies should read their work, however it is categorized). We shouldn't be too literalistic in staking out boundaries—defining a field is tricky and too often gets overtaken by contests for academic authority. It would be both wrong and insulting to say that the current generation of scholars has invented the academic study of sound. It would be even more ridiculous for a single scholar to claim to have invented or defined the field. Figuring out a point of prior origin or a proper center is equally difficult. The field can claim antecedents in philosophy, acoustic ecology, radio studies, cinema studies, science and technology studies, media theory, art history and art practice, music, ethnomusicology and popular music studies, history and literature, anthropology, and many other fields.

Even as it owes a huge debt to its intellectual antecedents, the current generation of sound studies work is defined by its conjuncture. More work on sound is being published in more fields than ever before, and many of these authors are self-consciously aware of being part of a group of scholars interested in sonic problems. Sociologist Robert Merton pointed out long ago that the normal process of science is simultaneous discovery. As people confront similar problems and conditions, they work out similar or related solutions.[40] The same is true even for fields that are not nearly as coherent as sciences. I am part of a generation of scholars who first published on or came to the topic in or around the 1990s, and in casual conversation, many of us tell similar stories about turning to sound as an academic subject in an effort to reconcile some element of practical knowledge of sound we brought with us to into university with academic discourses that seemed to have difficulty dealing with sonic problems and was unfriendly to sonic projects. The range of work since then has been characterized by much greater freedom and abundance, as there are new histories of almost every imaginable sound medium, a pile of new periodizations of electronic music and sound art, several excellent reconsiderations of hearing and deafness, and yet another pile of books that turn to sound to understand particular problems in new ways. This collection offers its readers a path into this growing and exciting field of thought.

The Sound Studies Reader is arranged around a set of problematics that I have found useful for organizing my teaching, thinking and research. Each of the section introductions will offer a brief reading of the ideas and debates covered by the authors (and those covered by authors I could not include). Those issues orient the section introductions and my selections in each section. I emphasize the problems that my students and I most often wrestle with. Each section is organized chronologically, and while there are many ways to read across sections—which is to say that many pieces belong in more than one section—there is some conceptual development from one part to the next. *Hearing, Listening, Deafness* focuses on the conditions of possibility and impossibility for audition. *Space, Sites, Scapes* explores the environments in which sound culture happens, ranging from physical space and the built environment to much larger spaces of sonic circulation. *Transduce and Record* and *Collectivities and Couplings* turn to the fundamental questions of media theory, asking after the technological and cultural conditions that shape and are shaped by the possibility of reproducing sound over time, across distances and for new publics and exclusions. The writers featured in *The Sonic Arts* consider sound as an aesthetic problem, or they consider the conditions under which aesthetic discussions happen. I have placed the section on *Voices* last for strategic reasons—as the essays in this section debate this most basic of human faculties, they also argue over what it means to be human, a question I believe is best addressed only after we think through culture, space, technology and aesthetics, and not before. Rather than giving a unified intellectual history of the field as a whole—a difficult enterprise best left to more deliberate intellectual histories—I have used the section introductions to allude to a few possible histories of the field (out of many more), which change depending on the problems and questions at hand.

Readers like this one are full of compromises, a fact that requires a few closing caveats. Apart from the extent that I have taken helpful advice from others, the essays and subjects in this reader are shaped by my own habits as a scholar. There are now a growing number of collections that can lay a legitimate claim to sound studies as a mantle, and each conceives of the field quite differently from the next. Some emphasize the work of sound artists and sound art (over and against music), some emphasize a musical or technological bent, and still others are grouped by method or topic of interest. A person interested in gaining a foothold in the field ought to be acquainted with many of them.[41]

This reader is heavy on theory, history, culture and technology because those are the areas in which its editor is most engaged. The reader also has a heavy North American bias (or perhaps a "Western" bias with its inclusion of European and Australian texts) in its subject matter which results both from gaps in my knowledge, gaps in the kinds of literature suitable to include in a book like this, the ready availability of English translations of work in other languages, and also from some tendencies in scholarly publishing (not the least being the politics and mechanics of permissions and the cost of space—I began with over 100 essays and excerpts that I wanted to include and I find new ones every week). Many of the readings are excerpted in the service of brevity and diversity, as I felt it important to offer newcomers many flavors of thought as prelude to digesting larger works in the field. In cases where the edits substantially change the orientation of the piece, I have titled the selection to give a sense of the excerpt. Nevertheless, *The Sound Studies Reader* aims at a kind of situated transcendence. It is impossible to assemble a truly encyclopedic reader, but like all readers it is defined by the doomed effort. My hope is that you will find the book expansive, engaging and occasionally inspiring, but also unsatisfying enough that it will push you back into the unedited primary sources, classic and forgotten work in the field in its original milieus, and into other areas of scholarship that the authors featured in these pages haven't yet imagined.

Notes

1   For comments on ideas in this intro, many thanks to Mara Mills, Dylan Mulvin, Emily Raine, Carrie Rentschler, the members of my fall 2011 sound studies seminar in AHCS, and the participants in the Sound in Media Culture workshop at Humboldt University, Berlin, 29 October 2011. Too many other people to list have contributed ideas that shaped this reader and my sense of the field, so they must accept my thanks in the abstract and my apology in the concrete.

2   Attali, *Noise: The Political Economy of Music*, 87.

3   Gopinath, "Ringtones, or the Auditory Logic of Globalization"; Théberge, *Any Sound You Can Imagine: Making Music/Consuming Technology*.

4   The quote is from Cockayne, *Hubbub: Filth, Noise and Stench in England, 1600–1770*, 107; Plato, "Republic"; Jackson, *Harmonious Triads: Physicists, Musicians and Instrument-Makers in Nineteenth-Century Germany*.

5   See, for instance, Chow and Steintrager, "In Pursuit of the Object of Sound: An Introduction"; Pinch and Bijsterveld, "Sound Studies: New Technologies and Music"; Stadler, "Introduction"; Kara Keeling and Josh Kun, "Introduction"; Schedel and Uroskie, "Writing about Audiovisual Culture." See also the special section "In Focus: Sound Studies" in *Cinema Journal* 48: 1 (Fall 2008).

6   As I complete this introduction, two new interdisciplinary, international, open access sound studies journals have just launched (*The Journal of Sonic Studies* based in the Netherlands and *Sound Effects,* based in Denmark), and there is talk in Europe of forming a new professional association.

7   Du Bois, Gates, and Oliver, *The Souls of Black Folk: Authoritative Text, Contexts, Criticism*, 177–78.

8   Heidegger, *Being and Time*, 98; Freud and Gay, *Civilization and Its Discontents*, 43.

9   In addition to the many works cited elsewhere in this volume, see, e.g., Carpenter and McLuhan, *Explorations in Communication: An Anthology*; Ong, *The Presence of the Word: Some Prolegomena for Cultural and Religious History*; Truax, *Acoustic Communication*; Silverman, *The Acoustic Mirror: The Female Voice in Psychoanalysis and Cinema*; Kahn and Whitehead, *Wireless Imaginations: Sound, Radio and the Avant-Garde*; Berland, "Cultural Technologies and the 'Evolution' of Technological Cultures"; Théberge, *Any Sound You Can Imagine: Making Music/Consuming Technology*; Kahn, *Noise, Water, Meat: A History of Sound in the Arts*.

10   Despite calling this book "The Sound Studies Reader" and having used the term in research and teaching over a decade, I only privilege it because it rolls off the tongue easily (I love the term "aural" but spoken with most Anglophone accents it is easily confused with "oral," which has a more vexed history), has nice alliteration, and pretty well describes the range of work it covers. It also puts one of its central terms up for debate immediately.

11   Hilmes, "Is There a Field Called Sound Culture Studies? And Does It Matter?," 249.

12   *Oxford English Dictionary*, sv "student." See Gitlin, "The Anti-political Populism of Cultural Studies"; and for a critique of Gitlin's position, see Rodman, "Subject to Debate."

13   Like any definition of an academic field, this is a working definition, imperfect and incomplete(able). But it is useful insofar as it helps us carve out a space between "all work by all writers on sound" and something more specific, situated and intellectually forceful.

14   The institutional conditions of sound studies remain for now an open question, and will vary across nations. Given today's transnational financial crises and changing conditions for people in higher education—from skyrocketing tuition to changing funding schemes to the casualization of the professoriate—the question of a field's institutional existence is not simply a matter of styles of inquiry and theoretical commitments. In many cases, institutional decisions are tied to much more practical matters like ensuring we and our students have space, freedom and resources to do the work, fair working conditions to do it in, and the academic freedom to do it well.

15   There can never be a single sonic imagination: "We can and must presuppose a multiplicity of planes, since no one plane could encompass all of chaos without collapsing back into it; and each retains only movements which can be folded together." Deleuze and Guattari, *What is Philosophy?*, 50.

16   Eliot, *The Use of Poetry and the Use of Criticism*, 11.

17   Mills, *The Sociological Imagination*, 5, 7.

18   I use "conjuncture" to describe a unit of context that is made up of different kinds of relations of force, which themselves may derive from any number of factors. Writers in the cultural studies tradition generally use it to invoke ideas descending from Antonio Gramsci, Michel Foucault, and others who argued that we cannot know ahead of time what is given in a particular context, which factors determine others and which factors are determined by others. For instance, Gramsci wrote "A common error in historico-political analysis consists in an inability to find the correct relation between what is organic and what is conjunctural. This leads to presenting causes as immediately operative which in fact only operate indirectly, or to asserting that the immediate causes are the only effective ones." Gramsci, *Selections from the Prison Notebooks*, 178. See also, Foucault, "Questions of Method"; Grossberg, *Cultural Studies in the Future Tense*.

19   Ihde, *Listening and Voice: A Phenomenology of Sound*, 28. Later in the book Ihde uses a much more restricted notion of "auditory imagination" than what I propose here, to describe imagining heard sounds.

20   Paul Fauconnet and Marcel Mauss, "Sociology: Object and Method" (1901): "Une recherche sérieuse conduit à réunir ce que le vulgaire sépare, ou à distinguer ce que le vulgaire confound," Bourdieu, Chamboredon, and Passeron, *The Craft of Sociology: Epistemological Preliminaries*, 15; Ihde, *Listening and Voice: A Phenomenology of Sound*, 29.

21   Balsamo, *Designing Culture: The Technological Imagination at Work*, 6–7.

22   Kahn to author, 18 September, 2011.

23   Hall, Morley, and Chen, *Stuart Hall*; Frow and Morris, *Australian Cultural Studies: A Reader*, xviii.

24   Sterne, *The Audible Past: Cultural Origins of Sound Reproduction*, 12.

25   Pinch and Bijsterveld, "New Keys to the World of Sound," 10 (ms); Bull and Back, "Introduction: Into Sound," 1–4.

26   Dyson, *Sounding New Media: Immersion and Embodiment in the Arts and Culture*, e.g., 27, 77, 114.

27   Friedner and Helmreich, "When Deaf Studies meets Sound Studies," 7 (ms).

28   Erlmann, *Reason and Resonance: A History of Modern Aurality*, 17–18.

29   Rodgers, *Pink Noises: Women on Electronic Music and Sound*, 6; see also McCartney, "Gender, Genre and Electroacoustic Soundmaking Practices."

30   Oliveros, *Deep Listening*.

31   Feld and Brenneis, "Doing Anthropology in Sound," 482.

32   Feld, "Aesthetics as Iconicity of Style (uptown title) or (downtown title) 'Lift-Up-Over-Sounding': Getting into the Kaluli Groove"; Helmreich, "An Anthropologist Underwater: Immersive Soundscapes, Submarine Cyborgs and Transductive Ethnography."

33   Sterne, *MP3: The Meaning of a Format*.

34   Mills, "Deaf Jam: From Inscription to Reproduction to Information."

35   Wurtzler, *Electric Sounds: Technological Change and the Rise of Corporate Mass Media*; Gouk, *Music, Science, and Natural Magic in Seventeenth-Century England*; Schmidt, *Hearing Things: Religion, Illusion and the American Enlightenment*; Collins, *Game Sound: An Introduction to the History, Theory and Practice of Video Game Music and Sound Design*; Bijsterveld, "Acoustic Cocooning: How the Car became a Place to Unwind."

36   Crawford, "Following You," 526–27.

37   Sterne, *The Audible Past: Cultural Origins of Sound Reproduction*, 15.

38   Schmidt, *Hearing Things: Religion, Illusion and the American Enlightenment*, 7.

39   Friedner and Helmreich, "When Deaf Studies meets Sound Studies."

40   Merton, *The Sociology of Science: Theoretical and Empirical Investigations*, 371.

41   This is only a partial list but it gives a sense of the range of work already out there: Abel and Altman, *The Sounds of Early Cinema*; Altman, *Sound Theory / Sound Practice*; Augaitis and Lander, *Radio Rethink: Art, Sound and Transmission*; Ayers, *Cybersounds: Essays on Virtual Music Cultures*; Braun, *Music and Technology in the Twentieth Century*; Bull and Back, *The Auditory Culture Reader*; Cox and Warner, *Audio Culture: Readings in Modern Music*; Drobnick, *Aural Cultures*; Erlmann, *Hearing Cultures: Essays on Sound, Listening and Modernity*; Gopinath and Stanyek, *The Oxford Handbook of Mobile Music*; Greene and Porcello, *Wired for Sound: Engineering and Technologies in Sonic Cultures*; Hilmes and Loviglio, *The Radio Reader: Essays in the Cultural History of Radio*; Kahn and Whitehead, *Wireless Imaginations: Sound, Radio and the Avant-Garde*; Kelly, *Sound*; LaBelle and Roden, *Site of Sound: Of Architecture and the Ear*; Morris, *Sound States: Innovative Poetics and Acoustic Technologies*; Pereira de Sá, *Rumos da Cultura da Música: Negócios, Estéticas, Linguagens e Audibilidades*; Pinch and Bijsterveld, *The Oxford Handbook of Sound Studies*; Rodgers, *Pink Noises: Women on Electronic Music and Sound*; Smith, *Hearing History: A Reader*; Squier, *Communities of the Air: Radio Century, Radio Culture*; Strauss, *Radiotext(e)*.

References

Abel, Richard, and Rick Altman, eds. *The Sounds of Early Cinema*. Bloomington: Indiana University Press, 2001.

Altman, Rick. *Sound Theory/Sound Practice*. New York: Routledge, 1992.

Attali, Jacques. *Noise: The Political Economy of Music*. Minneapolis: University of Minnesota Press, 1985.

Augaitis, Daina, and Dan Lander. *Radio Rethink: Art, Sound and Transmission*. Banff: The Walter Philips Gallery, 1994.

Ayers, Mike. *Cybersounds: Essays on Virtual Music Cultures*. New York: Peter Lang, 2006.

Balsamo, Anne. *Designing Culture: The Technological Imagination at Work*. Durham [N.C.]: Duke University Press, 2011.

Berland, Jody. "Cultural Technologies and the 'Evolution' of Technological Cultures." In *The World Wide Web and Contemporary Cultural Theory*, 235–58. New York: Routledge, 2000.

Bijsterveld, Karin. "Acoustic Cocooning: How the Car became a Place to Unwind." *The Senses and Society* 5, no. 2 (2010): 189–211.

Du Bois, W. E. B., Henry Louis Gates, and Terri Hume Oliver. *The Souls of Black Folk: Authoritative Text, Contexts, Criticism*. New York: W.W. Norton, 1999.

Bourdieu, Pierre, Jean-Claude Chamboredon, and Jean-Claude Passeron. *The Craft of Sociology: Epistemological Preliminaries*. New York: Walter de Gruyter, 1991.

Braun, Hans-Joachim. *Music and Technology in the Twentieth Century*. Baltimore: The Johns Hopkins University Press, 2000.

Bull, Michael, and Les Back. "Introduction: Into Sound." In *The Auditory Culture Reader*, 1–18. New York: Berg, 2003.

——. *The Auditory Culture Reader*. New York: Berg, 2003.

Carpenter, Edmund, and Marshall McLuhan. *Explorations in Communication: An Anthology*. Boston: Beacon Press, 1960.

Chow, Rey, and James Steintrager. "In Pursuit of the Object of Sound: An Introduction." *Differences* 22, no. 2–3 (2011).

Cockayne, Emily. *Hubbub: Filth, Noise and Stench in England, 1600–1770*. New Haven: Yale University Press, 2007.

Collins, Karen. *Game Sound: An Introduction to the History, Theory and Practice of Video Game Music and Sound Design*. Cambridge: MIT Press, 2008.

Cox, Christoph, and Daniel Warner. *Audio Culture: Readings in Modern Music*. New York: Continuum, 2004.

Crawford, Kate. "Following You: Disciplines of Listening in Social Media." *Continuum* 23 (August 2009): 525–35.

Deleuze, Gilles, and Felix Guattari. *What is Philosophy?* New York: Columbia University Press, 1994.

Drobnick, Jim. *Aural Cultures*. Toronto: YYZ Books, 2004.

Dyson, Frances. *Sounding New Media: Immersion and Embodiment in the Arts and Culture*. Berkeley: University of California Press, 2009.

Eliot, Thomas Stearns. *The Use of Poetry and the Use of Criticism: Studies in the Relation of Criticism to Poetry in England*. Cambridge: Harvard University Press, 1986.

Erlmann, Veit. *Hearing Cultures: Essays on Sound, Listening and Modernity*. New York: Berg, 2004.

——. *Reason and Resonance: A History of Modern Aurality*. Cambridge: Zone Books, 2010.

Feld, Steven. "Aesthetics as Iconicity of Style (uptown title) or (downtown title) 'Lift-Up-Over-Sounding': Getting into the Kaluli Groove." In *Music Grooves*. Chicago: University of Chicago Press, 1996.

Feld, Steven, and Donald Brenneis. "Doing Anthropology in Sound." *American Ethnologist* 31, no. 4 (November 1, 2004): 461–74.

Foucault, Michel. "Questions of Method." In *The Foucault Effect: Studies in Governmentality*, 73–86. Chicago: University of Chicago Press, 1991.

Freud, Sigmund, and Peter Gay. *Civilization and Its Discontents*. The Standard Edition. W. W. Norton & Company, 1989.

Friedner, Michele, and Stefan Helmreich. "When Deaf Studies meets Sound Studies." *Senses and Society* 7, no. 1 (forthcoming 2012).

Frow, John, and Meaghan Morris. *Australian Cultural Studies: A Reader*. Urbana: University of Illinois Press, 1993.

Gitlin, Todd. "The Anti-political Populism of Cultural Studies." *Dissent* 44, no. 1 (Spring 1997): 77–82.

Gopinath, Sumanth. "Ringtones, or the Auditory Logic of Globalization." *First Monday* 10, no. 12 (2005). http://firstmonday.org/htbin/cgiwrap/bin/ojs/index.php/fm/article/view/1295/1215.

Gopinath, Sumanth, and Jason Stanyek, eds. *The Oxford Handbook of Mobile Music*. New York: Oxford University Press, Forthcoming.

Gouk, Penelope. *Music, Science, and Natural Magic in Seventeenth-Century England*. New Haven: Yale University Press, 1999.

Gramsci, Antonio. *Selections from the Prison Notebooks*. Translated by Quentin Hoare, and Geoffrey Nowell Smith. London: Lawrence and Wishart, 1971.

Greene, Paul D., and Thomas Porcello. *Wired for Sound: Engineering and Technologies in Sonic Cultures*. Middletown: Wesleyan University Press, 2005.

Grossberg, Lawrence. *Cultural Studies in the Future Tense*. Durham: Duke University Press, 2010.

Hall, Stuart, David Morley, and Kuan-Hsing Chen. *Stuart Hall: Critical Dialogues in Cultural Studies*. Routledge, 1996.

Heidegger, Martin. *Being and Time: A Translation of Sein and Zeit*. New York: State University of New York Press, 1996.

Helmreich, Stefan. "An Anthropologist Underwater: Immersive Soundscapes, Submarine Cyborgs and Transductive Ethnography." *American Ethnologist* 34, no. 4 (2007): 621–41.

Hilmes, Michelle. "Is There a Field Called Sound Culture Studies? And Does It Matter?" *American Quarterly* 57, no. 1 (2005): 249–59.

Hilmes, Michelle, and Jason Loviglio. *The Radio Reader: Essays in the Cultural History of Radio*. New York: Routledge, 2001.

Ihde, Don. *Listening and Voice: A Phenomenology of Sound*. Athens: Ohio University Press, 1974.

Jackson, Myles. *Harmonious Triads: Physicists, Musicians and Instrument-Makers in Nineteenth-Century Germany*. Cambridge: MIT Press, 2006.

Kahn, Douglas. *Noise, Water, Meat: A History of Sound in the Arts*. Cambridge: MIT Press, 1999.

Kahn, Douglas, and Gregory Whitehead. *Wireless Imaginations: Sound, Radio and the Avant-Garde*. Cambridge: MIT Press, 1992.

Kara Keeling, and Josh Kun. "Introduction: Listening to American Studies." *American Quarterly* 63, no. 3 (2011): 445–59.

Kelly, Caleb. *Sound*. 1st ed. Cambridge: MIT Press, 2011.

LaBelle, Brandon, and Steve Roden. *Site of Sound: Of Architecture and the Ear*. Los Angeles: Errant Bodies, 2000.

McCartney, Andra. "Gender, Genre and Electroacoustic Soundmaking Practices." *Intersections: Canadian Journal of Music* 26, no. 2 (2006): 20–48,130.

Merton, Robert K. *The Sociology of Science: Theoretical and Empirical Investigations*. Chicago: University of Chicago Press, 1973.

Mills, C. Wright. *The Sociological Imagination*. New York: Oxford University Press, 1959.

Mills, Mara. "Deaf Jam: From Inscription to Reproduction to Information." *Social Text* 28, no. 1 (2010): 35–58.

Morris, Adalaide. *Sound States: Innovative Poetics and Acoustic Technologies*. Chapel Hill: University of North Carolina Press, 1997.

Oliveros, Pauline. *Deep Listening: A Composer's Sound Practice*. iUniverse, 2005.

Ong, Walter J. *The Presence of the Word: Some Prolegomena for Cultural and Religious History*. New Haven: Yale University Press, 1967.

Pereira de Sá, Simone. *Rumos da Cultura da Música: Negócios, Estéticas, Linguagens e Audibilidades*. Porto Allegre: Editoria Meridional Ltda., 2010.

Pinch, Trevor, and Karin Bijsterveld. "New Keys to the World of Sound." In *The Oxford Handbook of Sound Studies*. New York: Oxford University Press, 2011.

—. "Sound Studies: New Technologies and Music." *Social Studies of Science* 34, no. 5 (2004): 635–48.

—. eds. *The Oxford Handbook of Sound Studies*. New York: Oxford University Press, 2011.

Plato. "Republic." In *The Collected Dialogues of Plato*, 575–844. Princeton: Princeton University Press, 1961.

Rodgers, Tara. *Pink Noises: Women on Electronic Music and Sound*. Durham: Duke University Press, 2010.

Rodman, Gilbert B. "Subject to Debate: (Mis)Reading Cultural Studies." *Journal of Communication Inquiry* 21, no. 2 (October 1, 1997): 56–69.

Schedel, Margaret, and Andrew V. Uroskie. "Writing about Audiovisual Culture." *Journal of Visual Culture* 10, no. 2 (2011): 137–44.

Schmidt, Leigh Eric. *Hearing Things: Religion, Illusion and the American Enlightenment*. Cambridge: Harvard University Press, 2000.

Silverman, Kaja. *The Acoustic Mirror: The Female Voice in Psychoanalysis and Cinema*. Bloomington: Indiana University Press, 1988.

Smith, Mark M. *Hearing History: A Reader*. Athens: University of Georgia Press, 2004.

Squier, Susan Merrill. *Communities of the Air: Radio Century, Radio Culture*. Durham: Duke University Press, 2003.

Stadler, Gustavus. "Introduction: Breaking Sound Barriers." *Social Text*, no. 102 (Spring 2010). http://www.socialtextjournal.org/journal/issue102/introduction-breaking-sound-barriers.php.

Sterne, Jonathan. *MP3: The Meaning of a Format*. Durham: Duke University Press, 2012.

—. *The Audible Past: Cultural Origins of Sound Reproduction*. Durham: Duke University Press, 2003.

Strauss, Neil. *Radiotext(e)*. New York: Semiotext(e), 1993.

Théberge, Paul. *Any Sound You Can Imagine: Making Music/Consuming Technology*. Hanover: Wesleyan University Press, 1997.

Truax, Barry. *Acoustic Communication*. Norwood: Ablex, 1984.

Wurtzler, Steve J. *Electric Sounds: Technological Change and the Rise of Corporate Mass Media*. New York: Columbia University Press, 2007.

PART I

Hearing, Listening, Deafness

HEARING AND LISTENING SURFACE as problems in almost every discipline, and they are where we begin our reader, for any discussion of sound implies both audition and its limits. Writers in this section address issues of audition from diverse perspectives ranging from philosophy to cultural studies, aesthetics, anthropology, science and technology studies, and media studies.

While "the gaze," as an act of seeing, is a central trope in studies of visual culture, there is no central auditory trope equivalent to "the listen." In its place, there are dozens of figures and figurations of audition, even though all structures of listening, whether interpersonal, institutional or mediatized are also configurations of power. As Jean-Luc Nancy writes, "to be listening will always, then, be to be straining toward or in an approach to the self." But what does that mean for those who do not or cannot listen, or whose listening is shaped by forces beyond themselves? While Michel Foucault's most famous diagram of power was the panopticon, a vision of the prison as a seeing machine, in *The History of Sexuality, Volume 1,* he cites the confessional as an auditory technology of power through which the West produced sexuality. In the confessional, "the agency of domination does not reside in the one who speaks (for it is he who is constrained), but in the one who listens and says nothing; not in the one who knows and answers, but in the one who questions and is not supposed to know." Jacques Attali's essay in this section offers perhaps the most expanded conceptualization of listening, suggesting that it is the ear, not the eye, that offers a path into relations of power. More recent work like that of Mark Smith offers finely-grained analysis of power relations as they are heard, documenting how 19th-century U.S. elites heard themselves, each other, and their others, whether industrial workers or slaves.[1] Listening can be an act, a field of action, or a metaphor through which we can better understand social activity. Kate Crawford's essay in this section explores listening as a metaphor for social media practice, which helps her better characterize its nature as both ambiance and surveillance.

The line between hearing/hard-of-hearing/Deaf is perhaps the limit case of a sonic culture registering power relations on the bodies of its members. Neither celebration of nor critique of hearing must become too absolute. For either position risks fetishizing Deafness, or using it as what David Mitchell and Sharon Snyder call a "narrative prosthesis," where the stigmatized, pathologized figure of a person with a disability is used to advance a narrative, usually as a metaphor for something else. Too often we find that tendency in sound theory. In *The Third Ear*, Joachim-Ernst Berendt approvingly cites Aristotle's claim that "the blind are more understanding than the deaf because hearing exerts a direct influence on the formation of moral character, which is not immediately true of what is seen. The human soul can also become diffused by way of the eye whereas what is heard results in focus and concentration." He does this not in an effort to understand the social stigmas applied to the Deaf and hard-of-hearing, but rather to use those stigmas to advance his own argument about the importance of hearing. This kind of audism, the chauvinism of the hearing, would not be taken seriously today in scholarship if authors used people of a particular gender, race, sexuality or age in that fashion.[2]

In fact, the Deaf and hard-of-hearing are everywhere in sound history, both as objects and subjects. Alexander Graham Bell's model of the telephone was built on top of a machine he designed to hear for the Deaf. His lab wound up building a machine that heard for the hearing instead. As Peter Szendy reminds us, Wagner fetishized Beethoven's deafness as having the capacity of total focus to which hearing listeners could only aspire.[3] And as Mara Mills's contribution to this section shows, the Deaf and hard-of-hearing were never very far from research into sound technologies in the 20th century. Steve Goodman's essay, meanwhile, suggests that it is not just a question of the limits of hearing for those who are Deaf or hard-of-hearing, but rather that sonic thought needs to move toward the edges of sound itself—and beyond—to consider sound as a particular moment in a broader ontological and political field of vibration.

To understand the faculty of audition is, then, simultaneously to understand its possibilities and its limits, its status as embedded in real social relations and its power as a figurative and imaginative metaphor for other registers of human action. Each of the readings in this section help move us through different aspects of that ambitious project. Don Ihde's classic phenomenology of sound offers a philosophically informed account of what it means to hear and how auditory experience might have a certain specificity. Jody Berland's essay adds the crucial dimension of positionality to our understandings of what it means to hear, considering both the social position of the listener, and her place in a sonic and mediatic culture. Michel Chion further stratifies listening by thinking through it in terms of modes—not all listening is the same, and any aesthetic theory of listening will have to account for the plurality of the process (indeed, Chion represents in this collection a long line of thinkers who have developed typologies of listening).[4] Charles Hirschkind expands this modal approach to listening by thinking in terms of Islamic cultures, rather than the West, and in so doing offers a powerful alternative description of what it means to listen in modernity.

Notes

1   Nancy, *Listening*, 9; Foucault, *The History of Sexuality, Volume 1: An Introduction*, 62; Smith, *Listening to Nineteenth-Century America*; see also Levin, *The Listening Self: Personal Growth, Social Change and the Closure of Metaphysics*; Schwartz, *Listening Subjects: Music, Psychoanalysis, Culture*; Corbett, *Extended Play: Sounding Off from John Cage to Dr. Funkenstein*.
2   Mitchell and Snyder, *Narrative Prosthesis*; Berendt, *The Third Ear*, 12.
3   Szendy, *Listen: A History of Our Ears*, 120.
4   See, e.g., Adorno, *Introduction to the Sociology of Music*; Stockfelt, "Adequate Modes of Listening."

References

Adorno, Theodor W. *Introduction to the Sociology of Music*. New York: Continuum, 1988.

Berendt, Joachim-Ernst. *The Third Ear: On Listening to the World*. New York: H. Holt, 1992.

Corbett, John. *Extended Play: Sounding Off from John Cage to Dr. Funkenstein*. Durham: Duke University Press, 1994.

Foucault, Michel. *The History of Sexuality, Volume 1: An Introduction*. New York: Vintage Books, 1978.

Levin, David Michael. *The Listening Self: Personal Growth, Social Change and the Closure of Metaphysics*. New York: Routledge, 1989.

Mitchell, David T., and Sharon L. Snyder. *Narrative Prosthesis: Disability and the Dependencies of Discourse*. Minneapolis: University of Michigan Press, 2000.

Nancy, Jean-Luc. *Listening*. New York: Fordham University Press, 2007.

Schwartz, David. *Listening Subjects: Music, Psychoanalysis, Culture*. Durham: Duke University Press, 1997.

Smith, Mark M. *Listening to Nineteenth-Century America*. Chapel Hill: University of North Carolina Press, 2001.

Stockfelt, Ola. "Adequate Modes of Listening." In *Keeping Score: Music, Disciplinarity, Culture*, 129–46. Charlottesville: University of Virginia Press, 1997.

Szendy, Peter. *Listen: A History of Our Ears*. New York: Fordham University Press, 2008.

Chapter 2

Don Ihde

THE AUDITORY DIMENSION

WHAT IS IT TO LISTEN *phenomenologically*? It is more than an intense and concentrated attention to sound and listening, it is also to be aware in the process of the pervasiveness of certain "beliefs" which intrude into my attempt to listen "to the things themselves." Thus the first listenings inevitably are not yet fully existentialized but occur in the midst of preliminary approximations.

Listening begins with the ordinary, by proximately working its way into what is as yet unheard. In the process the gradual deconstruction of those beliefs which must be surpassed occurs. We suppose that there are significant contrasts between sight and sound; thus in the very midst of the implicit sensory atomism held in common belief we approximate abstractly what the differences might be between the dimensions of sight and of sound.[1] We "pair" these two dimensions comparatively. First we engage in a hypothetical and abstract mapping which could occur for ordinary experience with its inherent beliefs.

Supposing now two "distinct" dimensions within experience which are to be "paired," I attend to what is seen and heard to learn in what way these dimensions differ and compare, in what ways they diverge in their respective "shapes," and in what ways they "overlap."

I turn back, this time imaginatively, to my visual and auditory experience and practice a kind of free association upon approximate visual and auditory possibilities, possibilities not yet intensely examined, which float in a kind of playful revery.

Before me lies a box of paper clips. I fix them in the center of my vision. Their shape, shininess, and immobility are clear and distinct. But as soon as I pair their appearance with the question of an auditory aspect I note that they are also *mute*. I speculatively reflect upon the history of philosophy with recollections of pages and pages devoted to the discussion of "material objects" with their various qualities and upon the "world" of tables, desks, and chairs which inhabit so many philosophers' attentions: *the realm of mute objects*. Are these then the implicit standard of a visualist metaphysics? For in relation to stable, mute objects present to the center of clear and distinct vision, the role of *predication* seems easy and most evident. The qualities adhere easily to these material objects.

A fly suddenly lands upon the wall next to the desk where the paper clips lie and begins to crawl up that wall. My attention is distracted and I swat at him. He quickly, almost too quickly for the eye, escapes and flies to I know not where. Here is a moving, active being upon the face of the visual "world." With the moving, active appearance of the fly a second level or grouping of objects displays itself. This being which is seen is active and is characterized by motion. Movement belongs to the verb. *He walks, he flies, he escapes.* These are not quite correctly properties but activities. Who are the "metaphysicians" of the fly? I recall speculatively those traditions of "process" and movement which would question the dominance of the stable, mute object, and which see in motion a picture of the world. The verb is affirmed over the predicate.

But the metaphysicians of muteness may reply by first noting that the moving being appears against the background of the immobile, that the fly is an appearance which is discontinuous, that motion is an occasional "addition" to the stratum of the immobile. The fly's flight is etched against stability, and the arrow of Zeno, if it may speed its way at all, must do so against the ultimate foundation of the stable background. Even motion may be "reduced" to predication as time is atomized.

But what of sound? The mute object stands "beyond" the horizon of sound. Silence is the horizon of sound, yet the mute object is silently *present*. Silence seems revealed at first through a visual category. But with the fly and the introduction of motion there is the presentation of a buzzing, and Zeno's arrow whizzes in spite of the paradox. Of both animate and inanimate beings, motion and sound, when paired, belong together. "Visualistically" sound "overlaps" with moving beings.

With sound a certain liveliness also makes its richer appearance. I walk into the Cathedral of Notre Dame in Paris for the first time. Its emptiness and high arching dark interior are awesome, but it bespeaks a certain monumentality. It is a ghostly reminder of a civilization long past, its muted walls echoing only the shuffle of countless tourist feet. Later I return, and a high mass is being sung: suddenly the mute walls echo and reecho and the singing fills the cathedral. Its soul has momentarily returned, and the mute testimony of the past has once again returned to live in the moment of the ritual. Here the paired "regions" of sight and sound "synthesize" in dramatic richness.

But with the "overlapping" of sight and sound there remains the "excess" of sight over sound in the realm of the mute object. Is there a comparable area where listening "exceeds" seeing, an area beyond the "overlapping" just noted where sight may not enter, and which, like silence to sound, offers a clue to the horizon of vision?

I walk along a dark country path, barely able to make out the vague outlines of the way. Groping now, I am keenly aware of every sound. Suddenly I hear the screech of an owl, seemingly amplified by the darkness, and for a moment a shock traverses my body. But I cannot see the bird as it stalks its nocturnal prey. I become more aware of sound in the dark, and it makes its presence more dramatic when I cannot see.

But night is not the horizon of sight, nor Dionysius the limit of Apollo. I stand alone on a hilltop in the light of day, surveying the landscape below in a windstorm. I hear its howling and feel its chill, but I cannot see its contorted writhing though it surrounds me with its invisible presence. No matter now hard I look, I cannot see the

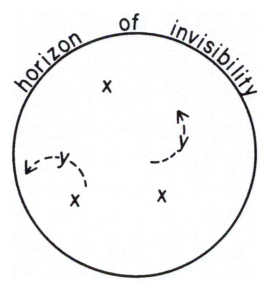

Fig. 2.1

wind, *the invisible is the horizon of sight.* An inquiry into the auditory is also an inquiry into the invisible. Listening makes the invisible *present* in a way similar to the presence of the mute in vision.

What metaphysics belong to listening, to the invisible? Is it also that of Heraclitus, the first to raise a preference for vision, but who also says, "Listening not to me but to the Logos, it is wise to acknowledge that all things are one."[2] Is such a philosophy possible beyond the realm of mute objects? Or can such a philosophy find a way to give voice even to muteness? The invisibility of the wind is indicative. What is the wind? It belongs, with motion, to the realm of verb. The wind is "seen" in its *effects,* less than a verb, its visible being is what it has done in passing by.

Is anything revealed through such a playful association? At a first approximation it seems that it is possible to map two "regions" which do not coincide, but which in comparison may be discerned to have differing boundaries and horizons.

In the "region" of sight there is a visual field which may be characterized now as "surrounded" by its open horizon which limits vision, and which remains "unseen." Such a field can be diagrammed [see Figure 2.1].

Here, where the enclosed circle is the present visual field, within this presence there will be a vast totality of entities which can be experienced. And although these entities display themselves with great complexity, within the abstraction of the approximation we note only that some are stable (x) and usually mute in ordinary experience, and that some (—y—) move, often "accompanied" by sounds. Beyond the actually seen field of presence lies a horizon designated now as a horizon of invisibility.

A similar diagram can be offered for a "region" of sound presences [see Figure 2.2].

Although once we move beyond this approximation, the "shape" of the auditory field will need to be qualified. Within the limits of the first approximation we note that the auditory field contains a series of auditory presences which do not, however,

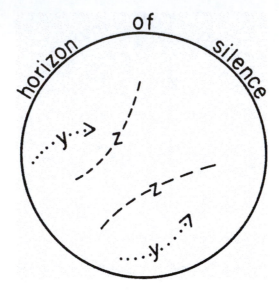

Fig. 2.2

perfectly overlap those of the visual field. There are sounds which "accompany" moving objects or beings (—y—), but there are some for which no visible presence may be found (—z—). Insofar as all sounds are also "events," all the sounds are, within the first approximation, likely to be considered as "moving." Again, there is also a horizon, characterized by the pairing as a horizon of silence which "surrounds" the field of auditory presence.

It is also possible to relate, within the first approximation, the two "regions" and discern that there are some overlapping and some nonoverlapping features of each "region." Such a "difference" may be diagrammed [see Figure 2.3].

In this diagram of the overlapping and nonoverlapping "regions" of sight and sound we note that what may be taken as horizonal (or absent) for one "region" is taken as a presence for the other.

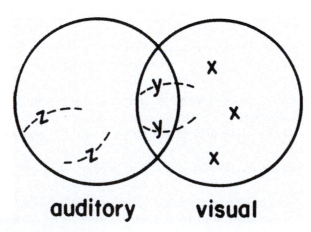

Fig. 2.3

Thus while the area of mute objects (x) seems to be closed to the auditory experience as these objects lie in silence, so within auditory experience the invisible sounds (—z—) are present to the ear but absent to the eye. There are also some presences which are "synthesized" (—y—) or present to both "senses" or "regions."

This pairing when returned to the revery concerning the associated "metaphysics" of the "senses" once more reveals a way in which the traditions of dominant visualism show themselves. If we suppose that any metaphysics of worth must be one which is at least comprehensive, then a total visualist metaphysics must find a way to account for and to include in its description of the world all those invisible events which at this level seem to lie beyond the reach of the visible horizon, but which are nevertheless present within experience.

This may be done in several ways. First, one can create some hermeneutic device which, continuing the approximation of the "regions," *functionally* makes the invisible visible. This implies some "translation" of one "region" into the terms of the favored "region." Such is one secret of the applied metaphysics often found in the sciences of sound. Physically, sound is considered a wave phenomenon. Its wave characteristics are then "translated" into various visual forms through instruments, which are the extended embodiments of the scientific enterprise. Voice patterns are "translated" into visual patterns on oscillographs; sound reverberations are mapped with Moire patterns; even echo-location in its practical applications is made a matter of seeing what is on the radar screen; the making or "translating" of the invisible into the visible is a standard route for understanding a physics of sound.

In the case of the sciences of sound this translation allows sound to be measured, and measurement is predominantly a matter of spatializing qualities into visible quantities. But in ordinary experience there is often thought to be a similar role for sound. Sounds are frequently thought of as anticipatory clues for ultimate visual fulfillments. The most ordinary of such occurrences are noted in locating unseen entities.

The bird watcher in the woods often first hears his bird, then he seeks it and fixes it in the sight of his binoculars. The person hanging a picture knows where to look for the dropped tack from the sound it made as it rolled under the piano. And although not all noises yield a visual presence for example the extreme case of radio astronomy may yield the presence of an unsuspected "dark" star which may never be seen—the familiar movement from sound to sight may be discerned.

The movement from that which is heard (and unseen) to that which is seen raises the question of its counterpart. Does each event of the visible world offer the occasion, even ultimately from a sounding presence of mute objects, for silence to have a voice? Do all things, when *fully* experienced, also sound forth?

In ordinary experience this direction is also taken. The bird watcher may be an appreciative bird listener. He awaits quietly in the hopes that the winter wren will sing his long and complicated "Mozart" song. But only in more recent times has this countermovement become conspicuous. The amplified listening which now reveals the noise of lowly ant societies gives voice to the previously silent. Physically even molecules sound, and the human ear comes to a threshold of hearing almost to the point of hearing what would be incessant noise.

Notes

1   A phenomenological warning must be issued here. There is a strict difference between empty supposing and what is intuitionally fulfilled. Thus the exercise at this point is not strictly phenomenological but proceeds toward strict phenomenology by approximations.

2   Philip Wheelwright. *The Presocratics* (New York: Odyssey Press. 1966), p 79.

Chapter 3

Jacques Attali

NOISE: THE POLITICAL ECONOMY OF MUSIC

FOR TWENTY-FIVE CENTURIES, Western knowledge has tried to look upon the world. It has failed to understand that the world is not for the beholding. It is for hearing. It is not legible, but audible.

Our science has always desired to monitor, measure, abstract, and castrate meaning, forgetting that life is full of noise and that death alone is silent: work noise, noise of man, and noise of beast. Noise bought, sold, or prohibited. Nothing essential happens in the absence of noise.

Today, our sight has dimmed; it no longer sees our future, having constructed a present made of abstraction, nonsense, and silence. Now we must learn to judge a society more by its sounds, by its art, and by its festivals, than by its statistics. By listening to noise, we can better understand where the folly of men and their calculations is leading us, and what hopes it is still possible to have.

In these opening pages, I would like to summarize the essential themes of this book [see original publication]. The supporting argument will follow.

Among sounds, music as an autonomous production is a recent invention. Even as late as the eighteenth century, it was effectively submerged within a larger totality. Ambiguous and fragile, ostensibly secondary and of minor importance, it has invaded our world and daily life. Today, it is unavoidable, as if, in a world now devoid of meaning, a background noise were increasingly necessary to give people a sense of security. And today, wherever there is music, there is money. Looking only at the numbers, in certain countries more money is spent on music than on reading, drinking, or keeping clean. Music, an immaterial pleasure turned commodity, now heralds a society of the sign, of the immaterial up for sale, of the social relation unified in money.

It heralds, for it is *prophetic*. It has always been in its essence a herald of times to come. Thus, as we shall see, if it is true that *the political organization of the twentieth century is rooted in the political thought of the nineteenth, the latter is almost entirely present in embryonic form in the music of the eighteenth century.*

In the last twenty years, music has undergone yet another transformation. This mutation forecasts a change in social relations. Already, material production has been supplanted by the exchange of signs. Show business, the star system, and the hit parade signal a profound institutional and cultural colonization. Music makes mutations audible. It obliges us to invent categories and new dynamics to regenerate social theory, which today has become crystallized, entrapped, moribund.

Music, as a mirror of society calls this truism to our attention: society is much more than economistic categories, Marxist or otherwise, would have us believe.

Music is more than an object of study: it is a way of perceiving the world. A tool of understanding. Today, no theorizing accomplished through language or mathematics can suffice any longer; it is incapable of accounting for what is essential in time—the qualitative and the fluid, threats and violence. In the face of the growing ambiguity of the signs being used and exchanged, the most well-established concepts are crumbling and every theory is wavering. The available representations of the economy, trapped within frameworks erected in the seventeenth century or, at latest, toward 1850, can neither predict, describe, nor even express what awaits us.

It is thus necessary to imagine radically new theoretical forms, in order to speak to new realities. Music, the organization of noise, is one such form. It reflects the manufacture of society; it constitutes the audible waveband of the vibrations and signs that make up society. *An instrument of understanding, it prompts us to decipher a sound form of knowledge.*

My intention here is thus not only to theorize *about* music, but to theorize *through* music. The result will be unusual and unacceptable conclusions about music and society, the past and the future. That is perhaps why music is so rarely listened to and why—as with every facet of social life for which the rules are breaking down (sexuality, the family, politics)—it is censored, people refuse to draw conclusions from it.

In the chapters that follow [see original publication], music will be presented as originating in ritual murder, of which it is a simulacrum, a minor form of sacrifice heralding change. We will see that in that capacity it was an attribute of religious and political power, that it signified order, but also that it prefigured subversion. Then, after entering into commodity exchange, it participated in the growth and creation of capital and the spectacle. Fetishized as a commodity, music is illustrative of the evolution of our entire society: deritualize a social form, repress an activity of the body, specialize its practice, sell it as a spectacle, generalize its consumption, then see to it that it is stockpiled until it loses its meaning. Today, music heralds—regardless of what the property mode of capital will be—the establishment of a society of repetition in which nothing will happen anymore. But at the same time, it heralds the emergence of a formidable subversion, one leading to a radically new organization never yet theorized, of which self-management is but a distant echo.

In this respect, music is not innocent: unquantifiable and unproductive, a pure sign that is now *for sale,* it provides a rough sketch of the society under construction, a society in which the informal is mass produced and consumed, in which difference is artificially recreated in the multiplication of semi-identical objects.

No organized society can exist without structuring differences at its core. No market economy can develop without erasing those differences in mass production. The self-destruction of capitalism lies in this contradiction, in the fact that music leads a deafening life: an instrument of differentiation, it has become a locus of repetition. It itself becomes undifferentiated, goes anonymous in the commodity, and hides behind the mask of stardom. It makes audible what is essential in the contradictions of the developed societies: *an anxiety-ridden quest for lost difference, following a logic from which difference is banished.*

Art bears the mark of its time. Does that mean that it is a clear image? A strategy for understanding? An instrument of struggle? In the codes that structure noise and its mutations we glimpse a new theoretical practice and reading: *establishing relations between the history of people and the dynamics of the economy on the one hand, and the history of the ordering of noise in codes on the other; predicting the evolution of one by the forms of the other; combining economics and aesthetics; demonstrating that music is prophetic and that social organization echoes it.*

This book [see original publication] is not an attempt at a multidisciplinary study, but rather *a call to theoretical indiscipline,* with an ear to sound matter as the herald of society. The risk of wandering off into poetics may appear great, since music has an essential metaphorical dimension: "For a genuine poet, metaphor is not a rhetorical figure but a vicarious image that he actually beholds in place of a concept."[1]

Yet music is a credible metaphor of the real. It is neither an autonomous activity nor an automatic indicator of the economic infrastructure. It is a herald, for change is inscribed in noise faster than it transforms society. Undoubtedly, music is a play of mirrors in which every activity is reflected, defined, recorded, and distorted. If we look at one mirror, we see only an image of another. But at times a complex mirror game yields a vision that is rich, because unexpected and prophetic. At times it yields nothing but the swirl of the void.

Mozart and Bach reflect the bourgeoisie's dream of harmony better than and prior to the whole of nineteenth-century political theory. There is in the operas of Cherubini a revolutionary zeal rarely attained in political debate. Janis Joplin, Bob Dylan, and Jimi Hendrix say more about the liberatory dream of the 1960s than any theory of crisis. The standardized products of today's variety shows, hit parades, and show business are pathetic and prophetic caricatures of future forms of the repressive channeling of desire.

The cardinal importance of music in announcing a vision of the world is nothing new. For Marx, music is the "mirror of reality"; for Nietzsche, the "expression of truth";[2] for Freud, a "text to decipher." It is all of that, for it is one of the sites where mutations first arise and where science is secreted: "If you close your eyes, you lose the power of abstraction" (Michel Serres). It is all of that, even if it is only a detour on the way to addressing man about the works of man, to hearing and making audible his alienation, to sensing the unacceptable immensity of his future silence and the wide expanse of his fallowed creativity. Listening to music is listening to all noise, realizing that its appropriation and control is a reflection of power, that it is essentially political.

The Sounds of Power

Noise and Politics

More than colors and forms, it is sounds and their arrangements that fashion societies. With noise is born disorder and its opposite: the world. With music is born power and its opposite: subversion. In noise can be read the codes of life, the relations among men. Clamor, Melody, Dissonance, Harmony; when it is fashioned by man with specific tools, when it invades man's time, when it becomes sound, noise is the source of purpose and power, of the dream—Music. It is at the heart of the progressive rationalization of aesthetics, and it is a refuge for residual irrationality; it is a means of power and a form of entertainment.

Everywhere codes analyze, mark, restrain, train, repress, and channel the primitive sounds of language, of the body, of tools, of objects, of the relations to self and others.

All music, any organization of sounds is then a tool for the creation or consolidation of a community, of a totality. It is what links a power center to its subjects, and thus, more generally, it is an attribute of power in all of its forms. Therefore, any theory of power today must include a theory of the localization of noise and its endowment with form. Among birds a tool for marking territorial boundaries, noise is inscribed from the start within the panoply of power. Equivalent to the articulation of a space, it indicates the limits of a territory and the way to make oneself heard within it, how to survive by drawing one's sustenance from it.[3] And since noise is the source of power, power has always listened to it with fascination. In an extraordinary and little known text, Leibnitz describes in minute detail the ideal political organization, the "Palace of Marvels," a harmonious machine within which all of the sciences of time and every tool of power are deployed.

> These buildings will be constructed in such a way that the master of the house will be able to hear and see everything that is said and done without himself being perceived, by means of mirrors and pipes, which will be a most important thing for the State, and a kind of political confessional.[4]

Eavesdropping, censorship, recording, and surveillance are weapons of power. The technology of listening in on, ordering, transmitting, and recording noise is at the heart of this apparatus. The symbolism of the Frozen Words,[5] of the Tables of the Law, of recorded noise and eavesdropping—these are the dreams of political scientists and the fantasies of men in power: to listen, to memorize—this is the ability to interpret and control history, to manipulate the culture of a people, to channel its violence and hopes. Who among us is free of the feeling that this process, taken to an extreme, is turning the modern State into a gigantic, monopolizing noise emitter, and at the same time, a generalized eavesdropping device. Eavesdropping on what? In order to silence whom?

The answer, clear and implacable, is given by the theorists of totalitarianism. They have all explained, indistinctly, that it is necessary to ban subversive noise because it betokens demands for cultural autonomy, support for differences or marginality: a concern for maintaining tonalism, the primacy of melody, a distrust of new languages, codes, or instruments, a refusal of the abnormal—these characteristics are common to all regimes of that nature. They are direct translations of the political importance of cultural repression and noise control. For example, in the opinion of Zhdanov (according to a speech he gave in 1947 and never really disclaimed), music, an instrument of political pressure, must be tranquil, reassuring, and calm:

And, indeed, we are faced with a very acute, although outwardly concealed struggle between two trends in Soviet music. One trend represents the healthy, progressive principle in Soviet music, based upon recognition of the tremendous role of the classical heritage, and, in particular, the traditions of the Russian musical school, upon the combination of lofty idea content in music, its truthfulness and realism, with profound, organic ties with the people and their music and songs—all this combined with a high degree of professional mastery. The other trend is that of a formalism alien to Soviet art; it is marked by rejection of the classical heritage under the cover of apparent novelty, by rejection of popular music, by rejection of service to the people, all for the sake of catering to the highly individualistic emotions of a small group of aesthetes. . . . Two extremely important tasks now face Soviet composers. The chief task is to *develop* and perfect Soviet music. The second is to *protect* Soviet music from the infiltration of elements of bourgeois decadence. Let us not forget that the U.S.S.R. is now the guardian of universal musical culture, just as in all other respects it is the *mainstay of human civilization and culture against bourgeois decadence and decomposition of culture.* . . . Therefore, not only the musical, but also the political, ear of Soviet composers must be very keen. . . . Your task is to prove the superiority of Soviet music, *to create great Soviet music.*[6]

All of Zhdanov's remarks are strategic and military: music must be a bulwark against difference; for that, it must be powerful and protected.

We find the same concern, the same strategy and vocabulary, in National Socialist theorists. Stege, for example:

If Negro jazz is banned, if enemies of the people compose intellectual music that is soulless and heartless, and find no audience in Germany, these decisions are not arbitrary. . . . What would have happened if the aesthetic evolution of German music had followed the course it was taking in the postwar period? The people would have lost all contact with art. It would have been spiritually uprooted, all the more so since it would find little satisfaction in degenerate and intellectual music that is better suited to being read than heard. The gulf between the people and art would have become an unbridgeable abyss, the theater and concert halls would have gone empty, the composers working counter to the soul of the people would have been left with only themselves for an audience, assuming they were still able to understand their own wild fancies.[7]

The economic and political dynamics of the industrialized societies living under parliamentary democracy also lead power to invest art, and to invest in art, without necessarily theorizing its control, as is done under dictatorship. Everywhere we look, the monopolization of the broadcast of messages, the control of noise, and the institutionalization of the silence of others assure the durability of power. Here, this channelization takes on a new, less violent, and more subtle form: laws of the political economy take the place of censorship laws. Music and the musician essentially become either objects of consumption like everything else, recuperators of subversion, or meaningless noise.

Musical distribution techniques are today contributing to the establishment of a system of eavesdropping and social surveillance. Muzak, the American corporation that sells standardized music, presents itself as the "security system of the 1970s" because it permits use of musical distribution channels for the circulation of orders. The monologue of standardized, stereotyped music accompanies and hems in a daily life in which in reality no one has the right to speak any more. Except those among the exploited who can still use their music to shout their suffering, their dreams of the absolute and freedom. What is called music today is all too often only a disguise for the monologue of power. However, and this is the supreme irony of it all, never before have musicians tried so hard to communicate with their audience, and never before has that communication been so deceiving. Music now seems hardly more than a somewhat clumsy excuse for the self-glorification of musicians and the growth of a new industrial sector. Still, it is an activity that is essential for knowledge and social relations.

Science, Message and Time

"This remarkable absence of texts on music"[8] is tied to the impossibility of a general definition, to a fundamental ambiguity. "The science of the rational use of sounds, that is, those sounds organized as a scale"—that is how the *Littré,* at the end of the nineteenth century, defined music in order to reduce it to its harmonic dimension, to confuse it with a pure syntax. Michel Serres, on the contrary, points to the "extreme simplicity of the signals," "the message at its extreme, a ciphered mode of communicating universals" as a way of reminding us that beyond syntax there is meaning. But which meaning? Music is a "dialectical confrontation with the course of time."[9]

Science, message, and time—music is all of that simultaneously. It is, by its very presence, a mode of communication between man and his environment, a mode of social expression, and duration itself. It is therapeutic, purifying, enveloping, liberating; it is rooted in a comprehensive conception of knowledge about the body, in a pursuit of exorcism through noise and dance. But it is also past time to be produced, heard, and exchanged.

Thus it exhibits the three dimensions of all human works: joy for the creator, use-value for the listener, and exchange-value for the seller. In this seesaw between the various possible forms of human activity, music was, and still is, ubiquitous: "Art is everywhere, for artifice is at the heart of reality."[10]

Mirror

But even more than that, it is "the Dionysian mirror of the world" (Nietzsche).[11] "Person-to-person described in the language of things" (Pierre Schaeffer).

It is a mirror, because as a mode of immaterial production it relates to the structuring of theoretical paradigms, far ahead of concrete production. It is thus an immaterial recording surface for human works, the mark of something missing, a shred of Utopia to decipher, information in negative, a collective *memory* allowing those who hear it to record their own personalized, specified, modeled meanings, affirmed in time with the beat—a collective memory of order and genealogies, the repository of the word and the social score.[12]

But it reflects a fluid reality. The only thing that primitive polyphony, classical counterpoint, tonal harmony, twelve-tone serial music, and electronic music have in common is the principle of giving form to noise in accordance with changing syntactic structures. The history of music is the "Odyssey of a wandering, the adventure of its absences."[13]

However, the historical and musicological tradition would still, even today, like to retain an evolutionary vision of music, according to which it is in turn "primitive," "classical," and "modern." This schema is obsolete in all of the human sciences, in which the search for an evolution structured in a linear fashion is illusory. Of course, one can perceive strong beats, and we will even see later on that every major social rupture has been preceded by an essential mutation in the codes of music, in its mode of audition, and in its economy. For example, in Europe, during three different periods with three different styles (the liturgical music of the tenth century, the polyphonic music of the sixteenth century, and the harmony of the eighteenth and twentieth centuries), music found expression within a single, stable code and had stable modes of economic organization; correlatively, these societies were very clearly dominated by a single ideology. In the intervening periods, times of disorder and disarray prepared the way for what was to follow. Similarly, it seems as though a fourth (and shorter) period was ushered in during the 1950s, with a coherent style forged in the furnace of black American music; it is characterized by stable production based on the tremendous demand generated by the youth of the nations with rapidly expanding economies, and on a new economic organization of distribution made possible by recording.

Like the cattle herd of the Nuer discussed by Girard,[14] a herd that is the mirror and double of the people, music runs parallel to human society, is structured like it, and changes when it does. It does not evolve in a linear fashion, but is caught up in the complexity and circularity of the movements of history.

This simultaneity of economic and musical evolution is everywhere present. We can, for example, toy with the idea that it is not by chance that the half-tone found acceptance during the Renaissance, at precisely the same time the merchant class was expanding; that it is not by coincidence that Russolo wrote his *Arte Dei Rumori* ("The Art of Noise") in 1913; that noise entered music and industry entered painting just before the outbursts and wars of the twentieth century, before the rise of social noise. Or again, that it is not by coincidence that the unrestricted use of large orchestras came at a time of enormous industrial growth; that with the disappearance of taboos there arose a music industry that takes the channelization of desire into commodities to such an extreme as to become a caricature; that rock and soul music emerged with the youth rebellion, only to dissolve in the cooptation of the young by light music programming; or finally, that the cautious and repressive form of musical production condoned today in countries with State-owned property designates "socialism" (if that is truly what it is) as simply the successor to capitalism, slightly more efficient and systematic in its normalization of men and its frantic quest for sterilized and monotonous perfection.

At a time when values are collapsing and commodities converse in place of people in an impoverished language (which in advertising is becoming increasingly musical), there is glaring evidence that the end of aesthetic codes is at hand. "The musical odyssey has come to a close, the graph is complete."[15]

Can we make the connections? Can we hear the crisis of society in the crisis of music? Can we understand music through its relations with money? Notwithstanding, the political economy of music is unique; only lately commodified, it soars in the immaterial. It is an economy without quantity. An aesthetics of repetition. That is why the political economy of music is not marginal, but premonitory. The noises of a society are in advance of its images and material conflicts.

Our music foretells our future. Let us lend it an ear.

Prophecy

Music is prophecy. Its styles and economic organization are ahead of the rest of society because it explores, much faster than material reality can, the entire range of possibilities in a given code. It makes audible the new world that will gradually become visible, that will impose itself and regulate the order of things; it is not only the image of things, but the transcending of the everyday, the herald of the future. For this reason musicians, even when officially recognized, are dangerous, disturbing, and subversive; for this reason it is impossible to separate their history from that of repression and surveillance.

Musician, priest, and officiant were in fact a single function among ancient peoples. Poet laureate of power, herald of freedom—the musician is at the same time within society, which protects, purchases, and finances him, and outside it, when he threatens it with his visions. Courtier and revolutionary: for those who care to hear the irony beneath the praise, his stage presence conceals a break. When he is reassuring, he alienates; when he is disturbing, he destroys; when he speaks too loudly, power silences him. Unless in doing so he is announcing the new clamor and glory of powers in the making.

A creator, he changes the world's reality. This is sometimes done consciously, as with Wagner, writing in 1848, the same year the *Communist Manifesto* was published:

> I will destroy the existing order of things, which parts this one mankind into hostile nations, into powerful and weak, privileged and outcast, rich and poor; for it makes unhappy men of all. I will destroy the order of things that turns millions into slaves of a few, and these few into slaves of their own might, own riches. I will destroy this order of things, that cuts enjoyment off from labor.[16]

A superb modern rallying cry by a man who, after the barricades of Dresden, would adopt "the attitude of the rebel who betrayed the rebellion" (Adorno). Another example is Berlioz's call to insurrection:

> Music, today in the flush of youth, is emancipated, free: it does as it pleases. Many of the old rules are no longer binding: they were made by inattentive observers or ordinary spirits for other ordinary spirits. New needs of the spirit, the heart, and the sense of hearing are imposing new endeavors and, in some cases, even infractions of the old laws.

Rumblings of revolution. Sounds of competing powers. Clashing noises, of which the musician is the mysterious, strange, and ambiguous forerunner—after having been long emprisoned, a captive of power.

Understanding through Music

If we wish to elaborate a theory of the relations between music and money, we must first look at the existing theories of music. Disappointment. They are a succession of innumerable typologies and are never innocent. From Aristotle's three kinds of music—"ethical" (useful for education), "of action" (which influences even those who do not know how to perform it), and "cathartic" (the aim of which is to perturb and then appease)[17]—to Spengler's distinction between "Apollonian" music (modal, monodic, with an oral tradition) and "Faustian" music (tonal, polyphonic, with a written tradition), all we find are nonfunctional categories. Today, the frenzy with which musical theories, general surveys, encyclopedias, and typologies are elaborated and torn down crystallizes the spectacle of the past. They are nothing more than signs of the anxiety of an age confronted with the disappearance of a world, the dissolution of an aesthetic, and the slipping away of knowledge. They are no more than collections of classifications with no real significance, a final effort to preserve linear order for a material in which time takes on a new dimension, inaccessible to measurement. Roland Barthes is correct when he writes that "if we examine the current practice of music criticism, it is evident that the work (or its performance) is always translated with the poorest of linguistic categories: the adjective."[18]

So which path will lead us through the immense forest of noise with which history presents us? How should we try to understand what the economy has made of music and what economy music foreshadows?

Music is inscribed between noise and silence, in the space of the social codification it reveals. Every code of music is rooted in the ideologies and technologies of its age, and at the same time produces them. If it is deceptive to conceptualize a succession of musical codes corresponding to a succession of economic and political relations, it is because time traverses music and music gives meaning to time.

In this book, I would like to trace the political economy of music as a succession of *orders* (in other words, differences) done violence by *noises* (in other words, the calling into question of differences) that are *prophetic* because they create new orders, unstable and changing. The simultaneity of multiple codes, the variable overlappings between periods, styles, and forms, prohibits any attempt at a genealogy of music, a hierarchical archeology, or a precise ideological pinpointing of particular musicians. But it is possible to discern who among them are innovators and heralds of worlds in the making. For example, Bach alone explored almost the entire range of possibilities inherent in the tonal system, and more. In so doing, he heralded two centuries of industrial adventure. What must be constructed, then, is more like a map, a structure of interferences and dependencies between society and its music.

In this book, I will attempt to trace the history of their relations with the world of production, exchange, and desire; the slow degradation of use into exchange, of representation into repetition; and the prophecy, announced by today's music, of the potential for a new political and cultural order.

Briefly, we will see that it is possible to distinguish on our map three zones, three stages, three strategic usages of music by power.

In one of these zones, it seems that music is used and produced in the ritual in an attempt to make people *forget* the general violence; in another, it is employed to make people *believe* in the harmony of the world, that there is order in exchange and legitimacy in commercial power; and finally, there is one in which it serves to *silence,* by mass-producing a deafening, syncretic kind of music, and censoring all other human noises.

Make people Forget, make them Believe, Silence them. In all three cases, music is a tool of power: of ritual power when it is a question of making people forget the fear of violence; of representative power when it is a question of making them believe in order and harmony; and of bureaucratic power when it is a question of silencing those who oppose it. Thus music localizes and specifies power, because it marks and regiments the rare noises that cultures, in their normalization of behavior, see fit to authorize. Music accounts for them. It makes them audible.

When power wants to make *people forget,* music is ritual *sacrifice,* the scapegoat; when it wants them to *believe,* music is enactment, *representation;* when it wants to *silence* them, it is reproduced, normalized, *repetition.* Thus it heralds the subversion of both the existing code and the power in the making, well before the latter is in place.

Today, in embryonic form, beyond repetition, lies freedom: more than a new music, a fourth kind of musical practice. It heralds the arrival of new social relations. Music is becoming *composition.*

Representation against fear, repetition against harmony, composition against normality. It is this interplay of concepts that music invites us to enter, in its capacity as the herald of organizations and their overall political strategies—noise that destroys orders to structure a new order. A highly illuminating foundation for social analysis and a resurgence of inquiry about man.

For Fear, Clarity, Power, and Freedom correspond in their succession to the four stages Carlos Castaneda distinguishes in his mysterious description of the initiatory teachings of his master, the sorcerer Don Juan Mateus. This convergence is perhaps more than coincidental, if music is a means of understanding, like the unbalanced relation to ecstasy created by drugs. Is the sorcerer speaking of drugs when he explains that:

> When a man starts to learn, he is never clear about his objectives. His purpose is faulty; his intent is vague. He hopes for rewards that will never materialize, for he knows nothing of the hardships of learning. He slowly begins to learn—bit by bit at first, then in big chunks. And his thoughts soon clash. What he learns is never what he pictured or imagined, and so

he begins to be afraid. Learning is never what one expects. Every step of learning is a new task, and the fear the man is experiencing begins to mount mercilessly, unyieldingly. . . . This is the time when a man has no more fears, no more impatient clarity of mind—a time when all his power is in check. . . . If a man . . . lives his fate through, he can then be called a man of knowledge, if only for the brief moment when he succeeds in fighting off his last, invincible enemy. That moment of clarity, power, and knowledge is enough.[19]

Don Juan's knowledge by peyote is reminiscent of the prophetic knowledge of the shaman, of the ritual function of the pharmakon. And of the interference between stages in the deployment of systems of music.

Music, like drugs, is intuition, a path to knowledge. A path? No—a battlefield.

Notes

1. Friedrich Nietzsche, *The Birth of Tragedy,* trans. Walter Kaufman (New York: Vintage, 1967), p. 63.
2. Nietzsche, *Birth of Tragedy,* p. 61.
3. "Whether we inquire into the origin of the arts or observe the first criers, we find that everything in its principle is related to the means of subsistence." Jean-Jacques Rousseau, *Essai sur l'inéqalité.*
4. Gottfried Wilhelm Leibnitz, "Drôle de pensée touchant une nouvelle sorte de représentation," ed. Yves Belaval, *La Nouvelle Revue Francaise* 70 (1958): 754 reverberations are mapped 68. Quoted in Michel Serres, "Don Juan ou le Palais des Merveilles," *Les Etudes Philosophiques* 3 (1966): 389.
5. [A reference to Rabelais, *Gargantua and Pantagruel,* b. 4, chap. 54. TR.]
6. [Andrei A. Zhdanov, "Music," address to a conference of leading musicians called by the Central Committee of the Communist party, 1947. Published in *Essays on Literature, Philosophy and Music* (New York: International Publishers, 1950), pp. 81, 95–96 (emphasis added). TR.]
7. Fritz Stege, *La situation actuelle de la musique allemande* (1938).
8. Michel Serres, *Esthétique sur Carpaccio* (Paris: Hermann, 1975).
9. Ibid.
10. Jean Baudrillard, *L'échange symbolique et la mort* (Paris: Gallimard, 1976), p. 116.
11. Nietzsche, *Birth of Tragedy,* p. 119.
12. See Dominique Zahan, *La dialectique du verbe chez les "Bambaras"* (Paris: Mouton, 1963).
13. Serres, *Esthétique.*
14. René Girard, *Violence and the Sacred,* trans. Patrick Gregory (Baltimore: Johns Hopkins University Press, 1977).
15. Serres, *Esthétique.*
16. Richard Wagner, "The Revolution," in *Prose Works,* trans. William Ashton Ellis, vol. 8 (New York: Broude Bros., 1966), p. 237.
17. [Aristotle, *Politics,* 1339a-1342b. TR.]
18. Roland Barthes, "Le grain de la voix," *Musique en Jeu* 9 (Nov. 1972): 51–63.
19. Carlos Castaneda, *The Teachings of Don Juan* (Berkeley and Los Angeles: University of California Press, 1971), pp. 57 and 60.

Chapter 4

Jody Berland

CONTRADICTING MEDIA: TOWARD A POLITICAL PHENOMENOLOGY OF LISTENING

THE NUMBER OF HUMAN HOURS, days, weeks spent listening to the radio is phenomenal. The number of radios purchased, possessed, listened to in Canada is phenomenal. It wouldn't be Canada without radio. Despite noises made with the introduction of TV, radio did not disappear between 1950 and 1960 (though of course it changed). If anything its constant presence became more constant, since the transistor (and freeways) appeared at about the same time. Radio hasn't gone away. What did disappear to a correspondingly phenomenal degree was critical attention to radio. Compare the number of publications on TV or film in your local bookstore to those on radio and the culture of sound technology. The last major research projects on radio content and listening habits were conducted in the 1940s. Only recently has this absence begun to register.

The "renaissance" of interest in broadcast sound can be attributed, to a small degree, to the emergence of alternative forms of radio broadcasting, which themselves owe their genesis to major shifts and consolidations in the international and local structuralization of technology, economics, power, and cultural production. Though alternative radio takes as many forms as there are cultural and political locations, these different forms of opposition articulate their strategies in relation to a common force: the global network of telecommunications whose musical arms have with unprecedented rapidity entered and transformed every social and cultural community in the world. It is said of music that it disdains all boundaries of language and location. If that can be argued, we are indebted for both its proof and its counterproof to the global explorations of the music industry. These explorations both transform boundaries and create the felt necessity for their rearticulation. Whether the "global village" toward which these powerful corporations drive us marks the end or the beginning of *autonomous* difference depends on a complex interaction of technology, power, and politics within which music plays a very central and unique role. Knowing how the struggle progresses means learning how to listen.

My own attentiveness to radio is logical enough, since I am a musician with a professional interest in media and politics. Also I am Canadian, and (even worse) a Canadian woman, which explains a certain paranoid ear for the discourses of power effected by technology, technological processes, mediated social relationships. At the same time, as I am completely inside of these, I am completely at the margin. But this logic would never have followed its apparently inevitable course were it not for the influence of CKLN, a campus-based alternative community FM station in Toronto. There I was one evening, sitting in the kitchen, reading Anthony Giddens of all things and listening to CKLN. Giddens was playing some fancy tricks with the terms "mob" and "mass" culture and I had just listened to about half an hour of uninterrupted music when I suddenly realized that what I was hearing was a totally different form of cultural/technological communication. I was being constituted as a member of a listening public in a way I hadn't experienced before (though similar stations in Australia first introduced me to such possibilities); most notably because the form of broadcasting had nothing to do with the usual injunction to recognize/desire/ purchase the record whose commodity form corresponded to what I was hearing. I didn't always know whose they were, for one thing; and the different relationship between me and the music corresponded to a different relationship between pieces of music, which "made sense" of them in a different way. I forgot to be annoyed by the absence of immediate author-information. I wasn't listening to advertisements; I was listening to radio.

Structure, Space, Time

Radio is an alteration of space and a structuring of time. It extends space if you're making music, shrinks it if you're listening. It both joins people together and reaches them where they are lonely, which may be why it was embraced so vigorously by Canadians from the beginning. Its centrality is clearly related to the geographic scale of the country. Though if we recognize considerations other than the physiological, we have to say that in other respects Canada is a very small country, and that smallness has had as determinant an impact on the development of its broadcasting as its largeness. Radio redefines space and structures time not only in its acoustic movement over distances but also in its format. R. Murray Schafer argues in *The Tuning of the World* that the joining of geographically and philosophically unrelated items in radio achieves an "irrationality of electroacoustic juxtapositioning" which we should refuse to take for granted. Though Schafer has done as much as anyone to analyze the experiential effects of what he calls the "schizophonia" of modern sound technology and its splitting of sound from source, we can go further by recognizing that the principles of juxtaposition that dominate ordinary radio programming are as "rational," i.e. motivated, as they are irrational, i.e. static.

Radio achieves this rational irrationality by its ability to place together sound messages that are disparate in terms of their location of origin, their cultural purpose, and their form, in order to create a continuous enveloping rhythm of sound and information. The rhythm's "reason" isn't about insight, originality, history, logic, or emancipation. It's about the market. Since the continuous rhythm of sound is more powerful than any single item enveloped in its progression, the reception of particular items is substantially determined by the larger discourse of radio programming, which teaches us addiction and forgetfulness. In commercial radio, the pleasures of location and identity, of specific recognitions or discoveries, are sacrificed to the (real) pleasures of the media's "boundless hospitality," which defends itself against anarchy by being totalitarian in its mode of address and in its structuring of program, genre, and rhythm. The tempo of events, information, pleasure, and interruption, with its prescribed balance of familiar and unfamiliar, is determined by economics, market research, and convention, before the DI ever gets there. Music is meted out by measure to reward the listener. The carefully managed rapidity and predictability of pattern maintains what might be called a community of listeners who identify with its generic classifications (Top 40, country, "easy listening," big band, classical, "new music," etc., all rigorously carved up by market research and broadcast regulation) and who share a certain locus of informed style.

Because of increased mobility, transience, fracturing of urban space via transportation, shopping centers, centralization, and marginalization—conditions that radio restructures but is simultaneously inseparable from—this listening community rarely exists today without radio having first brought it together. Imagine how different radio would be if there were real urban planning. The listening community is predominantly constituted, at least by ordinary radio, on the basis of a paradoxical and abstract relationship to depression, if I can use this precariously psychological term. We listen to radio, or rather, hear radio without always having to listen too closely (and in fact *hear* less and less) to keep from being depressed or isolated, to feel connected to something, to enfold ourselves in its envelope of pleasure, information, power; while the absence of any spontaneous or innovative event, or of any specific (vs. abstract) intimacy, contributes ultimately precisely to depression, which after all is merely a sideways description of powerlessness, of being prevented in various ways from achieving anything spontaneous or innovative, of having or living a new idea.

But this can be represented in economic terms, by locating the actual development of radio language in relation to the developing structural integration of the various sections of the communications industries.

The Play of Technology: Enter Economy, Center Stage

Radio entered the marketplace in the 1920s, the same decade in which American entertainment capital began the sweeping process of concentration and integration that now dominates the international production and dissemination of music. The first station networks were established in that decade and linked, via corporate ownership, to the production of radios, records, record players, music publishing, and film. The entertainment monopolies have triumphed through a process of continuous centralization and integration of all the stages of music production and dissemination; their imperatives of growth have marked the development of music technology and its communicative discourse from the beginning of broadcasting history.

Commercial broadcasting has become the dominant mode of promotion for musical commodities, i.e. records, and is totally dependent on the strategies of those record companies for its musical programming. DJs and local programmers have become a substantively irrelevant embellishment, and the medium of radio a totally instrumentalized form of communication. Record company profit is in turn dependent on the airtime acquired through various infamous strategies (though most communities have their own exceptions to point to). The profitability of record production contributes to the continuous *economic centralization,* which itself depends on exploiting the "strategical margins" of independent labels and innovative trends. But such centralization of profit also contributes to *symbolic centralization,* whereby the dynamics of technical innovation led by the big companies create more and more sophisticated sound production values, through which listeners learn to judge musical value. The changing modes of musical performance are, if not determined, certainly mediated by the evolving strategies of the big companies, who monopolize the development of new technologies and the marketing of music as a whole. In terms of the dominant discourse, there are only 30 "real" musical acts in the world. The rest are shadows, or so it would seem, flabby imitations, or marginal testimonies to the mythology of boundless hospitality by means of which the industrial powers weave their web.

Of course this is not the whole story, since behind this bland mask of boundlessness is the productivity of music itself, which is always also a social productivity. The traces of this are audible in the ruptures of rock, in black music, third world, or women's music, the "experiments" with space of new music, in all the spaces where location names itself and makes itself heard. The history of communications technology is not only that of the discourses of power, but also of opposition and difference, and of the interaction of these. At certain times the cultural productivity of making music becomes also an oppositional expression of new social formations and values. To work out when such cultural productivity becomes oppositional practice, it is important to understand more precisely how cultural domination works, and how it creates not only its own structures of imprisoned desire but also its own alternatives and oppositions.

American broadcasting has been officially private (with notable exceptions) since the 1927 Radio Act, a government decision of characteristically heroic self-denial which empowered the newly formed Federal Communications Commission to license and regulate radio communications "as public convenience, interest, or necessity requires." 1927 was also the year that NBC and CBS took control of programming and production. Obviously "public interest" offers a controversial framework for broadcast regulations, as indeed it has been in Canada since the federal government bestirred itself to create an alternative public broadcasting system in the 1930s. The American interpretation of "public interest" represented a clear victory for private interest and thus, explicitly, for direct broadcast advertising. The consequent strategical imperatives were imposed on broadcasters uniformly. They entailed the maximization of audience size in order to increase advertising revenue, and this meant both a continuous standardization of musical styles/forms and an increasing reliance on the mass-produced recorded music of the big companies. Such music, while cheaper, was produced through increasingly sophisticated processes, which encouraged the entrenchment of powerful implicit values of what constitutes "good" music. This control of technology is the real motor of symbolic centralization, rewarding listeners with continuous pleasure and thus continued confidence in the freedom of our pleasured ears.

But most of us, like our comrades in the "developing" nations, don't need to be reminded of what "free speech" really means in terms of American communications policy. As its horizons expand, we can enjoy wonderful things from Cuba, Warsaw, Liverpool, Kingston, Harlem, Nigeria, or Kamloops, British Columbia. We are in a particularly advantageous position to celebrate what McLuhan called the "global village." This privilege, like the Trojan horse, introduces the power dynamics of the technological conquering of space, and this has also been the case since broadcasting began.

Music In/Out of Canada

Canada—the space, the people, the airwaves—has had to deal far longer with the cultural and economic effects of the American communications empire than most other countries. We're not unique with respect to this challenge, but because the problem is a much older one here, it takes a different form. When the world hears African music, which it increasingly seems to want to do, our immanent recognition forms part of the pleasure and experience of listening to what is heard as African music (or, as music whose producers have heard African music and wanted to join in, which is also increasingly the case). African-ness can be heard. The music fills a specific symbolic and social space, that which is constructed as African-icity. Our hearing it is part of an international technological network by which African-ness, to us a symbol of preindustrial culture, is itself affected. As the tools of that network edge their way into the various centers of African music (which itself has never been a single style or discourse), they transform its social organization and, to some extent, its form. Africans themselves have, in response, begun to mobilize their own music production through various strategies of technological appropriation: cassette tapes and broadcasting policy in those countries, like many others, have become central to campaigns for cultural self-production. What we hear as "African" is increasingly inflected with the strategic language of such resistance/appropriation.

The same phenomenological representativeness marks American music, in a completely different sense. Its power signals not only the entrepreneurial prowess of the "big five" of the music industries, but also the symbolic powers attached to American formulations of the modern, the free, and the fun. American and African music articulate different kinds of aspirations for listeners in various locations. This difference is also a relationship, again not only economic, but also in terms of symbolized value systems struggling over formulations of the modern, the free, and the fun. Of course it is people who actually struggle, not symbolic systems. In all this global symbolic warfare, this "creative" tension between center and articulate margins, where does Canada stand?

When you hear Canadian music, its Canadian-ness doesn't often reach out and grab you as the first note sounds. It becomes an issue, so to speak, after the fact. This is part of how we are constituted as listeners. We may know that Rough Trade or Joni Mitchell or Burton Cummings or Anne Murray are Canadian, but we mainly know this factually, not musically. To ask whether the music we listen to is knowable musically as Canadian raises a number of questions that in themselves have been dubiously productive. Here I place native and Québecois music in brackets. In any case, hearing "prairies" or "Toronto" as a climactic aura framing the voice may be an externally informed part of the experience of listening, but it is part of it nonetheless. We still claim what we want of it as ours. What arises more readily as an immanent question from our historical experience as listeners concerns what we hear and how we hear what we hear. How we hear what we hear has, from the moment there was a listening "we," been predominantly from the radio. Because of this fact, and the specific patterns it implies, how we hear what we hear has been a question as long as we have heard it, and so this question is part of what we have always heard, though we haven't always heard it musically.

This historical centrality of radio to Canadian cultural experience is a function of geography, which was given, and of invention, which was made and which took form not long after American radio had firmly taken root, as a conscious strategy of public purpose in the name of national unity. Following the trail of the CNR, the CBC developed a radically different approach to broadcasting and specifically to music broadcasting. This is a rich and fascinating history of cultural self-defense (mediated by colonial elitism) that remains largely unwritten. For some decades, the CBC was the single most influential support system for the production and dissemination of Canadian music. Composers and historians maintain that without CBC radio there would not have developed a community of music producers able to conceive of the possibility of making music. The CBC organized, produced, and broadcast across the country a range of musical performances, from new operas to a prize-winning pipe band of CNR employees, from big bands to Irish folk songs, from commissioned compositions for radio and film documentaries and dramas to national talent-hunt singing contests.

No doubt it was an inspiring moment, that bringing together of so many voices under the protective rubric of the nation. Listeners congregated in rural living rooms and wrote letters about being truly thrilled by the sound of the bells ringing out from the Ottawa hilltop . . . In retrospect it may seem like so much state-funded maple syrup, but clearly something was happening in Canada in the '40s and '50s. Regions and communities had their voices and their voices could be heard. The CBC provided a space for this to happen in, if not a context for the larger implications to cohere in a political sense. They proved that when people themselves produce such complex sociality, the juxtaposition of sounds and messages starts to become intelligible (rather than "coherent," a term that implies singularity). The provision of resources for expressive social communication, and the making of such communication in a continually new and different way, rather than simply the making of new things to fill solidified frames: these are the bases of "value," if such a concept can be retrieved with respect to radio.

The CBC, however, could not grow to accommodate its own resources. Instead it was gradually transformed by a narrowing concept of public interest, with its related notions of "quality," and, equally important, by its growing vulnerability to commercial pressures and decreasing protection from the Canadian state. These pressures led to the consolidation of broadcasting conventions in which music airplay in urban centers (especially the more "serious" FM) has become largely as predictable and dead as it is predictable and transient on the private stations. The fertile interdependency of music production and broadcasting, which had found articulation in changing musical thinking, has mostly given way to the triumph of the economic and formal interdependency of broadcasting and prerecorded music. A former CBC music producer argues that this change has worked to discourage imagination, to decrease the producer's control over the final broadcast format, and to sever the relationship between host and musician. The effects of the transformed mode of musical packaging are passed on to the listener, to whom the daily spate of music becomes simply a component of the familiar daily environment. Music on radio ceases to matter. Against such an attitude it is all the more difficult for radio producers of imagination and originality to make their own demands on the time and special attentions of their potential audiences . . . The will to create, to experiment in imaginative and significant radiophonic forms, indeed to provide musical services as only radio can, seems to be far less influential than formerly.

It is no wonder, to add an apparent aside, that increased content quotas are treated with such aversion by the Canadian public. (Though, significantly, this is more true with respect to TV.) To suggest further restriction and regulation of the present petrified frameworks of broadcasting is bound to invite opposition in this context; not only because of the systematic training of cultural value through which American modernization effects its strategies, though this is important; but further, because "content" remains an empty formula for evoking public sympathy as long as the more essential "content" of media discourses—its unending, unbreakable flow—continues to reproduce itself through productive and regulatory processes that allow little participation other than consumptive choice (Coke or Pepsi?). The public chooses "freedom of choice." A militant defense of illusory freedom points to the absence of the real thing. So what else is new?

Reclaiming the Discourse

I said earlier that the recent emergence of alternative broadcasting is tied to major shifts in the international and local structuralization of technology, economics, power, and cultural production. While this structuralization works internationally, its local forms vary, as do strategies of local mobilization and cultural opposition. For many years "alternative" broadcasting in Canada took the form of a national public network (demanded and fought for by Canadians) whose mandate was to broadcast on behalf of a national community whose identity it simultaneously sought to build. That mandate could only have been fulfilled by allowing a far more complex and multiple concept of "public" than the dual imperatives of national (cultural) defense and the economy of dependency have permitted. The failure of the CBC joins with the simultaneous effects of a more universal colonization of musical resources, which make cultural opposition at once more international and more local. The "margins" reassert their power and find mutual recognition. The potential strength of CKLN is that it can exemplify and reinforce this dialectic of internationalism and localism; both are strengthened as it participates in the evolution of cultural self-determination within, and between, the various musical communities in Toronto.

As the station's manager explained to me, CKLN has no difficulty fulfilling Canadian content requirements because they like to play local music. A resource can be a catalyst; after a year of broadcasting, their library now contains 250 local cassette tapes. Without CKLN (I speak from experience!) many of these would not have been made. Many won't be heard elsewhere. The more complex and open the musical thinking of the station's programmers, the more autonomous, and "significant" as communication, can be the musical thinking that goes into making these tapes. It is not so much the individual authorship of music which is important within the programming discourse of the station, but the control and creative use of the medium as it mediates our musicality and our sociality. This can only evolve through an interaction between the station and the community, between listening and playing, and between music and other issues and activities.

The programs in which local tapes appear are not ordinarily organized around Canadian-ness, though there are special programs on local music (as on women's music, reggae, blues, imports, experimental music, jazz; musical "location" is a funny thing). Most frequently they are woven into a fabric of music discourse that draws connections in many different directions. Nowhere else would you hear the particular combinations and threads connecting those pieces of music. The juxtapositions cutting across time or space pull different sound thoughts together, as (for instance) when I heard the Birthday Party follow Janis Joplin, and suddenly recognized something about the voices of West Coast angst, or when I heard a series of pieces by the end of which I *really heard* the guitar. Such eventfulness can change as it responds to—is produced by—the community that is also the listening public. This process of enfranchisement has political effects, evident in the production of "documentary" talks on social issues in which the music intervenes, not (reduced) as illustration, not (inflated) as propaganda, but as a separate-but-equal movement of musically embodied expressive response to a politicized world. The station's evolving strategies of mediation make possible the development of a political phenomenology of listening, without which no emancipatory strategy in sound is possible.

Chapter 5

Michel Chion

THE THREE LISTENING MODES

Causal Listening

WHEN WE ASK SOMEONE TO SPEAK about what they have heard, their answers are striking for the heterogeneity of levels of hearing to which they refer. This is because there are at least three modes of listening, each of which addresses different objects.[1] We shall call them *causal listening, semantic listening,* and *reduced listening.*

Causal listening, the most common, consists of listening to a sound in order to gather information about its cause (or source). When the cause is visible, sound can provide supplementary information about it; for example, the sound produced by an enclosed container when you tap it indicates how full it is. When we cannot see the sound's cause, sound can constitute our principal source of information about it. An unseen cause might be identified by some knowledge or logical prognostication; causal listening (which rarely departs from zero) can elaborate on this knowledge.

We must take care not to overestimate the accuracy and potential of causal listening, its capacity to furnish sure, precise data solely on the basis of analyzing sound. In reality, causal listening is not only the most common but also the most easily influenced and deceptive mode of listening.

Identifying Causes: From the Unique to the General

Causal listening can take place on various levels. In some cases we can recognize the precise cause: a specific person's voice, the sound produced by a particular unique object. But we rarely recognize a unique source exclusively on the basis of sound we hear out of context. The human individual is probably the only cause that can produce a sound, the speaking voice, that characterizes that individual alone. Different dogs of the same species have the same bark. Or at least (and for most people it adds up to the same thing) we are not capable of distinguishing the barking of one bulldog from that of another bulldog or even a dog of a related breed. Even though dogs seem to be able to identify their master's voice from among hundreds of voices, it is quite doubtful that the master, with eyes closed and lacking further information, could similarly discern the voice of her or his own dog. What obscures this weakness in our causal listening is that when we're at home and hear barking in the back room, we can easily deduce that Fido or Rover is the responsible party.

At the same time, a source we might be closely acquainted with can go unidentified and unnamed indefinitely. We can listen to a radio announcer every day without having any idea of her name or her physical attributes. Which by no means prevents us from opening a file on this announcer in our memory, where vocal and personal details are noted, and where her name and other traits (hair color, facial features—to which her voice gives us no clue) remain blank for the time being. For there is a considerable difference between taking note of the individual's vocal timbre—and *identifying* her, having a visual image of her and committing it to memory and assigning her a name.

In another kind of causal listening we do not recognize an individual, or a unique and particular item, but rather a category of human, mechanical, or animal cause: an adult man's voice, a motorbike engine, the song of a meadowlark. Moreover, in still more ambiguous cases far more numerous than one might think, what we recognize is only the *general nature* of the sound's cause. We may say, "That must be something mechanical" (identified by a certain rhythm, a regularity aptly called "mechanical"); or, "That must be some animal" or "a human sound." For lack of anything more specific, we identify *indices*, particularly temporal ones, that we try to draw upon to discern the nature of the cause.

Even without identifying the source in the sense of the nature of the causal object, we can still follow with precision the *causal history* of the sound itself. For example, we can trace the evolution of a scraping noise (accelerating, rapid, slowing down, etc.) and sense changes in pressure, speed, and amplitude without having any idea of *what* is scraping against *what*.

The Source as a Rocket in Stages

Remember that a sound often has not just one source but at least two, three, even more. Take the sound of the felt-tip pen with which I am writing this draft. The sound's two main sources are the pen and the paper. But there are also the hand gestures involved in writing and, further, I who am writing. If this sound is recorded and listened to on a tape recorder, sound sources will also include the loudspeaker, the audio tape onto which the sound was recorded, and so forth.

Let us note that in the cinema, causal listening is constantly manipulated by the audiovisual contract itself, especially through the phenomenon of synchresis. Most of the time we are dealing not with the real initial causes of the sounds, but causes that the film makes us believe in.

Semantic Listening

I call semantic listening that which refers to a code or a language to interpret a message: spoken language, of course, as well as Morse and other such codes. This mode of listening, which functions in an extremely complex way, has been the object of linguistic research and has been the most widely studied. One crucial finding is that it is purely differential. A phoneme is listened to not strictly for its acoustical properties but as part of an entire system of oppositions and differences. Thus semantic listening often ignores considerable differences in pronunciation (hence in sound) if they are not *pertinent* differences in the language in question. Linguistic listening in both French and English, for example, is not sensitive to some widely varying pronunciations of the phoneme *a*.

Obviously one can listen to a single sound sequence employing both the causal and semantic modes at once. We hear at once what someone says and how they say it. In a sense, causal listening to a voice is to listening to it semantically as perception of the handwriting of a written text is to reading it.[2]

Reduced Listening

Pierre Schaeffer gave the name *reduced listening* to the listening mode that focuses on the traits of the sound itself, independent of its cause and of its meaning.[3] Reduced listening takes the sound—verbal, played on an instrument, noises, or whatever—as itself the object to be observed instead of as a vehicle for something else.

A session of reduced listening is quite an instructive experience. Participants quickly realize that in speaking about sounds they shuttle constantly between a sound's actual content, its source, and its meaning. They find out that it is no mean task to speak about sounds in themselves, if the listener is forced to describe them independently of any cause, meaning, or effect. And language we employ as a matter of habit suddenly reveals all its ambiguity: "This is a squeaky sound," you say, but in what sense? Is "squeaking" an image only, or is it rather a word that refers to a *source* that squeaks, or to an unpleasant *effect*?

So when faced with this difficulty of paying attention to sounds in themselves, people have certain reactions—"laughing off" the project, or identifying trivial or harebrained causes—which are in fact so many defenses. Others might avoid description by claiming to objectify sound via the aids of spectral analysis or stopwatches, but of course these machines only apprehend physical data, they do not designate what we hear. A third form of retreat involves entrenchment in out-and-out subjective relativism. According to this school of thought, every individual hears something different, and the sound perceived remains forever unknowable. But perception is not a purely individual phenomenon, since it partakes in a particular kind of objectivity, that of shared perceptions. And it is in this objectivity-born-of-intersubjectivity that reduced listening, as Schaeffer defined it, should be situated.

In reduced listening the descriptive inventory of a sound cannot be compiled in a single hearing. One has to listen many times over, and because of this the sound must be fixed, recorded. For a singer or a musician playing an instrument before you is unable to produce exactly the same sound each time, she or he can only reproduce its general pitch and outline, not the fine details that particularize a sound event and render it unique. Thus reduced listening requires the fixing of sounds, which thereby acquire the status of veritable objects.

Requirements of Reduced Listening

Reduced listening is an enterprise that is new, fruitful, and hardly natural. It disrupts established lazy habits and opens up a world of previously unimagined questions for those who try it. Everybody practices at least rudimentary forms of reduced listening. When we identify the pitch of a tone or figure out an interval between two notes, we are doing reduced listening; for pitch is an inherent characteristic of sound, independent of the sound's cause or the comprehension of its meaning.

What complicates matters is that a sound is not defined solely by its pitch; it has many other perceptual characteristics. Many common sounds do not even have a precise or determinate pitch; if they did, reduced listening would consist of nothing but good old traditional solfeggio practice. Can a descriptive system for sounds be formulated, independent of any consideration of their cause? Schaeffer showed this to be possible, but he only managed to stake out the territory, proposing, in his *Traité des objets musicaux,* a system of classification. This system is certainly neither complete nor immune to criticism, but it has the great merit of existing.

Indeed, it is impossible to develop such a system any further unless we create new concepts and criteria. Present everyday language as well as specialized musical terminology are totally inadequate to describe the sonic traits that are revealed when we practice reduced listening on recorded sounds.

In this book I am not about to go into great detail on reduced listening and sound description. The reader is encouraged to consult other books on this subject, particularly my own digest of Pierre Schaeffer's work published under the title of *Guide des objets sonores.*

What Is Reduced Listening Good For?

"What ultimately is the usefulness of reduced listening?" wondered the film and video students whom we obliged to immerse themselves in it for four days straight. Indeed, it would seem that film and television use sounds solely for their figurative, semantic, or evocatory value, in reference to real or suggested causes, or to texts—but only rarely as formal raw materials in themselves.

However, reduced listening has the enormous advantage of opening up our ears and sharpening our power of listening. Film and video makers, scholars, and technicians can get to know their medium better as a result of this experience and gain mastery over it. The emotional, physical, and aesthetic value of a sound is linked not only to the causal explanation we attribute to it but also to its own qualities of timbre and texture, to its own personal vibration. So just as directors and cinematographers—even those who will never make abstract films—have everything to gain by refining their knowledge of visual materials and textures, we can similarly benefit from disciplined attention to the inherent qualities of sounds.

The Acousmatic Dimension and Reduced Listening

Reduced listening and the acousmatic situation share something in common, but in a more ambiguous way than Pierre Schaeffer (who first developed both notions) gave us to understand. Schaeffer emphasized how acousmatic listening, which we shall define further on [see original publication] as a situation wherein one hears the sound without seeing its cause, can modify our listening. Acousmatic sound draws our attention to sound traits normally hidden from us by the simultaneous sight of the causes—hidden because this sight reinforces the perception of certain elements of the sound and obscures others. The acousmatic truly allows sound to reveal itself in all its dimensions.

At the same time, Schaeffer thought the acousmatic situation could encourage reduced listening, in that it provokes one to separate oneself from causes or effects in favor of consciously attending to sonic textures, masses, and velocities. But, on the contrary, the opposite often occurs, at least at first, since the acousmatic situation intensifies causal listening in taking away the aid of sight. Confronted with a sound from a loudspeaker that is presenting itself without a visual calling card, the listener is led all the more intently to ask, "What's that?" (i.e., "What is causing this sound?") and to be attuned to the minutest clues (often interpreted wrong anyway) that might help to identify the cause.[4]

When we listen acousmatically to recorded sounds it takes repeated hearings of a single sound to allow us gradually to stop attending to its cause and to more accurately perceive its own inherent traits.

A seasoned auditor can exercise causal listening and reduced listening in tandem, especially when the two are correlated. Indeed, what leads us to deduce a sound's cause if not the characteristic form it takes? Knowing that this is "the sound of x" allows us to proceed without further interference to explore what the sound is like in and of itself.

Active and Passive Perception

It seemed important, in the context of this book on audio-vision, to draw clear distinctions among the three modes of listening. But we must also remember that these three listening modes overlap and combine in the complex and varied context of the film soundtrack.

The question of listening with the ear is inseparable from that of listening with the mind, just as looking is with seeing. In other words, in order to describe perceptual phenomena, we must take into account that conscious and active perception is only one part of a wider perceptual field in operation. In the cinema to look is to explore, at once spatially and temporally, in a "given-to-see" (field of vision) that has limits contained by the screen. But listening, for its part, explores in a field of audition that is given or even imposed on the ear; this aural field is much less limited or confined, its contours uncertain and changing.

Due to natural factors of which we are all aware—the absence of anything like eyelids for the ears, the omnidirectionality of hearing, and the physical nature of sound—but also owing to a lack of any real aural training in our culture, this "imposed-to-hear" makes it exceedingly difficult for us to select or cut things out. There is always something about sound that overwhelms and surprises us no matter what—especially when we refuse to lend it our conscious attention; and thus sound interferes with our perception, affects it. Surely, our conscious perception can valiantly work at submitting everything to its control, but, in the present cultural state of things, sound more than image has the ability to saturate and short-circuit our perception.

The consequence for film is that sound, much more than the image, can become an insidious means of affective and semantic manipulation. On one hand, sound works on us directly, physiologically (breathing noises in a film can directly affect our own respiration). On the other, sound has an influence on perception: through the phenomenon of added value, it interprets the meaning of the image, and makes us see in the image what we would not otherwise see, or would see differently. And so we see that sound is not at all invested and localized in the same way as the image.

Notes

1.   English lacks words for two French terms: *le regard,* the fact or mode of looking, which has been translated in film theory as both "the look" and "the gaze," and its aural equivalent *l'écoute.* Here, *l'écoute* alternately appears in English as as "mode of listening" and "listening."—TRANS.

2.   Linguistics distinguishes perception of meaning from perception of sound by establishing the different categories of phonetics, phonology, and semantics.

3.   Pierre Schaeffer, *Traité des objets musicaux,* p. 270, and Michel Chion, *Guide des objets sonores,* p. 33. The adjective "reduced" is borrowed from Husserl's phenomenological notion of reduction.

4.   See Rick Altman on the "sound hermeneutic," in "Moving Lips," pp. 67–79.—TRANS.

References

Altman, Rick. "Moving Lips,"

Chion, Michel. *Guide des objets sonores*

Schaeffer, Pierre. *Traité des objets musicaux*

Chapter 6

Charles Hirschkind

CASSETTE SERMONS, AURAL MODERNITIES AND THE ISLAMIC REVIVAL IN CAIRO

I climb into a taxi cab just outside of the Ramses Mosque in the city center. The driver steers onto the busy thoroughfare of Ramses Street, and listens. A sermon struggles out through the frayed speakers and dust-encrusted electronics of a tape player bolted under the taxi's dashboard, just beneath a velvet-covered box holding a small Quran. The voice careens and crescendos along its rhetorical pathways, accompanied by the accumulated vibration, static, hiss, and squeak inherited from the multiple copies that have preceded the one now in the machine. Street noise picked up by the microphone continually rises up to engulf the speaking voice, redoubling the sonic jumble of horns, shouts, the rattles and pops of rusted exhaust pipes now buffeting the car. In the back seat, two friends joke and laugh together, their bodies pushed and pulled as the car proceeds through the congested alleyways, jerking, braking, jumping forward. Billboards advertising computer parts, soft drinks, and the latest films loom above the storefronts and crowded sidewalks. The driver hits the horn at a car attempting to cut in front of him, as the voice on the tape intones a Quranic verse on the inescapability of death: "Every soul tastes death . . ." (kullu nafs dha'iqa al-mawt). A wave of cries from the mosque assembly pierce through the background noise and the thick layer of reverb, the driver's lips lightly and inaudibly tracing the contours of the words "There is no God but the one God," as he accelerates ahead of the car seeking to pass him. One of the men in the back stops his conversation to comment: "That preacher must be Saudi. They're the ones who really know how to scare you." The recorded voice begins a series of supplications as the cab passengers go back to their previous conversation and the driver adjusts the volume knob: "May God lessen the death throes for us. May God light our graves. May God protect us on Judgment Day." The speakers rattle as the crowd roars "Amin" after each supplication. The taxi stops at the entrance to the 26th of July Bridge, named in celebration of Egypt's 1973 war with Israel, and the two passengers pay the driver and get out. Merging back into traffic, the driver heads for the onramp to the bridge that will take him to the upper-middle-class suburb of Muhandesin. As he approaches the ramp, the voice on the tape is asking "How will you feel when the grave closes tightly around you from all of the evil deeds you have done?" The bass line to a Michael Jackson hit sweeps in from the open window of a passing car and quickly fades away. "C'mon shaykh, get to the three questions," the driver implores as he accelerates, anxious for the scene of divine interrogation that he knows from experience will soon arrive. Heading over the bridge, he is still listening.

THIS BOOK IS A STUDY of a popular Islamic media form that has had a profound effect on the configuration of religion, politics, and community in the Middle East [see original publication]. As a key element in the technological scaffolding of what is called the Islamic Revival (*al-Sahwa al-Islamiyya*), the cassette sermon has become an omnipresent background of daily urban life in most Middle Eastern cities, accompanying and punctuating the mundane toils of men and women like the taxi driver whose journey through Cairo and the hereafter I began with above. As I will argue, the contribution of this aural medium to shaping the contemporary moral and political landscape of the Middle East lies not simply in its capacity to disseminate ideas or instill religious ideologies but in its effect on the human sensorium, on the affects, sensibilities, and perceptual habits of its vast audience. The soundscape produced through the circulation of this medium animates and sustains the substrate of sensory knowledges and embodied aptitudes undergirding a broad revival movement within contemporary Islam. From its inception in the twentieth century, this movement has centered on a critique of the existing structures of religious and secular authority. For those who participate in the movement, the moral and political direction of contemporary Muslim societies cannot be left to politicians, religious scholars, or militant activists but must be decided upon and enacted collectively by ordinary Muslims in the course of their normal daily activities. The notions of individual and collective responsibility that this movement has given rise to have come to be embodied in a wide array of institutions, media forms, and practices of public sociability. In doing so, they have changed the political geography of the Middle East in ways that have vast implications for the future of the region. This book examines the contribution of the cassette-recorded sermon to the revival movement and to the transformations it has engendered. Although the listening practices I explore inhabit a counter-history—counter to the modernist formations of politics and religion and the ideologies that sustain and legitimate them—this history nonetheless exerts forcible claims on the contemporary, and thus on the futures imaginable from its shores.

Islamic cassette sermons are commonly associated with the underworld of militants and radical preachers, a world quite distinct from one centered in the popular quarters of Cairo that I will describe in this book. Turn to any recent news item about a violent attack undertaken by Muslim radicals and chances are that there among the artifacts left behind by the perpetrators lies a taped sermon, inciting, propagandizing, working its insidious causality. "Bin Laden's Low-Tech Weapon," as a recent *New York Times* article dubs this media form, "well suited to underground political communication . . . easy to use and virtually impossible for governments to control" (Nunberg 2004). This menacing image of the cassette sermon as a symbol of Islamic fanaticism goes back to the 1979 Iranian Revolution, when the circulation of

Ayatollah Khomeini's recorded missives played a key role in the mobilizations leading up to the overthrow of the Shah (Mohammedi and Mohammedi 1994).[1] The Islamic cassette resurfaced again in 1993 at the trial of Shaykh Omar Abdul Rahman, the Egyptian cleric convicted of inciting and conspiring with the Muslim radicals who undertook the first attack on the World Trade Center. The prosecution relied heavily on Abdul Rahman's recorded sermons in making its case.[2] Since then, cassette sermons have appeared again and again among the personal effects of Muslim militants gathered up by investigators in the wake of an arrest or attack. "The cassette tapes tossed casually in a cardboard box would normally not arouse too much suspicion," an Australian journalist reports, "It was these recordings which the suicide bomber who detonated a massive car bomb outside the Australian Embassy last month and the members of his group listened to and learned from in the past year" (Wockner 2004). At once a tool of ideological indoctrination and a vehicle for the transmission of militant directives, cassettes, it would seem, are to fundamentalist Islam what the press was to the bourgeois public sphere of the European Enlightenment—its media form par excellence.

Scholars of contemporary Islam have also alerted us to the central role of the cassette sermon within fundamentalist or radical Islam. The following comment by a well-known investigator of Islamic militancy echoes popular journalistic accounts:

> Since Ayatollah Khomeini's movement in Iran in the mid-1970s, the cassette has played a crucial role in the spread, survival, and success of fundamentalist Islamic movements. Tapes have such an important role because in the absence of a Comintern-style hierarchical structure, they constitute a resilient web that holds together a plethora of local movements and groups, operating mostly within national borders. The constant flow of tapes in the area from Afghanistan to Morocco knits like-minded Muslims into a larger whole. Indeed, tapes even flow into Europe and North America.
>
> (Sivan 1995:13)

In this view, it is the cassette's capillary motion, its ability to proliferate beneath the radar of law enforcement, that has rendered this media form so useful to the task of international Islamic insurgency. The ominous web that cassette technology weaves— able to "flow," as this author warns, even across the borders of Europe and North America—recalls the hydra-headed image of al-Qaeda described by Western security agencies, with its loose network of hate-filled conspirators.

In this book I take issue with many of the assumptions and judgments through which the image of the militant or, to use more recent vocabulary, "the terrorist," has come to be sutured with the phenomenon of Islamic media and especially with the cassette sermon [see original publication]. Apart from the fact that the vast majority of these tapes do not espouse a militant message, listening to cassette sermons is a common and valued activity for millions of ordinary Muslims around the world, men and women who hold regular jobs, study at the university, send their kids to public schools, and worry about the future of their communities. As I will describe in the chapters that follow [see original publication], for almost all of those who listen to them, these tapes are not part of a program of radical mobilization but, instead, part of a complex ethical and political project whose scope and importance cannot be contained within the neat figure of the militant or terrorist. Islamic sermon tapes have helped craft and give expression to a religious sensibility moored in a set of ethical and social problems whose rationale deserves a serious engagement by anyone concerned with the future of Muslim societies or, for that matter, with the much-espoused goal of "promoting democracy" in the Middle East. To read the cassette sermon primarily as a technology of fundamentalism and militancy reduces the enormous complexity of the life world enabled by this medium, forcing it to fit into the narrow confines of a language of threat, fear, rejection, and irrationality.

This should not be taken to mean, of course, that these popular cassette media are devoid of political content. On the contrary, cassette sermons frequently articulate a fierce critique of the nationalist project, with its attendant lack of democracy and accountability among the ruling elites of the Muslim world. The form of public discourse within which this critique takes place, however, is not oriented toward militant political action or the overthrow of the state. Rather, such political commentary gives direction to a normative ethical project centered upon questions of social responsibility, pious comportment, and devotional practice. In addition, the styles of use that characterize this media form also bear the imprint of popular entertainment media and some listeners intersperse sermon and music tapes in their listening habits. These diverse strands that are conjoined in Islamic cassette media—the political, the ethical, and the aesthetic—at times sit in some tension with one another, provoking intense debate and contestation among their consumers about issues ranging from the appropriate use of such media to broader questions about the ethical and political bases upon which the future of the community should be established.

Much of the scholarly literature on contemporary Islam centers on the question, "Is the Islamic Revival movement compatible with democracy?" While I do discuss forms of public reason and critique that show a clear debt to democratic thinking and its institutional norms, my interest in these forms extends beyond the question of their relationship to that particular tradition of political thought. The line of investigation I pursue, in this regard, reflects my conviction that the analytical standpoint afforded by the notion of democracy is inadequate for grasping the articulations of politics, ethics, and religion in postcolonial contexts like Egypt, and for assessing the possibilities of social and political justice they may enfold. As scholars of postcolonialism have increasingly brought to our attention, the abstract principle of popular sovereignty stands in a complex and often contradictory relation to the norms and regulatory institutions of the modern nation-state—to the moral and political disciplines that Foucault refers to as technologies of governmentality.[3] Practices of democratic political participation cannot be understood solely by reference to the formal rights enjoyed by legally defined citizens, nor by reference to the democratic culture that such rights are understood to engender. The conditions of citizenship that allow for the development and exercise of democratic prerogatives also depend upon the techniques of social disciplines—the institutional networks of welfare, education, health, religion, and so on—through which the actual capacities of citizens are fashioned.[4] In this light, even to begin to think about what a democratic *practice* might look like in a context such as postcolonial Egypt requires careful attention to the complex and contingent linkages between discourses of collective agency and the specific forms of associational life, community, and authority within which those discourses are deployed.

The Politics of Sound

From the inception of the practice in the late 1960s and early 1970s, cassette-sermon audition has been an important and integral part of the Islamic Revival. While this movement encompasses a wide variety of phenomena, from political parties to underground militant organizations, in Egypt its broadest section has always remained grounded in grassroots efforts to revitalize Islamic forms of knowledge, pedagogy, comportment, and sociability.[5] As a result of this movement, many in Egypt from across the class spectrum, and particularly younger people, have increasingly found it important to deepen their knowledge of the Quran and the multiple disciplines it mediates, to participate in mosque study groups, to acquire competence in preaching and recitation techniques, and, more generally, to abide by the dictates of what they consider to be virtuous Muslim conduct in both their religious and nonreligious activities.

The effects of this movement are evident throughout Egypt but most strikingly and pervasively in the popular quarters of Cairo's lower-middle and lower classes, where a renewed concern with Islam is visible in everything from dress styles to mosque attendance to the prevalence of Islamic welfare organizations.[6] Indeed, networks of Islamic charitable, service, educational, and medical associations, many of them directly affiliated with local mosques, have increasingly proliferated in such popular quarters and have further enhanced the function of mosques as centers of neighborhood life. These developments have been accompanied by the creation of what might be called Islamic soundscapes, ways of reconfiguring urban space acoustically through the use of Islamic media forms. Rooted in this amalgam of forms of association, practice, learning, and sensibility, the Islamic Revival has exerted a profound effect on Egypt as well as other Middle Eastern societies over the last few decades. Its paradigmatic media form is the cassette sermon.

In Cairo, where I spent a year and a half exploring this common media practice, cassette-recorded sermons of popular Muslim preachers, or *khutaba'* (sing, *khatib*), have become a ubiquitous part of the contemporary social landscape. The sermons of well-known orators spill into the street from loudspeakers in cafes, the shops of tailors and butchers, the workshops of mechanics and TV repairmen; they accompany passengers in taxis, minibuses, and most forms of public transportation; they resonate from behind the walls of apartment complexes, where men and women listen alone in the privacy of their homes after returning home from the factory, while doing housework, or together with acquaintances from school or office, invited to hear the latest sermon from a favorite preacher. Outside most of the larger mosques, following Friday prayer, thriving tape markets are crowded with people looking for the latest sermon from one of Egypt's well-known *khutaba'* or a hard-to-find tape from one of Jordan's prominent mosque leaders. The popularity of sermon tapes has given public prominence to these orators that the Egyptian state, despite its attempts to silence such figures through rigid censorship policies, has been able to do little about.

During my stay in Egypt, I spent much of my time meeting both with the *khutaba'* who produced sermon tapes and with young people who listened to them on a regular basis. Ibrahim was one of the men who would often take time to listen to sermon tapes with me and explain their significance. A recent graduate of Cairo University now working for a small publishing company, Ibrahim had first become an enthusiast of sermon tapes while he was a student. He would often listen to them when he came home from work, either alone in his room or together with his younger sister and his parents. His sister, Huda, a university student herself at the time, also greatly appreciated cassette sermons and would frequently bring home new tapes she had borrowed from friends at school. As her brother had when he was a student, Huda participated in a study group at the university in which she and other students would sit and discuss current issues and events they considered germane to their lives as Muslim men and women. Like many of the young Egyptians who make up the backbone of the Islamic Revival, the siblings both condemned the violent tactics of Egypt's militant Islamic groups while agreeing with many of their social and political critiques. For both brother and sister, and many others like them, cassette sermons were at once entertaining, politically informative, educational, and ethically nourishing, a media form consonant with the challenge of living as a Muslim in today's world.

This book explores the practice of listening to such taped sermons and the forms of public life this practice serves to uphold in contemporary Egypt [see original publication]. In the popular neighborhoods of Cairo, sermon tapes are part of the acoustic architecture of a distinct moral vision, animating and sustaining the ethical sensibilities that enable ordinary Muslims to live in accord with what they consider to be God's will. Recorded and rerecorded, passing through worn-out electronics, bustling crowds, and noisy streets, the vocal performances resonate both within the sensorium of sensitive listeners and outside, around them and between them. In doing so, they create the sensory conditions of an emergent ethical and political lifeworld, with its specific patterns of behavior, sensibility, and practical reasoning. To call this lifeworld "fundamentalist," to chalk it up to the contortions of the religious mind in a secular age, misses the point of this ethicopolitical project. The reduction enacted by such terms blinds us to a variety of ambitions, goals, and aspirations, foremost among them the desire on the part of ordinary Muslims to live in accord with the demands of Islamic piety within a context of rapidly changing social, political, and technological conditions. As I show in chapter 4 [see original publication], this attempt entails the creation of new discursive forms for collectively arguing about and acting upon the conditions of social and political life. The emergent public arena articulated by the circulation of cassette-recorded sermons connects Islamic traditions of ethical discipline to practices of deliberation about the common good, the duties of Muslims in their status as national citizens, and the future of the greater Islamic community (the *umma*). These deliberative practices are not oriented toward *politics* as it is conventionally understood: their purpose is not to influence the formation of state policy or to mobilize voting blocs behind party platforms. Rather, the activities that constitute the public arena I describe are political in a way close to the sense Hannah

Arendt (1958) gives to the term: the activities of ordinary citizens who, through the exercise of their agency in contexts of public interaction, shape the conditions of their collective existence. As conceived by its participants, this arena constitutes that space of communal reflexivity and action understood as necessary for perfecting and sustaining the totality of practices upon which an Islamic society depends.

To explore this lifeworld requires that we confront the inadequacies of such binaries as moral/political, disciplinary/deliberative, and emotion/reason, that have shaped our normative understandings of both political life and the public sphere wherein aspects of that life are explicitly thematized and worked upon. Indeed, one of the central arguments of this book is that the affects and sensibilities honed through popular media practices such as listening to cassette sermons are as infrastructural to politics and public reason as are markets, associations, formal institutions, and information networks.[7] My analysis, in this sense, follows upon a growing recognition by scholars that the forms of thinking and reasoning that constitute our political discourses are profoundly indebted to evaluative dispositions outside the purview of consciousness, to what political theorist William Connolly refers to as "visceral modes of appraisal" (Connolly 1999). This book is a study of the contribution of a popular media practice to the fashioning of such modes of appraisal, and of the religious and political constellations this practice sustains within Egypt today [see original publication].

Subterranean Sounds

Within the modernist discourse on the ear, movements such as the one I discuss in this book [see original publication]—grounded in sensory practices unrepresentable and imperceptible within regnant constructions of public memory—constitute the noncontemporary within the contemporaneous. It is not surprising, therefore, that the dominant analysis of the Islamist movement either views it as a nostalgic gesture in the face of the psychological disorientation brought by modernization or as an attempt to give historical authenticity to a form of life without actual historical roots. When Muslims argue for the traditional Islamic status of the headscarf, Islamic conceptions of political pluralism, or the idea of an Islamic state, for example, the objective historian unmasks such claims as strategic moves within a modern politics of cultural authenticity, and thus as not really—historically—authentic (see, for example, Kepel 1993; al-Azmeh 1993; Roy 1993).[8] One paradoxical aspect of this argument, it might be noted, is that while cultural authenticity is often criticized as a reactionary form of modern politics, it is assumed that there is an *authentic* relation to the past (not nostalgic, invented, or mythological), and that Islamists are in some sense living falsely not to acknowledge it and adjust to its demands.[9]

One of the key difficulties encountered in complicating such a picture lies in what I consider to be an inadequate theorization of the senses within modernity and the extent to which our notion of tradition derives from a particular encoding and hierarchization of the senses that structures our experience of the past in accord with the precepts of secular historical consciousness. Can one speak of the ethical sensibilities cultivated by contemporary consumers of aural media without anachronistically resurrecting the nostalgic figure of the monastic listener? For the modern observer, one trained to be skeptical of the epistemological claims of the ear, such practices and the forms of life they inhabit must be recoded through the temporal figure of nostalgia and therefore interpreted as evidence of an alienated consciousness, a reactive gesture by those struggling to secure identity in a disenchanted and unstable world. Indeed, nostalgia is one of the terms by which secular forms of memory secure their privilege: in recoding nonsecular forms of memory as romantic sentimentality, the term secures the transparency and authority of secular historical practice. As the anthropologist Nadia Seremetakis notes, "Nostalgia, in the American sense, freezes the past in such a manner as to preclude it from any capacity for social transformation in the present, preventing the present from establishing a dynamic perceptual relationship to its history" (1994:4). Where such a dynamic relationship to the past is asserted, the skeptical analyst uncovers invention and fabrication.[10]

The historian Dipesh Chakrabarty describes how the methods of the discipline of history function to relegate certain forms of memory to the margins of modern historical consciousness:

> Some constructions and experiences of the past stay "minor" in the sense that their very incorporation into historical narratives converts them into pasts "of lesser importance" vis-à-vis dominant understandings of what constitutes fact and evidence (and hence vis-à-vis the underlying principle of rationality itself) in the practices of professional history. Such "minor" pasts are those experiences of the past that always have to be assigned to an "inferior" or "marginal" position as they are translated into the academic historian's language. These are pasts that are treated, to use an expression of Kant's, as instances of human "immaturity," pasts that do not prepare us for either democracy or citizenly practices because they are not based on the deployment of reason in public life.
>
> (2000:100–101)

The recoding and marginalization of these subjugated (or what Chakrabarty calls "minority") histories marks the historical discipline's insertion within modern juridical and bureaucratic modes of reason and the positivist epistemologies they deploy.[11] In writing against this evaluative stance, Chakrabarty argues that the historian's ability to historicize in this manner is, paradoxically, enabled by her own participation in nonmodern relationships to the past; it is the fact that much of her daily experience—generally relegated to the sphere of private life—does not accord with the protocols of secular historical consciousness that allows the historian to recognize nonmodern forms of life as such, even though such experience must be effaced in the moment of historicizing (2000:101). Chakrabarty's point may be read, I want to suggest, to imply that the historical time of the senses is not the same as that valorized by the social scientific criteria of the historian or the anthropologist. The senses are not a stable foundation upon which a singular and unassailable truth can be erected, as an empiricist epistemology would claim, but rather a space of indeterminacy, heterogeneity, and possibility. Both perceived objects and perceiving subjects are sensorially plural, enfolding a set of possibilities that take on a determinant but not final form in a moment of perceptual completion (Seremetakis 1994; see also

Benjamin 1969; Buck-Morss 1989). Modernity itself encompasses "plural ways of being in the world," forms of reason, memory, and experience grounded in histories other than those authorized by dominant secular rationalities. Modernity is not a functionally integrated totality governed by a singular overarching logic but rather a constellation of practices and technologies contingently connected within discontinuous formations of power.[12]

Scholars attentive to the heterogeneous temporalities of modernity have begun to chart an alternative history of the senses, one in which, not surprisingly, listening emerges as an important site of inquiry, pervading the modern in both overt and unacknowledged ways.[13] I want to briefly trace three moments in this account of listening that are of particular relevance to my analysis of cassette sermons and the forms of self, sociability, and politics they have helped create in contemporary Egypt. The first concerns the prevalence of "subterranean" listening practices within modern sensory landscapes: entwinings of sound and subject that are often ignored or misrecognized within modern spaces due to our dominant sensory epistemologies. Steven Connor, one of the most original scholars working on the topic of the modern sensorium, argues that within modern cities, often understood as spaces of intense visuality, we rely on a vocal-auditory consciousness to orient ourselves and find our way around. In his reading of such modernist classics as Joyce's *Ulysses* and Woolf's *Mrs. Dalloway,* Connor notes: "The unsteadiness of the ways of looking and seeing characteristic of city life—the glance or the glimpse rather than the sustained gaze—goes along with a sense of shifting and saturated space of which the plural, permeable ear can evidently make more sense than the eye" (1997:210; on this point, also see Jay 1994). Connor's work throws into question the assumption that listening cannot find a place for itself within the cacophony of the urban soundscape. Much of our capacity, he argues, to navigate the city, to enjoy its pleasures and be attentive to its dangers, relies crucially on subterranean forms of auditory knowledge and skill frequently ignored by analysts of urban life. This work alerts us to the way traditions of sound and listening have been articulated in changing and unpredictable ways with the constellation of sensory aptitudes and practices inhabiting contemporary cultural-historical formations, as an often unrecognized undercurrent emerging into and out of perceptual experience.

The epigraph to this chapter highlights the aurally saturated urban environment within which the practice of cassette-sermon listening takes place. If the solitary listener ensconced in the relative silence of his home represents one end of the spectrum of contexts within which this practice takes place, then the taxi driver struggling through the roar of downtown Cairo represents the other. In chapter 4 [see original publication], I address listening as it is practiced in such conditions of sonic intensity. Played in public transport, in shops, garages, and cafes, sermon tapes reconfigure the urban soundscape, imbuing it with an aural unconscious from which ethical reasoning and action draw sustenance. In other words, beyond their utility as a distraction from toil, such media create the intensifying sensory background for the forms of social and political life that the Islamic Revival has sought to promote and extend. Sermon tapes enable their listeners to orient themselves within the modern city *as a space of moral action,* with its characteristic challenges, threats, and daily problems. The style of listening that tape consumers bring to the practice render this media form something very different from a popular distraction or an instrument of religious propaganda, a difference, I argue, that has profound implications for collective life within contemporary Egypt.

A second key moment in this counterhistory (aimed at displacing an ocular-centric account of modernity) concerns the place of auditory practices within techniques of self-fashioning, most notably psychoanalysis. In the elaboration of Freud's call for a "calm, quiet attentiveness—of 'evenly hovering attention'" on the part of the analyst (Freud [1912] 1958:118), listening, with its therapeutic and transformative capacities, acquires its modern disciplinary function. Listening establishes the conditions of intersubjectivity, of the transference, of affect and unconscious, enabling the reorganization of psychic elements by the analysand (see Stein 1999).[14] For these reasons, the practice has remained a subject of inquiry and experimentation within the broader field of psychology. The philosopher and psychologist Peter Wilberg, for example, elaborates a notion of therapeutic audition—what he terms "maieutic listening"—on the model of musical sensibilities:

> The medium of maieutic listening is not the airy medium of words but the fluid medium of feeling tone—the tones of silence that communicate "through the word," radiate from the listener and underlie all verbal communication. These may or may not be echoed in the tone of a person's language or their tone of voice. Rather, speech itself may be regarded as a type of song, one that provides a more "tuned in" expression of the silent music of the soul—the music of feeling tone.
>
> (2004:8)

Not unlike psychoanalysis, as I will show, cassette-sermon audition is also a technique of self-fashioning predicated on the therapeutic capacities of listening, albeit one elaborated in ethical (rather than psychological) terms and in relation to a theologically based form of reasoning. Wilberg's attention to the affective and intersubjective dimensions of listening, as captured in his notion of "feeling tone," bears a distinct resemblance to the agential and sensorially rich form of listening practiced by those I worked with in Cairo. Of particular relevance is his understanding of communication not as the transmission of thought from the speaker to the listener through the medium of words but as a collective performance, founded upon an affective dynamic for which both the speaker and the listener are responsible. In chapter 2 [see original publication], I will flesh this out by exploring the structure of affect relevant to sermon audition and to the forms of public speech and sociability promoted by the Islamic Revival.

The last aspect of the modern ear that I want to address concerns the important role that technologies of listening—the gramophone, the telephone, the radio, and the tape recorder among them—have played in the fashioning of modern subjectivity.[15] As the religious historian Leigh Eric Schmidt has recently shown, auditory technologies were essential to the formation of the sensory dispositions and aptitudes characteristic of a modern secular subject (2000). Schmidt's book provides an account of the attenuation of what, up through the seventeenth and eighteenth centuries, had been the commonplace Christian experience of hearing God's direct speech, an account centered not on the familiar tropes of disenchantment and the triumph of reason but on auditory discipline. The silencing of God's voice was achieved, Schmidt argues, through a retraining of the ear, one part of a broader disciplinary undertaking aimed at educating the senses in the service of polite sociability, civic virtue, and scientific knowledge.

Emerging in the seventeenth century, the field of acoustics invented by Francis Bacon and his contemporaries was profoundly influenced by pursuits in natural magic and the hermetic traditions revived during the Renaissance. The development of auditory technologies was therefore often driven by an interest in the illusionist effects of natural magic, such as talking statues, speaking trumpets, and the arts of ventriloquism. By the eighteenth century, demonstrations of the technological means by which voices could be projected across distances and located within inanimate objects were increasingly used to undermine claims to divine communication: oracular voices, the whispering of demons, the ringing of invisible bells—all long a part of Christian experience—were unmasked as the effects of artificial contrivances cunningly deployed by priests to deceive and control their followers (Schmidt 2000:78–134). As Schmidt shows, the revealing of priestly power in acoustic illusionism provided the basis for a natural history of religion. Importantly, such demonstrations, performed by natural philosophers, magicians, and ventriloquists, rapidly became a popular form of entertainment, one that served to cultivate the pleasure of auditory suspicion. Reproduced in spectacles, carnivals, and exhibits throughout Europe and North America, these events were meant to educate audiences in the "deceits of the senses" and the dangers to which the unrefined ear remained an heir (Schmidt 2000:101–24).

Schmidt's work emphasizes the important relationship between technologies of auditory discipline and the historical redefinition and repositioning of religion central to the emergence of secular modernity. As he persuasively demonstrates, the technological extension and attunement of the ear have provided the conditions for modernity's unique forms of reason and experience. In this book [see original publication], I extend Schmidt's analytic to the Egyptian context by exploring the way new media practices have helped bring about the discursive relocation of Islamic traditions within Egyptian social, political, and religious life. Schmidt's historical work provides more than just a useful point of comparison for such an inquiry: the techniques and technologies of modern aurality whose development Schmidt traces in the early-modern American context have been a key component within the nationalist project in postcolonial societies like Egypt. As I describe in chapter 2, radio—an important precursor of the cassette and one that powerfully shaped its context of reception—was perhaps the single most important technology in the effort to mold a national citizenry throughout much of the twentieth century. The impact of sermon tapes on the perceptual habits of their vast audience, I argue, has produced a unique religiopolitical configuration that simultaneously compliments and challenges both the secular-bureaucratic rationalities of the state and Egypt's longstanding institutions of religious authority. My discussion of styles of cassette use in chapter 3 centers on how the functional possibilities peculiar to the cassette medium (such as rewind, pause, and home duplication) affect the sensory habits acquired in the course of listening practices.

Another aspect of Schmidt's account that carries great relevance for my own analysis lies in his exploration of religious responses to the secular retraining of the ear. As Schmidt relates, the Enlightenment assault on the ear did not result in a complete victory by any means. Swedenborgians, Methodists, Shakers, Mormons, and others sought to counter the charge of ocular deception in various ways— scientifically, theologically, as well as practically—through an ongoing emphasis on the disciplines of prayer, meditation, and spiritual listening that attuned the ear to divine sound. Even though the claim to hear voices from beyond, from the early nineteenth century on, would never free itself from the threat posed by the Enlightenment judgment of the ear's propensity for illusion, voices continue to be heard. One of the critical interventions of the Islamic Revival movement, in this regard, has been precisely an attempt to sustain certain virtues of the ear in the face of their threatened dissolution or obsolescence, an attempt carried out, in part, through the creation of new forms of social and political engagement consonant with the practice of such auditory virtues. Through these efforts, forms of sensory memory and experience pushed to the margins of daily life by the dominant perceptual regime have been renewed and redirected to meet a set of present challenges.

Notes

1. Michel Foucault, in a series of articles on the Iranian revolution written for the Italian newspaper *Corriere della Sera,* also noted the important role of the cassette in enabling the mass uprising of ordinary Iranians: "If the shah is about to fall, it will be due largely to the cassette tape. It is the tool par excellence of counterinformation" (2005:219).

2. For a discussion of this case and the significance of Abdul Rahman's recorded sermons for the prosecution, see the articles by Joseph Fried (1995) and Chris Hedges (1993) in the *New York Times.*

3. For recent works that address the contingent and contradictory aspects of the unfolding horizon of democratic politics in postcolonial societies, see Partha Chatterjee, *Politics of the Governed* (2004); Dipesh Chakrabarty, *Provincializing Europe* (2000); Thomas Blom Hansen, *The Saffron Wave* (1999); and David Scott, *Conscripts of Western Civilization* (2005).

4. Burchell has pointed to this lacuna within liberal scholarship regarding the place of discipline in preparing the citizen for public life: "What is altogether missing from this kind of controversy [over the conditions of political participation] is a sense of the citizen as a social creation, as an historical persona, whose characteristics have been developed in particular times and places through the activities of social discipline, both externally on the part of governments and internally by techniques of self-discipline and self formation" (1995:549). Burchell's own work focuses on how early-modern forms of civility and public life were understood to depend upon Christian techniques of ethical discipline, enacted through education and institutions of social discipline (e.g., police, schools, factories), as well as through techniques of self-fashioning promoted in manuals and treatises. In this book (see original reading), I take up Burchell's suggestion through an exploration of the place of ethical discipline in creating the nondiscursive background of sentiments and habits upon which contemporary forms of Islamic public deliberation depend.

5. Useful discussions of this dimension of the Islamic Revival in Egypt can be found in Baker 2003; Mahmood 2006; Salvatore 2001a, 2001b. For works focusing outside the Egyptian context and relevant to the dimensions of contemporary Islam that I explore here, see Asad 1993, 2003; Burgat and Dowell 1997; Bowen 1993; Hefner 2000.

6. Two of the neighborhoods in Cairo where I worked extensively, Imbaba and Bulaq Dukrur, are composed primarily of lower-income families. In contrast, Ain Shams and Zaytun, two other quarters I came to know well, encompass a mix of both middle- and lower-middle-class homes.

7.   There is a growing body of literature addressing the contribution of affect to politics. Among the scholars whose insights into the complex relationship between affect and political reasoning have most shaped my own thinking, see Asad 2003; Chakrabarty 2000; Connolly 2002; Deleuze 1988; Massumi 2002; Seremetakis 1994.

8.   For a fully developed critique of this position, see Hirschkind 2001.

9.   Seremetakis notes, and criticizes, a similar form of analysis in the context of historical writings on Greece: "The notions of authenticity and inauthenticity are symbiotic concepts that equally repress and silence non-contemporaneous and discordant cultural experiences and sensibilities. Thus the modernist critic would look at Greek society and dismiss any residues and incongruities emanating from the pre-modern as both romantic and invented. In both cases, static impositions of the polarity authentic/inauthentic led to the dismissal of important discontinuous cultural systems and sensibilities that have been repositioned within the modern as non-synchronous elements" (1994:17).

10.   See Hobsbawm and Ranger 1992 for one influential account of this kind of reasoning.

11.   In *The Names of History: On the Poetics of Knowledge* (1994), Jacques Rancière examines some of the narrative tropes by which forms of religious reasoning are effaced in accord with the precepts of secular history. His specific focus is on some of the classical texts of the historians of the Annales School.

12.   Even the objects, methods, and forms of practical reason within the natural sciences, as historians of science have long asserted, are, to a certain extent, incommensurable from one field to the next (Hacking 1983; Rouse 1987; Latour 1993).

13.   For studies into modern listening practices, see Bull and Back 2003; Corbin 1998; Drobnick 2004; Erlmann 2004; Kahn 1992; Smith 1999.

14.   As the historian of media Douglas Kahn notes, the ability of sound to pervade, encompass, and integrate—in contrast to the distance and separation established by vision—made it "the privileged figure of sensory interchange" within romantic thought: "Wherever sound occurred, it was always manifested elsewhere, or other things were manifested through it; a sound had no autonomy but was always relational, being somewhere or something else, a constant deflection that ultimately stretched out to spiritually organize everything from essence to cosmos, always ringing with the voice and music" (1992:15).

15.   For works on the role of auditory technologies in extending human capacities of sensory experience and refashioning modern soundscapes, see Corbin 1998; Kahn 1992; Smith 1999.

References

Anderson, Benedict. 1991. *Imagined Communities: Reflections on the Origin and Spread of Nationalism*. New York: Verso.

Arendt, Hannah. 1958. *The Human Condition*. Chicago: University of Chicago Press.

Asad, Talal. 1993. *Genealogies of Religion: Discipline and Reasons of Power in Christianity and Islam*. Baltimore, Md.: Johns Hopkins University Press.

— 2003. *Formations of the Secular: Christianity, Islam, Modernity*. Stanford, Calif.: Stanford University Press.

al-Azmeh, Aziz. 1993. *Islams and Modernities*. New York: Verso.

Baker, Raymond. 2003. *Islam Without Fear: Egypt and the New Islamists*. Cambridge, Mass.: Harvard University Press.

Benjamin, Walter. 1969. *Illuminations*. Ed. Hannah Arendt. Trans. Harry Zohn. New York: Schocken Books.

Bowen, John. 1993. *Muslims Through Discourse: Religion and Ritual in Gayo Society*. Princeton, N.J.: Princeton University Press.

Buck-Morss, Susan. 1989. *The Dialectics of Seeing: Walter Benjamin and the Arcades Project.* Cambridge, Mass.: MIT Press.

Bull, Michael. 2000. *Sounding Out the City: Personal Stereos and the Management of Everyday Life.* Oxford: Berg Press.

Bull, Michael, and Les Back. 2003. *The Auditory Cultures Reader.* Oxford: Berg Press.

Burchell, David. 1995. "The Attributes of Citizens: Virtue, Manners, and the Activity of Citizenship." *Economy and Society* 24 (4): 540–58

Burgat, Francois, and William Dowell. 1997. *The Islamic Movement in North Africa.* New ed. Austin: University of Texas at Austin Press.

Chakrabarty, Dipesh. 2000. *Provincializing Europe: Postcolonial Thought and Historical Difference.* Princeton, N.J.: Princeton University Press.

Chamberlain, Michael. 1994. *Knowledge and Social Practice in Medieval Damascus, 1190–1350.* Cambridge: Cambridge University Press.

Chatterjee, Partha. 2004. *The Politics of the Governed: Reflections on Popular Politics in Most of the World.* New York: Columbia University Press.

Connolly, William. 1999. *Why I Am Not a Secularist.* Minneapolis: University of Minnesota Press.

—. 2002. *Neuropolitics: Thinking Culture, Speed.* Minneapolis: University of Minnesota Press.

Connor, Steven. 1997. "The Modern Auditory 'I.'" In *Rewriting the Self: Histories from the Renaissance to the Present,* ed. Roy Porter, 203–23. New York: Routledge.

Corbin, Alain. 1998. *Village Bells: Sound and Meaning in the Nineteenth-Century French Countryside.* New York: Columbia University Press.

Deleuze, Gilles. 1988. *Bergsonism.* Trans. Hugh Tomlinson and Barbara Habberjam. New York: Zone Books.

Drobnick, James, ed. 2004. *Aural Cultures: Sound Art.* Toronto: YYZ Books.

Erlmann, Veit. 2004. *Hearing Cultures: Essays on Sound, Listening and Modernity.* Oxford: Berg Press.

Foucault, Michel. 2005. "The Challenge of the Opposition." In *Foucault and the Iranian Revolution: Gender and the Seductions of Islam,* by Janet Afary and Kevin B. Anderson, 213–20. Chicago: University of Chicago Press.

Freud, S. [1912] 1958. "Recommendations to Physicians Practising Psychoanalysis." In *Complete Psychological Works.* Standard ed. 12:109–20. London: Hogarth Press.

Fried, Joseph P. 1995. "Closing Arguments Start Tuesday in Terror Bomb Trial." *New York Times,* September 3.

Greene, Paul D. 1999. "Sound Engineering in a Tamil Village: Playing Audio Cassettes as Devotional Performance." *Ethnomusicology* 43 (3): 459–89.

Habermas, Jurgen. 1989. *The Structural Transformation of the Public Sphere.* Cambridge, Mass.: MIT Press.

Hacking, Ian. 1983. *Representing and Intervening: Introductory Topics in the Philosophy of Natural Science.* New York: Cambridge University Press.

Hansen, Thomas Blom. 1999. *The Saffron Wave: Democracy and Hindu Nationalism in Modern India.* Princeton, N.J.: Princeton University Press.

Hedges, Christopher. 1993. "A Cry of Islamic Fury, Taped in Brooklyn for Cairo." *New York Times,* January 7.

Hefner, Robert W. 2000. *Civil Islam: Muslims and Democratization in Indonesia.* Princeton, N.J.: Princeton University Press.

Hertz, Robert. 1909. *Death and the Right Hand.* Glencoe, Ill: The Free Press.

Hirschkind, Charles. 2001. "Tradition, Myth, and Historical Fact in Contemporary Islam." *ISIM Newsletter* 8:18.

Hobsbawm, Eric, and Terence Ranger, eds. 1992. *The Invention of Tradition.* Cambridge: Cambridge University Press.

Jay, Martin. 1994. *Downcast Eyes: The Denigration of Vision in Twentieth-Century French Thought.* Berkeley: University of California Press.

Kahn, Douglas. 1992. "Introduction: Histories of Sound Once Removed." In *Wireless Imagination,* ed. Douglas Kahn and Gregory Whitehead, 2–29. Cambridge, Mass.: MIT Press.

Kepel, Gilles. 1993. *Muslim Extremism in Egypt: The Prophet and the Pharaoh.* Berkeley: University of California Press.

Khalif, Abdul-Rahman. 1986. *Kayfa takun khatiban.* Mecca: Da'wat al-haqq.

Latour, Bruno. 1993. *We Have Never Been Modern.* Cambridge, Mass.: Harvard University Press.

Mahmood, Saba. 2006. "Secularism, Hermeneutics, Empire: The Politics of Islamic Reformation." *Public Culture* 18 (2): 323–47.

Manuel, Peter. 1993. *Cassette Culture: Popular Music and Technology in North India.* Chicago: University of Chicago Press.

Massumi, Brian. 2002. *Parables for the Virtual: Movement, Affect, Sensation.* Durham, N.C.: Duke University Press.

Mohammedi, Annabelle, and Ali Mohammedi. 1994. *Small Media, Big Revolution.* Minneapolis: University of Minnesota Press.

Nunberg, Geoffrey. 2004. "Bin Laden's Low-Tech Weapon." *New York Times,* April 18.

Ong, Walter. 1982. *Orality and Literacy: The Technologization of the Word.* London: Methuen Press.

Rancière, Jacques. 1994. *The Names of History: On the Poetics of Knowledge.* Trans. H. Melehy. Minneapolis: University of Minnesota Press.

Rouse, Joseph. 1987. *Knowledge and Power: Toward a Political Philosophy of Science.* Ithaca, N.Y.: Cornell University Press.

Roy, Olivier. 1996. *The Failure of Political Islam.* Cambridge, Mass.: Harvard University Press.

Salvatore, Armando. ed. 2001a. *Muslim Traditions and Modern Techniques of Power.* Münster: Lit Verlag.

—. 2001b. "Mustafa Mahmud: A Paradigm of Public Islamic Entrepreneurship?" In *Muslim Traditions and Modern Techniques of Power,* ed. A. Salvatore, 211–23. Münster: Lit Verlag.

Schmidt, Leigh Eric. 2000. *Hearing Things: Religion, Illusion, and the American Enlightenment.* Cambridge, Mass.: Harvard University Press.

Schulze, Reinhard. 1987. "Mass Culture and Islamic Cultural Production in Nineteenth-Century Middle East." In *Mass Culture, Popular Culture, and Social Life in the Middle East,* ed. G. Stauth and S. Zubaida. Boulder, Colo.: Westview Press.

Scott, David. 2005. *Conscripts of Modernity: The Tragedy of Colonial Enlightenment.* Durham, N.C.: Duke University Press.

Seremetakis, C. Nadia, ed. 1994. *The Senses Still: Perception and Memory as Material Culture in Modernity.* Boulder, Colo.: Westview Press.

Sivan, Emmanuel. 1995. "Eavesdropping on Radical Islam." *Middle East Quarterly* 2 (1): 13–24.

Smith, Bruce. 1999. *The Acoustic World of Early Modern England: Attending to the O-Factor.* Chicago: Chicago University Press.

Stein, Alexander. 1999. "Well-Tempered Bagatelles—a Mediation on Listening in Psychoanalysis and Music." *American Imago* 56 (4): 387–416.

Taussig, Michael. 1993. *Mimesis and Alterity: A Particular History of the Senses.* London: Routledge.

Warner, Michael. 1990. *The Letters of the Republic: Publication and the Public Sermon in Eighteenth-Century America.* Cambridge, Mass.: Harvard University Press.

Wilberg, Peter. 2004. "Charging the Question: Listening, Questioning, and the Counseling Dialogue." http://www.meaningofdepression.com/Charging%20 The%20Question.doc.

Wockner, Cindy. 2004. "Converting Good Men into Killers." *Daily Telegraph* (Sydney), October 9

Chapter 7

Steve Goodman

THE ONTOLOGY OF VIBRATIONAL FORCE

That humming background sound is ancient—the ringing of a huge bell. Exploding into a mass of intensely hot matter, pulsing out vast sound waves, contracting and expanding the matter, heating where compressed, cooling where it was less dense. This descending tone parallels the heat death of the universe, connecting all the discrete atoms into a vibrational wave. This cosmic background radiation is the echo of the big bang.

OUTLINING THE AFFECTIVE MICROPOLITICS of sonic warfare demands a specifically tuned methodology. Drawing from philosophy, cultural studies, physics, biology, fiction, and military and musical history, an ontology of vibrational force can be pieced together that traverses disciplines.[1] An ontology of vibrational force delves below a philosophy of sound and the physics of acoustics toward the basic processes of entities affecting other entities. Sound is merely a thin slice, the vibrations audible to humans or animals. Such an orientation therefore should be differentiated from a phenomenology of sonic effects centered on the perceptions of a human subject, as a ready-made, interiorized human center of being and feeling. While an ontology of vibrational force exceeds a philosophy of sound, it can assume the temporary guise of a sonic philosophy, a sonic intervention into thought, deploying concepts that resonate strongest with sound/noise/music culture, and inserting them at weak spots in the history of Western philosophy, chinks in its character armor where its dualism has been bruised, its ocularcentrism blinded.

The theoretical objective here resonates with Kodwo Eshun in *More Brilliant Than the Sun* when he objects to cultural studies approaches in which "theory always comes to Music's *rescue*. The organization of sound interpreted historically, politically, socially. Like a headmaster, theory teaches today's music a thing or two about life. It subdues music's ambition, reins it in, restores it to its proper place."[2] Instead, if they are not already, we place theory under the dominion of sonic affect, encouraging a conceptual mutation. Sound comes to the rescue of thought rather than the inverse, forcing it to vibrate, loosening up its organized or petrified body. As Eshun prophetically wrote at the end of the twentieth century, "Far from needing theory's help, music today is already *more* conceptual than at any point this century, pregnant with thought probes waiting to be activated, switched on, misused."[3]

An ontology of vibrational force objects to a number of theoretical orientations. First, the linguistic imperialism that subordinates the sonic to semiotic registers is rejected for forcing sonic media to merely communicate meaning, losing sight of the more fundamental expressions of their material potential as vibrational surfaces, or oscillators.

Despite being endlessly inspired by intensive confrontation with bass frequencies, neither should an ontology of vibrational force be misconceived as either a naive physicalism in which all vibrational affect can be reduced scientifically. Such a reductionist materialism that merely reduces the sonic to a quantifiable objectivity is inadequate in that it neglects incorporeal affects. A concern for elementary vibrations must go beyond their quantification in physics into primary frequencies. On the other hand, the phenomenological anthropocentrism of almost all musical and sonic analysis, obsessed with individualized, subjective feeling, denigrates the vibrational nexus at the altar of human audition, thereby neglecting the agency distributed around a vibrational encounter and ignoring the nonhuman participants of the nexus of experience.

Rather, it is a concern for potential vibration and the abstract rhythmic relation of oscillation, which is key. What is prioritized here is the in-between of oscillation, the vibration of vibration, the virtuality of the tremble. Vibrations always exceed the actual entities that emit them. Vibrating entities are always entities out of phase with themselves. A vibratory nexus exceeds and precedes the distinction between subject and object, constituting a mesh of relation in which discreet entities prehend each other's vibrations. Not just amodal, this vibrational anarchitecture, it will be suggested, produces the very division between subjective and objective, time and space.

If this ontology of vibrational force can help construct a conception of a politics of frequency, then it must go beyond the opposition between a celebration of the jouissance of sonic physicality and the semiotic significance of its symbolic composition or content. But enough negative definitions.

If affect describes the ability of one entity to change another from a distance, then here the mode of affection will be understood as vibrational. In *The Ethics,* Spinoza describes an ecology of movements and rest, speeds and slownesses, and the potential of entities to affect and be affected.[4] This ecology will be constructed as a vectorial field of "affectiles" (affect + projectile), or what William James refers to as pulsed vectors of feeling. As an initiation of a politics of frequency, it resonates with the ballistics of the battlefield as acoustic force field described by the futurists. This vectorial field of sonic affectiles is aerodynamic, but it can also be illuminated by rhythmic models of liquid instability that constitute a kind of abstract vorticism.

This vibrational ontology begins with some simple premises. If we subtract human perception, everything moves. Anything static is so only at the level of perceptibility. At the molecular or quantum level, everything is in motion, is vibrating. Equally, objecthood, that which gives an entity duration in time, makes it endure, is an event irrelevant of human perception. All that is required is that an entity be felt as an object by another entity. All entities are potential media that can feel or whose vibrations can be felt by other entities. This is a realism, albeit a weird, agitated, and nervous one. An ontology of vibrational force forms the backdrop to the affective agency of sound systems (the sonic nexus), their vibrational ontology (rhythmanalysis), and their modes of contagious propagation (audio virology). In its primary amodality and secondary affinity to the sonic, a discussion of vibrational ecologies also helps counter ocularcentric (modeled on vision as dominant sensory modality) conceptions of cyberspace, contributing to a notion of virtual space that cuts across analog and digital domains.

This ontology is concerned primarily with the texturhythms of matter, the patterned physicality of a musical beat or pulse, sometimes imperceptible, sometimes, as cymatics shows, in some sensitive media, such as water or sand, visible. While it can be approached from an array of directions, the ontology of vibrational force will be explored here by three disciplinary detours: philosophy, physics, and the aesthetics of digital sound. In each, the stakes are fundamental. Philosophically, the question of vibrational rhythm shoots right to the core of an ontology of things and processes and the status of (dis)continuities between them. In physics, the status of the rhythms of change, the oscillation between movement and rest, plays out in the volatile, far-from-equilibrium zones of turbulent dynamics. While the modeling of turbulence has become the computational engineering problem par excellence for control, within the domain of digital sound design, the generation of microsonic turbulence by the manipulation of molecular rhythms accessible only through the mesh of the digital has become a key aesthetic and textural concern. Each of these fields will be mined to construct a transdisciplinary foundation to the concept of sonic warfare and its deployments of vibrational force.

Notes

1. It attempts to retain the exactness of concepts while leaving them vulnerable, open enough to resonate in unpredictable fashion outside of their home discipline. As Brian Massumi has argued, such an approach, for example, forces cultural studies to become vulnerable to the effects of scientific concepts, compelling change to the degree that culture is (as if it ever was not) subject to the forces of nature. He calls such a method, following Deleuze and Guattari, *machinic materialism. Machinic* designates not a technological fetishism but rather a preoccupation with rhythmic relation, process, connection, and trade. But it is also inflected by Baruch Spinoza's ethology, Alfred North Whitehead's process philosophy, and William James's pragmatist radical empiricism.
2. Kodwo Eshun, *More Brilliant Than the Sun* (London: Quartet, 1998), p. 4.
3. Ibid., p. 3.
4. B. Spinoza, *The Ethics* (Indianapolis, Ind.: Hackett, 1992).

Chapter 8

Mara Mills

HEARING AIDS AND THE HISTORY OF ELECTRONICS MINIATURIZATION

I N THE APRIL 1965 ISSUE OF *Electronics,* Gordon Moore announced an exponential increase in the number of components that could be "crammed" onto integrated circuits (ICs). This ongoing small-scale process, he predicted, would result in a corresponding acceleration of technological breakthroughs in computing, medicine, and communications. "The object," Moore explained, is "to miniaturize electronics equipment to include increasingly complex electronic functions in limited space with minimum weight."[1] Smaller parts meant smaller equipment as well as the promise of increased reliability and processing speed. Moore's law famously became a self-fulfilling prophecy, a prescription for his company (Intel) and the rest of the microelectronics industry to double the number of components on a single chip every one to two years.[2]

Although Moore dated miniaturization to the development of integrated electronics in the 1950s, other engineers and historians have located the origins of the phenomenon in discrete components. In *Crystal Fire: The Invention of the Transistor and the Birth of the Information Age,* Michael Riordan and Lillian Hoddeson track what they call the "relentless progress of miniaturization" following the 1948 invention of the transistor.[3] To the contrary, Eric Hintz claims that the "button" mercury battery preceded the transistor and "was just as important, if not more so, for the progress of miniaturization."[4] In 1961, James Nall of Fairchild Semiconductor insisted that "printed electronic circuits and subminiature tubes encouraged our modern day electronic revolution"—he defined miniaturization as "a media in which there is a high degree of order and efficiency."[5] That same year, George Senn and Rudolph Riehs of the US Army agreed that "the philosophy of miniaturization" took hold during World War II, as subminiature vacuum tubes began to be adopted for a range of devices.[6]

In fact, the language and ideals of miniaturization can be traced to the first decade of the 20th century, just prior to the development of electronics. In philosophy and literary studies, Gaston Bachelard and Susan Stewart describe the *miniature* as a universal aesthetic and perceptual category, characterized by cuteness and charm, manipulability and control.[7] Doubtless, electronic miniaturization shares some of these qualities; however, it is historically framed by the modern industrial ideals of efficiency, rationalization, mechanical reproduction, mobility, individualism (and the rising interest in "personal" technology), and global communication.[8] And as Nall indicates, the phenomenon cannot be understood by looking at discrete components; it is a theory of infrastructure for electronic media. The interconnections between components have been miniaturized in conjunction with the components themselves; the steady increase in circuit complexity was always tied to new methods for compact assembly.[9]

Today, Moore's law is frequently reduced to the "prediction that the speed of computers will double every year or two."[10] Processing speed—due to number of transistors and their proximity to one another—was a relative latecomer to the "philosophy of miniaturization," which slowly accumulated features, starting with small size, and eventually including density, ruggedness, reliability, reduced power requirements and decreased production costs. In 1965, moreover, Moore had anticipated transformations across electronics quite broadly, from computing to telephone systems to radar.

"Personal portable communications equipment"—one of Moore's forecasts—predates computing and in many respects facilitated the emergence of microelectronics.[11] The hearing aid—the first such "personal portable" device—was a key site for component innovation during the first half of the 20th century. Many histories of microelectronics emphasize military demand beginning in World War II.[12] Yet as Michael Brian Schiffer has demonstrated, the interwar consumer market for portable radios fed components into military communications.[13] "Only the hearing aid"—which began to be miniaturized as early as 1900—"drove miniaturization harder."[14] In the opening decades of the 20th century, subminiature vacuum tubes originated in the hearing aid industry, as did strategies for compact assembly and the "wearability" of electronic devices.

Ross Bassett has described Moore's law as "technological trajectory," a focusing mechanism that "took advantage of an existing technological base and developed with relentless incrementalism."[15] Hearing aids were critical to the establishment of this base. Before the personal computer or other personal electronics were obvious commodities—and before reliable production techniques had made miniaturization economical—hearing aids incubated the technique and the "philosophy" of miniaturization.[16] Hearing aids were always "personal"—tools for daily life that were carried on the body and intimate to an individual user.

During World War II, Handie-Talkies and other lightweight electronics equipment for military use became crucial to component miniaturization (although they arguably did not require the drastic size reduction demanded by hearing aid users). Technologies developed during the war—such as the button battery and printed circuit—later made their first commercial appearances in hearing aids, as would the transistor and IC. With its relatively simple circuitry, the postwar hearing aid served as a testbed for mass production techniques, component longevity, and consumer interest in miniaturized products.[17] It also served as a standard of reference for other industries interested in miniaturization.[18]

New components could be introduced to this "luxury" consumer product with little regard to increases in cost. Although demographic trends (and methods) have varied across the 20th century, today the National Institute on Deafness and other Communication Disorders (NIDCD) maintains that nearly 30 million Americans have either permanent hearing loss or deafness.[19] This broad statistic includes members of Deaf culture who use sign language as well as hard of hearing individuals who experience their hearing loss as an impairment. Approximately one in five wears a hearing aid—a fact attributable to personal preference, device performance, social stigma, and cost.[20] Throughout the 20th and 21st centuries, hearing aids have only rarely been covered by health insurance. Lack of regulation, outright corruption, and the willingness of well-off (or occasionally desperate) customers have led to persistent overpricing of these devices.[21]

Beyond portability, the predominant trend in hearing aid design has always been invisibility, which propelled extreme miniaturization of components and assembly, even in the absence of immediate functional or economic gains.[22] The paradox of hearing aids is that they are designed to rehabilitate an invisible impairment, yet the devices themselves visibly mark and even socially disable their wearers. Although hearing aid users did not always demand miniaturized components outright, the longstanding "cultural imperative" of an in-the-ear or otherwise undetectable device motivated innovation in the early 20th century and, later, made hearing aids a ready site for the refinement of materials developed in scientific or military contexts.[23]

William Aspray and Martin Campbell-Kelly have demonstrated that in the 1950s and 1960s, when electronics and computing were separate industries, "computers appropriated the new electronics technologies as they became available."[24] Transistors were initially used within computers as substitutes for hot, fragile vacuum tubes. However, electronics and computing truly converged in the 1970s with the development of the microprocessor. With the IC thus transformed into a programmable "computer on a chip," hearing aids no longer remained at the fore of miniaturization. For one thing, the microprocessor was more than just a revamped vacuum tube; new algorithms for speech processing had to be devised to make use of this technology.[25] In this case, more importantly, the imperative for invisible aids undermined early adoption—Moore's law held true for ICs, but the first digital hearing aids themselves were many times larger than analog models.

The long history of miniaturization calls into question its "relentless progress"— the notion that technical changes in electronics are somehow autonomous or continuous. The exponential line of Moore's law is often extrapolated from microprocessors to devices and used to predict accelerating, technology-induced changes in human capabilities and social norms. Size reduction has been the overall trend in communications equipment, but it never held to a straight course. For the case of hearing aids, stronger amplifiers sometimes entailed an increase in component or circuit size, and different models of mechanical, electric, and electronic devices coexisted rather than cleanly succeeding one another. Consumers have always been forced to weigh trade-offs among cost, function, size, and style.

More importantly, although the enduring stigmatization of deafness often led to unhappy relationships between individuals and their prosthetics—and sometimes to fraudulence in the hearing aid field—it did not necessarily result in passivity or dependence. Deaf and hard of hearing people played shaping roles as early adopters, inventors, retailers, and manufacturers of miniaturized components—even though advertisements and the popular press have historically portrayed "the deaf" as patients, "guinea pigs," recipients of charity, or hapless consumers of technology. Even in the vast literature on "users" in technology studies over the past 30 years, people with disabilities have only rarely been ascribed the competence or the relevance to figure centrally in narratives of technological change.[26]

Concealed Trumpets and Tubes

The first dedicated hearing aid firm, Frederick Rein of London, began to manufacture ear trumpets, hearing fans, and conversation tubes in 1800.[27] Trumpets and tubes "amplified" by collecting and concentrating sound waves that would otherwise disperse. As such, their design was an ongoing compromise between amplification and portability—the longer the trumpet and the wider its bell, the greater the magnification of sound.

In Europe and the US, the number of hearing aid firms increased at the end of the 19th century, matched by a rising emphasis on concealment.[28] Age-related hearing loss was, at the same time, becoming pathologized due to new audiometric techniques. Moreover, in 1880 the International Congress of Milan endorsed oralism as the most effective pedagogical strategy for deaf schools—a censure of sign language, which amounted to a vote against deafness in all its forms. More broadly, the emerging ideals of mechanized communication and rationalized design dictated the treatment of hearing loss with unobtrusive technical aids.[29] Finally, as argued by many disability historians, urbanization and the growth of the middle class encouraged 19th-century individuals to take advantage of anonymity and manage their self-presentations. For people with disabilities in particular, becoming "unremarkable" was an aid to social mobility.[30]

Beyond portability or wearability, then, invisibility was established as the design standard for hearing aids. Trumpets, tubes, and other mechanical hearing devices might be disguised as clothing, accessories, or furniture. In the last quarter of the century, "inserts," "invisibles," and artificial eardrums became tremendously popular, despite their limited efficacy. Cathy Sarli and a team of researchers from the Central Institute for the Deaf recently measured the gain from a range of 19th-century instruments; they concluded that "the majority of the population wanted and would pay for increasingly inconspicuous devices even if they were of little benefit to their hearing."[31]

Notes

1.   G.E. Moore, "Cramming More Components onto Integrated Circuits," *Electronics,* vol. 38, Apr. 1965, p. 1.

2.   D. MacKenzie, *Knowing Machines,* MIT Press, 1996, pp. 54–59. Moore's initial prediction was one year, but in practice the doubling has occurred every 1.5 to two years.

3.   M. Riordan and L. Hoddeson, *Crystal Fire: The Invention of the Transistor and the Birth of the Information Age,* W.W. Norton, 1998, pp. 205, 9.

4.   E.S. Hintz, "Portable Power: Inventor Samuel Ruben and the Birth of Duracell," *Technology and Culture,* vol. 50 Jan. 2009, pp. 24–57. Although the button battery was produced before

the transistor, to claim that it was more important to the history of miniaturization—and to the development of electronic devices such as the calculator—is to misunderstand the technique of miniaturization and its advantages. With the transistor, especially as it evolved into the microprocessor, smallness was linked not only to literal size, but to increased density, processing speeds, and reliability.

5. J.R. Nall, "Miniaturization for Military Equipment," *Miniaturization,* H. Gilbert, ed., Reinhold Publishing, 1961, p. 14. Nall acknowledged the tradition of watch making as a nonelectronic example of the same "media."

6. G. Senn and R. Riehs, "Miniaturization in Communications Equipment," *Miniaturization,* H. Gilbert, ed., Reinhold Publishing, 1961, p. 94.

7. G. Bachelard, "Miniature," *The Poetics of Space,* M. Jolas, trans., Beacon Press, 1969; S. Stewart, *On Longing: Narratives of the Miniature, the Gigantic, the Souvenir, the Collection,* Duke Univ. Press, 1993.

8. M.B. Schiffer notes the rise of assorted "pocket" devices in the early 20th century for Americans who were newly mobile due to cars and increased leisure time. M.B. Schiffer, *The Portable Radio in American Life,* Univ. of Arizona Press, 1991, p. 38.

9. E. Mollick explains that "the increase in chip density" is today attributable to a number of factors, including circuit design, substrate materials, techniques for increasing surface area, and techniques for reducing the width of etched connections. E. Mollick, "Establishing Moore's Law," IEEE *Annals of the History of Computing,* vol. 28, no. 3, 2006, p. 63.

10. Mollick, "Establishing Moore's Law," p. 62.

11. Standard surveys of mobile phone and mobile media history similarly argue that portable handsets were the result of miniaturized electronics, rather than considering the ways that portable electroacoustic media drove component miniaturization. See, for instance, R. Ling and J. Donner, *Mobile Communication,* Polity, 2009, or G. Goggin, *Cell Phone Culture: Mobile Technology in Everyday Life,* Routledge, 2006.

12. T. Misa explains that military interest in miniaturized electronics began with the walkie-talkie in the late 1930s. T. Misa, "Military Needs, Commercial Realities and the Development of the Transistor," *Military Enterprise and Technological Change*, M. Roe Smith, ed., MIT Press, 1985, pp. 253–87. See also C. Lécuyer, *Making Silicon Valley: Innovation and the Growth of High Tech, 1930–70,* MIT Press, 2005.

13. Miniature tubes and other "diminutive components" specifically "made possible military transceivers of unprecedented portability," such as Handie-Talkies. Schiffer, *The Portable Radio in American Life,* p. 130.

14. Schiffer, *The Portable Radio in American Life,* p. 123. Although the dream of a pocket radio dates to the 19th century, Schiffer argues that radios truly began to be miniaturized during the Depression. "Prior to this time [the 1930s], there had been no effort to reduce the size of volume controls, tuning capacitors, intermediate frequency transformers, and so forth. But once it became a priority, miniaturization was readily accomplished." Interestingly, miniaturized radios were less expensive; the opposite was often true for hearing aids (Schiffer, p. 103).

15. According to Ross Bassett, this incrementalism was not necessarily linear. Bassett, *To the Digital,* p. 284.

16. Or what E. Braun and S. MacDonald call "the general ethos of miniaturisation." E. Braun and S. MacDonald, *Revolution in Miniature,* Cambridge Univ. Press, 1982, p. 94. By 1959, industry experts recognized that "more advances have been made in the miniaturization of hearing aids than in any other consumer product." D.A. Findlay, "Miniaturization of Consumer Products," *Miniaturization,* H.D. Gilbert, ed., Reinhold, 1961, p. 183.

17. Whereas the military demand for reliable electronics encouraged the development of the planar transistor in 1959, early and even provisional versions of the transistor (as well as other components) found their way into hearing aids. Thank you to the anonymous reviewer who pointed this detail out to me.

18. "The standard of reference for most miniaturization steps is the original vacuum-tube circuitry represented by the full size octalbase vacuum tube and its associated circuitry. The

first stage of miniaturization—which usually means a size reduction of the order of 10 times—was effected by the use of subminiature vacuum tubes, printed wiring, some component size reduction, and more efficient component integration." J.J. Staller and A.H. Wolfsohn, "Miniaturization in Computers," *Miniaturization*, H.D. Gilbert, ed., Reinhold, 1961, p. 115. The article by Nall in the same volume also places hearing aids at the start of a timeline that leads to ICs.

19. J. F. Battey, "Testimony to the Senate Subcommittee on Labor-HHS-Education Appropriations," Nat'l Inst. on Deafness and Other Common Disorders (NIDCD), 26 Mar. 2007, http://www.nidcd.nih.gov/about/plans/congressional/battey20070326.htm.

20. "The Basics: Hearing Aids," NIDCD, 2010, http://www.nidcd.nih.gov/health/hearing/thebasics_hearingaid.asp.

21. Quackery was less rampant in the field of electrical hearing aids than in that of "deafness cures." Nevertheless, the longstanding lack of legal and medical oversight in this industry has often permitted the fraudulent marketing of inexpensive as well as expensive aids. Am. Medical Assoc. Bureau of Investigation, *Deafness Cures*, Am. Medical Assoc., 1912.

22. To be sure, hearing aid miniaturization has often resulted in decreased amplification and/or options for customization.

23. I intend both meanings of "cultural imperative" here: the general definition of a compulsory cultural norm, as well as M.B. Schiffer's concept for "a product fervently believed by a group—its constituency—to be desirable and inevitable, merely awaiting technological means for its realization." M.B. Schiffer, "Cultural Imperatives and Product Development: The Case of the Shirt-Pocket Radio," *Technology and Culture*, vol. 34, no. 1, 1993, pp. 98–113.

24. "In the early 1970s, these electronics-based industries, and the traditional computer industry, were quite distinct sectors, with very little crossover between them. By the late 1970s, however, they would all converge around a single product—the personal computer—built around the microprocessor, which was a true computer." W. Aspray and M. Campbell-Kelly, *Computer: A History of the Information Machine*, Basic Books, 1997, p. 199.

25. In Braun and MacDonald's account, the history of miniaturized electronics switches from "market-pull" to "technology-push" with the transistor. Similarly, Bassett argues that with the microprocessor "digital electronics . . . proliferated into almost every area of American life, through the small unseen computers that do their work in appliances and automobiles as well as through personal computers." Bassett, *To the Digital*, p. 251.

26. For a survey of this literature, see N. Oudshoorn and T. Pinch, eds., *How Users Matter: The Co-Construction of Users and Technologies*, MIT Press, 2003, especially the introduction.

27. For a more detailed discussion of mechanical hearing aids, and their significance to the history of electroacoustics, see M. Mills, "When Mobile Communication Technologies Were New," *Endeavour*, vol. 33, no. 4, 2009, pp. 141–47. R. Hüls offers a broad history of hearing aids in *Die Geschichte der Hörakustik*, Median-Verlag Heidelberg, 1999. See also K. Berger, *The Hearing Aid: Its Operation and Development*, Nat'l Hearing Aid Soc., 1970.

28. C. Sarlie, et. al., "19th-Century Camouflaged Mechanical Hearing Devices," *Otology and Neurotology*, vol. 24, no. 4, 2003, pp. 691–98.

29. On the history of mechanization and rationalization across many domains of human life, see S. Giedion, *Mechanization Takes Command: A Contribution to Anonymous History*, Norton, 1969.

30. See S. Mihm, "'A Limb Which Shall be Presentable in Polite Society': Prosthetic Technologies in the Nineteenth Century," *Artificial Parts, Practical Lives: Modern Histories of Prosthetics*, ed. K. Ott, D. Serlin, and S. Mihm, eds., New York Univ. Press, 2002, pp. 282–99; D.D. Yuan, "Disfigurement and Reconstruction in Oliver Wendell Holmes's 'The Human Wheel, Its Spokes and Felloes,'" *The Body and Physical Difference: Discourses of Disability*, D.T. Mitchell and S.L. Snyder, eds., Univ. of Michigan Press, 1997, pp. 71–88; R. Garland-Thomson, *Staring: How We Look*, Oxford Univ. Press, 2009.

31. Sarli et al., "19th-Century," pp. 692–93. Here they restate the argument found in S.D. Stephens and J.C. Goodwin, "Non-electric Aids to Hearing: A Short History," *Audiology*, vol. 23, no. 2, 1984, pp. 215–40.

Chapter 9

Kate Crawford

FOLLOWING YOU: DISCIPLINES OF LISTENING IN SOCIAL MEDIA

Introduction

IN HIS BOOK ON ATTENTION AND MODERN CULTURE, *Suspensions of Perception*, Jonathan Crary reminds us that 'the ways in which we intently listen to, look at, or concentrate on anything have a deeply historical character' (1999, 1). He observes that the ways in which we pay attention – and what we pay attention to – shift over the centuries, as part of a larger shaping of subjectivity. Along with new technological forms of display, communication, recording and playback come new forms of looking, listening and interacting; they afford new ways of focusing as well as defocusing attention. In doing so, they also become part of the ongoing reconstruction of the limits of human capacities. They contribute to the sense of what is possible, as well as to the qualities of being.

My aim here is to engage with a set of emerging modes of paying attention online, and to propose that they be considered practices of listening. As a metaphor, listening is useful; it captures some of the characteristics of the ongoing processes of receptivity that mark much online engagement. Nick Couldry argues that aural terms are more able 'to register media's social presence' as they have distinct 'advantages as a source of metaphors for thinking about the social world' (2006, 6). He writes of the 'reciprocal, embodied nature of listening; its embeddedness always in an intersubjective space of perception' (6). This intersubjectivity is important to the functioning of many online spaces. It is my hope that the concept of listening will allow us to analyse the various affordances of online attention, and to assess the ways in which we listen also shape us as late modern subjects.

Listening online could be considered in any number of contexts: be it wikis, MUDs, blogs, mailing lists, and even RSS feeds. For my purposes here, I am taking the example of social media, and Twitter in particular, as spaces where we can observe various types of listening. Twitter is fruitful territory, as it offers a relatively young platform (having launched in 2006), where the norms of use are nascent and contested. It also functions for many users as a continuous background presence, a steady stream of messages that can be briefly focused on then returned to the peripheries of attention. This kind of ongoing yet diffuse engagement is increasingly common, with studies indicating that since early 2009, Internet users were spending more time on social networking services than email (Nielsen Online 2009).

Listening is not a common metaphor for online activity. In fact, online participation has tended to be conflated with contributing a 'voice'. 'Speaking up' has become the dominant metaphor for participation in online spaces such as blogs, wikis, news sites and discussion lists (Karaganis 2007; Bruns 2008). Little research has been done into other forms of participation, such as private email discussions or behind-the-scenes direct messaging in social media environments (Nonnecke and Preece 2001, 2), and even less to the act of simply witnessing the comments of others. 'Lurking' is a common pejorative term for those who are present in public online spaces but do not prominently speak up. I would argue that this term has hampered our understanding of online spaces, and that the concept of listening offers more open and critically productive ground.

There are three categories of listeners that I will address in this paper – individuals, politicians, and corporations. Each faces a set of disciplinary imperatives about developing a social media presence, and how to listen to others when using a service such as Twitter. As individuals, politicians and companies develop a greater capacity to listen to multiple others online, and more people come to expect this form of attention, a greater sense of responsibility to listen emerges. This contributes to the creation of different qualities of listening. I will consider three modes here: reciprocal listening, background listening, and delegated listening, when the act of online listening is outsourced altogether. These modes are not exclusive, nor are they singular: they can be adopted by any category of user, be they representing themselves or acting on behalf of a company or political party. Further, Internet users may regularly switch between modes of listening throughout a day, and listen to particular individuals and groups with varying degrees of attention. But by recognizing distinct modes, we can begin to develop a more granular assessment of the ways in which listening functions in social media.

In my view, social media powerfully invoke an efficient listening subject, drawing together the divergent spaces of modernity in one location – while simultaneously creating a gap between this ideal and what is humanly manageable. A Twitter user, for example, is functionally able to manage an online presence for friends, family and co-workers – and possibly also voters or customers. But there are complex ramifications for how this capacity can be managed across one's working life, family and social life, and political life. Disparities emerge between what users are technically able to do, and the limits of their schedules, desires and bodies. While this is not the place to delve into the detail of how this can be negotiated by individual users, I aim to develop some theoretical paths that will lead to a better understanding of the multivalent nature of listening online.

From Lurkers to Listeners

Since the days of what Geert Lovink calls 'the techno-utopianism storm' of the 1990s, there has been a glorification of 'voice' as the prime form of participation online (2002, 113). Not only has the metaphor of voice become the sine qua non of 'being' online, but it has been charged with all the political currents of democratic practice. Voice is closely tied to the libertarian model of online democracy that was championed by the likes of *Wired* magazine, and writers such as John Perry Barlow, Howard Rheingold and Stewart Brand. Expression is paramount for many US-centric techno-libertarians, as Barbrook and Cameron explain: 'they want information technologies to be used to create a new "Jeffersonian democracy" where all individuals will be able to express themselves freely within cyberspace' (1997, 45).

This privileging of voice, and particularly voice-as-democratic-participation, still influences critical accounts of online activity. In Henry Jenkins and David Thorburn's *Democracy and New Media*, the authors argue that the Internet 'is politically important because it expands the range of voices that can be heard in a national debate, ensuring that no one voice can speak with unquestioned authority' (2003, 2). This 'speaking truth to power' model is a prominent feature of much media and cultural studies analysis, but it has limited the recognition of the variety and reach of the practices of listening online. Listening has not been given sufficient consideration as a significant practice of intimacy, connection, obligation and participation online; instead, it has often been considered as contributing little value to online communities, if not acting as an active drain on their growth.

For example, in the Internet research of the 1990s, lurkers – meaning those who prefer to inhabit the margins of debates, rarely or never contributing in public – were commonly defined as non-participants online. This group has been described as more like readers than writers (Sharf 1999), as more akin to passive TV viewers (Morris and Ogan 1996), and as freeloaders who leech the energy of online communities without offering anything in return (Kollock and Smith 1996). However, there was little by way of substantial studies of lurking during this period. This was an interesting oversight, as lurkers have always constituted the large majority of individuals in most online spaces. Researchers have claimed that over 90% of an online community will only practise light public activity, if any (Mason 1999; Zhang and Storck 2001; Nonnecke and Preece 2003).

More recently greater attention has been paid to lurking, with some studies observing that lurkers have an important role to play in online communities (Nonnecke and Preece 2003; Lee, Chen, and Jiang 2006). Rather than freeloading, lurkers are actively logging in and tracking the contributions of others; they contribute a mode of receptiveness that encourages others to make public contributions. While they may not be contributing public posts, they do not deprive regular commenters of resources nor do they detract from the community (Lee, Chen, and Jiang 2006). They directly contribute to the community by acting as a gathered audience: neither agreeing nor disagreeing, but listening (even if distractedly).

There have been some efforts to replace the term 'lurking' with less derogatory labels such as 'peripheral participants' (Zhang and Storck 2001) and 'non-public participants' (Nonnecke and Preece 2003). While these terms attempt to remove the stigma from lurking, they continue to define this majority group by what they are not: not public, not at the centre. As terms, they fail to offer a sense of what is being done, and why it is important to online participation.

The concept of listening, on the other hand, invokes the more dynamic process of online attention, and suggests that it is an embedded part of networked engagement – a necessary corollary to having a 'voice'. If we reconceptualize lurking as listening, it reframes a set of behaviours once seen as vacant and empty into receptive and reciprocal practices. Moreover, as a metaphor for attending to discussions and debates online, listening more usefully captures the experience that many Internet users have. It reflects the fact that everyone moves between the states of listening and disclosing online; both are necessary and both are forms of participation.

A consideration of listening practices allows for a more acute assessment of online engagement, and decentres the current overemphasis on posting, commenting and 'speaking up' as the only significant forms of participation. Additionally, it allows for the deep sense of connection that listening participants can feel in online spaces, rather than diminishing this form of presence as lurking, with all its linguistic connotations of a sense of threat, ambiguity or concealment. 'Listening in', a term derived from older media forms, can also be understood as a process that operates in most online spaces, a vector that runs through user-cultures. The modes of listening have always been present online, and it is a critical (if under-researched) part of the process of experiencing being in networked space.

On Background Listening

In early 2009, Jay Rosen, a professor of journalism at New York University, posed a question to his 12,000 followers on the micro-blogging service Twitter. He wanted to know why they twittered. Of the almost 200 responses that he initially received via his blog and Twitter account, he noticed an important similarity. 'Surprise finding from my project', he wrote on Twitter on 8 January, 'is how often I wound up with radio as a comparison.'

The comparison may have been unexpected, but it is provocative. Twitter is a social networking service where users send and receive text-based updates of up to 140 characters. They can be delivered and read via the web, instant messaging clients or mobile phone as text messages. Unlike radio, which is a one-to-many medium, Twitter is many-to-many. People choose whom they will follow, which may be a small group of intimates, or thousands of strangers – they then receive all updates written by those people. Perhaps the most obvious difference from radio is that there is no sound broadcast on Twitter. It is simply a network of people scanning, reading and occasionally posting written messages. Yet the radio analogy persists. As MSN editor Jane Douglas writes, 'I see Twitter like a ham radio for tuning into the world' (cited in Rosen 2009).

The act of 'tuning in' reflects part of the process of engagement with social media. A Twitter user follows a range of people, some of whom will post updates that offer useful advice, amusing anecdotes, or interesting links. But many messages will simply be scanned quickly, not focused on, something closer to being tuned out rather than tuned in. I have described this as a kind of background listening (Crawford 2009), where commentary and conversations continue as a backdrop throughout the day, with only a few moments requiring concentrated attention. The conversational field of activity in these online spaces is dispersed and molecularized, a constant flow of small pieces of information that accrete to form a sense of intimacy and awareness about the patterns of speech, activity and thought across a group of contacts. Like radio, they can circulate in the background: a part of the texture of the everyday. Twitter is itself a word that implies the sonic in both its derivations: either as the calling of birds, or the 'idle' chatter of humans.

It is the access to the details of someone's everyday life, as prosaic as they often are, which contributes to the sense of 'ambient intimacy' in social media (Reichelt 2007). The process of background listening is critical to the sense of affinity generated in these spaces; access to the minutiae of a person's life is something normally reserved for family, close friends and lovers. The intimacy of social media contexts is not always pleasant or positive; it can generate discomfort, confusion and claustrophobia, amongst a range of negative affects. People often express anger, sadness, fear and resentment. They may also misrepresent themselves and lie. Nonetheless, the disclosures made in social media spaces develop a relationship with an audience of listeners. Further, those background listeners are necessary to provoke disclosures of any kind.

The act of listening to several (or several hundred) Twitter users requires a kind of dexterity. It demands a capacity to inhabit a stream of multilayered information, often leaping from news updates to a message from a friend experiencing a stressful situation, to information about what a stranger had for lunch, all in the space of seconds. Some will require attention; many can be glimpsed and tuned out. The popular desktop clients for receiving Twitter updates, such as Tweetie and Twitterific, provide 'pop up' messages on the user's screen whenever Twitter messages ('tweets') are received, acting as an irregular interruption. With the emergence of 'always on' broadband Internet, messages can be appearing night and day, for as long as an individual's computer is active and connected. This requires a certain loss of volition over when messages are seen, and it differs in important ways from consciously logging on to a website in order to check and read updates.

This relinquishing of control necessitates a 'tuning in/tuning out' response that corresponds with radio listening. As David Goodman has noted, the phonograph made it possible to select sounds in bounded time – a record might play for four minutes and then stop. The invention of radio 'created the possibility of abandonment of choice – you could just let it play on and hear whatever came along' (Goodman 2009, 17). People could clean the house, work, or socialize while the radio played continuously in the background, audible but not focused on. This kind of listening generated considerable concern. In the 1930s, distracted listening was seen as a risky practice, as listening to the radio in an indiscriminate, ongoing way could make people into easy prey for propaganda (31). At other times, public anger has focused on the disruptions of radio noise leaking from homes and cars, or portable transistor radios in public parks. Theodor Adorno once expressed concern that background radio could impair digestion (42). Gradually, normative frameworks developed about what constituted the appropriately attentive listener, and where and how radios should be played.

Currently, debates are emerging about the appropriate uses of Twitter, where it should be used, how it is best employed, and where responsibility lies when engaging with it. Apart from the mainstream media's interest in the service, there are numerous online guides to becoming a better Twitter user, with titles like '5 Ways to Use Twitter for Good' and '20 Twitter Tips to Make You a Better Twitter User' (Brogan 2007; Morgan 2008). Such 'how-to' guides contribute to the development of communication norms, as do more heated debates about 'good' versus 'bad' twittering. One example is the contention over 'retweeting': whether reposting someone else's message is an acceptable way of sharing something important or funny, or contributing an echo chamber of repeated information (Kaplan 2009).

Through guides, debates and habituated patterns of use, a range of disciplinary norms are manifesting: be it about how to respond to messages, where and when to check them, who to follow or friend (or unfollow or unfriend). These norms vary with the type of user. Having considered some of the emerging listening practices of individuals using Twitter, and background listening in particular, I will now briefly consider the listening experiences of politicians and corporations. Each faces expectations about how they will engage with others, and what kinds of listening are expected of them.

On Reciprocal Listening: Social Media Politics

Many heads of state currently use social media services to update their activities, shill for support and advise of policy announcements. Barack Obama, Gordon Brown and Kevin Rudd all have a presence on Twitter, and it has become a significant communications method during election campaigns. Social media platforms give politicians access to millions of users and offer the capacity to build a sense of camaraderie and connection with a wide constituency. But as the popularity of social media increases amongst politicians, important differences are emerging in the ways in which they engage in these spaces. In particular, some politicians engage in 'reciprocal listening' with their followers – which I define as hearing and responding to comments and direct messages – while some continue to adopt a broadcast-only model, leaving no room for dialogue with their contacts.

President Obama used Twitter extensively to send updates about the location and content of speeches and rallies prior to his election in 2008. After that time, restrictions commenced in regard to presidential use of digital technologies, and updates have slowed. But even during the times of heaviest use, Obama's campaign did not reply to followers, or indicate that direct messages were being heard. Australia's Prime Minister Rudd has adopted a similar approach – primarily issuing policy and press conference updates, with only occasional messages to reply to individual users. In the case of Prime Minister Gordon Brown, his 'Downing Street' Twitter presence is updated frequently, with a focus on the multi-platform content issued during the week: linking to video updates, transcripts, Flickr pages and policy news flashes. Further, many direct questions and comments from followers are publicly answered, generating an impression that responses are being read and considered.

There are also groups that continuously track national politicians using Twitter, such as Twixdagen in Sweden and Tweetminister in the United Kingdom.

Tweetminister, for example, re-streams all British politicians using Twitter, observing which topics are most popular, and allowing users to search for their local member online. According to the Tweetminister site, its aims are to 'connect the public with politics' and 'promote better and more transparent communications between voters and Members of Parliament through open conversations'. Yet it remains unclear just how much feedback via Twitter is being heard by political leaders, or if it is taken seriously as a form of communication and public accountability.

As Jason Wilson writes, many politicians using social media services are more like animated corpses – with little personality or life – which amounts to an enormous lost opportunity. 'Users of social media expect, rightly or wrongly, a much more conversational and unaffected style of political communication', writes Wilson, observing that 'there is visible frustration on services like Twitter and Facebook when politicians will not engage in the dialogue that many users take to be the key function these spaces afford' (Wilson 2009). Of course, it is difficult for politicians who have a high follower rate to ensure that a dialogue is maintained. Nonetheless, by maintaining a presence in social media networks, politicians are held accountable. If they fail to respond actively, they will lose followers and run the risk of alienating the very people they are seeking to reach.

It is particularly difficult to define the use of Twitter by politicians as a 'conversation' if a politician is not personally writing the messages, but requiring staffers to reply and engage with online responses. While it may come as no surprise that a politician's communications staff are actually updating a Twitter profile, it produces a degree of distance that is antithetical to genuine communication. Further, when a politician's face and name are connected to an online profile which is clearly being used as a public relations arm by unknown staffers, it evokes something akin to ventriloquism – a pretence of presence, or a consultation puppet-show.

As social media develop and mature, astute politicians will become more adept at providing voters with the sense that they are being heard and acknowledged. Joe Trippi, the campaign manager for US presidential candidate Howard Dean, argues that politicians now have no choice but to engage fully with social media, and be highly responsive (Trippi 2009). But the difficulty remains: politicians that outsource their online presence to staff are not really listening, nor are they fully engaging with that community of users. They are subject to disciplinary regimes of attentiveness, yet are performing a kind of engagement-at-arm's-length. This could be described as 'delegated listening' – a mode where the participant is seen to be listening (and observing the bare minimum of what Trippi suggests) while not spending the considerable amount of time required to be fully present in social media space. This mode of listening – different from background listening and reciprocal listening – can also be observed in the corporate sector.

Corporations and 'Listening In'

The corporate sector was quick to see the benefits of using social media to forge a closer relationship with customers, gain information about products, and enhance public personae. While some politicians enjoin staffers to update Twitter accounts, many companies allocate this task to employees. Some choose to hire the services of professional microbloggers to craft a presence for them online. Companies such as Twit4Hire.com update microblogs for clients who are, as they explain on their website, 'too busy to add yet another daily task to their burgeoning agendas, but who still want to proactively reach out to their customer base'.

But it remains difficult to outsource the act of listening. When professionals are hired to simulate the presence of a company or celebrity online, communications are commonly reduced to the level of an impersonal, unidirectional marketing broadcast. The benefit of being able to hear customers' views, rapidly respond to their comments and concerns, and gain insight into how the company is being discussed is sharply reduced. Delegated listening is not a perfect analogue for being there.

Dell is one company that has embraced social media, to the extent of appointing a Vice President of 'Communities and Conversations'. The employee with that title, Bob Pearson, is a strong advocate of the need for companies to become ideal listeners. 'Quite frankly, one of the most important things we do with Twitter is listen', Pearson argues. 'I don't think you can hire someone to listen for you' (Soller 2009).

However, a commitment to background listening comes at a cost – the cost of human attention. A senior executive at Dell may underscore the importance of listening to customers, but in practice this means that more than 130 Twitter feeds emanate from Dell Corp., and each is connected back to a staff member who must personally maintain that account while adhering to corporate communication protocols (Soller 2009). This is the labour of listening. But how is this labour to be quantified? As long as listening is not considered to be an important part of online participation, of 'low value' in the process of online engagement, it is difficult for it to be recognized as an important and value-generating form of work. Employees commonly maintain a microblog presence for their company, NGO or university department without financial compensation. Further, there is little by way of research or data to quantify what the value might be of this presence that both discloses information and listens.

For companies, the value of listening could be considered in three ways: being seen to participate in a community and hearing people's opinions; utilizing a rapid and lower-cost form of customer support (as compared to the telephone); and gaining a dispersed global awareness of how a brand is discussed and the patterns of consumer use and satisfaction. Services such as Facebook and Twitter can, in effect, be used as giant focus groups, where companies can listen in to positive and negative views of their products.[1] While companies may derive a range of direct benefits from their engagement in social media space, they also hold particular forms of responsibility. Corporations are increasingly expected to function in social media spaces in highly responsive and attentive ways: not only do they have new powers to 'listen in' but also they must be vigilant with rapid and targeted responses.

Disciplines of Listening

While online technologies are contributing to the development of varieties of listening subjects, they are also revealing the limits of these disciplines. Jonathan

Crary has argued that it is possible to think of modernity as 'an ongoing crisis of attentiveness':

> . . . in which the changing configurations of capitalism continually push attention and distraction to new limits and thresholds, with an endless sequence of new products, sources of stimulation, and streams of information, and then respond with new methods of managing and regulating perception . . . But at the same time . . . the articulation of a subject in terms of attentive capacities simultaneously disclosed a subject incapable of conforming to such disciplinary imperatives. (1999, 13–14)

Certainly, social networks could be considered as configurations that push our attention and distraction to new limits, and we are already witnessing the creation of new agencies to outsource this work of presence and perception. Crary has noted the emergence of pathologies of attention in the nineteenth century, where subjects were seen as deficient, even sociopathic, if they failed to internalize new disciplinary structures. If networked technologies in general, and social media in particular, generate ideal listening subjects of the twenty-first century – for individuals, politicians, consumers, parents and corporations – they also reveal the human limits of attention.

The emerging use of social media in working environments and educational institutions (e.g. the use of Twitter in university courses) is part of instructing workers and students in the more efficient management and regulation of their social presence. Students learn the regimen of maintaining a social media profile: it can be a research tool, and also a method of maintaining a strong network of contacts and potential employment opportunities. Workers might develop the social face of a corporation by maintaining its Twitter presence (with attentive eyes and ears), but they also develop the ability to stay in touch with their friends, lovers and family while at work.

If the hours are long, a worker can perform a kind of presence, using the ambient awareness of the goings-on in the lives of their loved ones to feel connected, despite being physically removed in an office or work site. At the same time, they may come to feel an increasing *expectation* that they should be using these services, regularly updating and never away too long. If they are not paying attention, are they still a maximally effective student, worker, partner or parent?

Technologies of listening impact not only on the ways in which we can connect with others, but also materially influence the ways in which we account for our own subjectivity. Imperatives of attentiveness impinge on all areas of life, but there is also a force of resistance, a point at which individuals can no longer sustain expectations. This interplay of expanding disciplinary imperatives and human limitations contributes to the formation and evolution of normative structures, as well as flows of capital and information, which gradually shift as technologies and subjects adapt.

The social practices and normative frameworks for listening in networked media are in their early stages, but the rapid uptake of social media services will result in an accelerated development of norms, habits and conventions. People will find ways to negotiate the terms of their engagement online, how and with whom they engage, and when to switch off and be unavailable, unhearing and unheard. As Don Ihde writes, 'If there is an ethics of listening, then respect for silence must play a part in that ethics' (1976, 180). But equally, there will be advancing demands for increased and multi-channelled attention, and the ability to listen – even if only in the background – to a chorus of voices.

We are still discovering what the thresholds of human listening might be, quantitatively and qualitatively. The study of the listening subject is just beginning: as work on the practices of surveillance and the disciplinary gaze produced an understanding of the observed and observing subject, so we need a better understanding of the listened to and listening subject. While I have sought to introduce some of these ideas here, further work needs to be done in the ways in which online listening constitutes a recognition of others, and how the qualities of listening differ between users and between services.

To my mind, there is considerable value in researching listening practices in relation to online media, as it opens up new ways of understanding the nuances of connection and communication that these spaces afford. For media studies, this requires a re-evaluation of how agency and subjectivity are expressed and developed through listening as much as through voice. Couldry's view that metaphors of listening possess a greater flexibility and capacity for registering the shifting nature of contemporary media seems percipient when applied to services such as Twitter. Such social media platforms are among the many forms of networked space that are already offering us a glimpse of how the boundaries of human attention and subjectivity are being reconstituted.

Note

1.   This capacity is already being sold as a service by some social media companies. At the World Economic Forum in 2009, Facebook launched its 'engagement ads' system, which allows companies to selectively target Facebook users and pose questions about their products and services (Neate and Mason 2009). This effectively allows Facebook to be used as an enormously powerful and immensely customizable database for market research.

References

Barbrook, R., and A. Cameron. 1997. The Californian ideology. *Science as Culture* 26: 44–72.

Brogan, C. 2007. 5 ways to use Twitter for good. *Lifehack,* 10 March. http://www.lifehack.org (accessed 12 February 2009).

Bruns, A. 2008. *Blogs, Wikipedia, Second Life, and beyond: From production to produsage.* New York: Peter Lang.

Couldry, N. 2006. *Listening beyond the echoes: Media, ethics and agency in an uncertain world.* Boulder: Paradigm.

Crary, J. 1999. *Suspensions of perception: Attention, spectacle, and modern culture.* Cambridge, MA: MIT Press.

Crawford, K. 2009. These foolish things: On intimacy and insignificance in mobile media. In *Mobile technologies: From telecommunications to media,* ed. G. Goggin and L. Hjorth, 252–66. New York: Routledge.

Goodman, D. 2009. Distracted listening: On not making sound choices in the 1930s. In *Sound in the era of mechanical reproduction,* ed. David Suisman and Susan Strasser, 17–44. Philadelphia: University of Pennsylvania Press.

Ihde, D. 1976. *Listening and voice: A phenomenology of sound.* Athens, OH: Ohio University Press.

Jenkins, H., and D. Thorburn, eds. 2003. *Democracy and new media.* Cambridge, MA: MIT Press.

Kaplan, E. 2009. Retweeting is killing Twitter, and more histrionics. Blackrim Glasses, 17 February. http://blackrimglasses.com

Karaganis, J., ed. 2007. *Structures of participation in digital culture.* New York: Social Science Research Culture.

Kollock, P., and M. Smith. 1996. Managing the virtual commons: Cooperation and conflict in computer communities. In *Computer-mediated communication: Linguistic, social, and cross-cultural perspectives,* ed. S. Herring, 109–28. Amsterdam: John Benjamins.

Lee, Y., F. Chen, and H. Jiang. 2006. Lurking as participation: A community perspective on lurkers' identity and negotiability. Making a difference: Proceedings of the 7th International conference on Learning Sciences, 404–10. Bloomington, IN: International Society of the Learning Sciences.

Lovink, Geert. 2002. *Uncanny networks: Dialogues with the virtual intelligentsia.* Cambridge, MA: MIT Press.

Mason, B. 1999. Issues in virtual ethnography. In *Esprit 13: Workshop on ethnographic studies in real and virtual environments: Inhabited information spaces and connected communities,* ed. K. Buckner. Edinburgh: Queen Margaret College.

Morgan, J. 2008. 20 Twitter tips to make you a better Twitter user. Jacob Morgan blog, 16 August. http://www.jmorganmarketing.com

Morris, M., and C. Ogan. 1996. The Internet as mass medium. *Journal of Computer-Mediated Communication* 46, Winter: 39–50.

Neate, R., and R. Mason. 2009. Networking site cashes in on friends. *Daily Telegraph* (UK), 2 February.

Nielsen Online. 2009. *Global faces and networked places: A Nielsen report on social networking's new global footprint.* http://www.nielsen-online.com

Nonnecke, B., and J. Preece. 2001. Why lurkers lurk. In *AMCIS 2001 Proceedings,* paper 295, http://aisel.aisnet.org/amcis2001/294 (accessed 12 March 2009).

—. 2003. Silent participants: Getting to know lurkers better. In *From Usenet to CoWebs: Interacting with social information spaces,* 110–32. ed. C. Lueg and D. Fisher. Amsterdam: Springer.

Reichelt, L. 2007. Ambient intimacy. Disambiguity, posted 1 March. http://www.disambiguity.com/ambient-intimacy

Rosen, J. 2009. Help me explain Twitter to eggheads. Press think, posted 4 January. http://journalism.nyu.edu/pubzone/weblogs/pressthink/2009/01/04/chronicle_hlp.html

Sharf, B.F. 1999. Beyond netiquette: The ethics of doing naturalistic discourse research on the Internet. In *Doing Internet research,* 243–56. ed. S. Jones. London: Sage.

Soller, K. 2009. Twitter unmasked. *Newsweek Online,* 13 February. http://www.newsweek.com/id/184656.

Trippi, J. 2009. Campaigning with the Internet. Address to the Sydney Institute, Sydney, 24 February.

Wilson, J. 2009. Not another political zombie. *New Matilda Online*, 25 February. http://newmatilda.com/2009/02/25/not-another-political-zombie

Zhang, W., and J. Storck. 2001. Peripheral members in online communities. In AMCIS 2001 Proceeding, paper 117. http://aisel.aisnet.org/amci2001/117 (accessed 12 March 2009).

PART II

Spaces, Sites, Scapes

THERE IS SOME DEEPER TRUTH to the tagline for the first *Alien* movie: in space, no one can hear you scream. Sound does not exist in a vacuum; it implies space, as does hearing. "Space," John Mowitt once said, "is the grain of sound." To Peter Sloterdijk, "the ear is the organ that connects the intimate and the public. Whatever might present itself as social life, it initially comes about only as the specific width of an acoustic bell over the group—a bell whose sonorous presences, especially in European cultures, are capable of textualization." His bell-ringing hyperbole aside, Sloterdijk follows on the heels of historian Alain Corbin, who read the politics of the French countryside through village bells. Social space *is* sonic space. Space is the register in which sound can happen and sound can have meaning. But space is not a static thing. It is in constant formation, dissolution and reformation. According to Deleuze and Guattari's notion of the refrain, sound is a means of *territorialization*: "to draw a circle around that fragile center, to organize a limited space." But it also de- and re-territorializes: "one ventures from home on the thread of a tune."[1]

The most enduring spatial figure in sound studies is without question R. Murray Schafer's concept of the *soundscape*. As his essay in this section states, a soundscape can be "any acoustic field of study" but he clearly meant it as a total social concept to describe the field of sounds in a particular place, or an entire culture, "a total appreciation of the sonic environment."[2] Schafer used tools like ear cleaning and soundscape recording to get students to behold their cultures' soundscapes in new ways, with the ultimate hope that in so doing they would both begin to notice the transformation of soundscapes and eventually become active in improving their cultures' soundscapes.[3] As a concept, soundscape has been taken up by writers in acoustic ecology, the field that descended from Schafer's work and one important historical source of the contemporary interest in sound, but also in history, anthropology, literature, and dozens of other fields. More recently, David W. Samuels, Louise Meintjes, Ana Maria Ochoa and Thomas Porcello have promoted the idea of soundscape as a master concept for the anthropology of sound, because it "provides some response to the ephemerality dilemma by offering a means to materialize sounds, their interrelations, and their circulation."[4]

Schafer has, in turn, come under modification and criticism from a number of directions. Hildegard Westerkamp has elegantly demonstrated the problems with treating a soundscape recording as pure documentarity in her soundwork "Kitts Beach Soundwalk"; Mitch Akiyama has criticized Schafer's division between hearing and seeing, and his importation of problematic concepts of landscape from visual art.[5] Others have conceptualized soundscape differently. Emily Thompson uses the concept of soundscape to organize her history of architectural acoustics, but does not make use of Schafer's epistemology or methods. Instead, his ideas appear as an artifact of the history she traces out. Barry Blesser and Linda Ruth Salter use the term "aural architecture" to denote "the composite of numerous surfaces, objects and geometries in a complicated environment."[6] Their contribution and Richard Rath's address the functions of built sonic space, especially as it mediates between the everyday and the expectional. Stefan Helmreich's essay extends those concerns to the present and submerges them underwater, troubling anthropological and sonic ideas of immersion in the process.

There is, also, a politics to space that occurs at many levels. John Picker explores problems of difference as they register in written text and thereby considers the representation of sonic space in terms of power. Picker and Karin Bijsterveld also touch on the enduring issue of noise as both a physical experience and its own point of entry into the politics of sonic space, for the definition of noise is always an operation of power and knowledge. As Michel Serres writes of it, "background noise may well be the ground of our being. . . . Noise cannot be a phenomenon; every phenomenon is separated from it, a silhouette on a backdrop, like a beacon against the fog, as every message, every cry, every call, every signal must be separated from the hubbub that occupies silence, in order to be, to be perceived, to be known, to be exchanged." Noise is the backdrop of activity and sociability, even as its designation also hints at sociability's limits, and writers across the human sciences have explored it at length.[7]

Although acoustic space has never simply or naturally existed in sympathy with physical space, the separation of acoustic space from other kinds, especially as a phenomenal concern, is captured particularly well in the case of mobile technologies. The essays by Shuhei Hosokawa and Michael Bull take up this issue directly as they also explore experiences of moving through urban space. Their work also suggests an aspiration for sound scholarship more broadly: their lines of inquiry are rooted in particular places and moments but outlive the specific technologies and cultural forms on which they are based. Hosokawa and Bull's attention to mobility also returns us to a fundamental challenge when considering sonic spaces, whatever they may be: space is not just a container nor just a context for action. It is generative and always in flux, as are our perceptions of it.[8]

Notes

1   Sloterdijk, *Bubbles*, 520; Corbin, *Village Bells: Sound and Meaning in the 19th-Century French Countryside*; Deleuze and Guattari, *A Thousand Plateaus: Capitalism and Schizophrenia, Volume 2*, 311.

2   Schafer, *The Soundscape: Our Sonic Environment and the Tuning of the World*, 8, 4 (in order of citation).
3   Ibid., 209–11.
4   Samuels et al., "Soundscapes," 338.
5   Westerkamp, *Kits Beach Soundwalk*; Akiyama, "Transparent Listening"; I have also critiqued Schafer for his antimodernism – Sterne, *The Audible Past: Cultural Origins of Sound Reproduction*; Kelman, "Rethinking the Soundscape."
6   Blesser and Salter, *Spaces Speak, Are You Listening?: Experiencing Aural Architecture*, 2.
7   Serres, James, and Nielson, *Genesis*, 13; see also, e.g., Bailey, "Breaking the Sound Barrier"; Bijsterveld, *Mechanical Sound: Technology, Culture, and Public Problems of Noise in the Twentieth Century*; Radovac, "The 'War on Noise': Sound and Space in La Guardia's New York"; Weheliye, *Phonographies: Grooves in Sonic Afro-Modernity*; Schwartz, *Making Noise*.
8   Augoyard and Torgue, "Introduction, An Instrumentation of the Sonic Environment"; Labelle, *Acoustic Territories: Sound Culture and Everyday Life*.

References

Akiyama, Mitchell. "Transparent Listening: Soundscape Composition's Objects of Study." *Revue d'art canadienne/Canadian Art Review* 35, no. 1 (July 14, 2010): 54–62.

Augoyard, Jean-François, and Henry Torgue. "Introduction, An Instrumentation of the Sonic Environment." In *Sonic Experience: A Guide to Everyday Sounds*, 3–18. Montréal: McGill-Queens University Press, 2005.

Bailey, Peter. "Breaking the Sound Barrier: A Historian Listens to Noise." *Body & Society* 2, no. 2 (June 1, 1996): 49–66.

Bijsterveld, Karin. *Mechanical Sound: Technology, Culture, and Public Problems of Noise in the Twentieth Century*. Cambridge: MIT Press, 2008.

Blesser, Barry, and Linda-Ruth Salter. *Spaces Speak, Are You Listening?: Experiencing Aural Architecture*. Cambridge, Mass.: MIT Press, 2007.

Corbin, Alain. *Village Bells: Sound and Meaning in the 19th-Century French Countryside*. New York: Columbia University Press, 1998.

Deleuze, Gilles, and Felix Guattari. *A Thousand Plateaus: Capitalism and Schizophrenia, Volume 2*. Minneapolis: University of Minnesota Press, 1987.

Kelman, Ari Y. "Rethinking the Soundscape: A Critical Genealogy of a Key Term in Sound Studies." *The Senses and Society* 5, no. 2 (2010): 212–34.

Labelle, Brandon. *Acoustic Territories: Sound Culture and Everyday Life*. New York: Continuum, 2010.

Radovac, Lilian. "The 'War on Noise': Sound and Space in La Guardia's New York." *American Quarterly* 63, no. 3 (2011).

Samuels, David W., Louise Meintjes, Ana Maria Ochoa, and Thomas Porcello. "Soundscapes: Toward a Sounded Anthropology." *Annual Review of Anthropology* 39 (October 21, 2010): 329–45.

Schafer, R. Murray. *The Soundscape: Our Sonic Environment and the Tuning of the World*. Rochester, Vermont: Destiny Books, 1994.

Schwartz, Hillel. *Making Noise: From Babel to the Big Bang and Beyond*. Cambridge: MIT Press, 2011.

Serres, Michel, Geneviève James, and James Nielson. *Genesis*. University of Michigan Press, 1997.

Sloterdijk, Peter. *Bubbles: Spheres – Microspherology*. Translated by Wieland Hoban. Cambridge, MIT Press, 2011.

Sterne, Jonathan. *The Audible Past: Cultural Origins of Sound Reproduction*. Durham: Duke University Press, 2003.

Weheliye, Alexander. *Phonographies: Grooves in Sonic Afro-Modernity*. Durham: Duke University Press, 2005.

Westerkamp, Hildegard. *Kits Beach Soundwalk*. ElectroCD, 2010. http://www.electrocd.com/en/oeuvres/select/?id=14313.

Chapter 10

R. Murray Schafer

THE SOUNDSCAPE

Now I will do nothing but listen. . .
I hear all sounds running together, combined, fused or following.
Sounds of the city and sounds out of the city, sounds of the day
and night. . . .

WALT WHITMAN, *Song of Myself*

THE SOUNDSCAPE OF THE WORLD is changing. Modern man is beginning to inhabit a world with an acoustic environment radically different from any he has hitherto known. These new sounds, which differ in quality and intensity from those of the past, have alerted many researchers to the dangers of an indiscriminate and imperialistic spread of more and larger sounds into every corner of man's life. Noise pollution is now a world problem. It would seem that the world soundscape has reached an apex of vulgarity in our time, and many experts have predicted universal deafness as the ultimate consequence unless the problem can be brought quickly under control.

In various parts of the world important research is being undertaken in many independent areas of sonic studies: acoustics, psychoacoustics, otology, international noise abatement practices and procedures, communications and sound recording engineering (electroacoustics and electronic music), aural pattern perception and the structural analysis of language and music. These researches are related; each deals with aspects of the world soundscape. In one way or another researchers engaged on these various themes are asking the same question: what is the relationship between man and the sounds of his environment and what happens when those sounds change? Soundscape studies attempt to unify these various researches.

Noise pollution results when man does not listen carefully. Noises are the sounds we have learned to ignore. Noise pollution today is being resisted by noise abatement. This is a negative approach. We must seek a way to make environmental acoustics a *positive* study program. Which sounds do we want to preserve, encourage, multiply? When we know this, the boring or destructive sounds will be conspicuous enough and we will know why we must eliminate them. Only a total appreciation of the acoustic environment can give us the resources for improving the orchestration of the world soundscape. For many years I have been fighting for ear cleaning in schools to eliminate audiometry in factories. Clairaudience not ear muffs. It is an idea over which I do not wish to exercise permanent ownership.

The home territory of soundscape studies will be the middle ground between science, society and the arts. From acoustics and psychoacoustics we will learn about the physical properties of sound and the way sound is interpreted by the human brain. From society we will learn how man behaves with sounds and how sounds affect and change his behavior. From the arts, particularly music, we will learn how man creates ideal soundscapes for that other life, the life of the imagination and psychic reflection. From these studies we will begin to lay the foundations of a new interdiscipline—acoustic design.

From Industrial Design to Acoustic Design

The most important revolution in aesthetic education in the twentieth century was that accomplished by the Bauhaus, that celebrated German school of the twenties. Under the leadership of architect Walter Gropius, the Bauhaus collected some of the great painters and architects of the time (Klee, Kandinsky, Moholy-Nagy, Mies van der Rohe), together with craftsmen of distinction. At first it seemed disappointing that the graduates of this school did not rise to rival their mentors as artists. But the purpose of the school was different. From the interdisciplinary synergy of faculty skills a whole new study field was created, for the school invented the subject of industrial design. The Bauhaus brought aesthetics to machinery and mass production.

It devolves on us now to invent a subject which we might call acoustic design, an interdiscipline in which musicians, acousticians, psychologists, sociologists and others would study the world soundscape together in order to make intelligent recommendations for its improvement. This study would consist of documenting important features, of noting differences, parallels and trends, of collecting sounds threatened with extinction, of studying the effects of new sounds before they are indiscriminately released into the environment, of studying the rich symbolism sounds have for man and of studying human behavior patterns in different sonic environments in order to use these insights in planning future environments for man. Cross-cultural evidence from around the world must be carefully assembled and interpreted. New methods of educating the public to the importance of environmental sound must be devised. The final question will be: is the soundscape of the world an indeterminate composition over which we have no control, or are *we* its composers and performers, responsible for giving it form and beauty?

Orchestration Is a Musician's Business

Throughout this book [see original publication] I am going to treat the world as a macrocosmic musical composition. This is an unusual idea but I am going to nudge it forward relentlessly. The definition of music has undergone radical change in recent years. In one of the more contemporary definitions, John Cage has declared: "Music is sounds, sounds around us whether we're in or out of concert halls: cf. Thoreau." The reference is to Thoreau's *Walden,* where the author experiences in the sounds and sights of nature an inexhaustible entertainment.

To define music merely as *sounds* would have been unthinkable a few years ago, though today it is the more exclusive definitions that are proving unacceptable. Little by little throughout the twentieth century, all the conventional definitions of music have been exploded by the abundant activities of musicians themselves. First with the huge expansion of percussion instruments in our orchestras, many of which produce nonpitched and arhythmic sounds; then through the introduction of aleatoric procedures in which all attempts to organize the sounds of a composition rationally are surrendered to the "higher" laws of entropy; then through the opening-out of the time-and-space containers we call compositions and concert halls to allow the introduction of a whole new world of sounds outside them (in Cage's *4'33" Silence* we hear only the sounds external to the composition itself, which is merely one protracted caesura); then in the practices of *musique concrète,* which inserts any sound from the environment into a composition via tape; and finally in electronic music, which has revealed a whole gamut of new musical sounds, many of them related to industrial and electric technology in the world at large.

Today all sounds belong to a continuous field of possibilities lying *within the comprehensive dominion of music.* Behold the new orchestra: the sonic universe!

And the musicians: anyone and anything that sounds!

Dionysian Versus Apollonian Concepts of Music

It is easier to see the responsibilities of the acoustical engineer or the audiologist toward the world soundscape than to understand the precise manner in which the contemporary musician is supposed to attach himself to this vast theme, so I am going to grind my axe on this point for a moment longer.

There are two basic ideas of what music is or ought to be. They may be seen most clearly in two Greek myths dealing with the origin of music. Pindar's twelfth Pythian Ode tells how the art of aulos playing was invented by Athena when, after the beheading of Medusa, she was touched by the heart-rending cries of Medusa's sisters and created a special *nomos* in their honor. In a Homeric hymn to Hermes an alternative origin is mentioned. The lyre is said to have been invented by Hermes when he surmised that the shell of the turtle, if used as a body of resonance, could produce sound.

In the first of these myths music arises as subjective emotion; in the second it arises with the discovery of sonic properties in the materials of the universe. These are the cornerstones on which all subsequent theories of music are founded. Characteristically the lyre is the instrument of Homer, of the epos, of serene contemplation of the universe; while the aulos (the reed oboe) is the instrument of exaltation and tragedy, the instrument of the dithyramb and of drama. The lyre is the instrument of Apollo, the aulos that of the Dionysian festivals. In the Dionysian myth, music is conceived as internal sound breaking forth from the human breast; in the Apollonian it is external sound, God-sent to remind us of the harmony of the universe. In the Apollonian view music is exact, serene, mathematical, associated with transcendental visions of Utopia and the Harmony of the Spheres. It is also the *anāhata* of Indian theorists. It is the basis of Pythagoras's speculations and those of the medieval theoreticians (where music was taught as a subject of the quadrivium, along with arithmetic, geometry and astronomy), as well as of Schoenberg's twelve-note method of composition. Its methods of exposition are number theories. It seeks to harmonize the world through acoustic design. In the Dionysian view music is irrational and subjective. It employs expressive devices: tempo fluctuations, dynamic shadings, tonal colorings. It is the music of the operatic stage, of *bel canto,* and its reedy voice can also be heard in Bach's Passions. Above all, it is the musical expression of the romantic artist, prevailing throughout the nineteenth century and on into the expressionism of the twentieth century. It also directs the training of the musician today.

Because the production of sounds is so much a subjective matter with modern man, the contemporary soundscape is notable for its dynamic hedonism. The research I am about to describe represents a reaffirmation of music as a search for the harmonizing influence of sounds in the world about us. In Robert Fludd's *Utruisque Cosmi Historia* there is an illustration entitled "The Tuning of the World" in which the earth forms the body of an instrument across which strings are stretched and are tuned by a divine hand. We must try once again to find the secret of that tuning.

Music, the Soundscape and Social Welfare

In Hermann Hesse's *The Glass Bead Game* there is an arresting idea. Hesse claims to be repeating a theory of the relationship between music and the state from an ancient Chinese source; "Therefore the music of a well-ordered age is calm and cheerful, and so is its government. The music of a restive age is excited and fierce, and its government is perverted. The music of a decaying state is sentimental and sad, and its government is imperiled."

Such a theory would suggest that the egalitarian and enlightened reign of Maria Theresa (for instance, as expressed in her unified criminal code of 1768) and the grace and balance of Mozart's music are not accidental. Or that the sentimental vagaries of Richard Strauss are perfectly consistent with the waning of the same Austro-Hungarian Empire. In Gustav Mahler we find, etched in an acid Jewish hand, marches and German dances of such sarcasm as to give us a presentiment of the political *dance macabre* soon to follow.

The thesis is also borne out well in tribal societies where, under the strict control of the flourishing community, music is tightly structured, while in detribalized areas the individual sings appallingly sentimental songs. Any ethnomusicologist will confirm this. There can be little doubt then that music is an indicator of the age, revealing, for those who know how to read its symptomatic messages, a means of fixing social and even political events.

For some time I have also believed that the general acoustic environment of a society can be read as an indicator of social conditions which produce it and may tell us much about the trending and evolution of that society. Throughout this book [see original publication] I will suggest many such relationships, and though it is probably in my nature to do this emphatically, I hope the reader may continue to regard the method as valid even if some of the equations seem disagreeable. They are all open to further testing.

The Notation of Soundscapes (Sonography)

The soundscape is any acoustic field of study. We may speak of a musical composition as a soundscape, or a radio program as a soundscape or an acoustic environment as a soundscape. We can isolate an acoustic environment as a field of study just as we can study the characteristics of a given landscape. However, it is less easy to formulate an exact impression of a soundscape than of a landscape. There is nothing in sonography corresponding to the instantaneous impression which photography can create. With a camera it is possible to catch the salient features of a visual panorama to create an impression that is immediately evident. The microphone does not operate this way. It samples details. It gives the close-up but nothing corresponding to aerial photography.

Similarly, while everyone has had some experience reading maps, and many can draw at least significant information from other schematics of the visual landscape, such as architects' drawings or geographers' contour maps, few can read the sophisticated charts used by phoneticians, acousticians or musicians. To give a totally convincing image of a soundscape would involve extraordinary skill and patience: thousands of recordings would have to be made; tens of thousands of measurements would have be taken; and a new means of description would have to be devised.

A soundscape consists of events *heard* not objects *seen*. Beyond aural perception is the notation and photography of sound, which, being silent, presents certain problems that will be discussed in a special chapter in the Analysis section of the book [see original publication]. Through the misfortune of having to present data on silent pages, we will be forced to use some types of visual projection as well as musical notation, in advance of this discussion, and these will only be useful if they assist in opening ears and stimulating clairaudience.

We are also disadvantaged in the pursuit of a historical perspective. While we may have numerous photographs taken at different times, and before them drawings and maps to show us how a scene changed over the ages, we must make inferences as to the changes of the soundscape. We may know exactly how many new buildings went up in a given area in a decade or how the population has risen, but we do not know by how many decibels the ambient noise level may have risen for a comparable period of time. More than this, sounds may alter or disappear with scarcely a comment even from the most sensitive of historians. Thus, while we may utilize the techniques of modern recording and analysis to study contemporary soundscapes, for the foundation of historical perspectives, we will have to turn to earwitness accounts from literature and mythology, as well as to anthropological and historical records.

Earwitness

The first part of the book will be particularly indebted to such accounts [see original publication]. I have always attempted to go directly to sources. Thus, a writer is trustworthy only when writing about sounds directly experienced and intimately known. Writing about other places and times usually results in counterfeit descriptions. To take an obvious instance, when Jonathan Swift describes Niagara Falls as making "a terrible squash" we know he never visited the place; but when Chateaubriand tells us that in 1791 he heard the roar of Niagara eight to ten miles away, he provides us with useful information about the ambient sound level, against which that of today could be measured. When a writer writes uncounterfeitingly about directly apprehended experiences, the ears may sometimes play tricks on the brain, as Erich Maria Remarque discovered in the trenches during the First World War when he heard shells exploding about him followed by the rumble of the distant guns that fired them. This aural illusion is perfectly accountable, for as the shells were traveling at supersonic speeds they arrived in advance of the sounds of their original detonations; but only someone trained in acoustics could have predicted this. *All Quiet on the Western Front* is convincing because the author was there. And we trust him when he describes other unusual sound events—for instance, the sounds made by dead bodies. "The days are hot and the dead lie unburied. We cannot fetch them all in, if we did we should not know what to do with them. The shells will bury them. Many have their bellies swollen up like balloons. They hiss, belch, and make movements. The gases in them make noises." William Faulkner also knew the noise of corpses, which he described as "little trickling bursts of secret and murmurous bubbling."

In such ways is the authenticity of the earwitness established. It is a special talent of novelists like Tolstoy, Thomas Hardy and Thomas Mann to have captured the soundscapes of their own places and times, and such descriptions constitute the best guide available in the reconstruction of soundscapes past.

Features of the Soundscape

What the soundscape analyst must do first is to discover the significant features of the soundscape, those sounds which are important either because of their individuality, their numerousness or their domination. Ultimately some system or systems of generic classification will have to be devised, and this will be a subject for the third part of the book [see original publication]. For the first two parts it will be enough to categorize the main themes of a soundscape by distinguishing between what we call *keynote sounds, signals* and *soundmarks*. To these we might add *archetypal* sounds, those mysterious ancient sounds, often possessing felicitous symbolism, which we have inherited from remote antiquity or prehistory.

Keynote is a musical term; it is the note that identifies the key or tonality of a particular composition. It is the anchor or fundamental tone and although the material may modulate around it, often obscuring its importance, it is in reference to this point that everything else takes on its special meaning. Keynote sounds do not have to be listened to consciously; they are overheard but cannot be overlooked, for keynote sounds become listening habits in spite of themselves.

The psychologist of visual perception speaks of "figure" and "ground," the figure being that which is looked at while the ground exists only to give the figure its outline and mass. But the figure cannot exist without its ground; subtract it and the figure becomes shapeless, nonexistent. Even though keynote sounds may not always be heard consciously, the fact that they are ubiquitously there suggests the possibility of a deep and pervasive influence on our behavior and moods. The keynote sounds of a given place are important because they help to outline the character of men living among them.

The keynote sounds of a landscape are those created by its geography and climate: water, wind, forests, plains, birds, insects and animals. Many of these sounds may possess archetypal significance; that is, they may have imprinted themselves so deeply on the people hearing them that life without them would be sensed as a distinct impoverishment. They may even affect the behavior or life style of a society, though for a discussion of this we will wait until the reader is more acquainted with the matter.

Signals are foreground sounds and they are listened to consciously. In terms of the psychologist, they are figure rather than ground. Any sound can be listened to consciously, and so any sound can become a figure or signal, but for the purposes of our community-oriented study we will confine ourselves to mentioning some of those signals which *must* be listened to because they constitute acoustic warning devices: bells, whistles, horns and sirens. Sound signals may often be organized into quite elaborate codes permitting messages of considerable complexity to be transmitted to those who can interpret them. Such, for instance, is the case with the *cor de chasse,* or train and ship whistles, as we shall discover.

The term *soundmark* is derived from landmark and refers to a community sound which is unique or possesses qualities which make it specially regarded or noticed by the people in that community. Once a soundmark has been identified, it deserves to be protected, for soundmarks make the acoustic life of the community unique. This is a subject to be taken up in Part Four of the book, where the principles of acoustic design will be discussed.

I will try to explain all other soundscape terminology as it is introduced. At the end of the book [see original publication] there is a short glossary of terms which are either neologistic or have been used idiosyncratically, in case doubt exists at any point in the text. I have tried not to use too many complex acoustical terms, though a knowledge of the fundamentals of acoustics and a familiarity with both musical theory and history is presupposed.

Ears and Clairaudience

We will not argue for the priority of the ear. In the West the ear gave way to the eye as the most important gatherer of information about the time of the Renaissance, with the development of the printing press and perspective painting. One of the most evident testaments of this change is the way in which we have come to imagine God. It was not until the Renaissance that God became portraiture. Previously he had been conceived as sound or vibration. In the Zoroastrian religion, the priest Srosh (representing the genius of hearing) stands between man and the pantheon of the gods, listening for the divine messages, which he transmits to humanity. *Samā* is the Sufi word for audition or listening. The followers of Jalal-ud-din Rumi worked themselves into a mystical trance by chanting and whirling in slow gyrations. Their dance is thought by some scholars to have represented the solar system, recalling also the deep-rooted mystical belief in an extraterrestrial music, a Music of the Spheres, which the attuned soul may at times hear. But these exceptional powers of hearing, what I have called clairaudience, were not attained effortlessly. The poet Saadi says in one of his lyric poems:

> I will not say, my brothers, what *samā* is
> Before I know who the listener is.

Before the days of writing, in the days of prophets and epics, the sense of hearing was more vital than the sense of sight. The word of God, the history of the tribe and all other important information was heard, not seen. In parts of the world, the aural sense still tends to predominate.

> . . . rural Africans live largely in a world of sound—a world loaded with direct personal significance for the hearer—whereas the western European lives much more in a visual world which is on the whole indifferent to him. . . . Sounds lose much of this significance in western Europe, where man often develops, and must develop, a remarkable ability to disregard them. Whereas for Europeans, in general, "seeing is believing," for rural Africans reality seems to reside far more in what is heard and what is said. . . . Indeed, one is constrained to believe that the eye is regarded by many Africans less as a receiving organ than as an instrument of the will, the ear being the main receiving organ.

Marshall McLuhan has suggested that since the advent of electric culture we may be moving back to such a state again, and I think he is right. The very emergence of noise pollution as a topic of public concern testifies to the fact that modern man is at last becoming concerned to clean the sludge out of his ears and regain the talent for clairaudience—clean hearing.

A Special Sense

Touch is the most personal of the senses. Hearing and touch meet where the lower frequencies of audible sound pass over to tactile vibrations (at about 20 hertz). Hearing is a way of touching at a distance and the intimacy of the first sense is fused with sociability whenever people gather together to hear something special. Reading that sentence an ethnomusicologist noted: "All the ethnic groups I know well have in common their physical closeness and an incredible sense of rhythm. These two features seem to co-exist."

The sense of hearing cannot be closed off at will. There are no earlids. When we go to sleep, our perception of sound is the last door to close and it is also the first to open when we awaken. These facts have prompted McLuhan to write: "Terror is the normal state of any oral society for in it everything affects everything all the time."

The ear's only protection is an elaborate psychological mechanism for filtering out undesirable sound in order to concentrate on what is desirable. The eye points outward; the ear draws inward. It soaks up information. Wagner said: "To the eye appeals the outer man, the inner to the ear." The ear is also an erotic orifice. Listening to beautiful sounds, for instance the sounds of music, is like the tongue of a lover in your ear. Of its own nature then, the ear demands that insouciant and distracting sounds would be stopped in order that it may concentrate on those which truly matter.

Ultimately, this book is about sounds that matter [see original publication]. In order to reveal them it may be necessary to rage against those which don't. In Parts One and Two I will take the reader on a long excursion of soundscapes through history, with a heavy concentration on those of the Western world, though I will try to incorporate material from other parts of the world whenever it has been obtainable. In Part Three the soundscape will be subjected to critical analysis in preparation for Part Four, where the principles of acoustic design will be outlined—at least as far as they can be determined at the moment.

All research into sound must conclude with silence—a thought which must await its development in the final chapters. But the reader will clearly sense that this idea also links the first part of the book to the last, thus uniting an undertaking that is above all lyrical in character.

One final warning. Although I will at times be treating aural perception and acoustics as if they were abstractable disciplines, I do not wish to forget that the ear is but one sense receptor among many. The time has come to move out of the laboratory into the field of the living environment. Soundscape studies do this. But even they must be integrated into that wider study of the total environment in this not yet best of all possible worlds.

References for quotes

Music is sounds Quoted from R. Murray Schafer, *The New Soundscape,* London and Vienna, 1971, p. 1.

Rural Africans J. C. Carothers, "Culture, Psychiatry and the Written Word," *Psychiatry,* November, 1959, pp. 308–10.

Terror Marshall McLuhan, *The Gutenberg Galaxy,* Toronto, 1962, p. 32

The days are hot Erich Maria Remarque, *All Quiet on the Western Front,* Boston, 1929, see Chapter 4, p. 126 [in original publication].

Therefore the music Hermann Hesse, *The Glass Bead Game,* New York, 1969, p. 30.

When a writer Erich Maria Remarque, *All Quiet on the Western Front,* Boston, 1929, see Chapter 4 [in original publication].

Chapter 11

Shuhei Hosokawa

THE WALKMAN EFFECT

THE WALKMAN – A CASSETTE recorder for headphone listening. This gadget, originally invented and marketed by Sony in the spring of 1980 in Japan, and soon exported, has become known throughout the West, however awkward its Japanese-made English may sound. As its use has proliferated, so have the arguments about its effects. One example, a report in *Nouvel Observateur,* was cited by Philippe Sollers (Sollers 1981, p. 50). The interviewer, apparently, asks young people (eighteen to twenty-two years old) the following: whether men with the walkman are human or not; whether they are losing contact with reality; whether the relations between eyes and ears are changing radically; whether they are psychotic or schizophrenic; whether they are worried about the fate of humanity. One of the interviewees replies: your question is out-of-date. All of these problems of communication and incommunicability, according to him, belong to the sixties and the seventies. The eighties are not the same at all. They are the years of *autonomy,* of an intersection of *singularities* in the construction of discourses. Soon, he says, you will have every kind of film on video at home, every kind of classical music on only one tape. This is what gives me pleasure.

The attitude of the inquirer is a common one: people once lived happily in harmonious contact with nature, but with industrialisation and urbanisation, especially in recent decades, they lose that healthy relationship with the environment, become alienated and turn into David Riesman's 'lonely crowd', suffering from incommunicability. The walkman, for such an interviewer, is taken as encouraging self-enclosure and political apathy among the young, under a structure of mass control. Such 'cultural moralists', as Umberto Eco calls them, are apt to adjust something novel or extraordinary to the normative epistemological system based on the known, on standardised factors. Therefore, they either cannot explain clearly the socio-cultural change brought about by something new, or more typically, they simply fear and refuse any attempt at clarification. Even for those with a keener interest, the new thing is considered as deviant or inappropriate to their ready-made framework of thought.

Our wise interviewee swiftly dodges the stereotyped questions: the eighties are the years of *autonomy*. It is not purely coincidental that the walkman appeared in the first spring of this decade. The walkman is neither cause nor effect of that autonomy, neither evokes nor realises it. It *is* the autonomy, or rather *autonomy-of-the-walking-self*. J.-F. Lyotard rightly remarks the position of the self in the 'post-modern' era: 'The *self* is small, but it is not isolated: it is held in a texture of relations which are more complex and more mobile than ever before' (1979, p. 31). The walkman represents parasitic and/or symbiotic *self* which has now become autonomous and mobile. Consequently we should analyse it not as a phenomenon in itself or as one of the examples which represent the latest developments in musical life, but as an *effect* (not in a causal sense) or *effect-event* in the pragmatic and semantic transformation of the urban. To think about it is to reflect on the urban itself: walkman as urban strategy, as urban sonic/musical device.

Musica Mobilis

I define *musica mobilis* as music whose source voluntarily or involuntarily moves from one point to another, coordinated by the corporal transportation of the source owner(s). One can describe its short history as comprising four successive and accumulative steps; the fourth does not exclude the preceding three but coexists with them (see Hosokawa 1981).

(a) First of all, there is the tone of urban life in general. In a city, there is no clear frontier between music and noise. Music becomes noise (the terrifying volume of the jukebox for some people); noise becomes music (the *Cries of London* of Thomas Weekes and of Luciano Berio, *Salt Peanuts* of Dizzy Gillespie; the voices of vendors in Oriental markets cannot be imagined without a kind of 'noisy music' or 'musical noise') (see Bosseur 1977). The same acoustic event can be considered as music or noise by different observers. Most of this 'music' is made involuntarily or without motive, in other words, without any conscious aesthetic motivation. The sound is nothing but one of the secondary consequences of other non-music-making activities (to promote, to vend and so on). It only shows that those involved *live together* (see *Musique en jeu* 1976).

(b) Besides the *musicien malgrè lui,* the city nourishes a group of voluntary musicians: so-called street musicians. In the subway or on the corner of the street, they play in order to earn money. Some people just pass by, others stop. As in a concert hall (though maybe less strictly), the participants are divided into two groups, musicians and audience—passers-by, and linked together (more closely and intimately) because both groups share their inner and outer time, 'tuning each other'. They share the ongoing flux of time and consciousness, and thus feel a recovery of the lost links of social life. Though the music is transmitted mono-directionally, the two groups react and 'communicate' bi-directionally: a mutual tuning-in relation is maintained even if it is very transitory. The aesthetic or artistic quality of the performed music is usually less important than the ephemeral we-feeling which is produced. These people are in the world of Schutz's *making-music-together* (see Schutz 1964, 1976; Prato 1983).

(c) We find also in the city other people who are involved with the music, or rather, who live with it. They do not play but listen to it through technological 'instruments'. A portable radio (or cassette) listener in a street disperses the music as he walks. Passers-by are obliged to hear it for a few seconds. Sometimes two or three machines cross the street, emitting different tunes. Here, people do not always share their inner and outer time. On the contrary, they usually have in common only their outer, measurable time, without penetrating or communicating with one another. They seem to live in the world of *listening-to-the-music-together*. A car stereo system (or radio) can be considered one of the variants of this type. A car is often taken to be a 'secondary house' or 'mobile home' in metropolitan life. The situation, however, goes beyond this. Now, it is a house which is a 'fixed car' or 'permanent parking area'. A garage does not function as a place to anchor a car but as a place through which to pin the house to the route of the car.[1] The car, consequently the car radio too, is an intermediary between social and personal life: it concerns the semi-social and/or semi-personal, in a word, *family*. If one switches it on, other 'family', if any, are forced to hear/listen to it, as is the case with 'street listening man'. But, unlike him, the family is capable of stopping it if it doesn't please.

(d) Finally there is the walkman listener, who is found in the world of *listening to music alone*. This listener seems to cut the auditory contact with the outer world where he really lives: seeking the perfection of his 'individual' zone of listening, he is the *minimum, mobile and intelligent unit* (Robert Fripp) for music listening. One cannot imagine any further advance (even 'body sound', the latest product in 1983, which is a sort of jacket furnishing two 'speakers' for feeling musical vibration anytime and anywhere) which constitutes more than examples of secondary 'progress', such as the invention of lighter, smaller and higher fidelity apparatus, of a wireless headphone, of waterproof (listen + swim) or hybrid gadgets (walkman + alarm clock + calendar + calculator + video game + bio-rhythm indicator + exposure meter + small light + holoscope + . . .). The walkman is doubtless the ultimate object for private listening, even though the proliferation of such 'secondary functions' (J. Baudrillard) will certainly progress right up to the vanishing point of the object, that is, to the point at which infinite differentiation makes them unrecognisable within the sea of objects, or at which the process of differentiation reaches the stage of a universe with no differences.

Technological Regression

It is interesting that, from the technical and technological point of view, the 'progress' from portable radio-cassette or car stereo to walkman is very minor, contrary to the conspicuous transformation on the level of praxis. Rather, the change seems to be a kind of 'devolution' because the walkman is a cassette recorder *minus* the recording function and the speaker. It is technologically a simpler object. Generally the technical development of an object is regarded as involving functional multiplication. When one type of object can do two things simultaneously, the user considers it more convenient (even if one of the two is quite useless to him, or, at least, if he has no need – is not able – to use both at the same time). For 'frivolous' consumers, then, differentiation of the secondary functions must be thought more important than the primary one (if any). The walkman, however, appears to be outside this law. It represents functional reduction, technological regression. According to the President of Sony, the idea of this reduction, which first came to him while walking in New York, was disliked intensely by the technical department because of its regressiveness. The engineers were in fact exclusively occupied with the 'techneme' level of the object, the President with the 'praxeme' level. He, well known for his ordinary-man-makes-good career and rationalistic approach, won the debate, risking capital and reputation, and came out on top in the commercial war. Needless to say, Sony was followed by many competitors (Toshiba, Aiwa, Philips. . .) who named their similar gadgets in more or less similar ways (*Walky, Cassette Boy*. . .). Some have a radio, some a recording function, others a battery meter: thus a refunctionalisation process. These products differ in only trifling ways. The war has already become less total than local, the old story of technical competition focusing upon the secondary functions. We can compare this with Kuhn's argument on the scientific revolutions (the relationship of paradigmatic change and ordinary science). The walkman constitutes a new paradigm owing to its 'revolutionary' effects on the pragmatic – not technical – aspects of urban musical listening, with the result that the technical assumptions come to seem ordinary. Sony had prepared a set of pragmatic presuppositions which were then 'taken for granted' (in Schutz's terms) by those who followed as 'knowledge at hand'. The walkman has become 'object at hand'.

A Walking Gadget

The short history of *musica mobilis* sketched previously suggests several specificities of the walkman:

(a) *Miniaturisation.* The more compact, the more portable . . . Technology always wants to make an object something *more:* its universe is one of teleological but endless comparisons. If a thing can be done in a more efficient way, people approve it as 'progress' or 'development'. In the history of technology, miniaturisation is one of the most obsessional goals. Imagine the space taken up by the now obsolete radio or gramophone. Miniaturisation allows us to make use of the space which the older objects occupied; and to take the objects outdoors more easily and with more mobility. It, therefore, contributes not only to a strategy of more efficient use of space but also to an urban strategy, that is, to the way of life. The portable radio and car stereo, for example, made possible on the road an experience which had previously only been feasible indoors. So, without doubt, did the walkman; however, in a much more thorough way, as will be discussed below.

(b) *Singularisation.* Miniaturisation as double strategy – spatial and urban – is deeply connected with another feature of the walkman, singularisation, for it enables our musical listening to be more occasional, more incidental, more contingent. Music can be taken wherever and whenever we go. The walkman produces or constitutes a musical *event* which is characterised as unique, mobile and singular. According to Gilles Deleuze, this singularity is radically different from being individual and personal. It is rather anonymous, impersonal, pre-individual and nomadic: 'A consciousness is nothing without some synthesis of unification, but there is no such synthesis for the consciousness without the form of the "I" or the point of view of the self (*Moi*). What is not individual nor personal, on the contrary, are the emissions of singularities in so far as these are constructed on an unconscious surface and enjoy an immanent mobile principle of auto-unification, through their *nomadic distribution*. These are radically distinct from the fixed and sedentary distributions which are the conditions for the unification of consciousness' (Deleuze 1969, pp. 124f.). The walkman obviously corresponds to such a 'singular' position of the self. It is not necessary to inquire into the causal relation between the birth of this consciousness and that of the walkman. What we must confirm here is the positional correspondence between them.

(c) *Autonomy*. Deleuze continues: 'The singularities enjoy a process of auto-unification which is always mobile and displaced by virtue of a paradoxical element which traverses and resonates the series, enveloping the corresponding singular points in the same aleatory space' (ibid. p. 125). Autonomy is not always synonymous with isolation, individualisation, separation from reality; rather, in apparent paradox, it is indispensable for the process of *self-unification*. Walkman users are not necessarily detached ('alienated' to use a value-laden term) from the environment, closing their ears, but are unified in the autonomous and singular moment – neither as persons nor as individuals – with the real. One instance may be quoted from the film starring Sophie Marceau entitled *La boom II*. At a party, a boy hesitates to approach the girl he loves, but finally manages to dance with her. He silently approaches her and puts a headphone on her head playing the same music as his. Their own exclusive music begins flowing between them. The happy pair dance to the different music, to the different rhythm. Is their dance an escape from reality? No, it is an 'incompossible' (Deleuze)[2] communication which establishes a radically *positive distance:* 'The idea of positive distance is topological and superficial, and excludes any depth or height which would lead the negative back to the pole of identity . . . Distance is . . . the affirmation of that which it distances' (ibid. p. 203).

To make this concept of 'positive distance' more precise, we may compare within the flood of objects the walkman with the polaroid, with respect to speed of act, immediacy of effect, simplicity of mechanical construction, verisimilitude of output, low-fidelity (lower than the ordinary stereo or camera) of reproduction, ease of operation, non-specificity of territory, anonymity of subject, and contingency of event.[3] The walkman is to the auditory domain what the polaroid is to the visual domain. If walkman is an ocular polaroid, polaroid is an optic walkman: *La boom II* versus *Alice in der Städten*. These two 'minor' objects are often taken as frivolous by those who avoid the surface, searching for the depth and the height. But if the surface is the 'place of meaning' (*le lieu du sens*) (ibid. pp. 87ff., 126, 151), then the autonomy, typically assigned to these two objects, can also give rise to a play of meanings.

(d) *Constructing / deconstructing meanings*. Walkman praxis focuses musical meaning on the surface of music, or generalises the surface to the whole: 'Musical meaning is . . . a *surface effect,* an effect of the resistant density of the sonorous' (Parret 1983, p. 30). With the walkman, the surface-ness of the music stands out, owing to the walkman's singularity and autonomy, realised by its miniaturisation. Creating meaning, in this case, goes parallel with objectification, in so far as we define an object as 'a status of meaning and a form' (Baudrillard 1972, p. 230). We are not interested here in the object in itself, but the object under use, not the lexical meaning but the practical one. The walkman, in fact, has no meaningless context; at the same time, paradoxically, no context is strictly appropriate for it. Every context (or no context) can be justified, appropriated and legitimated by its singularity and autonomy. Fellini once observed a boy with a walkman watching a film in a cinema: an example of a particular function of the *and:*

> AND . . . AND . . . AND . . . There was always a fight in the language between the verb 'to be' (*être*) and the conjunction 'and' (*et*), between *est* and *et*. These two terms only agree and combine together in appearance, because the one acts in the language as a constant forming the diatonic scale of language (*langue*), whilst the other puts all into variation, constituting the lines of a generalised chromaticism . . . We cannot be satisfied with the analysis of the 'and' as a conjunction; it is rather a very special form of every possible conjunction, which establishes a logic and language itself.
>
> (Deleuze and Guattari 1980, p. 124)

The practical meaning of the walkman is generated in the distance it poses between the reality and the real, the city and the urban, and particularly between the others and the I. It decontextualises the given coherence of the city-text, and at the same time, contextualises every situation which seemingly does not cohere with it. Though this double-faced work had already been partially achieved in the previous history of *musica mobilis,* it is the walkman that completes the process of the deconstruction of meaning which is inevitably coupled with its construction.

Walkman *Versus* Urbanism

So far the argument has been, more or less, from the point of view of the object. Now we shall look at the walkman from the point of view of the urban context. These two views are not separate and are often indistinguishable. They are, rather, complementary and only different accentuations will be found.

More significant to our research on the urban environment than its planning or description is a theory of its use; we shall proceed, in other words, not from the generative end (taking the part of the addresser of the urban message, roughly identifiable with the planner) but the interpretative end (taking the part of the addressee, the habitant). The latter approach permits us to deal with a city as 'a set of interrelations and of interactions between the subjects and the objects' (Greimas 1976, p. 144): 'The reception of spatial messages is not (or not only) their perception in terms of what is called "living" the city, reacting in significant ways to all spatial stimulations . . . To live in the city signifies for the individual . . . being in that space towards which all spatial messages converge, but also reacting to these messages, by dynamically engaging in the multiple programmes and mechanisms which attract and constrain one' (ibid. p. 153). As we shall see, the walk act consists precisely in the 'interrelations and interactions between the subjects and the objects' which Greimas mentions, for the walking subject is always in the un-predetermined process of the visual, auditive, olfactive, gustative, tactile transformation of his integral experience through the ongoing change of his point of view: The point of view is open to a divergence which it affirms. There is another city which corresponds to each point of view, each point of view is another city, the cities being united only by their distance and resonating only through the divergence of their series, of their houses and their streets. And always another city in the city' (Deleuze 1969, p. 203).

Not only the subject but also the environment is susceptible to transformation through this act, for the act can only be defined in terms of mutual and interdependent actions. It is not sufficient to say whether his interpretation of the spatial messages is pertinent to the environment or not: better to say that the pertinence of that interpretation is progressively adjusted by the progress of the act (see Sbisà and Fabbri 1980). Certainly his act presupposes several codes which have been socio-culturally conditioned, and he has a series of 'knowledges at hand' about his conduct provided partially by his experiences, partially and more implicitly by the urban planner who has hypothetically programmed and built the space and the place where he lives; but he, as walking subject, transforms these presuppositions, their knowledge, and, in consequence, his own self in a dynamic transaction with the environment: dynamic, because, as Baudrillard has noted, he himself does not confront the environment, but virtually and/or actually is a part of it (see Baudrillard 1972, p. 255). He is included in his environment, so his act and his environment are in a relationship like the structure of a Russian doll: inside out and outside in. This transaction progresses in line with the self-metamorphoses of the transactional world. If one assumes the city as a text, the habitants must be considered as a 'blank' within it, which should be completed by their interpretative acts, that is, their 'acts of reading' of the city-text-event (see Greimas 1976, pp. 151ff). The urbanist can only prepare this blank text to be read, though he sometimes fancies that he provides the integral text of a city and that the habitants should live almost wholly under the normative rules he has presupposed.

Planners are in many cases exclusively engaged in the planning of the spatial dimension of their city, leaving the acoustic aspect to one side. Every urbanist takes care, for example, of the proportion between habitant and window, trees and street, architecture and green zone and so on, neglecting what kind of tone the city has, that the habitants (are obliged to) hear. A city is not only unseen by the planner who observes it from outside – as noted critically by many humanists – but also unheard. 'The blind zone' (Henri Lefèbvre's *le champ aveugle*) is also the dumb zone. This is the case not only with modern urbanism, but also traditional city-planning, as well as, in a sense, the history of *Utopia* and *Città ideale*. From Plato and Piero della Francesca up to Fourier or Le Corbusier, most such schemes tell us very little about how the authors conceived the acoustic life of their cities, what kind of sounds the *habitante ideale* produces and is surrounded by. Are they monotonous or 'polytonous'? Maybe the ancient 'urbanists' did not feel they suffered from their acoustic ambience, nor imagined that each city had its own urban tone.

It was not until recent decades that urbanists began to care about this tone and to become actively involved in acoustic problems. The Canadian composer, Murray

Schafer, though not a professional urbanist, carried out the first research worthy of note into the total theory of acoustic design or, in his terms, the *soundscape:*

> Today, when the slop and spawn of the megalopolis invite a multiplication of sonic jabberware, the task of the acoustic designer in sorting out the mass and placing society again in a humanistic framework is no less difficult than that of the urbanologist and planner, but it is equally necessary. The problem of redefining the acoustic community may involve the establishment of zoning regulations; but to limit it to this, as is common today, is to mistake the trajectories of the soundscape for the property lines of the landscape. Only when the outsweep and interpenetration of sonic profiles is known and accepted as the operative reality will the acoustic zone rise to the level of an intelligent understanding.
>
> (Schafer 1977, p. 216; see also Sansot 1973, 1983)

Unlike Schafer's reconstruction of the past soundscape, which makes interesting use of history, literature and ethnography, his principal argument about the present urban soundscape seems to fall short of its reality, that is, of its necessary artificiality, which appears to him as something to be restored to a more natural, therefore a more 'human' state. His 'humanistic framework', supported by the ravishing neologisms, aims only at the improvement *ad hoc* of the soundscape in question on the perceptual level (for example, 'ear cleaning') or on the situational one (for example, 'soniferous garden'); there is no consideration of the underlying social interactions or of the process whereby the soundscape itself is institutionalised. His point of view still derives, against his wish, from that of the 'urbanist or planner', or that of the 'teacher', rather than of the user or habitant. One example: his 'acoustic ecology' is in fact based on an acute sensitivity to the existing soundscape; it is connected with the 'soundwalk' – which produces a report 'with specific reference to the sounds heard during the walk' – and presupposes that the given soundscape in a city is potentially pleasant. This presupposition appears quite doubtful except for those who feel pleasure when comparing the 'pitches of different cash registers or the duration of different telephone bells' or 'the pitches of drainpipes on a city street', singing 'tunes around the different harmonies of neon lights', or 'entering a store and tapping the tops of all tinned goods (Caribbean steel band!)' (Schafer 1977, p. 213). All of these are highly important as didactic experiments or exercises, but also miss the 'lived structure of praxis' (H. Lefèbvre), and, more particularly, are filled with the lament for a lost noise, a lost Nature. Baudrillard speaks against the sentimental ecologist:

> To speak of ecology is to signal the death and total abstraction of 'nature' . . . the great Signified, the great Referent. Nature is dead and replacing it is the environment which designates both the death of nature and its restitution as a model of simulation . . . As nature, air, water, after having been simple productive forces, become rare commodities and enter into the field of value, it is men themselves who are inscribed more deeply in the field of political economy.
>
> (Baudrillard 1972, p. 253)

What is lacking in Schafer is, on the one hand, reflection on this quality of simulation, based on that knowledge of political economy which is indispensable if we are to think of the total artificiality of our irreversible environment; on the other, the concept of plurality, as described by Michel de Certeau: 'Planning the city means simultaneously to *think of the plurality* of the real itself and to *confer effectivity* on this pluralised thought. It is both knowing how, and being able, to articulate' (de Certeau 1980b, p. 175). We do not live, as Schafer implicitly assumes, in a one-layered 'sonoferous' reality, in which one factor can exercise its influence on total reality homogeneously, but in a multi-layered structure, in which one layer, even if identifiable as such, shifts away from another and no definite causality is found, no heroic height or spiritual depth permitted.

If Schafer's proposed manner of listening can be thought of as 'territorialised listening', because he intends that urban space should be a 'space of familiar and known noises', a 'space of security' (Barthes 1982, p. 218), then walkman listening on the street appears as 'de-territorialised listening'. It intends that every sort of familiar soundscape is transformed by that singular acoustic experience coordinated by the user's own ongoing pedestrian act, which induces an autonomous 'head space' between his Self and his surroundings in order to distance itself from – not familiarise itself with – both of them. The result is a mobility of the Self. Thus the walkman crosses every predetermined line of the acoustic designers. It enables us to move towards an autonomous pluralistically structured awareness of reality, but not towards a self-enclosed refuge or into narcissistic regression.

You may ask yourself how the walkman, while making no substantial contribution to the public soundscape, can intervene in the urban tone, how it can interfere with the urban acoustic without having a material effect. The answer is: through the *walk act*.

Walk Act

Though the walkman can be used with various types of act, the walk act will be the most privileged, as suggested by the strange name, walk-man. Walking is the most primitive, the most immediate, the most corporal medium for human transportation. All expressive corporal practices, especially dance, theatre, certain sports, derive from the human walk act (see Charles 1979). The walkman connects it with music. De Certeau is right to compare the walk act with the speech act:

> The act of walking is to the urban system what enunciation (the *speech act*) is to language or to the system of available utterances. At the most elementary level it has a triple 'enunciative' function: it is a process of *appropriation* of the topographical system by the pedestrian (in the same way that the speaker appropriates and assumes language for himself); it is a spatial *realisation* of place (as the speech act is sonorous realisation of language); and finally it implies certain *relations* between differentiated positions, that is, certain pragmatic 'contracts' in the form of movements (in the same way as verbal enunciation is an 'allocation', a 'positioning of

the other' in relation to the speaker, and establishes a contract between speakers). Walking would therefore find its primary definition as a site of enunciation . . . Walking . . . creates a mobile organicity of the environment, a succession of phatic *topoi*.

(de Certeau 1980b, p. 180)

Jean-François Augoyard also thinks of the *poetics* of the walk, because the walk act is not the progressive totalisation of a given space to be traversed, but the articulation of a movement which constructs the lived experience of the space in a very perplexing manner (Augoyard 1979, pp. 28, 71; see also Bollnow 1963, Norberg-Schultz 1971, Sansot 1973).

The walkman may make the walk act more poetic owing to its 'stuttering' function of the Deleuzian *and*. One walks *and* listens (and inversely). One experiences *walk'n'listen,* or even walk'n'eat'n'drink'n'play'n' . . . 'n'listen (boy with roller skates eating McDonald, drinking Coke, and listening to Michael Jackson through walkman . . .). The pleasure of walkman, as the *Nouvel Observateur* interviewee was, consciously or unconsciously, aware can be found in the way that listening is incidentally overlapped by and mixed up with different acts: as a listening act, it is not exclusive but inclusive, not concentrated but distracted, not convergent but divergent, not centripetal but centrifugal. In an *additional* listening act, as opposed to a *subtractional* one (for example, a classical concert), music is incorporated with alien elements which are usually taken as non-musical. In walkman praxis, compared with other types of *musica mobilis* or with the dance-theatre of disco music, it is tightly conjoined with the corporality of the walk act itself. For, while in the disco the theatrical devices have been prepared before we enter and our body only dances in that pre-programmed circuit (even if the corporal movement itself is very fierce and almost sportive), with the walkman an amalgam composed of music and body is brought about and its user invents the art of their coordination on a daily level in order to figure out a 'short circuit' in the place he is walking around. Whether it is the walkman that charges the body, or, inversely, the body that charges the walkman, it is difficult to say. The walkman works not as a prolongation of the body (as with other instruments of *musica mobilis*) but as a built-in part or, because of its intimacy, as an intrusion-like *prosthesis* (see *Traverses* 1979). The walkman holder *plays* the music and listens to the sound come from his own body (see Barthes 1982, p. 265). When we listen to the 'beat' of our body, when the walkman intrudes inside the skin, the order of our body is inverted, that is, the surface tension of the skin loses its balancing function through which it activates the interpenetration of Self and world: a *mise en oeuvre* in the body, through the body, of the body (see Tibon-Cornillot 1982, p. 120). Through the walkman, then, the body is opened; it is put into the process of the aestheticisation, the theatricalisation of the urban – but *in secret.*

Walkman as Secret Theatre

What surprised people when they saw the walkman for the first time in their cities was the evident fact that they could know *whether* the walkman user was listening to something, but not *what* he was listening to. Something *was* there, but it did *not appear:* it was secret (see *Traverses* 1984). Until the appearance of the walkman, people had not witnessed a scene in which a passer-by 'confessed' that he had a secret in such a distinct and obvious way. They were, in fact, aware that the user was listening not only to something secret but also to the secret itself, a secret in the form of mobile sound: an open, public secret.

As to the user, he employs the 'manners of the poacher' (de Certeau 1980b, p. 10). Secrets proceed according to a relationship of communication and incommunication. The secret-holder always has an advantage over the secret-beholder, in so far as the former 'confesses' to the latter only that he has something hidden, something unknown to the latter. And the secret must vanish when the holder leaks its contents. So it is effective only between the first utterance – which reveals its existence – and the second – which removes the mask to reveal the truth. Before that it is too latent, after this, too manifest to function as a secret. The walkman holder has just finished the first confession. He lets people know that he is listening to a secret. He neither refuses communication nor is isolated from reality, but continues enunciating the existence of his secret in this simple way. He lets people know voluntarily that he has the *truth* which, nevertheless, does *not appear.* Verification may be guaranteed in so far as *it* does not appear, in sum, in so far as it is secret. François Truffaut, in Spielberg's *Close Encounters of the Third Kind,* thinks that the incomprehensible message from space must be true because it appears to him intuitively as a secret. This story is interesting to us for two reasons: (a) he imitates the received message-as-secret, when he, in his turn, emits it back to space; (b) the message is sonorous and almost 'musical' (d–e–c–C–G). ((a) can be seen also in *ET* when the boy and ET, in their first close encounter, imitate each other's gestures, as if both regressed to the mirror-phase of Lacan's psychoanalysis.) Truffaut's belief in imitation as the key to resolving the secret is also familiar among walkman holders. Their curiosity to know the secret the others guard in public makes the gadget circulate all over the world. Certainly it is an article of fashion, but more particularly of a fashion for secrecy. The superiority felt by the holder to the beholder is far from the casual satisfaction of acquiring something fashionable, but relates to receiving the visa for the secret garden of the walkman in which people communicate with one another through the form – not the content – of the secret. He neither knows the content of others' secrets nor cares about them. He just knows that others have secrets *as he does* and that they will know that he himself also has something different with respect to the content, but similar in its form: the cryptic. I know that he knows that I know that he knows it . . . They openly exhibit the form of their secrets to one another: this is the first level of 'expression' of the walkman act. The second level is the expressivity of the music tied up with that of corporal movement, of the walk act. Expression of the third level concerns what even the holders do not know exactly, that is the top secret of the walkman act, or rather of the music in general: 'What is listened to . . . is the *secret:* that which, enmeshed in reality, can only come to human consciousness by way of a code which simultaneously serves to encode and decode this reality' (Barthes 1982, p. 221).

Euphoric and dysphoric experiencing (to borrow Greimas' terms) of the urban by way of the walkman must be understood in terms of the network of that triple cryptic expressivity. These are two sides of a coin called 'aestheticisation', which may be defined as 'the act of a perception which attaches to the appearance of the object and tastes it as "sensible"' (perceptible by the senses) (Dufrenne 1979, p. 131). When the sensible is positive, we may call the result 'euphoria', when negative, 'dysphoria'. The important point is that what is aestheticisable is what can be *mise en ordre sensible*, rather than concerning any judgement of the beauty of the object in question. The walkman is 'aestheticisable' in so far as it concerns the *sensible*, provoking certain reactions, either dysphoric or euphoric, and transforming decisively each spatial signification into something else. The aesthetic aspects are, at least in this case, also linked with *semantic* and *theatrical ones*: the former because the walkman is able to construct and/or deconstruct the network of urban meaning; the latter, because it can organise an open and mobile theatre by means of its clandestine manoeuvres, which transform the spatial constellation of the urban, communicate autonomously, surreptitiously, tacitly, and present the user as a possible stranger who speaks an incomprehensible pedestrian language (for certain dysphoric persons, he looks like ET, that is, the *Extra-Tangible*). The beholders feel as if they were spectators in a theatre because the 'dialogue' on the stage would still apparently continue without their actual presence. But they soon come to know that in effect they also participate in the theatrical process since the dialogue on the stage presupposes, if one takes theatre as *text*, the existence and the reaction of the spectators themselves. They are indispensable for the textual process of theatre, and – why not? – of the walkman. Thus, with the appearance of this novel gadget, all passers-by are inevitably involved in the walkman-theatre, as either actors (holders) or spectators (beholders): 'There is no difference which separates passivity and activity, but only that which distinguishes the different ways of socially *marking* the space effected in a given (*un donné*) by a practice' (de Certeau 1980a, p. 248).

The walkman effect must be measured in terms of this practical mode of operation. Even when one switches off, or leaves it behind, theatrical effects are still active. The show must go on till the death of the gadget-object. We all live in the *Société ludique* (Alain Cotta), which is incessantly threatened by boredom and invaded by the play/game (*jeu*). It is up to you to choose your 'role' in this 'society of spectacle': actor or spectator.

Notes

1. As suggested in the films of Wim Wenders, *Im Lauf der Zeit* and *The State of Things*.
2. 'Incompossible' is untranslatable but means roughly a combination of 'impossible', 'incomprehensible' and 'uncomposable'.
3. In Wenders' *Alice in der Städten* a man with a polaroid incessantly photographs the things which attract him. The little girl accompanying him reacts immediately to the images. The reality is instantly duplicated by the image; the image multiplies reality.

References

Augoyard, J.-F. 1979. *Pas à pas. Essai sur le cheminement quotidien en milieu urbain* (Paris)
Barthes, R. 1982. *L'Obvie et l'obtus* (Paris)

Baudrillard, J. 1972. *Pour une critique de l'économie politique du signe* (Paris)

Bollnow, O. F. 1963. *Mensch und Raum* (Stuttgart)

Bosseur, J.-Y. 1977. 'Geographic musicale de la ville', *Revue d'Esthétique,* special number: *La Ville n'est pas en lieu,* pp. 207–14

de Certeau, M. 1980a. *La Culture au pluriel* (Paris)

—1980b. *L'Invention du quotidien* (Paris)

Charles, D. 1979. 'Flux de marche avec piétinement', *Traverses,* 14–15, pp. 81–92

Deleuze, G. 1969. *Logique du sens* (Paris)

Deleuze, G. and Guattari, F. 1980. *Mille plateaux* (Paris)

Dufrenne, M. 1979. 'Le champ de l'esthétisable', *Revue d'Esthétique,* special number: *Pour l'object,* pp. 131–43

Fabbri, F. 1980. 'Du secret', *Traverses,* 18, pp. 76–83

Greimas, A. J. 1976. *Sémiotique et sciences sociales* (Paris)

Hosokawa, S. 1981. 'Considérations sur la musique mass-médiatisée', *International Review of the Aesthetics and Sociology of Music,* XII: 1, pp. 21–50

Lyotard, J.-F. 1979. *La Condition postmoderne* (Paris)

Musique en Jeu. 1976. 24 (*La Musique, les sons et la ville*)

Norberg-Schultz, C. 1971. *Existence, Space and Architecture* (London)

Parret, H. 1983. 'Postface', in E. Tarasti, *De l'Interprétation musicale, Actes semiotiques – documents,* 42, EHESS (Paris), pp. 23–31

Prato, P. 1983. 'La fenomenologia della musica di Alfred Schutz', *Rivista di Estetica,* 11, pp. 129–40

Sansot, P. 1973. *Póetique de la ville* (Paris)

—1983. *Variations paysagéres* (Paris)

Sbisà, M. and Fabbri, P. 1980. *Models for a Pragmatic Analysis* (Urbano)

Schafer, M. 1977. *The Tuning of the World* (New York)

Schutz, A. 1964. 'Making music together', in *Collected Papers* vol. 2 (The Hague), pp. 159–78

— 1976. 'Fragments on the phenomenology of music' *Music and Man,* 2: 1/2, pp. 23–71

Sollers, P. 1981. 'Seul contre tous . . .! Entretien avec Philippe Sollers', *Magazine littéraire,* 171 (April), pp. 50–52

Tibon-Cornillot, M. 1982. 'Du maquillage aux prothèses', *Confrontation,* 7 (Spring), pp. 119–36

Traverses, 1979. 14/15 (*Panoplies du corps*)

—1984. 30/31 (*Le secret*)

Chapter 12

Emily Thompson

SOUND, MODERNITY AND HISTORY

THE SOUNDSCAPE OF MODERNITY is a history of aural culture in early twentieth-century America. It charts dramatic transformations in what people heard, and it explores equally significant changes in the ways that people listened to those sounds. What they heard was a new kind of sound that was the product of modern technology. They listened in ways that acknowledged this fact, as critical consumers of aural commodities. By examining the technologies that produced those sounds, as well as the culture that consumed them, we can begin to recover more fully the texture of an era known as "The Machine Age," and we can comprehend more completely the experience of change, particularly technological change, that characterized this era.

By identifying a soundscape as the primary subject of the story that follows, I pursue a way of thinking about sound first developed by the musician R. Murray Schafer about twenty-five years ago. Schafer defined a soundscape as a sonic environment, a definition that reflected his engagement with the environmental movements of the 1970s and emphasized his ecologically based concern about the "polluted" nature of the soundscape of that era.[1] While Schafer's work remains socially and intellectually relevant today, the issues that influenced it are not what has motivated my own historical study, and I use the idea of a soundscape somewhat differently. Here, following the work of Alain Corbin, I define the soundscape as an auditory or aural landscape. Like a landscape, a soundscape is simultaneously a physical environment and a way of perceiving that environment; it is both a world and a culture constructed to make sense of that world.[2] The physical aspects of a soundscape consist not only of the sounds themselves, the waves of acoustical energy permeating the atmosphere in which people live, but also the material objects that create, and sometimes destroy, those sounds. A soundscape's cultural aspects incorporate scientific and aesthetic ways of listening, a listener's relationship to their environment, and the social circumstances that dictate who gets to hear what.[3] A soundscape, like a landscape, ultimately has more to do with civilization than with nature, and as such, it is constantly under construction and always undergoing change. The American soundscape underwent a particularly dramatic transformation in the years after 1900. By 1933, both the nature of sound and the culture of listening were unlike anything that had come before.

The sounds themselves were increasingly the result of technological mediation. Scientists and engineers discovered ways to manipulate traditional materials of architectural construction in order to control the behavior of sound in space. New kinds of materials specifically designed to control sound were developed, and were soon followed by new electroacoustic devices that effected even greater results by converting sounds into electrical signals. Some of the sounds that resulted from these mediations were objects of scientific scrutiny; others were the unintended consequences—the noises—of an ever-more mechanized society; others, like musical concerts, radio broadcasts, and motion picture sound tracks, were commodities consumed by an acoustically ravenous public. The contours of change were the same for all.

Accompanying these changes in the nature of sound were equally new trends in the culture of listening. A fundamental compulsion to control the behavior of sound drove technological developments in architectural acoustics, and this imperative stimulated auditors to listen more critically, to determine whether that control had been accomplished. This desire for control stemmed partly from new worries about noise, as traditionally bothersome sources of sound like animals, peddlers, and musicians were increasingly drowned out by the technological crescendo of the modern city. It was also driven by a preoccupation with efficiency that demanded the elimination of all things unnecessary, including unnecessary sounds. Finally, control was a means by which to exercise choice in a market filled with aural commodities; it allowed producers and consumers alike to identify what constituted "good sound," and to evaluate whether particular products achieved it.

Perhaps the most significant result of these physical and cultural changes was the reformulation of the relationship between sound and space. Indeed, as the new soundscape took shape, sound was gradually dissociated from space until the relationship ceased to exist. The dissociation began with the technological manipulations of sound-absorbing building materials, and the severance was made complete when electroacoustic devices claimed sound as their own. As scientists and engineers engaged increasingly with electrical representations of acoustical phenomena, sounds became indistinguishable from the circuits that produced them. When electroacoustic instruments like microphones and loudspeakers moved out of the laboratory and into the world, this new way of thinking migrated with them, and the result was that sounds were reconceived as signals.

When sounds became signals, a new criterion by which to evaluate them was established, a criterion whose origins, like the sounds themselves, were located in the new electrical technologies. Electrical systems were evaluated by measuring the strength of their signals against the inevitable encroachments of electrical noise, and this measure now became the means by which to judge all sounds. The desire for clear, controlled, signal-like sound became pervasive, and anything that interfered with this goal was now engineered out of existence.

Reverberation, the lingering over time of residual sound in a space, had always been a direct result of the architecture that created it, a function of both the size of a room and the materials that constituted its surfaces. As such, it sounded the acoustic signature of each particular place, representing the unique character (for better or worse) of the space in which it was heard. With the rise of the modern soundscape this would no longer be the case. Reverberation now became just another kind of noise, unnecessary and best eliminated.

As the new, nonreverberant criterion gained hold, and as the architectural and electroacoustic technologies designed to achieve it were more widely deployed, the sound that those technologies produced now prevailed. The result was that the many different places that made up the modern soundscape began to sound alike. From concert halls to corporate offices, from acoustical laboratories to the soundstages of motion picture studios, the new sound rang out for all to hear. Clear, direct, and nonreverberant, this modern sound was easy to understand, but it had little to say about the places in which it was produced and consumed.

This new sound was modern for a number of reasons. First, it was modern because it was efficient. It physically embodied the idea of efficiency by being stripped of all elements now deemed unnecessary, and it exemplified an aesthetic of efficiency in its resultant signal-like clarity. It additionally fostered efficient behavior in those who heard it, as the connection between minimized noise and maximized productivity was convincingly demonstrated. Second, it was modern because it was a product. It constituted a commodity in a culture increasingly defined by the act of consumption, and was evaluated by listeners who tuned their ears to the sounds of the market. Finally, it was modern because it was perceived to demonstrate man's technical mastery over his physical environment, and it did so in a way that transformed traditional relationships between sound, space, and time. Technical mastery over nature and the annihilation of time and space have long been recognized as definitive aspects of modern culture. From cubist art and Einsteinian physics to Joycean stream-of-consciousness storytelling, modern artists and thinkers were united by their desire to challenge the traditional bounds of space and time. Modern acousticians shared this desire, as well as the ability to fulfill it. By doing so, they made the soundscape modern.

Telling the story of the complicated transformations outlined above presents its own challenge to the writer who strives to control a narrative that moves through historical time and space. The story that follows begins in 1900 and ends in 1933, but it traverses this chronological trajectory several times over, returning to the start to explore new themes and phenomena, reexamining recurrent phenomena along the way, reiterating central themes, and ultimately—I hope—creating a resounding whole in which all the disparate elements combine to characterize fully and compellingly the construction of the modern soundscape.

I begin at the turn of the century with opening night at Symphony Hall in Boston, and I end with Radio City Music Hall in New York, which opened just as the Machine Age in America came to a grinding halt at the close of 1932. Symphony Hall was a secular temple in which devout listeners gathered to worship the great symphonic masterpieces of the past, particularly the music of Ludwig van Beethoven, whose name was inscribed in a place of honor at the center of the gilded proscenium. Radio City Music Hall, in contrast, was a celebration of the sound of modernity. Its gilded proscenium was crowned, not with the name of some long-dead composer, but with state-of-the-art loudspeakers that broadcast the music of the day to thousands of auditors gathered beneath it.

Yet, even as Symphony Hall was dedicated to the music of the past, it heralded a new acoustical era, an era in which science and technology would exert ever-greater degrees of control over sound. Symphony Hall was recognized as the first auditorium in the world to be constructed according to laws of modern science. Indeed, it not only embodied, but instigated, the origins of the modern science of acoustics. When a young physicist at Harvard University named Wallace Sabine was asked to consult on the acoustical design of the hall, he responded by developing a mathematical formula, an equation for predicting the acoustical quality of rooms. This formula would prove crucial for the subsequent transformation of the soundscape into something distinctly modern.

While Radio City Music Hall was intended to celebrate that soundscape, facing optimistically toward the future rather than gazing longingly back at the past, it actually signaled the end of this period of change. Radio City demonstrated an unprecedented degree of control over the behavior of sound, but this demonstration was no longer compelling in a culture now facing far greater challenges. In America in 1933, the technological enthusiasm that had fed the long drive for such mastery was fundamentally shaken. The Machine Age was over, and Radio City was immediately recognized as a relic of that bygone era.

Since Wallace Sabine's work on Symphony Hall was recognized at the time as something distinctly new, it must be examined closely in order to understand its significance for what would follow. Chapter 2 presents this examination by exploring the scientific details of Sabine's research and his application of those results to the design of Symphony Hall [see original publication]. The equations and formulas he developed are crucial historical artifacts for the story that follows and it would be inappropriate not to include them, but their importance will be fully explained in nonmathematical prose, for readers not accustomed to confronting scientific equations.

Just as important for understanding the nature and reception of Sabine's work is the context in which it took place, so chapter 2 also presents a brief survey of earlier efforts to control sound, and it considers why Sabine's work was perceived to be valuable by both architects and listeners. Finally, an examination of the critical reception of the acoustics of Symphony Hall demonstrates the complicated combination of social, cultural, and physical factors that go into the process of defining, as well as creating, "good sound."

Chapters 3 through 6 cover the period 1900–1933 from four different perspectives. Chapter 3 focuses on the work of the scientists who, following Sabine's lead, devoted their careers to the study of sound and its behavior in architectural spaces. Like Sabine before them, these men were initially frustrated by a lack of suitable scientific tools for measuring sound. With the development of new electrical instruments in the 1920s, not only did it become possible to measure sound, but the tools also stimulated new ways of thinking about it. Scientists drew conceptual analogies between the sounds that they studied and the circuits that measured those sounds, and the result was a new interest in the signal-like aspects of sound. By 1930, new tools, new techniques, and a new language for describing sound had fundamentally transformed the field of acoustics. "The New Acoustics" was proclaimed, and its success as a science and a profession was acknowledged with the founding of the Acoustical Society of America.

The New Acousticians of the modern era sought a larger sphere in which to apply their science, to attract public attention to that science and to earn respect for their expertise and their efforts. The problem of city noise provided a challenging and highly visible forum. Chapter 4 thus moves out into the public realm and charts changes in the problem and meaning of noise.

While noise has been a perennial problem throughout human history, the urban inhabitants of early-twentieth-century America perceived that they lived in an era unprecedentedly loud. More troubling than the level of noise was its nature, as traditional auditory irritants were increasingly drowned out by the din of modern technology: the roar of elevated trains, the rumble of internal combustion engines, the crackle and hiss of radio transmissions. As the physical nature of noise changed, so, too, did attempts to eliminate it. At the turn of the century, noise abatement was a type of progressive reform where influential citizens attempted to legislate changes in personal behavior to quiet the sounds of the city. As the sounds of modern technology swelled, it became clear that only technical experts could quell these sounds, and in the 1920s, acousticians were called upon to reengineer the harmony of the modern city.

While the majority of those who engaged with noise sought to eliminate it, some were stimulated more creatively by the sounds that surrounded them. The modern soundscape was filled with music as well as noise, and chapter 4 considers how both jazz musicians and avant-garde composers redefined the meaning of sound and the distinction between music and noise. Acousticians did much the same thing, but with scientific, rather than musical, instruments.

Noise abating engineers ultimately failed, however, to master the modern urban soundscape. Their new ability to measure noise only amplified the problem and did not translate into a solution within the public sphere of legislation and civic action. Nonetheless, a private alternative would succeed where this public approach did not, and chapter 5 retreats back indoors to consider how the technology of architectural acoustics was deployed to alleviate the problem of noise and to create a new modern sound.

Chapter 5 follows the rise of the acoustical materials industry, charting the development of a range of new building technologies dedicated to isolating and absorbing sound. Acousticians devised new materials and supervised their installation in offices, apartments, hospitals, and schools, as well as in traditional places of acoustical design like churches and auditoriums. These sound-engineered buildings offered refuge from the noise without, and transformed quiet from an unenforceable public right into a private commodity, available for purchase by anyone who could afford it.

Acoustical building materials demonstrated technical mastery over sound and embodied the values of efficiency. By minimizing reverberation and other unnecessary sounds, the materials created an acoustically efficient environment and engendered efficient behavior in those who worked within it, and began the process by which sound and space would ultimately be separated. Through a series of case studies of representative materials and the buildings in which they were installed, chapter 5 will describe the architectural construction of modern sound and will conclude by demonstrating how that sound made an integral contribution to the establishment of modern architecture in America.

With the silencing of space came a desire to fill it with a new kind of sound, the sound of the electroacoustic signal. Chapter 6 examines how electroacoustic technology moved out of the lab and into the world, and, by returning to performance spaces, emphasizes how much things had changed since 1900. Microphones, loudspeakers, radios, public address systems, and sound motion pictures now filled the soundscape with new electroacoustic products. Consumers of those products, like acoustical scientists and engineers, learned to listen in ways that distinguished the signals from the noise. This distinction became a basis for defining what constituted good sound: clear and controlled, direct and nonreverberant, denying the space in which it was produced.

This modern sound was not exclusively the product of electrical technologies, and it was constructed architecturally in auditoriums where loudspeakers were neither required nor desired. Nonetheless, most Americans heard this sound most often on the radio or at the movies, and chapter 6 focuses on the transformation of motion picture theaters and studios as both were wired for sound.

The technologies of electroacoustic control that were developed in the sound motion picture industry highlighted questions about the relationship between sound and space, forcing sound engineers and motion picture producers alike to decide just what their new sound tracks should sound like. The technology also provided new means by which to construct the sound of space, as engineers learned to create electrically a spatialized sound that we would call "virtual." The sound of space was now a quality that could be added electrically to any sound signal in any proportion; it no longer had any relationship to the physical spaces of architectural construction. This new sound bore little resemblance to that which had been heard in 1900. It was so different, Wallace Sabine's fundamental reverberation equation failed to describe it. Sabine's equation was revised to fit the modern soundscape, and with this revision, the transformation was complete.

The revision of Sabine's equation expressed the transformation of the soundscape in a cryptic mathematical language that spoke only to acousticians and sound engineers. That same transformation was more widely and unmistakably heard in the sounds and structures of Rockefeller Center, and *The Soundscape of Modernity* closes by examining the critical reception of the center in order to understand the conclusion of the era that defined the modern sound.

From the office spaces of the RCA tower to the NBC studios to the auditorium of Radio City Music Hall, the modern soundscape was epitomized and celebrated. Even before the construction of the center was complete, however, such celebration was immediately perceived to be inappropriate and outdated. New economic conditions and new attitudes regarding the previously unquestioned promise of modern technology brought the era of modern acoustics to a close. The Machine Age was now over, and the modern soundscape would begin to transform itself again into something new.

With the basic outline of the story in place, it is useful to consider briefly how this story will relate to others doubtlessly more familiar to its readers. What does *The*

Soundscape of Modernity accomplish, beyond providing a sound track to a previously silent historiography? Most basically, my story builds and expands upon past histories of the science and technology of acoustics. Much of this work has been written by practitioners, and they have constructed a solid foundation upon which I have built my own understanding of the intellectual developments of the field.[4] Historians of science have only recently begun to turn their attention to the science of sound, and have so far focused on periods that precede my own.[5] These studies have offered important insights into general questions concerning the rise of modern science and the role of scientific instruments in its creation. The history of twentieth-century acoustics similarly addresses fundamental questions about the relationships between science, industry, and the military, and it elucidates the instrumental connections between the material culture of science and its intellectual accomplishments.[6] My work only begins to examine these issues, but it demonstrates the fruitfulness of the history of acoustics in a way that may encourage others to follow.

As a contribution to the history of technology, my story is situated at the intersection of two different, but equally important, strands of scholarship. While some of the best work in this field has been devoted to the history of radio, the accomplishments of Hugh Aitken and Susan Douglas have recently been complemented by the output of an emerging community of scholars focusing upon a whole range of technological topics associated with music and sound.[7] My work adds architectural acoustics to this mix, but perhaps more importantly addresses the history of listening in a way that may influence our understanding of the entire range of acoustical technologies currently being explored.[8]

The environmental trend in the history of technology is equally vibrant and particularly valuable for its consideration of the urban context.[9] My examination of the problem of noise in American cities builds upon the work of others who have explored this phenomenon, but my perspective is distinct. Instead of drawing upon late-twentieth-century concerns about pollution and the degradation of the environment, I turn instead to the cultural meaning of noise in the early decades of the century, to demonstrate how musicians and engineers created a new culture out of the noise of the modern world.[10] By doing so, I hope to argue more generally that culture is much more than an interesting context in which to place technological accomplishments; it is inseparable from technology itself.

The history of acoustics intersects with the history of the urban environment not only through the problem of city noise, but also through technologies of architectural construction, and my work addresses an aspect of construction long neglected by visually oriented architectural historians. I challenge these historians to listen to, as well as to look at, the buildings of the past, and I thereby suggest a different way to understand the advent of modern architecture in America. As an outsider to this field, I leave it to others to evaluate the usefulness of my approach and its conclusions.[11]

I am similarly an outsider to the field of film studies, but some of the most interesting and thoughtful work on the history of sound technology and the culture of listening is found here, and my own work has benefitted enormously from the insights of this scholarship.[12] Still, here, as in architectural studies, many historians continue to operate with a predominantly visual orientation, understanding sound film primarily in its relation to the earlier traditions of silent film production. In contrast, I approach sound film from the perspective of the wider range of acoustical technologies that were developed and deployed alongside it. By doing so, I am able to demonstrate that, in deciding what sound film should sound like, filmmakers functioned in a larger cultural sphere. The decisions they made reflected not only the conditions of their own industry, but the larger soundscape in which that industry flourished.

Any exploration of a soundscape should ultimately inform a more general understanding of the society and culture that produced it. The reverberations of aural history within the larger intellectual framework of historical studies are just beginning to be heard, but the successes already accomplished speak well for the future of this approach. Leigh Schmidt, for example, has examined the meaning of sound in the American Enlightenment, and has thereby not only recovered the sensory experience of religion in American history, but also documented the forging of both science and popular culture out of those experiences. Mark Smith has identified a previously unacknowledged site of sectional tension in antebellum America by reconstructing the soundscapes of slaves, masters, and abolitionists.[13] And such studies of soundscapes are by no means limited to the American context. Bruce Smith has restored the lost sound of Shakespearian drama as it originally reverberated through the Globe Theatre and across Early Modern England, and in those reverberations he hears the transition from oral to literate culture. James Johnson has detected the rise of romanticism and bourgeois sensibility within the soundscape of the French concert hall, and Alain Corbin has perceived in the peals of village bells in nineteenth-century France the changing structures of religious and political authority.[14]

Clearly, these histories have much to say about the larger historical processes at work within their soundscapes, and all highlight themes and issues that historians have long considered to be constitutive of the rise of modern society and culture in the West.[15] Until recently, that long-term process of modernization was perceived as a particularly visual one, but the new aural history now demonstrates that, to paraphrase Schmidt, there is more to modernity than meets the eye.[16] This is particularly true for the period of so-called high modernism, and the long-standing absence of the aural dimension in cultural histories of the late nineteenth and early twentieth centuries is perhaps most striking of all.

"Modernism has been read and looked at in detail but rarely heard," concludes Douglas Kahn, in spite of the fact that this culture "entailed more sounds and produced a greater emphasis on listening to things," and on "listening differently" than ever before.[17] Those new sounds, and that different way of listening, were created and constructed through new acoustical technologies. James Lastra also asserts that "the experience we describe as 'modernity'—an experience of profound temporal and spatial displacements, of often accelerated and diversified shocks, of new modes of society and of experience—has been shaped decisively by the technological media."[18] To exclude acoustical technologies and sound media from scrutiny is to miss the very nature of that experience. Scholars who assume that consideration of the visual and textual is sufficient for understanding modernity, seem, well, shortsighted to say the least.

Restoring the aural dimension of modernity to our understanding of it promises not only to render that understanding "acoustically correct," it also provides a means by which to understand, more generally and significantly, the role of technology in the construction of that culture. This, after all, was the era in which the adjective *modern* achieved a new resonance through the self-conscious efforts of artists, writers, musicians, and architects, all of whose work was characterized by a pervasive engagement with technology.

Histories of modernism have long recognized the importance of technology as inspiration to the artists who are credited with creating the new culture. But these histories have too seldom engaged with technology as intensely as did those artists. Too often, the machines of the Machine Age are characterized as the uninteresting products of naive engineers that only achieved cultural significance when transmitted through the lens of art. "The impact of technology" upon these artists, not the technology itself, is what drives these accounts.[19]

It is not my intent to deny the importance of those artists and their work; indeed their music and architecture are crucial elements of the story that follows. But by juxtaposing the creations of mundane engineers with those of extraordinary artists, I implicitly argue that the works of both were equally significant and equally modern. Unremarkable objects like sound meters and acoustical tiles have as much to say about the ways that people understood their world as do the paintings of Pablo Picasso, the writings of John dos Passos, the music of Igor Stravinsky, and the architecture of Walter Gropius. All are cultural constructions that epitomized an era defined by the shocks and displacements of a society reformulating its very experience of time and space.

Karl Marx had these displacements in mind when he famously summarized the condition of modernity by proclaiming, "All that is solid melts into air."[20] Marx had very particular ideas about the material aspects of life and their role in historical change, ideas not necessarily at play in the story that follows. Nonetheless, like Marx, I believe that the essence of history is found in its material. I argue against the idea of modernity as a cultural Zeitgeist, a matrix of disembodied ideas perceived and translated by great artists into material forms that then trickle down to a more popular level of consciousness. In the story that follows, modernity was built from the ground up. It was constructed by the actions and through the experiences of ordinary individuals as they struggled to make sense of their world.[21]

If modern culture is not a Zeitgeist, not an immaterial cluster of ideas somehow "in the air," it must be acknowledged that sound most certainly is there, in the air. This ephemeral quality of sound has long frustrated those who have sought to control it, and the architect Rudolph Markgraf expressed the frustrations of many when he complained in 1911 that "sound has no existence, shape or form, it must be made new all the time, it slumbers until it is awaken[ed], and after it ceases its place of being it is unknown."[22] Markgraf was perplexed by "the mysteries of the acoustic," and historians of soundscapes are similarly challenged by sound's mysterious ability to melt into air, its tendency—even in a postphonographic age—to efface itself from the historical record. But if most sounds of the past are gone for good, they have nonetheless left behind a rich record of their existence in the artifacts, the people, and the cultures that once brought them forth. By starting here, with the solidity of technological objects and the material practices of those who designed, built, and used them, we can begin to recover the sounds that have long since melted into air. Along with those sounds, we can recover more fully our past.

Notes

1. R. Murray Schafer, *The Soundscape: Our Sonic Environment and the Tuning of the World* (Rochester, Vt.: Destiny Books, 1994), definition on 274–75. This edition is a largely unrevised version of material originally written in the 1960s and 1970s. See also Schafer, *The New Soundscape* (Scarborough, Ont., and New York: Berandol Music and Associated Music Publishers, 1969); and *The Book of Noise* (Wellington, N.Z.: Price Milburn, 1970). Equally stimulating in more theoretical ways is Jacques Attali, *Noise: The Political Economy of Music,* trans. Brian Massumi (1977; Minneapolis: University of Minnesota Press, 1985).

2. Alain Corbin, *Village Bells: Sound and Meaning in the 19th-century French Countryside,* trans. Martin Thorn (1994; New York: Columbia University Press, 1998), ix.

3. See Barry Truax, *Acoustic Communication* (Norwood, N.J.: Ablex, 1984), for a similarly contextualized study of the contemporary soundscape.

4. Dayton Clarence Miller, *Anecdotal History of the Science of Sound* (New York: Macmillan, 1935); Frederick Vinton Hunt, *Origins in Acoustics: The Science of Sound from Antiquity to the Age of Newton* (1978; Woodbury, N.Y.: Acoustical Society of America, 1992), and *Electroacoustics: The Analysis of Transduction, and Its Historical Background* (1954; n.p.: Acoustical Society of America, 1982); Robert Bruce Lindsay, "Historical Introduction" to J. W. S. Rayleigh, *The Theory of Sound,* 2d ed. (1894; New York: Dover, 1945), v–xlii; John W. Kopec, *The Sabines at Riverbank: Their Role in the Science of Architectural Acoustics* (Woodbury, N.Y.: Acoustical Society of America, 1997); Robert T. Beyer, *Sounds of Our Times: Two Hundred Years of Acoustics* (New York: Springer-Verlag, 1999); and the numerous historical articles that have appeared in the *Journal of the Acoustical Society of America* since its founding in 1929. An equally compelling and beautifully illustrated historical account by the architect Michael Forsyth is *Buildings for Music: The Architect, the Musician, and the Listener from the Seventeenth Century to the Present Day* (Cambridge, Mass.: The MIT Press, 1985).

5. Penelope Gouk, *Music, Science and Natural Magic in Seventeenth-Century England* (New Haven: Yale University Press, 1999); Thomas L. Hankins and Robert J. Silverman, *Instruments and the Imagination* (Princeton: Princeton University Press, 1995); Timothy Lenoir, "Helmholtz and the Materialities of Communication," *Osiris,* 2d ser., 9 (1994): 184–207; Robert Jacob Silverman, "Instrumentation, Representation, and Perception in Modern Science: Imitating Human Function in the Nineteenth Century," Ph.D. Dissertation, University of Washington, 1992; H. F. Cohen, *Quantifying Music: The Science of Music at the First Stage of the Scientific Revolution, 1580–1650* (Dordrecht: D. Reidel, 1984); Sigalia Dostrovsky, "Early Vibration Theory: Physics and Music in the Seventeenth Century," *Archive for History of Exact Sciences* 14 (December 1975): 169–218. Although not situated within the traditions of the history of science, a thoughtful survey of the inscriptive practices of eighteenth- and nineteenth-century investigators of sound is found in James Lastra, *Sound Technology and the American Cinema: Perception, Representation, Modernity* (New York: Columbia University, 2000).

6. My interest in the material practice of science has been stimulated particularly by the works of Peter Galison, Robert Kohler, and Angela Creager. See Peter Galison, *Image and Logic: A Material Culture of Microphysics* (Chicago: University of Chicago Press, 1997); Robert E. Kohler, *Lords of the Fly: Drosophila Genetics and the Experimental Life* (Chicago: University of Chicago Press, 1994); and Angela N. H. Creager, *The Life of a Virus: Tobacco Mosaic Virus as an Experimental Model, 1930–1965* (Chicago: University of Chicago Press, 2002). I began to explore this approach in my article, "Dead Rooms and Live Wires: Harvard, Hollywood, and the Deconstruction of Architectural Acoustics, 1900–1930," *Isis* 88 (December 1997): 597–626.

7.   Hugh G. J. Aitken, *Syntony and Spark: The Origins of Radio* (1976; Princeton: Princeton University Press, 1985), and *The Continuous Wave: Technology and American Radio, 1900–1932* (Princeton: Princeton University Press, 1985); Susan J. Douglas, *Inventing American Broadcasting, 1899–1922* (Baltimore: Johns Hopkins University Press, 1987), and *Listening In: Radio and the American Imagination* (New York: Times Books, 1999). See also the essays collected in Hans-Joachim Braun, ed., *"I Sing the Body Electric": Music and Technology in the 20th Century* (Hofheim: Wolke Verlag, 2000); David Morton, *Off the Record: The Technology and Culture of Sound Recording in America* (New Brunswick: Rutgers University Press, 2000); Alexander Boyden Magoun, "Shaping the Sound of Music: the Evolution of the Phonograph Record, 1877–1950," Ph.D. Dissertation, University of Maryland, College Park, 2000; James P. Kraft, *Stage to Studio: Musicians and the Sound Revolution, 1890–1950* (Baltimore: Johns Hopkins University Press, 1996); Andre Millard, *America on Record: A History of Recorded Sound* (Cambridge: Cambridge University Press, 1995); Joseph O'Connell, "The Fine-Tuning of a Golden Ear: High-End Audio and the Evolutionary Model of Technology," *Technology and Culture* 33 (January 1992): 1–37; and Susan Schmidt Horning, "Chasing Sound: The Culture and Technology of Recording Studios in the United States, 1890–1979," Ph.D. Dissertation, Case Western Reserve University, 2001.

8.   I began to develop this emphasis in "Machines, Music, and the Quest for Fidelity: Marketing the Edison Phonograph in America, 1877–1925," *Musical Quarterly* 79 (spring 1995): 131–71. My ability to expand upon this aspect of my work in the current study has been directly inspired by Douglas, *Listening In.*

9.   For a survey of this literature, see Jeffrey K. Stine and Joel A. Tarr, "At the Intersection of Histories: Technology and the Environment," *Technology and Culture* 39 (October 1998): 601–40; and Stine and Tarr, "Technology and the Environment: The Historians' Challenge," *Environmental History Review* 18 (spring 1994): 1–7, introduction to a special issue dedicated to "Technology, Pollution and the Environment." See also Martin V. Melosi, "The Place of the City in Environmental History," *Environmental History Review* 17 (1993): 1–23, and Melosi, ed., *Pollution and Reform in American Cities, 1870–1930* (Austin: University of Texas Press, 1980).

10.   See, most notably, the works of Raymond W. Smilor: "Toward an Environmental Perspective: The Anti-Noise Campaign, 1893–1932," pp. 135–51 in Melosi, ed., *Pollution and Reform;* "Personal Boundaries in the Urban Environment: The Legal Attack on Noise: 1865–1930," *Environmental Review* 3 (spring 1979): 24–36; and "Confronting the Industrial Environment: The Noise Problem in America, 1893–1932," Ph.D. Dissertation, University of Texas at Austin, 1978. More in tune with my own approach is Warren Bareiss, "Noise Abatement in Philadelphia, 1907–66: The Production of a Soundscape," M.A. Thesis, University of Pennsylvania, 1990. See also Hillel Schwartz, "Beyond Tone and Decibel: The History of Noise," *Chronicle of Higher Education* (9 January 1998): B8.

11.   One vocal exception to the general silence on the topic of acoustics in architectural history is Reyner Banham, *The Architecture of the Well-tempered Environment,* 2d ed. (Chicago: University of Chicago Press, 1984). My own understanding of the emergence of modern architecture was initially presented in "Listening to/for Modernity: Architectural Acoustics and the Development of Modern Spaces in America," pp. 253–80 in Peter Galison and Emily Thompson, eds., *The Architecture of Science* (Cambridge, Mass.: The MIT Press, 1999). See also Forsyth's specialized study, *Buildings for Music;* Cecil D. Elliott, *Technics and Architecture: The Development of Materials and Systems for Buildings* (Cambridge, Mass.: The MIT Press, 1992); and James Marston Fitch, *American Building 2: The Environmental Forces That Shape It,* 2d ed. (New York: Schocken Books, 1971) for historical works that have considered the acoustic elements of architectural design.

12.   See particularly the essays collected in Rick Altman, ed., *Sound Theory / Sound Practice* (New York: Routledge, 1992), and in Elisabeth Weis and John Belton, eds., *Film Sound: Theory and Practice* (New York: Columbia University Press, 1985). See also Lastra, *Sound Technology and the American Cinema;* Donald Crafton, *The Talkies: American Cinema's Transition to Sound, 1926–1931* (New York: Charles Scribner's Sons, 1997); Scott Eyman, *The Speed of Sound:*

Hollywood and the Talkie Revolution, 1926–1930 (New York: Simon and Schuster, 1997); and Michel Chion, *Audio-Vision: Sound on Screen,* trans. Claudia Gorbman (New York: Columbia University Press, 1994).

13. Leigh Eric Schmidt, *Hearing Things: Religion, Illusion, and the American Enlightenment* (Cambridge, Mass.: Harvard University Press, 2000), and "From Demon Possession to Magic Show: Ventriloquism, Religion, and the Enlightenment," *Church History* 67 (June 1998): 274–304; Mark M. Smith, "Listening to the Heard Worlds of Antebellum America," *Journal of the Historical Society* 1 (spring 2000): 65–99, and "Time, Sound, and the Virginia Slave," pp. 29–60 in John Saillant, ed., *Afro-Virginian History and Culture* (New York: Garland, 1999).

14. Bruce R. Smith, *The Acoustic World of Early Modern England: Attending to the O-Factor* (Chicago: University of Chicago Press, 1999); James H. Johnson, *Listening in Paris: A Cultural History* (Berkeley: University of California Press, 1995): Corbin, *Village Bells.* See also Corbin, *Time, Desire and Horror: Toward a History of the Senses,* trans. Jean Birrell (Cambridge: Polity Press, 1995); and Constance Classen, *Worlds of Sense: Exploring the Senses in History and Across Cultures* (London: Routledge, 1993).

15. This perspective is enhanced by comparing these works to ethnomusicological studies of aural culture in non-Western societies. Most notable here is Steven Feld, *Sound and Sentiment: Birds, Weeping, Poetics, and Song in Kaluli Expression,* 2d ed. (Philadelphia: University of Pennsylvania Press, 1990). See also Feld, "Sound Structure as Social Structure," *Ethnomusicology* 28 (September 1984): 383–409. For ethnographic studies of contemporary Western soundscapes, see Jonathan Sterne, "Sounds Like the Mall of America: Programmed Music and the Architectonics of Commercial Space," *Ethnomusicology* 41 (winter 1997): 22–50; and Thomas Porcello, "The Ethics of Digital Audio-Sampling: Engineers' Discourse," *Popular Music* 10 (1991): 69–84.

16. Schmidt, *Hearing Voices,* 28. For explorations of modernity and visual culture, see the essays collected in David Michael Levin, ed., *Modernity and the Hegemony of Vision* (Berkeley: University of California Press, 1993); and in Hal Foster, ed., *Vision and Visuality* (Seattle: Bay Press, 1988); Jonathan Crary, *Techniques of the Observer: On Vision and Modernity in the Nineteenth Century* (Cambridge, Mass.: The MIT Press, 1993); and Barbara Maria Stafford, *Artful Science: Enlightenment, Entertainment, and the Eclipse of Visual Education* (Cambridge, Mass.: The MIT Press, 1994). Crary's *Suspensions of Perception: Attention, Spectacle, and Modern Culture* (Cambridge, Mass.: The MIT Press, 1999) recognizes the role of aural as well as visual culture in modernity, as does Steven Connor's essay, "The Modern Auditory I," pp. 203–23 in Roy Porter, ed., *Rewriting the Self: Histories from the Renaissance to the Present* (London: Routledge, 1997).

17. Douglas Kahn, *Noise Water Meat: A History of Sound in the Arts* (Cambridge, Mass.: The MIT Press, 1999), 4, 9. See also Kahn, "Sound Awake," *Australian Review of Books* (July 2000): 21–22.

18. Lastra, *Sound Technology and American Cinema,* 4.

19. See, for example, Stephen Kern, *The Culture of Time and Space, 1880–1918* (Cambridge: Harvard University Press, 1983), quote on 119. See also Terry Smith, *Making the Modern: Industry, Art, and Design in America* (Chicago: University of Chicago Press, 1993); Anson Rabinbach, *The Human Motor: Energy, Fatigue, and the Origins of Modernity* (Berkeley: University of California Press, 1990); Miles Orvell, *The Real Thing: Imitation and Authenticity in American Culture, 1880–1940* (Chapel Hill: University of North Carolina Press, 1989); and Cecelia Tichi, *Shifting Gears: Technology, Literature, Culture in Modernist America* (Chapel Hill: University of North Carolina Press, 1987).

20. "All fixed, fast-frozen relations, with their train of ancient and venerable prejudices and opinions, are swept away, all new-formed ones become antiquated before they can ossify. All that is solid melts into air, all that is holy is profaned, and men at last are forced to face. . . . The real conditions of their lives and their relations with their fellow men." Quoted in Marshall Berman, *All That Is Solid Melts into Air: The Experience of Modernity* (1982; New York: Penguin, 1988), 21.

21.   Here my own work is particularly inspired by the material histories of Wolfgang Schivelbusch, whose studies of the technologies of travel and light are both moving and illuminating. Schivelbusch, *The Railway Journey: The Industrialization of Time and Space in the 19th Century* (1977; Berkeley: University of California Press, 1986); and *Disenchanted Night: The Industrialization of Light in the Nineteenth Century* (1983; Berkeley: University of California Press, 1988).

22.   Wallace Clement Sabine Correspondence Files, Rudolph Markgraf to Professor G. W. Stewart (6 September 1911); copy sent to Wallace Sabine (8 September 1911). Courtesy of Riverbank Acoustical Laboratories, Illinois Institute of Technology Research Institute, Geneva, 111. The Harvard University Archives hold photocopies of Sabine's correspondence, the originals of which are held at the Riverbank Acoustical Laboratories.

Chapter 13

Richard Cullen Rath

NO CORNER FOR THE DEVIL TO HIDE

As both a musician and someone who studies sound, I have the odd habit of clapping once sharply or speaking in a loud staccato voice or humming to no one in particular when I enter what appears to be an acoustically interesting space. I was glad, then, that the Birmingham meeting of the Society of Friends was just about to start their worship when I asked to go into the old hexagonal-shaped schoolroom: I was given permission to go alone. The room responded to my claps and vocal probes with a "live" sound because the ceilings are made of hard plaster and shaped in such a way that sounds bounce immediately back with little in the way of complex echoes typically produced by the high, steep, two-sided ceiling in a gothic chapel. Today, shape-note singers, with their emphasis on the participation of all and their accentuation of the mid-range timbres of the voice, value these old Quaker halls for their participatory acoustics. Later users of the room, annoyed by the same acoustics, installed hooks in the ceiling from which to hang thick, sound-absorbing drapes to muffle the reverberation. The "live" sound of the undraped room was akin to the slap-back echo popularized on old rockabilly and rhythm and blues records from the late 1950s, but when I was there it sounded the same as it and other hexagonal Quaker schoolhouses and meetinghouses had sounded for centuries. The acoustics amplified everyone's voice, with no echoes building up anywhere because the shallow-ceilinged, obtuse-angled rooms had, according to one folk explanation, "no corner for the devil to hide."

THIS CHAPTER CONSIDERS WHAT eighteenth-century encyclopedists called "catacoustics," the study of how sound was instrumentally projected, reflected, dissipated, and otherwise manipulated once it had been produced.[1] By manipulating reflected sounds, early Americans added layers of meaning that enriched and reinforced deeply held beliefs. They carefully attended to the audible world when they created and shaped public—and in some cases, not so public—spaces. Acoustical spaces reflected the beliefs underlying social order as well as vocal and instrumental sounds. Thinking about acoustics, we can still hear the echoes of those social orders and begin to notice how people created and maintained ranked points of contact within their communities and nations, across divides of ethnicity, race, gender, and class, and (perhaps most important) between visible and invisible worlds.

Acoustic spaces and the quality of the sounds made therein are remarkably durable even though the particular sounds are ephemeral. Anyone who has ever tested the reverberation in an old high-ceilinged church knows the power and durability of acoustic design and the shape of the sounds made within it. Our everyday acoustics are now filtered through electronic amplifiers and speakers, giving us soft voices at loud volumes and problems of distortion, feedback, and tone unfathomable in the seventeenth century. And in many ways, it is difficult for people today to imagine a world where sounds with no visible source were necessarily other-worldly: our radio, television, and film voice-overs, as well as music recordings, routinely fragment sounds to the point that disembodiment is mundane. Yet the gap between our worlds and theirs can—at least in part—be breached, as a study of church acoustics makes clear.

European Church Acoustics

In order to understand Anglo-American acoustical soundways, we must begin with a baseline of European church acoustics. While the two traditions are parallel in many respects, we need to pay attention to the fact that colonists did not have to face the preexisting institutions and acoustic spaces with which Europeans contended during the Reformation.

Older church designs emphasized high ceilings made of hard, sound-reflecting materials. The priest stood within a semi-enclosed wing of the church, the chancel, facing the altar, his back to the chancel screen separating the altar from the rest of the churchgoers in the nave. The priest was nearly invisible to his auditors. He spoke and chanted in Latin, indecipherable to most from the outset. Language, however, formed only the last barrier to comprehension. Facing away from the congregation, the priest's voice never carried directly to listeners in the nave. It began its trip toward them as an echo, reflected several more times before reaching any ears.

While the medieval chancel is often negatively construed as an impediment to vision and acoustic clarity separating priest from congregants, it can also be considered a beautifully executed, very large musical instrument, somewhat like the body of a lute. The priest's voice provided the initial signal, like the plucked string of the lute. Unlike a lute string, however, the priest's voice was located inside the body of the instrument rather than outside, and it was carefully directed toward the back of the instrument, the concave eastern wall of the chancel, rather than being a diffuse signal such as that from a lute string. The chancel walls collected and directed the sound forward to the listeners like the back of the lute's body. En route, the signal encountered a set of vertical barriers. On the floor was the chancel-screen, topped with a crucifix or rood. The chancel screen was often carved so that people in the nave could partly see through it. While it made the priest's actions vaguely visible, the chancel screen's open tracery or perforations acted as an acoustic baffle, muffling and deflecting the floor-level sound waves emanating from the chancel. This would make the sound that did escape seem to come more from above than across. Directly above the chancel screen was an opening occupied by the rood, through which sounds passed more freely, something like the sound holes of the lute. Above that, hanging down from the ceiling, was the tympanum, named after a drum head or the eardrum. In effect, the tympanum acted like the sounding board of our hypothetical lute, vibrating when struck by the signal but also bouncing sounds back into the chancel until they were directed out of the opening where the rood was situated. Taken together, the chancel and its parts constituted a sort of reverberant sound amplifier. Because the signal was already reverberating before it left the chancel and because a chancel is much larger than a guitar, the sound emitting from it at any moment was a compendium of echoes, the sources of which overlapped in time much more so than those coming from a lute.[2]

Once this complex signal reached the nave, where the congregants were seated, the crosslike construction of medieval churches bounced it around more, creating cascades of echoes. The high, acoustically reflective ceilings added sonic power to the priest's voice, reverberating and reinforcing it, while at the same time further muddying it with the echoes that constituted the nave's reverberation. The steep incline of the high ceilings increased the reverberation time. Long after the first echoes faded, the last ones would still be escaping from the cavernous ceilings of a typical church. Sounds bounced around echo upon echo upon echo rather than reaching the listener's ears all at once. This created a powerfully moving effect, one that amplified the voice and enriched the tone, but at the cost of clarity. Acoustician Hope Bagenal somewhat derisively describes the emphasis on reverberant sound found in Catholic churches as the "acoustics of the cave," comparing it with the acoustics of the open air exemplified by Greek amphitheaters and, implicitly, Protestantism.[3]

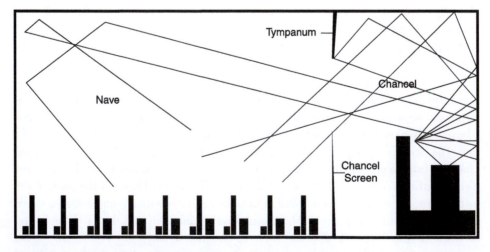

Fig. 13.1 Acoustics of a medieval chancel.

The Reformation changed the acoustics of existing churches. Graven sounds as well as graven images had to be removed. Clarity of voice rather than fullness became the goal. The *Book of Common Prayer* instructed Anglican ministers to speak from the place where they would be heard most clearly. The foremost late-seventeenth-century British church architect, James Wren, took as his guiding design principle the creation of buildings where the minister could be seen and heard clearly by all. Martin Bucer had mapped out this position a century before, and it was adopted in the second edition of the *Book of Common Prayer* in 1552, so Wren's conservative position was hardly an innovation.[4] The pulpit and reading desk directed the sanctioned voices of authority emanating from the reader and the minister directly across the room to the ears of the congregation, amplifying the signal in the process. The first and loudest sound was the original, unreflected signal. The reflecting surfaces of the pulpit were so close to the speaker that the reflected sounds were perceived as part of the original signal, slightly "fattening" it and giving the impression of amplification rather than gothic reverberation.[5]

The flow of this direct signal was nonreciprocal, from the pulpit to the congregation. Testers did little to amplify the sounds coming from the congregation, which made whispering and murmuring—particularly in the farthest reaches, where the lowest status people sat—a dangerous, even seditious activity. Whisperers stole the minister's rightful audience. The congregants literally absorbed most of the direct signal with their bodies. High and steep ceilings were permissible, however, and whatever part of the signal was not absorbed would reverberate slightly as it faded off, a tone that would be perceived as a sharp ring to loud or staccato utterances.

The Thomaskirche in Leipzig illustrates the typical process of reforming a church's acoustics well. In the pre-Reformation church, the priest's voice would take a full eight seconds to fade away. Sometime in the mid-sixteenth century, the Thomaskirche was refitted for Lutheran services. The high ceilings were draped over to muffle reverberation. Galleries were added that further dampened resonance. The center of aural focus was moved away from the narrow side where the old altar can still be seen; it moved forward in the chancel and was stripped of its images and statues. Instead, a capsule-like pulpit was placed at the center of the widest side. The minister's voice was directly projected over the shorter distance to the congregants below and to those in the galleries rather than beginning as a reflected sound. The sounding board or "tester" above the minister's head and the wooden board immediately behind him served to amplify his voice and direct it onto the congregation. Longer echoes were muffled by the bodies of the audience and the drapes on the ceiling. Reverberation time was one-fifth that of the pre-Reformation church, taking only about 1.6 seconds to fade away. These "reformed" acoustics made it possible for one of the church's eighteenth-century cantors, Johann Sebastian Bach, to write intricate organ and voice music full of nuances that would have been lost in the old church. They also made it possible for congregants to comprehend the sermons and readings of the minister.[6]

Reformed church acoustics also resembled those of open theaters, where again clarity of voice was more important than fullness. Compare the Thomaskirche to the old Globe Playhouse in London, for example. Both sought clarity by stacking up as many seats as possible at the closest distance from the aural center. Draping the ceilings of the church served the same purpose as the open air above the Globe: sound went up but never came back down as an echo. Bruce Smith calls the wooden stage a sounding board for the actors, making the comparison with the pulpit furnishings explicit. But Reformation churches differed from London theaters in ignoring vision, placing a number of benches facing away from the pulpit, though still within good auditory range.[7]

North American Houses of Worship

The acoustics of meetinghouses and churches reflected early American methods of constructing and maintaining social order both within a society and between the heavens and that society. Chesapeake churches, hewn closest to the Church of England, became the most hierarchical. Quaker meetinghouses began as the most egalitarian, but the years led inexorably to acoustic hierarchies, though Friends maintained a reciprocity that others lacked. Puritan meetinghouses also began with egalitarian acoustics, but in ordering their interior acoustic spaces they, like Chesapeake Anglicans, became more hierarchic and unidirectional, with sound and the authority to make it flowing from heaven through the pulpit and onto the audience. For it to flow back in any but sanctioned forms was a transgression and a threat to social order in both the Chesapeake and New England.

All the early houses of worship shared certain characteristics as a result of their common origin as well as circumstance. Unlike Roman Catholicism, worship was in English, so all three denominations sought a degree of acoustic clarity, although how much and for whom differed in important ways. Seventeenth-century churches and meetinghouses were usually of the "auditory" or "hall" type rather than the larger, cross-shaped, and more reverberant basilicas that tended to be the pre-Reformation urban norm in old England.[8] Communities began small and so it was with their churches and meetinghouses. They all started from scratch so Reformation acoustics could be built in rather than added on. Despite their commonalities, the differences show us much about the pluralistic construction of social order and semi-public space in seventeenth-century British North America.

Chesapeake Churches and Chapels

Jamestown's settlers carefully constructed the soundscape within the chapel that marked the center of their day-to-day existence. They were particularly proud of their cedar pulpit. While no mention is made of a canopy or tester, the pulpit was probably raised somewhat and placed near a reflective wall in the 1610 chapel.

By the early eighteenth century, American Anglican pulpits generally raised the minister above the audience to make him easier to hear. A sounding board or tester was usually part of the pulpit, particularly in larger churches. It would be either carved out of the same block as the pulpit or suspended overhead. It concentrated and reflected the minister's voice, amplifying it to make him seem louder than an untreated voice. At the bottom of the pulpit would be the "reading desk" from which the bulk of the service would be read out. At the ground level was another desk from which psalms and hymns were "lined out" from a book. From the reading desk the voice would reflect from the walls of the pulpit, giving the reader an acoustic position almost as prominent as when the minister spoke.[9]

Like their brethren across the Atlantic, Chesapeake Anglicans focused the sounds that came from positions of authority. The Jamestown chapel itself was two and a half times longer than wide, and the pulpit and communion table were most likely situated at the eastern end, particularly if there was a chancel screen. The chancel, at the east end of the chapel, was in the building rather than attached to it, which leads Dell Upton to think that the chapel was of the auditory type.[10] Sounds were projected along the length rather than the breadth of the chapel. Where one was seated was an indicator of social standing.[11] Those in the front heard more of the direct signal. Those in the back heard less of it, and thus more reverberation. This may have reinforced social assumptions. The people seated in the back from lower social standings were assumed more likely to be taken in by the power of the sounds rather than the articulated words. Although we know little about the height of the earliest Jamestown chapels, the brick church built there in the late seventeenth century had high, steep, reverberant ceilings.[12]

The congregation's job was to listen rather than see. As early as 1610, the Jamestown chapel may have attenuated the visual with a cedar chancel screen that blocked the view of the communion table. Chancel screens were the norm in later Chesapeake Anglican churches.[13] The primacy of listening over seeing was also reflected in seating. Rude benches probably gave way to box pews for many elite churchgoers sometime in the seventeenth century. Box pews had high walls to keep out drafts. Seating was on three or four sides of the box so that many auditors were facing away from the pulpit and reading desk or unable to see because of the walls. Poorer folk and, later, slaves found seats in single pews in the back or in the rear galleries. The box pews partially obstructed the views of those in back at ground level.

The congregants were supposed to make a "joyful noise unto the Lord" at the appropriately sanctioned times. The emphasis on noise rather than sound meant that articulation was not as important as volume. God knew the words; it was the sincerity and affect of the response that was important. Here the high ceilings played an important role. They strengthened the congregation's joyful noise, which, unlike the minister's voice, was not directed away from the ceiling by the sounding board or pulpit and would thus reverberate more, but at the expense of clarity. The vigorous ritual sounding of the congregation's set responses placed the community in its proper relation to itself and the heavens. The reader and the minister had to be clear because the congregation—unlike God and the speakers—could not be assumed to know all of what was being spoken from the desk and the pulpit. The congregation was supposed to be loud and powerful, and the high ceilings helped.

Chesapeake church acoustics shifted toward the end of the seventeenth century. Brick churches began to replace the smaller wooden chapels, though the dimensions remained the same. These in turn gave way to larger, more familiar churches of the eighteenth century.[14] The later churches were no longer at the center of Chesapeake daily life, replaced by the peculiar rhythms of the plantation. Less care was given to the placement of the pulpit for good hearing in plantation-era Chesapeake churches. Rather than placing the pulpit against a wall, it would be on a corner of the chancel with open air behind it. The testers themselves became more decorative and less functional, with fancier ones having no acoustically reflective surfaces at all.[15] Eighteenth-century Anglican ministers often read their sermons in a nearly inaudible mumble to avoid being associated with their more evangelical brethren. High ceilings and the lengthwise orientation of the church remained. Cross-shaped churches, usually with chancel screens, began to be built again. All these tendencies reinforced a loss of interest in acoustic clarity, as the importance of the Chesapeake's visible world waxed in the eighteenth century.

Quaker Meetinghouses

Many early Quaker meetinghouses were square or nearly so, hexagonal or octagonal. The earliest meetinghouse for which we have evidence was hexagonal, with a hexagonal roof. This was the first Burlington meetinghouse, built in 1683. It hosted the yearly meeting for the East and West Jersey and Philadelphia every other year from 1683 to the mid-eighteenth century.

The Burlington meetinghouse's shape acoustically instituted Quaker notions of egalitarianism. From the inside of the building, the ceiling panels acted as a set of six sounding boards, equally amplifying voices originating anywhere in the room. While the Burlington Meetinghouse is gone, other octagonal and hexagonal buildings are still extant. From one of these, the hexagonal Quaker schoolhouse in Birmingham, Pennsylvania, we can reconstruct the acoustics of an earlier time. The acoustics are very crisp. The decay time for reverberation is quick, much less than a second, because of the relatively shallow pitch of the roof. The walls and roof echo the voice directly back into the audience rather than reverberating like a steeper roof. Because the delay time of the echo is so short, the echo is experienced as a fullness to the voice that does not impede clarity. A round room or a dome might seem even more equitable, and in fact earlier Protestant architectural reformers thought it to be the best shape, but acoustically a round room or a dome would direct sound too narrowly, conveying a voice from one point to another without diffusing it. This would create "listening spots" rather than making voices clear and audible to all. The flat surfaces of square, hexagonal, or octagonal buildings would be just uneven enough to refract the voice rather than concentrating it, so these shapes were preferred over circular walls and ceilings.

The efficacy of these rooms in conveying the voice is attested in two ways. The Birmingham schoolhouse has hooks in the ceiling for draperies in order to dampen sound. Apparently, the combined voices of a roomful of children were amplified so well that they had to be countered to make the room more conducive to learning. Also, shape-note singers today often seek out Quaker hexagonal and octagonal rooms for their singing. Shape-note singing is usually done with a roomful of participants— there is no audience per se, just as everyone is a potential participant at a Quaker meeting. The emphasis in shape-note singing is on the mid-range frequencies that mark a clearly articulated voice, the same frequencies emphasized in Quaker plain styles of speech.[16]

Quakers were not alone in their use of hexagonal meetinghouses. The eighteenth century witnessed the construction of several others among Wesleyan, Congregationalist, and Dutch reformed congregations, but the early and most emblematic use was by the Quakers. The old folk saying that attributed the hexagonal design to the notion that there was no corner for the devil to hide is perhaps a way to think about reverberation. Other early Quaker meetinghouses tended to be square and have galleries, much like the early Puritan meetinghouses, but with no pulpit.[17]

The soundscape of the room was critical to Quaker worship, and its delicate interplay of silence and speech rested uneasily in a bustling urban center like Philadelphia. Maintaining silence was often a challenge. The "Great Meeting House" at Second and Market Street in Philadelphia was driven into disuse in the eighteenth century because the street noise became too much. Iron hooves and cartwheels on cobblestones and pavement made a tremendous racket, much louder than present-day automobiles. Even with specially designed roadways with cobblestones in the middle to give the horse traction and smooth paving stones for the wheels, the noise in an urban environment could quickly overwhelm a meeting. Noisy children and barking dogs posed another set of problems, which meetinghouses tried to solve with gates and gatekeepers.[18]

Inside the room, careful attention was paid to acoustics above and beyond the shape of the room. Since everyone was in theory a potential preacher, the minister-audience dichotomy of other denominations would not work. Acoustics had to be clear and sharp everywhere, for all speakers and hearers alike. In practice, however, certain concessions to hierarchy were made as the meetings grew larger. A set of "facing benches" was set above the other seats and often had a curved wall behind them to both collect and project voices. Although acoustically favored, the seats were sometimes called a gallery to make them seem less elite. The acoustic differences between these seats and the New England or Chesapeake minister's pulpit were significant. Obviously, more people were seated in these seats than in the pulpit. But more important, there was an element of reciprocity to the facing benches. Other denominations focused the sounds of the minister's voice sharply and directed it toward the audience. No care was taken to clarify the audience's joyful noise, and no effort was made to make the minister's pulpit a favored place for *listening*. The size of the sounding boards behind the facing benches did just that, though, collecting and amplifying sounds coming in from the room as well as projecting the voices of the "elders" who sat there. The importance of being able to listen was underscored in 1763 when a new stairway impaired the acoustics of the High Street Meeting in Philadelphia, and the meeting found it necessary to "fix up a suitable board for the conveyance of the voice when Friends are concerned in public testimony."[19]

During the eighteenth century all denominations introduced more hierarchy and emphasized visual over auditory elements in reinforcing social order. Sounding boards fell into disrepair, with some ministers fearing injury so much as to have them removed from the pulpit. Slanted, acoustically effective testers were reset parallel to the floor, which improved them visually but defeated their sonic purpose. Churches were introduced into Congregationalist architecture, so that the Chesapeake and New England acoustic soundways converged. Quakers maintained some amount of reciprocity but sacrificed the primitive egalitarianism of the early meetings to a de facto system of elders who were expected to speak more often and non-elders who were expected to remain for the most part silent.

Perhaps because of its very nature, sound remained difficult to regulate and order. Rather than improving regulations, diminishing the importance of sound was ultimately how early Americans made their soundscapes more manageable. Before they did so, however, they spent a tremendous amount of effort on governing each other's tongues, with ever-diminishing returns.

Notes

1. *Encyclopedia Brittanica,* s.v. "Acoustics." The source document was torn from the original volume and is not labeled. The attribution to the 1787 edition is from the finding aid, the attribution to 1792 from the archivist; in Warshaw Collection, Acoustics box, folder 2, Archive Center, National Museum of American History, Smithsonian Institution, Washington, D.C. "Diacoustics" included the generation of voices as well as sounds of instruments, "Catacoustics" often concerned the manipulated reflection of voices as well as other sounds. Today this field is known as architectural acoustics.

2. I have reconstructed the acoustics of the chancel from descriptions found in G. W. O. Addleshaw and Frederick Etchells, *The Architectural Setting of Anglican Worship: An Inquiry into the Arrangements for Public Worship in the Church of England from the Reformation to the Present Day* (London, 1948), 15–22. The lute analogy is my own. For the tympanum, see *OED Online,* s.v. "tympanum."

3. Michael Forsyth, *Buildings for Music: The Architect, the Musician, and the Listener from the Seventeenth Century to the Present Day* (Cambridge, Mass., 1985), 4–13; Hope Bagenal, "Bach's Music and Church Acoustics," *Journal of the Royal Institute of British Architects* 37, no. 5 (1930): 154–63.

4. Stephen Palmer Dorsey, *Early English Churches in America, 1607–1807* (New York, 1952), 16; Addleshaw and Etchells, *Architectural Setting of Anglican Worship,* 54, 245–53; Marian C. Donnelly, *The New England Meeting Houses of the Seventeenth Century* (Middletown, Conn., 1968), 36.

5. In fact they are two separate signals, with the original louder than the reflection, but if an echo occurs about one-thirtieth of a second or less after the original sound, the ear cannot distinguish them. The two together are perceived as a single "fat" signal that is louder than the unreflected one because it consists of the unreflected plus the reflected signal.

6. Forsyth, *Buildings for Music,* 9; Addleshaw and Etchells, *Architectural Setting of Anglican Worship,* 22–63, 68–86, 245–53. Dell Upton makes the case that the cover over the pulpit was an ornament indicating power, and that it was called a "type" or "canopy" rather than a tester or sounding board. I believe that both Upton's definition and a definition that treats them as acoustic devices can be sustained simultaneously. It is true that many testers, particularly in larger churches built at later dates in the eighteenth century, were ineffective both in their construction and placement as acoustic devices. It is equally true that many of them were built and placed in such a way as to direct the voice and amplify it. Where, how, and when testers were used acoustically is the focus of this study, not whether. The earliest reference to "sounding board" referring specifically to the apparatus over the pulpit in the *OED Online* is from 1766, which would place it in the colonial period. It is important to remember that vernacular usage of the term no doubt antedated the first published citation. References to musical instrument "sound boards" occur throughout the sixteenth and seventeenth centuries, including one referring to a musician's attempt to play the harmonic stops of a monochord in which "none wold speke" because "Þe sownd~borde was to hy," This shows that the speech and sound boards were at least conceptually related in the sixteenth century. The *OED Online* dates "testers" with the meaning of pulpit coverings to

1908. Prior to that the word referred to bed canopies or canopies placed over dignitaries, which would support Upton's usage if earlier references are found. The "tipe" or "type" is not listed in the *OED Online* as a pulpit cover in any of the references used to support the definition. Although the etymology of "tipe" as a canopy is regarded by the *OED Online* as unknown, the evidence presented points toward the same etymology as for other entries for "type," which share the same Greek root, *τυφτειυ*, meaning "to strike or beat, as in a drum," from which "tympanum" is derived. See Dell Upton, *Holy Things and Profane: Anglican Parish Churches in Colonial Virginia* (Cambridge, Mass., 1986), 134–35; and *OED Online,* s.v. "type," "tipe," "tympanum," "tester," "sound-board," and "sounding board."

7. For an excellent discussion of the Globe's acoustics, as well as the acoustics of other Elizabethan theaters, see Bruce R. Smith, *The Acoustic World of Early Modern England: Attending to the O-factor* (Chicago, 1999), 206–17. I disagree with Smith's formulation of "two liturgical ideas—one [Catholicism] based on vision, the other [Protestantism] on audition." The Reformation adopted soundways that valued characteristics of the sonic pallette different from those valued by Catholicism, as the Catholic emphasis on forcefulness and reverberation compared to the Protestant emphasis on clarity underscores. Arguments could be made for Protestantism to be more visual than Catholicism, in that a much greater proportion of the devout were expected to be literate enough to read the Bible than in Catholicism, where only the clergy were expected to be able to do so. Although vision was plainer for Protestants, with images removed as objects of learning, reading is still the taking in of language through the eyes. Again, the better argument would show *how* vision ways differed between the two branches of Christianity rather than asserting the primacy of one sense over another. The difference does not affect the main thrust of Smith's argument. See Smith, *Acoustic World of Early Modern England,* 261.

8. For the distinction between "auditory" and "Basilica" type churches, see Addleshaw and Etchells, *Architectural Setting of Anglican Worship,* 52–62, and Upton, *Holy Things and Profane,* 56–59.

9. William Strachey, *A True Reportory of the Wreck and Redemption of Sir Thomas Gates, Knight, upon and from the Islands of Bermudas,* in *A Voyage to Virginia in 1609,* ed. Louis B. Wright (Charlottesville, 1964), 80; and Dorsey, *Early English Churches in America,* 16–23.

10. Upton, *Holy Things and Profane,* 59.

11. Ibid., 59, 175–96.

12. Ibid., 59, 175–96. Jamestown's old brick church was forty-six feet at the tip of the ceiling. See James Scott Rawlings, *Virginia's Colonial Churches: An Architectural Guide; Together with Their Surviving Books, Silver & Furnishings* (Richmond, 1963), 19. Compare this to the twelve-to-seventeen foot average height of seventeenth-century New England Puritan meetinghouses.

13. For the importance of chancel screens to Anglican services and their use in Virginia, see Dorsey, *Early English Churches in America,* 16–17. For Jamestown's chancel see Strachey, *True Reportory,* 80. The evidence for a chancel screen at Jamestown is ambiguous, but they were common in later Virginia churches.

14. Upton, *Holy Things and Profane,* 74.

15. Upton argues that testers were not acoustically reflective but were merely for show. Many testers earlier in the century, however, even some that he presents, did serve an acoustic purpose, in part because of their placement. Upton's decorative testers became more prevalent as the decibel level of preaching styles diminished and pulpits were moved to visual rather than acoustic centers. The process was never complete, and acoustically effective pulpits were still prevalent later in the eighteenth century, particularly in more rural churches such as Christ Church in Broad Creek Hundred, near Laurel, Delaware.

16. The material on octagonal and hexagonal acoustics is derived from a visit to a Birmingham meeting in Pennsylvania in February 1998. Also see T[homas] Chalkley Matlack papers, Haverford College Quaker collection, mss 1106, box 1 book 4: "Friend's meeting Houses in Pennsylvania: Columbia, Delaware, and Lycoming Counties," s.v. "Cheyney: the Shelter."

17. Donnelly, *New England Meeting Houses of the Seventeenth Century,* 79; John Thomson Faris, *Old Churches and Meeting Houses in and around Philadelphia* (Philadelphia, 1926), 79–80; "Bank

Street Meeting House," Haverford College Quaker Collection, Philadelphia Meeting houses, 911 A-F Box 1; David A. Barton, *Discovering Chapels and Meeting Houses* (Aylesbury, Bucks, [1975]), 56; Hubert Martin Lidbetter, *The Friends Meeting House: An Historical Survey of the Places of Worship of the Society of Friends (Quakers), from the Days of Their Founder George Fox, in the Seventeenth Century, to the Present Day* (York, [Eng.], [1961]), 21.

18.   George Vaux, "The Great Meeting House," *Friend* 63 (1890): 148, Division of Community Service Programs, Pennsylvania Historical Survey, Works Project Admnistration, *Inventory of Church Archives, Society of Friends in Pennsylvania* (Philadelphia, 1941), 63.

19.   Division of Community Service Programs, Pennsylvania Historical Survey, Works Project Admnistration, *Inventory of Church Archives, Society of Friends in Pennsylvania,* 63.

Chapter 14

John Picker

THE SOUNDPROOF STUDY

I remember a funny dinner at my brother's, where, amongst a few others, were Babbage and Lyell, both of whom liked to talk. Carlyle, however, silenced every one by haranguing during the whole dinner on the advantages of silence. After dinner, Babbage, in his grimmest manner, thanked Carlyle for his very interesting Lecture on Silence.

(Charles Darwin, *Autobiography*)

Scatterbrain London

LATE IN OCTOBER 1864, during a dinner with family and friends, Charles Dickens received a telegram that read simply "LEECH DEAD." Marcus Stone, a guest at the dinner, later recalled, "silence fell upon us. . . . No one said a word. What was there to say?"[1] In the following weeks, as Dickens struggled to complete another monthly installment of *Our Mutual Friend* (1864–65), he made an unusual confession to John Forster: "I have not done my number. This death of poor Leech (I suppose) has put me out woefully. Yesterday and the day before I could do nothing; seemed for the time to have quite lost the power; and am only by slow degrees getting back into the track to-day."[2] Dickens's biographers have described these lines as a "cry of personal lamentation," a sign that Dickens felt "desiccated, unable to work" after the death of John Leech, his close friend and, more famously, his illustrator for *A Christmas Carol* (1843) and other Christmas stories.[3] As the words of the novelist and Stone indicate, however, Leech's death caused Dickens more than "personal" pain. It brought on a professional crisis, for it reduced the characteristically prolific author to an unfamiliar state of nonproductivity. Leech's death, if only temporarily, stopped Dickens's hand and silenced him.

That the passing of Leech brought such silence is ironic, since what precipitated his death was noise. Clanging bells, cracking whips, clattering carriages, clamoring hawkers and cabmen, roaring crowds, barking dogs—these sounds regularly accosted Leech and other Londoners, but scattered about the streets stood the worst offenders of all: the itinerant musicians, in Dickens's words, those "brazen performers on brazen instruments, beaters of drums, grinders of organs, bangers of banjos, clashers of cymbals, worriers of fiddles, and bellowers of ballads."[4] Driven nearly mad by street music over his final years, Leech allowed this to exacerbate what already was for him a serious heart condition and nervous temperament. His final words to his fellow artist and future biographer William Powell Frith indicate the depth of his misery: "'Rather, Frith,'" Leech bitterly commented the month of his death, "'than continue to be tormented in this way, I would prefer to go to the grave where there is no noise.'"[5] Days later, he got his wish, bringing him the quiet he felt he had been unjustly denied in life.

In his antipathy toward street music in Victorian London, Leech had plentiful company. Throughout the city, artisans, academics, musicians, clergy, and doctors and their patients shared Leech's suffering and railed against what an author of a leading article from a May 1856 *Times* called "the noisy, dizzy, scatterbrain atmosphere of London."[6] As tempers flared, the fight against the oppression of street noises mounted in print and Parliament. With predictable indignation, another *Times* leader emphatically declared for the exasperated many, "there is no London nuisance equal to that of out-door music! . . . O for a little quiet in London!"[7] Anger and disgust among the middle classes soon found its outlet and target. The prolonged war of words and images that ensued not only resulted in new legal restrictions upon music-makers but also accelerated what Peter Bailey has identified as "a continuing struggle between refinement and vulgarity."[8] For the battle revealed a midsection of later Victorian society in the process of making one of its more elaborate, fierce efforts toward collective action and self-definition.

What can loosely be considered the anti–street music movement represents a critical aspect of the context in which much if not most of the major artwork and literature of the period developed. The influential urban historian H. J. Dyos was among the first to suggest the specifically acoustic nature of this context. He observed that in cities of the modern era, silence had become a commodity of precious value, while the impact of sensory overstimulation remained unclear: "What is less certain [than the modern value put upon silence]," Dyos wrote, "is whether the combined assault on the senses of a profusion of sights, smells, noises, crowds, moving objects, changing levels, constraints, commands, is an important source of disturbance to people."[9] Without doubt—with urgency, in fact—the excessiveness of one of the urban qualities Dyos mentioned, noise, evolved into "an important source of disturbance" during the latter half of the Victorian age. On a larger scale than before, noise began in this period to alter the agents, subjects, and conditions of artistic and intellectual occupations as well as much other professional employment.

Beginning at midcentury, advocates for silence on the streets waged a battle to impose the quiet tenor of interior middle-class domesticity upon the rowdy terrain outside. Thomas Carlyle's renowned attack on noise served as a kind of overture to those that followed. Carlyle's long-standing aversion to noises of all kinds, ranging from piano-playing neighbors to crowing roosters and chickens, is legendary; Thea Holme, among others, relates the facts in amusing detail.[10] By 1853, nearly two decades after moving to Cheyne Row in Chelsea, the "UNPROTECTED MALE," as Carlyle referred to himself, had had enough of "Demon Fowls" and other disturbances to issue bloodthirsty responses in defense of his territory: "Those Cocks must either withdraw or die. That is a fixed point;—and I must do it myself if no one will help: it is really too bad the 'celebrated man,' or any *man,* or even a well-conditioned animal (of any size) should be submitted to such scandalous paltrinesses."[11] He reserved special venom for his nemesis, a "vile yellow Italian" organ grinder: "The question arises, Whether to go out and, if not assassinate him, call the Police upon him, or to take myself away to the bath-tub and the other side of the house? Of course, I *ought* to chuse the latter alternative,—and do, for the wretch's organ is a *horse* one, I hear; drawn by a horse; and, one w[oul]d think, played by one!"[12] "All summer I have been more or less annoyed with *noises,* even accidental ones, which get free access thro' my open windows . . . henceforth I hope to be independent of all men and all dogs, cocks and household or street noises." he wrote later that year, as his limited patience reached its end.[13] For Carlyle, to rest, but more important to *work,* depended upon denying outdoor commotion "free access" to interior professional space.

Carlyle's solution to the problem made spatially evident the complications that many Victorian intellectuals in London faced as they struggled for both professional differentiation and quiet. Carlyle sought to create a personal space that outside sounds could not infiltrate, a sanctum in which he would go on to write *Frederick the Great* (1858–65). Although the idea of a soundproof attic study had occurred to him at least a decade earlier, events of 1853 revived his hope in it: "Masons (who have already *killed* a year of my life, in a too sad manner), are again upon the roof of the house,—after a dreadful bout of resolution on my part,—building me a SOUNDLESS ROOM! 'The world, which can do me no good, shall at least not torment me with its street and backyard *noises.'*"[14] The construction of Carlyle's study provided an intriguing juncture for a number of Victorian concerns. With new double walls, skylights, and slated roof with muffling air chambers beneath, the room signified what Carlyle referred to as his "glorious conquest": a professional seizure of urban space, and an architectural tactic by which to expel the threat of the noisy rabble and thereby preserve an authorial career.[15] Yet it was also a tactic that encapsulated the oddly positioned existence of silence-seeking professionals whose living and working spaces overlapped.

In her formative study of the Victorian home, Jenni Calder writes of the drive of the middle classes to escape urban realities and attain a degree of separateness and self-definition within the home: "Society itself was ugly. The aspect of the urban world was not nice to look upon. There was dirt, there was noise, there was human excrement, there was starvation, there was crime, there was violence, all on the surface, all very close to the senses of all who ventured beyond their front doors. . . . To have an interior environment that enabled such things to be forgotten was a priority of middle-class aspiration."[16] In one sense, then, Carlyle's plan for the soundproof study was another—even the definitive—step toward self-identification with members of the professional class, whose emerging sense of group identity directly conflicted with the problem of street noise. Carlyle's construction of a room specifically designed to keep out city noises provided a spatial reinforcement of a vocational identity, even as it kept the threats of the base distractions of society at bay.

At a cost of some £200 to construct, however, the silent space did not come cheaply. Such a price lends support to Dyos's observation about the gradual commodification of silence in urban areas. At the same time, Carlyle's soundless room demonstrates how that shift could manifest itself domestically, or, in more general terms, territorially, as a phenomenon particular to an emerging stratum of professionals who sought through silence to localize, even spatially contain, noise.

Changing productions and conceptions of noise have tended to be overlooked or, more precisely, underheard in standard social and literary histories, but there are signs this is starting to change, as scholars have begun reconstructing "auditory landscapes" of the past to discern "the elaboration of collective and territorial identities."[17] Along similar lines, Jacques Attali's politicized history of music remains a provocative study of the relations between sound and power, and it offers a theoretical perspective from which to consider the street music problem. Attali writes that "all music, any organization of sounds is then a tool for the creation or consolidation of a commodity, of a totality . . . [and] any theory of power today must include a theory of the localization of noise and its endowment with form."[18] Noise, Attali goes on to claim, "indicates the limits of a territory and the way to make oneself heard within it, how to survive by drawing one's sustenance from it" (6). If Attali is correct to see throughout history an ongoing conflict between makers of music and those of noise, then the events under scrutiny in this chapter provide an especially suitable opportunity for testing the resonance of his claims. It follows that the anti–street music movement can be considered an urban territorial campaign, a conflict for control between regions of harmony and those of dissonance. That conflict often manifests itself in legal action, for "the institutionalization of the silence of others assure[s] the durability of power" (8). Noise, then, in a definition quite relevant to this discussion, "*is violence:* it disturbs. To make noise is to interrupt a transmission, to disconnect, to kill. It is a simulacrum of murder" (26). Attali's claim captures the underlying message in Leech's final words to Frith, in which the ailing artist expressed his belief that he was being violently driven to the only quiet place left him. And in Attali's terms, Carlyle's soundproof chamber institutionalized silence to "assure the durability" of the author's literary ability and power.[19]

While Attali offers a compelling theory of the relationship between sound and silence, that theory only represents a starting point for what follows. Later nineteenth-century Londoners' deliberations over street music served as a gauge of an urban community's explicit demands and entrenched biases. During the period under discussion, fights for silence repeatedly emerged as regional struggles against street music, insofar as they attempted not only to protect literal neighborhoods and city blocks from intrusive noises but also to defend more abstract regions of identity, those critical domains of nationality, professionalism, and the body. Hence, these ongoing battles over sounds were concretely as well as conceptually territorial. Even as those opposed proclaimed as their principal goal the removal of music from the streets throughout the City and West London, including Belgravia, Kensington, and Chelsea, they endeavored to maintain clear boundaries in three principal areas that necessarily interrelated and at times overlapped: first, defending the purity of English national identity and culture against the taint of foreign infiltration; second, upholding economic and social divisions between the lower classes and middle-class professionals;

and third, protecting the frail, afflicted bodies of (English, middle-class) invalids from the invasive, debilitating effects of (foreign, lower-class) street music. What might have seemed a harmless entertainment thus came to represent a rallying point for the large numbers of Londoners, including Carlyle, Leech, and ultimately even Dickens himself, who heard in street music the strains of a powerful threat.

"Blackguard Savoyards and Herds of German Swine"

> Seedy Savoyard, wherefore art thou grinding?
> Rough blows the wind, thy pipes are out of order,
> Old is thy tune, thy monkey is a nuisance,
>   So is thy organ.
> ("Friend of tranquillity," in *The Owl*)

To refer to the anti–street music attacks as such is perhaps misleading, for generally speaking, they were directed less against all outdoor music and performers than at certain types of music and particular players. Isolated published indictments of London street musicians appeared as early as the first decade of the nineteenth century, but the frequency of the reports rose significantly in the 1840s, when the *Times* began to print complaints against street noise on a regular basis. Scholars have noted that "the decibel count seemed to have increased from mid-century on" in London streets, in part from higher rates of immigration and commercial growth, and that street trading in the middle decades of the century was "augmented by a rare audibility."[20] In *London Labour and the London Poor* (1861), Henry Mayhew described the array of nationalities of what he estimated were upward of one thousand street musicians in London during the period, including English violin-players, street bands, and a harpist, Irish and Scotch pipers, a German brass-bandsman, a French hurdy-gurdy player, a host of Italian street entertainers, and numerous percussionists and minstrel-singers from England, India, and the United States.[21] The increasing number and variety of musicians throughout the 1850s brought an escalation of published letters of attack and one of the first appearances, in an 1851 *Times* headline, of the phrase "organ nuisance" to designate the larger problem of noisy street music.[22] This move by the *Times* allowed the press and public to simplify a larger problem by singling out a particular type of performer upon which to place blame for the interruptions of daily life. As a consequence, the street music nuisance of the 1840s resolved itself, through synecdoche, into the "organ-grinding nuisance" of the 1850s and 1860s. The Italian organ grinders came to be seen as the repulsive source of virtually all noise in the city, and their eradication the task of every "Friend of Tranquillity."[23]

This development was complicated by the fact that a number of the outraged had legitimate grievances against those street musicians who in essence used extortion to make their living. To get certain organ grinders to stop playing or go elsewhere, a noticeable segment of the complainants regularly had to pay them off, and this understandably only fueled the anger against them. Street music had few defenders, and these could do little to offset the quantity of outbursts of the incensed majority. In his *London* (1841), Charles Knight published an early defense in response to the

1839 Metropolitan Police Act, which attempted to legislate street noise. Knight openly sympathized with the musicians; street music, he wrote, "ought now to be left alone, if it cannot be encouraged by the State." Over two decades later, during the 1864 street music debates in Parliament, aristocratic MPs spoke out on behalf of the working classes, paternalistically claiming that doing away with organ grinders would deprive the poor of one of their few forms of entertainment. Also that year, the journal *Good Words* published a short article and illustration sympathetic toward the organ grinders, claiming they were "discoursing the best music of the day, and educating the ear of hundreds for a few halfpence."[24] Minor and infrequent as defenses such as these were, they failed to counteract the prevailing hostility toward street music. Perhaps of greater significance, the grinders, many of whom had only a rudimentary command of English, were for the most part not able to speak, let alone publish, for themselves. With the possible exception of interviews by Mayhew and some scant police reports, the words and sentiments of the musicians, when noted at all, were presented by intermediaries whose antipathy, fear, and ignorance shaped their depictions.

The noise itself was a very real and potent concern to those who felt the force of it. An early article by Charles Manby Smith that analyzed the problem echoed Mayhew (or perhaps foreshadowed him) by imposing external order in the form of nine separate "classes" upon the seemingly jumbled collection of "Music-Grinders of the Metropolis." One of the first authors explicitly to single out the organ grinders for their particular brand of disturbance, Smith used terms that other critics soon adopted when he described them as "the incarnate nuisances who fill the air with discordant and fragmentary mutilations and distortions of heaven-born melody, to the distraction of educated ears and perversion of the popular taste."[25] Smith's groupings of the grinders included "hand organists," "monkey-organists," "blind bird-organists," "flageolet-organists," and "the horse-and-cart organists." Under this last heading, Smith provided one of the most colorful of the many descriptions of the jarring sounds of organs during the period:

> The piercing notes of a score of shrill fifes, the squall of as many clarions, the hoarse bray of a legion of tin trumpets, the angry and fitful snort of a brigade of rugged bassoons, the unintermitting rattle of a dozen or more deafening drums, the clang of bells firing in peals, the boom of gongs, with the sepulchral roar of some unknown contrivance for bass, so deep that you might almost count the vibrations of each note—these are a few of the components of the horse-and-cart organ, the sum total of which it is impossible to add up. (199)

While the performances of smaller organs did not approach the magnitude of these massive productions, they ranged from dulcet and charming to more often, in the words of one scholar, "loud and coarse . . . [like that] of a monstrously amplified ice-cream van."[26] Smith's relatively early attempt to convey the cacophony of the horse-and-cart organ focused on the difficulty of scouting the vast territory of the machinery of the organ itself, which seemed beyond the reach of rational observation, a mechanism "impossible" to grasp. Curiously, his description evokes the bewildering sound and effect of the "iron horse" of the locomotive, which, along with the street organ, was a significant component of early industrial urban noise. Smith provided a spirited sense of organ-induced confusion while hinting at the damning tone that came to dominate ensuing arguments about the street music problem.

Smith's article was most important because it drew attention to the performers as distinctly alien to London. Smith's classifications included the grinder who was "nearly always a foreigner," or "not uncommonly some lazy Irishman, if he be not a sickly Savoyard," as well as "little hopping, skipping, jumping, reeling Savoyard or Swiss urchins" (198–99). Smith concluded that "with respect to all these grinders, one thing is remarkable: they are all, with the exception of a small savour of Irishmen, foreigners. . . . Scarcely one Englishman, not one Scot, will be found among the whole tribe" (201). Mayhew's comments on an "Italian with Monkey" who was formerly an organ grinder reiterated Smith's emphasis on foreignness in more insidious ways: "He wore the Savoy and broad-brimmed felt hat, and with it on his head had a very picturesque appearance, and the shadow of the brim falling on the upper part of the brown face gave him almost a Murillo-like look. There was, however, an odour about him,—half monkey, half dirt,—that was far from agreeable, and that pervaded the apartment in which he sat."[27] This pointed description of the stench of the man who might "almost" have emerged from a Spanish painting reveals a not-so-subtle contempt for an "uncivilized" foreigner, one of equal parts beast and earth.

As Smith's and Mayhew's comments suggest, those describing the "organ nuisance" repeatedly fell back on epithets such as the catch-all term "Savoyard," the use of which might easily be dismissed as a matter of convention. Yet in this case, such a convention is especially interesting and revealing. The *Oxford English Dictionary* traces the English adoption of the French word "Savoyard" back to the mid-eighteenth century and notes that it refers to "a native or inhabitant of Savoy. Well known in other countries as musicians itinerating with hurdy-gurdy and monkey." Although this latter meaning might appear to refer to the nineteenth-century influx of street musicians, it does not.[28] As the Italian musicians arriving in the nineteenth century were from the Duchy of Parma, not, as the earlier Savoyards had been, from the Duchy of Savoy, Victorians used an outdated term, one complicated even more by the events of 1860, in which France permanently annexed Savoy from the Italian kingdom of Piedmont-Sardinia, to delineate those who were in reality Parmesan immigrants. The distinction is a significant one: Parma went on to join Italy proper, while Savoy became part of France, and, as the "new Savoyards" used Savoy as a stopping-point on their way from Parma to London, it is likely that many Victorians in writing about the Parmesan musicians conflated the two places or just never knew the difference, unthinkingly applying an old term to a new phenomenon.[29] That they attributed the players' origins to Savoy, a province that alternated allegiance to Italy and France, is itself symptomatic of a heightened xenophobia, a fear of intrusion from those who are made to seem, in the wake of the events of 1860, doubly foreign.[30] Juggled as a political pawn between Cavour and Napoleon III, Savoy held a status that Cavour described to English visitors as the "Ireland of Italy."[31] The analogy resonated back home, for Victorian Londoners expressed toward the so-called Savoyards a degree of contempt similar to what they showed those others who provoked territorial and racial anxieties, those from the "Savoy of Britain," the loathed Irish.

A contemporary full-page *Punch* cartoon by John Tenniel fuses the political significance of the Savoy region with the "organ nuisance" of London in a provocative image. The illustration [see original publication] alludes both to the French acquisition of Savoy and to the growing sense that England was being overrun by itinerant musicians. In the cartoon, a respectably dressed Mr. Punch herds a group of organ grinders and hurdy-gurdy players to the edge of a cliff and bats at them forcefully with his umbrella, his top hat and spectacles flying off from the force of the swing. The foreigners, longhaired, unshaven, and wearing the "Savoy hat" noted by Mayhew, topple off the cliff and presumably into the sea below, their instruments still strapped to their backs and chests. The one organ grinder whose eyes are visible grimaces leeringly toward viewers and his evictor, while Punch glares back at him in agitation, his eyes open wide and hair on end; the caption reads "Mr. Punch Surrenders the Savoyards." Using these terms, the artist invokes the literal surrender of Savoy to France even as he represents the expulsion of the "new Savoyards" (the Parmesans) over the cliffs of Dover. Grafting a territorial fantasy onto a territorial reality, he transforms a controversy about offensive sounds into one of invaded spaces. And his proposed solution is the purging of foreign performers from England, a musical decontamination.

Representations of the street music problem as a type of foreign infestation became commonplace in the 1850s, and few illustrations expressed more malice than the work of the premier *Punch* artist and enemy of street sounds, John Leech. A number of sketches particularly attested to his acute xenophobia. In the first [see original publication], while itinerant musicians wander in the background, "Field Marshall" Punch earnestly presents a recoiling organ grinder with a bayonet, with the comment, "'Here's an instrument for you, go play upon it in your own country!'" In the second [see original publication], an organ grinder occupies center stage in a double-page procession of "Some Foreign Produce That Mr. Bull Can Very Well Spare." Both illustrations portrayed the street musicians as haggard, shabbily dressed, dirty—as clearly foreign, even when surrounded, as in the second image, by other foreigners. Further, both expressed the desire for the street musicians' deportation by capitalizing on their status as aliens and suggested that itinerants ought to be turned away and immigrants surrendered to their "own country" or simply refused. In his work, Leech used his subjects' foreignness against them, as a means to single them out as undesirables and advocate their expulsion.

As calls for the legislation of street noise increased during the late 1850s and into the 1860s, insults directed at the "organ nuisance" became more pointed and defensive, and many characterized the musicians as aliens who were less than human, indeed, bestial. A letter to the *Times* in January 1864 bemoaned the fact that "we consider ourselves compelled to endure the most deafening rows, conducted for the most part, if not universally, *by foreigners*," while editorials from the *Examiner* consistently represented the musicians as no better than degenerates and animals: they were "blackguard Savoyards and herds of German swine," "with sounds like those of a pig, to which they are so near akin"; their music recalled "the grunts and squeaks of a herd of filthy German swine."[32] Likewise, a writer for the *City Press* characterized the musicians as "filthy Germans—as filthy in speech as in looks . . . they howl like so many apes and baboons escaped from the Zoological Gardens, and looking much like these creatures too." The only way to deal with escaped wild animals, the author concluded, was to hunt them down: "no Londoner should sally forth to business without first spiking, or hanging, or shooting one of the howlers of the streets."[33] Depicting the musicians as filthy animals, and ultimately urging urban self-defense, this position drew upon language of the hunt to demonstrate among other things the persistence of territorial concerns, of metaphors of invasion and containment, in the gathering opposition to street music. But it was for an emerging segment of middle-class professionals—authors, artists, and other "brain-workers"—that the notion of territory took on new meanings, and their attacks reflected the added strains of having simultaneously to define and defend their newfound socioeconomic turf.

Notes

1. From a manuscript in the Dickens House Museum, quoted in Fred Kaplan, *Dickens: A Biography* (New York: William Morrow, 1988), 450.
2. Letter to Forster, [?1 November 1864], *The Letters of Charles Dickens,* Pilgrim edition, ed. Madeline House, Graham Storey, Kathleen Tillotson, et al., 12 vols. (Oxford: Clarendon, 1965–2002), 10:447. Unless otherwise noted, all references to Dickens's letters will be to this edition and cited by volume and page number.
3. Edgar Johnson, *Charles Dickens: His Tragedy and Triumph,* 2 vols. (New York: Simon and Schuster, 1952) 2:1017; Kaplan, *Dickens,* 451. A good discussion of Leech's professional relationship with Dickens on the Christmas books can be found in Jane R. Cohen, *Charles Dickens and His Original Illustrators* (Columbus: Ohio State University Press, 1980), 142–49.
4. Letter to M. T. Bass, [May 1864], in Michael T. Bass, *Street Music in the Metropolis: Correspondence and Observations on the Existing Law, and Proposed Amendments* (London: Murray, 1864), 41.
5. Quoted in W. P. Frith, *John Leech: His Life and Work,* 2 vols. (London: Bentley, 1891), 2:297.
6. *Times* (London), 2 May 1856, 9.
7. *Times,* 2 July 1860, 8–9.
8. Peter Bailey, "Breaking the Sound Barrier," in his *Popular Culture and Performance in the Victorian City* (Cambridge: Cambridge University Press, 1998), 206.
9. H. J. Dyos, "Some Historical Reflections on the Quality of Urban Life," in *Exploring the Urban Past: Essays in Urban History,* ed. David Cannadine and David Reeder (Cambridge: Cambridge University Press, 1982), 69.
10. These can be found in the chapter "Neighbours and Nuisances" in Thea Holme, *The Carlyles at Home* (London: Oxford University Press, 1965), 58–76. Holbrook Jackson claims that Carlyle "was probably pathological" in his attitude toward noise, but then there were many other urban workers echoing the same pathology ("Listening to Reading," *The Reading of Books* [London: Faber and Faber, 1946], 118).
11. From Thomas Carlyle's letter to Jane Welsh Carlyle, 28 July 1853, in *The Collected Letters of Thomas and Jane Welsh Carlyle,* ed. C. R. Sanders, K. J. Fielding, et al., 29 vols. to date (Durham, N.C.: Duke University Press, 1970), 28:231; his note to a letter from Jane Welsh Carlyle, 19 December 1853, 28:342; and his letter to Jane Welsh Carlyle, 29 July 1853, 28:233. All references to Thomas and Jane Welsh Carlyle's letters will be to this edition and cited by volume and page number.
12. Letter to Jane Welsh Carlyle, 8 July 1853, 28:185; to Jean Carlyle Aitken, 8 February 1853, 28:38.
13. Letter to Jean Carlyle Aitken, 11 August 1853, 28:245.
14. From Carlyle's journal, c. 17 August 1853, quoted in *Froude's Life of Carlyle,* ed. and abr. John Clubbe (Columbus: Ohio State University Press, 1979), 521.
15. Letter to Charles Redwood, 5 August 1853, 28:240.
16. Jenni Calder, *The Victorian Home* (London: Batsford, 1977), 15.

17.   Alain Corbin, *Village Bells: Sound and Meaning in the 19th-Century French Countryside,* trans. Martin Thom (New York: Columbia University Press, 1998), x, xii; see also Brace R. Smith, *The Acoustic World of Early Modern England: Attending to the O-Factor* (Chicago: University of Chicago Press, 1999); Mark M. Smith, *Listening to Nineteenth-Century America* (Chapel Hill: University of North Carolina Press, 2001); and Emily Thompson, *The Soundscape of Modernity:Architectural Acoustics and the Culture of Listening in America, 1900–1933* (Cambridge, Mass.: MIT Press, 2002).

18.   Jacques Attali, *Noise: The Political Economy of Music,* trans. Brian Massumi (Minneapolis: University of Minnesota Press, 1985), 6; hereafter cited in text.

19.   For approaches that are complementary to Corbin's and Attali's claims, see Eric Wilson ("Plagues, Fairs, and Street Cries: Sounding Out Society and Space in Early Modern London," *Modern Language Studies* 25.3 [1995]: 1–42), who studies "chapbooks, plague pamphlets, street cries, and ballads" as well as "the economic rhythms of voice and sound" in the soundscapes of Tudor and Stuart London (8–9). See also Bruce Smith, *The Acoustic World,* which offers "an ecology of voice, media, and community" for the primarily oral culture of early modern England (29). Mark M. Smith shows in *Listening to Nineteenth-Century America* "how important aurality, listening, and hearing were to the process of creating real and abiding notions of slavery and freedom, North and South, especially during the last three decades prior to the Civil War" (6–7). In *The Soundscape of Modernity* Thompson studies the ways, in tandem with urban industrialization, "new kinds of noises began to offend" in the early decades of the twentieth century (116–17).

20.   James Winter, *London's Teeming Streets, 1830–1914* (London: Routledge, 1993), 71; Lucio Sponza, *Italian Immigrants in Nineteenth-Century Britain: Realities and Images* (Leicester: Leicester University Press, 1988), 163–65; David R. Green, "Street Trading in London: A Case Study of Casual Labour, 1830–60," in *The Structure of Nineteenth-Century Cities,* ed. James H. Johnson and Colin G. Pooley (London: Croom Helm, 1982), 138. For an early account of street trader cries and music, see Charles Knight, "Street Noises," in *London,* ed. Charles Knight (London: Knight, 1841), 129–44. Knight's predictions are optimistic but fail to account for rising immigration and decreasing middle-class patience: "we are still advancing; and in a few years the [1839] Act which protects housekeepers from the nuisance of street musicians will be a dead letter" (142, 144).

21.   Henry Mayhew, *London Labour and the London Poor* (1861; reprint New York: Dover. 1968), 3:158–204.

22.   Medicus, "The Organ Nuisance," *Times,* 20 March 1851, 6.

23.   The most detailed study of Italian immigration in Victorian London is Sponza, *Italian Immigrants.* For a survey that primarily focuses on the twentieth century, see Terri Colpi, *The Italian Factor: The Italian Community in Great Britain* (Edinburgh: Mainstream, 1991). The literature on English views toward foreigners and immigrants during the period is, of course, vast; a very selective list of studies includes Robin Cohen, *Frontiers of Identity: The British and the Others* (London: Longman, 1994), especially chapter 1, "Six Frontiers of a British Identity," 5–36; Panikos Panayi, *Immigration, Ethnicity, and Racism in Britain, 1815–1945* (Manchester: Manchester University Press, 1994); and Colin Holmes, *John Bull's Island: Immigration and British Society, 1871–1971* (London: Macmillan Education, 1988).

24.   Knight, *London,* 142; "A Paterfamilias," "An Unneighbourly Act," *Good Words* (1864): 698. This is indeed one of the only published defenses of the musicians in this period of which I am aware.

25.   [Charles Manby Smith], "Music-Grinders of the Metropolis," *Chambers's Edinburgh Journal,* n.s., 17 (27 March 1852): 197; hereafter cited in text.

26.   Ronald Pearsall, *Victorian Popular Music* (Newton Abbot, U.K.: David and Charles, 1973), 192. For those who want to gauge the accuracy of the responses for themselves, performances of restored barrel organs, organettes, and a barrel piano are included on the recording *Music of the Streets,* Saydisc CSDL 340 (1983).

27.   Mayhew, *London Labour,* 3:180.

28. In fact, as John Zucchi explains, the first Savoyards of note in England were children who arrived in the sixteenth century as chimney-sweeps and also played hurdy-gurdies, exhibited animals native to Savoy such as groundhogs, and put on magic lantern shows. However, unlike their predecessors, "the new Savoyards [those arriving in the later nineteenth century] were not from the Duchy of Savoy but from the Duchy of Parma." See John Zucchi, *The Little Slaves of the Harp: Italian Child Street Musicians in Nineteenth-Century Paris, London, and New York* (Montreal: McGill-Queen's University Press, 1992), 18.

29. For more on the confusion over "Savoyard" origins, see Sponza, *Italian Immigrants,* 40–41. Savoy's and Nice's surrender was the result of a series of secret treaties in 1859–60 between Napoleon III and Cavour, who all the while publicly vowed not to give up the regions. An enthusiastic supporter of Italian unity, England responded to the decision with shock: Lord Palmerston began to regard Cavour "as a puppet of imperial France and thoroughly untrustworthy" (*The Making of Italy, 1796–1870,* ed. Denis Mack Smith [New York: Walker and Company, 1968], 304).

30. David Thomson provides a summary of the events leading up to the unification of Italy in 1871. with details about the role of Cavour in Savoy, in *Europe since Napoleon,* 2nd ed. (New York: Knopf 1962), 263–71. Details can be found in Arthur James Whyte, *The Evolution of Modern Italy* (New York: Norton, 1959), 129–30; Denis Mack Smith, *Italy: A Modern History,* 2nd ed. (Ann Arbor: University of Michigan Press, 1969), 24–25; and Harry Hearder, *Cavour* (London: Longman, 1994), 155–59. Still not surpassed for its focus is Derek Beales's *England and Italy 1859–60* (London: Nelson, 1961), which devotes an entire chapter to the Savoy controversy (131–62).

31. Cavour's epithet is taken from Denis Mack Smith, *Cavour* (New York: Knopf, 1985), 200.

32. Letter from "Chelone," reprinted in Bass, *Street Music,* 76; *Examiner* articles quoted in Bass, 70, 92, 96.

33. Quoted in Bass, *Street Music,* 109–10.

Chapter 15

Karin Bijsterveld

LISTENING TO MACHINES: INDUSTRIAL NOISE, HEARING LOSS AND THE CULTURAL MEANING OF SOUND

IN 1887, AN INQUIRY BY the Dutch parliament into the alarming working conditions in the nation's factories revealed that young boys employed in the boilermaking industry often had to stand inside the boilers holding back rivets as they were hammered in. Willem Ansing, a former smith, socialist and active trade union president was one of the people interviewed. 'Imagine', he reported, 'what it does to the brains of these children: they stay in the boilers all day long; it drives you crazy. Although I am not a boilermaker, I became deaf from it myself.'

'I noticed!', the president of the committee exclaimed, apparently responding to Ansing's raised voice. Another member of the parliamentary committee seemed to be unimpressed by the union leader's horror story:

> I admit that it is not desirable to leave a boy in a boiler for an entire day. Yet I am familiar with men who have done this work from the age of 13 to 16 . . . and who are very vigorous workers now. . . . But wouldn't it be possible to do something about it, for instance by putting wadding into one's ears? . . . [D]on't you know of bosses who do something in order to fight the adverse consequences?

'No', Ansing answered. And 'to put wadding in one's ears won't do, since the boys also need to listen to the things the men standing outside say to them.'[1]

Another interviewee, Heinrich Struve, a forty-year-old engineer, didn't see a problem at all. For two years he had maintained an office in a boiler workshop with about a hundred workers. 'Yet,' he stated, 'it did not do me any harm, I even regretted the moments the knocking was absent.' And Hendrik Suyver, aged fifty-two, manufacturer of boilers and a former boiler-boy himself, needed only a few words to answer the question of the link between his past profession and his impaired hearing: 'All of us get deaf.'[2]

That the engineer did not 'hear' the problem of noise, or unwanted sound, is understandable. Although his office was in the workshop, he did not have to enter the boilers. Neither is it surprising that a manufacturer was relaxed about getting hard of hearing: the noise was a sign of his business. What is remarkable, though, is that even the union leader, whose clear aim was to draw attention to the poor working conditions in Dutch industry, declared the use of wadding to be a mission impossible. His observation about the need to stay in touch with one's supervisor provides a straightforward explanation for this view, and one underlining the major significance of the act of listening on the shop-floor. Similarly revealing is the committee member's claim that boiler-boys had grown up into 'vigorous' workers, suggesting that the ability to stand noise was a sign of toughness. The remarks of both men point to the relevance of the symbolism of sound and cultures of listening for understanding why the use of earplugs was not unambiguously welcomed by workers.

Workers were questioning the need for ear protection for many decades to come. The aim of this paper is, then, to demonstrate the role of the cultural meaning of sound in the clash between the dramatisation of the industrial noise problem by experts, notably physicians, and the response to this dramatisation by shop-floor labourers. By focusing on pro-earplug campaigns in the Netherlands and Germany, I will illustrate what the sound of machines 'said' to both experts and laymen. By staging my account in the wider context of the Western history of industrial noise and noise abatement, I will also analyse the significance of the cultural meaning of sound for the position of hearing protection among alternative industrial noise abatement strategies, such as quieting machines and masking noise with music.

In so doing, I make use of and hope also to contribute to two distinct strands of research in science and technology studies concerned with science and sound: studies focusing on *sound in science*, and those concentrating on the *science of sound*. The first aims to understand the role of sound in science and technology development,[3] a focus related to the rising area of research analysing the role of embodied practice, and thus the senses, in generating scientific knowledge.[4] Works in the second tradition are cultural histories of the sciences of sound, such as acoustics and audiology, and their coevolution with public problems of noise.[5] Both sorts of research need to be involved in answering my key question – areas of research that are, in turn, deeply indebted to the cultural history and anthropology of the senses.

The Chaos of Industrial Noise: Restoring Rhythm and Distracting Attention

To the cultural history and anthropology of the senses we owe our knowledge of the longstanding association between noise and chaos. In war, revolution and ritual, the irregular and extremely loud use of drums and bells usually expresses intimidation, change and chaos, whereas a restoration of rhythm stands for situations being in control.[6] These are the kinds of cultural convention that are implied in what I have called 'the symbolism of sound'. Such a symbolism of sound co-constitutes 'the cultural meaning of sound', yet this cultural meaning of sound encompasses, at least in my use of the phrase, more than symbolism. It also includes cultures, or practices, of listening – cultures that have changed over time, partly in response to the introduction of new audio technologies.[7]

In line with age-old connotations of noise, the public problem of noise was initially — that is before the widespread introduction of instruments measuring the intensity and loudness of sound in the mid 1930s — often defined as a problem situated in the chaos of simultaneously perceived sounds and the absence of a univocal rhythm. At the end of the 1920s, the Noise Commission of London for instance claimed that street noise was a much more serious problem than industrial noise, because street noise, unlike industrial noise, had no rhythm. This made the clatter of traffic harder to adjust to than the cadence of industrial machines. Such difficulty of habituating to the chaos of street noise created angry emotions and added to fatigue.[8] Lack of rhythm thus made street noise more distressing than industrial noise.

Experts focusing on industrial noise, however, took quite a different stand. Although work had once been rhythmical, the introduction of modern machines had brusquely unbalanced the sound of the shop-floor. The beat of the machine was more rapid and fixed than human rhythms. Even worse, a standard workshop had not one, but a multitude of machines, with varying rhythms that, taken together, produced sonic chaos. Clearly, the experts' experience of factory sounds departed from the anti-street noise activists' ideas of industrial noise. Yet the arguments underpinning their positions were remarkably similar: rhythmic sound was the thing to strive for, whereas the absence of unambiguous rhythm — the most dangerous side of noise — was the situation to be avoided.

As early as 1913, Josephine Goldmark, chair of the Committee on the Legal Defense of Labor Laws of the US National Consumers' League, was quite clear on the dangers of noise. Noise, she claimed, 'not only distracts attention but necessitates a greater exertion of intensity or conscious application, thereby hastening the onset of fatigue of the attention.' According to her description of the textile trade, some kinds of motor sewing machine

> now carry 12 needles, others set almost 4000 stitches a minute. Let any observer enter a modern roaring, vibrating workroom where several hundred young women are gathered together, each at her marvelous machine, which automatically hems, tucks, cords, sews, seams together . . . Her attention cannot relax a second while the machine runs its deafening course . . . The roar of the machines is so great that one can hardly make oneself heard by shouting to the person who stands beside one.[9]

Investigations into the psychological and physiological effects of auditory stimuli on humans in the late 1910s, 20s and early 30s seemed to substantiate Goldmark's straightforward statements on noise and fatigue. Experiments of the American John J. B. Morgan in 1916/7, for instance, focused on the effect of noise on subjects translating a code on a typewriter. 'An increase in muscular tones, vocalization and marked changes in breathing disclosed that noise raised energy expenditure in order for the subjects to overcome the auditory distractions.'[10] And the work of the industrial psychologist Donald A. Laird showed a faster breath and raised systolic blood pressure in response to unexpected noise, as well as 'a lowering of efficiency in action and mental processes when noise is introduced'.[11]

In the context of the Taylorisation of the West's industrial life in the 1920s and 30s, suggestions of inefficiency in workers operating noisy machines clearly rang a bell. Enhancing employees' efficiency by restoring the sensation of rhythm on the shop-floor therefore became one of the strategies used to reduce the negative effects of noise. Playing the phonograph, the gramophone or the radio on the shop-floor was seen as a promising way of recreating such a rhythmic feel within the factory walls.

This strategy started out from the assumption that the rhythm of music facilitated effective performance. Initially, arguments for the significance of musical rhythm for work were of a historical-anthropological nature. In 1896, the German historical and anthropological economist Karl Bücher claimed that the origins of work were to be found in the rhythmical character of physical labour. Since *Naturvölker* (primitive peoples) had a natural disinclination for work, but loved to dance, only rhythm could explain why people had learned to endure simple, fatiguing tasks to an extent beyond that needed for basic survival. From and intertwined with the lust- and fantasy-evoking rhythm of bodily movement, music had evolved to facilitate the performance of individual work and the synchronisation of the communal. Rhythm had thus raised the productivity of labour. Art and technology, now differentiated domains of life, had once been two sides of the same coin.[12] As Goldmark put it:

> Not the poetry of existence only, but all the daily offices of life – spinning, weaving, sowing the grain, harvesting, and the rest – inspired song and dance, their own rhythms. Even today innumerable survivals persist . . .
> In the midst of discordant city traffic, workmen who are mending the pavements drive steel wedges with rhythmic shouts and rhythmic alternating blows of their sledges. They know, instinctively, that the rhythm makes the work easier.[13]

In contrast, the fast movements of modern machines, so Bücher asserted, produced a 'confusing, deafening noise' in which one could 'hear' but not 'experience' rhythm, thus evoking 'merely a sense of frustration'.[14] And, as Goldmark added: 'Not only is the beat of the machine much more rapid and regular than the more elastic human rhythms; it is often wholly lost in the chaos of different rhythms of the various machines, belts, and pulleys in one workroom.'[15] In the future, Bücher suggested, one might hopefully succeed in combining technology and art once more 'into a higher rhythmical unity'.[16]

It is not immediately obvious what unity of art and technology Bücher had in mind. Yet Thomas Edison seemed in a sense to make his dreams come true. In 1915, Edison 'used a programmed selection of phonographic music for factories to determine the extent to which it would mask hazardous drones and boost morale. But the infant loudspeaker and transmission technology was still too weak'.[17] The idea itself, however, continued to fascinate researchers from the field of industrial psychology. *The Influence of Music on Behavior*, a Princeton doctoral thesis of 1926 by Charles M. Diserens, summarised practices already existing, such as the speeding up of typewriting with the help of music, as well as new experiments. The results of controlled laboratory studies on the effects of tones and tonalities on blood circulation and muscular force were far from clear-cut. Yet many other reports, often based on questionnaires, claimed simply that music in the workplace led to an increased rate of work, fewer errors, better temper and lower fatigue. Theoretically, Diserens claimed, these phenomena could be explained by saying that 'by lending regularity to muscular reaction [rhythm] eliminates the strain of voluntary attention, and reduces fatigue. It is a conservative factor. Tone, on the other hand, lends force to muscular movements.'[18]

Numerous reports and studies followed those discussed by Diserens, both in the United States and Europe, and all claiming an increase in output under the influence of music.[19] 'It diverted the mind from the monotonous conditions of work, provided an attractive aim, made time seem to pass more quickly, and created a more cheerful attitude towards work', one famous British study from the second half of the 1930s explained. It took some discussion, however, to decide what *kind* of music was most suited to the job. The quick rhythm of one-steps coincided with high output, yet made 'the workers feel "lively and restless"', and the rhythm of marches 'clashed with some of the movements involved' in factory work.[20]

According to a report published in 1938 by the Philips firm, the music should not be too sentimental since the daydreams of the factory girls were already leaning too much towards the sentimental and sexual. On the other hand, jazz didn't fit because of its 'sudden variations in high and low tones' and because of the 'very pronounced rhythm' that conflicted with the rhythm of work and led to 'stammering' of hands and feet.[21] Similarly, the people behind the BBC programme *Music While You Work* explicitly banned 'hot' music with complex rhythms since such music created 'a confusion of sound'.[22]

Precisely because of the rhythmic character of factory work, the music should be 'more than rhythm', a Dutch author stressed in 1950. 'A clear, easily appealing melody should expound, as it were, the difference from the noise.'[23] By all means music needed 'to create order in the chaos of sound',[24] yet, as many authors claimed, one did not need to adjust the rhythm of the music to the rhythm of the machines. Nor would employing fast music necessarily speed up work. Less than through tempo, music rather influenced the worker by claiming attention and affecting mood. The speed of work simply varied too much to be dependent on the tempo of the music.[25] Moreover, both European and American studies found that the clatter of machines seemed to adjust to the rhythm of the music, and that even amidst terrific din, the music stood out.[26] As pianist and music journalist Doron K. Antrim clarified, 'the ear tends to follow' the agreeable 'regular tonal pulsations' of music and 'to forget' the irritating and fatiguing 'irregular pulsations' of noise.[27] Even if the 'hum' and 'shrieks' of machines mixed with the sound of music, a Dutch commentator stated, the music still had a positive effect.[28] Music of relatively high frequency, others explained, did not have to be very loud in order to be audible above the low-frequency noise produced by many machines.[29]

Many factory managers enthusiastically embraced music on the shop-floor, and so did most workers – judging by the published questionnaires and the success of radio programmes such as *Music While You Work*. Workers even introduced audio sets at work themselves.[30] The managers aimed to restore the rhythm of work within a chaos of mechanical din, thus following a deeply rooted symbolism of sound which associated noise with chaos and rhythm with order. They also contributed to a culture of listening in which listening to the radio became increasingly combined with other activities – something already quite common, so Susan Douglas has claimed for North America, by the 1930s.[31] Yet playing music was not the only conceivable way of dealing with industrial noise. Reducing the noise of the machines themselves and providing workers with earplugs were two alternative options.

Turning a Deaf Ear to Industrial Hearing Loss

Ever since the Middle Ages, physicians have pointed out the potential damage noise can inflict on the ear.[32] The danger of sudden and traumatic deafness connected with gunpowder was being mentioned as early as the late sixteenth century, and coppersmiths and blacksmiths were among the first groups of workers identified as getting hard of hearing and deaf because of their professional activities. Particularly famous are Bernardino Ramazzini's remarks on the coppersmiths of Venice in his *Diseases of Workers* of 1713:

> . . . these workers . . . are engaged all day in hammering copper to make it ductile . . . From this quarter there rises such a terrible din, that only these workers have shops and homes there; all others flee from that highly disagreeable locality . . . [As a result] the ears are injured by that perpetual din, and in fact the whole head, inevitably, so that workers of this class become hard of hearing and, if they grow old at this work, completely deaf.[33]

From the 1830s onwards, studies on 'blacksmiths' disease' and subsequently on artillerymen, sheet-iron workers, miners, coppersmiths, coopers, millers, metal-workers, locksmiths, boilermakers and railway workers appeared in European and American medical journals.[34] Over the course of the nineteenth and twentieth centuries, ever new groups, such as telephone-switchboard operators, were added. By 1938, 'over 560 occupations' had been classified by the Detroit Health Department as 'noisy occupations'.[35]

Quieting the machines that made these occupations noisy may seem to be a logical response to the problem of hearing loss. Yet, as medical historian Allard Dembe has illustrated for the United States, when such noise control was introduced it was probably not because of the danger of noise-induced hearing loss, but out of considerations of efficiency – as had been the rationale behind the use of music on the shop-floor. Around 1900, engineers began with the reduction of noise from production equipment since they realised that 'noisy machinery' could be 'an indication of mechanical inefficiency that ultimately can result in lower productivity and increased cost'.[36] Somewhat later, sound deadening foundations that reduced the vibration of machines, as well as the exclusion of machinery noise from particular areas through insulation, came to be discussed and introduced.[37] Quieting machines by suppressing the causes of noise at source was usually seen as the most effective approach. This focused on oiling moving parts, fixing defective ones, improving gearing, balancing machinery, reducing vibration and resonance caused by magnetic pulsation, and preventing sudden discontinuities in the motion of machines.[38]

Wearing 'personal protective devices in or around the ears to control exposure to industrial noise', however, did not become common until at least the 1950s. In the United States, this only happened after a rapid growth in workers' compensation claims, itself partly a consequence of the recognition of the war-related hearing loss suffered by forty thousand veterans of the Second World War.[39] The adoption of legislation with respect to industrial noise standards, with threshold limit values for noise, was delayed right up until the introduction of federal noise standards in 1969. In Europe, financial recognition of occupational hearing loss came even later. Apart from Germany, Sweden and the Soviet Union, before the second half of the 1960s most European countries provided compensation for hearing loss solely in cases where hearing problems affected the ability to work.[40] Before the Second World War, the Netherlands had introduced legislation determining that workers should be provided with some means of ear protection and that their use of earplugs should be assessed. Yet, codes of practice and legislation proclaiming such practices and noise exposure time limits did not become established before the 1960s (in Germany) and the 1970s (in the Netherlands and the UK).[41]

One reason for the delay in legislation regulating hearing protection and compensation for hearing loss, so Dembe says, was the need for specific evidence of injuries. Such proof could only be gathered through large-scale audiometric testing, which started in the 1930s – a few years after the introduction of the decibel in the 1920s. In the United Kingdom, a report commissioned by the government was claiming even as late as 1963 that 'the present knowledge of this complex problem', such as the variation in susceptibility of individuals to hearing loss, provided no 'sufficient basis for legislation'.[42]

In the United States, such legislation was further impeded by the fact that 'for most occupations, a partial loss of hearing [was] not critical to the performance of the job'.[43] Employers' perceptions of the costs of prevention and the economic crisis of the 1930s did not help either. In 1929, a German study defined hearing loss as an occupation-related disease in cases where a worker was unable to understand colloquial speech at a distance greater than four metres. Under this condition, the worker should be entitled to receive a moderate allowance. Since the authors considered this a substantial burden on the economy, however, they warned readers to be aware of the risk of simulation by workers. One of the results of this warning was that hearing loss became anchored in the revised German Workmen's Compensation Act of 1929 for the metals industry alone.[44]

Also unhelpful to large-scale interventions was the fact that the noise abatement societies of the 1910s and 20s, dominated by the bourgeoisie, gave a higher priority to street than to industrial noise.[45] Since the nineteenth century the bourgeois elite had largely welcomed the sound of industry as the sound of progress, and so it was no coincidence that street and transport noise rather than industrial noise became the primary target of the first civil noise abatement campaigns. As was illustrated above with the arguments of the London Noise Commission, the people behind such noise abatement initiatives legitimised their priorities by referring to street noises's lack of rhythm compared with the putative regularity of industrial noise. According to Dembe, such symbolism of sound also hampered recognition in the United States of noise-induced hearing loss as a disorder warranting compensation. The 'cultural association of loud industrial noise with admired societal traits', such as 'strength', 'progress', 'prosperity' and 'prowess', complicated the case for obligatory industrial noise control, hearing protection and financial compensation for hearing loss.[46] And as physicians would discover from the 1960s onwards, this not only explained the perspective of the industrialists, but also in part the behaviour of the workers.

Education on the Dangers of Noise

In the meantime, German and Dutch physicians and industrial hygienists focused on educating workers about the need to employ earplugs. As early as 1928, the German Society of Industrial Hygiene published a pamphlet on industrial noise and the prevention of hearing loss. The pamphlet explained to workers that '[i]mpairment of hearing caused by continuous, moderate occupational noise develops gradually and is at first hardly noticed'. Initially, the ability to perceive high frequencies would become affected. Later, 'the perception of lower tones' might become problematic. Workers should not stop their ears 'with plugs of cotton or of flax fibre', but were to employ 'compact plugs made of gauze saturated with petroleum or wax'. Neither should they postpone consulting a physician 'until serious disturbances become noticeable, such as ringing in the ears or attacks of dizziness'.[47] Limiting industrial noise on the shop-floor needed to be fostered, the pamphlet noted. Yet it did not go into detail in this respect – an approach more in line with the preference of employers for individual hearing protection than with that of trade unions for more comprehensive noise abatement measures.[48] 'Relaxation in quiet surroundings when away from work is the most helpful means of preventing ear problems', the pamphlet concluded.[49]

In the Netherlands, physicians taught workers similar kinds of lessons. Through audiometric testing they revealed the problems of such diverse groups as concrete workers, boilermakers and weavers. Yet labourers, a medical officer claimed during a debate on industrial noise in 1958, 'show hardly any inclination to use ear plugs'.[50] In order to improve this, he tried to 'cultivate' a small group of workers ready to wear earplugs permanently so as to be an example to others, in particular young workers. But it wasn't an easy job. 'We continuously have to harp on the same string', he added (without a trace of irony). An engineer also contributing to the discussion even claimed that workers, unconsciously or not, created more noise than was strictly necessary. The workers were thus in dire need of education.[51]

A few months later, a short movie entitled *Dangerous Noise* had its premiere. The film had been commissioned by the Dutch Department of Social Affairs and Public Health and aimed at providing workers with knowledge of the causes and consequences of hearing impairment. The problem was, as an accompanying note said, that being hard of hearing wasn't painful. Staying in noisy environments, in fact, became less annoying to the victims over time: they simply didn't hear the noise any more. Even worse, experienced workers ridiculed the use of earplugs. 'Elderly weavers jeer at youthful colleagues who wish to protect themselves against the noise. A nail boy wearing earplugs will never become a man, judges the riveter.'[52] In response, the film attempted to dramatise the danger of impaired hearing and deafness in everyday life by showing a near-fatal accident. In addition, it explained the workings of the ear and the character of audiometric examinations. The film also mentioned technical forms of noise control in industry, yet underlined that in case these were insufficient one simply had to wear earplugs. Such was the plight of the employees themselves. According to one of the film's medical advisers, it had been hard to plot a course between being scientifically accurate and educational. They thought they had succeeded, though.

Notwithstanding their satisfaction with the message of *Dangerous Noise*, Dutch doctors kept complaining about the fact that workers refused to wear earplugs, such 'a small inconvenience' in the medical experts' view. Of the hundreds of plastic earplugs provided to workers at a weaving factory, only a few actually came to be used for extended periods. The workers simply did not understand their personal 'interest' in hearing protection, so the medical officers claimed. Under such conditions, they grumbled, one could hardly expect employers to invest in noise abatement.[53] Workers considered industrial deafness as a fact of life.[54]

As late as 1972, Dutch physicians were stressing that it was hard to sustain the use of earplugs on the shop-floor.[55] German publications similarly pointed to the opposition of workers to personal hearing protection.[56] The medical officers considered their way of dramatising the problem of industrial hearing loss crystal clear, and implicitly blamed the workers for not speaking their abstract language of early causes and late effects. In contrast, the medical experts barely grasped how sound spoke to the workers themselves.

Sounds Reassuring, Impressive and Revealing: Listening to Machines

It took years before researchers hit on the idea of actually examining – by talking and listening to the workers themselves – why the men and women on the shop-floor were far from enthusiastic about wearing earplugs. It was only after this change of strategy that the public voice of workers sang more tunes than mere objections to hearing protection. Diving into the world of workers suddenly amplified the positive meanings industrial sound could embody for those working on the shop-floor.

A study published in 1960 showed that hearing protection made workers feel insecure about the direction from which sounds came, and caused communication problems as well as 'a nasty feeling'. The workers also reported that wearing earplugs meant 'a kind of embarrassment' in relation to their 'comrades'. Moreover, they did not believe the earplugs to be of any help and considered the cleaning of hearing protection too much trouble. In contrast, the sound of machines represented important opportunities. Industrial noise, for instance, enabled young workers to 'sing away to their heart's content' without disturbing their fellow workers. By doing so the youngsters produced, one could say, the music-while-you-work labourers had so often welcomed. Just as significant was that the noise acted as a kind of reassurance: the sounds signified that the machines were running normally.[57]

The study reporting these workers' experiences did not go into the details of such reassuring sounds. Other primary and secondary sources, however, suggest what mechanical sounds could say to those operating machines. As we have seen, engineers had often considered industrial noise as a sign of inefficiently running machines. What is more, the specific character of the mechanical noises informed them about the inefficiencies' causes. This practice of listening to machines in order to diagnose the origins of mechanical faults was also evident in car repair. At a Dutch anti-noise meeting in the mid 1930s, an engineer talked at length about the rattling, puffing, whistling, clicking, tapping, crashing, screeching, howling, crying, grinding, cracking, sneezing and whizzing of cars. He asserted that the analysis of motor sounds could reveal deviations from normal function before these could be detected visually.[58]

Car handbooks for the early generations of mass motorists often included sections explaining to drivers how to listen to their cars. These books literally clarified how the car 'spoke' to the driver. A 'sneezing' car had something to 'tell' about an obstruction in the spray nozzle of the tube from the carburettor's mixing chamber. A 'trained ear' could hear that this sneezing never started overnight, but announced itself by a change of engine pitch and rhythm. 'Pinking' and 'conking' recounted more serious problems.[59] A German author compared the sounds of cars to those of musical instruments, assuming that this would help with identification: 'Engine is pounding (muffled timpano): bearings disrupted. Car needs to be *dragged* to the workshop for testing! Oil consumption?'[60] He stressed that drivers should in principle mistrust every peep or crack: such could be a sign of damage.

Listening to machines was thus not a practice confined to factory life. And while unusual noises suggested mechanical faults, familiar sounds were a comfort to both drivers and workers: the machines were behaving as they were supposed to. This reassuring effect of machines sounding normally is also known from work by Cyrus Mody and Gerard Alberts on laboratory environments. In the laboratory for surface and materials science studied by Mody, sounds could contaminate experiments and disturb personnel, but they could also become 'epistemologically relevant'. Many of the scientists' instruments made specific sounds, such as the 'whirr of micrograph plates' being moved inside a transmission electron microscope, or the 'chuk-chuk of a probe being lowered on an atomic force microscope': 'When things run smoothly, these sounds unfold regularly, marking out the running of a clean experiment. Learning these sounds, and the experimental rhythm they indicate, is part of learning the proper use of the instrument.' Some laboratory employees, Mody adds, consider data such as those expressing 'periodicity' to be much better processed with one's ears than with the eyes. The sounds – whether 'beautiful', 'cool', 'neat' or 'ugly' – may even have aesthetic value, for listening 'is felt to increase embodied interaction with the instrument', enhancing the 'craft status' of operating microscopes.[61] Or as Arnold Pacey has noted, we talk about the 'tuning' of an engine, 'because we know that when it sounds "sweet", it is likely to be running well'.[62]

Similarly, Gerard Alberts has explained how in the 1950s the operators of the pioneer computers at the Philips Physical Laboratory in the Netherlands amplified the sounds of their equipment because they missed the 'trustworthy' rattling sounds of mechanical calculators. In contrast, the radio tubes and transistors of the new computers were comparatively silent. Adding amplifiers and loudspeakers to the computers created an 'auditory monitor', thus restoring a sensory relation with the equipment.[63] Philips even published a gramophone record with these sounds – sounds which were, in fact, employed to create music.[64]

The flip side of the reassuring sounds of well running machines, as Mody illustrates for 'his' laboratories, was and is 'the tacit knowledge of the sounds made when tools are not operating smoothly'. Such sounds help 'to diagnose problems, particularly with mechanisms hidden inside the instrument', while the deliberately created sounds of singing, stomping and clapping can be used to test both the instruments' sensitivity and acoustic isolation.[65] Alberts' Philips engineers gradually learned to hear that each computer problem had its 'own rhythm'. Thus they 'auralised' the inner workings of the computers in order to debug them.[66]

Yet, the sounds of machines not only warned and reassured their operators. To piece-rate workers, the German physician Gunther Lehmann claimed in 1961, a higher level of noise simply stood for an increase in income, while lower levels indicated reduced earnings.[67] The same phenomenon, Mark M. Smith has recently stressed, explains the ambivalence of workers in the early nineteenth-century North American textile industry in relation to the noise of machinery. He refers to a female factory worker who felt intimidated by the 'great groaning joints and wizzing fan' of a new machine, and mentions that most factory operatives aimed to be far from the deafening noise in their free time. The very same noise, though, was enjoyed by the workers as an indicator of the employment opportunities that allowed them to share in the region's progress.[68]

Moreover, and in contrast to the female worker just mentioned, men often appreciated noise for its very loudness. To whoever controlled the noisiest machine on the shop-floor, so Gunther Lehmann stated, noise was the expression of his importance and his power over others. This was similar to the meaning noise had for young drivers, Lehmann added, expressing the motorist's strength and masculinity.[69] This may explain the embarrassment workers felt when wearing earplugs: these would do their position in the masculine hierarchy no good at all. How significant such signs of toughness could be is also illustrated by a study into British shop-floor cultures of the 1970s. This study quoted a foundryman who proudly reported on his work 'on the big hammer', a 'six-tonner'. It was 'bloody noisy', the man said, but he got used to it. At home, he was considered to be a 'silly deaf old codger'. He could 'hear perfectly well in the factory', though. 'If I see two managers at the end of the shop, I know . . . just about what they're saying to each other.'[70]

According to another investigator, employees were much more afraid of losing their sight than their ability to hear, since hearing loss only became a social handicap after many years. Furthermore, wearing earplugs could be painful or irritating to the ear, and using them was an attention-taking and time-consuming affair. Workers needed to take care not to lose their earplugs, to clean them and to store them correctly. Since labourers such as weavers worked on piece-rate, taking care of earplugs was simply 'too much'. Moreover, a sloppy use of earplugs had no consequences for the group of weavers as a whole, whereas leaving weaving looms untidy did. The researcher therefore experimented with glass fluff that the weavers could easily draw from an automaton and throw away afterwards. This automaton also reduced their sense of being controlled by their bosses. Thereupon, acceptance rates rose to about seventy per cent.[71]

Workers supposed, as the authors of a 1973 paper regretted, that earplugs reduced their capacity to understand speech. Theoretically, the researchers claimed, this was impossible, since the signal-to-noise ratio remained the same with or without plugs. To their surprise, however, a subsequent study into this phenomenon substantiated the workers' knowledge in terms of the experts' methodologies. This was in particular true for those workers already suffering from hearing loss, which the authors put down to problems with recognising the high-frequency consonants in signals below a certain level. Workers, so the researchers concluded, should therefore be educated to shout even if they didn't hear much noise because of their earplugs.[72]

Taking seriously the opinions of the workers thus recognised their 'indigenous knowledge' of sound and communication.[73] In this light, the remark by Willem Ansing with which this paper started gets a new twist: the union leader's stress on the potential communication problems caused by using ear protection acknowledged the workers' indigenous knowledge of their trade. More than that, listening to the workers and to how these workers listened to the hum of machines opened up the labourers' particular expertise in what the sounds of machines had to say about their functioning, as well as about the workers' share in progress and importance.

Conclusion

In sum, until the legislation of the late 1960s and 70s it was largely left to industrial workers themselves whether or not to employ hearing protection. Medical officers did not succeed in dramatising the problem of industrial hearing loss in such a way that it convinced the workers. Their notions of today's risks and future problems clashed with the cultural values of the workers, the meaning sound had for them, and the routines of the shop-floor. Physicians combined an abstract discourse with a rather individualising strategy, considering the workers responsible for their own ears. The workers, on the other hand, turned a deaf ear to the physicians' rhetoric. To them, the hum of a machine could be a comforting sound since it informed them of its proper functioning. The noise enabled them to sing as loud as they wanted, and reminded them of their earnings. Putting up with the noise enabled them to parade their toughness, and controlling a noisy machine signified a position of power. They wanted to communicate with their comrades, and not to indulge in time-consuming cleaning and storing of their own earplugs if the collectivity of the workers demanded something else.

Cultural meanings of sound – both expressed in a particular symbolism of noise and a shop-floor culture of listening to machines – thus largely explain the lack of workers' enthusiasm for hearing protection. Similarly significant is the cultural meaning of sound in the rise of the two other available strategies for handling industrial noise. A striving for efficiency fostered both the initial quieting of machines, and the introduction of music on the shop-floor. Yet the music was legitimised by reference to longstanding positive connotations of rhythm, versus the negative ones of the irregular chaos of industrial sounds.

This does not mean that the cultural meanings of sound have not changed over time. While some of the symbolic meanings of noise may have been quite stable, routines and cultures of listening on the shop-floor have certainly evolved. Just as car drivers have increasingly learnt to trust visual displays rather than sound for information on their cars' performance, so industrial machines have been improved with new mechanisms of computer-based feedback. This is, for now, speculation, but these new forms of feedback may indeed have affected the eventual, late-twentieth-century advance of ear protection across the shop-floor just as much as the new legislation of the 1970s and after has done.

One last remark. Given the workers' ear for the informative and reassuring sounds of machines, it may seem strange that factory music was welcomed so warmly. Knowing that the music was supposed to cut through rather than to suppress mechanical noise, however, it becomes clear that the workers could both enjoy the music *and* listen to their machines. In this sense, the cheery British foundryman was right. Outside the walls of the factory, he was hard of hearing. Yet on the shop-floor, he could hear perfectly well.

Notes

1.   J. Giele: *Een kwaad leven. Heruitgave van de 'Enquête betreffende werking en uitbreiding der wet van 19 September 1874 (Staatsblad No. 130) en naar den toestand van fabrieken en werkplaatsen' (Sneek, 1887), bezorgd en ingeleid door Jacques Giele. Deel I Amsterdam*, 118; 1981, Nijmegen, Link. This and all other translations from Dutch and German originals are the author's.

2.   J. Giele: *Een kwaad leven*, pp. 64 and 366 (see Note 1).

3.   C. C. M. Mody: 'The sounds of science: listening to laboratory practice', *Science, Technology & Human Values*, 2005, 30, 175–98. See also G. Alberts: 'Computergeluiden', in *Informatica & Samenleving*, (ed. G. Alberts and R. van Dael), 7–9; 2000, Nijmegen, Katholieke Universiteit Nijmegen, and G. Alberts: 'Een halve eeuw computers in Nederland', *Nieuwe Wiskrant*, 2003, 22, 17–23.

4.   See for such research L. Roberts: 'The death of the sensuous chemist: the "new" chemistry and the transformation of sensuous technology', *Studies in the History and Philosophy of Science*, 1995, 26, 503–29, and C. C. M. Mody: 'The sounds of science' (see Note 3).

5.   E. Thompson: *The Soundscape of Modernity: Architectural Acoustics 1900–1933*; 2002, Cambridge, MA, MIT Press. See also A. E. Dembe: *Occupation and Disease: How Social Factors Affect the Conception of Work-Related Disorders*; 1996, New Haven, CO/London, Yale University Press.

6.   See for an overview K. Bijsterveld: 'The diabolical symphony of the mechanical age: technology and symbolism of sound in European and North American noise abatement campaigns, 1900–40', *Social Studies of Science*, 2001, 31, 37–70.

7.   See J. H. Johnson: *Listening in Paris*; 1995, Berkeley, CA, University of California Press; S. J. Douglas: *Listening in: Radio and the American Imagination from Amos 'n' Andy and Edward R. Morrow to Wolfman Jack and Howard Stern*; 1999, New York, NY, Times Books; M. Bull: *Sounding out the City: Personal Stereos and the Management of Everyday Life*; 2000, Oxford, Berg; J. Sterne: *The Audible Past: Cultural Origins of Sound Reproduction*; 2003, Durham, NC, Duke University Press; M. Bull and L. Back (ed.): *The Auditory Culture Reader*; 2003, Oxford/New York, NY, Berg; V. Erlman (ed.): *Hearing Cultures: Essays on Sound, Listening and Modernity*; 2004, Oxford/New York, NY, Berg; M. M. Smith (ed.): *Hearing History: A Reader*; 2004, Athens, GA/London, University of Georgia Press.

8.   E. F. Brown *et al.* (ed.): *City Noise: The Report of the Commission Appointed by Dr. Shirley W. Wynne, Commissioner of Health, to Study Noise in New York City and to Develop Means of Abating It*, 18, 106–7; 1930, New York, NY, Noise Abatement Commission, Department of Health.

9.   J. Goldmark: *Fatigue and Efficiency: A Study in Industry*, 71, 54; 1913, New York, NY, Survey Associates.

10.   R. W. Smilor: *Confronting the Industrial Environment: The Noise Problem in America, 1893–1932*, PhD thesis, University of Texas, Austin, TX, 1978, 145–46.

11.   R. W. Sherman: 'Sound insulation in apartments', *Architectural Forum*, 1930, 53, 373–78, at 373. See also D. A. Laird and K. Coye: 'Psychological measurements of annoyance as related to pitch and loudness', *Journal of the Acoustical Society of America*, 1929, 1, 158–63, and D. A. Laird: 'The effects of noise', *Journal of the Acoustical Society of America*, 1930, 1, 256–62.

12.   K. Bücher: *Arbeit und Rhythmus*, 80ff; 1896, Leipzig, S. Hirzel.

13.   J. Goldmark: *Fatigue and Efficiency*, p. 80 (see Note 9).

14.   K. Bücher: *Arbeit und Rhythmus*, p. 115 (see Note 12).

15.   J. Goldmark: *Fatigue and Efficiency*, p. 82 (see Note 9).

16.   K. Bücher: *Arbeit und Rhythmus*, p. 116 (see Note 12).

17.   J. Lanza: *Elevator Music: A Surreal History of Muzak, Easy-Listening, and Other Moodsong*, 13; 1994, New York, NY, Picador. See also R. L. Cardinell: *Music in Industry, No. 1–5*, No. 1, 5; 1944, New York, NY, American Society of Composers, Authors and Publishers.

18.   C. M. Diserens: *The Influence of Music on Behavior*, 122; 1926, Princeton, NJ, Princeton University Press. See for more contemporary arguments in favour of the beneficial effects of rhythm on work, W. McNeill: *Keeping Together in Time: Dance and Drill in Human History*; 1995, Cambridge, MA, Harvard University Press, and A. Pacey: *Meaning in Technology*; 1999, Cambridge, MA, MIT Press.

19.   See for instance S. Wyatt and J. N. Langdon: *Fatigue and Boredom in Repetitive Work*; 1937, London, HMSO; also D. K. Antrim: 'Music in industry', *Musical Quarterly*, 1943, 24, 275–90; H. Burris-Meyer: 'Music in industry', *Mechanical Engineering*, 1943, 65, 31–34; and 'Muziek in de fabriek', *De Nederlandse industrie*, 1955, (4), 66–67.

20.   S. Wyatt and J. N. Langdon: *Fatigue and Boredom*, pp. 40, 42 (see Note 19).

21.   H. Opdenberg: 'Music in worktime', Philips Concern Archives (hereafter PCA), File 642, Philips Bedrijfsomroep, 6. The report's year of publication is estimated to be 1938 by Philips archivist Ivo Blanken.

22.   W. Reynolds: *Music While You Work*, 6–7; 1942, London, British Broadcasting Corporation.

23.   M. Schröder: 'Muziek gedurende het werk', *Mens en Onderneming*, 1950/1, (4), 189–95, 192.

24.   M. Schröder: 'Muziek gedurende het werk', p. 191 (see Note 23).

25.   W. Reynolds: *Music While You Work*, p. 6 (see Note 22). See also J. Groen: 'Werk en werkomgeving: muziek', *Tijdschrift voor interne bedrijfsorganisatie*, 1948, 3, 144–48, at 145; and D. D. Halpin: 'Industrial music and morale', *Journal of the Acoustical Society of America*, 1943, 15, 116–23, at 118.

26.   R. Bergius: 'Die Ablenkung durch Lärm', *Zeitschrift für Arbeitspsychologie*, 1939, 12, 90–114, at 112–13.

27.   D. K. Antrim: 'Music in industry', p. 276 (see Note 19).

28.   A. J. van der Toorn: 'Over de invloed van muziek bij het werk op werknemer en productie', *Tijdschrift voor Efficiëntie en Documentatie*, 1949, 19, 203–7, at 206.

29.   M. Schröder: 'Muziek gedurende het werk', p. 191 (see Note 23) and R. L. Cardinell: *Music in Industry*, No. 1, p. 9 and No. 2, p. 6 (see Note 17).

30.   J. Lanza: *Elevator Music*, p. 13 (see Note 17), R. L. Cardinell: *Music in Industry*, No. 1, p. 6 (see Note 17).

31.   S. J. Douglas: *Listening in*, p. 84 (see Note 7).

32.   A. E. Dembe: *Occupation and Disease*, p. 163 (see Note 5).

33.   B. Ramazzini: *Diseases of Workers*, 437; 1964, New York, NY, Hafner Publishing (first published 1713 as *De Morbis Artificum*), quoted in G. Rosen: 'A backward glance at noise pollution', *American Journal of Public Health*, 1974, 64, 514–17, at 514.

34.   A. E. Dembe: *Occupation and Disease* (see Note 5). See also S. Krömer: *Lärm als medizinisches Problem im 19. Jahrhundert*; 1981, Mainz, Johannes Gutenberg-Universität, and E. Neisius: *Geschichte der arbeitsmedizinischen Lärmforschung in Deutschland*; 1989, Frankfurt am Main, Johann-Wolfgang-Goethe-Universität.

35.   G. Rosen: 'A backward glance', p. 514 (see Note 33).

36.   A. E. Dembe: *Occupation and Disease*, p. 195 (see Note 5).

37.   'Reducing noise in factories', *Scientific American*, 1921, 6 August, 96. See also E. G. Richardson: *Sound: A Physical Text-Book*; 1927, London, Edward Arnold; A. H. Davis: *Modern*

Acoustics; 1934, London, G. Bell & Sons; and K. W. Wagner: 'Praktische Wege der Lärmabwehr', *Forschungen und Fortschritte*, 1936, 12, 41–43.

38. E. J. Abbott: 'The role of acoustical measurements in machinery quieting', *Journal of the Acoustical Society of America*, 1936, 8, 133–42; H. Wigge: *Lärm: Die Grundtatsachen der Schalltechnik. Lärmstörungen — Lärmschütz*; 1936, Leipzig, Dr Max Jänecke Verlagsbuchhandlung; G. H. Ballot: 'Bestrijding van hinderlijk lawaai in fabrieken en werkplaatsen', *Bedrijf en Techniek*, 1948, 3, 54–56; W. Zeller: *Technische Lärmabwehr*; 1950, Stuttgart, Alfred Kröner Verlag.

39. A. E. Dembe: *Occupation and Disease*, p. 209 (see Note 5).

40. A. E. Dembe: *Occupation and Disease*, p. 203 (see Note 5). See also W. Passchier-Vermeer: Review of *Introduction to the Study of Noise in Industry*, *Tijdschrift voor Sociale Geneeskunde*, 1969, 47, 282; C. S. Kerse: *Noise*, 121; 1975, London, Oyez Publishing; E. Neisius: *Geschichte der arbeitsmedizinischen*, pp. 49–50 (see Note 34).

41. J. P. Kuiper: 'Veiligheidswet en lawaaibestrijding', *Tijdschrift voor Sociale Geneeskunde*, 1972, 50, Suppl. 2, 42–43 and 45; H. Wiethaup: 'Lärmbekämpfung in historischer Sicht. Vorgeschichtliche Zeit – Zeitalter der alten Kulturen usw.', *Zentralblatt für Arbeitsmedizin und Arbeitsschutz*, 1966, 16, 120–24; *Code of Practice for Reducing the Exposure of Employed Persons to Noise*; 1972, London, HMSO; C. S. Kerse: *Noise* (see Note 40).

42. A. H. Wilson: *Noise. Final Report. Presented to Parliament by the Lord President of the Council and Minister for Science by Command of Her Majesty, July 1963*, 128; 1963, London, Her Majesty's Stationery Office.

43. A. E. Dembe: *Occupation and Disease*, p. 203 (see Note 5).

44. E. Neisius: *Geschichte der arbeitsmedizinischen*, pp. 64–65 (see Note 34); K. Beck and F. Holzmann: *Lärmarbeit und Ohr: Eine klinische und experimentelle Untersuchung*, 31; 1929, Berlin, Verlag von Reimar Hobbing; H.-J. Braun: 'Lärmbelastung und Lärmbekämpfung in der Zwischenkriegszeit', in *Sozialgeschichte der Technik. Ulrich Troitzsch zum 60. Geburtstag*, (ed. G. Bayerl and W. Weber), 251–58, at 255–56; 1998, Münster, Waxmann.

45. K. Saul: 'Wider die "Lärmpest". Lärmkritik und Lärmbekämpfung im Deutschen Kaiserreich', in *Macht Stadt krank? Vom Umgang mit Gesundheit und Krankheit*, (ed. D. Machule, O. Mischer and A. Sywottek), 151–92, at 153; 1996, Hamburg, Dölling & Galitz.

46. A. E. Dembe: *Occupation and Disease*, pp. 203, 211 (see Note 5).

47. 'Combat against noise' (Foreign Letter, Berlin), *Journal of the American Medical Association*, 1929, 92, 2119.

48. E. Neisius: *Geschichte der arbeitsmedizinischen*, pp. 56, 60 (see Note 34).

49. 'Combat against noise' (see Note 47).

50. 'Lawaai-en beroepsdoofheid', *Tijdschrift voor Sociale Geneeskunde*, 1958, 36, 643–46, at 643. See also H. A. van Leeuwen: 'Bedrijfsgeneeskundige aspecten van de beroepsslechthorendheid', *Tijdschrift voor Sociale Geneeskunde*, 1958, 36, 623–31.

51. 'Lawaai-en beroepsdoofheid', pp. 644, 646 (see Note 50).

52. F. H. Bonjer: '"Gevaarlijk geluid". Een film', *Tijdschrift voor Sociale Geneeskunde*, 1959, 37, 733–34.

53. 'Lawaaibestrijding', *Tijdschrift voor Sociale Geneeskunde*, 1959, 37, 740.

54. B. Lammers: 'Gehoorbescherming in de textielindustrie', *Tijdschrift voor Sociale Geneeskunde*, 1964, 42, 248–52, at 248.

55. W. Passchier-Vermeer: 'Een grens tussen veilig en onveilig geluid', *Tijdschrift voor Sociale Geneeskunde*, 1972, 50, Suppl. 2, 26–32, at 26.

56. G. Kurtze: *Physik und Technik der Lärmbekämpfung*, 424; 1964, Karlsruhe, Verlag G. Braun, and H. Wiethaup: *Lärmbekämpfung in der Bundesrepublik Deutschland*, 573; 1967, Cologne, Carl Heymanns Verlag.

57. *De invloed van lawaai op groepen*, 24–25; 1960, Leiden, Instituut voor Gezondheidstechniek TNO.

58. *Verslag van het tweede Anti-Lawaai-Congres te Delft op 21 april 1936 georganiseerd door de Koninklijke Nederlandsche Automobiel Club en de Geluidstichting*, 77; 1936, Delft, Geluidstichting.

59.   H. Meyer: *Achter het Autostuur.Wenken in het belang van rijder en mechanisme*, 19, 20, 22, 24; [no year], Amersfoort, Valkenhoff & Co.

60.   H. Dillenburger: *Das praktische Autobuch*, 301–3; 1957, Gütersloh, G. Bertelsmann Verlag.

61.   C. C. M. Mody: 'The sounds of science', pp. 186, 188–89 (see Note 3).

62.   A. Pacey: *Meaning in Technology*, p. 18 (see Note 18).

63.   G. Alberts: 'Een halve eeuw computers in Nederland', pp. 17, 23 (see Note 3); see also G. Alberts: 'Computergeluiden', p. 9 (see Note 3).

64.   G. Alberts: 'Een halve eeuw computers in Nederland', p. 21 (see Note 3).

65.   C. C. M. Mody: 'The sounds of science', p. 186 (see Note 3).

66.   G. Alberts: 'Een halve eeuw computers in Nederland', pp. 20–21 (see Note 3).

67.   G. Lehmann: *Die Einwirkung des Lärms auf den Menschen*, 10; 1961, Cologne/Opladen, Westdeutscher Verlag.

68.   M. M. Smith: *Listening to Nineteenth-Century America*, 136, 137, 140–41; 2001, Chapel Hill, NC/London, University of North Carolina Press.

69.   G. Lehmann: *Die Einwirkung des Lärms*, p. 10 (see Note 67).

70.   P. Willis: 'Shop floor culture, masculinity and the wage form', in *Working-Class Culture: Studies in History and Theory*, (ed. J. Clarke, C. Critcher and R. Johnson), 185–98, at 189–90; 1980, New York, NY, St Martin's Press.

71.   B. Lammers: 'Gehoorbescherming in de textielindustrie', *Tijdschrift voor Sociale Geneeskunde*, 1964, 42, 248–52.

72.   H. E. Lindeman and P. van Leeuwen: 'Spraakverstaan en gehoorbeschermers', *Tijdschrift voor Sociale Geneeskunde*, 1973, 51, 331–35 and 347.

73.   See for an overview of research into 'indigenous' or 'local' knowledge H. Watson-Verran and D. Turnbull: 'Science and other indigenous knowledge systems', in *Handbook of Science and Technology Studies*, (ed. S. Jasanoff *et al.*), 115–39; 1995, London, Sage.

Chapter 16

Stefan Helmreich

AN ANTHROPOLOGIST UNDERWATER: IMMERSIVE SOUNDSCAPES, SUBMARINE CYBORGS AND TRANSDUCTIVE ETHNOGRAPHY

I AM PREPARING TO SINK into the sea, probably the first anthropologist to join the research submersible *Alvin* on a dive to the ocean floor. The three-person sub sits like a massive, oblong washing machine on the stern of the research vessel *Atlantis,* where a thick rope temporarily tethers it to an enormous metal A-frame rising from the ship's fantail. Clambering down a steep ladder into the submarine, I find pilot Bruce Strickrott already adjusting *Alvin*'s array of knobs, buttons, and computer screens. Geologist John Delaney is next to descend; delivering a foul-mouthed oath, he wedges his tall frame into a nook on the port side of the sub. As we are lowered into the waters of the northeastern Pacific on this cloudy June day in 2004, wet-suited escort swimmers survey the exterior of our capsule to make sure we do not go down gurgling. They snorkel past our individual four-inch-thick acrylic view ports, each window just wide enough to fit the features of a face.

In what I initially imagine to be an idle pun, graduate students on *Atlantis* have joked that I will now truly "immerse" myself in the culture of deep-sea oceanographers, seeing their preferred medium with my own anthropological eyes. As we begin our hour-long descent, my attention is, indeed, captured by such traditional icons of the deep as the evanescent jellies that flash past my window. But I am also fascinated by the sounds that accompany and enable our descent. The snug seven-foot-diameter interior of our titanium sphere is awash in the metallic and muffled pings of distant sonar devices, the echoes of telephone voices from the *Atlantis,* and the quiet pop music that percolates from *Alvin*'s stereo sound system. These bleep-blooping, burbling, and babbling sounds do, in fact, contribute, I find, to a feeling of immersion. Submerging into the ocean almost seamlessly merges with a sense of submerging into sound—and into a distinctively watery soundscape.

The easy image comes to me of *Alvin* as a ball of culture submerged in the domain of nature. After all, submarine settings often take "to an extreme the displacement of the natural environment by a technological one" (Williams 1990:4). As the noted vent biologist Cindy Van Dover suggests, in a more sensational turn of phrase, "descending the water column in a submarine is an unnatural act" (1996:16). But natural and cultural dynamics develop dense interrelations as well, feeding back into one another in *Alvin*'s immersion. The assemblage of the sub and its encapsulated scientists is clearly a cyborg, a combination of the organic and technical kept in tune and on track through the self-correcting dynamics of visual, audio, and tactile feedback. Positioned in the sub, our bodies are threaded into a media ecology of communication and control, networked into a semiotic order that extends, modulates, and conditions our senses. As an anthropologist on *Alvin,* I am anxious about my role in this circuit. Recalling an iconoclastic one-liner delivered by Chris Kelty (2003), another ethnographer of the hypertechnological, I ask myself, "What would Margaret Mead do?" Delaney unsuspectingly offers a possible answer, scripting me into the informatic loop, wisecracking that my research will constitute a "recursive study of ourselves studying." Mead, as readers may recall, was not only fascinated by sex in Samoa and trance and dance in Bali but was also a fan of feedback systems. In an article entitled "Cybernetics of Cybernetics" (Mead 1968), she called for anthropologists to become familiar with the vocabulary of information theory, to take seriously the possibilities and effects of systems thinking and doing.[1]

In this article, I take up that charge, paying special attention to the role of sound in constituting the experience of cybernetic and cultural immersion. I follow Steven Feld's recent call for "doing anthropology in sound" (Feld and Brenneis 2004)—which, for the setting that concerns me here, entails attending to the "sounds of science" (Mody 2005), placing "sound studies" at the center of investigations of technoscientific practice (Pinch and Bijsterveld 2004).[2] In asking after the sounds that float in and out of submariners' consciousness, however, I am less interested in the self-referential looping of a "cybernetics of cybernetics" than I am concerned with the technical transformations of sound and signal that support cybernetic sensibility and consciousness in the first place. I am curious about the cognitive, affective, and social effects of transducing—that is, converting, transmuting—sound from the medium of water into that of air, and about what an anthropology of such transduced sensing can make explicit about the conditions that permit immersion (and, I maintain, that create senses of presence as such), whether people speak of immersing themselves in water, sound, or the medium of culture. The *Oxford English Dictionary* (*OED*) defines *transduce* as follows: "To alter the physical nature or medium of (a signal); to convert variations in (a medium) into corresponding variations in another medium."

Such alterations and conversions are about the simultaneous structuring of matter and meaning. I counterpose, then, to the recursive recipes of reflexive ethnography the possibilities of a transductive ethnography—an inquiry motivated not by the visual rhetoric of individual self-reflection and self-correcting perspectivalism, but one animated by an auditorily inspired attention to the modulating relations that produce insides and outsides, subjects and objects, sensation and sense data. Rather than seeing from a point of view, then, I suggest tuning in to surroundings and to circumstances that allow resonance, reverberation, echo—senses, in brief, of presence and distance, at scales ranging from individual to collective. Using my dive in *Alvin* as a narrative vehicle, I meditate less on what I saw in the teensy patch of ocean floor I visited (mostly passing apparitions of flesh and rock) and more on what we in the sub (and sometimes, by extension, we in the ship–sub system) heard and listened to.

In operating the concept of "transduction," I develop and refine for anthropological purposes an exposition offered by historian of sound Jonathan Sterne, who argues in *The Audible Past* (2003) that mechanisms of transduction, built into such technologies as the telephone and radio, have been read back into the very nature of hearing; transduction is now imagined as a universal infrastructure for a range of cultures of hearing (see, e.g., Arehart 2005). I suggest that hearing cultures (cf. Erlmann 2004)—or, better, listening to social and cultural practices—can be sharpened by sounding out concretions of this infrastructure, pressing us as ethnographers toward discernments of material and semiotic relationships often washed out of attention by the all-encompassing idiom of immersion.

In adapting transduction for the anthropology of sound, I hope to illustrate how novel ethnographic results might follow from attending to the ways soundscapes are fashioned and to how hearing and listening are conceived and experienced. At various points during my dive narrative, I flag other ethnographies of sound I think zero in on transductive dynamics—or that might benefit from doing so. I also identify a loose constellation of anthropological scholarship that explicitly works with the notion of transduction (to anticipate: Fischer 2007; Myers 2006; Silverstein 2003) and that in some instances takes transduction beyond the realm of the auditory to consider a range of other sensory relays and transformations of matter and meaning. Drawing on phenomenological and philosophical treatments of transduction as a process of constituting, structuring, and modifying spatial and logical relations (Deleuze and Guattari 1987; Mackenzie 2002; Simondon 1992), I conclude that such ethnographies of transduction press toward considering ethnography *as* transduction.

Soundscapes

The *Alvin* dive I have joined will employ a high-resolution imaging sonar system called "Imagenex" to map portions of the Mothra Hydrothermal Vent Field, a seabed region of black smokers on the Endeavour Segment, a narrow submarine volcano situated on the Juan de Fuca Ridge, the edge of a major tectonic plate that sits some 200 nautical miles off the Pacific Northwest coast and about 2,000 meters down. I have talked my way into *Alvin* as part of ethnographic research into how oceanographers imagine and encounter such abyssal ecologies as hydrothermal vents (see Helmreich 2003). Chief scientist Deborah Kelley of the School of Oceanography at the University of Washington in Seattle, learned through colleagues about my project on the anthropology of contemporary marine biology, and when a berth opened up on *Atlantis* for this National Science Foundation (NSF)-funded trip, she invited me along. My dive will be a standard eight-or-so hours long. I have been able to sign on largely because no groundbreaking research is slated for this routine excursion, Dive #4020—an indication of the safe and steady rhythm into which *Alvin* dives have settled since the Woods Hole Oceanographic Institution in Massachusetts began operating the sub in 1964.[3]

As we drop down to the ocean floor, amidst a wash of submarine sounds, some questions surface: How did the domain that Jacques Cousteau (with Dumas 1953) once named "the silent world" become so sonorous? How did the underwater realm, this zone to which humans cannot have extended, unmediated access (without drowning, that is), become imaginable and accessible as a space of sound? What kinds of technical work have been necessary to bring this field into audibility for human ears? And what have been the cultural effects—for people in submarines, for example—of such work? Learning the answers requires dipping into some submarine history, tuning into the technical specifics of underwater listening, considering cybernetic networks of communication and control, and querying the multiple modes through which people imagine immersion: as a descent into liquid, as an absorption of mind and body in some activity or interest (such as music), and—in a meaning of relevance to anthropologists—as the all-encompassing entry of a person into an unfamiliar cultural milieu.

Key to thinking through how the sensation of auditory immersion is produced is the concept of a "soundscape." Ecologically minded musician R. Murray Schafer advanced the term in 1977 to call attention to his worry that natural sonic environments were being polluted by industrial noise. Historian Emily Thompson, in a more formal register, defines the soundscape as "an auditory or aural landscape . . . simultaneously a physical environment and a way of perceiving that environment; it is both a world and a culture constructed to make sense of that world" (2002:1). A soundscape includes what Feld calls an "acoustemology," a "sonic way of knowing and being" (Feld and Brenneis 2004:462; see also Feld 1996).[4]

There are, of course, many genres of such knowing and being, "diverse meanings of the auditory" (Mody 2005:193), and, although it may seem to go without saying, three-dimensional space has been central to the conception—the acoustemology—of the soundscape (Schafer's composition of soundwalks, in which sonic landscapes are experienced via movement through space, makes spatiality explicit). In *Village Bells* (1998), a lush history of sound in 19th-century rural France, Alain Corbin argues that the ringing and reverberation of church bells served to define the auditory circumference of village communities, rooting people in local territories by placing them in a soundscape that symbolically reinforced their social proximity to town centers. In "Sounding the Makassar Strait," Charles Zerner describes how Mandar fishermen off the southwestern coast of Indonesia's island of Sulawesi employ spells and calls—"prayers, exhortations, and instrumental performances" (2003:62)—to summon flying fish into floating traps they fasten to their small outrigger sailboats. The soundscape that fishers create across this stretch of water—made of their whispered speech, shouted songs to spirit guardians, and Koranic recitations—responds to and demarcates local maritime territories. Thompson's *The Soundscape of Modernity* (2002) tells yet another tale of space and sound; in the early 20th century, she reports, the rise of electroacoustic devices redescribed sounds as signals, which allowed for the measurement and standardization of soundscapes. In that machine age, the spatialization of sound came ideally to be dictated not by the acoustics of places (like concert halls) but by techniques of sound reproduction, aimed at making diverse places—from public auditoriums to private homes—all sound the same.

Corbin, Zerner, and Thompson describe sounds organized and perceived through air. But what about sound underwater? Technologically constructed transductive apparatuses are essential for the submarine medium to be rendered into a soundscape for humans. I attempt below to map out the phenomenologies that result from attending to—as well as from forgetting—such transductions. In aid of that inquiry, I develop the figure of the submarine cyborg—the cyborg in a deep-sea soundscape—to make explicit the material transformations across media that have to unfold for the seemingly seamless transfer of information in cybernetic systems to be accomplished. I argue that a transductive ethnography provides tools for making audible the conditions that produce what many people have come to think of as the self-evident experience of watery and auditory immersion.

Let me return to my ethnographic setting, inside the sub, from which seat I will spin stories of sounding, soundscaping, listening, hearing, not listening, immersion, and transduction.

Sounding

We are well into our descent, some 400 meters down. Pilot Bruce switches off *Alvin*'s exterior lights to save power, leaving the outside ink black. The phone rings. Kelley on *Atlantis* has a question for John about a grant proposal. Her voice, soaked with echo like a track on a Jamaican dub recording, bounces around the sub as she and Delaney agree about an e-mail she will send.

We continue to sound—in the sense of diving into and also investigating, fathoming—the deep. Such sounding employs devices, like sonar (sound navigation and ranging), that, in a confusing pun, capture and transmit sound (*sound* as fathoming has its etymological moorings in the Old English *sund,* "sea," whereas *sound* as vibration reaches back to Old English *swinn,* "melody"). With the interior lights dimmed, a cycle of blips and bleeps captures my attention. Bruce identifies these for me as a 9-kilohertz tracking pulse sent out from *Alvin* to *Atlantis* every three seconds, a 9.5-kilohertz response from the ship, and a steady metronome of "pings" from transponders dispatched to the seafloor by *Atlantis* in advance of *Alvin* dives. Transponders are spheres about the size of beach balls that, anchored and floating about 180 meters off the seafloor, transmit sonic signals that help the sub to continually locate itself in three dimensions using triangulation. Bruce tells me he thinks of transponder pings as background noise. But they are not exactly the meaningless patter that journalist Victoria Kaharl, who descended in *Alvin* in 1989, rendered in her dive narrative as occasional interruptions of "Wa WA wawa WAWA wowo wowo WOWO wawa WAWA" (1990:335–36) and "POP weewee wo WOP ka POP weewee wo" (1990:337). For Bruce, the noises secure a sense that the sub is somewhere rather than nowhere, supported in a web of sound rather than lost in a featureless void. Even though he jokes that the prattle of pings can be an "acoustic 'will-o'-the-wisp'"—"a thing that deludes or misleads by means of fugitive appearances" (*OED*)—for Bruce, these echoes are the warp and weft of a reassuring soundscape ("without them, it'd be too quiet," he offers). Far from being "noise" as "irrelevant or superfluous information" (*OED*), transponder pings constitute noise as the hum of a world, as what musician Aden Evens calls an "implicated reserve of sense" (2005:142).

In "The Sounds of Science: Listening to Laboratory Practice," Cyrus Mody writes that "labs are full of sounds and noises, wanted and unwanted, many of which are coordinated with the bodily work of moving through space, looking at specimens, and manipulating instruments" (2005:176). And so it is here in the oceanographic field, too; work in *Alvin* is coordinated by and through sound, even if we are not always fully tuned in to quite how. Indeed, our task this afternoon to map a tiny swath of the seafloor makes use of a system that translates sonic soundings (which we do not hear) into computer-generated topographic images. *Alvin* moves through and creates a multiplicity of soundscapes, at various frequencies and levels of accessibility to submariners' ears.

Transducing a Submarine Soundscape for Humans

How have underwater soundscapes come into audibility for humans? Devices that permit listening across different media—from water over into air environments (like the inside of the sub)—are key. *Alvin,* maintained at one atmosphere of pressure in its interior (i.e., at everyday, sea-level pressure), can only deliver to passengers a sense of an exterior soundscape because of such transducers.[5] What might be less obvious is why the underwater realm is not a soundscape for people unless such prosthetic technologies are made available to our naked ears.

Consider a skin diver. The sensation of floating in a three-dimensional net of sound is not immediately available to people swimming submerged in water. This is in part because it is nearly impossible for humans to use underwater acoustic vibration to locate themselves in space. For one thing, sound waves travel four times faster in water than in air. For another, human eardrums are too similar in density to water to provide the resistance that can interrupt many underwater vibrations so that they might be translated into tympanic movement—sound—in the ears; lots of vibrations pass right through our bodies. For humans, underwater sound is largely registered by bones in the skull, which allow enough resistance—*impedance,* to use the technical term—for vibrational motion to be rendered into resonances in the body. Moreover, conduction of sound by bone directly to the inner ear confounds any difference in signals received by left and right ears, making it impossible to compose what audiophiles call a "stereo image." Unaided human ears perceive underwater sound as omniphonic: coming from all directions at once (and, indeed, because of sound's seemingly instantaneous arrival, often as emanating from within one's own body). In this (transductively phrased) framing, the underwater world is not immediately a soundscape for humans because it does not have the textured spatiality of a landscape; one might, rather, think of it as a zone of sonic immanence and intensity: a soundstate.

A couple of acoustemologies can be imagined that correspond to this pheno-menology. One acoustemology might have the auditor feeling the immediate compressing power of an alien medium, perhaps experiencing a shock akin to that felt by 18th-century European cure seekers who traveled to the seashore to be suddenly immersed in cold water. Another acoustemology might posit a oneness, a sensory communion, with the medium, what Don Ihde in his "Auditory Imagination" calls a "'dissolution' of self-presence" (2003:62). Such a sensibility might regard the immediacy of sound as a sign that one is "merging with the elemental forces"—a phrase Corbin (1988:164) uses to describe the sensation desired by those Romantic poets who sought through swimming to achieve sublime union with the sea.

Neither of these two acoustemologies opens out into the dimensional topography of a soundscape. It takes technical and cultural translation to carve a soundscape for humans out of the subaqueous milieu, to endow submarine space with sonic distance and depth, to create immersive space. Equipment must first be constructed that can capture submarine vibrations in the audio register—hydrophones, for example, like the ones manufactured by the International Transducer Corporation in Santa Barbara, California, devices that can get hold of underwater vibrations, usually using a microphone fashioned of ceramic or another material sufficiently denser than water to allow propagating waves to be impeded (see International Transducer Corporation n.d.). Once sound has been received by a hydrophone, signals must then be transported into an airy medium for apprehension by human ears. Such sound can be rendered into stereo using devices that transform signals arriving at separate underwater receivers into "binaurally centered" impressions in headphones or from speakers, translating captured submarine sound into spatial relations dimensionally meaningful to hearing humans (Höhler 2003).[6]

With hydrophones and speakers, even such items as submerged bells might be assessed for their underwater reverberation: In 1901, the Submarine Signal Company of Boston sought robust methods for submarine communication, imagining "a network of underwater bells whose sonorous gongs would carry through the water at great distances" (Schlee 1973:246). The company, seeking an alternative to foghorns and responding to growing densities of ship traffic, built receivers to capture the resulting resonances for listeners on board ships, although it must be said that the system envisioned never came into focus; plans to use bells to send Morse code were swamped by the turbulent, scattering character of the submarine medium.

Bringing underwater sound into human-occupied air pockets like *Alvin* requires and entails transduction. Indeed, the possibility of imagining oneself immersed in a submarine soundscape depends on transduction—as, indeed, in its own way, does the sense of feeling omniphonically at one with a soundstate summoned forth by a skull-enveloping fluid.[7] The ear itself, it is crucial to note, has for the last century or so been understood as a transducing device, translating vibrations in air into corresponding motions in the eardrum (Sterne 2003), a description that, as I have already suggested, folds an engineering formulation into scientific understandings of the sense of hearing as such.[8] If, as Thompson suggests, the soundscape of modernity is patterned by sounds "increasingly the result of technological mediation" (2002:2), underwater soundscapes do not exist at all for humans without such mediation all the way down—or, more exactly, all the way across (and, in the case of *Alvin*'s pinging sonarscape, without first becoming *soundedscapes*—which, because sonar sounding depends on knowing the speed of sound in water, demonstrates that subs use "sound to map time into space" [Evens 2005:54]).

From Listening to Hearing

And so, transponder signals must be transduced to create the echoing sounds carried to listeners cocooned inside the sub. Bruce's joke about the "will-o'-the-wisp" character of these sounds speaks to the sometimes misleading nature of the aqueous vibrational field. Turbulence and refracting motions of water can produce fluctuating amplitudes, "frequency-smearing" effects, and "blobs of reverberation" that make directionality difficult to discern, even once sounds are converted across media (Urick 1983). Water waves—which form and even crash underwater, where liquid layers of different temperatures meet—can also change the contours of vibration, introducing such complexities as Doppler effects, even for submarine auditors staying "still."

Closer listening cannot really help when these factors pile up on one another, as they sometimes do. But none of us in *Alvin,* not even the pilot, really needs to listen to the sounds of sonar closely. These days, onboard computers process transponder and other sonar signals. "No one now wears headphones and a rapt, faraway look, attentive in ambient hush. For all that modern oceanography relies so much on acoustic techniques, it is the machines which do the listening" (Hamilton-Paterson 1992:21). On *Alvin,* sound has been so transposed (often into visual data) for more than a quarter of a century.[9] In the early 1980s, when computers were first installed in *Alvin,* they were divided into three kinds, collectors, listeners, and nodes, which— in sequence—gathered, sorted, and displayed data and allowed a human interface (Stetten 1984). Listeners were not strictly or only dedicated to sound processing but were so named because of their general interpretative, sorting functions; they were programmed to make data presentable, worthy of attention. The word *listening* is crucial. Listening has been associated with active, often highly technical, efforts to interpret or discern auditory sensation, whereas hearing has been imagined as passive, a letting of sounds wash over the ear (Carter 2004; Sterne 2003).[10] *Listening,* by this definition, is work. If listening to sonar on *Alvin* has been delegated to machines, the result is that we passengers now hear in a much more diffuse, less disciplined way than people may have in earlier days. The "sonic habitus" (Feld and Brenneis 2004:468) animating submariners' sensibilities has been transformed.

To be sure, *Alvin* pilots must remain attentive to rhythms of the sub. Bruce, after all, is able to describe sonar sounds once his attention is directed to them. But I gather he focuses most of his technical listening on the sounds of the vehicle's engines and thrusters, over which he has more control. It was incumbent on earlier generations of submarine pilots to be attentive auditors of sonar, and it was through such close listening that the crackling of crustaceans, snapping of shrimp, and singing of whales were first disclosed, providing a portrait of soundscapes already in existence for underwater creatures with the means to hear them—soundscapes likely altered by such sounds as *Alvin'*s transponder pitter-patter, to say nothing of the racket created by large-scale sonar surveys (on the *Alvin* dive I joined, animal sounds were nearly absent; in another ecology—warmer, closer to shore—the soundscape may have been quite different, with more organic components).[11] Scientists no longer think the deep is a quiet, meditative space, a silent world; as Delaney tells me, "The ocean is wired for sound" (*Alvin'*s depth rating, not incidentally, was originally guided by U.S. Navy specifications for a vehicle that could inspect seafloor arrays of sound-capturing, submarine-detecting hydrophones [Oreskes 2003]).[12] When it comes to the routine work of subs like *Alvin,* however, humans no longer need to listen closely to such sound.[13]

This is not to say that sound inside subs is no longer as present as it was back in the era of, say, WWII, when sonar headphones were standard equipment. But sound is now heard differently. At the risk of repeating myself, if it is made audible at all, sound is heard rather than listened to or for. One result of this shift is that sound from outside *Alvin* becomes a just-out-of-consciousness buoy for passengers' perception of floating presence. Because we do not need to work at the boundary between self and sound—that is, because we do not have to be actively aware of transducing—the boundary becomes imperceptible, inaudible; we become immersed, absorbed. Mody suggests that "the boundary between desirable sound and unwanted noise is very much a constructed, contingent, and historically variable one" (2005:177). So, too, with the boundary between sound listened to and heard, between meaningful sound and background hums. The building of this boundary into machinic and bodily techniques contours how people perceive their relation to spaces, places, and their own embodiment.

To amplify this point, let me offer an example from another anthropology of sound concerned with listening in the making of sense and sensibility, reception and presence. In "The Ethics of Listening: Cassette-Sermon Audition in Contemporary Egypt" (2001), Charles Hirschkind argues that listening to recorded Islamic sermons often helped the men in Cairo with whom he worked acquire modes of pious comportment. Audition is a practice through which "the perceptual capacities of the subject are honed and, thus, through which the world those capacities inhabit is brought into being, rendered perceptible" (Hirschkind 2001:624). This making of capacities can be construed as a transductive operation, a making, perhaps, of capacitances that permit a seamless flow between believers and religious messages— an interpretation made explicit in an Islamic digest Hirschkind quotes, which explains why some auditors of cassette sermons have difficulties being fully receptive: "The Quran is effective in itself," an article in the digest suggests, "just as the electrical current. If the Quran is present [to your ears], and you have lost its effect, then it is you yourself that you must blame. Maybe the conductive element is defective" (Hirschkind 2001:627). This writer is worried about transduction—a worry Hirschkind's interlocutors phrase in terms of the hearing-listening dyad: "The men I worked with often made a distinction between the verb commonly used for 'hearing,' *sam'*, and two other terms that suggest a more deliberate act: *ansat,* meaning to incline one's ear toward or pay close attention, and *aşghā,* to be silent in order to listen" (2001:633). A "moral physiology," argues Hirschkind, is "acquired through . . . listening exercises" (2001:628)—that is, through working at the boundaries that permit new worlds of experience to materialize, that smooth transductions to capacitate presence in an "ethical soundscape" (Hirschkind 2006).

. . . and Back to Listening (to Music, e.g.)

It is not all hushed, ambient techno in the world of *Alvin.* There is a more familiar, interior, air-pocketed soundscape, too. As we continue our descent, a quiet classic rock soundtrack accompanies us from Bruce's MP3 player, plugged into the sub. Sociologist Chandra Mukerji, in her analysis of videotapes from *Alvin* dives, suggests that music functions as a social and psychological means for "normalizing the process of working in a small sphere on the dark seafloor" (1989:71). This contention in mind, it might come as no surprise that the North Americans who are the overwhelming majority of users of *Alvin* often compare it to a car. Playing music in automobiles, as Michael Bull writes in "Soundscapes of the Car" (2003), often serves to sever drivers from the outside world, creating a private, interior space.[14] Such a severing operates to some extent in *Alvin,* keeping our sense of identity bathed in familiar melodies that shield us against the alien world outside. This musical soundscape creates a sense of absorption in the interior space of the sub, but because it mingles with the transduced soundscape of the outside, the effect is to feel at once inside a bubble and porously immersed in a wider world.

According to Sterne, the dominant phenomenology of Western science and religion holds that "hearing is concerned with interiors, vision is concerned with surfaces . . . hearing tends toward subjectivity, vision tends toward objectivity . . . hearing is a sense that immerses us in the world, vision is a sense that removes us from it" (2003:15). The sounds of *Alvin*—echoing from outside, trickling from inside— reinforce the notion that we are in an interior space that is itself both sonically and wetly immersed. The various pings and pongs create an echoing sense of being in a landscape that extends beyond the confines of the sphere, perhaps one reason few people become claustrophobic in the tight space of *Alvin.* The music gently bouncing off the walls of the sphere reinforces this sense of immersion. Music, of course, has often itself been imagined as immersive. David Toop writes in *Ocean of Sound* that "the image of bathing in sound is a recurrent theme of the past hundred years: Debussy's *Images* and Ravel's *Jeux d'eau* ripple around the listener; Arnold Schoenberg's *The Changing Chord-Summer Morning By a Lake-Colours* wraps us in flickering submarine light; Gyorgy Ligeti's *Atmospheres* envelops us in steam" (1995:271).[15] *Alvin* divers may not favor such modernist compositions, but they do go for soundscapy music: Pink Floyd's 1973 *Dark Side of the Moon* album is a perennial favorite on dives.[16]

When we arrive at the seafloor, Bruce turns on the sub's exterior lights, illuminating the rocky landscape around us. Spider crabs crawl lugubriously over brown boulders. The 300 atmospheres weighing on the sub outside are impossible to imagine from inside our tight titanium bubble. We scrabble around for words, metaphors, associations. The desert. National parks. Outer space.[17] My notepad scribbles are disappointing encounters with clichés about other planets, although the sheer fact of living through a sci-fi fantasy reminds me that "the boundary between science fiction and social reality is an optical illusion" (Haraway 1991:149). None of this is coming together as a narrative, even if it looks like one on this page. After all, the erasure of the boundary between ethnographic science fiction and social reality is also an illusion, and perhaps a partly auditory one. My use of the ethnographic present tense in this article has its own potentially immersive effects for you, reader, reading aloud or to yourself, and my calling attention to this device here means to direct your awareness to how ethnographic experience is always transduced into ethnographic text. I use *transduced* instead of *translated* here in resonance with the work of Michael Silverstein, who, in his intervention into linguistic anthropology, "Translation,

Transduction, Transformation," urges readers to imagine the work of rendering meaning from one milieu into another as akin to transduction:

> We should think seriously of the underlying metaphor of the energy transducer that I invoke, such as a hydroelectric generator. Here, one form of organized energy [e.g., the gravitationally aided downstream and downward linear rush of water against turbine blades] is asymmetrically converted into another kind of energy [electricity] at an energetic transduction site. . . . much of what goes into connecting an actual source-language expression to a target-language one is like such a transduction of energy. [2003:83–84, first set of brackets in original, second set of brackets mine]

For Silverstein, translations unfold within and across "configurations of cultural semiosis" (2003:91), and meaning is nearly always transduced—and sometimes radically transformed—in such transfers.[18] Just so with this text and its reception by various possible readers or auditors. And just so with the transduced sounds and signals in *Alvin*.

We approach a complex of hydrothermal vent chimneys called "Faulty Towers," after the British television sitcom, and John tells me, "What you're going to see is what you see on the poster in the *Atlantis* dining room." This reference to the composite photograph displayed in the mess hall of the ship gives me a template against which to judge my vision. I fiddle with one of the digital cameras provided in the sub. Delaney instructs me to look out the window, "Right now, if I were you, I'd be focusing exclusively on looking. Never mind the photography. I've got thousands of pictures. Just fill your eyes." Right. In this cyborg setting, we can play with the prosthetics that modulate and channel our sensing. We can also fiddle with the ratios between different senses. I take a picture at Faulty Towers despite Delaney's scold— of a fish whistling by a hydrothermal black smoker. It turns out blurry.

Yet another soundscape weaves through the sub, that of the fugitive speech of passengers. Not all speech is evanescent here, however, for each passenger is provided with a cassette player to make verbal notes about the trip. Delaney narrates some impressions into his tape recorder. I ask, "If you're doing all this tape recording, does that mean you spend a lot of time back on land listening to your own voice?" "Most scientists are very chatty with their machines, not each other," he replies. "Yeah, their auxiliary brains," adds Bruce. Or their externalized memories. After all, recording automatic speech allows for later listening, permitting *Alvin* divers to be "focusing exclusively on looking"; even so, the exteriorization of our inner voices contributes to the notion that sound is immediate, unmediated, ephemeral, a fleeting sign of reality itself. So, although James Clifford famously argued that, "once cultures are no longer prefigured visually—as objects, theaters, texts—it becomes possible to think of a cultural poetics that is an interplay of voices, of positioned utterances" (1986:12), this rhetorical gambit leaves open the work of comprehending how voices are imagined as signs of presence—and position—in the first place.[19] With *Alvin*'s tape players, the voice as a sign of presence is secured as a kind of back formation from the recording itself (cf. Kittler 1999).

And so, *Alvin* is a recording studio. Maybe this is not surprising. After all, a previous chief engineer for *Alvin* had substantial audio experience: "Jim Akens . . . joined the Alvin group in 1977 after a decade in the rock-and-roll business; he built state-of-the-art sound systems for Joan Baez, Jeff Beck, Sonny Rollins, Steely Dan, Joni Mitchell" (Kaharl 1990:273). By the 1970s, recording studios had become places that were standardized; they had become sites of signal routing, monitoring, and controlled feedback (Poynor 1986; Théberge 2004:770)—control and communications systems, like *Alvin*.

Notes

1. Also advocated by Gregory Bateson in the second edition of *Naven* (1958) and in *Steps to an Ecology of Mind* (1972).
2. Trevor Pinch and Karin Bijsterveld write that the field of sound studies is characterized by "a focus on the materiality of sound, its embeddedness not only in history, society, and culture, but also in science and technology and its machines and ways of knowing and interacting" (2004:636).
3. The U.S. Navy owns *Alvin,* although most research conducted by the sub is civilian, with access granted through the Office of Naval Research and NSF.
4. Feld's phrasing avoids Thompson's cleaving of the world into physical and cultural components.
5. A different circumstance obtains in saturation diving, which acclimatizes divers to pressures greater than one atmosphere for prolonged periods and requires extended decompression. Saturation diving allows people to live in air-filled undersea facilities maintained at ambient (high) pressure. To prevent oxygen poisoning, helium is often added to the mix, causing divers' voices to rise, making them sound like the 1950s novelty act Alvin and the Chipmunks (whose castrati songs were the result of speeding up tape recordings). Access Historic Naval Ships Association (n.d.) to listen to a 1965 recording of Commander Scott Carpenter of Sealab II leading his crew of saturation divers in a helium-voiced version of "Goodnight Irene."
6. Sabine Höhler writes that "acoustic methods of depth measurement based on the binaural technique relied on making humans and their sense of hearing a crucial part of the sounding technology" (2003:134).
7. This brings up the question of whether the inside of the head can be considered a soundscape. The long history of inner voices would suggest this possibility. Friedrich Kittler, however, in *Gramophone, Film, Typewriter* (1999), argues that the specifically stereo spatialization of cranial interiors arrives only with headphones. Roy Wagner, urging a biosemiotic take on the question, plays with the idea that the human is "an introversion of the bat, with its 'cave' on the inside" (2001:xiv). For me, this "echo-subject" is constituted through transduction.

    Another way to think about interior bodily soundscapes—and their commingling with exterior soundscapes—is through an oft-told story about composer John Cage's 1950s visit to an anechoic chamber, an acoustically insulated room that prevents sounds resonating within it. Left alone in this space, Cage reported hearing the sound of his own blood flowing and concluded that there was no such thing as silence. Douglas Kahn points out that, "although he had internalized acoustical space, he did not transform it to an 'inner space' of the mind" (2005:6)—at the same time that this melting of body boundaries required a transcendent, disembodied mind to take note of its own dissolution. Kahn argues that this Cagean epistemological armature "keeps the immersive edifice upright" (2005:7).
8. On the reading of transcriptional techniques into bodily ontologies, see Lenoir 1994. An early conference on sensation as transduction was held by the National Academy of Sciences

in 1962. In the foreword to the pamphlet published in connection with that meeting, the reader learns that

> engineers are becoming increasingly intrigued by the fact that biological transducers exhibit fantastic sensitivities. One species of fish can recognize a change of electrical field of 3/1000ths of a microvolt per millimeter in water; the rattlesnake has an infrared sensing device that recognizes temperature changes of 1/1000th of a degree Centigrade at the surface of the sensing organ. The B-17 airplane, developed in 1940, had some 2,000 electronic parts, but the present B-58 has 97,000 electronic elements. Functionally this is beginning to simulate in complexity a living system. [Cannan et al. 1962:v]

In 1992, a meeting on "sensory transduction" was held at Woods Hole; consult Block 1992 and Shepherd and Corey 1992. See also Borsellino et al. 1990. On hearing as transduction, consult Géléoc and Holt 2003.

9.   The transposition of sonic into visual data describes the historical trajectory of much oceanographic representation. Other sciences have lately seen moves to "sonify" rather than visualize data. NASA's sound representation of the Huygens probe's January 2005 entry into the atmosphere of Saturn's moon Titan results from bringing vibrations up in pitch (into the frequency range of human audition) and compressing them in time (see Johnson and Lecusay 2005). The "sonocytology" of University of California, Los Angeles, chemist Jim Gimzewski, meanwhile, brings vibrations of cells up in volume (amplitude) so that humans can hear them (see Roosth n.d.). One of Gimzewski's collaborators reports that the "frequency of the yeast cells the researchers tested has always been in the same high range, 'about a C-sharp to D above middle C in terms of music,' . . . Sprinkling alcohol on a yeast cell to kill it raises the pitch" (Wheeler 2004). Less mimetic versions of sonification are being considered for apprehending high-dimensional data (e.g., Hermann and Ritter 2004).

10. Hillel Schwartz notes that listening and hearing on occasion change places: "Listening itself might well be indiscriminate and automatic, as for example with telegraph and telephone operators, and hearing might well be specific and voluntary, as with hypnotic commands, only some of which would be 'heard' and acted upon" (2003:488).

11. For a thorough review of underwater acoustic ecology as it pertains to marine animals, see Stocker 2002–3. Research into vent sounds has begun, with the claim made that acoustic energy from these settings "may provide some local organisms with behavioral or navigational cues" (Crone et al. 2006:1).

12. Delaney reminds me of the SOFAR (SONAR Fixing and Ranging) channel, a layer of seawater in which the speed of sound reaches its underwater minimum. Low-frequency vibrations can travel long distances through this conduit (which sits about 800 to 1,000 meters deep at midlatitudes and higher toward the surface in temperate zones) before they dissipate. Marine scientists have been able to listen in on whale calls and other submarine sounds by placing hydrophones in this channel (consult Munk et al. 1995).

13. Sound remains important in marine bioacoustics research—although submarines like *Alvin* are too disruptive to be used as primary instruments in this enterprise. Sound is also key to ocean acoustic tomography, the study of ocean temperature using sound data, although human listeners are hardly necessary for this work.

14. And these days, for cars at least,

> designers of factory-installed stereos can know exactly what listening spaces and what speaker and listener positions they are dealing with, things they can't know when designing home systems. With this knowledge and a lot of detailed measurements, they can design systems that at least partially overcome that car's acoustical deficiencies. Systems can even be tailored to

the sound-reflecting character of the car interior's materials—leather or cloth upholstery, for example. [Berger 2003]

This tailoring, pioneered by Massachusetts Institute of Technology professor Amar Bose for 1983 General Motors cars (Bose 1984), engineers soundscapes into cars from the get-go.

15.   Some composers have attempted quite literally to fuse the immersively oceanic and the musical. Michel Redolfi (1989) has created pieces to be played underwater. His "Sonic Waters" was performed in the early 1980s just beneath and beyond the pier of the Scripps Institution for Oceanography in La Jolla, California. Listen also to David Dunn's 1992 "Chaos and the Emergent Mind of the Pond," a collage of underwater recordings of aquatic insects in ponds in North America and Africa.

16.   Musical atmospheres recall the more literal one atmosphere of pressure that obtains inside the sub, a necessary condition of our immersion in senses both poetic and technical; *atmos,* from the Greek *ατμοσ* (vapor) and the earlier Sanskrit *atman* (breath or spirit), signals the life-sustaining function of the air we breathe, and *sphere,* of course, finds a material housing in the titanium orb within which *Alvin* divers breathe.

17.   I leave aside in this piece metaphors that configure the deep as a primitive and hostile environment in which scientists quest for secret knowledge of a lost world—a formulation animating pronouncements such as the following, by Van Dover: "Raw and powerful, black smokers look like cautionary totems of an inhospitable planet" (1996:101).

18.   Compare Karen Barad's discussion of the "ongoing transduction between feminist and queer studies and science studies" (2001:102) in her "Performing Culture/Performing Nature: Using the Piezoelectric Crystal of Ultrasound Technologies as a Transducer between Science Studies and Queer Theories." Barad employs the piezoelectric transducer, similarly to the way I use the metaphor of transduction, "as a tool to examine the question of the relationship between the material and the discursive more generally" (2001:99).

19.   Insofar, too, as " 'culture' is always relational, an inscription of communicative processes that exist, historically, *between* subjects in relations of power" (Clifford 1986:15), more attention is needed to how this betweenness is made; transduction offers one tool.

References

Arehart, Kathryn H. 2005 The Nature of Hearing and Hearing Loss. Soundscape: The Journal of Acoustic Ecology 6(1):9–14.

Barad, Karen 2001 Performing Culture/Performing Nature: Using the Piezoelectric Crystal of Ultrasound Technologies as a Transducer between Science Studies and Queer Theories. *In* Digital Anatomy. Christina Lammar, ed. Pp. 98–114. Vienna: Turia and Kant.

Bateson, Gregory 1958 Naven. 2nd edition. Stanford: Stanford University Press.

—1972 Steps to an Ecology of Mind. Chicago: University of Chicago Press.

Berger, Ivan 2003 DRIVING; Body by Fisher, Sound by Bose. New York Times, April 25: 9.

Block, Steven M. 1992 Biophysical Principles of Sensory Transduction. *In* Sensory Transduction. Society of General Physiologists series, 47. David P. Corey and Stephen D. Roper, eds. Pp. 1–17. New York: Rockefeller University Press.

Borsellino, Antonio, Luigi Cervetto, and Vincent Torre, eds. 1990 Sensory Transduction. New York: Plenum Press.

Bose, Amar 1984 Hi-Fi for GM Cars. Lecture delivered to the Electrical Engineering and Computer Science seminar, March 19. Amar Bose Papers. MC 261. Institute Archives and Special Collections, MIT Libraries, Cambridge, Massachusetts.

Bull, Michael 2003 Soundscapes of the Car: A Critical Study of Automobile Habitation. *In* The Auditory Culture Reader. Michael Bull and Les Back, eds. Pp. 357–74. Oxford: Berg.

Cannan, R. Keith, H. Burr Steinbach, and Richard C. Jordan 1962 Foreword to Engineering and the Life Sciences: A Presentation of Papers. Pamphlet published in relation to a joint Annual Meeting of the Divisions of Biology and Agriculture, of Medical Sciences, and of Engineering and Industrial Research of the National Academy of Sciences and the National Research Council. Washington, DC: National Academy of Sciences and the National Research Council.

Carter, Paul 2004 Ambiguous Traces, Mishearing, and Auditory Space. *In* Hearing Cultures: Essays on Sound, Listening and Modernity. Veit Erlmann, ed. Pp. 43–63. Oxford: Berg.

Clifford, James 1986 Partial Truths. *In* Writing Culture: The Poetics and Politics of Ethnography. James Clifford and George Marcus, eds. Pp. 1–26. Berkeley: University of California Press.

Corbin, Alain 1988 The Lure of the Sea: The Discovery of the Seaside in the Western World 1750–1840. Jocelyn Phelps, trans. Berkeley: University of California Press.

—1998 Village Bells: Sound and Meaning in the Nineteenth-Century French Countryside. Martin Thom, trans. New York: Columbia University Press.

Cousteau, Jacques, with Frédéric Dumas 1953 The Silent World. New York: Harper and Brothers.

Crone Timothy J., William S. D. Wilcock, Andrew H. Barclay, and Jeffrey D. Parsons 2006 The Sound Generated by Mid-Ocean Ridge Black Smoker Hydrothermal Vents. PLoS ONE 1(1). Electronic document, http://www.plosone.org/article/fetchArticle.action?articleURI= info:doi/10.1371/journal.pone.0000133, accessed May 20, 2007.

Deleuze, Gilles, and Félix Guattari 1987 A Thousand Plateaus: Capitalism and Schizophrenia. Minneapolis: University of Minnesota Press.

Dunn, David 1992 Chaos and the Emergent Mind of the Pond. *From* Angels and Insects. Santa Fe: Nonsequitur/What Next Recordings.

Erlmann, Veit, ed. 2004 Hearing Cultures: Essays on Sound, Listening and Modernity. Oxford: Berg.

Evens, Aden 2005 Sound Ideas: Music, Machines, and Experience. Minneapolis: University of Minnesota Press.

Feld, Steven 1996 Waterfalls of Song: An Acoustemology of Place Resounding in Bosavi, Papua New Guinea. *In* Senses of Place. Steven Feld and Keith Basso, eds. Pp. 91–135. Santa Fe: School of American Research Press.

Feld, Steven, and Donald Brenneis 2004 Doing Anthropology in Sound. American Ethnologist 31(4):461–74.

Fischer, Michael M. J. 2007 Culture and Cultural Analysis as Experimental Systems. Cultural Anthropology 22(1):1–65.

Géléoc, Gwénaëlle S. G., and Jeffrey R. Holt 2003 Developmental Acquisition of Sensory Transduction in Hair Cells of the Mouse Inner Ear. Nature Neuroscience 6:1019–20.

Hamilton-Paterson, James 1992 The Great Deep: The Sea and Its Thresholds. New York: Random House.

Haraway, Donna 1991 A Cyborg Manifesto: Science, Technology, and Socialist-Feminism in the Late Twentieth Century. *In* Simians, Cyborgs, and Women: The Reinvention of Nature. Pp. 149–82. New York: Routledge.

Helmreich, Stefan 2003 Trees and Seas of Information: Alien Kinship and the Biopolitics of Gene Transfer in Marine Biology and Biotechnology. American Ethnologist 30(3):341–59.

Hermann, Thomas, and Helge Ritter 2004 Sound and Meaning in Auditory Data Display Proceedings of the IEEE 92(4):730–41.

Hirschkind, Charles 2001 The Ethics of Listening: Cassette-Sermon Audition in Contemporary Egypt. American Ethnologist 28(3):623–49.

—2006 The Ethical Soundscape: Cassette Sermons and Islamic Counterpublics. New York: Columbia University Press.

Historic Naval Ships Association n.d. HNSA-Historic Naval Sound and Video. Electronic document, http://www.hnsa.org/sound, accessed July 20, 2007.

Höhler, Sabine 2003 Sound Survey: The Technological Perception of Ocean Depth, 1850–1930. *In* Transforming Spaces: The Topological Turn in Technology Studies. Mikael Hård, Andreas Lösch, and Dirk Verdicchio, eds. Publication of the International Conference held in Darmstadt, Germany, March 22–24, 2002. Electronic document, http://www.ifs.tu-darmstadt.de/fileadmin/gradkoll//Publikationen/transformingspaces.html, accessed May 20, 2007.

Ihde, Don 2003 Auditory Imagination. *In* The Auditory Culture Reader. Michael Bull and Les Back, eds. Pp. 61–66. Oxford: Berg.

International Transducer Corporation n.d. Home Page. Electronic document, http://www.itc-transducers.com, accessed July 19, 2007.

Johnson, Emma, and Robert Lecusay 2005 In Space, NASA Can Hear You Scream. Paper presented at the Annual Meetings of the Society for the Social Studies of Science, Pasadena, CA, October 20–22.

Kaharl, Victoria A. 1990 Water Baby: The Story of *Alvin*. New York: Oxford University Press.

Kahn, Douglas 1999 Noise Water Meat: A History of Sound in the Arts. Cambridge, MA: MIT Press.

—2005 The Art of Anechoic Perception in Postwar America. Paper presented at the Amsterdam School of Cultural Analysis, Amsterdam, March 30.

Kelty, Chris 2003 Qualitative Research in the Age of the Algorithm: New Challenges in Cultural Anthropology. Lecture delivered at the Research Libraries Group 2003 Annual Meeting: Rethinking the Humanities in a Global Age, Boston Public Library, Boston, MA, May 5.

Kittler, Friedrich 1999[1986] Gramophone, Film, Typewriter. Geoffrey Winthrop-Young and Michael Wutz, trans. Stanford: Stanford University Press.

Lenoir, Timothy 1994 Helmholtz and the Materialities of Communication. Osiris 9:185–207.

Mackenzie, Adrian 2002 Transductions: Bodies and Machines at Speed. London: Continuum.

Mead, Margaret 1968 Cybernetics of Cybernetics. *In* Purposive Systems: Proceedings of the Fifth Annual Symposium of the American Society for Cybernetics. Heinz von Foerster, John D White, Larry J. Peterson, and John K. Russell, eds. Pp. 1–11. New York: Spartan Books.

Mody, Cyrus C. M. 2005 The Sounds of Science: Listening to Laboratory Practice. Science, Technology, and Human Values 30(2):175–98.

Mukerji, Chandra 1989 A Fragile Power: Scientists and the State. Princeton: Princeton University Press.

Munk, Walter, Peter Worcester, and Carl Wunsch 1995 Ocean Acoustic Tomography. Cambridge: Cambridge University Press.

Myers, Natasha 2006 Animating Mechanism: Animations and the Propagation of Affect in the Lively Arts of Protein Modeling. Science Studies 19(2):6–30.

Oreskes, Naomi 2003 A Context of Motivation: US Navy Oceanographic Research and the Discovery of Sea-Floor Hydrothermal Vents. Social Studies of Science 33(5):697–742.

Pinch, Trevor, and Karin Bijsterveld 2004 Sound Studies: New Technologies and Music. Social Studies of Science 34(5):635–48.

Poynor, Rick 1986 The Dynamics of the System. *In* More Dark than Shark. Brian Eno, Russell Mills, and Rick Poyner. Pp. 72–77. London: Faber and Faber.

Redolfi, Michel 1989 Sonic Waters #2 (Underwater Music) 1983–89. Therwil, Switzerland: Hat Hut Records.

Roosth, Sophia n.d. Sonic Eukaryotes: Sonocytology, Cytoplasmic Milieu, and the *Temps Intèrieur*. Doctoral Program in History, Anthropology, and Science, Technology and Society, Massachusetts Institute of Technology, Cambridge, MA.

Schafer, R. Murray 1977 The Tuning of the World. New York: Knopf.

Schlee, Susan 1973 The Edge of an Unfamiliar World: A History of Oceanography. New York: Dutton.

Schwartz, Hillel 2003 The Indefensible Ear. *In* The Auditory Culture Reader. Michael Bull and Les Back, eds. Pp. 487–501. Oxford: Berg.

Shepherd, G. M., and D. P. Corey 1992 Sensational Science. Sensory Transduction: 45th Annual Symposium of the Society of General Physiologists, Marine Biological Laboratory, Woods Hole, MA, USA, September 5–8, 1991. New Biologist 4(1):48–52.

Silverstein, Michael 2003 Translation, Transduction, Transformation: Skating "Glossando" on Thin Semiotic Ice. *In* Translating Cultures: Perspectives on Translation and Anthropology. Paula G. Rubel and Abraham Rosman, eds. Pp. 75–105. Oxford: Berg.

Simondon, Gilbert 1992[1964] The Genesis of the Individual. Mark Cohen and Sanford Kwinter, trans. *In* Incorporations. Jonathan Crary and Sanford Kwinter, eds. Pp. 296–319. New York: Zone.

Sterne, Jonathan 2003 The Audible Past: Cultural Origins of Sound Reproduction. Durham, NC: Duke University Press.

Stetten, George D. 1984 *Alvin*'s Memory. Oceanus 27(3):44–46.

Stocker, Michael 2002–3 Ocean Bio-Acoustics and Noise Pollution: Fish, Mollusks and Other Sea Animals' Use of Sound, and the Impact of Anthropogenic Noise on the Marine Acoustic Environment. Soundscape: The Journal of Acoustic Ecology 3(2)–4(1):16–29.

Théberge, Paul 2004 The Network Studio: Historical and Technological Paths to a New Ideal in Music Making. Social Studies of Science 34(5):759–81.

Thompson, Emily 2002 The Soundscape of Modernity: Architectural Acoustics and the
    Culture of Listening in America, 1900–1933. Cambridge, MA: MIT Press.

Toop, David 1995 Ocean of Sound: Aether Talk, Ambient Sound and Imaginary Worlds.
    London: Serpent's Tail.

Urick, Robert J. 1983 Principles of Underwater Sound. 3rd edition. New York:
    McGraw-Hill.

Van Dover, Cindy Lee 1996 Deep-Ocean Journeys: Discovering New Life at the Bottom
    of the Sea. Redwood City, CA: Addison-Wesley.

Wagner, Roy 2001 An Anthropology of the Subject: Holographic Worldview in New
    Guinea and Its Meaning and Significance for the World of Anthropology. Berkeley:
    University of California Press.

Wheeler, Mark 2004 Signal Discovery? Smithsonian, March. Electronic document,
    http://www.smithsonianmag.si.edu/smithsonian/issues04/mar04/phenomena.
    html, accessed May 1, 2005.

Williams, Rosalind 1990 Notes on the Underground: An Essay on Technology, Society,
    and the Imagination. Cambridge, MA: MIT Press.

Zerner, Charles 2003 Sounding the Makassar Strait: The Poetics and Politics of an
    Indonesian Marine Environment. *In* Culture and the Question of Rights: Forests,
    Coasts, and Seas in Southeast Asia. Charles Zerner, ed. Pp. 56–108. Durham,
    NC: Duke University Press.

Chapter 17

Barry Blesser and Linda-Ruth Salter

ANCIENT ACOUSTIC SPACES

OLDER CULTURES WERE not only aware that some of their revered objects and spaces had unusual acoustics; they also wove sound into the fabric of their religion. They made no distinction between objects actively producing sound, such as bells, and objects passively modifying those sounds, such as a caves. Aural experience resulted from a composite of all contributory elements. And that composite was an integral part of all experience, which included mythology, religion, and philosophy. Life was holistic, not segmented.

In remote sites around the world, scientists and nonscientists alike have observed unusual acoustics in the structures created by ancient and prehistoric cultures. Acousticians, archaeologists, and amateurs with an unfettered curiosity about human history have formally studied some of these sites. However, due to the highly speculative nature of acoustic evidence, support for this kind of research is limited. This has not, however, prevented those with a passion for the auditory sense from pursuing acoustic archaeology. Eventually, some speculations will no doubt be confirmed by scholars; others will be discarded as baseless. Nevertheless, the overall patterns in the aural architecture of these structures are too compelling to dismiss as accidental.

Aural Icons and Acoustic Spaces in Early Cultures

Existing in almost every culture, whether as pictures, as statues, or as small, unremarkable objects, icons have special meanings linked to particular ideas, people, events, or other objects. Icons are experienced through one or more of the senses— vision, hearing, touch, and smell—but the experience expands beyond immediate sensation by including cultural, religious, or collective memories and associations. As perceptible manifestations of abstractions, icons are especially prevalent in religions: they strengthen the relationship between believers and their beliefs. In our technological culture, computer icons, representing complex data and actions, link users to operating systems.

The aural analogue of a visual icon, an *earcon* is a sonic event that contains special symbolic meaning not present in the sound wave. The concept has recently appeared in specialized vocabularies but has not yet spread into ordinary lexicons. In a computer environment, special sonic signals such as spectrally chirped tones can represent user success, failure, or acknowledgment. These are earcons. In earlier cultures, earconic sounds merged religious and philosophic views of the cosmos with life on earth. Sound in general, and earcons in particular, connect the *here* with the *there,* be it spiritual leaders with their followers or heavenly spirits with earthly beings.

Earcons acquire symbolic meanings by repeated exposure to a particular event in a corresponding context, which then creates an associating linkage between the sound and its context. Subsequently, such sounds, even without the original context, trigger the thoughts, emotions, and memory associated with that context. Consider the family dinner bell. Its sound stimulates the appetite just because it is associated with the eating event in the family dining room. The symbolism is not deep, but it can still be considered an earcon. In this case, the linkage to food is acquired through family dining. And that particular bell sound might have no such symbolic meaning in another family. Similarly, the extended reverberation of a cathedral becomes an earcon to those who frequently attend religious services in that particular space.

We can hypothesize how the earcons of aural architecture come into existence. An architect designs a structure or a space for its visual or utilitarian properties, while being generally oblivious to its acoustic attributes or aural personality. Then, over time, with increasing exposure and familiarity, the aural attributes become associated with the visual attributes in the minds of those who use that structure or space, and, together, these attributes share a common symbolic meaning. An earcon has come into being.

To test our hypothesis that aural architecture is invested with symbolism, we would need to describe and analyze a wide variety of cultures whose objects and spaces manifest themselves as earcons. Ancient and prehistoric cultures, because of their mystical attitude toward sound in general, are more likely to have had earcons. Yet, whereas icons can survive for centuries, earcons disappear in a moment. Nevertheless, speculative evidence supports the concept of earconic sounds and earconic spaces.

For many ancient civilizations, sacred objects produced sacred sounds. When the tribes in pre-Columbian west Mexico discovered metallurgy, they treated their crafted objects as an extension of their aural religion (Hosier, 1994). Religious leaders used metallic bells as a novel replacement for early materials that did not produce pure resonances. The sounds of small bells were central to their rituals and served to celebrate human and agricultural fertility, to protect warriors from injury, and to create the garden of paradise. Bells and rattles figured prominently in ritual and ceremonies throughout indigenous American societies because of their special aural powers.

The early Greeks are credited with having invented the Aeolian harp, named after Aeolus, their god of wind, and often called a "wind harp." Although constructed like a harp, the Aeolian harp does not function as a musical instrument because its sounds are unpredictable, ethereal, and not under human control. As the wind passes over its taut strings, they vibrate in an oscillating vortex, with a series of overtones determined by the wind velocity. Its melodies and harmonies, if one could call them such, *sonify*—make audible—an otherwise inaudible natural phenomenon, in this case, the wind. Yet, for Aristotle, the sounds of this instrument were the spirit of the wind carrying the heavenly Muses to the earth, where they sang to their earthly children. Aeolian harps produced the music of the spheres.

The modern counterparts to Aeolian harps are wind chimes; some artists have constructed giant versions as acoustic sculptures. When large, the harplike wind chimes become aural architecture, creating an acoustic arena, with its own aural personality, within which people can move; when small, they are simply an "instrument," although earconic symbolism does not depend on size.

The religious structures of ancient Greece, like the Aeolian harp, also made connections between earth and heaven. To supplement their study of the few that have survived intact, S. L. Vassilantonopoulos and John M. Mourjopoulos (2001) used historical records to explain how acoustically complex spaces were transformed into aural expressions of religion. The Acheron Necromancy, which served as a temple around the eighth century B.C., was associated with a ceremony where the soul of a deceased person was separated from the body and led via chasms and caves to an underground world populated by the spirits of the dead. The temple, with its many acoustically coupled rooms, was situated over a cave that had been modified into an underground chamber. The exterior walls were 3 meters (10 feet) thick, thereby ensuring both structural integrity and acoustic isolation from the outside world. The rooms and chambers had minimal reverberation, which, when combined with the extreme acoustic isolation, let listeners hear even the softest whisper from a priest located in acoustically coupled but visually remote chambers. When the space was dark, listeners experienced the priest's disorienting voice as coming from a remote and unknown chamber, as if from another world. By separating the image of the priest from his aural manifestation, the aural architecture of the temple aurally separated the priest's spirit from its physical body. The temple's "spirit voices" would have been clear, enveloping, and intimate, yet invisible. Many mythical figures, such as Ulysses, Hercules, Theseus, and Orpheus, are said to have participated in such rituals.

Comparable auditory phenomena were also found in cultures that were unrelated to our Western tradition. The Mayan culture in Mexico and Central America had a relatively sophisticated grasp of mathematics, astronomy, agriculture, and social organization. Perhaps as early as 1500 B.C., the Mayans settled in small villages, which eventually grew into large cities containing ceremonial centers, temples, pyramids, palaces, courts for public games, and plazas; at its peak, the Mayan population exceeded 2 million. Unlike the Greek tradition, however, written evidence describing the meaning, purpose, or recognition of the acoustic attributes of structures at the Mayan sites is conspicuously missing.

Nevertheless, archaeological evidence supports the thesis that the Mayans had a heightened auditory spatial awareness. The Great Ball Court, a large gathering place of some 10,000 square meters (350,000 square feet) surrounded by sloped and vertical stone walls, contains a raised temple at one end. It hosted a combined sporting and religious event, where losers were sacrificed to the gods. Many visitors have noted the unexpected pleasant acoustics: a whisper at one end can be heard clearly at the other end, making it an ideal place for a ceremonial leader to guide the audience. By adding reflections and resonances, the Ballcourt augmented the perceived mass and size of the leader's voice, raising his stature and perceived power.

As the de facto, self-appointed chairman of amateur acoustic archaeologists collecting reports from tourists, Wayne Van Kirk (2002) compiled stories and testimonials about archaeological sites with notable acoustics. He described a series of stones shaped like artillery shells in a Mayan ruin upon which you could play a tune by tapping them with a wooden mallet. Other visitors observed distinct howls and whistles from stone structures when the wind arrived from a particular direction, as if it were giving early warning of imminent storms and hurricanes. The Mayans also had configured three pyramids such that you could conduct a three-way conversation when you and two others stood at their tops. In general, many Mayan structures and spaces possessed both religious meaning and distinctive acoustic properties. It seems highly likely that the aural experience of these structures and spaces also had religious interpretations.

David Lubman (1998), an acoustic consultant and a scientist with zeal for examining the acoustics of historical spaces, studied the chirplike echoes produced by the staircases of the Pyramid of Kukulkán at Chichén Itzá, shown in figure 3.3 [see original publication]. Although the echoes can be physically explained as a series of periodic sonic reflections from the small tread steps, their sound bears an uncanny resemblance to the call of the Mayans' sacred bird, the resplendent Quetzal. Both the call of this bird and the echoes from the staircases show the same decreasing frequency of the dominant formants. Chirplike echoes appear in many other Mayan sites where a long stone staircase faces an open plaza. The Quetzal, now near extinction, symbolized the spirit of the Mayans; however they came to be, the echoes could well have been heard by the Mayans as the call of their sacred bird immortalized in stone.

More than other acoustic artifacts, the Mayan staircases at Chichén Itzá have given rise to heated debate among scientists. Are the chirplike echoes of the staircases merely an accident with no religious meaning, or were they deliberately created as an earcon of the Quetzal? Those who have heard both the echoes and the call of the Quetzal concede that they do, indeed, sound alike. The following discussion presents a plausible justification for treating the sound of the staircases as an earcon of the Quetzal.

Consider the properties of the staircases from a scientific perspective. Wave interferences from evenly spaced regular geometric shapes, be they jars, tubes, or stair treads, create a frequency-dependent response in sound reflections or sound transmission. Nevertheless, we must also acknowledge that geometric regularity has aesthetic appeal in itself, quite apart from its acoustic consequences.

Acoustics and aesthetics aside, why might the Mayans have constructed staircases with such physical properties? Historians speculate that the shallow stair treads arose from the decision to construct four staircases of 91 steps each, together totaling 364, which, with the platform on top as a final step, equaled the number of days in the

Mayan year. There is ample evidence that the Mayans possessed considerable knowledge about astronomy and mathematics. The Mayan staircases, it would seem, are linked to astronomy.

With continuing interest in this ancient Mayan pyramid, Niko F. Declercq and colleagues (2004) explained why observers seated on the lowest steps of the pyramid hear the sound of raindrops falling in a water bucket instead of the footstep of people climbing the stairs. Somewhat later, it was observed that a mask of the Mayan rain god Chac was located at the top of the pyramid. We know that patterns can always be discovered when one looks for them, even if they are accidents, and yet we also know that older cultures often had a refined aural sensitivity to their environment. The Mayans could certainly have recognized the sound of raindrops, even if it resulted from an architectural accident, but once having perceived the sounds as that of raindrops, they might have then intentionally placed an image of their rain god at the top.

The frequency effects of both the Mayan staircases and Eusebio Sempere's stainless-steel tubes, described in chapter 2 [see original publication], required only a constrained relationship among the numerous physical parameters. Objects intended for a nonauditory purpose may still have interesting aural properties, and once recognized, they become earcons or acoustic sculptures with symbolic or artistic meaning. The sound of Sempere's tubes could just as easily have become a religious earcon if the sculpture had been embedded into a religious context, and if listeners had then become aware of its aural properties.

Lubman (2004) describes a perfect example of an aural embellishment arising from a religious context. As shown in figure 3.4 [see original publication], the shrine to Saint Werburgh, a seventh-century Saxon princess, located in England's Chester Cathedral contains six recesses where kneeling pilgrims inserted their heads while petitioning their saint. The geometry of these recesses, with their strong resonances and powerful amplification, created the feeling of an intimate encounter with the saint, whose spirit was visually and aurally accessible. Lubman's recorded demonstration of the acoustics of these recesses is dramatic. Resonances contribute to the sense of being in another world; amplification contributes to intimacy; visual isolation contributes to privacy. Absent any evidence that it was deliberately chosen, we assume that the earconic aspect of this embellishment was an incidental consequence of its religious context.

After the acoustic properties of a structure or space were recognized and integrated into the culture, the rules for replication would have been obvious: make copies or variants from the original reference. Architectural rules then become their own traditions—like religious rules. With a high tolerance for trial and error, even a scientifically unsophisticated culture can duplicate value-laden acoustic designs that originated from unrelated forces and ideas.

Following the accidental creation of a structure with unusual aural properties, it may then acquire earconic meaning, which induces the society to replicate the structure for its symbolic meaning. This conclusion requires only that the culture have an elevated sense of the aural experience, a well-documented characteristic of many early cultures. Knowledge of physical acoustics or recognition of aural architecture per se is unnecessary.

Religion and Philosophy Dominate Architecture

The ancient Greeks and Romans, who created the foundations of Western culture, believed in a unified cosmos; in their world philosophy, ideas and concepts fit together in glorified, harmonious unity. How did their harmonious view of the cosmos influence their aural architecture, and their legacies to modern society?

The ancient Greek belief in a universal and harmonious natural order was all-pervasive. "Works of art or of society were seen less as a contrivance of man than as a reflection of nature . . . and the natural world was viewed in terms of life and mind." With this comment, Edward A. Lippman (1964) captured the essence of this belief—everything was a reflection of a single unified and integrated cosmos—a grand, well-oiled assemblage of all elements of the universe. Theater, politics, music, religion, architecture, and government, along with the twelve gods of Mount Olympus, were all part of the integrated harmony.

From earliest Greek times, music was integral to religious ceremonies and closely connected to astronomy, both because of a shared mathematical foundation, and because of links to the harmony of the cosmos. As exemplified by Pythagoras's "music of the spheres" (James, 1993), early intellectuals held the ratios of integer numbers to be fundamental to understanding experience. Indeed, the numbers and integer ratios found in music and astronomy joined the harmony of the cosmos to that of human experience. Rather than being simply utilitarian means for creating physical comforts, arithmetic, geometry, and science were also vehicles for representing that harmony. Likewise, rather than being distinct pursuits in the own right, religion, the arts, music, dance, theater, and poetry were all natural parts of the harmonious universal whole. Much of ancient Greek art, science, philosophy, and technology served as the foundation for Christian culture. More than a thousand years later, the great Gothic cathedrals would still be designed on the basis of integer ratios (Wittkower, 1971).

In ancient Greece and in the succeeding Roman and Christian cultures, using abstract thinking as the means for attaining truth, philosophers influenced spatial concepts by elevating the importance of their cosmic rules; indeed, spatial concepts originated from religious philosophy.

This raises interesting questions. How did philosophy influence the design of the large basilicas and cathedrals? Were their acoustics, with long reverberation time and enveloping sound, an *intentional* imitation of God's house on earth? Why and how did early Christian spaces, which initially were small and clandestine, and which supported a spoken liturgy, evolve into grand cathedrals?

Although cathedrals may have been the first man-made structures of such great volume, large enclosed spaces also occurred in nature. Cathedrals were the acoustic equivalent of the largest natural caverns found in many countries. Some, such as the Kateřnská Jeskyně cavern in the Czech Republic, approaching 50,000 cubic meters (1,750,000 cubic feet), are comparable in volume to a cathedral. Caverns and cathedrals alike are large enclosed spaces with irregular geometries, randomly shaped surfaces, minimal acoustic absorption, and uniform diffusion of sound arriving from all directions.

Long before cathedrals, prehistoric cultures are known to have used large enclosed spaces. The underground Oracle Chamber at the Hal Salfieni Hypogeum on Malta is but one example of a natural space that had become a sacred space four millennia before the flowering of Greek culture. Archaeologists discovered a series of temples, large man-made caverns, carved into the solid limestone before the advent of metalworking tools. After settling on Malta, perhaps around 5000 B.C., this isolated agrarian civilization evolved skilled builders and engineers who constructed numerous megalithic temples, both below and above ground. The underground oracular and ritual burial chambers at the Hal Saflieni Hypogeum were the acoustic equivalents of Gothic cathedrals.[2]

Were the Gothic cathedrals an *intentional* extension of earlier cultures that used the acoustics of large enclosed spaces for their religious meaning? As a working hypothesis, the notion that religious spaces were designed or selected for long reverberation time is attractive. But at least in the case of Christianity, reliable evidence contradicts this intuitive conclusion.

Beginning in the fourth century, when Rome converted to Christianity, and continuing to the fifteenth century, when secular forces redefined music and space alike, the acoustic properties of cathedrals and churches were actually an *unintentional* consequence of religious, philosophic, and social forces. When Emperor Constantine proclaimed Christianity the official religion of the Roman Empire in the early fourth century, various basilicas, which had been designed using a style of Greek architecture of some two centuries earlier, and which had served as courthouses and as meeting places for commerce, were converted to churches. William Smith (1875), in describing the rectangular shape and two rows of columns of these early basilicas, noted that they had open sides. When Roman society became wealthier and more refined, outer walls were added to create an enclosed space, and the supporting columns became part of the interior. Although walls dramatically changed the acoustics, they were added for other reasons: to protect against the weather, to demonstrate political power, and to visually separate the space they enclosed from the external environment.

Thus basilicas were of utilitarian design, initially unrelated to art or religion. As the traditional architecture of the period, this style also became the model for early church buildings. Rapid construction of new religious spaces, many of which followed the shape, form, and size of public buildings, dispersed the basilica style of church architecture throughout the Roman Empire (Platner, 1929). The Christian view of architecture was not rigid, but adapted to local regions; with the rapid growth in new converts, church spaces grew large enough to hold thousands of congregants (Krautheimer, 1965). Thus, even though size was and is the dominant parameter of aural architecture, large church size actually reflected the desire to have large congregations share religious events and was unrelated to the resulting acoustics.

With their enormous floor area, dramatically high ceilings, and stone surfaces, cathedrals have a reverberation time at the theoretical limit of an enclosed space, often approaching 10 seconds for middle frequencies (1000– Hz), where air humidity begins to dominate acoustics. The three key components of such spaces, area, height, and surfaces materials, each arose from independent social forces. Whereas increasing floor area allowed churches to contain large congregations, increasing height, the other dimension of volume, was of no practical value, serving instead to express the grandeur of God's home. Thus, for example, the ceiling of the Basilica of Constantine is 34 meters (110 feet) from ground level. Stone surfaces, which replaced wood, resulted from advances in building technology. Stone buildings were durable, strong, and immune to the ravages of fire, a common event at a time when illumination was provided by torches and other flammable material. Hard, acoustically reflective surfaces were therefore incidental, a by-product of using stone as a building technology to avoid fire, and to support large heavy ceilings over large floor areas.

A thousand years after the founding of Christianity, architectural design reached its pinnacle with the construction of the majestic Gothic cathedrals of Europe. Beginning in the twelfth century, when Abbott Suger sponsored the cathedral at Saint-Denis, just north of Paris, cathedrals were built with volumes well over 200,000 cubic meters (7,000,000 cubic feet), compared to the early churches of the fourth century with less than 5,000 cubic meters (175,000 cubic feet). Although closely linked to religious traditions and building technology, these enormous sizes created overpowering and enveloping acoustics. Ultimately, they determined the acoustic scope and nature of liturgical music.

Early Christians (like many pre-Christians) believed that particular places were associated with God's presence. Even today, the word *church* retains its dual meaning of religious faith and building for religious services. Other religions have separate words to distinguish the place from the religion: notably, mosque and Islam, temple and Judaism. In his study of cathedrals, Otto Georg von Simson (1989) portrayed a religious culture dominated by a single conceptualization that merged all aspects of life into a unified view: as the "symbol of the kingdom of God on earth, the cathedral gazed down upon the city and its population, transcending all other forms of life as it transcended all its physical dimensions." The architecture and sculpture of the medieval sanctuary were images of heaven, while the music therein was its sounds. Everything was symbolic—objects were neither illusions nor allusions, but a representation of religious truth. The creative legitimacy of architects, sculptors, and musicians was determined by their ability to represent this truth.

Biblical descriptions represent church structures, mystically and liturgically, as a vision of the Celestial City with its Heavenly Mansions. In their role as heavenly architects, the designers of religious structures called on the cosmic geometries passed down through the ages from Pythagoras. For example, all of the ribs under the vault of the Reims Cathedral circumscribe equilateral triangles, a fact few observers are likely to notice. Surviving documents report debates about the religious meaning of squares or triangles as the basic geometric shape for cathedral design. As cited by von Simson (1989), Thierry of Chartres argued that geometry and arthmetic provided divine inspiration.

Similarly with music, Saint Augustine (387), though not denying that music could be produced by instinct or practical skill as a vulgar art suitable for popular audiences, asserted in his treatise *De musica* that music becomes an important expression of universal truth only when based on the science of arithmetic—ratios of integers. Without numbers, music and space return to chaos. For medieval Christians, "auditory and visual harmonies are actually imitations of the ultimate harmony which the blessed will enjoy in the world to come" (von Simson, 1989). The attitudes toward music and architecture arose from this concept, which permeated all aspects of Christian Rome and arose from the earlier Greek concept of harmony.

As the Roman Empire was dissolving and Christianity was spreading, the church gradually became the only central authority governing politics, spirituality, and artistic expression, eventually merging music, religion, and administration into a unified social system. In the Western heritage, auditory arts enjoying church support were fully incorporated into the Christian religion; their dedicated spaces determined the nature of music for a thousand years.

When music was linked to a dedicated space, it became stylized and constrained in order to fit with the unique acoustics of those spaces. Christianity was a prolific builder of dedicated spaces and an enthusiastic sponsor of dedicated music. Such spaces were expensive, and the costs had to be borne by a civil or religious organization with power, resources, and architectural vision. Just as Greek and Roman theaters were dedicated spaces supported by the state and wealthy patrons, Christian basilicas and cathedrals were dedicated spaces supported by an increasingly powerful church hierarchy.

As the church became the only viable social structure, its evolving concepts of space dominated architecture. Looking at several examples of basilicas and cathedrals that have survived, we see a progression in their size, shape, and design. The Rotunda of Thessaloniki, a unique fourth-century monument of Romanesque art, was typical of the kind of building that served early Christianity. As a modest-sized space with a volume of 15,000 cubic meters (530,000 cubic feet), it has a comfortable reverberation time at middle frequencies of about 2.5 seconds when fully occupied (Tzekakis, 1975). Its acoustics were acceptable for a wide range of uses. In contrast, Roman basilicas with volumes of over 100,000 cubic meters (3,500,000 cubic feet) have reverberation times that range from 5 to 10 seconds even when full (Raes and Sacerdote, 1953). Of the four Roman basilicas studied by Robert S. and H. K. Shankland (1971), Saint Peter's stands out in terms of sheer size; it is the largest church in the world with a length of 180 meters (600 feet) and a volume of 500,000 cubic meters (1,750,000 cubic feet). Because of its extensive interior surfaces, however, its reverberation time is only 7 seconds. Having fewer interior surfaces, the smaller San Paolo fuori le Mura, also in Rome, has a longer reverberation time.

Although most forms of music and vocalization do not work effectively in spaces with so much reverberation, the Gregorian chant does. A type of slow, monophonic, unison singing, it is believed to have originated as a dominant component of the Christian liturgy after a progressive series of simplifications of a more complex vocal tradition that had existed much earlier (Grout, 1960). However beautiful in themselves, Gregorian chants were a utilitarian adjunct to worship, as well as a functional music that defined the temporal prayer cycle of monastic life. Selecting such chants as the vocalization of choice was an inevitable consequence of the high reverberance of most cathedrals and monasteries (Lubman and Kiser, 2001). Only slow, simple singing would avoid the aural soupiness of reverberation that seemed to last forever. The more rapid and complex singing that had existed earlier (and would again later) would have been acoustically degraded to total unintelligibility by long reverberation. Even in the relatively small monastery at Santo Domingo de Silos, near

Burgos, Spain, with a volume of only 5,000 cubic meters (175,000 cubic feet), reverberation was excessive (Lopez and Gonzales, 1987). The simpler chants are so tightly linked to their original spaces, that in 1994, when the Benedictine monks of Santo Domingo de Silos recorded *Chant,* one of the best-selling albums of Gregorian chant music, they selected the same space their brethren had used some thousand years before.

Within the vast literature of the church, extensive theological discussions describe the intent and goals of church architects and spiritual leaders over a 1,500-year span. But, even though the forms of church music and liturgy alike clearly responded to its presence, there is no mention of *intentionally* creating reverberation for its theological relevance. Instead, evidence suggests that long reverberation was simply an unintentional consequence of the spatial grandeur of God's earthly home. Nevertheless, for those who repeatedly attended services in these religious spaces, aural and visual symbolism became tightly linked. In this context, long reverberation indirectly acquired its meaning from the religion, with its liturgy, icons, and visual designs. And this link was further strengthened by religious music written for this highly reverberant space.

Christianity was certainly not the first religion to give reverberation a theological meaning. The Temple of Zeus, constructed about 460 B.C. in Olympia, was one of the largest, most prominent religious structures of ancient Greece. Owing to a lack of sound-absorbent materials, its reverberation time was a relatively long 3 seconds, which impaired speech clarity. With sound arriving from all directions, the space created a listening experience similar to that of Christian churches of comparable size, where reverberation enveloped the listener with the grandeur of God's voice.

Thus the acoustics of temples, cathedrals, monasteries, and churches acted as cultural filters, excluding those art forms that were aurally inappropriate. Moreover, because the Christian church was the locus of literacy and power, other subcultures would not have been in a position to support alternate forms of the auditory arts, and they certainly were not in a position to leave a written record of their activities. For a thousand years of Western civilization, aural architecture was, in effect, the Christian view of their music in their spaces. We might argue that the symbolic meaning of reverberation, even in reduced amounts, was partially a legacy of Christianity. When spaces became that large, they had limited utility for theater, spoken liturgy, musical detail, and any aural form that required clarity and intelligibility.

Notes

1. Unlike *visualize, auralize* refers to an *external* process, namely, to a spatial simulation that produces real sound; the coinage is less than a decade old. Accordingly, and as explained in chapter 2, note 3, the term *aurally visualize* will be used to refer to the internal process.
2. To appreciate the physical scale of these ancient temples, see Daniel Cilia's archaeological review (2000) of the megalithic temples of Malta.
3. To appreciate, in detail, the explosive creativity in musical form and space during the eighteenth and nineteenth centuries, see Forsyth, 1985.

References

Augustine, Saint (387). De Musica Translated by R. C. Taliafero. In *The Writings of Saint Augustine*. Vol. 2, *Fathers of the Church*. New York: Cima Publishing, 1948.

Cilia, D. (2000). The Megalithic Temples of Malta. Found online at http://web.infinito. it/utenti/m/malta_mega_temples/index.html (accessed 12 April 2004).

Declercq, N., Degrieck, J., Briers, R., and Leroy, O. (2004). A theoretical study of special acoustic effects caused by the staircase of the El Castillo pyramid at the Maya ruins of Chichen-Itza in Mexico. *Journal of the Acoustical Society of America* 116(6): 3328–35.

Forsyth, M. (1985). *Buildings for Music: The Architect, the Musician, and the Listener from the Seventeenth Century to the Present Day*. Cambridge, Mass.: MIT Press.

Grout, D. (1960). *A History of Western Music*. London: Norton.

Hosier, D. (1994). *The Sounds and Color of Power: The Sacred Metallurgical Technology of Ancient West Mexico*. Cambridge, Mass.: MIT Press.

James, J. (1993). *The Music of the Spheres*. New York: Springer.

Krautheimer, R. (1965). *Early Christian and Byzantine Architecture*. Baltimore: Penguin Books.

Lippman, E. (1964). *Musical Thought in Ancient Greece*. New York: Columbia University Press.

Lopez, M., and Gonzales, C. (1987). Experimental study of the acoustics in the Church of the Monastery of "Santo Domingo de Silos." *Acustica* 62(3): 241–48.

Lubman, D. (1998). Archaeological acoustic study of chirped echo from the Mayan pyramid at Chichén Itzá. *Journal of the Acoustical Society of America* 104: 1763. Extended version available at www.ocasa.org/MayanPyramid.htm (accessed 6 June 2006) and www.ocasa.org/MayanPyramid2.htm (accessed 28 March 2006).

— (2004). Acoustics at the shrine of St. Werburgh. Paper presented to the 148th Meeting of the Acoustical Society of America, San Diego, November 15–19.

—, and Kiser, B. (2001). The history of Western civilization told through the acoustics of its worship spaces. Paper presented to the seventeenth International Conference on Acoustics, Rome, September 2–7.

Platner, S. (1929). *A Topographical Dictionary of Ancient Rome*. London: Oxford University Press.

Raes, A., and Sacerdote, G. (1953). Measurements of the acoustical properties of two Roman basilicas. *Journal of the Acoustical Society of America* 25(5): 954–61.

Shankland, R., and Shankland, H. (1971). Acoustics of St. Peter's and Patriarchal Basilicas in Rome. *Journal of the Acoustical Society of America* 50: 389–95.

Smith, W. (1875). *A Dictionary of Greek and Roman Antiquities*. London: John Murray.

Tzekakis, E. (1975). Reverberation time of the Rotunda at Thessaloniki. *Journal of the Acoustical Society of America* 57(6): 1207–9.

Van Kirk, W. (2002). The accidental (acoustic) tourist. Abstract. *Journal of the Acoustical Society of America* 112(5): 2284.

Vassilantonopoulos, S., and Mourjopoulos, J. (2001). Virtual acoustic reconstruction of ritual and public spaces of ancient Greece. *Acustica* 87(5): 604–9.

von Simson, O. (1989). *The Gothic Cathedral*. Princeton, N.J.: Princeton University Press.

Wittkower, R. (1971). *Architectural Principles in the Age of Humanism*. New York: Norton.

Chapter 18

Michael Bull

THE AUDIO-VISUAL IPOD

Whether at home or in some modern means of transportation, society's actions remain everywhere the same. Changes in the landscape, however, distract attention from the hypocrisy of societal events, whose monotony is forgotten in the adventure of the voyage . . . Travel is one of the best means for a society to maintain a permanent state of absentmindedness, which prevents that society from coming to terms with itself. It assists fantasy along mistaken paths; it occludes one's perspective with impressions; it adds to the wonder of the world, so that the world's ugliness goes unnoticed.

(Kracauer 1995: 299)

The consumer is engaged by his or her own mobility and imagination: movement and incompleteness equally energise the imagination; fixity and solidity equally deaden it.

(Sennett 2006: 149)

A fictitious world, as illusion it contains more truth than does everyday reality.

(Marcuse 1978: 154–155)

Cities are fabulous with a soundtrack. They morph so easily – to becoming super-modern places if you're listening to, say, Belle and Sebastian, or a sexual playground if you're listening to some hot R&B. Or a melancholy wasteland if indie rock. People change accordingly. Rural landscapes are best appreciated with ambient stuff, or, in the case of America, good classic rock. Irrespective of what music you listen to, it makes your environment seem 'super-real' or more animated – charged somehow with the life of the music. Banal things seem more significant or poetic. You feel 'cooler' too, in your soundtrack cocoon.

(iPod user)

ONE SET OF STRATEGIES EMBARKED upon by iPod users in their effort to deal with the contingent and chilly nature of urban space is to aestheticise it. This aesthetic colonisation of urban space is in part a technological tale whereby urban experience becomes synonymous with technological experience. This technological structure to experience is both pervasive and increasingly taken for granted in wide areas of daily life. The pervasiveness is simultaneously empowering and dependent for contemporary consumers. Technology as a medium of organisation seamlessly mediates urban experience for large numbers of citizens – whether it is through individualising technologies like the iPod, the mobile phone or the automobile or through the multitude of hidden technologies that enable everyday life to function.

This chapter focuses primarily upon the aestheticising potential of the most totalising of all of these technologies, the iPod. This aesthetics of the street is largely an audio-visual one in which iPod users are transported from one cognitive and physical space to another through the dominant organising potential of privatised sound. The aestheticisation of urban space represents one set of strategies undertaken by iPod users in their management of daily life. The use of an iPod enables users to create a satisfying aestheticised reality for themselves as they move through daily life.

The aestheticising strategies undertaken by iPod use differs from the traditionally accepted mode of urban aesthetics which goes by the name of flâneurism, which has become the romantic metaphor for city life in much urban analysis.[1] Flâneurism as a mode of urban appropriation is representative of the dominance of the visual in urban and cultural studies (Amin and Thrift 2002; Freidberg 1993; Jenks 1995; Tester 1994; Tonkiss 2005). The flâneur, in this literature, is understood as a rootless, displaced subject who places themself in the shoes of the 'other' – imagining what the world would be like from the position of the other. Flânerie is an act of alienated integration representing a quest to understand the other, albeit in imaginary terms, and *is* 'characterised by its very receptive disposition, a mode of embracing rather than of excluding external impulses' (Gleber 1999: 26). Benjamin understood the flâneur as representing the image of the outsider, yet in contemporary rhetoric flânerie has become universalised – we all become flâneurs in a sanitised image of urban relations in which flânerie becomes an integral part of the 'tourist' gaze.

Flâneurism is, however, an inappropriate concept for understanding the audio-visual world of the contemporary iPod user. The mundane and routine daily experience of the urban citizen is not primarily made up of the tourist gaze. Indeed, iPod culture embodies a directly contrary position to that of the flâneur. The aesthetic moment of urban experience within iPod use draws the 'other' numerically into the users own imaginary realm – theirs is a strategy in which all 'differences' are negated to become one with the user. iPod culture represents the aesthetics of mimicry; it is an audio-visual mimicry.

Visual epistemologies impose a silent gaze upon the city in a manner that mimics the 'purely visual *agora*' of the city, which itself is thought to 'provoke mutual withdrawal' (Sennett 1994: 358). Visual descriptions of the city often resemble the snapshot – the fragmentary distillation of urban life as if through the aperture of a camera (Benjamin 1973). iPod culture, by contrast, concerns the seamless joining together of experience in a flow, unifying the complex, contradictory and contingent nature of the world beyond the user. The success of these aestheticising strategies depends upon the creation of an all-enveloping wall of sound through which the user looks. Users report that iPod experience is at its most satisfying when no external sound seeps into their world to distract them from their dominant and dominating vision.

The Aesthetics of the Street

Urban citizens frequently ignore the physical environment through which they move. The mundane journeying through the city invariably does not evoke the 'tourist' gaze (Urry 1995), with city dwellers rarely mentioning the spaces that they daily pass through. City spaces are, rather, experienced as habitual, not meriting mention. iPod use provides one way in which the urban dweller navigates through the mundane spaces of the city, frequently preoccupied with their own mood and orientation rather than the spaces passed through. iPod users' inattention to the visual is true both of crowded city centres and of quiet suburban streets. When iPod users do choose to look, their attentiveness is an auditory attentiveness facilitated by the rhythm of sound pumped directly into their ears. iPod users aim to create a privatised sound world, which is in harmony with their mood, orientation and surroundings, enabling them to re-spatialise urban experience through a process of solipsistic aestheticisation. iPod users aim to habitually create an aesthetically pleasing urban world for themselves as a constituent part of their everyday life. The aesthetic appropriation of urban space becomes one cognitive strategy as users attempt to create a seamless web of mediated and privatised experience in their everyday movement through the city, enhancing virtually any chosen experience in any geographical location at will. In doing so they create an illusion of omnipotence through mediated proximity and 'connectedness' engendered by the use of their iPod.

Jason is thirty-five years old; he lives in New Orleans and works in online media distribution. He is married, with one young child, and has owned an iPod for over a year, never having possessed a mobile music player previously. He regularly listens to music and audio books on his iPod, and employs both in his aestheticising strategies. Jason describes listening to a talking book on his iPod whilst drinking a cup of coffee in a local café: 'I love the experience of listening to a work of fiction and being in a public place like a coffee store. I like to watch people around me and imagine them as the characters in the novel.' The aesthetic impulse transforms the mundane space of the café into the scenario of the novel being listened to, with its customers as unknowing characters. The aesthetic impulse energises the mundane space of the café, creating an audio-visual drama in which Jason becomes its active audio-visual master. Listening frees up the eyes to observe and imagine, thus differing from the traditional reading of a book, in which the reader is visually engaged in the text. Jason can look around the café, the movements of his body unconstrained by the act of reading. The text becomes a continuous flow of sound on to which he adds a level of physicality in the act of imagination. The sound print of the book is imposed on the silence of the world around him. Jason does not experience the café itself as an unpleasant environment – he chooses to enter and have refreshments, after all. The aesthetic impulse is triggered by the desire to heighten his experience. The mimetic character of iPod aesthetics occurs equally in music listening, as Jason explains, again in the café:

> My world looks better. I get more emotional about things, including the people I see and my thoughts in general. Sometimes I project the lyrical content of songs on to the people I see while I'm listening. For example, I can distinctly remember listening to U2's 'Stuck in a Moment' and I was looking at some of the people standing around me in a coffee shop, with the look of anxiety on their faces and general angst. It made me want to hug them and tell them it's OK . . . I would look at other people and they would smile at me, almost like they knew what I was thinking. . . . It's like it polarised my world into these hemispheres of those who understood Bono's message and those who didn't. I'm not a Bono worshipper or anything; it was just the first time I had really listened to the lyrics of the song. That's a very private moment (in public). . . . it's difficult to explain, but when he said the words 'I know it's tough, but you can never get enough of what you don't really need' it all just crystallised for me. I've had a lot of surreal moments like that listening to the music on my iPod and watching the world around me . . . It's almost like watching a movie, but you're in it.

The reference to iPod experience as being like that of a movie is common, although its meaning varies (Bull 2000). In Jason's account it refers to the world in which he lives, appearing as if it were a movie in which he is also placed. The U2 song heightens Jason's mood. Listening to the song, he recognises the superfluity of the ethics of consumption as articulated by Bono and seemingly etched upon the faces of the hapless customers in the café. The lyrics of the song appear to describe the cognitive state of the others, visually imagined and interpreted by Jason. The aesthetic principle serves to elevate Jason beyond mundane concerns – placing him in a position of an empowered interpreter of the world whilst remaining distant. In the act of interpretation Jason remains silent, impenetrable to others.

City life is invariably about surfaces, the superficial reading and the transitory clues involved in our observations of others, hence the overriding dominance of the visual in urban accounts of experience. The presentation of self is a largely visual one – the presence of the other is largely a silent presence in urban culture, even in the urban world of the mobile phone. Silence protects the urban subject from 'the harsh realities of the world'. It is this silence which promotes both isolation and the flowering of self; the richness of interiority contrasted with the blandness of the outside world. The flow of people moving through the street differs from that of those sitting or milling around a café. The café is also a place of talk, of snatched conversations, of potential exposure. The above account of iPod use re-imposes the purely visual on to the activity of others in order to construct them as significant, yet imaginary, others. Jason in drawing others into his 'enlightenment' vision is essentially saying, 'If you could hear what I hear, then you too would be transformed.' Jason's enlightenment, however, remains a mute and private enlightenment in which others are unaware as they move through space with their own unknown preoccupations. Jason's private revelations nevertheless cognitively empower him, heightening his sense of presence and purpose; his is an audio-visual mastery of the world:

> Sometimes I think I can calm people down just by looking at them when I'm listening to music. And sometimes, when they look at me, I think they do 'shift', because they recognise that I'm in a 'good place'.

Jason, in the act of private listening, imagines that he ceases to be a blank canvas, a mere surface that others look at uninterestedly. Meaning radiates from him, the internal becomes externalised, constructed through music and made transparent – immediate. He is transformed in the imagined eyes of others becoming the centre of a cognitive universe through which others reflect – his cognitive state becomes their cognitive state – though they are not privy to his sound world. The auditory 'look' is a sufficient tag, in the above account, for an 'imaginary' recognition to flow from the 'other'. Jason is not merely a part of this audio-visual world; he becomes its director, orchestrating meanings in which he imagines others as 'knowing' cast members. Jason is not alone in summoning up precise aesthetic re-creations through the creation of scenarios in which others play unwitting stand-up parts:

> For some reason, Talking Head songs seem to work best for this. Like, I will look at an old woman with a cane, and imagine her singing one lyric. Then move on to a hip-hop style teenage boy, and have him sing to the next line. My imagination really can take off. It sometimes makes me laugh and smile to myself – especially if a particularly amusing line comes up. It really does transform my surroundings. I sort of feel like I'm in my own music video.
>
> (Karen)

Underlying this virtual connectivity appears a playful narrative of invention in which users remain cognitively invisible. Alternatively, the personalisation of the user's sound world imbues the street and its atmosphere, indeed the whole world, with an intimacy, warmth and significance it otherwise lacks. The world mimics and moves to the rhythm of users. For iPod users the street is orchestrated to the predictable sounds of their favourite playlists:

> The world looks friendlier, happier, and sunnier when I walk down the street with my iPod on. It feels as if I'm in a movie at times. Like my life has a soundtrack now. It also takes away some of the noise of the streets, so that everything around me becomes calmer somewhat. It detaches me from my environment, like I'm an invisible, floating observer.
>
> (Berklee)

The process of auditory looking described above by the young Dutch user in Amsterdam mirrors that of users elsewhere. iPod users in their viewing strategies often describe themselves as 'not really there'. The solipsistic viewer is shielded by their iPod from a truly reciprocal gaze. Jason's description above, for example, was of the imaginary gaze of the other; a constituent part of his own imaginative construction. iPod users frequently engage in non-reciprocal gazing whereby they don't receive the gaze of others at all – the iPod acts as a virtual pair of sunglasses from which the user stares imperiously. Susan, a manager from Toronto, describes this transformative power of the iPod over her urban environment:

> I find when listening to some music choices I feel like I'm not really there. Like I'm watching everything around me happening in a movie. I start to feel the environment in the sense of the mood of the song and can find that I can start to love a street that I usually hate, or feel scared for no reason.
>
> (Susan)

The solipsism of the user is frequently referred to in terms of general feelings of separateness:

> I'm living in a world where music is going on and things are happening and everyone else who can't hear what I'm hearing is not really in that world or slightly less connected to it. There's something going on in my head that's for me and only me.
>
> (Kate)

> I see people like I do when I watch a movie . . . there is a soundtrack to my encounters . . . music to accompany my thought about others. It dramatises things a bit, it fills the silent void.
>
> (June)

Streets perceived as silent are in reality a complex of sounds. June's observation that her iPod filled the 'silent void' is indicative of users' experiencing the world solely as a function of mediated sound. The unmediated sound world of urban society is a place where nothing happens – devoid of interest, throwing the subject back into the world of contingency, isolation and incompleteness.

Richard Sennett has argued that feelings of subjective incompleteness in urban space might be conquered through the mere act of movement. To move becomes an end in itself, whilst to remain still is to be reminded of 'self' as 'object' rather than self as activity; as Paris Hilton was heard to comment, 'I walk, I don't think.' iPod users, however, display no such completeness through the mere act of movement. They experience unmediated experience as threatening, silence is associated with falling prey to the unmanageable and contingent nature of their own cognition. In addition to this cognitive frailty they also become aware of the chill of city spaces, which are perceived as inhospitable, without the warmth of desired communication. Whilst the use of a mobile phone makes for a temporary respite, iPod use provides the user with the power to transform their environment seamlessly and continuously. A sense of completeness arrives through mediation – not movement.

Sound Enhancement

To aestheticise, as Marcuse argued, is to simplify, to strip reality of its inessentials. The aesthetic principle is inherently one of transcendence. An essential component of this transcendence for iPod users is to replace the multi-rhythmic and hence unmanageable nature of urban life with their own manageable mono-rhythms. Mundane yet nevertheless unmanageable urban life is transformed through iPod use, creating movement and energy in the user where there was none before. Amy, a thirty-two-year-old who works in product design in Philadelphia, describes walking down the street with her iPod playing;

> My music drives my attitude as I walk down the street. If I'm listening to melancholy music my surroundings are a little greyer, a little more dismal, and the strangers I see on the street become a little more menacing. If I'm listening to upbeat music the strangers look friendlier and my surroundings are not as depressing. While living in a city is practical for many reasons, it can also be overwhelmingly depressing. Having cheerful music in my ears as I see a homeless person digging through garbage to find a meal is disconcerting. Sometimes the music acts as a buffer between me and the city, and other times the music draws such a sharp contrast between what I'm hearing and what I'm seeing that it's hard to take. Other times, when I'm walking through the city with a great song, one that's appropriate to my external surroundings and internal feelings, I feel like I'm the star of my own personal movie, strutting along to my theme song of the moment.

Common in iPod accounts of aesthetic experience is making the street mimic the mood engendered by the music playing on the iPod. In the above account the homeless that are observed are not so much aestheticised as recessed. The use of the iPod provides a 'buffer' between the user and the recognised reality of the city street, invoking Kracauer's observation that 'the world's ugliness goes unnoticed' in iPod culture. Negatives are transformed into positives as Amy describes her elation as she traverses the spaces of the city. Emily, a twenty-six-year-old worker in the advertising industry in London, paints a dystopian image of her experience of the city, highlighted by both her mood and her music:

> I'd just moved house, was going through a *very* tough patch in my life and particularly with my boyfriend. I decided to walk to a different Tube station, trying to find my way without the aid of a map. The song which came on was 'Roses' by Outkast. It's about a nasty woman whose boyfriend is fed up of her . . . You can see the resonance – there's a sense of lonely resignation to the song, and this transformed the surroundings. (I was getting lost and moved from Little Venice, where I live, to the grittiness of Edgware Road.) I was into dull and hideous. Crossing a huge road – filthy petrol fumes, etc. – it all became more intense, thanks to the music. Another time was when I was in Paris for work, and was feeling less than good about work, and wanted to be home, and listening to familiar upbeat

music (Basement Jaxx) made the surroundings seem even more melancholic and alien to me.

(Emily)

Ironically the comfort of listening to familiar music whilst in Paris highlighted her alienation from the streets of Paris – acting merely to remind her of her wish to be home. The following respondent also highlights this colonisation of space in which one's surroundings take on the ambience of the cognitive state of the user, mediated through their soundtrack:

I feel as though life is a movie and is playing especially for me. If I listen to sad music, which I only listen to when I'm down (boyfriend break-up, bad grade, just bad news) then everything sort of has a grey shadow over it, even when it's sunny outside.

(Betty)

The world experienced as a movie script in which the user takes a central role is a common description of iPod use. The selection of 'sad' music to match the user's mood transposes those feelings to the streets passed through. The world and the user's experience within it gain significance through their enveloping and privatised sound world. iPod users invariably prefer to listen to their music loud, thus providing them with an overwhelming sense of presence whilst simultaneously blocking out any sound from their enviornment that might sully the heightened and empowering pleasure of use. In their world of aesthetic euphoria, experience is simplified, clarified – the aesthetic impulse provides an unambiguous sense of purpose and meaning for users, creating a 'space' within which to unwind and unravel their emotions. When attended to, the street becomes a function of their mood and imagination, mediated through their iPod:

I like to crank angry, loud music at night; the city seems so much more dark and brutal in the dark if I do that. Walking home, I sometimes listen to more soaring, passionate melodies, and they make me see things differently. I listen to rhythmic and pulsating music sometimes, which makes me feel confident and secure – I don't have to do anything but 'following the beat', so to speak. Sometimes I listen to piano music, and because most of my piano music is kind of depressing/saddening (in a good way) it makes the world seem more fragile and on the verge of collapse. Delirium's music always strikes me in this emotional, soul-searching way, and elevates even the smallest details to some greater significance; every movement of the people in the streets seems spiritual and sacred.

(Brian)

If it's dark and gloomy and raining outside, I'll pick something that complements the weather, and that can alter the outlook on the world around me. I can take joy in otherwise gloomy, rainy, dank weather by putting on something wonderfully gloomy and dank, something I love to hear. It's a fine synergy of the visual and auditory environments. It makes me feel like I'm walking through my own movie, with my own soundtrack. The people around me look like extras on the set. Dark clouds look brighter and the smell of the rain gets stronger. I see myself in the third person.

(Kerry)

My iPod puts me in a place and time. It's very common for me to walk to the music, so to speak. What I am listening to affects how I see everything around me. I might listen to some classic soul while I walk and the city seems to have a very mellow vibe. On other occasions I might have on some Rage against the Machine or something like that, and the city seems chaotic, crazy, too fast. What I listen to always impacts the way I view my surroundings.

(Freedom)

Aesthetic enhancement is a central strategy of iPod use. Times of the day or weather conditions are complemented by and enhanced through the use of music played on the iPod. This might be predetermined through the construction of playlists made for these occasions or found whilst scrolling through the contents of the iPod. The contents of the iPod represent a repository of sensory and environmental stimuli.

Some iPod users play music at random, rather than sorting through their playlists to find a suitable track to harmonise or illuminate their surroundings. They have their iPod on shuffle, thereby forcing a level of contingency upon the juxtaposition of sound and street. None the less, the aestheticising impulse continues to throw up interesting options for users in which the world continues to be brought into harmony with the music:

I find that my iPod 'colours' my surroundings quite significantly; as it's on shuffle I don't know what's coming up next, and it often surprises me how the same street can look lively and busy and colourful one moment and then – when a different song starts – it can change to a mysterious and unnerving place. I like the sensation, though.

(Andy)

iPods are non-interactive in the sense that users construct fantasies and maintain feelings of security precisely by not interacting with others or their environment.

Sound both colonises the listener and actively recreates and reconfigures the spaces of experience. Through the power of a privatised sound world the world becomes intimate, known and possessed. Imagination is mediated by the sounds of the iPod becoming an essential component in the ability of users to imagine at all. Users are often unable to aestheticise experience without the existence of their own individual soundtrack acting as a spur to the imagination.

In this ordering of cognition the user surpasses the disjunction that exists between their own soundtrack, the movement of others and the environment passed through.

Without the iPod they experience the world out of sync. The polyrhythmic nature of the city relativises their own place within the world, making them just one more piece of an anonymous urban world.

Sound Utopias

If movement is itself a potentially transformative activity, then moving to sound is doubly so. Movement itself embodies an element of ideology as the subject moves through the city. In the modernist urban world of the city it was the subject who was traditionally colonised by the enticements of the city, interiorising the utopian dreams fabricated in the electronic lights and billboards of the city of which the subject became a constituent part. The representational spaces of the city fill up subjectivity, so to speak:

> Illuminated words glide on the rooftops, and already one is banished from one's own emptiness into the alien advertisement. One's body takes root in the asphalt, and, together with the enlightening revelations of the illuminations, one's spirit – which is no longer one's own – roams ceaselessly out of the night and into the night.
>
> (Kracauer 1995:332)

Kracauer's understanding of the urban colonisation of the subject is essentially Fordist, in which the dominant rhythms of the city create the cadences within which all citizens walk. Urban experience becomes mediated through the advertising technologies of commodity culture and the empowered dreams associated with the very act of movement itself. iPod culture reverses this phenomenon. The user is saturated with the privatised sounds of the iPod – the cultural imperative, fully commoditised, lies in the contents of the iPod itself. The world is drawn into the user's 'individual' narrative rather than the street drawing the user into its realm. The experiences of the city described by Kracauer and those of the iPod user remain mediated and commoditised. Both sets of descriptions are equally filmic. Kracauer's urban stroller lives in the polyrhythmic audio-visual world of the street, which presents itself to him as a spectacle in which the street becomes a commodified dream. iPod users, rather, construct a mono-rhythmic aesthetic narrative to the street deciphered from the sounds of the culture industry emanating from the iPod in their pocket. Theirs is a hyper-post-Fordist street of potentially multiple audio-visual scenarios – with each iPod user constructing their own singular mediated dream world simultaneously. Kracauer's subject is diminished, made smaller, by the scale of the street and its illuminated signs, whereas iPod users such as Sophie, a marketing manager from London, describes her iPod experience as

> making the world look smaller – I am much bigger and more powerful listening to music. The world is generally a better place, or at the very least it is sympathetic to my mood . . . you become part of the music and can take on a different persona.

iPod use inverts the relationship between the user and the world. Sophie occupies the centre of her world. Empowered, she looms large against the horizon. The world, in harmony with her mood, is a better world. The world is brought into line through the privatised yet mediated act of cognition. A potentially perfect mimetic fantasy that denies the contingent nature of the world.

iPod users resemble both the imaginative city dweller who aesthetically recreates any chosen urban space at will, enlivening it as they move through the city, whilst also, and equally, appearing to represent an urban subject in retreat from a bland and alienating urban environment. Accounts of the blandness of urban experience are invariably accounts of the solitary subject confronting the 'non-spaces' of the city (Augé 1995). In these portrayals the city is portrayed as semiotically void, in which the subject, without the ideological props of commodity culture, remains 'transcendentally homeless'.

Aestheticisation has utopian implications for users. To aestheticise is to transcend the mundane world as it is experienced. Aestheticisation remains an active mode of appropriating the urban, transforming that which exists, making it the user's own. The desire to engage in these aestheticising processes derive both from the habitual predispositions of users located in wider media use – for are not television and film viewers equally in positions of imaginary omnipotence whilst they watch from the comfort of their own home? (Morley 2000) – and as a response to the nature of urban space itself and the dislocation from it felt by the urban subject (Augé 1995; Sennett 1990).

In this process of aestheticisation iPod users transform the world in conformity with their predispositions. The world becomes part of a mimetic fantasy in which the 'otherness' of the world in its various guises is negated. This is an important strategy for iPod users, who subjectivise space – consume it, as if it were a commodity. In the process, immediate experience is fetishised. Technologised experience is fetishised experience. Experience becomes real or hyper-real precisely through its technologisation – through technological appropriation. The utopian impulse to transform the world occurs only in the imaginary: in its technologised instrumentality the world remains untouched. Users prefer to live in this technological space whereby experience is brought under control – aesthetically managed and embodied–whilst the contingent nature of urban space and the 'other' is denied. The concept of 'otherness' becomes increasingly redundant in iPod culture. Forms of urban reciprocity, of urban recognition, are denied within the very structure of iPod use. The empowerment of the subject implies an incipient crisis in the way in which users 'recognise' the other (Honneth 1995).

The aestheticisation of experience has traditionally been portrayed not merely as pleasurable, which it certainly is, but also as inconsequential in so far as the object of the gaze is left untouched – unsullied. 'Aesthetically, the city space is a spectacle in which amusement value overrides all other considerations' (Bauman 2000: 168). Yet, far from being inconsequential, this aestheticising mode of urban experience contains cognitive and moral resonances. The aestheticisation of experience remains relational, and, whilst the subjects of the aestheticisation process remain untouched, the aestheticising impulse highlights the underlying values of users in their relation to the 'other' and the spaces passed through. The aestheticising practices of iPod users contribute to our understanding of what it means to 'share' urban space with others from within an auditory bubble, immune to the sounds of others.

Notes

1. 'Flanerie is very closely related to other constructions of cultural modernity. Linked to the movements and images that belong to the processes of tourism, photography, and psychoanalysis, it ultimately charts the aesthetics of modernity that reveals its affinities to the medium of the cinema and its reception of external reality' (Gleber 1999: 6).

References

Amin, A. and Thrift, N. (2002) *Cities. Re-imagining the Urban*. Cambridge. Polity.

Augé, M. (1995) *Non-places. Introduction to Anthropology of Supermodernity*. London. Verso.

Bauman, Z. (2000) *Liquid Modernity*. Cambridge. Polity.

Benjamin, W. (1973) *Illuminations*. London. Penguin.

Bergson, H. (1998) *Introduction to Metaphysics*. London. Kessinger.

Bull, M. (2000) *Sounding out the City. Personal Stereos and the Management of Everyday Life*. Oxford. Berg.

Freidberg, A. (1993) *Window Shopping*.

Berkeley CA. University of California Press.

Gleber, A. (1999) *The Art of Taking a Walk. Flanerie, Literature and Film in Weimar Culture*. Princeton NJ. Princeton University Press.

Honneth, A. (1995) *The Fragmented World of the Social. Essays in Social and Political Philosophy*. New York. SUNY Press.

Jenks, C. (ed.) (1995) *Visual Culture*. London. Routledge.

Kracauer, S. (1995) *The Mass Ornament. Weimar Essays*. Cambridge MA. Harvard University Press.

Marcuse, H. (1978) *The Aesthetic Dimension*. Boston MA. Beacon.

Morley, D. (2000) *Home Territories. Media, Mobility and Identity*. London. Routledge.

Sennett, R. (1990) *The Conscience of the Eye*. London. Faber.

— (1994) *Flesh and Stone*. New York. Norton.

— (2006) *The Culture of the New Capitalism*. New Haven CT. Yale University Press.

Tester, K. (ed.) (1994) *The Flaneur*. London. Routledge.

Tonkiss, F. (2005) *Space, the City and Social Theory. Social Relations and Urban Forms*. Cambridge. Polity.

Urry, J. (1995) *Consuming Places*. London. Routledge.

PART III

Transduce and Record

THE PHILOSOPHICAL, CULTURAL and political questions raised by transduction—the transformation of sound into something else like grooves on a cylinder that can be turned back into sound—provide an inviting point of entry into sound studies. In his famous essay on technological reproducibility, Walter Benjamin wrote that it "can put the copy of the original into situations which would be out of reach for the original itself [...] The choral production, performed in an auditorium or open air, now resounds in the drawing room." More recently Friedrich Kittler used sound reproduction to call into question what it means to be human: "whereas (according to Derrida) it is characteristic of so-called Man and his consciousness to hear himself speak and see himself write, media dissolve such feedback loops [...] the phonograph does not hear as do ears that have long been trained immediately to filter voices, words, and sounds out of noise; it registers acoustic events as such."[1] His chapter in this section pursues the implications of that radical proposition.

Basic questions about reproducibility reverberate across the humanities and social sciences. Rick Altman's contribution to this section inquires into the nature of film sound. Altman's career was spent promoting sound studies as a part of film sound, but his edited collections and the work of his students and colleagues show the field's heterogeneity from the outset, as they deal with questions of recording and reproducibility more generally.[2] James Lastra's chapter explores how norms around the process of sound reproduction—fidelity and intelligibility—shape conceptions of what sound is and what it should do. In short, it inverts the older approach of starting with an a priori definition of sound that is then used to measure reproducibility. Lisa Gitelman takes another approach, examining early phonograph records *as records*, both of sound events and as pieces of tinfoil audience members took home from early exhibitions. Altman, Lastra and Gitelman all use specific media sites—cinema, phonograph exhibitions, 19th-century literary criticism—to ask after fundamental problems in media theory.

The power to reproduce sound is a central figure in classic writing on media. Previous generations of writers framed reproducibility in terms of separation between sounds and their sources. Pierre Schaeffer used the term "acousmatic sound"—sounds separated from their sources—to describe the unmoored condition of recorded sound, while Murray Schafer chose the more pathological language of "schizophonia" to describe the split between sound and source.[3] Both approaches replay Plato's old division between original and copy in *The Phaedrus*, where Socrates argues that living speech is better than dead painting or writing because they "stand before us as if they were alive, but if you question them, they maintain a most majestic silence . . . They go on telling you just the same thing forever." For Plato, reproducibility meant that speech would move out of its original context, and thereby could be transformed and abused.[4] Transposed to sound reproduction, this can take on many different possible meanings: for Schaeffer it was an aesthetic opportunity. For Schafer it was a problem, for Benjamin it had a dialectical potential, and for the many industry people in David Suisman's *Selling Sounds*, it was commercial opportunity first, a cultural problem second.[5] But as Jason Stanyek and Benjamin Piekut show in their essay in this section, all sounds are by definition separated from their sources by virtue of being sounds. The question, they ask, is what happens at the logical limit of reproducibility when the living and the dead can seem to be in collaboration. By examining deadness as a media phenomenon, they help reframe the meaning of liveness.[6]

When we talk about technology, agency often comes to the fore. Where does the power lie in human-technological relations and how do we think about the ability of technologies to act in the world, especially in relation to how we think about human action? These are huge questions that get re-asked every time someone considers technology as a cultural problem. Two intellectual antecedents of sound studies have bequeathed it a powerful constructivist tradition—science and technology studies and cultural studies. Writers in science and technology studies have articulated both constructivist approaches to technology in general, and to sound technologies in specific. As Trevor Pinch and Karin Bijsterveld write, Science and Technology Studies' engagement with sound "can be thought of as an extension of the field's continued examination of the detailed material practices that constitute technoscience." These approaches can take the form of laboratory ethnographies, histories of scientific and technical thought, and studies of particular disciplines and technologies as they relate to sound.[7] Trevor Pinch and Frank Trocco's chapter in this section asks how the Moog synthesizer came to have a keyboard. In the process they reveal the network of people, institutional and technical forms that helped shape modern sound synthesis. They also show how new interest in technology can be applied to the study of instruments as well as media, a project also taken up by writers like Paul Théberge and Steve Waksman.[8]

Apart from Kittler, for whom the phrase "cultural sciences" (kulturwissenschaft) means something very different from Anglo-American cultural studies,[9] the constructivist tradition coming out of cultural studies can be felt in the rest of the readings included in this section. While Science and Technology draws its constructivism from a critique of positivist epistemology, cultural studies draws its constructivism from critiques of power, derived from traditions like Marxism, feminism, anti-racism, postcolonial thought, queer studies, and poststructuralism. Their conclusions about technologies are often sympathetic to one another, but the paths they take to and from technologies are different.

Though it was originally published in 1987, John Mowitt's chapter is still one of the most incisive and creative analyses of digital audio that we have to date. By connecting ideas of the bit with older debates around originals and copies, sound fidelity, listening and the fragment, Mowitt develops an analysis of digital audio that attends to its digital character while holding out the technology as a social and cultural artifact. His essay is particularly salutary for updating two discussions that are fixtures of 20th-century media theory: Walter Benjamin's notion of *aura* as the rootedness of a work of art in time and space, and Benjamin and Theodor Adorno's ongoing debate over the politics of attention and distraction in a media culture where aura is superceded by mechanical and electronic reproducibility. While Mowitt's chapter comes out of the critical theory tradition, Louise Meintjes's essay asks after the artifactual character of sound technology from an ethnographic and acoustemological approach. Using the anthropological concept of fetishism, Meintjes examines the symbolic meaning of recording, recording equipment, and the recording studio as a space apart. In the process, she interrogates the various separations between production, music-making, consumption and listening that suffuse contemporary culture, and at the same time also examines how sound recording technology operates as "Western" technology in the global south. If Mowitt's piece seems oddly timely for an essay on such a dated moment in the history of sound technology, Meintjes's analysis seems impressively, perceptively portable for one so thoroughly attentive to its context. Their careful attention to present context and the intellectual ambition to transcend it is one of the most exciting aspects of their work.

Notes

1   Benjamin, "The Work of Art in the Age of Mechanical Reproduction," 221; Kittler, *Gramophone-Film-Typewriter*, 22–23.

2   See, e.g., Altman, *Sound Theory/Sound Practice*.

3   Schaeffer, *Traité des objets musicaux*; Schafer, *The Soundscape: Our Sonic Environment and the Tuning of the World*.

4   Plato, "Phaedrus"; see also Chang, *Deconstructing Communication: Representation, Subject and Economies of Discourse*; Peters, *Speaking into the Air: A History of the Idea of Communication*.

5   Suisman, *Selling Sounds: The Commercial Revolution in American Music*.

6   See also Auslander, *Liveness: Performance in a Mediatized Culture*.

7   Pinch and Bijsterveld, "Sound Studies: New Technologies and Music," 637; see also, e.g., Pinch and Bijker, "The Social Construction of Facts and Artefacts: Or How the Sociology of Science and the Sociology of Technology Might Benefit Each Other"; Mody, "The Sound of Science: Listening to Laboratory Practice"; Hankins and Silverman, *Instruments and the Imagination*; Roosth, "Screaming Yeast."

8   Théberge, *Any Sound You Can Imagine: Making Music/Consuming Technology*; Waksman, *Instruments of Desire: The Electric Guitar and the Shaping of Musical Experience*; see also Bayton, "Women and the Electric Guitar."

9   See John Durham Peters's introduction to Kittler, *Optical Media*.

References

Altman, Rick. *Sound Theory/Sound Practice*. New York: Routledge, 1992.

Auslander, Philip. *Liveness: Performance in a Mediatized Culture*. New York: Routledge, 1999.

Bayton, Mavis. "Women and the Electric Guitar." In *Sexing the Groove*, 37–49. New York: Routledge, 1997.

Benjamin, Walter. "The Work of Art in the Age of Mechanical Reproduction." In *Illuminations*, 217–52. New York: Shocken, 1968.

Chang, Briankle. *Deconstructing Communication: Representation, Subject and Economies of Discourse*. Minneapolis: University of Minnesota Press, 1996.

Hankins, Thomas L., and Robert J. Silverman. *Instruments and the Imagination*. Princeton: Princeton University Press, 1995.

Kittler, Friedrich. *Gramophone-Film-Typewriter*. Stanford: Stanford University Press, 1999.

—. *Optical Media: Berlin lectures 1999*. Translated by Anthony Enns. Polity, 2009.

Mody, Cyrus. "The Sound of Science: Listening to Laboratory Practice." *Science, Technology and Human Values* 30, no. 2 (2005): 175–98.

Peters, John Durham. *Speaking into the Air: A History of the Idea of Communication*. Chicago: University of Chicago Press, 1999.

Pinch, Trevor, and Wiebe Bijker. "The Social Construction of Facts and Artefacts: Or How the Sociology of Science and the Sociology of Technology Might Benefit Each Other." *Social Studies of Science* 14, no. 3 (1984): 399–441.

Pinch, Trevor, and Karin Bijsterveld. "Sound Studies: New Technologies and Music." *Social Studies of Science* 34, no. 5 (2004): 635–48.

Plato. "Phaedrus." In *The Collected Dialogues of Plato*, 475–525. Princeton: Princeton University Press, 1961.

Roosth, Sophia. "Screaming Yeast: Sonocytology, Cytoplasmic Milieus, and Cellular Subjectivities." *Critical Inquiry* 35, no. 2 (January 1, 2009): 332–50.

Schaeffer, Pierre. *Traité des objets musicaux*. Nouv. éd. Paris: Seuil, 1964.

Schafer, R. Murray. *The Soundscape: Our Sonic Environment and the Tuning of the World*. Rochester, Vermont: Destiny Books, 1994.

Suisman, David. *Selling Sounds: The Commercial Revolution in American Music*. Cambridge: Harvard University Press, 2009.

Théberge, Paul. *Any Sound You Can Imagine: Making Music/Consuming Technology*. Hanover: Wesleyan University Press, 1997.

Waksman, Steve. *Instruments of Desire: The Electric Guitar and the Shaping of Musical Experience*. Cambridge: Harvard University Press, 1999.

Chapter 19

John Mowitt

THE SOUND OF MUSIC IN THE ERA OF ITS ELECTRONIC REPRODUCIBILITY

> With every tool man is perfecting his own organs, whether motor or sensory, or he is removing the limits to their functioning. In the photographic camera he has created an instrument which retains the fleeting visual impressions, just as the gramophone disc retains the equally fleeting auditory ones; both are at bottom materializations of the power he possesses of recollection, his memory.
>
> (Sigmund Freud)

Is it 'Live' or is it Memorex?

TO EMPHASIZE THE IMPORTANCE of reproductive technology when analyzing the social significance of music is to privilege the moment of reception in cultural experience. What follows is organized around the acknowledgment of such a moment. Put succinctly, reception has acquired its analytic importance as a result of socio-historical developments within the cultural domain. I can best illustrate this by turning to a concrete example – an example that will indicate why music is a decisive reference point for an understanding of these developments. My aim in the analysis of this example will be to introduce the category of a structure of listening, on the basis of which I will argue for the priority of reception within the social determination of musical experience. Central to this argument is the notion that subjectivity acquires its irreducibly social character from the fact that experience takes place within a cultural context organized by institutions and practices. Today, these include institutions that technically fuse the contexts of cultural production and reception. I will elaborate this in terms of the problem of the place of memory in musical experience – a problem which has come to receive its strongest formulation within the phenomenological tradition. By drawing on a reading of the psychoanalytic account of memory, I will also reflect in detail on the social constitution of experience which is conspicuously underdeveloped in phenomenology. Once the socio-technological basis of memory is elaborated and used to establish the sociality of music, I will address the political issues raised by this development. By turning to the debates within critical theory, I will not only be able to specify these issues, but I will be able to sketch out the emancipatory dialectic of contemporary musical reception.

A recent advertising campaign for a major cassette tape producer underscores the key socio-historical developments that have shaped contemporary musical reception. I am thinking of the Memorex Corporation's well-known television commercial featuring Chuck Mangione and Ella Fitzgerald that centered on the interrogative phrase, 'Is it live or is it Memorex?' A brief reconstruction of the commercial's narrative and *mise en scène* will enable me to unpack the main points of my illustration.

The scene is a recording studio. The television audience arrives upon the scene just as the final cadence of Mangione's 'hit' fades. Two acoustic spaces are joined: the space of the recording and the space of the commercial. A cinematically fostered structure of identification situates us in the control room of the studio along with Fitzgerald who is watching and listening to the session. The juncture of acoustic spaces means that both Fitzgerald and the television audience are listening to Mangione's piece through the playback monitors in the control room. A voice-over narrator gives us the details of a test that is going to be conducted to establish the quality of the Memorex product.[1] Fitzgerald is to turn her back on the control room window and, simply by listening once again to the monitors, determine whether the music she is listening to is 'live' or Memorex, that is, electronically reproduced. Because of our proximity to her in the narrative space, we are being invited in effect to submit to the test and its conclusions as well. The melodic 'hook' of Mangione's piece returns on the audio track, Fitzgerald indicates uncertainty, and Mangione and his group resolve her dilemma by screaming to her from within the studio, 'It's Memorex!' The voice-over narration reaches closure with the requisite repetition of the product's name embedded in the memorable phrase: 'Is it live or is it Memorex?'[2]

Many themes and problems have been paraded before our eyes and ears: memory, fidelity, production, reception, music, looking and listening. In regard to these, the issue at stake in the ad is not, in fact, whether 'The First Lady of Song' is really deceived by the King of Memory (Memo Rex). Our basic precritical cynicism assures us that this is not worth caring about because we know that Fitzgerald is being paid by the Memorex Corporation to appear in the commercial. Instead, what made this commercial and its slogan one of the most successful in the industry was its accurate and reassuring evocation of a contemporary structure of listening, a structure that is now in decline. Detailing this structure will allow me to justify the importance I have attached to musical reception.

The recording studio is a cultural facility whose existence testifies to the technological advances that made the present priority of cultural consumption over cultural production possible. The social fact that more people listen to music rather than play it derives, in part, from the cultural impact of the operation of this facility. At the very core of the studio reside repetition and reproducibility. Indeed, in the contemporary musical world (and this is not restricted to the West) repetition now constitutes the very threshold of music's social audibility. In actual recording practice this phenomenon has penetrated musical material to the point where performances themselves are immanently shaped by both the fact and the anticipation of repetition.[3] Moreover, recording has profoundly altered the improvisational idioms in music essentially by providing them with a form of notation. Besides making it possible to study the 'scores' of jam sessions, reproduction – particularly in these instances – restricts interpretation to the recorded notation of specific performances of the piece. While this can be seen as contributing to the musicological temptation to reduce interpretation to execution, it is also important to recognize that the replacement of scores with records (and tapes) has been an indispensable component of the explosion in 'nonprofessional' composition.

Significantly, in the Memorex commercial we encounter music in the studio, ostensibly the site of its production. But consider again the drama that unfolds there. The primary reason Chuck Mangione appears in the ad is that he and his music are recognizable. They are recognizable – and therefore commercially valuable – because of the 'plugging' mechanism made possible by the impact of recording on musical performance. Mangione's very presence then derives from the location in which we find him. What is more important, though, is that by joining the two acoustic spaces I have delineated, the ad fuses our *recognition* of Mangione's 'hit' with a representation of the moment of its original inscription. What could be reduced here to an instance of mere temporal deception can be more fruitfully read as an indication of the radical priority of reception. The ad does not merely record a moment of musical production: it registers the social construction of music. To clarify this we need to re-enter Fitzgerald's dilemma.

When we join her she has just witnessed a 'take'. Together we are then confronted with another performance of Mangione's piece. This is a test. We have to remember what the performance our eyes told us was 'live' sounded like and compare that with what subsequently comes over the playback monitors for fidelity. Who or what controls Fitzgerald's memory and, therefore, her access to the telling difference in musical listening? Clearly it is the recording facility itself, since she is represented as never having heard Mangione's piece except as it has been mediated by the recording apparatus. But what has happened to those of us who took up the invitation to share her dilemma? I believe we end up baffling ourselves. The ad presents us with the fact that even a Black musician, who in our culture is still deemed genetically (rather than culturally) rooted in music, cannot tell the difference between a sound and its reproduction. But we screen ourselves from a recognition of the electronic colonization of listening by cynically consuming the *spectacle* of our fetishized listener's failure. In short, following Fitzgerald's example, we resort to listening with our eyes and reducing the qualitative significance of musical expression to the technical perfection of its reproduction. Put more emphatically, the baffle that protects us from having to acknowledge our 'loss of hearing' becomes a concrete visual (Baudelaire might have said 'synaesthetic') supplement to listening. As such, the scandal of contemporary hi-fidelity is not that one cannot actually hear it, but that we persist in regarding the perfection of listening as essentially beyond all forms of social determination.

If recording organizes the experience of reception by conditioning its present scale and establishing its qualitative norms for musicians and listeners alike, then the conditions of reception actually *precede* the moment of production. It is not, therefore, sufficient merely to state that *considerations* of reception influence musical production and thus deserve attention in musical analysis. Rather, the social analysis of musical experience has to take account of the radical priority of reception, and thus it must shift its focus away from a notion of agency that, by privileging the moment of production, preserves the autonomy of the subject. My argument, therefore, develops on the basis of two complementary assertions: (1) that individuals are made up of the society their associations produce and (2) that human subjectivity, as a general structure of experience, is socially engendered. The Memorex ad can serve as a convenient point of reference to highlight the problems that subjectivity raises when its authority is no longer taken for granted.

In the ad Fitzgerald is not shown hearing; she is shown listening, that is, paying a particular sort of attention to the performance of Mangione's 'hit'. What distinguishes her attention from mere hearing is its interpretive character – she is trying to make sense of what she hears. Barthes and Havas, in their essay entitled 'Listening', argue that it is precisely in the activity of interpretation that what distinguishes the 'human' from the 'animal' arises within the auditory realm.[4] It is certainly fair to say then that Fitzgerald recognizes herself as a human subject as she listens. But I can be more specific than that. Meanings not only occur to her, but her identity as a listener arises where these meanings occur. During the televised test Fitzgerald is listening to one set of sounds (a recording) while trying to remember another (a performance). As such, a human faculty, memory, is being solicited and delimited within the commercial. Significantly, at the very point where Fitzgerald's memory is shown to lack sufficient discriminating power, its proper functioning is at once defined (the flawless retrieval of an origin) and taken into custody by a facility upon which she, as a recording star, is obliged to rely for proper self-recognition. What is at stake here is less a particular memory than memory as such, since the commercial organizes her acts of listening around the philosophically charged abstractions of recollection and knowledge. That the commercial produces an experience of a faculty around which the subject organizes him- or herself – an experience which includes a specific technical and therefore social mediation – indicates how deeply experience is organized by the social process.

There is one last feature of the commercial's presentation of the structure of listening that requires elaboration: the conspicuous subordination of listening to looking that coincides with the subjugation of perception by the King of Memory. The Memorex Corporation has to find a way to manage the following problem: if Memorex is as good as it is claimed to be, then what good is the original? The original becomes necessary and therefore valuable solely as a means of notarizing the copy. However, if listening cannot be trusted to differentiate between the original and the copy, how are we to perceive the validity of the original's notarization of the copy since the aural original might always already be the copy from which it can no longer be aurally differentiated? This difficulty is resolved in the ad by invoking the priority of looking. Fitzgerald knows that the first time she listened she was listening to the original performance because she watched it. The television audience knows that

Memorex can replace the original, not because they heard it – that would have been impossible given the actual listening conditions – but because they saw that their representative could not tell the difference. The commercial's producers were in no danger of compromising themselves here because the ad is merely consolidating a social experience of the hierarchy of senses that came into being with the hegemony of typographic culture and that continues to ground the modern subject. That is, since the seventeenth century sight has acquired ever more primacy over hearing in the West.[5] The commercial addresses us as though we were subjects who should recognize ourselves in this hierarchy of senses. In recognizing ourselves as the addressees of the ad, we implicitly affirm that we must be the ones whose aural memories have come to rely on a prosthesis that can be seen but not heard.

Despite my declared aims, I have not really addressed the fact that Fitzgerald and the television audience are listening to a piece of music. It is thus time to remedy this. What I have stressed is that music, as an organization of noise or sound, arises within the structure of listening I have outlined. Music's social significance derives from the role it plays in the stabilization of this structure, that is, how it articulates and consolidates structurally necessary practices of listening. By sanctioning specific technical mediations of listening as subjectively normative, musical reception supplies the social order sponsoring such mediations with an experiential confirmation. There is therefore a political issue here which I have yet to pose adequately: an issue having to do with the concrete character of the social order that stands confirmed within the contemporary structure of listening. This will be easier to do once the proper context has been established. Most immediately then, music needs to be characterized in a manner that enables us to understand how it can meet these rather general social demands while at the same time providing in its texture the details that occasion listening pleasure. Such a characterization is provided in Jacques Attali's *Noise: the political economy of music,* where he writes, 'All music, any organization of sounds, is then a tool for the creation or consolidation of a community, of a totality.'[6] While this formulation clarifies the tremendous theoretical importance given to music by Attali, it does not clarify the way in which it belongs within the context I have established for it. We still need to know why the structure of listening evoked by the Memorex Corporation was organized around a piece of music rather than a fragment of ambient noise no less 'live' than Mangione's 'hit'.

Bits and Pieces

At the first New Music America Festival sponsored by The Kitchen in 1979, British composer Brian Eno gave a lecture on the topic, 'The studio as compositional tool'.[7] Aside from his fascinating remarks about the effects of recording on music listening and composing, the general question examined by Eno indicated the extent to which certain of Adorno's concerns were justified. The recording studio had become an instrument with its own peculiar musical idiom – an instrument that was also its own means of reproduction. As a consequence, repetition and the precondition for 'plugging' had advanced to the point of entering the musical material itself. For example, tape 'loops' in Eno's own work have come to be used for establishing everything from rhythm to chromatic texture, and while he did not refer to the practice of 'playing' or 'scratching' records characteristic of rap music, he could have. In most of his late discussions of 'new music', Adorno criticized this type of development from an uncharacteristically romantic position: one that exempted the opposition between conception and realization from the otherwise obligatory compositional demands for total musical integration.[8] As long as aura held out the promise of the mind's autonomy, Adorno was prepared to support it, even when doing so committed him to essentialist musical fantasies. What remains undecidable and therefore decisive is whether the developments cited by Eno are the consummation of the regressive tendencies identified by Adorno, or precisely the developments whose theoretical articulation enable us to understand that the technical penetration of music is a necessary development in the present effort to formulate a critical theory of society.

During the 1970s, the Sony Corporation introduced the Walkman cassette tape player. This device offers maximally portable hi-fidelity to listeners who are, through its use, radically reindividuated while they collectively recontextualize 'masterpieces' as (among other things) the sound-tracks for health routines. In effect, everything that Benjamin had defined as the revolutionary features of mechanically reproduced art is, if not contradicted, at least neutralized by the Walkman. The same might be said about television which is a device closer to the cinematic apparatus. It is nonetheless difficult to conclude that these historical developments entitle one to regard the technologies of mass culture as constitutive of fascistic subjectivity. On the contrary, our ability to theorize this possibility despite the hegemony of mass culture, underscores an aspect of the cultural tradition, *qua* tradition, that Benjamin's historical situation authorized him to set aside.

Taken together, the Walkman and the recording of the recording studio mark developments which in effect confirm the apparently antinomous diagnoses of Adorno and Benjamin by embodying the victory of what each of them opposed in the other. That is, these developments represent simultaneously the appropriation of 'serious' music by the technology of mass culture feared by Adorno and the political co-optation of the social possibilities embedded in our relation to that technology feared by Benjamin. This might suggest, in accordance with a certain dialectical perversity, that the theoretical recognition of the decay of aura – assumed by both writers – arises only once this decay is being reversed. The role of critical theory in this reversal deserves to be elaborated in accord with the reversal's dialectical character – a task far too ambitious to be attempted here. Nonetheless, critical theory should not avoid the task of attempting to articulate the conditions of the restoration of aura, even if it can be demonstrated that doing so involves a conflict of interest. If, as I have implied, aura returns through the systematization of the fragment, it is because its restoration presupposes the shift from mechanical to electronic reproduction.

The social character of the shift to electronic reproduction has been most rigorously addressed by Oskar Negt and Alexander Kluge in their *Öffentlichkeit und Erfahrung*.[9] In a provocative discussion of the change in the character of the traditional media wrought by the advent of electromagnetic technologies, they show how our daily-life contexts have become the objects of the media conglomerate, an institutional feature of contemporary capitalism. Their argument draws directly upon the Marxian notion that the way in which human beings associate for the purpose of transforming nature into that which satisfies their needs also serves as the organizing matrix for the human production of expressive forms. The media represent specific historical instances of the production and reproduction of expressive forms. As such, they can be correlated with various structural features of the prevalent mode of production that serves as the context for the cultural reproduction of human subjectivity. Towards the end of Marx's introduction to the *Grundrisse*,[10] for example, he argued that the expressive form of oral epic poetry is grounded in the level of control over nature attained by the Greeks. He stressed that the mythological deities central to the epic would lose their phantasmatic power in a world where subjects could fully harness natural forces. In the traditional media, which emerge in conjunction with the industrial harnessing of nature (examples being radio, photography, and cinema), subjects are predisposed towards a particular mode of cultural reception through their exposure to the segmentation and hierarchization of specific sensory tasks that characterized the mode of production within high capitalism. In the new media, which belong to the 'post-industrial' era, the practice of sensory reintegration (exemplified in the supervisory labor of the systems analyst) predisposes subjectivity towards the hegemonic mode of cultural reception. Computer-assisted video art is a good example of a medium that arises within the mode of production characteristic of this era. A dynamic correlation can thus be established between the structural organization of the institutions of media production and the sensory division of labor presupposed and reproduced by the products of these institutions.

For Negt and Kluge this represents a qualitatively new organization of the relationship between cultural production and reception, not merely at the level of structural complexity but at the level of lived experience itself. They argue that the as-yet-unmet and even unimagined needs of subjects are capable of being organized by the solicitations of the 'consciousness industry' to such an extent that what was typically defended by the protest of 'technological determinism' is reduced to the status of a collector's item. In short, they identify as a distinctive element of post-industrial capitalism the fact that it has become impossible to separate the subject from the technologies of cultural reception. Any political critique of capitalist culture that has recourse to a non-integrated subject as the agent of social change fails to engage its object. This is not, however, a recipe for political resignation. Negt and Kluge simply insist upon locating the contradictions of experience capable of holding a political charge in the only nature we have left – culture.

Negt's and Kluge's observations concerning the correlation between the division of sensory labor within production and cultural reception invite us to reconsider the contested opposition between contemplation and distraction. Put simply, their conclusions imply that this opposition is a feature of a hierarchy of senses that has been superceded. To argue, as Adorno and Benjamin did, that distraction in looking (at silent film) was progressive while distraction in listening (to 'modern' music) was regressive, belies a commitment to a division among the senses, where what is actually at stake is the sensory and cognitive order of the revolutionary subject itself. If what characterizes the subject today is the reintegration of its senses in the cultural domain, it is perhaps just as fruitless to retain the notion of 'hierarchy' as it is to map organs and faculties onto the opposition between contemplation and distraction. Since the name for aura arose within a reception context dominated by what Negt and Kluge call the 'traditional mass media' and was therefore fastened to the moment of aura's decay, its restoration implies that the question of aura must always be posed anew, even if the question means something different each time. But in what sense can it be said that aura has been restored? My response will take the form of an elaboration of the cultural and political implications of Negt's and Kluge's remarks as they bear on the status of the contemporary fragment.

Consider the most advanced form of the fragment, the bit or binary digit. It is the fundamental organizing structure of electronic information, and it is as indispensable to the surveillance mechanisms of the South African state as it is to the state-of-the-art digital recording techniques and 'simulcast' technologies that flourish in the 'advanced' countries. The bit is structured like a language. It is a doubly articulated sign that acquires its significance or value from within a matrix of differentiated values forming a synchronic system. In the categories of information theory, the bit may be said to represent the maximal rationalization of the noise/information polarity. The severely rationalized structure of the contemporary fragment facilitates the multiplication and inter-referencing of information systems. There is then a sense in which the bit is the monad come true. The most recent application of bit-centered technology in the domain of music listening, the compact disc player, promises not only to supercede the claims of reproductive fidelity made by Memorex, but to integrate, at the level of a technological continuum, the modes of production, reproduction and reception. When CD libraries match LP libraries, more of the world's music – both quantitatively and qualitatively – will be available for listening than at any other time in history. At that point the contrast between what is 'live' and what is Memorex will be irrelevant. The frayed fabric of tradition will be rewoven with optical fibers and the conditions for auratic reception will be restored.

The problematic aspects of this development are not difficult to enumerate since they are already making themselves felt. The ritual character of auratic art manifests itself in the triumphant cult of technology.[11] Simultaneously, the intellectual atmosphere created by this cult has redefined the role of tradition in the administration of cultural interpretation. On the one hand, tradition is now called upon to assure individual interpreters that the meaning they are incapable of assigning to their experience is in fact an accurate reflection of the general meaninglessness of culture. And on the other hand, tradition is invoked to reinforce the pluralistic constraint of repressive tolerance: any meaning an individual assigns to experience is valid provided it immediately renounces all claims of generality. Critical theory responded to these developments by converting the renunciation of generality into a stylistic principle – hence the fascination of Adorno, Benjamin and Horkheimer with the essay and the aphorism. This transformation of critical theory into a vanguard literary practice did not, however, protect it from the developments it sought to elude. The demise of critical theory as a vanguard discourse nonetheless allows one to perceive the possibility of a new collective cultural practice. If Marx could regard the proletariat as a concrete manifestation of theory, then perhaps contemporary music can be seen as a gateway to the new collectivity, since it situates subjects within an emergent structure of listening which offers experiential confirmation of a social configuration.

In closing I will turn once again to Attali's remarkable book. Early in the chapter entitled 'Listening', while sketching the parameters of his project, he argues that it is 'necessary to imagine radically new theoretical forms, in order to speak new realities. Music, the organization of noise, is one such form.'[12] If we connect this citation to the earlier one in which Attali linked music and community, then it is possible to articulate why music emerges as a decisive cultural practice in the social order of the bit.

Electronically reproduced art has radicalized noise by seeking to eliminate it. Standard cassette players and stereo receivers contain the various Dolby formats for noise reduction which operate according to a systematic logic that produces information out of suppressed noise. There are two levels of production here. Musical information is produced out of noise that can be rendered informative through various strategies of signal enhancement – redundancy, for example. And noise, as a *category* of sound, is produced (though at a different level) by what is made to differ from it, namely, information. As a consequence, noise arises everywhere information is produced. With the increasing cultural hegemony of bit-oriented systems, noise even functions to name that which stands opposed to the information system as a whole. The political character of this development is reflected in the history of contemporary music where the fetish of noise reduction has gone hand in hand with the aggressive marketing of distortion boosters and other less obvious instrumental sources of noise. In a reception context increasingly dominated by the media conglomerates, noise is thus proliferated only to be recaptured and channelled in a manner that allows the industry to profit from it. However, this does not result in total control for the industry, because it is operating within a mode of production that continually produces new needs while failing to satisfy those it is ostensibly attempting to meet. This general dynamic has its structural basis in the binary fragment. The 'post-industrial' mode of production, in its effort to convert our life-contexts into usable information, seeks to extend the domain organized by bit-centered technologies. However, just as the production of needs always exceeds the capacity of the mode of production, the production of information always proliferates noise which exceeds the organizing capacity of the bit-centered system. As a collective organization of noise, contemporary music (classical and popular alike) is profoundly marked by this situation. The generality of the impact on music is due to the fact that the production and reception of all music is mediated by the same reproductive technologies. However much two listeners may differ in their tastes, they are likely to share standards of hi-fidelity. Even so, it is certainly the case that only specific producers and consumers of music act so as to realize the critical potential of the emerging structure of listening. It is striking though that those who *do,* typically see themselves as 'cross-overs' (that is, as members of several of the various communities of performers and listeners).

What characterizes the work of those musicians radicalized by their relation to bit-oriented reproductive technologies is the effort to raise the technical preconditions of their musical material to the level of cultural expression. That is to say, they struggle to make audible the noise/information polarity that both grounds contemporary listening and undermines its present boundaries. When Laurie Anderson played the Orpheum Theater in Minneapolis, she opened her show with an opaque projection of a digital representation of the very lyrics she would soon 'sing' through the Vocoder (a computerized voice synthesizer). Anderson's work, which is only one example among many, can be understood as an attempt to communicate or socialize the general material character of the contemporary mode of reproduction. To the extent that the material character of reproduction currently rests on the boundless noise/ information opposition, the effort to socialize it gives socio-political significance to all those musics that have hitherto been listened to as noise. These musics stand forth now as the costs of the canons.

If, as I have argued earlier, subjectivity is engendered within the social process, then there are clear implications for subjects in what has been said here concerning the forms of community that circulate in contemporary music. In analyzing the Memorex Corporation's solicitation of the faculty of memory, I noted that the delimitation of this faculty went hand in hand with a structuring of subjectivity that subordinated the sense of hearing to the sense of seeing. This subordination of hearing permitted the social mediations of listening to become part of the very structure of the competent listener. The structure of listening that arises with contemporary music cannot center itself on a subject ordered by the sensing hierarchy that emerged with the art of memory embodied in printing. This is because the classical subject, whose limits had precise internal and external coordinates, came into being through cultural experiences (like reading to oneself) that have been overrun by the institutional practices and technologies of the current modes of cultural reproduction.

The bit as contemporary fragment relocates the limits of the subject in two decisive ways. Because it is fundamental to a cultural technology that can be used to communicate the material preconditions of reproduction, the bit orientates subjectivity towards what, in this case, makes the experience of listening possible. The form of community that arises within this experience situates the subjects it comprises at their very limits, that is, at the very points where the institutions and practices that precede them give them shape. Second, because the logic of the bit indicates that the system of information can condition but not determine its outside, the subject that arises under its influence stands within a potentially multicultural field where it is exposed to 'others' who are not the convenient foils of the classical subject. Even if we acknowledge, as we must, that the social order circulated within music performed under the regime of the bit bears a corporate imprint, we need not conclude that this condemns music to a conservative political role, for to do so would be to ignore the specificity of the current mode of reproduction. Since our reception of music cannot escape the institutions and technologies that mediate it, the collectivity which Attali insists takes form within music must then articulate the peculiar logic of the bit – a logic which forces this collectivity into a relation with its technical preconditions and the experiences that necessarily elude it. The subjects that are engendered under these conditions are themselves informed by this double relation: they listen most closely to the noises they do not recognize. Because music takes us in these unheard-of directions it can be understood to function as a cultural practice whose oppositional character derives from its ability to engender subjects who are predisposed towards others. Music's critique of society takes the post-theoretical form of a symbolically constructed collectivity. Here the estrangement and totalization we associate with theoretical discourse return as the social experience of cultural production. At a time when the aestheticization of theory is becoming increasingly prevalent, music has responded by sensualizing cultural politics. I am not sure it is possible to have greater social significance than that.

The structure of listening that confirmed the primacy of looking is in decline, as the Memorex Corporation inadvertently illustrated. What our new organization of memory and its accompanying sensory apparatus will feel like is difficult to define, but is prefigured in Reik's notion of the 'third ear', inspired by Freud, who thought a great deal about memory while listening to others. Rather than an organ, it was a location where listening took place, registering what the speaker had forgotten. In psychoanalysis, what is forgotten gives the speaker his or her identity; as Freud said, 'Where it was, I shall become.'[13] Because the syntax of this formulation evokes so strongly the logic of the bit-centered mode of production, it strikes me as a particularly suggestive way to imagine the emerging experience of listening. Music permits us to experience this form of listening through 'ears' that feel more like tangled resonating bodies than the folds of flesh situated on both sides of the head. If I have likened listening to festive dancing, it is because what is crucially new about contemporary listening is its irreducibly communal character. What joins festive dancing to the psychoanalytic notion of the third ear is the fact that the experience of collective interdependence is precisely what was forgotten by the classical subject.

The memory that will form through the new experience of listening may well enable us to grasp its ongoing relation to the moments of danger described by Benjamin in his 'Theses on the philosophy of history'.[14] What threatened memory, according to Benjamin, was the fact that the tradition resulting from its gathering necessarily put memory at the disposal of the ruling classes. In Benjamin's hands, historical materialism was thus forced to confront the fact that the future would be under the control of those who could edit the past. Missing from this discussion of historical materialism, however, was an adequate reflection on the role of the medium of cultural memory in the constitution of historical subjects. What I have argued here is that contemporary music, as an embodiment of memory structured by the bit-centered matrix, obliges memory to register its relation with precisely what threatens it: the material conditions of its communication. However much tradition may endanger memory, if the socially organized inscription of memory preserves the problematic character of its present institutionalization, then subjects may form who expect a different future. The memory produced in this context deserves to be called 'popular' as does the music that organizes it. The problem today, in the era of music's electronic reproduction, is not, as Foucault suggests, that we have failed to decapitate the King of Memory, but that in desiring to do so we continue to locate memory in our heads.[15] The continued politicization of music will involve recognizing that the memory it organizes is no longer contained in the minds of autonomous subjects and that, in fact (to paraphrase Freud), we may be becoming who we will be where it is going.

Notes

1.   The test organizing the Memorex commercial strongly evokes the 'blindfold test' that has been a feature in the monthly music magazine *Downbeat* for decades. Used as a forum for critical exchange, the 'blindfold test' pits a recognized musician against a record whose jacket has been kept hidden. The featured musician listens to the record and is then asked to

identify the performers while commenting on their performances. Crucial to one's performance in the test is the ability to remember someone's 'sound'. Beyond the fact that musical reproduction is central to this test, it is important to stress that musical recognition is again situated here within the opposition between looking and listening.

2.   Prior to the advertisement featuring Ella Fitzgerald and Chuck Mangione, Memorex ran a commercial that featured Fitzgerald and Melissa Manchester. Two fundamental differences characterized the earlier example. First, the generational scheme was reversed: Manchester listened to two versions of a performance by Fitzgerald. Second, the race and gender of the 'original' were respectively transformed and reversed: a white woman listened to a black woman. While the reversal of the generational scheme in the second commercial introduced the appropriate but unorthodox theme of an inverted temporality (the younger man coming before the older woman), its recoding of the 'original' invoked a tradition begun in the recording industry by RCA Victor's slogan, 'His Master's Voice'.

3.   I am thinking here, first, of the relatively common recording practice of splicing different takes together to assemble the 'right' performance, where repetition establishes the very texture of the recorded surface; and second of the well-known temporal restraints that organize composition around the anticipated strictures of the radio 'plugging' format.

4.   Roland Barthes and Roland Havas. 'Listening'. *The responsibility of forms,* trans. Richard Howard (New York. 1985), pp. 245–60.

5.   Donald Lowe, *The history of bourgeois perception* (Chicago, 1982), chapter 6. There is also an important summary of the issues at stake here in the introductory chapter.

6.   Jacques Attali, *Noise: the political economy of music,* trans. Brian Massumi (Minneapolis, 1985), p. 6. The entire chapter entitled 'Repeating' is worth consulting if one is interested in another analysis of the issue I am examining in this paper.

7.   Brian Eno, *Downbeat* (July, 1983), pp. 56–57 and (August, 1983), pp. 50–52.

8.   Adorno discusses this problem even in the 1930s. See 'On the social situation of music', trans. Wesley Blomster, *Telos,* 35 (Spring, 1978), pp. 124–38. Two examples of his later writing specifically devoted to the problems of technology and technique in the new music are, 'Music and technique', trans. Wesley Blomster, *Telos,* 32 (Winter, 1977), pp. 78–94, and 'Music and new music; in memory of Peter Suhrkamp', trans, Wesley Blomster, *Telos,* 43 (Spring, 1980), pp. 124–38.

9.   An English translation of this important work is forthcoming from the University of Minnesota Press. To date only one chapter has appeared in English, See Oskar Negt and Alexander Kluge, 'The context of lift as object of production of media conglomerates', *Media, Culture and Society,* 5 (1981), pp. 65–74.

10.   Karl Marx, *Grundrisse,* trans, Martin Nicotaus (New York, 1973), p. 110.

11.   Jürgen Habermas, 'Technology and science as "ideology"', *Toward a rational society,* trans. Jeremy Shapiro (Boston, 1970), pp. 81–122.

12.   Attali, *Noise,* p. 4.

13.   Sigmund Freud, 'Dissection of the personality', *New introductory lectures,* trans. James Strachey (New York, 1965), p. 80.

14.   Walter Benjamin, 'Theses on the philosophy of history', *Illuminations,* p. 255.

15.   Michel Foucault, 'Truth and power', *Power/knowledge; selected interviews and other writings 1972–1977,* ed. Colin Gordon, trans. Colin Gordon, *et al.* (New York, 1980), p. 121.

Chapter 20

Rick Altman

FOUR AND A HALF FILM FALLACIES

LOGICALLY, EVERY THEORY OF CINEMA should address the problem of film sound. Practically speaking, such has hardly been the case. On the contrary, a surprising number of theoreticians blithely draw conclusions about the nature of cinema simply by extrapolating from the apparent properties of the moving image. If this were just a question of oversight, the problem would be rapidly corrected. In fact, the theoreticians who overlook sound usually do quite self-consciously, proposing what they consider strong arguments in favour of an image-based notion of cinema. Indeed, some of these arguments have reached the level of truisms, uninterrogated assumptions on which the entire field is based. In the pages that follow, I propose to reopen the cases of these arguments, cross-examining the very assumptions that have guided cinema theory over the years.

The Historical Fallacy

The late twenties' worldwide conversion to synchronized sound was received by many film-makers as an affront (Clair, Eisenstein, and Pudovkin, among others). Intent on exacting satisfaction, they found a clever method of disenfranchising the offending sound track. Cinema was cinema before the sound track was added, they said, so sound cannot be a fundamental component of the cinematic experience. Historically, sound is an add-on, an afterthought, and thus of secondary importance.

Ironically, it is precisely because of insufficient historical knowledge and reflection that these avengers err. As a purely historical argument, the notion of sound-as-afterthought cannot stand careful scrutiny. Apparently convinced that "silent" film had always conformed to the mid-twenties model of standardized organ or orchestral accompaniment, sound's critics set up an all-or-nothing opposition that has been perpetuated by generations of critics. On one side an ethereal cinema of silence, punctuated only by carefully chosen music; on the other side, the talkies, with their incessant, anti-poetic dialogue. Too heavily dependent on the practice of the twenties, this is an unacceptable assessment of the first thirty years of cinema history.

Here, for example, is a pop quiz that is not likely to be passed by sound's detractors. In what year did the following editorial appear? "In our opinion the singing and talking moving picture is bound sooner or later to become a permanent feature of the moving picture theater." 1926? 1927? 1928? Wrong by a wide margin. This 1910 *Moving Picture World* editorial came at the height of sound film's expansion. Cameraphone, Chronophone, Cinephone and dozens of other competing systems were not only invented in this period; during the end of the century's first decade they were installed in hundreds of theaters across Europe and from coast to coast in the United States. Their competition came, by the way, not from silent films, with or without musical accompaniment, but from road shows with extremely sophisticated and carefully synchronized effects (a technique originated by Lyman Howe), and from the many "wheels" (vaudevillelike circuits) of human-voice-behind-the-screen companies, with colorful names like Humanovo, Actologue, Humanophone, Humano-scope, Natural Voice Talking Pictures, Ta-Mo-Pic, and Dram-o-tone. In short, the world did not wait until *Don Juan* and *The Jazz Singer* to discover the entertainment (and financial) value of synchronized sound. From a purely historical point of view, the notion that sound is a Johnny-come-lately add-on to a thirty-year-old silent medium simply will not stand.

Even if the historical information had been correct, however, the claims of sound's early critics would still have been fallacious. Though their appeal is apparently to history, these unconditional lovers of "silent" cinema actually close themselves off from history, refusing to recognize that the identity and form of the media are in no sense fixed. Why do we identify the human appendix as vestigial? Because we recognize that it is possible for evolution to redefine the structure and even the nature of the human body. How can we tell when one system has given way to another? This we can do only by analyzing the functioning of the system. The fact that one element appeared before or after another carries no weight in this evaluation. At stake here is the very ability to take into account historical change in theoretical arguments. It is regularly assumed that a single term (like cinema) covers a single object. If our theories are to become sufficiently sensitive to historical concerns, we must abandon that assumption, recognizing instead that historical development regularly occurs within an apparently single object, thus often hiding under a single name two or more historically distinct objects. In other words, even if silent film were the object that sound's detractors claim, the sound-as-afterthought argument would still not hold up. Cinema changes, and the action of sound is one of the prime reasons for that change.

The Ontological Fallacy

Though they continue to influence cinema studies, historical fallacy arguments were especially popular among the filmmakers of the late twenties and early thirties. Later in the thirties, a new argument appeared in the writings of such influential critics as Rudolf Arnheim and Bela Balazs. Eschewing historical arguments, they make the formal case that the image without sound still constitutes cinema, while sound without an image is no longer cinema. Clearly assuming that cinema is a firm, unchanging category, immune to history, these critics present their arguments as logical and permanent. Indeed, so strong is the apparent appeal of this ontological claim that it regularly reappears in the writings of current theoreticians.

Two primary considerations undermine the ontological argument. The first is a practical concern relating to the way in which ontological critics use their claims. Like the historical case, the ontological argument seeks to disenfranchise sound, to prove that sound has (or should have) little effect on overall film structure. Even if we were to accept the notion that film is a fundamentally image-oriented medium, this conclusion begs the larger question of the relationship between ontology and structure. May we affirm with confidence that an object's structure can be predicted from its nature? The answer to this question depends on the way in which we construe the term "nature." If nature is defined through structure, that is, if all claims about the nature of a class of objects are derived from analysis of the structures characteristic of the objects, then we can treat nature as predictive of structure. But this is precisely what sound's ontological critics do not do. On the contrary, they base their claims about cinema on a single surface aspect rather than on a careful inspection of the structure of actual films and the system that produces them. Indeed, the acerbic vocabulary and prescriptive exhortations of these critics suggests that they are more interested in influencing the structure of future films than they are in analyzing the structure of existing ones.

What about the truth value of ontological critics' claims? The problem with these apparently rock solid claims, I would suggest, is that they are actually built on sand. Presented as absolute and unchanging, appeals to the nature of cinema appear to be independent of history. In spite of appearances, however, the evidence actually offered is all historically specific. To say that a particular configuration would not be recognized as cinema, while another would, is to affirm that *in the present conditions* these conclusions would be reached. Present conditions, though, have to do with the way in which a given configuration has been used, and not with some transhistoric category. The ontological argument, it turns out, is only falsely ontological.

Even in the absence of a properly ontological argument, however, the historical claim would remain: cinema has indeed been exploited as a visual medium, to the point where audiences identify the medium with the image rather than the sound. To the extent that it represents a carefully documented historical argument, this position has a certain amount of merit (however unontological it may be). Even when the ontological argument is reduced to its historical evidence, however, hesitations must still remain. For the historical circumstances assumed by ontological critics have not always obtained. During the many periods when cinema was heavily marked by its relation to the music industry, for example, music accompanied by a blank screen has regularly been recognized as cinema: the long overtures to the early Vitaphone sound-on-disk features, the introduction of a film's theme song before the images or its continuation after the post-credits (as in *Nashville*), and the use of a totally black screen in recent music videos. These examples hardly prove that cinema is regularly taken as a sound-based medium, but they do suggest the *historical* possibilities of cinema as an audio-visual medium, in which sound-oriented proclivities regularly confront image-based tendencies, thus producing a varied history belying claims of a solely image-oriented ontology.

Since first pointing out the ontological fallacy in *Cinema / Sound,* I have become aware of an even more problematic appeal to ontology in the study of sound. Surprisingly, this dependency on ontological arguments comes not from the enemies of sound, but from its greatest defenders. In their celebrated book on *Composing for the Films,* Theodor Adorno and Hanns Eisler attribute to hearing a privileged relation to pre-individualistic collective times; music thus has a pre-capitalistic nature, being more direct and more closely connected to the unconscious. While their other arguments are by and large well attuned to historical differences, this approach to hearing and sound edges dangerously close to an ontological claim, apparently capable of predicting sound's nature in any given situation, but actually able only to locate sound's action in certain past situations.

A similar danger lurks in the work of Mary Ann Doane, Kaja Silverman, Michel Chion, Claudia Gorbman, and other critics who have leaned heavily on the psychoanalytic theories of Guy Rosolato and Didier Anzieu, who characterize the voice as archaic, based on the notion that we hear the soothing voice of the mother from the womb long before we are able to see. It is not surprising that such a transhistoric proposal, apparently predictive of sound's role in any situation whatsoever, should lead to such conclusions as Doane's claim that "the aural illusion of position constructed by the very approximation of sound perspective and by techniques which spatialize the voice and endow it with 'presence' *guarantees* the singularity and stability of a point of audition, *thus* holding at bay the potential trauma of dispersal, dismemberment, difference" (Doane 1980, 171; my emphasis). Yet we know from actual listening that very few films construct an approximation of sound perspective. Can it then be said that "the subordination of the voice to the screen as the site of the spectacle's unfolding makes vision and hearing work together in manufacturing the 'hallucination' of a fully sensory world"? (Doane 1980, 171) The problem here is that an apparently ontological claim about the role of sound has been allowed to take precedence over actual analysis of sound's functioning. (In my article "Sound Space," later in this volume [see original publication], I suggest a different approach to the same question, based not on an assumption of unity and concordance, but on a perceived conflict between sound scale and image scale.) While it would be unreasonable to cut short speculation on the sources of sound's attraction, it is essential that such speculation not be taken as a prescription, as a binding assumption about the way sound must work in all cases. If we are fully to restore a sense of sound's role in creating our sense of the body, we must depend on historically grounded claims and on close analyses of particular films rather than on ontological speculations that presume to cover all possible practices.

The Reproductive Fallacy

In spite of the fact that, as a storage medium, sound recording lags behind the image by tens of thousands of years, recorded sound has from its very beginnings held a great fascination for critics. Whereas the image, however carefully rendered, clearly reduces a three-dimensional original to two dimensions, sound appears to reproduce the original faithfully, in its full three-dimensionality. By no means limited to early admirers of the newfangled technology, this position was until recently held by a majority of sound critics (many of whose pronouncements are quoted at the beginning of Jim Lastra's article, below [see original publication]). By and large, critics remain convinced that sound is literally *reproduced* by a high quality recording and playback system, in spite of Alan Williams' demonstration of the contrary in his *Cinema/Sound* article ("Is Sound Recording Like a Language?").

Sound, it is worth recalling, cannot be construed independently of the volume of air (or other medium) in which it is heard. Typically, we notate sound (through writing or musical notation) as if sounds were ideal entities. But volume, frequency, and timbre cannot exist independently of several material factors which preclude reproduction as such. To be sure, in some sense a G# is a G#, whether it is played at home or on stage, but that does not make the two sounds identical. By restricting our description of sounds to familiar musical terminology, we have bamboozled ourselves into believing that sound itself is restricted to those characteristics. Does the G# have a slow attack? a long decay? an echo? reverberation? Does it bounce around like a superball in a hollow cavity? Or does it rapidly lose its force, like a beanbag hitting a pillow? If all we want to know about a sound is that it was a G#, then all G#s are the same, but if we care about the material differences between two sounds, and the spatial configurations that cause them, then we must recognize that no recording can possibly reproduce an original sound.

Recordings do not reproduce sound, they represent sound. According to the choice of recording location, microphone type, recording system, postproduction manipulation, storage medium, playback arrangement, and playback locations, each recording proposes an interpretation of the original sound. To be sure, one of the common strategies involved in this process is an attempt to convince the audience that they are listening not to a representation but to a reproduction. We must not, however, be taken in by advertisements for "high fidelity" sound. The notion of "fidelity" is not a measure of success in reproduction, but a way of assessing a recording's adherence to a set of evolving conventions, like the parallel standards established for such culturally important qualities as "realism," "morality," or "beauty." The concept of fidelity is thus a strange hybrid of engineers' aspirations and ideology, serving to mask recording's representational nature.

Considered as a reproduction, recording seems to fall under the aegis of technology and engineering. Construed as a representation, however, sound inherits the double mantle of art. Simultaneously capable of misrepresentation and of artistically using all the possibilities of representation, sound thus recovers some of the fascination lost to its reputation as handmaiden of the image. Indeed, it is recording's very ability to manipulate sound that makes it so amply worthy of our interest.

The Nominalist Fallacy

In order to show that recording cannot possibly reproduce the original sound, critics (Williams, Levin, Altman) have regularly made the following points: (1) sound exists as pressure within a volume; (2) it is impossible to collect all the sound of a particular performance, since it disperses differently into the various parts of the theater or other surrounding space; (3) even at a live performance, different spectators hear different sounds, depending on where they are seated and which way they and the performers are turned; (4) sound systems always enforce a particular set of values in selecting microphone type and location, frequency response, volume levels, and many other recording and playback characteristics; (5) playback involves the same set of differences and choices involved in recording.

Within this apparently coherent argument lurks a potential danger. Stressing the material nature of sound in order to counter fundamentally idealist assumptions, this approach fragments sound to the point where the emission of a single sound apparently gives rise to the perception of a multiplicity of different sounds. By concentrating on the differences between the sound as heard in the orchestra and the "same" sound as heard from the balcony, this argument has rendered the important service of sensitizing critics to the materiality, complexity, and context-based nature of sound. At the same time, however, these defenses against the reproductive fallacy have failed to address the problem of the communicative language used by auditors having heard the "same" sound to overcome the fact that they actually perceived physically different sounds.

This is an old problem, closely identified with the weaning of philosophy from theology in the latter part of the Middle Ages. When I pick up two different rocks and call them "rocks," what is the status of the name that I attribute to them? Is the name itself real? Or is the name just a convenient label? To put it another way, is the shared category to be understood as actually existing, or are the objects themselves the only things that exist? Is there such a thing as the category "rock," or are there only objects, on which for the sake of convenience we confer names (such as "rock") which have no existence independent of the objects they represent? The traditional position, usually identified with Plato and Augustine, is termed "realism," because it takes the general category as real; the radical position, championed by William of Ockham and generally thought to have been instrumental in paving the way for Renaissance individualism, is known as "nominalism," because it considers that the general category is just a convenient name. Especially concerned to recognize individual difference (and thus the value of the created world), the nominalists accused the realists of subordinating the entirety of creation to a set of preexisting universals.

This is precisely where we stand today with regard to sound. As Jim Lastra demonstrates so well in his article, below [see original publication], the critics of the reproductive fallacy have edged dangerously close to an ultra-nominalism in which differing auditor perceptions make a single original sound appear like so many different rocks with no common identity save their common name. The very names used to identify sounds are suspect, disrespectful of sound's material heterogeneity. Yet we do discuss the film as we file out of the theater. In spite of the fact that we have literally, really heard different sounds, we still manage to find a common ground on which to base our conversation.

At this point in time, the study of sound shares the position of reception studies. I once witnessed an interchange that says a great deal about the project of reception studies. After demonstrating that neither the author nor the text can possibly determine readings, that each reader may read the text in differing ways, Tony Bennett opened the floor to questions. Said Paul Hernadi: "This is all well and good, but if what you say is true, how did I understand what you just said?" Taking an ultra-nominalist stance (which, by the way, he has toned down since), Bennett laid such heavy emphasis on our freedom of interpretation from textual constraints that he jeopardized the very notion of understanding. Even today, reception studies need to concentrate more fully on the bridges, the terms, the categories, the reading formations that permit a Paul Hernadi to understand a Tony Bennett.

A similar situation holds in sound studies. While not abandoning for a moment the notion that every auditor of the "same" performance actually hears different sounds, we need actively to interrogate the cultural phenomena that permit us to compose sentences, frame ideas, and ultimately communicate about the sounds which are heard. A decade or two ago, it would no doubt have been politically essential to defend at all costs the free play of the signifier; today it seems far more important to remember with Saussure that signification can occur only through the repression of the signifier and to call for increased sensitivity to the many strategies adopted by various cultures to assure the repression of sound's differences in favor of language's communicative value.

Indexicality: Half a Fallacy Working on the Other Half

Inherited from photography, one of the most deeply ingrained notions about cinema is that it depends primarily on recording. Unlike painting or writing, it is commonly supposed, cinema uses motion picture photography and sound recording to fix and retain in memory a physical image of the pro-filmic scene. Whereas representational painting is based largely on iconic resemblances, and writing is built around symbolic relationships (according to the terminology of Charles Sanders Peirce), cinema is thought to depend especially strongly on indexical connections, that is, those revealing a particularly close existential relationship between the represented item and its representation (such as that which exists when light rays bouncing off an object expose motion picture film, or when sound waves either drive the stylus of a disk recorder or, once transformed into light, expose the sound track portion of the film). This close connection of course creates an iconic relationship between the pro-filmic object or sound and its filmic representation (that is, the object and its representation have the same shape), but critics and theoreticians have consistently stressed the indexical ties over the iconic resemblance. In particular, André Bazin's realist criticism has been especially influential in popularizing an indexical approach to cinema. For Bazin, cinema is like a mold that takes each scene's impression; cinema thus works like a death mask or the Shroud of Turin, recording as it were by sacred contact.

During the early history of photography, photographs could be produced only through indexical relationships. As photography matured, however, photographers discovered various methods of "correcting" nature, typically adding painted-in iconic details to the photograph's indexical base. From the very start, however, such techniques were roundly condemned. Offering ontological arguments about photography's nature, critics insisted that certain types of retouching constituted a highly undesirable form of "cheating." The moralistic tone of this argument carried over intact to motion picture. In spite of early cinema's non-indexical display of color, "silent" cinema's iconic and symbolic approach to sound, or the late twenties' creation of the falsely indexical playback system, critics and theorists continued to stress the ability of the motion picture camera, like that of its still picture cousin, to take snapshots of reality. As cinema developed, to be sure, the scenes recorded by the camera began to depend on an increasing amount of manipulation (through set design, costuming, makeup, and so forth), and the final film image was increasingly constructed from a combination of separate images (through mattes, background projections, and other processes). For all this prestidigitation, however, the basic assumption was never jeopardized: cinema is primarily an indexical medium, directly dependent on the photographic recording of each pro-filmic scene (or scene fragment).

Throughout the history of cinema, the image has by and large corresponded to this indexical, recording-oriented definition (with the exception of special cases like scratch-animation, computer graphics, or electronically generated images). Cinema sound, on the other hand, has rarely been the result of straightforward indexical recording. Long before the cinema industry converted to sound, the market for telephonic communication, phonograph records, public address systems, and radio entertainment had led engineers to investigate the possibilities of "enhancing" sound in order to achieve greater volume, presence, or intelligibility, while reducing unwanted characteristics. At first, engineers concentrated on the recording process itself, laboring to increase the indexical fidelity of the sound recording apparatus. Soon, however, sound's capacity for post-recording transformation became apparent. Why *record* the reverberation associated with sounds produced in a large hard-walled room if you can simply process the reverb in later? Throughout the thirties, parallel developments in electronics and film sound led to the creation of myriad devices designed to produce final-release sound differing radically from the sound originally recorded on the set.

Little by little, the indexical nature of film sound became compromised by the ability of acoustic networks and electronic circuits to alter or simulate sound. Once the sole province of high-end sound production facilities (such as those found in New York, Hollywood, and a few other important centers around the world), the electronic revolution has now made it possible to produce all the music and effects for a film sound track without recording a single cricket or musical instrument. For a decade, film sound has been heavily influenced by digital systems like MIDI and the Synclavier. Even the most inexpensive films feature sound tracks that are no longer primarily recorded. In cinema, television, and disk production, sound has definitely surpassed the era of indexicality.

Today, the customary electronic manipulation and construction of sound has begun to serve as a model for the image. Though the film image currently depends primarily on a chemical (and thus indexical) technology, the electronic nature of the television image provides a different model, whose influence is increasingly felt in the cinema world. In order to create Mickey Mouse, Walt Disney had to do more than just make thousands of drawings; he had to record them with the same (indexical) motion picture process used for live actors. Today's animators work in an entirely different fashion. While most still depend in part on drawing, they make heavy use of electronics and its ability to produce iconic relationships without depending on the indexicality of recording. A similar shift has taken place in color technology. Whether two- or three-strip, whether additive or subtractive, traditional color processes systematically depended on indexical relationships: the color was fixed by the existential contact of the object with the film. Today, films are colorized by an electronic process that owes nothing to recording. It is only a matter of time before the plunging prices of all electronic processes turn colorization from a postproduction technique into a production device.

In short, the recording medium that cinema once was has now been massively transformed and risks ultimate obsolescence. However accurate it may once have been to understand cinema as recording its object by sacred contact, we must recognize that three-quarters of a century of electronics has radically desacralized cinema, substituting circuitry for direct contact, constructed iconicity for recorded indexicality, and the infinite imagined possibilities of the keyboard for the restricted immediacy of recording reality. Not so very long ago, treating cinema as *écriture* was a radical move; the technology itself is now turning this metaphor into a reality. Once, cinema was recorded with a camera; now, it is increasingly written with a keyboard.

So far, it is only half a fallacy to treat cinema as a recording medium. By the end of the century, however, cinema will be well on its way toward full digitalization. The end of the indexical era looms large. Perhaps it is time to revise our theories and our vocabulary to take this transformation into account. More experienced in this domain than the image, sound must lead the way.

Reference

Doane, Mary Anne (1980) "The Voice of Cinema: The Articulation of Body and Space," in Rick (Charles F.) Altman (ed) *Cinema/Sound*, special issue of *Yale French Studies* 60: 33–50.

Chapter 21

Friedrich Kittler

GRAMOPHONE

"**H**ULLO!" EDISON SCREAMED INTO the telephone mouthpiece. The vibrating diaphragm set in motion a stylus that wrote onto a moving strip of paraffin paper. In July 1877, 81 years before Turing's moving paper strip, the recording was still analog. Upon replaying the strip and its vibrations, which in turn set in motion the diaphragm, a barely audible "Hullo!" could be heard.[1]

Edison understood. A month later he coined a new term for his telephone addition: phonograph.[2] On the basis of this experiment, the mechanic Kruesi was given the assignment to build an apparatus that would etch acoustic vibrations onto a rotating cylinder covered with tinfoil. While he or Kruesi was turning the handle, Edison once again screamed into the mouthpiece—this time the nursery rhyme "Mary Had a Little Lamb." Then they moved the needle back, let the cylinder run a second time—and the first phonograph replayed the screams. The exhausted genius, in whose phrase genius is 1 percent inspiration and 99 percent perspiration, slumped back. Mechanical sound recording had been invented. "Speech has become, as it were, immortal."[3]

It was December 6, 1877. Eight months earlier, Charles Cros, a Parisian writer, bohemian, inventor, and absinthe drinker, had deposited a sealed envelope with the Academy of Sciences. It contained an essay on the "Procedure for the Recording and Reproduction of Phenomena of Acoustic Perception" (*Procédé d'enregistrement et de reproduction des phénomènes perçus par l'ouïe*). With great technological elegance this text formulated all the principles of the phonograph, but owing to a lack of funds Cros had not yet been able to bring about its "practical realization." "To reproduce" the traces of "the sounds and noises" that the "to and fro" of an acoustically "vibrating diaphragm" leaves on a rotating disk—that was also the program of Charles Cros.[4]

But once he had been preceded by Edison, who was aware of rumors of the invention, things sounded different. "Inscription" is the title of the poem with which Cros erected a belated monument to honor his inventions, which included an automatic telephone, color photography, and, above all, the phonograph:

Comme les traits dans les camées
J'ai voulu que les voix aimées
Soient un bien qu'on garde à jamais,
Et puissent répéter le rêve
Musical de l'heure trop brève;
Le temps veut fuir, je le soumets.

Like the faces in cameos
I wanted beloved voices
To be a fortune which one keeps forever,
And which can repeat the musical
Dream of the too short hour;
Time would flee, I subdue it.[5]

The program of the poet Cros, in his capacity as the inventor of the phonograph, was to store beloved voices and all-too-brief musical reveries. The wondrously resistant power of writing ensures that the poem has no words for the truth about competing technologies. Certainly, phonographs can store articulate voices and musical intervals, but they are capable of more and different things. Cros the poet forgets the noises mentioned in his precise prose text. An invention that subverts both literature and music (because it reproduces the unimaginable real they are both based on) must have struck even its inventor as something unheard of.

Hence, it was not coincidental that Edison, not Cros, actually built the phonograph. His "Hullo!" was no beloved voice and "Mary Had a Little Lamb" no musical reverie. And he screamed into the bell-mouth not only because phonographs have no amplifiers but also because Edison, following a youthful adventure involving some conductor's fists, was half-deaf. A physical impairment was at the beginning of mechanical sound recording—just as the first typewriters had been made by the blind for the blind, and Charles Cros had taught at a school for the deaf and mute.[6]

Whereas (according to Derrida) it is characteristic of so-called Man and his consciousness to hear himself speak[7] and see himself write, media dissolve such feedback loops. They await inventors like Edison whom chance has equipped with a similar dissolution. Handicaps isolate and thematize sensory data streams. The phonograph does not hear as do ears that have been trained immediately to filter voices, words, and sounds out of noise; it registers acoustic events as such. Articulateness becomes a second-order exception in a spectrum of noise. In the first phonograph letter of postal history, Edison wrote that "the articulation" of his baby "was loud enough, just a bit indistinct . . . not bad for a first experiment."[8]

Wagner's *Gesamtkunstwerk,* that monomaniacal anticipation of modern media technologies,[9] had already transgressed the traditional boundaries of words and music to do justice to the unarticulated. In *Tristan,* Brangäne was allowed to utter a scream whose notation cut straight through the score.[10] Not to mention *Parsifal*'s Kundry, who suffered from a hysterical speech impairment such as those which were soon to occupy the psychoanalyst Freud: she "gives a loud wail of misery, that sinks gradually into low accents of fear," "utters a dreadful cry," and is reduced to "hoarse and broken," though nonetheless fully composed, garbling.[11] This labored inception of language has nothing to do with operas and dramas that take it for granted that their figures can speak. Composers of 1880, however, are allied with engineers. The undermining of articulation becomes the order of the day.

In Wagner's case this applies to both text and music. The *Rheingold* prelude, with its infinite swelling of a single chord, dissolves the E-flat major triad in the first horn melody as if it were not a matter of musical harmony but of demonstrating the physical overtone series. All the harmonics of E-flat appear one after the other, as if in a Fourier analysis; only the seventh is missing, because it cannot be played by European instruments.[12] Of course, each of the horn sounds is an unavoidable overtone mixture of the kind only the sine tones of contemporary synthesizers can avoid. Nevertheless, Wagner's musico-physiological dream[13] at the outset of the tetralogy sounds like a historical transition from intervals to frequencies, from a logic to a physics of sound. By the time Schoenberg, in 1910, produced the last analysis of harmony in the history of music, chords had turned into pure acoustics: "For Schoenberg as well as for science, the physical basis in which he is trying to ground all phenomena is the overtone series."[14]

Overtones are frequencies, that is, vibrations per second. And the grooves of Edison's phonograph recorded nothing but vibrations. Intervals and chords, by contrast, were ratios, that is, fractions made up of integers. The length of a string (especially on a monochord) was subdivided, and the fractions, to which Pythagoras gave the proud name *logoi,* resulted in octaves, fifths, fourths, and so on. Such was the logic upon which was founded everything that, in Old Europe, went by the name of music: first, there was a notation system that enabled the transcription of clear sounds separated from the world's noise; and second, a harmony of the spheres that established that the ratios between planetary orbits (later human souls) equaled those between sounds.

The nineteenth century's concept of frequency breaks with all this.[15] The measure of length is replaced by time as an independent variable. It is a physical time removed from the meters and rhythms of music. It quantifies movements that are too fast for the human eye, ranging from 20 to 16,000 vibrations per second. The real takes the place of the symbolic. Certainly, references can also be established to link musical intervals and acoustic frequencies, but they only testify to the distance between two discourses. In frequency curves the simple proportions of Pythagorean music turn into irrational, that is, logarithmic, functions. Conversely, overtone series—which in frequency curves are simply integral multiples of vibrations and the determining elements of each sound—soon explode the diatonic music system. That is the depth of the gulf separating Old European alphabetism from mathematical-physical notation.

Which is why the first frequency notations were developed outside of music. First noise itself had to become an object of scientific research, and discourses "a privileged category of noises."[16] A competition sponsored by the Saint Petersburg Academy of Sciences in 1780 made voiced sounds, and vowels in particular, an object of research,[17] and inaugurated not only speech physiology but also all the experiments involving mechanical language reproduction. Inventors like Kempelen, Maelzel, and Mical built the first automata that, by stimulating and filtering certain frequency bands, could simulate the very sounds that Romanticism was simultaneously celebrating as the language of the soul: their dolls said "Mama" and "Papa" or "Oh," like

Hoffmann's beloved automaton, Olympia. Even Edison's 1878 article on phonography intended such toy mouths voicing the parents' names as Christmas presents.[18] Removed from all Romanticism, a practical knowledge of vowel frequencies emerged.

Continuing these experiments, Willis made a decisive discovery in 1829. He connected elastic tongues to a cogwheel whose cogs set them vibrating. According to the speed of its rotation, high or low sounds were produced that sounded like the different vowels, thus proving their frequency. For the first time pitch no longer depended on length, as with string or brass instruments; it became a variable dependent on speed and, therefore, time. Willis had invented the prototype of all square-curve generators, ranging from the bold verse-rhythm experiments of the turn of the century[19] to *Kontakte*, Stockhausen's first electronic composition.

The synthetic production of frequencies is followed by their analysis. Fourier had already provided the mathematical theory, but that theory had yet to be implemented technologically. In 1830, Wilhelm Weber in Gottingen had a tuning fork record its own vibrations. He attached a pig's bristle to one of the tongues, which etched its frequency curves into sooty glass. Such were the humble, or animal, origins of our gramophone needles.

From Weber's writing tuning fork Edouard Leon Scott, who as a Parisian printer was, not coincidentally, an inhabitant of the Gutenberg Galaxy, developed his phonautograph, patented in 1857. A bell-mouth amplified incoming sounds and transmitted them onto a membrane, which in turn used a coarse bristle to transcribe them onto a soot-covered cylinder. Thus came into being autographs or handwritings of a data stream that heretofore had not ceased not to write itself. (Instead, there was handwriting.) Scott's phonautograph, however, made visible what, up to this point, had only been audible and had been much too fast for ill-equipped human eyes: hundreds of vibrations per second. A triumph of the concept of frequency: all the whispered or screamed noises people emitted from their larynxes, with or without dialects, appeared on paper. Phonetics and speech physiology became a reality.[20]

They were especially real in the case of Henry Sweet, whose perfect English made him the prototype of all experimental phonetics as well as the hero of a play. Recorded by Professor F. C. Donders of Utrecht,[21] Sweet was also dramatized by George Bernard Shaw, who turned him into a modern Pygmalion out to conquer all mouths that, however beautiful, were marred by dialect. To record and discipline the dreadful dialect of the flower girl Eliza Doolittle, "Higgins's laboratory" boasts "a phonograph, a laryngoscope, [and] a row of tiny organ pipes with a bellows."[22] In the world of the modern *Pygmalion,* mirrors and statues are unnecessary; sound storage makes it possible "to inspect one's own speech or discourse as in a mirror, thus enabling us to adopt a critical stance toward our products."[23] To the great delight of Shaw, who saw his medium or his readability technologically guaranteed to all English speakers,[24] machines easily solve a problem that literature had not been able to tackle on its own, or had only been able to tackle through the mediation of pedagogy:[25] to drill people in general, and flower girls in particular, to adopt a pronunciation purified by written language.

It comes as no surprise that Eliza Doolittle, all of her love notwithstanding, abandons her Pygmalion (Sweet, a.k.a. Higgins) at the end of the play in order to learn "bookkeeping and typewriting" at "shorthand schools and polytechnic classes."[26] Women who have been subjected to phonographs and typewriters are souls no longer; they can only end up in musicals. Renaming the drama *My Fair Lady,* Rodgers and Hammerstein will throw Shaw's *Pygmalion* among Broadway tourists and record labels. "On the Street Where You Live" is sound.

In any event, Edison, ancestor of the record industry, only needed to combine, as is so often the case with inventions. A Willis-type machine gave him the idea for the phonograph; a Scott-type machine pushed him toward its realization. The synthetic production of frequencies combined with their analysis resulted in the new medium.

Edison's phonograph was a by-product of the attempt to optimize telephony and telegraphy by saving expensive copper cables. First, Menlo Park developed a telegraph that indented a paraffin paper strip with Morse signs, thus allowing them to be replayed faster than they had been transmitted by human hands. The effect was exactly the same as in Willis's case: pitch became a variable dependent on speed. Second, Menlo Park developed a telephone receiver with a needle attached to the diaphragm. By touching the needle, the hearing-impaired Edison could check the amplitude of the telephone signal. Legend has it that one day the needle drew blood—and Edison "recognized how the force of a membrane moved by a magnetic system could be put to work." "In effect, he had found a way to transfer the functions of his ear to his sense of touch."[27]

A telegraph as an artificial mouth, a telephone as an artificial ear—the stage was set for the phonograph. Functions of the central nervous system had been technologically implemented. When, after a 72-hour shift ending early in the morning of July 16, 1888, Edison had finally completed a talking machine ready for serial production, he posed for the hastily summoned photographer in the pose of his great idol. The French emperor, after all, is said to have observed that the progress of national welfare (or military technology) can be measured by transportation costs.[28] And no means of transportation are more economical than those which convey information rather than goods and people. Artificial mouths and ears, as technological implementations of the central nervous system, cut down on mailmen and concert halls. What Ong calls our secondary orality has the elegance of brain functions. Technological sound storage provides a first model for data streams, which are simultaneously becoming objects of neurophysiological research. Helmholtz, as the perfecter of vowel theory, is allied with Edison, the perfecter of measuring instruments. Which is why sound storage, initially a mechanically primitive affair on the level of Weber's pig bristle, could not be invented until the soul fell prey to science. "O my head, my head, my head," groans the phonograph in the prose poem Alfred Jarry dedicated to it. "All white underneath the silk sky: They have taken my head, my head—and put me into a tea tin!"[29]

Which is why Villiers de l'Isle-Adam, the symbolist poet and author of the first of many Edison novels, is mistaken when, in *Tomorrow's Eve,* he has the great inventor ponder his delay.

> What is most surprising in history, almost unimaginable, is that among all the great inventors across the centuries, not one thought of the Phonograph! And yet most of them invented machines a thousand times more complicated. The Phonograph is so simple that its construction owes nothing to materials of scientific composition. Abraham might have

built it, and made a recording of his calling from on high. A steel stylus, a leaf of silver foil or something like it, a cylinder of copper, and one could fill a storehouse with all the voices of Heaven and Earth.[30]

This certainly applies to materials and their processing, but it misses the historical a priori of sound recording. There are also immaterials of scientific origin, which are not so easy to come by and have to be supplied by a science of the soul. They cannot be delivered by any of the post-Abraham candidates whom Villiers de l'Isle-Adam suspects of being able to invent the phonograph: neither Aristotle, Euclid, nor Archimedes could have underwritten the statement that "The soul is a notebook of phonographic recordings" (but rather, if at all, a tabula rasa for written signs, which in turn signify acts of the soul). Only when the soul has become the nervous system, and the nervous system (according to Sigmund Exner, the great Viennese neurophysiologist) so many facilitations (*Bahnungen*), can Delboeuf's statement cease to be scandalous. In 1880, the philosopher Guyau devoted a commentary to it. And this first theory of the phonograph attests like no other to the interactions between science and technology. Thanks to the invention of the phonograph, the very theories that were its historical a priori can now optimize their analogous models of the brain.

Jean-Marie Guyau, Memory and Phonograph (1880)

Reasoning by analogy is of considerable importance to science; indeed, in as far as it is the principle of induction it may well form the basis of all physical and psychophysical sciences. Discoveries frequently start with metaphors. The light of thinking could hardly fall in a new direction and illuminate dark corners were it not reflected by spaces already illuminated. Only that which reminds us of something else makes an impression, although and precisely because it differs from it. To understand is to remember, at least in part.

Many similes and metaphors have been used in the attempt to understand mental abilities or functions. Here, in the as yet imperfect state of science, metaphors are absolutely necessary: before we *know* we have to start by *imagining* something. Thus, the human brain has been compared to all kinds of objects. According to Spencer it shows a certain analogy to the mechanical pianos that can reproduce an infinite number of melodies. Taine makes of the brain a kind of print shop that incessantly produces and stores innumerable clichés. Yet all these similes appear somewhat sketchy. One normally deals with the brain at rest; its images are perceived to be fixed, *stereotyped*; and that is imprecise. There is nothing finished in the brain, no real images; instead, we see only virtual, potential images waiting for a sign to be transformed into actuality. How this transformation into reality is really achieved is a matter of speculation. The greatest mystery of brain mechanics has to do with dynamics—not with statics. We are in need of a comparative term that will allow us to see not only how an object receives and stores an imprint, but also how this imprint at a given time is reactivated and produces new vibrations within the object. With this in mind, the most refined instrument (both receiver and motor in one) with which the human brain may be compared is perhaps Edison's recently invented phonograph.

For some time now I have been wanting to draw attention to this comparison, ever since I came across a casual observation in Delboeuf's last article on memory that confirmed my intentions: "The soul is a notebook of phonographic recordings."

Upon speaking into a phonograph, the vibrations of one's voice are transferred to a point that engraves lines onto a metal plate that correspond to the uttered sounds—uneven furrows, more or less deep, depending on the nature of the sounds. It is quite probable that in analogous ways, invisible lines are incessantly carved into the brain cells, which provide a channel for nerve streams. If, after some time, the stream encounters a channel it has already passed through, it will once again proceed along the same path. The cells vibrate in the same way they vibrated the first time; psychologically, these similar vibrations correspond to an emotion or a thought analogous to the forgotten emotion or thought.

This is precisely the phenomenon that occurs when the phonograph's small copper disk, held against the point that runs through the grooves it has etched, starts to reproduce the vibrations: to our ears, these vibrations turn back into a voice, into words, sounds, and melodies.

If the phonographic disk had self-consciousness, it could point out while replaying a song that it remembers this particular song. And what appears to us as the effect of a rather simple mechanism would, quite probably, strike the disk as a miraculous ability: memory.

Let us add that it could distinguish new songs from those already played, as well as new impressions from simple memories. Indeed, a certain effort is necessary for first impressions to etch themselves into metal or brain; they encounter more resistance and, correspondingly, have to exert more force; and when they reappear, they vibrate all the stronger. But when the point traces already existing grooves instead of making new ones, it will do so with greater ease and glide along without applying any pressure. The *inclination* of a memory or reverie has been spoken of; to pursue a memory, in fact: to smoothly glide down a slope, to wait for a certain number of complete memories, which appear one after the other, all in a row and without shock. There is, therefore, a significant difference between impressions in the real sense and memory. Impressions tend to belong to either of two classes: they either possess greater intensity, a unique sharpness of outline and fixity of line, or they are weaker, more blurred and imprecise, but nevertheless arranged in a certain order that imposes itself on us. To *recognize* an image means to assign it to the second class. One *feels* in a less forceful way and is aware of this emotion. A memory consists in the awareness, first, of the diminished intensity of an impression, second, of its increased ease, and third, of the connections it entertains with other impressions. Just as a trained eye can see the difference between a copy and the original, we learn to distinguish memories from impressions and are thus able to recognize a memory even before it has been located in time and space. We project this or that impression back into the past without knowing which part of the past it belongs to. This is because a memory retains a unique and distinguishing character, much like a sensation coming from the stomach differs from an acoustic or visual impression. In a similar manner, the phonograph is incapable of reproducing the human voice in all its strength and warmth. The voice of the apparatus will remain shrill and cold; it has something imperfect and abstract about it that sets it apart. If the phonograph could hear itself, it would learn to recognize the difference between the voice that came from the outside and forced itself onto it and the voice that it itself is broadcasting and which is a simple echo of the first, following an already grooved path.

A further analogy between the phonograph and our brain exists in that the speed of the vibrations impressed on the apparatus can noticeably change the character of the reproduced sounds or recalled images. Depending on whether you increase or decrease the rotation of the phonographic disk, a melody will be transposed from one octave to another. If you turn the handle faster, a song will rise from the deepest and most indistinct notes to the highest and most piercing. Does not a similar effect occur in the brain when we focus our attention on an initially blurred image, increasing its clarity step by step and thereby moving it, as it were, up the scale? And could this phenomenon not be explained by the increased or decreased speed and strength of the vibrations of our cells? We have within us a kind of scale of images along which the images we conjure up and dismiss incessantly rise and fall. At times they vibrate in the depths of our being like a blurred "pedal"; at times their sonic fullness radiates above all others. As they dominate or recede, they appear to be closer or farther away from us, and sometimes the length of time separating them from the present moment seems to be waning or waxing. I know of impressions I received ten years ago that, under the influence of an association of ideas or simply owing to my attention or some change of emotion, suddenly seem to date from yesterday. In the same way singers create the impression of distance by lowering their voice; they merely need to raise it again to suggest the impression of approaching.

These analogies could be multiplied. The principal difference between the brain and the phonograph is that the metal disk of Edison's still rather primitive machine remains deaf to itself; there is no transition from movement to consciousness. It is precisely this wondrous transition that keeps occurring in the brain. It remains an eternal mystery that is less astonishing than it appears, however. Were the phonograph able to hear itself, it would be far less mystifying in the final analysis than the idea of our hearing it. But indeed we do: its vibrations really turn into impressions and thoughts. We therefore have to concede the transformation of movement into thought that is always possible—a transformation that appears more likely when it is a matter of internal brain movement than when it comes from the outside. From this point of view it would be neither very imprecise nor very disconcerting to define the brain as an infinitely perfected phonograph—a conscious phonograph.

It doesn't get any clearer than that. The psychophysical sciences, to which the philosopher Guyau has absconded, embrace the phonograph as the only suitable model for visualizing the brain or memory. All questions concerning thought as thought have been abandoned, for it is now a matter of implementation and hardware. Thus memory, around 1800 a wholly "subordinate inner power,"[31] moves to the fore eighty years later. And because Hegel's spirit is thereby ousted from the start, the recently invented phonograph, not yet even ready for serial production, is superior to all other media. Unlike Gutenberg's printing press or Ehrlich's automatic pianos in the brain metaphors of Taine and Spencer, it alone can combine the two actions indispensable to any universal machine, discrete or not: writing and reading, storing and scanning, recording and replaying. In principle, even though Edison for practical reasons later separated recording units from replaying ones, it is one and the same stylus that engraves and later traces the phonographic groove.

Which is why all concepts of trace, up to and including Derrida's grammatological *ur*-writing, are based on Edison's simple idea. The trace preceding all writing, the trace of pure difference still open between reading and writing, is simply a gramophone needle. Paving a way and retracing a path coincide. Guyau understood that the phonograph implements memory and thereby makes it unconscious.

It is only because no philosopher, not even one who has abandoned philosophy for psychophysics, can rid himself of his professional delusions that Guyau attempts to crown or surpass the unconscious mnemonic capabilities of the phonograph at the end of his essay by contrasting them with conscious human abilities. But consciousness, the quality that Guyau ascribes to the brain in order to celebrate the latter as an infinitely perfected phonograph, would result in an infinitely inferior one. Rather than hearing the random acoustic events forcing their way into the bell-mouth in all their real-time entropy, Guyau's conscious phonograph would attempt to understand[32] and thus corrupt them. Once again, alleged identities or meaning or even functions of consciousness would come into play. Phonographs do not think, therefore they are possible.

Guyau's own, possibly unconscious example alludes to the imputation of consciousness and inner life: if a phonograph really possessed the consciousness attributed to it and were able to point out that it remembered a song, it would consider this a miraculous ability. But impartial and external observers would continue to see it as the result of a fairly simple mechanism. When Guyau, who had observed the brain simply as a technical apparatus, turns his experimental gaze inward, he falls short of his own standards. It was, after all, an external gaze that had suggested the beautiful comparison between attention and playback speed. If the focusing of blurred mental images by way of attention amounts to nothing more or less than changing the time axis of acoustic events by increasing playback speed or indulging in time axis manipulation (TAM), then there is no reason to celebrate attention or memory as miraculous abilities. Neither gramophone needles nor brain neurons need any self-consciousness to retrace a groove faster than it was engraved. In both cases it boils down to programming. For that reason alone the diligent hand of the phonograph user, who in Edison's time had difficulties sticking to the correct time while turning the handle, could be replaced by clockworks and electronic motors with adjustable speed. The sales catalogues of American record companies warned their customers of the friend who "comes to you and claims that your machine is too slow or too fast. Don't listen to him! He doesn't know what he is talking about."[33]

But standardization is always upper management's escape from technological possibilities. In serious matters such as test procedures or mass entertainment, TAM remains triumphant. The Edison Speaking Phonograph Company, founded two months after Edison's primitive prototype of December 1877, did its first business with time axis manipulation: with his own hand the inventor turned the handle faster than he had during the recording in order to treat New York to the sensational pleasure of frequency-modulated musical pieces. Even the modest cornet of a certain Levy acquired brilliance and temperament.[34] Had he been among the delighted New

Yorkers, Guyau would have found empirical proof that frequency modulation is indeed the technological correlative of attention.

Of course Europe's written music had already been able to move tones upward or downward, as the term "scale" itself implies. But transposition doesn't equal TAM. If the phonographic playback speed differs from its recording speed, there is a shift not only in clear sounds but in entire noise spectra. What is manipulated is the real rather than the symbolic. Long-term acoustic events such as meter and word length are affected as well. This is precisely what von Hornbostel, albeit without recognizing what distinguished it from transposition, praised as the "special advantage" of the phonograph: "It can be played at faster and slower speeds, allowing us to listen to musical pieces whose original speed was too fast at a more settled pace, and accordingly transposed, in order to analyze them."[35]

The phonograph is thus incapable of achieving real-time frequency shifts. For this we need rock bands with harmonizers that are able to reverse—with considerable electronic effort—the inevitable speed changes, at least to deceivable human ears. Only then are people able to return simultaneously and in real time from their breaking voices, and women can be men and men can be women again.

Time axis reversal, which the phonograph makes possible, allows ears to hear the unheard-of: the steep attack of instrumental sounds or spoken syllables moves to the end, while the much longer decay moves to the front. The Beatles are said to have used this trick on "Revolution 9" to whisper the secret of their global success to the tape freaks among their fans:[36] that Paul McCartney had been dead for a long time, replaced on album covers, stage, and in songs by a multimedia double. As the Columbia Phonograph Company recognized in 1890, the phonograph can be used as machine for composing music simply by allowing consumers to play their favorite songs backwards: "A musician could get one popular melody every day by experimenting in that way."[37]

TAM as poetry—but poetry that transgresses its customary boundaries. The phonograph cannot deny its telegraphic origin. Technological media turn magic into a daily routine. Voices that start to migrate through frequency spectra and time axes do not simply continue old literary word-game techniques such as palindromes or anagrams. This letter-bending had become possible only once the primary code, the alphabet itself, had taken effect. Time axis manipulation, however, affects the raw material of poetry, where manipulation had hitherto been impossible. Hegel had referred to "the *sound*" as "a disappearing of being in the act of being," subsequently celebrating it as a "saturated expression of the manifestation of inwardness."[38] What was impossible to store could not be manipulated. Ridding itself of its materiality or clothes, it disappeared and presented inwardness as a seal of authenticity.

But once storage and manipulation coincide in principle, Guyau's thesis linking phonography and memory may be insufficient. Storage facilities, which according to his own insight are capable of altering the character of the replayed sounds (thanks to time manipulation), shatter the very concept of memory. Reproduction is demoted once the past in all its sensuous detail is transmitted by technical devices. Certainly, hi-fi means "high fidelity" and is supposed to convince consumers that record companies remain loyal to musical deities. But it is a term of appeasement. More precise than the poetic imagination of 1800, whose alphabetism or creativity confronted an exclusively reproductive memory, technology literally makes the unheard-of possible. An old Pink Floyd song spells it out:

> When that old fat sun in the sky's falling
> Summer ev'ning birds are calling
> Summer Sunday and a year
> The sound of music in my ear
> Distant bells
> New mown grass smells
> Songs sweet
> By the river holding hands.
> And if you see, don't make a sound
> Pick your feet up off the ground
> And if you hear as the wall night falls
> The silver sound of a tongue so strange,
> Sing to me sing to me.[39]

The literally unheard-of is the site where information technology and brain physiology coincide. To make no sound, to pick your feet up off the ground, and to listen to the sound of a voice when night is falling—we all do it when we put on a record that commands such magic.

And what transpires then is indeed a strange and unheard-of silver noise. Nobody knows who is singing—the voice called David Gilmour that sings the song, the voice referred to by the song, or maybe the voice of the listener who makes no sound and is nonetheless supposed to sing once all the conditions of magic have been met. An unimaginable closeness of sound technology and self-awareness, a simulacrum of a feedback loop relaying sender and receiver. A song sings to a listening ear, telling it to sing. As if the music were originating in the brain itself, rather than emanating from stereo speakers or headphones.

That is the whole difference between arts and media. Songs, arias, and operas do not rely on neurophysiology. Voices hardly implode in our ears, not even under the technical conditions of a concert hall, when singers are visible and therefore discernible. For that reason their voices have been trained to overcome distances and spaces. The "sound of music in my ear" can exist only once mouthpieces and microphones are capable of recording any whisper. As if there were no distance between the recorded voice and listening ears, as if voices traveled along the transmitting bones of acoustic self-perception directly from the mouth into the ear's labyrinth, hallucinations become real.

And even the distant bells that the song listens to are not merely signifiers or referents of speech. As a form of literature, lyric had been able to provide as much and no more. Countless verses used words to conjure up acoustic events as lyrical as they were indescribable. As rock songs, lyric poetry can add the bells themselves in order to fill attentive brains with something that, as long as it had been confined to words, had remained a mere promise.

In 1898, the Columbia Phonograph Company Orchestra offered the song "Down on the Swanee River" as one of its 80 cylinders. Advertisements promised Negro songs and dances, as well as the song's location and subject: pulling in the gangplank, the sounds of the steam engine, and, 80 years before Pink Floyd, the chiming of a steamboat bell[40]—all for 50 cents. Songs became part of their acoustic environment. And lyrics fulfilled what psychoanalysis—originating not coincidentally at the same time—saw as the essence of desire: hallucinatory wish fulfillment.

Notes

1. Chew 1967, 2. When Kafka's captured ape delivers his "Report to an Academy," the scene depicting his animal language acquisition quotes both Edison's "Hullo" and his storage technology: On board the ship "there was a celebration of some kind, a gramophone was playing"; the ape drank the schnapps bottle "that had been carelessly left standing" in front of his cage; and, "because I could not help it, because my senses were reeling, [I] called a brief and unmistakable 'Hallo!' breaking into human speech, and with this outburst broke into the human community, and felt its echo: 'Listen, he's talking!' like a caress over the whole of my sweat-drenched body" (Kafka 1917/1948, 162).

2. Three months later (and independently of Edison) the same word appeared in an article on Charles Cros. See Marty 1981, 14.

3. *Scientific American,* 1877, quoted in Read and Welch 1959, 12.

4. Cros 1877/1964, 523–24.

5. Cros 1908/1964, 136; trans. Daniel Katz, in Kittler 1990, 231.

6. See Cros 1964, x.

7. See Derrida 1967/1976, 240.

8. Bruch 1979, 21.

9. See the documents from the *Gründerzeit* in Kaes 1978, 68–69, 104 (the scriptwriter H. H. Ewers on Wagner as "teacher").

10. See Friedheim, 1983, 63: "Wagner is probably the first dramatist to seriously explore the use of scream."

11. Wagner 1882/1986, 101.

12. Wagner, *Das Rheingold* (1854), mm. II–20.

13. See Wagner 1880/1976, 511–12.

14. Jalowetz 1912, 51.

15. See Rayleigh 1877–78, I: 7–17.

16. Lévi-Strauss 1964/1969, 23.

17. See Kylstra 1977, 7.

18. See Bruch 1979, 26, and Kylstra 1977, 5.

19. See Stetson 1903.

20. See Marage 1898.

21. See Bruch 1979, 3–4. Ong (1982, 5) even hailed Sweet (1845–1912) as the progenitor of Saussure's phoneme concept.

22. Shaw 1912/1972, 684.

23. Lothar 1924, 48–49.

24. See Shaw 1912/1972, 659–64.

25. For details, see Kittler 1985/1990, 27–53.

26. Shaw 1912/1972, 795. [*My Fair Lady* is by Lerner and Loewe.—Trans.]

27. Lothar 1924, 12, and Kylstra 1977, 3, respectively.

28. See Knies 1857, iii.

29. Jarry 1895/1975, 4: 191.

30. Villiers 1886/1982, 19.

31. "Hähnische Litteralmethode" 1783/1986, 156–57.

32. On understanding as a measurable source of noise parallel to hearing, see Gutzmann 1908.

33. Lothar 1924, 51–52.

34. See Gelatt 1977, 27–28.
35. Abraham and Hornbostel 1904, 229.
36. On rock music and secret codes, see Kittler 1984, 154–55.
37. Gelatt 1977, 52.
38. Hegel 1830/1927–40, 10: 346.
39. Pink Floyd 1976, 10–11.
40. Gelatt 1977, 72.

References

Abraham, Otto, and Erich Moritz von Hornbostel. 1904. "Über die Bedeutung des Phonographen für vergleichende Musikwissenschaft." *Zeitschrift für Ethnologie* 36: 222–36.

Bruch, Walter. 1979. "Von der Tonwalze zur Bildplatte: 100 Jahre Ton- und Bildspeicherung." *Funkschau,* special issue.

Chew, Victor Kenneth. 1967. *Talking Machines 1877–1914: Some Aspects of the Early History of the Gramophone.* London.

Cros, Charles. 1964. *Oeuvres complètes.* Ed. Louis Forestier and Pascal Pia. Paris.

Derrida, Jacques. 1976. *Of Grammatology.* Trans. Gayatri Chakravorty Spivak. Baltimore.

Friedheim, Philip. 1983. "Wagner and the Aesthetics of the Scream." *19th-Century Music* 7: 63–70.

Gelatt, Roland. 1977. *The Fabulous Phonograph 1877–1977. From Edison to Stereo.* 2d rev. ed. New York

Gutzmann, Hermann. 1908. "Über Hören und Verstehen." *Zeitschrift für angewandte Psychologie und psychologische Sammelforschung* 1: 483–503.

"Die Hähnische Litteralmethode." 1986. In *Karl Philipp Moritz: Die Schriften in Dreissig Bänden,* ed. Petra and Uwe Nettelbeck, vol. i, pt. 2, 157–58. Nördlingen.

Hegel, Georg Wilhelm Friedrich. 1927–40. *Sämtliche Werke.* Ed. Hermann Glockner. 26 vols. Stuttgart.

Jalowetz, Heinrich. 1912. "Die Harmonielehre." In *Arnold Schönberg,* 49–64. Munich.

Jarry, Alfred. 1975. *Les minutes de sable mémorial.* In *Oeuvres complètes,* ed. René Massat, vol. 4, 169–268. Geneva.

Kaes, Anton, ed. 1978. *Kino-Debatte: Texte zum Verhältnis von Literatur und Film 1909–29.* Munich.

Kafka, Franz. 1948. *The Penal Colony: Stories and Short Pieces.* Trans. Willa and Edwin Muir. New York.

Kittler, Friedrich. 1984. "Der Gott der Ohren." In *Das Schwinden der Sinne,* ed. Dietmar Kamper and Christoph Wulf, 140–55. Frankfurt a. M.

Kittler, Friedrich. 1990. *Discourse Networks, 1800/1900.* Trans. Michael Metteer, with Chris Cullens. Stanford, Calif.

Knies, Karl. 1857. *Der Telegraph als Verkehrsmittel.* Tübingen.

Kylstra, Peter H. 1977. "The Use of the Early Phonograph in Phonetic Research." *Phonographic Bulletin* 17: 3–12.

Lévi-Strauss, Claude. 1969. *The Raw and the Cooked.* Trans. John and Doreen Weightman. New York.

Lothar, Rudolph. 1924. *Die Sprechmaschine: Ein technisch-ästhetischer Versuch.* Leipzig.

Marage, René M. 1898. "Les phonographes et l'étude des voyelles." *L'année psychologique* 5: 226–44.

Marty, Daniel. 1981. *Grammophone: Geschichte in Bildern.* Karlsruhe.

Ong, Walter J. 1982. *Orality and Literacy: The Technologizing of the Word.* London.

Pink Floyd. 1976. *Song Book: Ten Songs from the Past.* London.

Read, Oliver, and Walter L. Welch. 1959. *From Tin Foil to Stereo: Evolution of the Phonograph.* Indianapolis, Ind.

Rayleigh, Lord John William Strutt. 1877–78. *The Theory of Sound.* 2 vols. London.

Shaw, George Bernard. 1972. *Collected Plays with Their Prefaces.* Ed. Dan H. Laurence. London.

Stetson, Raymond Herbert. 1903. "Rhythm and Rhyme." *Harvard Psychological Studies* 1: 413–66.

Villiers de l'Isle-Adam, Philippe Auguste Mathias, Comte de. 1982. *Tomorrow's Eve.* Trans. Robert Martin Adams. Urbana, Ill.

Wagner, Richard. 1976. *Mein Leben.* Ed. Martin Gregor-Dellin. Munich.

Wagner, Richard. 1986. *Parsifal.* Trans. Andrew Porter. London.

Chapter 22

James Lastra

FIDELITY VERSUS INTELLIGIBILITY

THE TWO GENERAL MODELS of sound recording that dominated—and to a remarkable degree continue to dominate—technicians' ideas about sound representation could be called the "phonographic" (or "perceptual fidelity") model and the "telephonic" (or "intelligibility") models. Like its nineteenth-century predecessor, perceptual simulation, the former sets as its goal the perfectly faithful reproduction of a spatiotemporally specific musical performance (as if heard from the best seat in the house); the latter, like writing, intelligibility or legibility at the expense of material specificity, if necessary. A recording of an orchestra, for example, should try to preserve the reverberant space within which the sounds were produced, while a telephone, being designed with a very different social function in mind, would never be suitable for this. However, a "phonographic" recording could just as easily represent one of the "worst" seats, while still remaining "faithful" or specific. A telephone, in contrast, sacrifices acoustic specificity in favor of rendering speech clearly under widely varying conditions.

For each model articulated by sound engineers and researchers, the very conception of what a sound "is" differs in important ways. The "fidelity" approach assumes that all aspects of the sound event are inherently significant, including long or short reverberation times, ratios of direct to reflected sound, or even certain peculiarities of performance or space. The "telephonic" approach, not literally limited to telephones and voices, assumes that sound possesses an intrinsic hierarchy that renders some aspects essential and others not. As with our academic theorists, the relevant terms of comparison are uniqueness versus recognizability or event versus structure, and consequently, these terms presume different ideals of "good" representation.

Within the classical Hollywood style, we can find instances of both the "telephonic" and "phonographic" approaches to sound representation. According to the principle of narrative priority, dialogue recording tends almost uniformly from the early thirties on toward the telephonic, minimizing the amount of reverberation, background noise, and speech idiosyncrasy, while simultaneously maximizing the "directness" or "frontality" of recording, and the intelligibility of the dialogue.[1] Even when a speaker appears to turn away, a high level of direct sound often implies that he or she is still speaking "to" the auditor, because speech is understood not simply as an abstract sound but as a sound with a specific social and narrative function.[2] This statistically dominant form of recording differs markedly from the less common technique that has been dubbed point-of-audition (POA) sound, which tends to correspond more closely to the phonographic model of represented hearing.

In spite of its relative rarity as a technique, the phonographic or simulation model ruled the theoretical roost. This should not surprise us, since it lent itself easily to the reigning theoretical orthodoxies of the day. By insisting on a physically real observer as the principle of representational coherence, it was easily understood as a variation on the "invisible witness" model of narration. From Hugo Münsterberg and V. Pudovkin to André Bazin, classical film theorists have tried to account for narration by claiming that editing (for example) mimicked the perceptions of an "invisible observer." In this view, edits reflect the shifting attention of a real witness, and filmmaking becomes the process of moving that witness around through space to the most salient details of a scene. The frequently impossible spatial leaps and changes of perspective characteristic of standard continuity editing give the lie to this model, but it persisted nonetheless. As David Bordwell notes, this theoretical expedient allowed filmmakers and critics to collapse the observer with both the camera and the narrator. Furthermore, the ambiguity of the term "point of view" (POV) allowed the conflation of both its optical and intellectual senses. Thus, he argues, "the invisible-witness model became classical film theory's all-purpose answer to problems involving space, authorship, point of view, and narration."[3] Whatever inconsistencies (sometimes a real observer, sometimes an "ideal" one, sometimes an "omniscient" one, etc.) or outright silliness the invisible observer produced, the model died hard.

In addition to its conceptual and rhetorical benefits, the invisible observer's insistence on the foundational importance of POV responded to other pressures. If we look back to the nineteenth and early twentieth centuries and remember the extent to which the technical media disrupted customary understandings of the relationship between perception and representation, the model makes even more sense. While a filmmaker like Dziga Vertov might celebrate the machine-vision produced by the camera and editing, and extol its modernity and superhuman capacities, the experience of radical shifts of space and time made possible by the cinema (and even the gentler dislocations of continuity editing) presented the spectator with an unsettling and profoundly inorganic experience of the visible world.

Even a conventionally edited scene might offer microscopic or bird's-eye perspectives, and it would almost certainly jump back and forth across the shoulders of couples engaged in intimate conversation. Even if not literally shocking, this was a novel and potentially confusing experience. By assimilating these obviously inhuman processes to a thoroughly (if problematical) human model, critics, theorists, and classical filmmakers carved a space for subjectivity in film narration and "anthropomorphized" its more perplexing possibilities. In essence, POV "humanized" machine perception. In a larger sense, by focusing on character, adjusting framing to the human body, and emphasizing psychological interiority and character-motivated

POV, the classical cinema systematically worked to minimize the more disturbing tendencies of the new medium. It is therefore even less surprising that variations on this "anthropomorphism" would creep into technical discussions.

POA sound (like the POV shot) attempts to represent the experience of hearing within the diegesis, normally the hearing of a character. Sometimes this is indicated by muffling sounds, as if hearing them through a wall, by including a Doppler effect to indicate the rapid passage of a sound source (by an increase or decrease in volume indicating the approach or retreat of the source), or perhaps by giving a clear sense of the acoustics specific to a particular location. All of these different characteristics can be assimilated under Altman's term "spatial signature," which includes all those indicators of the spatial and temporal specificity of sound production and reception that characterize any recording as unique, and that create an effect of simulated perceptual presence.[4] Both the POV shot and POA sound represent spaces that are to be taken as diegetically "real," and as heard by an embodied perceiver within that space. It therefore implicitly confirms the classical cinema's emphasis on the human character, while simultaneously rendering its other historical norms more apparently "human." In a rather straightforward fashion, it simultaneously embodies the idea of representation as perceptual simulation and responds to the same pressures that elicited its appearance in the nineteenth century. The difference between a sonic space whose principal goal is the intelligibility of some sounds at the expense of others (foregrounding narratively important information against a reduced, generic background), and a space that is constructed in order to represent a particular real act of audition, embodies the basic difference between the telephonic and phonographic models.

In a typical Hollywood film, visual space, when not explicitly marked as a POV shot, is primarily a marker of the narrative or enunciative level of the presentation. In other words, its dimension, angle, framing, etc. are typically not understood as someone's actual vision (neither narrator nor character), but as an index of narrative emphasis. Unlike the POV shot, which is marked as a unique perception in a specific, diegetically real space, a typical shot can usually be replaced by another shot that represents a noticeably different view of the space. A typical shot's index of substitutability is much higher than that of a POV shot since it presents *narratively important* information rather than *perceptually specific* information. It is indicative, however, that sound technicians who call for perceptual fidelity in sound and image representation often call for an "invisible witness" model of cinematic narration as well. Such a heuristic seems obviously to encourage one to think of filmmaking as a stringing together of unique perceptions.[5] The sonic specificity implied by the standard of perceptual fidelity was quickly pressed into a carefully defined, and carefully delimited, role. It was soon harnessed almost exclusively to particular characters within a fictional world.

Sound recorded as if heard by a character—POA sound—became the primary instance within the classical system where the spatial characteristics of sound might manifest themselves (often, significantly, for narrative purposes). This however, was the exceptional case. In general, close frontal miking of actors, which minimizes reflected and indirect sound, became the norm for dialogue since, as one researcher put it, "In no case did an increase in reverberation cause an increase in articulation [i.e., intelligibility]."[6] Or as another phrased a related observation, "The quality of a recording is effectively independent of the reverberant characteristics of the set if the microphone is within approximately three feet of the speaker."[7]

Together, the two quotations indicate that in certain contexts a "good" recording could be associated with recognizable speech sounds, and dissociated from any strict sense of fidelity.[8] In fact, some researchers from the period began to argue that perceived "naturalness" seemed to be correlated with the presence of reflected sound, while "articulation" was associated with direct sound.[9] In other words, these articles suggest that indications of spatial specificity and naturalness were linked to certain forms of *unintelligibility,* or at least suggest the possibility that fidelity and intelligibility are not necessarily related. Although my argument here focuses heavily on speech, I would suggest that terms such as "intelligibility" have analogs in the case of sound effects as well, where something like "recognizability" or "identifiability" performs roughly the same function—that of comprehension.[10] A recording with a high degree of reflected sound, or some other indicator of spatial signature and temporal specificity, corresponds to an approach that considers sound an *event,* while closely miked sound, with a relatively "context-less" signature, corresponds to sound considered as an intelligible *structure*—as a signifying element within a larger system.

According to a 1931 article by Carl Dreher, there need not be any irresolvable conflict between the two approaches, however.

> Since the reproduction of sound is an artificial process, it is necessary to use artificial devices in order to obtain the most desirable effects. For example, it is normal procedure to reproduce dialog at a level higher than the original performance. This may entail a compromise between intelligibility and strict fidelity.[11]

Clearly at stake are not the sounds "themselves," but as Alan Williams says, the signs of those sounds—even in the case of supposedly strictly accurate recordings. Nevertheless, the problem of strict fidelity arises again and again in other contexts. John L. Cass, for example, complains that the "illusion" is destroyed when a spectator becomes aware that despite changes in shot scale, the recordist has maintained "close-up" sound in order to ensure intelligibility, thereby violating the presumed norms of "sound perspective." Since "the resultant blend of sound may not be said to represent any given point of audition," the spectator is left feeling that he is experiencing the "sound which would be heard by a man with five or six very long ears, said ears extending in various directions."[12]

Here Cass is, of course, assuming that film narration works by the "invisible observer" method, stringing together a series of unique and spatiotemporally real perceptions. However, filmic narration, as Bordwell points out, does *not* need the supposition of a flesh-and-blood observer to perceive every element *for* us.[13] "Real" space, as it is perceived in actuality, is simply not an issue for most images on the screen: their scale and angle are functions of narrative emphasis, not of more or less precise perception. Cass's symptomatic insistence on the model of narration as perception, however, indicates the extent to which a model of precise perceptual duplication ruled the imaginative world of film professionals, helping to shape the practices of sound representation for decades to come, even if it was ultimately to be marginalized or rejected. A legacy of earlier encounters with technology, the illogical but persistent "invisible auditor" served to rehumanize the cinema when it most threatened to become inhuman. The resilience of this persuasive but misleading model also illustrates how reigning notions of filmic representation may come into conflict with institutional and industrial demands.

Notes

1.   It might be argued that, ultimately, "voices" (be they Al Jolson's, Bert Lahr's, or Mischa Elman's violin) were the only sounds that Hollywood had an inherent *need* to reproduce accurately in synchronization. Although the theoretical discourse promoted the importance of recording music (an emphasis derived from the Vitaphone's "disc" format?), almost every "problem" with the apparatuses involved either synchrony or dialogue—rarely if ever inaccurate rendering of instrumental timbre.

2.   Although in the Vitaphone shorts (e.g., the *Tannhäuser* overture) the moving violin bow, the cymbal crash, and various other visible manifestations of sync replace the moving lips, it is not difficult to see the analogy between these types of sounds and speech.

3.   Recorded musical accompaniment for films such as *Don Juan* (1926) and *Old San Francisco* (1927) was important to the extent that it further standardized the commodity, but the added cost to producers could not have been an effective inducement to convert to sound. The musical and sound effects accompaniment typical of both films was not necessarily any better synchronized than that provided by a gifted theater orchestra, so novelty was minimal. Warner stood to profit most through the presentation of vaudeville and concert acts who were salable precisely by providing their signature sounds in a manner which left no doubt that the persons depicted on the screen were producing those sounds. Concern with sound source was prominent in Bell Labs' Public Address research as well. See, e.g., T. A. Dowey, "Public-Address Systems," *Bell Laboratories Record* 3.2 (October 1926): 50–56.

4.   Aside, that is, from certain forms of (narrative-driven) ethnic accent. The importance of these deviances from the King's (or rather Bell Labs') English is their ability to provide motivations for certain forms of melodramatic narrative. Warner's *Old San Francisco, Noah's Ark* (1929), and *The Jazz Singer* (1927) all attest to this use of accent (the first only in intertitles). Moreover, such accents rarely if ever impede dialogue intelligibility, while they often provide important character information and plot complication.

5.   See Rick Altman's discussion of "for-me-ness" in "The Technology of the Voice" (Part 1), *Iris* 3.1 (1985): 3–20.

6.   David Bordwell, *Narration in the Fiction Film* (Madison: University of Wisconsin Press, 1985), 9.

7.   Rick Altman, "Sound Space," in Altman, ed., *Sound Theory/Sound Practice* (New York: Routledge), 46–64.

8.   Interestingly, the tendency to think of sound representation as records of perception duplicates the early tendency to treat the individual shots of, say, a chase film as autonomous wholes whose unity is provided by point of view rather than a higher-level narrative unity. See Tom Gunning, "Non-Continuity, Continuity, Discontinuity: A Theory of Genres in Early Film," *Iris* 2.1 (1984): 101–12; Charles Musser, "The Travel Genre in 1903–4: Moving Towards Fictional Narrative," *Iris* 2.1 (1984): 47–60; and André Gaudreault, "The Infringement of Copyright Laws and Its Effects (1900–906)," *Framework* 29 (1985): 2–14.

9.   J. C. Steinberg, "Effects of Distortion Upon the Recognition of Speech Sounds," *Journal of the Acoustical Society of America* (hereafter, *JASA*) 2.4 (October 1930): 132.

10.   Franklin L. Hunt, "Sound Pictures: Fundamental Principles and Some Factors Which Affect Their Quality," *JASA* 2.4 (April 1931): 482.

11.   For example, Hunt, "Sound Pictures," 481–82. It also makes clear that very "normal" kinds of sound recording paid no heed to the credo which claimed that the "eyes and ears" of the recording apparatuses had to be linked like those in a real body. It further indicates that at least a portion of the technicians involved in research around problems in sound film were aware that Hollywood was primarily in the business of selling narratives, not optical and acoustic effigies of real experience. For a good example of a technician grappling with the pair intelligibility/naturalness, see Carl Dreher, "Recording, Re-recording, and Editing of Sound," *Journal of the Society of Motion Picture Engineers* 16.6 (June 1931): 756–65.

12.   Hunt, "Sound Pictures," 499.

13.   A notable exception are those sound effects that require a strong dose of spatial acoustics in order to be genetically recognizable. Hence we often get sound/image scale mismatches which do not disturb us in the least because the rendering of the sound stresses its "name" rather than its actuality.

Chapter 23

Trevor Pinch and Frank Trocco

SHAPING THE SYNTHESIZER

The Moog filter design is as unique to the sounds of the synthesizer as the Steinway steel frame is to the piano.
Herb Deutsch, "The First Moog Synthesizer," excerpt from NAHO, fall 1981, New York State Museum, The State Education Department. Available at www. Moogarchives.com.

BOB MOOG WAS EXCITED. He may have been only a graduate student, but he had made a start in the electronic music instrument business. He had built his first synthesizer modules, he had three precious orders, and he had his beloved shop. And the shop was soon going to expand.

The Modular Moog synthesizer, which was advertised for the first time as a "synthesizer" in 1966, emerged over a period of time from a thousand different design decisions and a thousand conversations. It was an *innovation* rather than an invention.

The history of technology tells us that inventions are two a penny. There are many, many people who invent new things: machines, processes, tools, gizmos, gadgets, widgets, and the like. Such people are often portrayed as unsung heroes, ahead of their field, unrecognized in their own time. But singing in the bath is not the same as singing on stage. There are very few people who successfully turn their inventions into a real product that can be manufactured, marketed, and sold. The field of electronic music instruments is littered with inventions, but there have been very few true innovations.

One of the most spectacular inventions is Thaddeus Cahill's Telharmonium, developed in 1901.[1] This enormous instrument, which weighed 200 tons, generated sound from giant alternators. It was installed in Telharmonium Hall in downtown Manhattan, and its sound was piped to nearby hotels and restaurants. Technical problems of crosstalk with the ordinary telephone cables and a rather annoying timbre led to its failure. It was, however, a precursor to one of the few true musical innovations—the immensely popular Hammond organ invented by Laurens Hammond in 1933.[2] Hammond used a series of spinning tone wheels (a miniaturized form of the Telharmonium sound source) and took advantage of tube amplifiers and loud speakers (unavailable to Cahill).

Another notable inventor was Friedrich Trautwein, who in 1928 developed the trautonium (which Goebbels was keen to use for Nazi propaganda) and who, with composer Oskar Sala, went on to produce the mixturtrautonium used for the sound effects in Hitchcock's *The Birds* (1963).[3] Maurice Martenot developed the Ondes Martenot in 1928; it was used in classical performance and had a special repertoire written for it, including works by Varese, Messiaen, Boulez, and Ravel. To this day it is still used in France. Luigi Russolo, a member of the Italian futurists, in 1914 developed an early mechanical form of the synthesizer. His *intonarumori* (noise instruments) provoked scandal but remained as oddities.[4] However, like the theremin and the Ondes Martenot, Russolo's *intonarumori* found a home in movies.

The Listening Strategy

Bob's success as an innovator can be traced to one key factor: he listened to what his customers wanted and responded to their needs. Rather than telling them "this is the way things are going to be," he devised a strategy over the years for learning how other people wanted things to be. He learned from going on the road, entering their homes and studios, and bringing them to Trumansburg, first for a summer workshop and later to his own factory studio. He saw more clearly than anyone that his own fate as a manufacturer was tied to the success of the field as a whole, and he devised ways of nurturing that field, such as by starting his own magazine for electronic music.

Moog's strategy does not appear to have been deliberate. It was not that on the bus ride home from the 1964 Audio Engineering Society meeting Bob planned out the next three years. As he constantly reminded us, "I didn't know what the hell I was doing." He fell into what he was doing, but he learned as he fell. He learned from what he found happening to him, around him, and in the culture. And above all it was fun. Bob had a blast during those early years. What he enjoyed doing most we know already—fiddling, diddling, and futzing with electronics. But he soon discovered he enjoyed something else—meeting his customers, many of whom became his life-long friends. Moog: "Nikolais and Siday and Hillar and all the people I did business with in the early days have remained collaborators and friends and customers throughout the years. I've gotten to know them all . . . They've been very valuable to me both as personal friendships and as guidance in refining synthesizer components."

That guidance began with his first three customers. Alwin Nikolais, Lejaren Hillar, and Eric Siday represented a spectrum of needs. Nikolais wanted a bunch of modules on which to make avant-garde music for the dance troupe he choreographed. He had previously used tape loops. Hillar was an academic composer who headed the well-known University of Illinois electronic music studio, and Siday was a commercial musician. Moog formed a particularly close relationship with Siday, whose order turned out to be important for the future of the synthesizer. Siday wanted not just modules but a complete system, and he had the money to pay for it.

Eric Siday

Eric Siday was one of the best-paid commercial musicians of the day. Trained as a violinist at the London Royal Academy of Music in the 1920s, he played in silent films before moving to the United States in 1938. When radio and TV came along, he helped invent a new occupation: creating electronic jingles, sound signatures, and sound logos that, in five seconds, identify a product or corporation on TV or radio. He used oscillators, tape loops, splicing, and any other technique he could lay his hands on to ply his new trade. One of his best-known signatures was the burps of coffee percolating in a Maxwell House coffee commercial. The little electronic ditty that introduced every CBS television show as an announcer said "CBS presents this Program in Color" was heard by millions, and it earned him $5,000 for each second of sound.[5]

After Moog's AES presentation, Siday and his technician came to Trumansburg. Moog: "We sat down and conceived on paper a whole modular system that was going to cost him $1,400. It was an incredible load of stuff . . . something like ten or twelve modules." As far as Bob can recall, "this is the first time when a system the size of a synthesizer was actually talked about between me and a central customer." Bob had already designed many of the modules Siday wanted. He had voltage-controlled oscillators, amplifiers, and filters, and he had envelope generators. But now he had to put them all together into one system. He had to design a workable keyboard and a cabinet in which to house everything. He also had to come up with a price. "I knew about what the material would cost. I thought I had an idea of how much work would go into it, once we knew how to build them. Well, I didn't know! A lot of time it was just feeling and guesswork. I was not a businessman at the time . . . I literally didn't know what a balance sheet was." The business side of things was something Moog never enjoyed or mastered. "Feeling and guesswork," as he was to discover the hard way, didn't keep a business running.

After six months' work the system was ready for delivery. Siday's studio was in his home, a grand ten-room apartment in an Upper West Side building, the Apthorp. Siday had taken over the elegant living room and maid's bedroom for his work. "It was completely filled up with instruments and half-instruments and stuff taken apart and stands and whatnot." It was to this home studio that Bob was to deliver his first complete system. There was just one problem: How was he going to get this rather large synthesizer down to New York?

Bob did what he always did—he rode the bus: "We worked months and months and we sweated it out. First product, and we were very proud of it. My coworkers and I packed it up into some cardboard cartons and I took it on a bus—a big synthesizer—it takes two men to carry each box . . . I got it into a taxi after the bus and got it to the Apthorp." It was now morning and Bob was a "little bit strung out" after his night on the bus:

> It's eight o'clock in the morning and Edith [Eric's wife] is watching this like a shy child . . . from one of the doorways. I put one of the boxes down and take the lid off and take all the packing out and spread it on the hall floor. Take one of the instruments out and set it up. Begin to unpack

the next box and I didn't realize this, but Edith is slowly losing control of herself. She's watching this. I was busy unpacking. I'm setting the second box up . . . All of a sudden she loses control of herself completely. She screams out, 'Eric, more shit in this house. All you ever do is bring shit in this house. One piece of shit after the other!' . . . and somehow I got the instrument set up and [got] out of there that day.

Over the years Moog designed many customized modules for Siday, including a keyboard where each note was individually tunable, although he had trouble delivering them on schedule. On another famous occasion, Edith (who by now had become close with Shirleigh Moog) bawled Bob out for keeping Eric waiting for a piece of equipment. Bob found it hard to make a deadline—he was nearly always late.

Other customers were important for the future of the synthesizer, and none more so than Wendy (formerly Walter) Carlos, who pushed Bob to perfect the technology. It was at her urging that Bob designed his first touch-sensitive keyboard. She also came up with the idea of adding the portamento control and the fixed filter bank (a form of graphic equalizer), which eventually became standard features. The portamento control, which allows the voltage generated by one key to slide smoothly to the next, was particularly important for live performance. It was rock performer Keith Emerson's favorite feature of the Moog.

To Key or Not to Key?

Listening to what customers wanted was all very well, but what if customers disagreed over what they wanted? Moog soon faced this problem. In 1965 Vladimir Ussachevsky contacted Moog and expressed interest in buying some of his modules, but in the end he bought very few. Instead, he bought three complete systems from Don Buchla, which, unlike Moog's synthesizers, had no keyboard. Ussachevsky was well-known for opposing the keyboard. The standard keyboard just did not fit with his conception of how electronic music should be made. And Ussachevsky was not someone Bob could easily ignore. Ussachevsky had started off as an engineer and switched to music later. He spoke the language of engineering, and the way to Bob's heart was, of course, through circuitry.

Soon Ussachevsky and Bob were discussing one specific circuit—the envelope generator. Normally such a module is used with a keyboard as a trigger to make the sound of, say, a plucked string. Ussachevsky wanted an envelope generator, but he didn't want it to be triggered by a keyboard. Instead, he planned to use it with tapes to shape recorded sounds. Moog designed him a special module with the envelope triggered by an external switch rather than by a keyboard.

Moog's interaction with Ussachevsky was important not only because it conveyed to him the depth of hostility toward the keyboard that existed among some serious composers but also because it led to the standard way to describe the main functions of an envelope generator in terms of T_1 (attack time), T_2 (initial decay time), E_{SUS} (sustain level), and T_3 (final decay time). Eventually ARP simplified this to the ADSR (attack, decay, sustain, and release) nomenclature still in current usage.

That Ussachevsky had purchased his rival's synthesizers and was opposed to the keyboard gave Moog food for thought. Moog was not strongly wedded to the keyboard as a controller; it was just one option. After all, he built theremins, and these were about as far removed as you could get from a keyboard-controlled instrument. But not everyone agreed with Ussachevsky. One composer who saw things rather differently was Herb Deutsch, who had been Moog's first collaborator: "Bob didn't want to have a keyboard, because he had talked to Vladimir Ussachevsky, and Vladimir said, 'Oh, no, you don't want a keyboard, because then people are going to think of it more traditionally. You'll be, it'll be dominated by the need to be tonal, or at least relate to tonal design' . . . And I simply thought, Well, it didn't bother Schoenberg to have a keyboard. I mean, he still created atonal music and you still have the freedom to do anything you want. And I persuaded Bob to do a keyboard on it." Deutsch felt, in other words, that a serious composer would be able to overcome any conventional associations the keyboard evoked.

The commercial appeal of the keyboard was something Deutsch and Moog both recognized as well. Walter Sear also put pressure on Moog to stick with the keyboard: "Buchla's [synthesizer] had nothing to do with musicians. I kept saying without a keyboard it's not anything that a musician [could use], you know, all musicians, in those days, had to have some background in keyboard." And commercial musicians were voting with their feet—or rather their hands. Eric Siday had wanted keyboards. So too did other commercial musicians.

For many musicians, the simpler-to-operate Moog with its keyboard interface was more appealing. Moog, no doubt impressed by what most of his customers wanted, decided to stay with the keyboard, himself regarding it as a "general controller" with which to adjust a variety of modules on the synthesizer and not simply as a way to play melodic music.

Keyboard Culture

As the Moog synthesizer evolved, it increasingly became seen as a keyboard instrument. Many of the photographs of the Moog (in the media, on record albums, and in promotional literature) show the keyboards prominently displayed. In these early pictures the right hand of the operator is usually on the keyboard while the left hand is outstretched adjusting the knobs. We asked Bob about these pictures: "The keyboards were always there, and whenever someone wanted to take a picture, for some reason or other it looks good if you're playing a keyboard. People understand that then you're making music. You know [without it] you could be tuning in Russia! This pose here [acts out the pose of the left arm extended] graphically ties in the music and the technology. So there are probably a zillion pictures like that."

The need to show that "you're making music" was something of which Bob was all too well aware. The modular Moog synthesizer is a very odd musical instrument, because, unlike most instruments, you cannot immediately get a sound out of it. It first has to be plugged in, patched up, and connected to an amplifier and loudspeaker. On first encountering the synthesizer, people often expect to hear a tune. Jon Weiss discovered this when he brought the synthesizer on the set for Mick Jagger's use in the movie *Performance:* "I had to go through this with the English workers, saying 'Agh it's a fabulous sanitizer and what does it do?' You know, 'Play us a tune' . . . Moog heard that so much that in one series of synthesizers he put a little speaker and amplifier in one so that you could actually hear something. People couldn't conceive that this is an instrument but it doesn't do anything."

A keyboard is immediately recognizable; it's an icon and "looks good" and invites people to come and play it. And it is here that the wider culture and particularly the dominance of the piano played a role in shaping the synthesizer. Over time, almost inexorably, the Moog synthesizer became a keyboard synthesizer. By the time the Minimoog was developed in 1970, it was, de facto, a keyboard instrument.

Moog has eventually come to see the wisdom of not following the strict approach of Ussachevsky and Milton Babbitt, another giant of electronic music composition who co-directed the Columbia-Princeton studio in Princeton and was closely associated with composing on the RCA synthesizer. Moog: "Ussachevsky and Babbitt have always talked as if they were the light and the way and everyone else should follow them. But actually their concept is very narrow, I think. They have dictated that certain things shall not be. There shall not be keyboards and that sort of thing."

With hindsight, we can see that Bob's decision to design his system around a keyboard was a propitious one. But again, hindsight should not mislead. At the time, this was just one of many little decisions being made. It was not that Moog looked into his crystal ball and foresaw that the synthesizer would become a keyboard instrument. It was just that if musicians wanted keyboards, who was he to stop them having what they wanted? His strategy of listening and responding to customers meant that the synthesizer as a keyboard instrument was being shaped by the wider culture. And that culture would, in turn, be shaped and changed by the Moog.

The Ribbon Controller

Although Moog went down the keyboard path, he also developed other sorts of interfaces such as the ribbon controller (also known as the linear controller or stringer).[6] This two-foot-long narrow rectangular box has a taut gold-plated metal band strung over a resistance strip running along its length. By moving a finger along the band and pushing down the musician can vary the control voltage smoothly in direct proportion to the point of contact. The ribbon can be used to control the pitch of an oscillator in a similar way to moving a finger up and down a violin string. It can also be used for vibrato, or to control other modules like the filter.

Musicians came to value the ribbon, especially in live performance. One such musician was Chris Swansen, a Trumansburg-based jazz musician. By rapidly sliding his finger backward and forward along the controller, Swansen produced the same effect as a trombonist sliding the arm of his trombone in and out. Swansen played the ribbon with one hand while he played keyboards with the other. It was also useful in the studio. Malcolm Cecil and Bob Margouleff used the ribbon controller with Stevie Wonder to produce the classic "burump" of the bass on "Boogie on, Reggae Woman," and Paul McCartney used it on the Beatles track "Maxwell's Silver Hammer."

Rock keyboardists took to the controller with a vengeance for live performance. For Keith Emerson, it was an indispensable part of his stage act. The shape of the ribbon controller evokes the guitar, and Keith Emerson wielded it like an axe. Videos of Emerson, Lake and Palmer in performance show Keith standing on stage in all the pomp rock regalia of the day lifting his ribbon controller upward from his groin as the music swells and climaxes. Keith even had toy rocket motors attached to the ribbon controller to fire up at such moments for added pyrotechnic effect (once in rehearsal he was demonstrating the rockets to a fire marshal and was lucky to have had only his thumbnail blown off).

But in the middle of all these pyrotechnics Keith stumbled upon a new use for his ribbon controller: "The ribbon got so worn down, and I was almost complaining, 'Oh God, I've worn this out. I should really call Bob up and get a new ribbon.' But then I realized that by short-circuiting my thumb across the ribbon and the actual bar it made these machine-gun sounds. I thought, 'No, this is great!' There again, it was just, the instrument wore out, but I got other sounds out of it as a consequence." Even in the Moog's imperfections musicians could often find a use.

Running around with a big electronic phallus in live performance is not always easy. Keith's ribbon controller usually had a hundred feet of cable, but on one occasion he was limited to twenty-five feet and he forgot how far he could go. Will Alexander, Keith's keyboard technician, recalls what happened next: "During the Japan tour, the band was playing in Osaka at a baseball stadium. They were set up in the outfield and the audience was 150 feet away, up where the home plate was. So Keith started playing with the ribbon controller and he went running at the audience, when all of a sudden he reached the end and it knocked him down. It made the Moog go berserk."[7] Keith, always the consummate showman, was able to deal with the incident with aplomb: "He got up, turned and bowed to the audience, and went running back to the stage."[8] By, in effect, turning the ribbon controller into a guitar, Emerson and his audience (mainly made up of young men) were reproducing all the cultural and gender symbolism that the guitar as "technophallus" in rock music evokes.[9]

Music seems to be one of the most conservative areas of cultural production. Here was a new instrument, the synthesizer, one of the few new instruments ever to come along, and people seemed obliged to perceive it in terms of instruments with which they were familiar, the piano and guitar. Escape from these shadows would be difficult.

The Moog Ladder Filter

Moog's voltage-controlled oscillators, amplifiers, filters, and envelope generators were initially based on standard circuits. Sometime during late 1965 and early 1966 Moog came up with a novel design for a filter, known as the low-pass filter or ladder filter (after the ladder of transistors in the circuit). This filter is the crown jewel of the Moog synthesizer—it is the "rich," "fat," "juicy" tone that nearly everyone refers to as the Moog sound. This is the filter that Moog's rivals at ARP and EMS were most envious of and which they tried to copy.

Filters, which control the higher harmonics of sound, were not new; they had been used since the days of radio. Bob seems to have designed his unique low-pass filter from a combination of book knowledge and his usual tinkering. He presented the design in a paper delivered to the AES convention on October 11, 1965. A year later, on October 10, 1966, he filed for a patent, which was granted on October 28, 1969. It is the only item on the whole synthesizer that Moog ever patented.[10]

A low-pass filter can be thought of as a gate in a stream. The higher it is raised, the higher the harmonic frequencies that pass through it—or, more correctly, under it, since it's a low-pass filter. If you speak into a long pipe, your voice will be muffled because the pipe is acting as a low-pass filter; talking into a pillow has the same effect. Where the cutoff occurs—that is, how high the gate is raised—depends on where the cutoff control is set. By varying the height of the gate, the timbre or tone color of the sound can be varied. (Timbre is what allows you to distinguish a pitch played by a clarinet from the same pitch played by an oboe.) By voltage-controlling the gate, the musician can sweep the filter through its range, changing the timbre of the sound by emphasizing some harmonics and attenuating others.

Bob found a novel circuit to do this, using pairs of transistors connected by capacitors arranged in a ladder. This makes the filter balanced, because the signals can go up both sides of the ladder at the same time. The signals enter the bottom of the ladder, and those with higher frequencies find it hard to make their way up the ladder because of the electrical properties of the transistors and capacitors.[11] One of the main factors in the quality of the sound from the Moog filter is a characteristic called the cutoff slope. A filter doesn't actually chop the high harmonics off completely but rather attenuates them. The cutoff slope refers to how abruptly the amplitudes of the high frequencies taper off. The Moog filter has a much sharper cutoff slope than almost any other synthesizer filter.[12]

The filter has many other qualities, such as a sharp resonance around the cut-off frequency. When the filter is overdriven—which means that the amplitudes of the signals going into the filter are too large—it produces a rich form of distortion that is characteristic of the fat Moog sound. Jim Scott, a Moog engineer who worked extensively with the ladder filter, adapting it for use on the Minimoog, commented, "This filter defies analysis. There are lots of subtle things going on that almost defy mathematical treatment."[13] The best analog components in sound nearly always have this quality of not being quite understood and nearly always involve some not quite specifiable resonances and distortions that occur at high frequencies beyond the audible range but that produce audible effects.

When the filter is used with an envelope generator in the bass range, the resonant deep sound is particularly appealing and was soon discovered by synthesists.[14] Over the years it has become a staple of pop and rock music, as has the bass sound of the Minimoog (which uses a similar filter). Bob Moog was himself a witness to the power of his bass sound when he was invited to bring his synthesizer to a New York studio session where Simon and Garfunkel were recording their album *Bookends* (1968). Moog set up the bass sound himself for the track "Save the Life of a Child," which opens with this sound: "One sound I remember distinctly was a plucked string, like a bass sound. Then it would slide down—it was something you could not do on an acoustic bass or an electric bass . . . a couple of session musicians came through. One guy was carrying a bass and he stops and he listens, and listens. He turned white as a sheet." The significance of the Moog bass sound was not lost on this session musician. The Moog not only sounded like an acoustic or electric bass, but it also sounded *better.*

Moog liked to repeat this story; he felt that at last he was "getting somewhere." At last the Moog was finding a home among musicians at large, rather than being an instrument merely for the avant-garde. Session musicians were some of the first to see the writing on the wall; their livelihoods were under threat. This threat was something that the powerful musicians' union would eventually take up.

But is it a Synthesizer?

In the early accounts of his work, Moog refers to "electronic music modules" and a "system" of such modules, but he does not use the word "synthesizer." In 1966 he used the term "synthesizer" for the first time in print, and in 1967 he introduced the "Synthesizer Concept."[15] The classical meaning of "to synthesize" is to assemble a whole out of parts. A synthesizer assembled parts of a sound into a complete sound. Moog, like Buchla, thought long and hard about whether to use the term. The name was associated with the RCA synthesizer, but Moog's synthesizer, unlike the RCA, worked in real time and had a keyboard. Moog and Deutsch debated this a lot. Reynold Weidenaar, a composer based at the Moog factory, joined the debate: "I remember when he told me that was his decision, to call it a synthesizer . . . I said, 'You can't do that, you know, the RCA device is the synthesizer, and every-body's going to think of the RCA synthesizer if you use this word, so you're going to have to think of another word.' And he said, 'Well, no, it's a synthesizer and that's what it does and we're just going to have to go with it.' And so he was obstinate, and good thing, too."

By the time other manufacturers like ARP and EMS got going in the late sixties and early seventies, "synthesizer" had become the standard name. Buchla held out longest against the usage, but even he at some point recognized that this was the name that most people were using.

What's in the Moog Name

For a short while in the late 1960s and early 1970s, the Moog became the brand name for any synthesizer, in much the same way that the Hoover was synonymous with vacuum cleaners.[16] Branding—making customers aware of your brand, above all of its competitors—can be crucial for the success of a product, as marketers are well aware.

Moog is a Dutch name and rhymes with "rogue," not "fugue." Many people, including musicians, continue to this day to mispronounce the name. Bob even used to have a placard on his desk telling people how to pronounce his name. Several people unfamiliar with the existence of the real Bob Moog have told us that they assumed the name was made up to resemble the sound of the synthesizer itself—MOOOOOOOOOOOG! Cows moo, but synthesizers moog, and as David Van Koevering (the best Moog salesman ever) once said, paraphrasing the sixties lyric by Jonathan King; "Everyone's gone to the Moog [Moon]." The name not only sounds right, it also looks right in distinctive letters adorning a piece of equipment.

And here Moog was extremely lucky. If his name had been Larry Smith or Dusan Bjelic, it is unlikely that his make of synthesizer would have become the brand name.[17] Naming a synthesizer is no trivial matter, as the Japanese, who would later dominate the market, were well aware. Ikutaro Kakehashi, the founder of Roland, the most successful synthesizer company in the world today, told us that he came up with the name by looking through an American telephone directory. Having found the name, he wrote it on piece of paper and attached it to an organ (in those days the company made organs) for a week to see if it felt right. It did![18]

The 900 Series

By October 1965 Moog had standardized the different modules, which became known as the 900 series.[19] The modules varied in price from $195 for a 901 VCO to $475 for a 904 filter. In April 1967 Moog introduced for the first time a catalog with complete "synthesizers."[20] He offered three different models (I, II, and III) ranging in price from $2,800 to $6,200. The most expensive model cost a sizable chunk of money—enough to buy a small house. A more elaborate system with a tape recorder and amplifier could set you back a lot more. Even rock stars were known to balk at the cost. Keith Emerson tried hard to get his for free, and Mick Jagger, on being told the price, famously remarked, "Man, that's a lot of bread."

The first Moog catalog listed numerous customers who had bought Moog equipment, and on the inside back and front covers were endorsements from 21 composers and directors of studios, including Siday, Carlos, Ciamanga, Deutsch, and Nikolais. This impressive list shows that Moog was reaping the benefit of his close links with his customers if for no other purpose than to promote his equipment. The catalog was directed almost exclusively at the electronic music composers who made up the bulk of Moog's customers. "Moog synthesizers are designed to meet the requirements of composers of all types of electronic music."[21] These requirements were "based on discussions with over 100 composers." The first requirement was that "the synthesizer should perform all of the basic generating and modifying operations of the classical studio, and provide additional resources with the state of the art."

Moog had the name, and by 1967 he had the product. Also, the culture around him was slowly changing, becoming ever more receptive to his innovation. We now turn to look at how this culture was experienced in one funky factory, and how Moog set out to change it [see original publication].

Notes

1. Reynold Weidenaar, *Magic Music from the Telharmonium* (Metchuen, NJ: Scarecrow Press, 1995).

2.   Laurens Hammond, like Bob Moog, was a Cornell alumnus (he graduated in mechanical engineering in 1917). See Mark Vail, *The Hammond Organ* (San Francisco: Miller Freeman, 1997). Hammond worked closely with W. L. Lahey, a church organist, in the development of his instrument See Théberge, *Any Sound You Can Imagine* (Hanover, NH: Wesleyan University Press, 1997), p. 45.

3.   Goebbels followed new developments in music technology and was very keen on the sound of the trautonium. He advocated regular trautonium concerts on the radio for propaganda purposes. See Hans-Joachim Braun, "Technik im Spiegel der Musik des fruehen 20. Jahrhunderts," *Technikgeschichte* 59 (1992); 109–31.

4.   Karin Bijsterveld, "A Servile Imitation: Disputes about Machines in Music, 1910–30," in Braun *"I Sing the Body Electric:" Music and Technology in the 20th Century.* (Hofheim: Wolke, 2000), pp. 121–34.

5.   *Time,* November 4, 1966, p. 44.

6.   The Ondes Martenot and trautonium both used a form of ribbon controller to produce continuous changes in pitch.

7.   Vail, ed., *Vintage Synthesizers* (Montclair, NJ: Backbeat Books, 2000), p. 121.

8.   Ibid.

9.   See, Waksman, *Instruments of Desire* (Cambridge, MA: Harvard University Press, 2001), p. 188.

10. Patent No. 3,475,623, "Electronic high-pass and low pass filters employing the base to emitter diode resistance of bipolar transistors."

11. The ladder of paired transistors with capacitors in between permits low-frequency signals to pass up the ladder unattenuated, since the reactance of the capacitors is highest at low frequencies. At higher frequencies the signal is shunted around the emitter-emitter input and is sharply attenuated.

12. The cutoff slope is 24 dB/octave, which means that frequencies one octave above the cut-off point are reduced 24 dB over those at the cutoff frequency.

13. Quoted in Steve Smith, "The Best Filter Built," *Imooginations* (Chicago: Norlin, 1976), p. 10. Our description of the operation of the Moog filter is based upon this article.

14. A good example is Malcolm Cecil's and Bob Margouleff's track "Cybernaut" on *Zero Time* (1971).

15. At the 1966 AES fall convention Moog presented in the exhibit hall his "System A" studio synthesizer, *Journal of the Audio Engineering Society* 14 (1966): 364.

16. The Hoover is also one of the few inventions whose name onomatopoeically suggests the sound of the invention.

17. Dusan Bjelic is an acquaintance of one of the authors. When he applied for U.S. citizenship, it was recommended that he change his name to Larry Smith!

18. The other Japanese synthesizer giant, Korg, has a similar made-up name. Korg's founder, Tsutomu Katoh, was a nightclub proprietor who teamed up with Tadahi Osanai, an engineer and noted Japanese accordionist, to form Keio Electronic Laboratories (representing the combination of the first initials of Katoh's and Osanai's names). In 1967 they produced their first organ with programmable voices and adopted the company name Korg, a combination of the words Keio and Organ.

19. Moog's 1965 "Ultra-Short Form Catalog of Electronic Composition Instruments" lists a VCO, 901; a VGA, 902; a white sound source, 903; a filter, 904; a reverberation unit, 905; a fixed filter bank, 907; an envelope generator, 911; a keyboard controller, 950; and a linear controller, 955, as well as other subsidiary modules.

20. R. A, Moog Co., "Short Form Catalog," 1967. Moog also offered a complete range of 900-series modules and other devices, including a frequency shifter and ring modulator made under license from Harald Bode.

21. Ibid.

Chapter 24

Louise Meintjes

THE RECORDING STUDIO AS FETISH

Gear

DOWNTOWN STUDIOS IS ONE of the best-equipped and most abundantly staffed state-of-the-art recording facilities in South Africa. In the early 1990s it was run by five in-house engineers, a programmer who also engineered, a programmer-trainee/tape operator, a technician, and a team of administrative and executive personnel. Freelancing engineers also used the facility. The engineers and the trainee were young men (early twenties to mid-thirties), South African except for one Briton and white except for one African.[1] Two of the seven were also performing musicians. With the exception of Humphrey Mabote, the African engineer, none spoke local languages other than English or Afrikaans. Of the South Africans, three had had no overseas experience in engineering and three had trained (short-term) and/or worked briefly in the United States or Britain. The British engineer, a recent immigrant to South Africa, had trained in London.

The studio complex comprises three 24-track studios. Each houses a superb console. The capacity of these analog facilities is enhanced by hard disc and DA8 digital equipment. Additional facilities are provided by a sixteen-track studio, a digital editing suite, and an analog dubbing-editing suite.[2]

The differences in the size, design, and equipment of the four studios offer functional versatility. Studios 1 and 2 are the bigger spaces designed for projects with large choral groups and bands, and for general mixing; Studio 3 is smaller and ideal for overdubs, vocals, MIDI tracking, and final mixing; and Studio 4, the sixteen track, is intended as a programming, demo, and budget album space.

Over the course of my primary research period in 1991 and 1992, the use of DAT tape superseded analog tape in the studios. Songs were either recorded directly onto DAT or onto half-inch analog tape (in Studio 4) or onto two-inch analog tape and then transferred to DAT for final editing. Most recordings were released on LP and cassette, CDS were reserved for big-budget products at this time.

The studios own an extensive array of outboard gear that gets stacked and trolleyed into the studios, plugged in, yanked out, and shunted around. A full range of MIDI Equipment, keyboards, and professional microphones are available, including prized old equipment.[3] Drum kits and guitars are also retained, though these are rarely used in mbaqanga and "trad" (traditional) recording sessions. The studios sold the Sotho trad drum, a steel bin with a rubber tire stretched over its opening and rattling bottletops wired up across it, along with the shabby furniture in their garage sale in the basement. Its disappearance was part of the building's facelift and the technological revamping of the studios.

The choice item in the studio makeover, an SSL4048 G Series Console with total recall, arrived late in 1991. This console was the top of the range, the Mercedes Benz 560SEL of the studio world. Downtown's SSL was the first of its kind installed in South Africa.[4] The solid state logic of its internal electronics enables the engineer to store within it all the settings of a particular recording session. The settings can thereby be recalled with absolute ease, precision, and speed from one session to the next. The SSL is especially valued by sound engineers for two features that have a direct bearing on the recorded sound: the accuracy of its input-output relationship and the flexibility with which it can handle sound manipulation. It is said to have the capacity to deliver the very cleanest scientifically accurate sound while still matching the warmth and personality of older consoles.[5] The SSL is a form of technological capital. In transnational studio discourse, merely to work on this console indexically suggests something about the professional sophistication of the engineer, the quality of his (or her) production, and the particular kind of sound a product can attain. Simply by owning an SSL, Downtown indexes the internationally competitive quality of its technicians and the elevated positioning of the studio within the hierarchy of the domestic recording industry.

With superb studios, an array of excellent analog and digital equipment, and fine engineers, Downtown Studios is able to accommodate a wide range of recording and production projects. Musicians touring with Paul Simon on his *Rhythm of the Saints* tour laid down some tracks in Studio 1 for an album by New York-based Tony Cedras in December 1991. Shangaan musician Thomas Chauke traveled down from the north of the country and—like no other local musician—booked fourteen open weeks for his next Shangaan hit album. Rock band the Get Out traveled up from East London for three weeks to produce a CD. While week in and week out Lance or Neil or sometimes Darryl or Richard took their dreaded turns recording texts for automated phone-in services. "Ah!" exhales programmer-trainee Lance in exasperation. "I've been sitting there for *hours* and *days* doing horoscopes and tarots and medical lines and now, now I'm doing Indian [horoscope] lines. All it is it's finger PT [physical training]—hey, that tape machine. . . . " He pecks repeatedly at his thigh with one finger while rolling his eyes and contorting his mouth. "Play and record—they make a mistake—rewind, drop them in, carry on. It's hideous! It's crazy! It's a total jungle!"

The bulk of the studio's income comes from recording "black stuff," as I heard many an engineer and white person in the music industry call the stream of low-budget productions geared toward the mostly regional, sometimes national market that provides most of studio's bookings.[6] Such productions usually take up to a week of studio time and use programmed rhythm and percussion tracks. They are worked by one sound engineer, though he is often interchangeable with the others. Trad, mbaqanga, gospel, and "bubblegum" (township pop) music generally fall into this category. Session musicians are frequently called in on the spur of the moment to do an overdub. The musicians are often not present during mixing. Sometimes even the producer is absent for some or almost all of the mixing. The engineer is usually not informed until the beginning of the first session about the particularities of a production.

The production of Isigqi Sesimanje's *Lomculo Unzima* fits squarely and clearly with the bulk of its genre as a run-of-the-mill studio project. It was recorded, mixed, and edited in seven days, 18–21 November 1991 and 30 March – 1 April 1992. (Not all days were full.) Different production tasks were assigned to appropriate studio spaces: the basic backing was laid down in Studio 2; the overdubs and mixing happened in the smaller Studio 3. The editing was completed in the editing suite, downstairs, as is the procedure for all studio product. Peter Pearlson was assigned to engineer the project, with producer West Nkosi's approval. Neil Kuny substituted for him for some sessions. In the course of engineering, Neil also played some of the percussion overdubs, such as the steel drum (on an electronic drum pad) on the title song, "Lomculo Unzima." Session musicians were called in midsession a couple of times to overcome hitches in the band's performance.

> Standby . . . rolling. . . .
>
> The backing male chorus resorts to one by one practice in front of the microphone in the studio. Right—on. No, it's off. Again. It's still out of tune. Again, three, four. "Where's Mandla?" asks West, getting bored. "He'll sing it right quickly." He calls him up at old Gallo's in Kerk Street while Bheki runs downstairs to check if he's hanging out in the sun outside, with Fakes and Ebony's backing singers and Harare.

The somewhat haphazard organization of *Lomculo Unzima's* studio production—an extended intercession, shifts in location, and engineer and musician substitutions midproduction—would be far less likely to occur during the course of prominent projects. Musicians had minimal input during mixing; few were even present. They were, of course, all present and on time the morning of the first day of recording.

Take 1: The Studio as Fetish

Open the door to the left of Florence and Liza's reception desk. Head down the tunnel-like passage for the double doors at the end. Unless the red "session in progress" light above the double door prohibits interruptions, enter the black box that is Studio 3.[7] It is an enclosed space, a dark-bounded interior, a private space with a secret life. Its physical placement in the company's floor plan and its architectural design separate the studio from the outside world.

Inside, the studio's decoration and the specialized objects and their arrangement within the space lend it its distinction. Black walls, low black ceiling, and overhead lighting make the small, square control-room space close in on itself. The previous session's cigarette smoke sits invisibly on your eyebrows. The electronic equipment reflects in the double-paned, vacuum-sealed windows connecting/separating the control room and the two recording booths. The reflections cast more techno images into the multiply machined studio space. Technology fills the floor area and stacks up against the walls. "U sho ukuthi yonke le'mishini uma kure-khodwa iyasebenza? Yonke le'mishini?" (Are you sure all these machines work when something is recorded? *All* these machines?) asks guitarist-producer Hansford Mthembu. The machines gleam magnificently. Their newness and sophistication seem to balance the space on the edge of the sonic future. Is this a mirror image of Apollo and Sputnik with their cramped and awesome technical interiors?

Iconicity is there to be noticed in the look of the studio. Panels of instruments— as in cockpits, luxury cars, rockets, and space stations—situate the studio alongside similar developments of the military-industrial complex. Music-makers' talk about the studio in terms of space research metaphorizes a particular relation of subjects to instrumentation and subjects to time. That space capsules take precedence over luxury cars and cockpits as the metaphorical reference is due to the way space has historically been presented to the public as the site of the future and how space scientists have been presented as the leaders preparing the way to that future through their technological design and operation.[8]

Phenomenological links between space travel and other kinds of movement enabled by the studio are also there to be sensed and elaborated by those who work in its space. Indeed, by means of successful recording, music-makers may well rocket upward through the star system, just as they may travel out to new places in the listening, dancing, sociopolitical world. And while working within the confines of the studio itself, they may be propelled into inner worlds, expressive worlds—art worlds—in the process of composition and production.[9] All right, gents, let's see where we're going.

Inner worlds? Elements of the studio's design and decoration point to the existence of interiors within interiors in the physical enclosure that they make and mark. The presence of these complex interiors play a part in generating an atmosphere of mystery and hidden potency, for they can be revealed—always only in part—to those who know how to access them, while they are hidden from ordinary view.

I'm isolating that track.

Master maskandi Thembinkosi Ntuli is overdubbing his own backing vocals on his self-produced recording. His singing style is taut and nasal. When in top form, he glides on and off tones like a swinging acrobat in an extravagant circus. But tonight he's struggling with the tuning, for the chorus lies awkwardly in his upper vocal range.

Take. Erase. Take. Erase. Lee directs and advises from the engineer's chair. He gets up and dims the lights in Ntuli's booth. 'Let's get some atmosphere in here!' he quips. He darkens the edges and back of the control room. The world outside disappears; the extremities of the studio hide in shadow. Now only Lee listening piercingly, and the mixing console, will be illuminated.

Around the black walls of Studio 3's control room dances an airsprayed luminous yellow, pink, and green path. Scattered graffiti-like lines depict the scientific transformation of sound from airwaves through the recording process to magnetic flux. It is as minimalist a representation of the recording process as a look at the studio is of its intricate sonic workings or as a dissection of its electronic workings is of its artistic expressive activity.

It is day one, session one, of Isigqi Sesimanje's recording.

In Studio 2 engineer Peter Pearlson and West are laying backing tracks with the instrumentalists and the drum box. Mkhize and Mzwandile, the guitar and bass players, are stuffed into the smaller sound booth with their amps. The women—Jane, Joana, and Janet—and Michael sing along in the larger booth, rehearsing into the microphone. They each cover one ear with a headphone cup. The second cup hangs open on their necks, leaving their other ear free for in-booth communication. The singers and players watch one another through the glass door partitioning their booths.

A plate bored with holes for mike and amp chord jacks is set into the front wall of the recording booths, ready to transmit audio lines into the control room. The space is carpeted, air conditioned, double-doored. Soundproofing pads the walls in sophisticated patches, visually drawing attention to the sonic difference of the space. On the ceiling, panels slant at odd angles to enhance the acoustics.

In the control room, West leans his elbows on the mixing console, listening, watching the musicians through the wide double-paned and vacuum-sealed windows that separate the control room and the booths. Peter sits alongside him listening, watching likewise, gesturing an entry to the musicians. He reaches across the enormous desk spread with knobs and buttons and sliding sound-level controls to tweak a button on the far side. He hawkeyes the lit gauges of the VU meters. He flips a switch.

The pair are seamed in between the mixing console in front, the outboard effects rack behind, the telephone, the ashtray, the remote control for the tape deck, the MIDI rack holding the drum synthesizer machine, the MIDI clock/tape synchronizing converter, a trigger converter, a sequencer or two perhaps, a thru box or a patcher. These loose components are all stacked on wheeled trolleys, drawn in close enough for Peter to swivel and reach. Signal-processing devices are sleekly stacked, floor-to-rib height, in the outboard effects console, hierarchically ordered in terms of the frequency of their use: echo, decay, delay, and reverberation machines; limiters, expanders, compressors; phasing and flanging units; exciters and pitch shifters; graphic and parametric equalizers and noise gates. The multinationals are wired into the studio system. They name their indelible presence—Lexicon, Roland, Yamaha, Korg, Technics, Amcron—on the faces of their products.

Along the side wall of the studio are more pieces of equipment, more lights, more dials. The latest Dolby SR/A noise-reduction machines are packed into a rack as tall as Peter. Alongside, at waist height, sits the mastering tape recorder and the multitrack recording deck. Two-inch tape wound onto a large, fat reel snakes around tension levers, past the recording head, onto a second reel. If the new portable Tascam DAT recorder is used instead, it is placed on top of the outboard effects console along with any keyboard in use.

Jane, Joana, Janet, and Michael's voices, Mkhize's guitar, Mzwandile's bass, and the MIDI-ed rhythm tracks rain down from the huge speakers mounted high on the wall in front of the console. The speakers are angled downward. On the ledge of the main recording console, middle-sized monitors mimic the large ones. Between them sit two tiny ones that replicate the sound of a cheap ghetto blaster.

My two microphones, perched below the little monitors, face West and Peter. I hang over the desk, facing them too. Sometimes I move to the back of the studio and lean on the rib-height console with the keyboard players and any cruising visitors. Sometimes I perch on West's or Peter's shoulders like a parakeet.

Mandla, the drummer; Bethwell the band's regular bass player whom West has replaced with Mzwandile for some of the sessions; and Phatiswe, Oscar, and Bheki, the backing vocalist dancers, lounge on the couch against the back wall. They watch, they listen, they chat, they read the Sowetan newspaper.

> Stand by, I'm dropping this in.
> West and his musical colleagues from the old days are recording a sax jive CD for the international market.[10] West is the producer and principal artist. I want to listen in one day. West hesitates. He defers to the others sitting around the canteen table, lunching on goat's head and stiff maize porridge. 'Why, of course she can come in,' answers Hansford. 'She's part of the family!' Hansford turns to tease me: 'Do you like *ipapa nembuzi* [stiff porridge and goat's meat]?'

The studio is remote and exclusive. It is closed to outsiders except for haphazard, enticing ingressions like mine and those of friends of the music-makers who might drop in for a session or a moment. 'If the studios had their shit together, you'd never have got in!' Wry engineer Neil half laughs, warning that 'overseas your story would be different, hey!' As Michael Taussig writes about the image of Cuna women, their very inaccessibility to outsiders (foreigners), which is controlled by mediating figures (Cuna men in Taussig's case, studio workers in this case) who make access tauntingly erratic, invests them with aura (1993, 182). Cuna women and recording studios are invested with something potent, unknowable, and desirable.

What is this something? In the words of Susan Stewart writing on miniatures, a "thing" with a "secret life," if opened up, can reveal "a set of actions and hence a narrativity and history outside the given field of perception" (1993, 54).

Take 2: The Studio's Technology Fetishized

It is not a long leap to link Apollo and Sputnik and a space station on the moon to the studio via the look of things. But the studio's awe emanates not only from the spatial encapsulation and glossy technics that promise travel, discovery, excellence, and accumulation in their design. Housed inside its machines are the fetishized worlds of science and sound. Just as the studio's technology plays a part in fetishizing the sound it produces, so do the complexity and beauty of the sound in turn intensify the aura of the technology.[11]

Fast-forward to day five, session five of Isigqi Sesimanje's recording, on 30 March 1992: In Studio 3 engineer Neil Kuny and West have just triple-tracked the backing male vocals on the first chorus of the song "South Africa is on Fire." The backing singers—Phatiswe, Oscar, and Bheki—cluster around their microphone, listening through their headphones for further instruction from West and Neil, and watching through the window for their gestures. The women, Bethwell, and Michael hang around the control room. West decides to check the newly recorded section. They listen through the huge speakers up on the wall.

Joana enthuses, "Uyezwa ukuthi bayicula kamnandi njani? Imnandi!" (Can you hear how nicely they sing it? It's nice!)

West and Neil discuss how they will sequence this chorus of the male voices to insert wherever it's needed in the song, rather than recording it anew each time. Joana chats on. She stands alongside the MIDI rack.

"Eyi! Lento"—she loosens her folded arms and points at the MIDI clock on the top deck—"ungaze uyibone incane, iphethe yonke inhlobo yento ezakure-khodwa manje sikulekwaya." (Eyi! This thing, you might see it small as it is, [but] it is carrying all different types of things in it, which are going to be recorded. Now we are on this choir.)

With the choir triple-tracked, nine men's voices are captured in that small machine. But Joana implies more than this: nine men's voices, plus twelve women's voices (their verses also being triple-tracked), a solo voice, and all the instrumental backing now reside in that small machine.

Neil and West move on with the session. They turn to the weak bass drum sound. West wants more weight in it. They extract it from the small box to change its frequency profile and perhaps to add effects.

The MIDI clock does not actually house the sounds to which Joana refers. Rather it is a central node for entering information into the MIDI system. It synchronizes the digitally processed sounds with the sounds recorded on tape. However, its positioning for quick and easy access right next to the console at Neil's right hand and its constant use readily give it the appearance of being the central housing unit for the recorded sound, from Joana's point of view. For her, there is a whole sonic world packed into that sleek machine, which registers the presence of its precious contents only as digitized figures in a tiny control window and as a steady, red "power on" light the size of a pinhead. It is a world to which Joana can point, but that she cannot enter herself. This sonic world encoded in complex electronics is more extensive than the object within which it resides. It is invisible but sensed to be of enormous proportion. The mathematical and electronic processes that encode it are as sophisticated as the face of their component's casing is simple. This interior world—the extensive and ephemeral residing in the complex and mathematical, yet presented as the small, intact, and simple—imbues the technology with an affecting presence. Its presence is further enhanced by the complex user interface that surrounds it. The multiple steps required for its operation (and these steps are far from transparent) and the elaborate lexicon that accompanies them inhibit contact with the object by all but the specialist. Technical lexicons enshroud objects and already opaque processes in mystery.

Standby.

"There's the DBX. These are the URIs, which should go across the desk. Six! I wasn't using six. SCAMPS—which go across the guitars. What?!"

Peter sucks in his lips, creases his eyebrows together. "Okay. Vocal is going into thirty-three."

Take 2 interrupted in favor of a third more similar to Take 1.

Take 3: Studio Sound Fetishized

Open the door to the left of Florence and Liza's reception desk. Head down the tunnel-like passage. The carpet creeping up the walls muffles your footsteps. You can hear music stopping and starting, stopping and starting behind those double acoustic doors at the end of the passage. Enter the music box that is Studio 3. It is a space of sonic control, clarity, and separation, a space in which you notice yourself hearing and you miss the everyday reverb on your voice.

The acoustics mark the studio as a space out of the ordinary. But its distinction is not only derived from its focus around a sense other than the eye, the sense privileged in the metalanguage of the everyday (Stoller 1989; Minh-Ha 1991; Taussig 1993; Feld 1996). The studio also draws enchantment from the very quality of the sense it privileges. For "sound is a very special modality. We cannot handle it. We cannot push it away. We cannot turn our backs to it. We can close our eyes, hold our noses, withdraw from touch, refuse to taste. We cannot close our ears though we can partly muffle them. Sound is the least controllable of all sense modalities" (Jaynes 1976, quoted in Alten 1986). In their notion of musical groove, Keil and Feld extend this idea of sound as an uncontrollable modality to one of an infusing, embodied social sensibility (Schutz 1967; Keil and Feld 1994). Because sound as groove is participatory, feelingful, and experiential, its power is essentially unpredictable, unprogrammatic, in a sense, uncontrollable. Both the purely physiological uncontrollability of sound that Jayne recognizes and its social and sensual unboundedness, which Keil and Feld discuss, imbue sound with a particular— and heightened—quality.

The studio both houses and (re)produces sound's physiological, social, and sensual dimensions. The material structure of the studio seals the space acoustically, studio technology can open up and shut down the sounds within it. Engineers control and manipulate the science of sound in order to release and play with that social/ sensual uncontrollability. Their function is to harness and fix sounds momentarily in new combinations in order to create new grooves and thereby, eventually, to prompt new social and sensual experiences for those who listen (see Bendix 2000).

Studios regulate and optimize the physical and physiological conditions of listening in multiple ways. They are designed to isolate the internal sonic environment from the noise of the outside world.[12] The hubbub of the vicinity is dampened or extinguished. The world out there sounds far away.

I'm dropping this in. . . .

The telephone shrieks like a panic-stricken cricket noticing it's crouched near the console. "Hello?" Peter flicks down the master fader to hear the faint telephone voice. His takeout chicken-and-cheese has arrived at reception.

Inside the studio, the facility is insulated as tightly as possible from the noise of its own operation, for both recording and monitoring purposes. Clean sound separation is an ideal in studio design, from the overall structure of the rooms down to the minute electronic circuitry. Ambient sound from such sources as the ventilation is minimized through design and specialized insulating materials. Soundproofing in the booths and control room blocks out as much external sound as possible and absorbs unwanted internal frequencies. Specialized double-paned acoustic windows visually connect booths and the control room, while blocking the sound. Additionally, in a booth large enough to record more than one source at a time, movable, acoustically insulated baffles partition the area to limit leak-through from the sound source of one microphone into another.[13] To further minimize the effects of ambient sounds and leak-through, gating circuits are installed on microphone lines. These amplifier circuits cut out all signals below a selected threshold, thereby cutting out low-level noise. They are controlled from the outboard effects rack behind the engineer.

In addition to isolation and insulation procedures, other structural and technological features reproduce and monitor sound with minimal sonic disturbance. Music studios are designed to be acoustically dry.[14] An ideal control room is one that is itself acoustically neutral and uniform, so that there is as small a discrepancy as possible between a sound as it is laid onto tape and as it is heard through the monitors. Acoustic uniformity ensures that the quality of the sound is not affected by the spatial positioning of the listener or the live sound source. Sounds produced within this acoustic space can be isolated and listened to for and in themselves with minimal intervention, interruption, contamination, or transformation. Individual high-end headphones can further isolate external noise. The sound piped into each set can be individually mixed to accommodate a single listener's aural balance and volume needs.

Within this fantastically regulated sonic environment, by means of more technology, the infinitely "secret life" of sounds inside space, space inside sounds, and sounds inside sounds can be revealed. The studio becomes a space of sonic virtuosity, of movement, of experimentation, of creative expression let loose through the seemingly mad science of electronics. That is to say, by means of electronic processes that seem as impenetrable as sound itself, one voice is turned into many or into Mickey Mouse; dry sounds echo like a cavern; real becomes more than real; matter is transformed into something more than matter, into symbol, feeling, and aesthetic form.

"You can just take voices," West says. "You can make them sound like Mickey Mouse—you can make them sound anyhow you want them to. That is a producer's job."

Composite or single sounds seemingly fixed on tape or captured in computers can be minutely manipulated. Peter can control every sound parameter by means of the electronic technology available in the studio. He can manipulate the sound as a whole, or he can dissect and change it track by track or motive by motive. He can erase, shift, add, or precisely repeat any musical feature within the backing. In the mixing process, he can position each track acoustically in any given relation to the other tracks by cutting or boosting their relative volumes, channeling them to the left and/or right farther or nearer from the center for a stereo playback, and adding effects to and shaping the individual complex waveforms of their component tones in order to give a particular sense of dimension, color, and form to the overall sound.

"I like space in music," he tells me. "When I produce I try to create as much space as I can, in the tracks, because I find that you get a lot of relief from a track that is enormous and then just breaks down into absolutely nothing—there's all this space there, and it just gives you a chance to feel what is happening in the track." Peter can manipulate the wave components of a tone in multiple ways. He can play with its shape in time to effect textural features such as the attack and decay of tones. He can alter its fundamental frequency and hence its pitch. He can play with the composite frequency profile in order to shape timbre. He does so by extracting particular frequencies or frequency bands from within the composite signal or by increasing or diminishing their prominence. He can add effects to a tone or series of tones. He has at his electronic fingertips multiple versions of multiple effects programmed in the outboard gear—the signal processing devices—and linked through the MIDI systems into the programmed and recorded tracks.

With this facility, the life within a single sound can be revealed to an extent impossible outside in the everyday. With the studio's scientific precision, the technical skills of its engineers and the aural sophistication of its artists (including the engineers), sounds can be teased out of their surrounding sounds. From the macro to the micro, they are separated out for analysis, reworked, then reinserted in a transformed whole.

Studio music-makers with their superior aural competence can imagine composite sonic wholes, new sound worlds, and set about creating them with the technical expertise of their sound engineer. They can hear the details of complex sounds and set about reshaping them.[15] They can manipulate waveforms in order to give the impression of weight, density, movement, and space. That is to say, they can manipulate scientific technological processes and sound for metaphysical effect. I like space in music. Space here, inside the tracks, is at once a material band on a magnetic tape, a metaphor of that tape band extended to describe digital "space" in a computer, and an illusion and feeling of space.

By its function and the quality of its form, the studio marks sound as privileged, fantastic, enchanted, and enchanting.

Take 4: Studio Artistry Fetishized

Like the patchbay to the board, the studio is the nerve center of the creative process, the mad scientist, the head of the industry, which 'you'll never be able to figure out by observing.'

Sometimes I irritated engineer Neil, just staring at what he was doing, this face always there, in front of him, behind him, over his shoulder, squeezed into an unused space. Not that I was in the way, he reassured me. 'But I reckoned that however much you watched you'd never know what's *really* going on. You could never know what's in my head when I make adjustments on the desk.' I would never be able to detail the creative thought of an artist scientifically analyzing the sound components of what he hears on the monitors, choosing from multiple options for how to improve it, and registering the changes through microelectronic analog or digital adjustments on the equipment in front of him. What does he hear? How does he translate it into science? Why does he boost the upper mids on the DI (direct input) bass line, change the vocal-plate settings on the solo voice, at this moment, in this combination, to these degrees?[16]

I cannot know his head. It is another unknowable, illimitable interior present in the studio and essential to music production. It is a significant phenomenological studio space, similar to the physical and metaphysical realms I have described. His head is a Cuna woman, to whom he grants me, as ethnographer, some alluring access until it appears I might claim to know and describe his creative self.

While I can account for and measure some of the adjustments he makes on the sound gear and console, I cannot necessarily anticipate or explain his choices. Neil is so deeply immersed in a set of engineering practices that his hands can race intuitively across the outboard gear. Much of his manipulation of the controls is felt, learned but not or no longer rationalized. He plays, improvises, and experiments with the technical options his instrument offers, much as performers do with their skills and sonic materials.

Though I cannot know his head, nor systematize his musical-technological body knowledge, I can link him as agent and voice into the creative process and trace the pathways of composition through him as through the other studio realms I have characterized. The sound passes through his artistic sensibility into the technology of the mixing console; transformed into magnetic flux, it passes onto studio tape, then off it, out again through the monitors mounted on the wall, and back into the body. I like spaces in music. There's all this space there, and it just gives you a chance to feel what is happening in the track. While each space is of a different order since each resides in a different kind of material body, they are all similarly imagined in terms of their formal qualities and spatial dimensions. The musical shape of the sound is transformed in the course of flowing.

The merging of these sites for moments and the flows between them are present in the conversation of music-makers, in their perceptions of what it is they do, and their presentations of how they do it.

Fast-forward again.

It is the seventh and last day of Isigqi Sesimanje's recording, 1 April 1992. West and Peter are mixing.

Peter reaches for the logging chart to set up the board for "South Africa is on Fire."

"Heyi! It's very difficult, this one. It's not easy!" comments West as he anticipates the work ahead.

Peter agrees. They have already programmed and overdubbed the song extensively. Janet's original song, titled "Omhlaba wonke," has been translated in part into English, retitled, and transformed lyrically, rhythmically, and in its arrangement during the recording process.

"I've changed the drums, everything, you know. I've changed a lot of things," West begins to explain. *His mind is in the song.* "Now we must start putting them back together. The problem is I did not have the whole cassette for these things, to work out lines."[17] *The song is on the demo cassette, in its tracks.* "So I had to work out lines every night, you know, by thinking, you know, imagining the whole thing." *The song is in West's mind. It exists in his creative sensibility as an ephemeral entity.*

He chuckles a little. Peter is still transferring information from the logging chart onto the console controls. He's not really listening to West's patient rambling.

"So, I'm not sure where we're going!" West muses on. "But I'll pick it up. . . . And then also this one we need to pick a spot [vacant recording track] again."

"What? To clear?" asks Peter, suddenly alerted.

"Ja, to clear."

"Okay," replies Peter, "maybe we use the computer, let's see."

The song also exists in the recording tracks and in the computer. They will empty out some of its sonic clutter to make way for new signals, for new ideas. Increasingly, the computer is becoming the mind of the studio; it controls the sound-shaping tools and stores and manipulates creative ideas. However much you observed, you'd never really be able to figure out what's going on.

While Peter leaves the studio for a moment, West turns to talk to me.

"This one is very difficult!" he says again.

"'South Africa on Fire'?" I ask.

Then in Zulu he repeats the same story to Jane, Michael, Joana, and Janet.

Reshaped each night by the thoughtful inspiration of an artist churning over forms and ideas, the song eludes him in the daylight of everyday-ness, returning to him only in the interior presence of the studio with its technical facility to realize the nuance of his ideas in sound.

"Yes, it's difficult! The problem is I never had a cassette to set it up, you see," he explains to the musicians.

Hansford who is hanging around in the studio backs his friend up with intermittent sounds of agreement as West continues.

"Now I was building it up every night. When I get home, I try it, I work on it. Now some things I forget, and [then] remember when I'm here. Eyi! But to put them together—I've laid them down—but to put them together, it's difficult, I'm telling you! This thing is very difficult! It's not easy! Because now I have to open it up [in order to change the patterns again]. And I don't know which spot I'm going to find."

Jane is thirsty. She diverts the conversation and goes to get a cup of tea.

West presents his own creativity as interiorized, elusive, as unending, as part of his artistic personhood, and as an essential part of the production process. As Howard Becker writes, those activities that are regarded as gifted, as requiring an artistic sensibility to conduct them with excellence, are the "core activities" that are taken to distinguish an artwork from industrial product or natural object within the ideology of capital. This distinction is accompanied by certain status and privileges awarded to the artist (Becker 1982, 16). The charisma of the gifted persona, when present in the studio, lends its quality also to the space(s) of artistic production.

West's story notices distinct spaces occupied in the process of creating and producing expression—his head or imagination, the tape, the form of the song itself, which must be opened up again, the interior of the technology. There are tensions that at times fracture these spaces: "it is very difficult" to hold them together and to negotiate the moves between them. For example, West says it would be easier to rework the song in conjunction with hearing the cassette, albeit a demo of poor recording quality. He has to work with Peter "to find a spot," using the computer. This pull between the self-sufficient interiorized personhood of the artist and factors external to him or her that need to be negotiated is always present in the production process.[18]

> Stand by, I'm dropping this in. . . .
> I want to listen in in the studio one day. West hesitates. 'Because we are composing,' he says. As if by witnessing his compositional process I would intrude too far into his creative interior; as if I then might expose and disseminate his artistic secrets and thereby publicly deconstruct his aura, lay him open to imitation, and diminish his uniqueness.[19] He defers to the others sitting around the canteen table. 'Why of course she can come in,' answers Hansford. 'She's part of the family!' 'Do you like *ipapa nembuzi?*'

It is in the momentary merging of these spaces—the mind roving into the song, the song into the mind or into the figurative and literal spaces in the machine and on the tape—as well as in the fracturing of these spaces and in the movement between them that creativity resides.

Mix

Downtown Studios's historical lineage, its size, its position in the industry, its array of contemporary electronics, and the hits produced there, all bring renown to the facility, for professionals and outsiders alike. That history is celebrated, documented, and disseminated by Gallo Africa itself.

In addition, the studio is made to feel special by the people who make music within it. For them, it is more than a functional physical space: creative agents work it into another status that derives from and contributes to the aesthetic and symbolic value of the sounds they produce.[20]

The structural design of the studio and music-makers' discourse about it together constitute the space as magical and as a fetish. The basis for the depiction of the studio in this way arises from the idea that there are complex interiors housed within it. The interior of the place itself, the internal workings of electronic machines, the components of sounds, and the interiority of the artist are each enchanting in and of themselves. Together, they enhance the aura of the studio as a whole while they are mutually enhanced.

Once inside, the specialness of the artists and of artistry itself is made palpable for being set in the studio's rarefied atmosphere. In turn, the magic of the studio space is dialogically animated by the enigma of the artists. West considers excluding me from his studio session in order to preserve the studio's aura. The studio's creative processes would be disclosed, the studio's aura would be unsettled, and West's compositional processes would be demystified by the intrusion of an outsider. He protects his own mystique as a musician as well as the symbolic value of the studio by closing it to outsiders. Similarly, it is to infuse the atmosphere of the studio's space into the sound of Ntuli's singing that Lee dims the recording booth and control room lights when Ntuli is struggling to lay down fine vocals. He wants the feeling of the darkened room to inspire focus and quality in Ntuli's performance.

The lure of the studio, like that of the fetish, lies in the coupling of the promise of the revelation of its secrets with the knowledge of their infinite unknowability (Taussig 1993). Within the material body of the studio and of the bodies within it—its technology, its artists, and its sound—there is a wealth of ever-discoverable pathways. The boundaries of the creative possibilities in the studio are unfixed, unknown, and unending. There is always another possible way to change the sound. This is both a physical and metaphysical condition.

In these four takes, I have presented the mysteriousness of the studio as a phenomenon. There is a set of conditions that renders it possible to experience the space in this way. But is the studio only mysterious to people who don't have better knowledge? Is it mysterious because people in power make it that way? Or does it only appear to be mysterious?

Notes

1 Some women apprentice at the South African Broadcasting Corporation and work as sound engineers there. None had moved into commercial recording by the early 1990s, though some of their male counterparts had, such as Downtown engineer Lee Short.

2 The studios are all fitted out with Dolby SR/A, JBL monitoring, and Studer A 827 tape machines. They have soft-front/hard-back acoustic design. The three main studios house different consoles: an SSL4048 G Series, a Sony, and a Harrison. A TS 12 Soundcraft console is installed in the sixteen-track Fostex studio. The digital editing suite features an Apple Mac and Digimix software.

3 Among the prized old equipment retained by the studio are Pultec EQPIA valve equalizers, a Manley variable MU stereo compressor, a Focusrite stereo equalizer, Neuman u67s, and AKGC12 valve microphones.

4 The South African Broadcasting Corporation was the second to install an SSL, although its use was restricted to the SABC until the late 1990s when producers began to book it on a freelancing basis.

5 Tom Porcello, personal communication, January 1995.

6 Low studio budgets range from approximately S.A. R4,500–514,000 (U.S. $1,500 – $4,700). In contrast, West's prize domestic projects in 1991, reggae group O'Yaba and soul singer Walter D, each enjoyed R20,000 ($6,600) of studio work. The production budgets for Mahlathini and the Mahotella Queens would have been much higher than this. (U.S. dollar equivalents are based on the approximate currency exchange rate in 1991, the time of these productions.)

7 The red warning lights above the double studio doors are rarely used. The lights nevertheless mark a boundary. Porcello suggests that these lights are a holdover from an earlier recording era when sound editing was less sophisticated and interruptions could more easily ruin a take (personal communication, January 1996).

8 See Taylor 2001 for a fascinating look at the discursive and technological interfaces between music and the military-industrial complex in postwar America. While much postwar technology developed out of military research and design, it was first and foremost space research that captured the imagination of the public and that was used in advertising campaigns for music technologies of the era.

9   Howard Becker's *Art Worlds* (1982) foregrounds the interconnectedness of institutions involved with art production. Here I extend his idea.

10   *Rhythm of Healing,* Virgin Records (U.K.) and Earthworks (USA), Carol 2427–2, mastered in the British Chop 'em Out Studios, released 1992 "overseas" and at home.

11   Walter Benjamin (1968) means something different by *aura,* although my thinking is prompted by his work. Aura, for Benjamin, emanates from the actual physical presence of an original artwork. It is that presence and the time/space situation it brings to the artwork that compels attention to the artwork. I use the term more loosely to represent an unspecifiable but compelling quality of an object. That quality appears to be natural or spiritual. This is perhaps closer to Robert Plant Armstrong's "affecting presence" (1971). The monetary expense of studio technology also contributes to its aura.

12   For description of the structural details of soundproofing, see Munro 1994; Burd 1994; Huber and Runstein 1995; and Nardantonio 1990.

13   See again Munro 1994; Burd 1994; Huber and Runstein 1995; and Nardantonio 1990 for technical specification. The amount of leak-through is also affected by the choice of microphone and the settings selected on it, which determine the shape and dimensions of its pick-up pattern.

14   There are, of course, variations in the ideal specifications of the acoustic environment of recording booths versus the control room in terms of ambient noise, sound isolation, absorbency, and acoustic character. Additionally, those specifications are also in part determined by the type of recording project for which the studio is principally constructed. However, preference for a dry environment holds as a general principle, especially for productions and musics that are aesthetically engaged with the technological manipulation of sound (see, e.g., Burd 1994, 112–16).

15   Here my generalization glosses over the differences in aural skill of different kinds of music-makers. Sound engineers' ears, for example, are trained and developed in a particular way, notably to listen analytically to the minutiae of timbre and separation, whereas musicians often do not pick up these differences per se. Tensions over discrepancies in aurality do arise during studio sessions. They are often expressed as judgments of another's musicality. Tom Porcello's recounting of a troubled wind quintet session in a studio in San Marcos, Texas, illustrates the communicative complexities and value judgments that arise from discrepancies in aural points of reference (Porcello 1996, 191–228). *Golden Ears* (Moulton 1995), an eight-CD ear-training program designed to develop the aural acuity engineering requires, lays out timbral nuances in fine detail.

16   In most mbaqanga and trad sessions I witnessed, two bass lines were recorded simultaneously: a DI line inserted directly into the console and a mike line set up at the bass amp. The two were either combined in the mix or the miked track was discarded. The mike line could be used as a backup while it acted as a means of reassuring bass players, used to recording their music via their amps, that the sound engineer knew what was appropriate to the music.

17   He is referring to a demo cassette. Isigqi had given him a copy of a tape I recorded during rehearsal. Few groups have the opportunity or budget to produce professional demo tapes of their songs.

18   The tension is further troubled by the difficulties of rendering matters of musical hearing and sound into speech.

19   Composition of his own work is qualitatively different from production, in terms of his desire for protection and privacy. West was altogether more hesitant about my taping in the control room than other producers I asked. He deferred to Isigqi's executive producer, Ali Mpofu, when I requested permission to tape Isigqi's production—the only studio production I taped with West, although I was present at many of his other sessions.

20   Despite their creative significance to twentieth-century music, technological gear, technological engagement, and studio production practices have rarely been addressed in music scholarship in any detail. In the 1980s when interest did begin to pick up, technology was lamented as a contaminating presence. A more positive, often celebratory discussion was first stimulated by the work of sociologists (Kealy 1979; Bennet 1980; Frith 1981) and culture

and media studies scholars (Frith 1986; Hennion 1989; Théberge 1989). Keil's seminal thought piece, "Music Mediated and Live in Japan" (Keil and Feld 1994), originally published in 1983, is the single ethnomusicological voice directly addressing the issue in the early 1980s.

Ethnomusicology has been particularly slow to recognize the creative potential and semiotic nuance of technology in music making and to include its analysis within the field's interpretive frameworks. This is in part an outcome of the facts that ethnomusicologists have privileged live performance, expected technology to take away from both creative processes and from the experience of music, and have focused historically on musics that have, or seem to have, a life of their own outside the music industry. In recent years ethnomusicologists have acknowledged the presence of technology, and scholars have begun to adopt a more agent-centered approach to technology's processes by looking at how music practitioners make, manipulate, understand, and experience technology.

Most of this new work (which claims ethnography as fundamental to its approach) has examined the engagement with technology at the moment of staged and public performance or of "reception" (Waterman 1990; Manuel 1993; Walser 1993; Fox 1992; Fox 1996; Sutton 1996; Rasmussen 1996; Gay 1998; Lee 1999; Greene 1999; Greene 2001; and others). These discussions focus especially on issues of distortion, amplification, the juxtaposition of styles facilitated by electronics, and the technologies of reproduction and circulation. Moments of recording have been less considered. Part of the problem is that the studio—a critical compositional site—has historically been treated as the black box in analyses of production. That is to say, its popular representation as secret, magical, and unknowable has been taken at face value. As long as the studio was thought of as a site into which creative agents and compositional ideas would go, get compromised by technological manipulation there, then emerge packaged for consumption, there was little need for detailed analysis of its processes.

However, there are important texts that carved a way into the studio from different angles. Robert Faulkner's work (1971) on Hollywood studio musicians situates session musicians within the institution of the industry and nuances issues of power and control over music making in studio environments. Edward Kealy's paper (1979) recognized the sound engineer as an artist in his own right and tied this new status to technological evolutions. Herman Gray (1988) entered the studio as a media and popular culture studies scholar. Though he does not address issues of style or unpack technological processes during the recording procedure, his work introduces the studio as a socially constructed space. Keith Negus (1992, 1999) lays out the nonlinearity in the organization of music production and discusses the interplay of creativity and market management in the industry. Norman Stolzhoff (2000) articulates the studio as a primary site in the production of Jamaican dance-hall culture. Thomas Porcello (1996, 1998) details studio discourse and artistry with a focus on sound engineers in the first extended and ethnographic study of the studio. Writing as a linguistic anthropologist, ethnomusicologist, and audio engineer, he develops an anthropology of production that places issues of music style and language poetics at the center of the study of the relationship between power, technology, and creativity. Along with Paul Théberge (1997), Porcello argues for a focus on sound, socially situated, rather than music, more narrowly conceived, as the object of study. He shows the studio to be at once a mundane workspace for sound engineers and a rarefied entity in the popular press. Sound engineers have also been recognized for their artistry in the popular press, with publications such as Richard Buskin's series of interviews (1991), and those by Terri Stone (1992).

While the scholars above began to develop ethnographic treatments, others such as Michael Chanan (1995), Théberge (1997), Mark Cunningham (1998), and Timothy Taylor (2001) have reexamined music histories, introducing technologies as a crucial component in the theorization of music styles and practices. Taylor combines field research and historical work. He argues for a practice-theory approach, with a focus on the relationship between people using technology for expressive purposes and the shifts in technological design and organization. While not studio-specific themselves, these works collectively contribute to studio research in their sophisticated theoretical thinking about technology and by drawing attention to a different way of listening to sound at the level of timbre.

References

Alten, Stanley R. 1986. *Audio in Media*. 2nd ed. Belmont: Wadsworth Publishing.

Armstrong, Robert Plant. 1971. *The Affecting Presence: An Essay in Humanistic Anthropology*. Urbana: University of Illinois Press.

Becker, Howard. 1982. *Art Worlds*. Berkeley: University of California Press.

Bendix, Regina. 2000. The Pleasures of the Ear: Toward an Ethnography of Listening. *Cultural Analysis* I: http://socrates.berkeley.edu/~caforum/.

Benjamin, Walter. 1968. *Illuminations*. New York: Harcourt, Brace, and World.

Bennet, Stith. 1980. *On Becoming a Rock Musician*. Amherst: University of Massachussets Press.

Burd, Alex. 1994. Studio Acoustics. In *Sound Recording Practice,* edited by J. Borwick. 4th ed. Oxford: Oxford University Press.

Buskin, Richard. 1991. *Inside Tracks: A First-Hand History of Popular Music from the World's Greatest Record Producers and Engineers*. New York: Avon Books.

Chanan, Michael. 1995. *Repeated Takes: A Short History of Recording and Its Effects on Music.* New York: Verso.

Cunningham, Mark. 1998. *Good Vibrations: A History of Record Production.* 2nd ed. London: Sanctuary Publishing.

Faulkner, Robert. 1971. *The Hollywood Studio Musician*. Chicago: Adline.

Feld, Steve. 1996. Waterfalls of Song: An Acoustemology of Place Resounding in Bosavi, Papua New Guinea. In *Senses of Place,* edited by S. Feld and K. H. Basso, 91–135. Santa Fe, N.M.: School of American Research.

Fox, Aaron. 1992. The Jukebox of History: Narratives of Loss and Desire in the Discourse of Country Music. *Popular Music* 11, no. 1: 53–72.

—. 1996. "Ain't It Funny How Time Slips Away": Talk, Trash, and Technology in a Texas Working-Class Bar. In *Knowing Your Place: Rural Identity and Cultural Hierarchy,* edited by Barbara Ching and Gerald Creed. New York: Routledge.

Frith, Simon. 1981. *Sound Effects: Youth, Leisure, and the Politics of Rock and Roll*. New York: Pantheon.

—. 1986. Art Versus Technology: The Strange Case of Popular Music. *Media, Culture, Society* 8, no. 3: 263–79.

Gay, Leslie C., Jr. 1998. Acting Up, Talking Tech: New York Rock Musicians and Their Metaphors of Technology. *Ethnomusicology* 42, no. 1: 81–98.

Gray, Herman. 1988. *Producing Jazz: The Experience of an Independent Record Company.* Philadelphia, Penn.: Temple University Press.

Greene, Paul. 1999. Sound Engineering in a Tamil Village: Playing Audio Cassettes as Devotional Performance. *Ethnomusicology* 43, no. 3: 459–89.

—. 2001. Mixed Messages: Unsettled Cosmopolitanisms in Nepali Pop. *Popular Music* 20, no. 2:169–88.

Hennion, Antoine. 1989. An Intermediary between Production and Consumption: The Producer of Popular Music. *Science, Technology, and Human Values* 14, no. 4: 400–424.

Huber, David Miles, and Robert E. Runstein. 1995. *Modern Recording Techniques*. 4th ed. Indianapolis, Ind.: Howard W. Sams.

Jaynes, Julian. 1976. *The Origin of Consciousness in the Breakdown of the Bicameral Mind*. Boston: Houghton Mifflin.

Kealy, Edward. 1979. From Craft to Art: The Case of Sound Mixers and Popular Music. *Sociology of Work and Occupations* 6, no. 1: 3–29.

Keil, Charles, and Steve Feld. 1994. *Music Grooves.* Chicago: University of Chicago Press.

Lee, Tong Soon. 1999. Technology and the Production of Islamic Space: The Call to Prayer in Singapore. *Ethnomusicology* 43, no. 1: 86–100.

Manuel, Peter Lamarche. 1993. *Cassette Culture: Popular Music and Technology in India.* Chicago: University of Chicago Press.

Minh-Ha, Trinh T. 1991. *When the Moon Waxes Red: Representation, Gender, and Cultural Politics.* New York: Routledge.

Munro, Andy. 1994. Studio Planning and Installation. In *Sound Recording Practice,* edited by J. Borwick. 4th ed. Oxford: Oxford University Press.

Nardantonio, Dennis. 1990. *Sound Studio Production Techniques,* 1st ed. Blue Ridge Summit, Pa.: TAB Books.

Negus, Keith. 1992. *Producing Pop: Culture and Conflict in the Popular Music Industry.* New York: Routledge.

—. 1999. *Music Genres and Corporate Cultures.* New York: Routledge.

Porcello, Thomas. 1996. Sonic Artistry: Music, Discourse, and Technology in the Sound Recording Studio. Ph.D. diss., University of Texas at Austin.

—. 1998. "Tails Out": Social Phenomenology and the Ethnographic Representation of Technology in Music-Making. *Ethnomusicology* 42, no. 3: 485–510.

Rasmussen, Anne K. 1996. Theory and Practice at the "Arabic Org": Digital Technology in Contemporary Arab Music Performance. *Popular Music* 15, no. 3: 345–65.

Schutz, Alfred. 1967. *The Phenomenology of the Social World.* Chicago: Northwestern University Press.

Stewart, Susan. 1993. *On Longing: Narratives of the Miniature, the Gigantic, the Souvenir, the Collection.* Durham, N.C.: Duke University Press.

Stoller, Paul. 1989. *The Taste of Ethnographic Things: The Senses in Anthropology.* Philadelphia: University of Pennsylvania Press.

Stolzhoff, Norman C. 2000. *Wake the Town and Tell the People: Dancehall Culture in Jamaica.* Durham, N.C.: Duke University Press.

Stone, Terri, ed. 1992. *Music Producers: Conversations with Today's Top Record Makers.* Emeryville, Calif.: Mix Books.

Sutton, R. Anderson. 1996. Interpreting Electronic Sound Technology in the Contemporary Javanese Soundscape. *Ethnomusicology* 40, no. 2: 249–68.

Taussig, Michael. 1993. *Mimesis and Alterity: A Particular History of the Senses.* New York: Routledge.

Taylor, Timothy D. 2001. *Strange Sounds: Music, Culture, and Technology in the Post-war Era.* New York: Routledge.

Théberge, Paul. 1989. The "Sound" of Music: Technological Rationalization and the Production of Popular Music. *New Formations* 8 (summer): 99–111.

—. 1997. *Any Sound You Can Imagine: Making Music / Consuming Technology.* Hanover, N.H.: Wesleyan University Press.

Walser, Robert. 1993. *Running with the Devil: Power, Gender, and Madness in Heavy Metal Music.* Hanover, N.H.: Wesleyan University Press.

Waterman, Christopher. 1990. *Juju: A Social History and Ethnography of an African Popular Music.* Chicago: University of Chicago Press.

Chapter 25

Lisa Gitelman

THE PHONOGRAPH'S NEW
MEDIA PUBLICS

1878: Tinfoil

L IKE ANY NEW MEDIUM, recorded sound could not but emerge according
to the practices of older media. Edison stumbled on the idea of sound recording
while working on telephones and telegraphs during the summer and fall of 1877, and
communication devices like these provided an initial context for defining the
phonograph. To the inventor and his contemporaries, the phonograph meant what it
did because of the ways it might resemble and—particularly—because of the ways it
might be distinguished from existing machines. As Edison (1878, 527) put it, what
made the phonograph so different was its "gathering up and retaining of sounds
hitherto fugitive, and their [later] reproduction at will." What had always been lost,
what had previously fled, could now be gathered up or "captured" and stored for
future use. And of course, the fugitive sounds captured by the phonograph meant
what they did because of the ways they might resemble and—particularly—because
of the ways they had to be distinguished from the only other snare available:
inscriptions made on paper.[1]

The torrent of accounts in the press that ensued all suggest that the first
phonographs were initially understood according to the practices of writing and
reading, particularly in their relation to speaking, and not, for instance, according to
the practices or commodification of musical notation, composition, and performance.
The really remarkable aspect of the "speaking phonograph" or "talking machine"
arose, as some of its earliest observers marveled, in "literally making it read itself." A
record was made and then played, as if, "instead of perusing a book ourselves, we
drop it into a machine, set the latter in motion, and behold! The voice of the author
is heard repeating his own composition."[2] Hidden here are what James Lastra (2000,
6–7) has identified as the two "tropes for understanding and normalizing" new media:
one of inscription, and the other of personification.[3] Assisting in the public
apprehension of the phonograph as a textual device and a metaphoric author and

reader were structural as well as functional comparisons: those first recordings were indented on sheets of tinfoil. Like some celebrated author-orator, Edison's phonographs went on the lyceum circuit during the summer of 1878, publicly "writing on" and "reading" or "speaking from" their sheets.

Audiences at the phonograph demonstrations were both enthusiastic and skeptical, responding simultaneously to the unprecedented marvel of recorded sound and the unreasoned hype surrounding its early, imperfect demonstration. Those early recordings were faint, flimsy, and full of scratchy surface noise. After the initial fanfare died down, the public had little opportunity to experience recorded sound again firsthand until 1889–93, when improved phonographs playing wax cylinder records were exhibited and started to become available for demonstration and as nickel-in-the-slot amusements, playing prerecorded musical records in public, urban locales and as diversions at fairs and summer resorts. These machines were met with more enthusiasm (lots of nickels) and skepticism, since neither the mechanisms nor the wax recordings delivered much of what they promised. Nonetheless, musical entertainment had become a presumed function of the new medium, though Edison and others continued to promote the devices as business machines for taking dictation.[4]

This chapter is about these early incarnations of the new medium. It is about the public life of phonographs at a time when publics and public life were the incumbent structures of print media. Americans of the day thought of themselves as constituents of a nation and nationally constituent localities according in part to their ritualized collocation as readers of a shared press, as private subjects within the same vast, public, and calendrical circulatory system for printed matter.[5] Even the most disadvantaged could occasionally self-enroll as members of society by dint of literacy acquisition. Frederick Douglass ([1892] 1976, 89) called the antiabolitionist Baltimore newspapers "our papers," when he recalled reading them as a youth, verbally including himself as a constituent of the very public, the very "us," that had attempted systematically to deny his humanity. Because it curiously pertained to "papers," the early history of recorded sound had something to do with "us" and "our." One of my points is that all new media emerge into and help to reconstruct publics and public life, and that this in turn has broad implications for the operation of public memory, its mode and substance. The history of emergent media, in other words, is partly the history of history, of what (and who) gets preserved—written down, printed up, recorded, filmed, taped, or scanned—and why.

The interrelated meanings of print and public speech have been the subject of intensive study by scholars of early U.S. literary history.[6] Such accounts, however, seldom encompass the nineteenth or twentieth centuries, when the liberal nation-state was more firmly in place.[7] As James Secord (2000, 523) explains in his study of early Victorian print production and reception, the West experienced an "industrial revolution in communication" during the mid-nineteenth century, stemming in large part from interconnected changes to the technology of print production and to "the form of public debate." At the broadest level, notes Secord, "the power of print lies in the [shared] assumption of its fixity," and in the nineteenth-century United States as in Britain, print came unglued.[8] The relative instability of nineteenth-century print may be glimpsed first in the sheer volume of print media, in what one observer remarked as "books in shoals [and] journals by the score" (Farmer, 1889, vii), but particularly in the profusion of cheaper monthly, weekly, and daily periodicals. By one account, there were 8,129 local newspapers in the United States and its territories in 1876.[9] Yet quantity is far less suggestive than quality. Under the U.S. "exchange" system (the subsidized postal swapping of issues across the country), newspapers and periodicals reprinted voraciously. Local papers culled each other's pages, assembling a national press. Meanwhile, without international copyright strictures, U.S. publishers pirated fervidly, particularly from the British press. The result was an unfixity of print perhaps unprecedented since the seventeenth century.[10]

Part of the most basic connection between print and *fact*—that transparent Enlightenment logic that operates (what Michel Foucault identified as) the "author function," and that lionizes textual authenticity and legitimates textual evidence[11]— eroded in practice: readers know today how frustrating it is to pick up an edition, even an authorized "complete works" from the period, or a newspaper column, not to say a copy of a British novel published piratically in the United States, and receive little or no indication of the provenance of the work it presents. Where and when was it originally published, and by whom? Whether newspaper "exchange editors" snipped it off or larcenous publishers obscured it as a matter of course, provenance came loose from texts amid the fertile chaos of industrial print production. Sometimes the most elaborately authenticated texts—framed by testimonials and prefaced by respected authorities—were encountered as the least trustworthy.[12] Even the Bible seemed newly unstable, widely and differently printed in English amid accelerated efforts toward revision and retranslation.[13] And if it was impossible to tell where a text had originally come from, it was increasingly difficult to tell where a text was eventually going. As literacy and reading publics expanded, potential readings did too. To make this point narrowly, studying literary texts before this period had much more to do with appreciation than with interpretation, because "a gentleman could be depended upon to understand intuitively what" such a text meant (Graff and Warner 1989, 4).[14] Once mass literacy met cheap editions, things were different. With provenance loose (bibliographically), reception unpredictable (sociologically), and questions of authorial ownership vexed, the fixity of print was in jeopardy and the social meanings of print were in flux.

No less fluid were the meanings of public speech in the nineteenth-century United States, though these meanings are notoriously hard to get at. The work of "governing the tongue" or speaking properly had long before ceased to be a matter of legality or the evidence of salvation, and had become a more subtle, more personalized "code distinguishing the refined from the vulgar," an "exercise in self-control" (Kamensky, 1997, 190, 182). By Reconstruction, keeping a "civil" tongue had nothing at all to do with the civil authorities—that is, with the notable exceptions of schoolchildren (particularly Native American and normative ones, whose "uncivilized" speech tended to be circumscribed) and President Andrew Johnson, who was impeached in 1868 partly because of allegedly "intemperate, inflammatory, and scandalous harangues" as well as "loud threats and bitter menaces" uttered in public against Congress. For others who were neither president nor pupil, speech possessed a less specific, if still public, valence.[15]

In bourgeois circles, "calls for plain speech remained a key component of demands for a democratic culture" (Lears 1994, 53), as successive generations of verbal critics fulminated against a decline in the standards of American usage.[16] The verbal critics were caught in a telling dilemma: they pointed to U.S. newspapers as their evidence of declining standards in usage, but they also pointed to them as the single most important cause of decline. So-called newspaper English was the "arch villain" in their campaign for rectitude (Cmiel 1990, 134–35). The logical conundrum of blaming as cause that which is also ascribed as effect was overlooked, I suspect, because readers experienced the newspaper as contradictorily bivalent, as printed speech. The fleeting currency of news, the ephemerality of the papers, rendered them more like speech acts and less like print artifacts, while their tangibility conversely rendered them "hard" evidence in black and white. Materially, newspapers were print. Legally, however, they tended to resemble vocal performances more than they did authored forms. According to a precedent established by the U.S. Supreme Court in 1829, nothing with "so fluctuating and *fugitive* a form" could possess copyright, which the Constitution reserved for "more fixed, permanent, and durable" expressions.[17] In this context, Edison's "capture" of "fugitive" sounds onto sheets of tinfoil offered nothing less than the renovation of newsprint.

Because the phonograph demonstrations of 1878 and the nickel-in-the-slot business of the early 1890s variously interrogated the normal habits of writing, reading, and speaking, they offer an opportunity to gauge the meanings of print media during the late nineteenth century. For sure, these same meanings may also be glimpsed in other, attendant experiences of text—for instance, in the ongoing legal construction of authorship, in the changing political economies of publishing, the additional subjectivities of late-century literacy, the shifting character and institutional status of criticism, and so on. The list is long. Against it, I will suggest here that tinfoil records, in particular, can profitably be read as *foils* in the literary or Schoolbook sense. They were historical characters important in their pairing function, defining by contrast, relative and mutually opposed to other characters—characters like authors, readers, publishers, and critics, but even more particularly the characters who "spoke" between quotation marks from the pages of U.S. newspapers. Subsequent adaptations of the phonograph into a musical amusement device involved corresponding adaptations to what Benedict Anderson (1991) has called "print capitalism," the cultural economies of print circulation and consumption that so powerfully helped to articulate a U.S. public, an "us," with "our" "own" national tradition and aspirations.

Along with the surrounding publicity, tinfoil records offered a profound and self-conscious experience of what "speaking" on paper might mean. Judging at least from the coincident popularity of verbal criticism, or the coincident quarrels between philologists and rhetoricians over the appropriate study of language, Edison's invention was less a causal agent of change than it was fully symptomatic of its time. Related issues of speaking on paper were also raised in contemporary promotions of simplified spelling, rampant competition between different shorthand systems, and published dialect and regional literatures as well as scholarly worries about the "correct" pronunciation of Latin, the probable pronunciation of English by Chaucer and Shakespeare, and the appropriate "collection" of non-Western tongues, "authentic" black spirituals, folktales, and English ballads.[18] This chapter tells the story of both a few, fragile sheets of tinfoil and then a short-lived nickel-in-the-slot amusement because these stories offer another, modest opportunity to look into the concerns of their time. In particular, the early history of sound recording makes visible the ways in which new media emerge as local anomalies that are also deeply embedded within the ongoing discursive formations of their day, within the what, who, how, and why of public memory, public knowledge, and public life.

In January 1878, Edison signed contracts assigning the rights to exhibit the phonograph (and to make clocks and dolls), reserving for himself the right to exploit its primary dictation function at a later time. Exhibition rights went to a small group of investors, some of them journalists and most of them involved already in the financial progress of Alexander Graham Bell's telephone. In April, they formed the Edison Speaking Phonograph Company, and they hired James Redpath as their general manager in May. A former abolitionist, Redpath had already helped to transform the localized adult-education lecture series of the early American lyceums into more formal, national "circuits" administered by centralized speakers' bureaus. He had just sold his Redpath Lyceum Bureau, and came to the phonograph company with a name for exploiting "merit" rather than what his biographer later dismissed as "mere newspaper reputation" (Horner 1926, 227, 185). The distinction was a blurry one throughout the ensuing months of phonograph exhibitions. Like so much entertainment then and now, phonograph exhibitors capitalized on novelty. Novelty wore off, of course, though it would be about a year until they had "milked the Exhibition cow pretty dry," as one of the company directors put it privately in a letter to Edison.[19]

The Edison Speaking Phonograph Company functioned by granting regional demonstration rights to exhibitors. Individuals purchased the right to exhibit a phonograph within a protected territory. They were trained to use the machine, which required a certain knack, and agreed to pay the company twenty-five percent of their gross receipts. This was less of a lecture circuit, then, than it was a bureaucratic one. Phonograph exhibitors were local; what tied them together into a national enterprise were corporate coordination and a lot of petty accountancy. Paper circulated around the country—correspondence, bank drafts, and letters of receipt— but the people and their machines remained more local in their peregrinations, covered in the local press, supported or not by local audiences and institutions in their contractually specified state or area. Admission was set at twenty-five cents, though soon there were exhibitors cutting that to a dime. Ironically, no *phonographically* recorded version of a phonograph exhibition survives. Despite wishful reports to the contrary, the tinfoil records did not last long and were difficult to replay. Instead, the character of these demonstrations can be pieced together from the many accounts published in local newspapers, letters mailed to Redpath and the company, and a variety of other sources, which include a minstrel burlesque of the exhibitions titled *Prof. Black's Phunnygraph, or Talking Machine.*

While the Edison Speaking Phonograph Company was getting on its feet, Edison along with his friends and associates made some of their own exhibitions, setting a pattern for Redpath's exhibitors to follow and raising the expectation of company insiders. Edison himself appeared *gratis* before an audience at the National Academy of Sciences in Washington, DC. The exhibition included an explanation of how the machine worked, and then Edison's assistant "sung and shouted and whistled and crowed" into its mouthpiece. As the *Washington Star* reported the next day, "There was something weird and uncanny about the little machine," as it then "expressed itself," and "the same sounds floated out upon the air faint but distinct." Later on, the demonstration was marred for an instant when the tinfoil ripped, but excepting this interruption, "the awful hush that preceded the phonograph's remarks was broken [only] by its far off utterances." As he had during the preceding months, Edison gladly granted an interview to reporters. He vaunted the promise of recorded sound for preserving speech or recording a famous diva, and reported that the American Philological Society had requested a phonograph "to preserve the accents of the Onondagas and Tuscaroras, who are dying out." According to the *Star,* Edison said, "One old man speaks the language fluently and correctly, and he is afraid that he will die. You see, one man goes among the Indians and represents the pronunciation of their words by English syllables. Another represents the same words differently. There is nothing definite. The phonograph will preserve the exact pronunciation."[20] Edison implied a distinction between one man and another, between "men" and "the Indians," which he mapped against a distinction between the contrivances of representation and the natural fluidity of spoken language.

Edison's friend Edward H. Johnson gave the first demonstrations for hire, pairing the phonograph with versions of the telephone. He charged theater managers one hundred dollars a night during a tour of New York State in January and February. Not all of his performances recouped the hundred dollars, but in Elmira and Cortland "it was a decided success," he claimed, and the climax of the evening was "always reached when the Phonograph first speaks." "Everybody talks Phonograph," Johnson reported, on "the day after the concert and all agree that a 2nd concert would be more successful than the first." Johnson's plan was a simple one. He categorized the fare as "Recitations, Conversational remarks, Songs (with words), Cornet Solos, Animal Mimicry, Laughter, Coughing, etc., etc.," which would be "delivered into the mouth of the machine, and subsequently reproduced." Johnson described getting a lot of laughs by trying to sing himself, but he also attempted to entice volunteers from the audience or otherwise to take advantage of local talent.[21] A month later, Professor J. W. S. Arnold half filled Chickering Hall in New York City, where his phonograph "told the story of Mary's little lamb," and then like Johnson's phonograph, rendered a medley of speaking, shouting, and singing. At the end of the evening, Arnold distributed strips of used tinfoil as souvenirs, and there was reportedly "a wild scramble for these keepsakes."[22]

By the time the Speaking Phonograph Company swung into action, New York City, at least, had been pretty thoroughly introduced to Edison's invention. Redpath complained (perhaps facetiously) that the city had endured more than three hundred demonstrations by the time of his own short season at Irving Hall, which was tepidly received. The company's contracted exhibitors sought less jaded audiences. Across the Hudson in New Jersey, for instance, a journalist named Frank Lundy owned demonstration rights, and his activities can be gauged in the local press. For example, Lundy came through Jersey City, New Jersey, in mid-June, where he gave one exhibition at a Methodist Episcopal church ("admission 25 cents"), and another at Library Hall as part of a concert given by "the ladies of

Christ Church." Both programs featured musical performances by community groups as well as explanations and demonstrations of the phonograph. Lundy reportedly "recited to" the machine, various "selections from Shakespeare and Mother Goose's melodies, laughed and sung, and registered the notes of [a] cornet, all of which were faithfully reproduced, to the great delight of the audience, who received pieces of the tin-foil as mementos." Poor Lundy's show on June 20 had been upstaged the previous day by a meeting of the Jersey City "Aesthetic Society," which met to wish one of its members bon voyage. Members of the "best families in Jersey City" as well as "many of the stars of New York literary society" were reportedly received at Mrs. Smith's residence on the eve of her departure for the Continent. One New York journalist had brought along a phonograph, and occupied part of the evening recording and reproducing laughter as well as song, along with a farewell message to Smith, and a certain Miss Groesbeck's "inimitable representation" of a baby crying. Of these recorded cries, "the effect was very amusing," and the journalist "preserved the strip" of foil, saving the material impressions of what were reported as Groesbeck's "mouth" impressions.[23]

Further from Edison and the company's orbit, demonstrations of the phonograph appear to have been similar affairs. In Iowa, George H. Iott of Des Moines owned exhibition rights. The *Iowa State Register* reported "The Phonograph in Des Moines" on July 3, 1878. Iott's demonstrations ran morning, noon, and night in one of the city's commercial blocks, for any who wished to visit "the wondrous machine of iron, steel and foil that can be made to talk, whistle, sing, crow, laugh or make any other vocal sound." Like Groesbeck in New Jersey, Iowans got a chance to make their own records. As the *Register* put it, "Quite a number of our people sung and talked to this phonograph yesterday." A lawyer recorded an argument to the court, another man recorded the Lord's Prayer, "several ladies sang to it," a professor spoke to it in foreign languages, and the machine "repeated" them all. The foreign languages sounded funny, and Iott's own renditions of "John Brown's Body" and "Whoop Her Up, Eliza Jane" proved to be crowd-pleasers. Two weeks later, during a horrible heat wave, the phonograph appeared in Dubuque. Iott probably operated it there too, though the local *Daily Times* called it only "Edison's" phonograph. In advance of the Dubuque exhibitions, someone else had already offered "a specimen of tinfoil," for display in town, it "being a section of the band which encircled the cylinder of an Edison phonograph," presumably at a public demonstration someplace else. Even without the phonograph to play it on, "the solidified, or rather materialized effects of voice" visible on the foil were "indeed a curiosity."[24]

Though there was obviously some variety among them, phonograph exhibitions all shared a similar form and content. Their structure was self-fulfilling, interactive, and based on a familiar rhetoric of educational merit. Lecturers introduced Edison's machine as an important scientific discovery by giving an explanation of how it worked, and then the "how" was confirmed in successive demonstrations of recording and playback. Audiences were edified, and they were entertained.[25] The demonstrations first involved recording a hodge-podge of sounds that ranged from shouting, singing, and recitation, to noises like coughing, laughing, and crowing, all by the lecturer and all reproduced by the machine to the silent assembly. Then, a few audience members got a chance to record sounds of their own, which were also reproduced. By making recordings themselves, audiences became part of the demonstration and party to the new medium—instrumental to the claims of each.

The exhibitions formed an intricate and spontaneous response to the contemporary cultural order of which they were also functioning ingredients. After the contested presidential election of 1876 and the great railroad strike of 1877, with the economy still recovering from a deep depression, the phonograph helped to encourage a "renewed optimism about America's future," serving as an early palliative within what historian Robert Wiebe (1967) has called the post-Reconstruction "search for order."[26] Though their meanings for different audiences must have been to some degree different, the exhibitions fostered consensus. They were local experiences—many audience members probably knew each other—yet they had extralocal significance. Like the exchange columns and wire stories of the local press, phonograph exhibitions pointed outward, toward an impersonal public sphere comprised of similarly private subjects. Audiences in the meanest church basements were recorded just like audiences in the grand concert halls of New York, Chicago, and New Orleans. In their very recordability, people were connected. Audience members might imagine themselves as part of an up-to-date, recordable community, an "us" (as opposed to some imagined and impoverished "them"), formed with similarly up-to-date recordable people they didn't know.

Phonograph exhibitions drew audiences together by flattering them in two different ways. On the one hand, the exhibitions offered tacit participation in technological progress to everyone in attendance. Audiences could be up to the minute, apprised of the latest scientific discovery, in on the success of the inventor whom the newspapers were calling the "Wizard of Menlo Park" and the "Modern Magician." Together, audiences might imagine and salute all of the useful functions the phonograph would serve, once Edison had improved the device as promised. On the other hand, the exhibitions provided a playful and collective engagement with good taste. In making their selections for recording and playback, exhibitors made incongruous associations between well-known lines from both Shakespeare and Mother Goose, between talented musicians and hacks like Edward Johnson, between animal and baby noises and the articulate sounds of speech. Audiences could draw and maintain their own distinctions, laugh at the appropriate moments, recognize impressions, and be in on the joke. They could participate together in the enactment of cultural hierarchy.

Cultural hierarchy was enacted partly through carnivalesque gestures—body sounds or animal noises—the negative of bourgeois identity, newly contained, captured, by the mimetic device. (One of the first Edison kinetoscope films offered, similarly, *The Record of a Sneeze,* in 1894.) Edison had proposed that his machine might preserve "our Washingtons, our Lincolns, [and] our Gladstones"—what Matthew Arnold called "the best that has been thought and *[literally]* said"—and yet the public capaciousness of the phonograph seemed to ask for the low, the other, and the infantile—the pro- or protosemiotic—all performed cathartically within the respectability of the middle-class lecture space and its rational, technocratic weal. Thus, recording was from the outset a complex "studio art," in the words of Jonathan Sterne, in which "both copy *and* original are products of the process of reproducibility" (2003, 236, 241; emphasis added).[27] Confronted by a machine that preserved and repeated speech, individuals reduced their own expressions to rote. They repeated bits that were already often repeated: a prayer, a lyric, a snippet from a common vocabulary of quotations (from Shakespeare), or a piece from a common past (from the nursery). They mimicked to the machine they knew would mimic them mimicking. They made themselves fully its subjects, recording themselves by phonograph at the same time that they acknowledged its rote "memory" by comparing it to theirs.

Something of the same carnival circulated in the press, where the phonograph was hailed sincerely as the most wondrous scientific invention of the age, but was also the source and butt of jokes. The most frequent were misogynist gibes, maintaining the masculinity of publics and public speech by assigning private and aberrant speech to women, gossips, harpers, nags, talking machines that never require any tinfoil, and so on. Other jokes proposed new, related devices for inscription: the smellograph for recording and reproducing odors, then ipograph for recording and reproducing inebriation, and so forth. Like the great variety of sounds recorded during demonstrations, such jokes hint at the hugely varied contexts within which public speech acts made sense as bodily cultural productions. If phonographs were "speaking," their functional subjects remained importantly diffuse among available spoken forms: lectures and orations as well as "remarks," "sayings," recitations, declamations, mimicry, hawking, barking, and so on. The sheer heterogeneity of public speech acts should not be overlooked any more than the diversity of the differently public speakers whose words more and less articulated a U.S. public sphere. The nation that had been declared or voiced into being a century before remained a noisy place.

More specific audience response is difficult to judge. There were some parts of the country that simply were not interested. Mississippi and parts of the South were experiencing one of the worst yellow fever epidemics in recent memory. Audiences in New Orleans were reportedly disappointed that the machine had to be yelled into in order to reproduce well, and there were other quibbles with the technology once the newspapers had raised expectations to an unrealistic level. Out in rural Louisiana, one exhibitor found that his demonstrations fell flat unless the audience heard all recordings as they were made. Record quality was still so poor that knowing what had been recorded made playback much more intelligible. Redpath spent a good deal of energy consoling exhibitors who failed to make a return on their investments, but he also spent his time fielding questions from individuals who, after witnessing exhibitions, wrote to ask if they could secure exhibition rights themselves. To one exhibitor in Brattleboro, Vermont, Redpath wrote sympathetically that "other intelligent districts" had proved as poor a field as Brattleboro, but that great success was to be had in districts where "the population is not more than ordinarily intelligent." Some areas of the country remained untried, while others were pretty well saturated, like parts of Pennsylvania, Wisconsin, and Illinois.[28]

But one response in particular seems to have been commonplace: audience members took souvenir scraps of indented foil home with them when the exhibitions were over. These partial and primitive records were in some way meaningful to the women and men who sought them, and who were probably asked at the break-fast table the next morning, "What does it say?" Without the phonograph for playback, the tinfoil records of course said nothing. Yet at the same time, as a few lines in the morning newspaper might help to report, the very same records said *something.* These "materialized effects of voice" were "indeed a curiosity": they were talismans of print culture, pure "supplement," in the language of literary study today, illegible and yet somehow textual, public, and inscribed. Exhibitors wrote back to the company for more and more tinfoil. The company kept a "foil" account open on its books to enter these transactions. Pounds of tinfoil sheets entered into national circulation, arriving in the possession of exhibitors only to be publicly consumed: indented, divided, distributed, and collected into private hands, and then saved. This saving formed a totally new experience of savability as well as the preservative effects of tinfoil. That is, tobacco and cheese were sometimes sold in tinfoil, but the commercial availability of foil for wrapping and saving leftovers would come much later.

Confirming much about the phonograph exhibitions was a "colored burlesque on the phonograph" titled *Prof. Black's Phunnygraph, or Talking Machine.* Frank Hockenbery's (1886) skit offers a comment on the phonograph lectures that it lampoons. The term *burlesque* did not then denote striptease as much as it indicated a topical, risqué comedy, full of witticisms pointed at events of the day, and the butt of Hockenbery's burlesque are the phonograph exhibitions of 1878. As a "colored" burlesque, *Prof. Black's Phunnygraph* also taps fifty years of blackface minstrelsy in its makeup. This was the era of the so-called mammoth minstrel shows, touring troupes of forty to sixty performers, and Hockenbery's *Phunnygraph* was probably intended as an interlude in one of these racist pageants, since its concluding stage directions call for a minstrel staple, "moving to half circle, [and as] soon as half circle is struck, begin negro chorus or plantation melody. Minstrel business."[29]

Whatever its origins and performance history, *Prof. Black's Phunnygraph* takes aim at phonograph exhibitors like Johnson, Lundy, and Iott. The burlesque develops in the form of a lecture "on de Phunnygraph, or Talking Machine, as she am called by de unsophisticated populace." "Professor" Black is its "sole inwentor, patenter, manufacturer an' constructioner," although there is passing and disparaging mention of a "Billy Addison." Professor Black is a character adapted as much from medicine shows as from men like Edison or his associate Arnold. A connection to patent medicines is made abundantly clear by the scenery, which consists in part of a sign announcing the lecture within the play:

> Admittance
> Adults   10 cents
> Children   ½ dose

The rest of the scenery is "a dry goods box large enough to hold three persons" to which has been attached a "sausage-grinder on top with crank," a household funnel, and "slips of white paper to run into [the] grinder to talk on." In the circumstances of its demonstration, the phunnygraph closely resembles the phonograph it mocks. Professor Black's lecture follows the formula of so many Edison Speaking Phonograph Company exhibitions. The professor explains how the machine works and then gives a demonstration. Just like the real phonograph exhibitors, the professor tries to record talk, recitations, animal mimicry, whistling, and song. But his phunnygraph is really just three people hiding in a box, and it proves impossible for them to remember and accurately repeat the words and noises that the professor shouts into the kitchen utensils on top of the box.

Professor Black fails in his efforts to "talk on[to]" paper. His three accomplices (literally) draw a blank. The substitution of empty "white paper" for tinfoil in the opening stage directions again identifies the phonograph as a kind of writing instrument and mnemonic machine at the same time that it serves to underscore that souvenir tinfoil sheets remained vexingly illegible, blank to the eyes of readers. Aural culture could suggestively be saved for posterity, but saving threw the experienced norms of savability into question.

If the tinfoil souvenirs were unreadable, they were also unauthored in important ways. Repeated explanations told how air was set in motion by the human voice, moving a diaphragm and a stylus, which in turn caused indentations in the foil. The author's voice authored. The *Iowa State Register* called it "incomprehensible." Added to what may have been a vague sense of how the machine worked, the phonograph exhibitions did plenty to confuse authorial agency in other ways. In each, the exhibitor was the author in evidence, responsible for manipulating the machine along with its stylus and sheets, and principally in charge of the substance of the recordings made. Audience members shared the exhibitor's authorial role when they made their own recordings. The machine, so readily personified, was an authorial subject too, to the extent that later exhibitors were chided to remember, "The audience is always more anxious to hear the machine than to hear you."[30] Finally, Edison remained author, a paradigmatic self-made man and maker, everywhere associated with his invention, sometimes occluding the phonograph's local exhibitor in the press. He received a royalty of 20 percent from the Edison Speaking Phonograph Company's net receipts, and the company tried to get Edison to control his image. One of the company's directors figured that they could sell a hundred thousand souvenir photographs of the inventor, if only he would carefully limit his exposure to photographers.[31] This gambit probably never came off, but the initial estimate of a hundred thousand was plausible; four years later, it was easy to sell eighty-five thousand souvenir photographs of Oscar Wilde as he made a lecture tour around the United States.[32]

The analogy so abundantly apparent between souvenir photos and souvenir tinfoil remained curiously absent from most early accounts of phonograph exhibitions. Though a few individuals had wondered before about the possibility of an "acoustic daguerreotype," and many were soon willing to compare Edison's phonograph to "its sister instrument, the camera," their analogy simply does not surface in accounts of 1878 with any great regularity.[33] If anything, Hockenbery's facetious analogy to patent medicines had more weight. Edison and others noted the miraculous power of his invention to "bottle up" speech for posterity, and bottling adapted well to the partially carnivalesque tenor of the exhibitions. Indeed, medicine shows also offered multiauthor fun and focused on inscrutable matter. As an itinerant "professor" lectured on the benefits of his pills or elixirs, the showman's company entertained the audience; James Whitcomb Riley remembered his youthful days sketching busts of Shakespeare and writing bad puns on two chalkboards while a "doctor" C. M. Townsend droned on about his miraculous Wizard Oil in 1875.[34] Like so many bottles of elixir, tinfoil promised much but delivered little. What the phonograph exhibitors were selling besides novelty was amazing curative potential as yet unrealized. The speculative future functions of Edison's device suggested social and cultural ills, or lacks that might soon be as fugitive as the fugitive sounds the phonograph would capture, once and for all.

The tinfoil was thus the site of enormous tension. Phonograph exhibitors ran through pounds of it, and audiences scrambled for keepsakes. In their sonic "capture" and later mute evocation of public experience, pieces of foil in private hands must have formed souvenirs of curious power. Like all souvenirs, they were belongings that vouched for belonging. They were artifacts that vouched for facts. Publicly made and privately held, their very material existence offered a demonstrable continuity of private and public memories, hard evidence of shared experiences. As Susan Stewart (1993, 133, 135) explains, "Within the development of culture under an exchange economy, the search for authentic experience and, correlatively, the search for the authentic object become critical." She adds,

> We might say that this capacity of objects to serve as traces of authentic experience is, in fact, exemplified by the souvenir. The souvenir distinguishes experiences. We do not need to desire souvenirs of events that are repeatable. Rather we need and desire souvenirs of events that are reportable, events whose materiality has escaped us, events that thereby exist only through the invention of narrative.

The desire for tinfoil must have been partly a desire for authenticity, for what had really transpired. More than any souvenir program or photograph, though, the tinfoil records suggested the authentication of actual sounds that had been shared. If they lacked real readers and real authors, the records were stunning harbingers of provenance. Each had a precise point of origin (recorded at one moment in "real time," according to today's parlance), and they were together defined by virtue of their precision, a new, more vivid indexicality.

Tinfoil offered a new, precise sort of quotation, in effect, or a way of living with the question of quotation as never before. To put it another way, the tinfoil souvenirs suggested that oral productions might be textually embodied as aural reproductions, rather than as the usual sort of graphic representation, spelled out and wedged between quotation marks on a page. What the phonograph demonstrations offered was not the special performance of texts (for example, a written declaration making a nation independent, paper instruments of law making law, or canonical texts making a national tradition). What had been witnessed was a special textualization of performance—quotation somehow made immanent, quotation *marks* of a new sort, which turned (or *re*turned, mechanically, magically) into the quotations themselves.

Tinfoil souvenirs offered the renovation of the souvenir as such, hinting at changes to the then normal connections between matter and event, stuff and utterance, text and speech act. The phonograph demonstrations were indeed only reportable, not repeatable, in Stewart's terms: it was devilishly hard to get a tinfoil record back onto the machine once it had been removed, and certainly impossible to reproduce anything from it when it had been ripped up and distributed among the audience. Still, what was reportable about the demonstrations was precisely repeatability. Narrating the meaning of the tinfoil at breakfast meant testifying to the pending usurpation of that very narrative. These were souvenirs about souvenirness. The desire for authenticity would finally be consummated, when some soon and now imaginable souvenir spoke for itself. The morning papers promised as much. Tinfoil scrap and newsprint squib lying side by side on the breakfast table served to interrogate that promise, if also to prompt the witness/auditor who owned them and formed part of their collective subject. Evidence is scanty, to be sure, and I must admit to having imagined U.S. breakfast table readers in 1878, somewhat in the manner that Benedict Anderson has imagined them imagining themselves as a national community. It should be noted, however, that part of my argument is precisely about that scantiness, about the necessity (then) if speculative (today) reciprocity of newsprint and tinfoil scraps as matters of evidence, where "matters of evidence" and the data of culture are constructed culturally as part of an ongoing dialectic with emergent media forms.

Keyword: Record

Although the exhibitions of 1878 were short-lived, Redpath quickly went on to fresh projects, and souvenir sheets of tinfoil were soon forgotten, the medium of sound recording had forever questioned the relative meanings of writing, print, and public speech. Other versions of related questions soon captured public attention as, for example, when the shooting and eventual death of President James Garfield in 1881 tested the incipient liveness of U.S. media, challenging the press to keep its bulletins up to date via telegraph communications while it followed the hapless use of Bell telephone technology to detect the assassin's bullet inside the president's body.[35] Whether it worked well now or later, recorded sound had disparaged print by implication, helping to suggest the artificiality of writing in comparison to speech. At the same time, the evident inadequacies of tinfoil records as permanent or indelible inscriptions helped to raise emphatic questions of loss within which the meanings of writing and print had long been enrolled. These questions of loss were narrowly a matter of words written down, printed up, and saved. But they were further suggestive of much broader matters of public memory, self-identification and corresponding exclusion, "our Washingtons" and "our Lincolns" saved against "our" uncertain future, for example, and Onondaga and Tuscarora "accents" "preserved" against "their" imminent demise. If their immediate subjects were the local and the semicarnivalesque, the first phonographs were more broadly the instruments of middle-class hegemony, of an Arnoldian "Culture" with its sacralizing functions directed at "our" traditions and its salvage mentality directed at "theirs."[36]

I am suggesting that the phonograph exhibitions formed vernacular experiences of the relationship between speech and writing—a relationship theorized only later by linguists and philosophers—and that such experiences had broad, if unexamined, consequences for cultural formations.[37] These experiences were certainly not unique to the phonograph exhibitions or 1878. They had been and continued to be habitual accessories to print. For instance, in 1869 a congressional committee investigated the treatment of Union prisoners held in the South during the Civil War. The committee canvased the North for testimony, oral and written, with the immediate aim to render those "transient and somewhat *fugitive* histories based on personal experiences and observations" into "an enduring *record,* truthful and authentic and stamped with the national authority." Oral and personal histories were captured and redeemed by the authoritative, textual operations of the incipient welfare state.[38] Diction makes this a particularly tidy example, but so too did the collectors of song, authors of regionalism, critics of idiom, and reporters of news seek to render personal and aural encounters into material, public records. Wherever it appeared, "speaking" on paper was party to precisely the tangle of concerns that Edison's phonograph newly helped adumbrate.

Edison boasted to the newspapers that his invention would ruin the market for books, reasoning that recordings were created naturally at no expense, by sound waves impinging on foil, rather than laboriously set in type by wage-hungry compositors. Authors and their audiences would win, even if printers and compositors would lose. But when the inventor's comments reached the readers of one paper in Philadelphia, set in type of course by compositors, the inventor was quoted as saying that a phonograph record "is not in tpye [*sic*], but in punctures" on tinfoil. The typographic error is exactly that: graphic. It produces an unpronounceable "utterance," which remains viable only on the page, seen and not said. The four individual pieces of type remain insistently, visually, sorts of type. They are emphatically t, p, y, and e, since they do not make the word *type*. "Pye" or "pie" is a printer's expression for jumbled type, yet there is no way to know for sure whether this was an accident or derision on the part of a compositor employed by the Philadelphia weekly (lazy or Luddite? rushed or radical?), and it is unlikely that many readers stumbled or that any noticed their dilemma.[39] One typo in a local paper is a trivial matter, then, but one that neatly captures the verbal-visual status of writing and print that the first phonograph records visited so unfamiliarly: errors can be quite telling, as chapter 4 will elaborate below [see original publication]. Consuming "speech" on paper requires eyes not ears. By the same token, early auditors wrote "Behold!" (instead of "Listen!" or "Hark!") "The voice of the author is heard repeating his own composition." They got the sensory apparatus wrong in their rush to celebrate the greater immediacy of a new medium within the contexts of its public exhibition.

Far less trivial than the typography of one word by Edison on the future of literature was Moses Coit Tyler's two-volume version of the American literary past. Tyler was one of the first professors of American literature. His *History of American literature, 1607–1765* (1878) was among the first works to put together a coherent narrative of early American literary history, and it helps characterize the specifically *cultural* status of writing and print at the moment Edison's phonograph was introduced to U.S. audiences. Tyler's volumes assumed as well as redacted a national literary tradition, offering long quotations from early authors.

As he himself described it, Tyler's (1878, xii) project sought to present an exhaustive history of those writings that "have some noteworthy value as literature, and some real significance in the unfolding of the American mind." His method had been to troll for years through libraries, seeking out neglected books, assessing their literary merits, and judging their pertinence to "the scattered voices of the thirteen colonies," which eventually and so importantly, in his view, "blended in one great and resolute utterance" (xi). It was a hugely ambitious project, and one Tyler everywhere portrays in terms that seem to mix the functions of speech and writing. He wanted to see just where "the first lispings of American literature" took their departure from their "splendid parentage, the written speech of England" (11). Tyler's "lisped literature" and "written speech" confirm the degree to which spoken and written language were integrally, mutually, defining. The substitution of "Behold!" for "Listen!" partook of an ancient tradition still current. Writing in general, and literary tradition in particular, lived and was valued in intricate association with speech acts.

The word *record* encapsulates these points. Tyler starts his first chapter proposing the intellectual history of the United States: "It is in written words that this people, from the very beginning, have made the most confidential and explicit record of their minds. It is these written records, therefore, that we shall now search for that record" (5). Despite his reputation as a "superb stylist," Tyler's double use of *record* is confusing.[40] Mental records are his broader category, within which written records stand preeminent as searchable traces. Confusion between the two is indicative of tensions surrounding the potentially national and literary character of textuality for Tyler, and more generally, the gap he seems anxiously to have sensed between minds and pages, between an author's conception and its written, printed expression. Whether or not Tyler composed these sentences just before, after, or in light of Edison's records, his diction partakes of the self-same context.

Not surprisingly perhaps, Tyler took liberties when quoting the literary tradition he established. Acting on a distinction that would be articulated in copyright law only a year later, Tyler sought and valued authors' ideas, but had to make do with their printed expression.[41] His literary criticism was aimed at works by authors, yet relied on texts by printers. Tyler (1878, xv) noted provenance sloppily, silently modernized spelling and punctuation, and considered that it was "no violation of the integrity of quotation" for him to expunge or correct any confusion, "extreme inaccuracy," or "palpable error of the press." Against such liberal quotation practices and mistrust of the press, and in keeping with his larger project to collect and preserve an explicitly American, explicitly literary tradition, Tyler's *record* is a keyword in the sense that Raymond Williams (1976) picked out his *Keywords*.[42] Like Williams's word *culture* (or *class,* or *media*), that is, Tyler's *record* seems to have "acquired meanings in response to the very changes he proposed to analyze."[43] The term cannot be defined without recourse to the very conditions it connotes: the lispings of literature and the construction of tradition. So too must Edison's "records" have emerged as meaningful according in part to the differently desired subjects of recording. Whether glimpsed here in American literary history or early sound recording, the subjects and the instruments of public memory cannot be pulled apart.[44]

Though obvious in Tyler, this reflexivity of the noun *record* proved fleeting. After some initial awkwardness, its use soon stabilized, broadening to include phonograph recordings as well as one other "curious perversion of meaning" noted by verbal critics. Whereas the word had long meant "an authentic register," including the abstract, immaterial, and impersonal register of public purview, it was now "perverted" to refer to a person's past performance. Originally applied to a candidate's past performance, this sense of the word soon applied colloquially to anyone. People had records. People had *permanent* records. These sorts of records were both personally derived and publicly constituted, possessing a curious instrumentality in the sense that "when a man breaks the RECORD he makes the RECORD" (Farmer 1889, 454).[45] These new records, somewhat like Edison's new ones, were performative. It was as if the frequent personifications of the phonograph had been inverted lexically, as (the meaning of) *record* now incorporated people. Phonographs had so readily become metaphoric authors, readers, and speakers, but people correspondingly became metaphoric machines.

Notes

1. The portion of this chapter on nickel-in-the-slot phonographs initially was a contribution to a conference at the Dibner Institute at MIT, and I am thankful to Paul Israel and Robert Friedel for their invitation to participate. The material on tinfoil phonographs has occupied me for a long time; different and much more partial versions have appeared as "First Phonographs: Writing and Reading with Sound" and "Souvenir Foils."
2. *Scientific American* 37 (December 1877): 384.
3. Lastra's (2000) first chapter, "Inscriptions and Simulations," is an account of the ways in which modern media were first imagined according to these tropes.
4. There is a widespread misapprehension that magnetic tape was the first medium for amateur recording. Actually, phonographs and graphophones (but not gramophones) could all record sound until electrical recording became the norm around 1920. See Morton (2000).
5. These are claims adapted from the work of Anderson (1991), Habermas (1989), and Warner (1990). On circulation, see also Henkin (1998); John (1995).
6. On public speech, for instance, see Looby (1996); Fliegelman (1993); Grasso (1999); Ruttenburg (1999).
7. The most notable exception is Cmiel (1990).
8. Secord (2000, 523) supposes that "relative stability in print reemerged from the mid- and later 1840s" in Britain, "with the laying of a groundwork for a liberal nation-state, based on imperial free trade and an economic future clearly within the factory system," though this was clearly not the case in the Victorian United States. Another factor unattended here, as in Secord, is electric telegraphy.
9. For the number of papers, see *Centennial Newspaper Exhibition* (1876), where the data were compiled in part from the 1870 census, and in the course of collecting a "monster reading room and an exchange for newspaper men" at the Centennial Exposition in Philadelphia, known as the Newspaper Pavilion, with collected issues from across the United States. According to the *U.S. Census of Manufactures,* in the twenty years between 1880 and 1900, the amount of capital involved in U.S. newspapers and periodicals rose by an estimated 400 percent, and the amount of paper consumed rose by 650 percent.
10. In this last claim, I am agreeing with Secord (2000). Like Secord, I am trying to stress that the fixity of print is a variable social construct rather than an inherent property of the medium, that media are always social before they are perceptual. This case has been stated most strongly by Johns (1998, 2, 19). For the U.S. context, see McGill (2003).
11. See de Grazia (1992, 7), who offers a wonderful account of how the Shakespearean canon emerged as a constituent of this logic, how it "came to be reproduced in a form that continues to be accorded all the incontrovertibility of the obvious."
12. A. Fabian (2000, 173, passim). Slave narratives offer a particularly good example of this.
13. See Gutjahr (1999, 110–11).
14. Secord (2000) makes this point more broadly and at much greater length in his study of the ways that different readers differently received *The Vestiges of the Natural History of Creation* (1844).
15. Article 10 of the *Articles of Impeachment* against Johnson (March 1868) reads, "That said Andrew Johnson . . . did attempt to bring into disgrace, ridicule, hatred, contempt and

reproach the Congress of the United States, . . . to excite the odium and resentment of all good people of the United States against Congress . . . and in pursuance of his said design and intent, openly and publicly and before divers assemblages of citizens . . . did . . . make and declare, with a loud voice certain intemperate, inflammatory, and scandalous harangues, and therein utter loud threats and bitter menaces . . . amid the cries, jeers and laughter of the multitudes then assembled in hearing." (The twentieth-century impeachment, by contrast, was less about what President Bill Clinton literally *said* than about what he *meant;* namely, it "depends what the meaning of is is")

16. In writing about plain speech, Lears relies on Cmiel (1990, 263–65), who counted books of verbal criticism and usage manuals listed in the *National Union Catalog* between S. Hurd's *A Grammatical Corrector* (1847) and R. H. Bell's *The Worth of Words* (1902); Cmiel notes 182 total editions of 34 titles.

17. Emphasis added; quoted in *Clayton v. Stone and Hall, 2* Payne 392 (1829), referring to "a newspaper or price-current," and cited in *Baker v. Seiden,* 101 U.S. 99 (1880). My thinking about the two cases is indebted in part to Meredith L. McGill, "Fugitive Objects: Securing Public Property in United States Copyright Law" (working paper, October 12, 2000).

18. On spirituals, I've been influenced by Cruz (1999).

19. Records of the Edison Speaking Phonograph Company exist at the Edison National Historic Site in West Orange, New Jersey, and at the Historical Society of Pennsylvania in Philadelphia. Documents from West Orange have been microfilmed and form part of the *Thomas A. Edison Papers: A Selective Microfilm Edition* (1987). These items are also available as part of the ongoing electronic edition of the Edison Papers; see <http://edison.rutgers.edu>. For the items cited here, like Uriah Painter to Thomas Edison, August 2, 1879 ("milked the Exhibition cow"), microfilm reel and frame numbers are given in the following form: TAEM 49:316. Documents from Philadelphia form part of the Painter Papers collection and have been cited as such. The company's incorporation papers are TAEM 51:771. The history of the company may be gleaned from volume 4 of *The Papers of Thomas A. Edison* (1998). Also see Israel (1997–98).

20. "An Interesting Session Yesterday: Edison, The Modern Magician, Unfolds the Mysteries of the Phonograph," *Washington Star,* April 19, 1878. The *New York Times* carried a shorter version of the same story on the same day.

21. Edward H. Johnson to Uriah H. Painter, January 27, 1878, in the Painter Papers; Johnson prospectus, February 18, 1878, TAEM 97:623. Both are transcribed and published in Edison (1998). I am grateful to the editors of the *Papers of Thomas A. Edison* for sharing this volume in manuscript as well as their knowledge of the Painter Papers.

22. "The Phonograph Exhibited: Prof. Arnold's Description of the Machine in Chickering Hall—Various Experiments, with Remarkable Results," *New York Times,* March 24, 1878, 2:5.

23. Accounts of Jersey City are reported in *the Jersey Journal,* June 13, 14, and 21, 1878, and the *Argus,* June 20, 1878.

24. *Iowa State Register,* July 3, 1878; *Daily Times* (Dubuque), July 16 and June 29, 1878.

25. For a discussion of this improving ethos at later demonstrations, see Musser (1991, chapter 3), where he adapts Neil Harris's idea of an "operational aesthetic" to the circumstances of Lyman Howe's career in "high-class" exhibitions. Differently germane is Cook (2001).

26. "Renewed optimism" is Musser (1991, 22), apropos of Wiebe. In thinking about the demonstrations as hegemonic forms, I have been influenced by Uricchio and Pearson's (1993) work on me "quality" films of 1907–10; on the pervasiveness and social function of Shakespeare in U.S. culture, see Uricchio and Pearson (1993, 74–78).

27. "Our Washingtons" is from Edison (1878). My carnivalesque touches on Friedrich A. Kittler's association of recorded sound and the Lacanian order of the real, since as Kittler (1999, 16) notes, the phonograph (unlike writing) can record "all the noise produced by the larynx prior to any semiotic order and linguistic meaning."

28. These details from the Painter Papers, Letter books, and Treasurer's books of the Edison Speaking Phonograph Company, including Smith to Hubbard, November 23, 1878; Mason

to Redpath, November 1, 1878; Cushing to Redpath, July 16, 1878; Redpath to Mason, July 10, 1878.

29.   The year 1878 also saw a bewildering number of versions of *H. M. S. Pinafore* on the U.S. stage, see Allen (1991). An original printed copy of Hockenbery is at the New York Public Library, available elsewhere in microprint as part of the English and American Drama of the Nineteenth Century series (New York: Redex Microprint, 1968). The production history of *Phunnygraph* is unknown.

30.   This refers to the second wave of phonograph demonstrations, when the machine had been "perfected," as Edison put it; *Proceedings of the Fourth Annual Convention of Local Phonograph Companies* (1893), 112. On authorship and exhibitions, see Musser (1991, 6–7).

31.   Uriah Painter to Thomas Edison in reference to the Matthew Brady Studio's photograph of the inventor with the phonograph; see TAEM 15:575.

32.   We know this figure for Wilde's photographs because they were in violation of copyright; *Burrow-Giles v. Sarony,* 111 U.S. 53 (1884).

33.   See Lastra (2000, 16). On sister instruments, see Andem (1892, 7). This point has been difficult for audiences to swallow when I have tried to make it at conferences. I am confident of its accuracy in specific reference to accounts of 1878: though present on occasion, phono/photo analogies are not typical in this first rush of news accounts.

34.   From Dickey (1919); noted in Lears (1989, 41), as part of his discussion of advertising and the "modernization of magic."

35.   See Menke (2005).

36.   "Sacralizing" is from Levine (1988); "salvage" is from James Clifford's "salvage ethnography," noted in Cruz (1999, 180). For the slightly later use of the phonograph in ethnography, see Brady (1999).

37.   Stated in the extreme, or too extremely, "All concepts of trace, up to and including Derrida's grammatological ur-writing, are based on Edison's simple idea. The trace preceding all writing, the trace of pure difference still open between reading and writing, is simply a gramophone needle" (Kittler 1999, 33).

38.   Quoted and further described in A. Fabian (2000, 132, 134; emphasis added). I am relying on recent scholarship that sees the federal support of Civil War widows, orphans, and veterans as the origin of the U.S. welfare state; see Skocpol (1992).

39.   *Weekly* (?), April (?), 1878; see TAEM 25:187. Pat Crain pointed out the "pye" pun to me

40.   On Tyler and his style, see Vanderbilt (1986, 81, 84); also see Spengemann (1994, 4–11).

41.   *Baker v. Selden* was heard by the U.S. Supreme Court in 1879. In its decision, the Court established the idea/expression dichotomy that has stood in copyright law since. The case involved bookkeeping manuals and asked whether an author's rights to the printed bookkeeping forms extended to cover the bookkeeping method they made possible. The answer was yes at first hearing (in 1874) and no on appeal (101 U.S. 99).

42.   An even better example of a similar mistrust of print was the ballad collectors' determination to value unpublished sources above published ones. Francis James Child devoted himself to locating manuscript sources and the sources that "still live on the lips of the people" (Kittredge, 1965, xxvii–xxviii). Childs's work appeared in parts, from 1883 to 1898. American "Folk-Lorists" felt the same way. "Negro" folklorist Alice Mabel Bacon urged, "Nothing must come in that we have ever seen in print" (1897); quoted in Cruz (1999, 170). A generation later, the "new bibliography" movement in literary studies set out to establish editions of canonical "works," salvaged from the (potentially corrupt) printed "texts" of the past.

43.   This is Marx (1997, 967) from his work on another keyword.

44.   More broadly put, "Production is indeed historiography's quasi-universal principal of explanation, since historical research grasps every document as the symptom of whatever produced it" (de Certeau 1988, 11).

45.   The *Oxford English Dictionary* seconds Farmer, noting in 1856 and 1879 the first uses of *record* to mean a person's record, and in 1883 and 1884 the first uses of *record* to mean best recorded achievement.

References

Allen, Robert C. 1991. *Horrible Prettiness: Burlesque and American Culture.* Chapel Hill: University of North Carolina Press.

Andem, James. 1892. *Practical Guide for the Use of the Edison Phonograph.* Cincinnati, OH: C. J. Krehbiel and Co.

Anderson, Benedict. 1991. *Imagined Communities: Reflections on the Origin and Spread of Nationalism.* Rev. ed. London: Verso.

Brady, Erika. 1999. *A Spiral Way: How the Phonograph Changed Ethnography.* Jackson: University Press of Mississippi.

Centennial Newspaper Exhibition, 1876. 1876. New York: Geo. P. Rowell and Co.

Cmiel, Kenneth. 1990. *Democratic Eloquence: The Fight over Popular Speech in Nineteenth-Century America.* Berkeley: University of California Press.

Cook, James W. 2001. *The Arts of Deception: Playing with Fraud in the Age of Barnum.* Cambridge: Harvard University Press.

Cruz, Jon. 1999. *Culture on the Margins: The Black Spiritual and the Rise of American Cultural Interpretation.* Princeton, NJ: Princeton University Press.

de Certeau, Michel. 1988. *The Writing of History.* Trans. Tom Conley. New York: Columbia University Press.

de Grazia, Margreta. 1992. *Shakespeare Verbatim: The Reproduction of Authenticity and the 1790 Apparatus.* Oxford: Clarendon Press.

Dickey, Marcus. 1919. *The Youth of James Whitcomb Riley: Fortune's Way with the Poet from Infancy to Manhood.* Indianapolis: Bobbs-Merrill.

Douglass, Frederick. [1892] 1976. *Life and Times of Frederick Douglass, Written by Himself.* New York: Collier Books.

Edison, Thomas. 1878. The Phonograph and Its Future. *North American Review* 126 (June): 527–36.

——. 1987–. *The Thomas A. Edison Papers: A Selective Microfilm Edition,* ed. Thomas E. Jeffrey et al. Bethesda, MD: University Publications of America.

——. 1998. *The Wizard of Menlo Park.* Vol. 4 of *The Papers of Thomas A. Edison,* ed. Paul B. Israel, Keith A. Nier, and Louis Carlat. Baltimore: Johns Hopkins University Press.

Fabian, Ann. 2000. *The Unvarnished Truth: Personal Narratives in Nineteenth-Century America.* Berkeley: University of California Press.

Fabian, Johannes. 1983. *Time and the Other: How Anthropology Makes Its Object.* New York: Columbia University Press.

Farmer, John S. 1889. *Americanisms Old and New.* London: Thomas Poulter.

Fliegelman, Jay. 1993. *Declaring Independence: Jefferson, Natural Language, and the Culture of Performance.* Stanford, CA: Stanford University Press.

Graff, Gerald, and Michael Warner. 1989. Introduction: The Origins of Literary Studies in America. In *The Origins of Literary Study in America: A Documentary Anthology,* ed. Gerald Graff and Michael Warner, 1–16. New York: Routledge.

Grasso, Christopher. 1999. *A Speaking Aristocracy: Transforming Public Discourse in Eighteenth-Century Connecticut.* Chapel Hill: University of North Carolina Press.

Gutjahr, Paul C. 1999. *An American Bible: A History of the Good Book in the United States, 1777–1880.* Stanford, CA: Stanford University Press.

Habermas, Jürgen. 1989. *The Structural Transformation of the Public Sphere: An Inquiry into a Category of Bourgeois Society.* Trans. Thomas Burger with Frederick Lawrence. Cambridge: MIT Press.

Henkin, David M. 1998. *City Reading: Written Words and Public Spaces in Antebellum New York.* New York: Columbia University Press.

Hockenbery, Frank. 1886. *Prof Black's Phunnygraph, or Talking Machine: A Colored Burlesque on the Phonograph.* Chicago: T. S. Denison.

Horner, Charles F. 1926. *The Life of James Redpath and the Development of the Modern Lyceum.* New York: Barse and Hopkins.

Israel, Paul. 1997–98. The Unknown History of the Tinfoil Phonograph. *NARAS Journal* 8 (Winter–Spring): 29–42.

John, Richard. 1995. *Spreading the News: The American Postal System from Franklin to Morse.* Cambridge: Harvard University Press.

Johns, Adrian. 1998. *The Nature of the Book: Print and Knowledge in the Making.* Chicago: University of Chicago Press.

Kamensky, Jane. 1997. *Governing the Tongue: The Politics of Speech in Early New England.* New York: Oxford University Press.

Kittler, Friedrich A. 1999. *Gramophone, Film, Typewriter.* Trans. Geoffrey Winthroup-Young and Michael Wutz. Stanford, CA: Stanford University Press.

Kittredge, G. L. 1965. Preface. In *The English and Scottish Popular Ballads,* ed. Francis James Child. 5 vols. New York: Dover.

Lastra, James. 2000. *Sound Technology and the American Cinema: Perception, Representation, Modernity.* New York: Columbia University Press.

Lears, Jackson. 1989. Beyond Veblen: Rethinking Consumer Culture in America. In *Consuming Visions: Accumulation and Display of Goods in America, 1880–1920,* ed. Simon J. Bronner, 73–98. New York: W. W. Norton.

Lears, Jackson. 1994. *Fables of Abundance: A Cultural History of Advertising in America.* New York: Basic Books.

Levine, Lawrence. 1988. *Highbrow/Lowbrow: The Emergence of Cultural Hierarchy in America.* Cambridge: Harvard University Press.

Looby, Chris. 1996. *Voicing America: Language, Literary Form, and the Origins of the United States.* Chicago: University of Chicago Press.

Marx, Leo. 1997. Technology: The Emergence of a Hazardous Concept. *Social Research* 64 (Fall): 965–88.

McGill, Meredith L. 2003. *American Literature and the Culture of Reprinting, 1834–1853.* Philadelphia: University of Pennsylvania Press.

Menke, Richard. 2005. Media in America, 1881: Garfield, Guiteau, Bell, Whitman. *Critical Inquiry* 31 (Spring): 638–64.

Morton, David. 2000. *Off the Record: The Technology and Culture of Sound Recording in America.* New Brunswick, NJ: Rutgers University Press.

Musser, Charles. 1991. *High-Class Moving Pictures: Lyman H. Howe and the Forgotten Era of Traveling Exhibition, 1880–1920.* Princeton, NJ: Princeton University Press.

Ruttenburg, Nancy. 1999. *Democratic Personality: Popular Voice and the Trial of American Authorship.* Stanford, CA: Stanford University Press.

Secord, James A. 2000. *Victorian Sensation: The Extraordinary Publication, Reception, and Secret Authorship of Vestiges of the Natural History of Creation.* Chicago: University of Chicago Press.

Skocpol, Theda. 1992. *Protecting Soldiers and Mothers: The Political Origins of Social Policy in the United States.* Cambridge: Harvard University Press.

Spengemann, William C. 1994. *A New World of Words: Redefining Early American Literature.* New Haven, CT: Yale University Press.

Sterne, Jonathan. 2003. *The Audible Past: Cultural Origins of Sound Reproduction.* Durham, NC: Duke University Press.

Stewart, Susan. 1993. *On Longing: Narratives of the Miniature, the Gigantic, the Souvenir, the Collection.* Durham, NC: Duke University Press.

Tyler, Moses Coit. 1878. *A History of American Literature, 1607–1765.* New York: Putnam's.

Uricchio, William, and Roberta E. Pearson. 1993. *Reframing Culture: The Case of the Vitagraph Quality Films.* Princeton, NJ: Princeton University Press.

Vanderbilt, Kermit. 1986. *American Literature and the Academy: The Roots, Growth, and Maturity of a Profession.* Philadelphia: University of Pennsylvania Press.

Warner, Michael. 1990. *The Letters of the Republic: Publication and the Public Sphere in Eighteenth-Century America.* Cambridge: Harvard University Press.

Wiebe, Robert H. 1967. *The Search for Order: 1877–1920.* New York: Hill and Wang.

Williams, Raymond. 1976. *Keywords: A Vocabulary of Culture and Society.* New York: Oxford University Press.

Chapter 26

Jason Stanyek and Benjamin Piekut

DEADNESS: TECHNOLOGIES OF THE INTERMUNDANE

IN LATE CAPITALISM, THE DEAD are highly productive. Of course, all capital is dead labor, but the dead also *generate* capital in collaboration with the living. What is "late" about late capitalism could be the new arrangements of interpenetration between worlds of living and dead, arrangements that might best be termed *intermundane*. As Joseph Roach writes, "modernity itself might be understood as a new way of handling (and thinking about) the dead," but the mechanisms and procedures through which this handling takes place are under constant revision (1996:14). While Roach is concerned with mapping "a revolutionary spatial paradigm: the segregation of the dead from the living" (48) in early modern Europe and its colonies, we are interested in a later arrangement of bio- and necroworlds, one centered on production of several kinds: social, economic, cultural, and affective. In this arrangement, the living do not one-sidedly handle the dead, but participate in an inter-handling, a mutually effective co-laboring.

"Death isn't the end," remarks Mark Roesler, the CEO of CMG Worldwide, an intellectual property management company that plays an important role in the growing field of "necromarketing" (in Hoffman 2005).[1] In what could be seen as a case of millennial anxiety over the reconfiguration of labor in a burgeoning necro market, *Forbes* in 2001 began publishing their annual list of "Top Earning Dead Celebrities," which for the past seven years has been fleshed out by a barely rotating cast of actors, writers, artists, and musicians: Marilyn Monroe, Charles Schultz, J.R.R. Tolkien, Andy Warhol, John Lennon, and Bob Marley, among others. Without doubt, Elvis is the king of the dead, topping the list for six of the past seven years, and earning between $35 and $50 million annually in publishing, Graceland tourism, and licensing and merchandising fees.[2]

The revivification of celebrities has become a key tactic in advertising campaigns for global product lines—John Wayne yuks it up with a pair of thirsty losers for Coors; Fred Astaire gets down with a Dirt Devil vacuum cleaner; Audrey Hepburn cuts a rug for the Gap; and Louis Armstrong, Humphrey Bogart, and Jimmy Cagney enjoy a wild Diet Coke party with Elton John. "Would you believe this little baby holds 30 gigs?" asks a digitally reanimated Orville Redenbacher (who crossed over in the pre-iPod 1990s) in one recent advertisement, hoping to capitalize on the rather oblique relationship between an ultra-thin MP3 player and ultra-fluffy popcorn (see Beard 1993 and 2001; and Anderson 2004/2005).

Music has been a particularly fertile growth market for dead talent. Although "Unforgettable," the 1991 Grammy Award–winning collaboration between Natalie Cole and her then almost 30-year-dead father, is undoubtedly the essential example of what has variously been referred to as "electronic deception," or "manufactured," "virtual," "simulated," or "studio-engineered" duets,[3] the recording capitalized on a tradition that included Hank Williams Jr. and Sr.'s "There's a Tear in My Beer" (which won a Grammy Award for "Best Country Vocal Collaboration" in 1990), and Jim Reeves and Patsy Cline's "Have You Ever Been Lonely (Have You Ever Been Blue)" of 1981 (Zimmerman 1989 and Hilburn 1981). The latter collaboration enjoys special status as perhaps the first duet to have been recorded after *both* of its partners were dead. The success of "Unforgettable" also set in motion a wave of collaboration CDs, including tributes to Bob Marley (*Chant Down Babylon*, 1999), Dean Martin (*Forever Cool*, 2007), and Notorious B.I.G. (*Duets:The Final Chapter*, 2005), as well as numerous individual tracks pairing David Byrne and Selena ("God's Child [Baila conmigo]," 1995), Kenny G and Louis Armstrong ("What a Wonderful World," 1999), The Beatles and John Lennon ("Free as a Bird," 1995), Brian and Carl Wilson ("Soul Searching," 2004), and a new track by Anita Cochran ("[I Wanna Hear] A Cheatin' Song," 2004) that used previously recorded material by Conway Twitty to construct new vocal lines that he had never actually sung in the first place.[4] Two dead artists have been particularly prolific. Frank Sinatra's 1999 duet with Celine Dion, "All the Way," and his more recent collaboration with Alicia Keys ("Learnin' the Blues," which kicked off the 2008 Grammy Awards show) pale in comparison to *Sinatra at the London Palladium*, a complete revue that ran for seven months in 2006 and featured Old Blue Eyes accompanied by a 24-piece orchestra.[5] 2Pac's posthumous albums have sold over 20 million copies and eight of these have been certified platinum. The bulk of these albums feature posthumous duets with living hip-hop artists and the soundtrack to the biopic film *Resurrection* even has him and the similarly deceased Notorious B.I.G. dueting on the track "Runnin' (Dying to Live)" (2003).[6]

Sound-recording technologies have always been associated with death. While Jonathan Sterne argues that sound recording in the 19th century "preserve[d] the bodies of the dead so that they could continue to perform a social function after life" (2003:292), we are concerned with a different arrangement of technologies and bodies that is less about preservation than it is about complex forms of rearticulation. If the late-19th-century urge was to embalm (sounds floating, inert, in the formaldehyde of tin, wax, or resin), since World War II, the tendency has been to recombine. This is the age of the splice, and this recombinatorial imperative emerges on the corporeal plane, broadly by the end of the 1950s, with the structural modeling of DNA, the standardization of life-support technologies, and the development of immunosuppressive organ transplant procedures. In the technosonic realm, the logics of recombination surface in multitrack tape technology and begin to recondition the very nature of global musical production. In each of these cases, technologies of the body refigure component parts—the DNA strand, the disabled or transplanted organ, the voice—into networks that extend beyond self-contained limits. In this essay we peer into this environment of emergent extensities to consider the recombinatorial sonics of intermundane collaboration.

We situate this project within a body of literature on the effective presence of the dead (Castronovo 2001; Derrida 1994; Fuss 2003; Gordon 1997; Peterson 2007; Rayner 2006; Verdery 1999; Jones and Jensen 2005). The general subject of post-humous duets engages and extends this literature by setting in motion a large number of concerns, including the poetics of modern bereavement; kinship patterns; the legal and commercial structures of celebrity and property; interanimations of voice, body, and identity; and medical discourses of cryogenics, cloning, transplantation, and bioethics. Though we address these concerns in a current book project, our prevailing interest in this article is the history of recording practices from the late 19th century until the early 1990s, and the contingent arrangements of bodies, technologies, and sounds that take shape through these practices.

Although countless posthumous duets have appeared in the last two decades, our touchstone here is the Coles' "Unforgettable" (Cole 1991a). The track is important for a number of reasons beyond its Grammy-winning, multiplatinum status. Recorded in 1991 at the moment when music production made its final transition to full digitality, "Unforgettable" is a liminal document. Although sampling, digital instruments, automated mixing consoles, and even digital audiotape were commonplace by this time, it was not until the early 1990s that most aspects of production became digitized. As we detail below, "Unforgettable" participates in some—but not all—of these changes. For example, had the song been produced just a few years later, engineers would have employed visual editing applications such as Pro Tools, in contrast to long traditions of aural editing.[7] "Unforgettable" thus stands at the end of a long history of analog recording reaching back to the late 19th century. Tracking this history to the early 1990s, our task here is not to give a complete overview of the posthumous duet phenomenon (intermundane collaboration in the digital era, for example, requires separate treatment), but to uncover a theoretical apparatus from the long history that culminates with "Unforgettable."

There is nothing new about selling the dead to the living. In the popular music marketplace of the early 1990s, one way this activity took shape was through re-releasing the stars of the early LP era on CD or repackaging their personas in novel ways. But "Unforgettable" is different. The song may appear to be a straightforward record that is, like much popular music produced in the US after the mid-1960s, the simple result of overdubbing new tracks on top of previously recorded tracks. Our analysis suggests, however, that "Unforgettable" raises questions that are much more profound.

Agency as Effectivity

One question we continually encounter when sharing our ideas about posthumous duets with other scholars should be addressed from the very beginning. That question is, How are these "collaborations" when the dead cannot respond, cannot change or adapt to their living counterparts? We contend that this question is already hemmed in by certain presuppositions about agency, many of which assume a stable and reduced ontological backdrop woven out of theories of resistance, reinscription, refiguration, and emancipation. For us, agency is not merely an individual's capacity to respond to changing conditions. "Crucially," as Karen Barad argues, "*agency is a matter of intra-acting; it is an enactment, not something that someone or something has*" (Barad 2007:178; emphasis in original). By "intra-action," Barad means to stress that "agencies are only distinct in a relational, not an absolute, sense, that is, *agencies are only distinct in relation to their mutual entanglement; they don't exist as individual elements*" (33). We take it as axiomatic that agency is always distributed and never coterminous with a single body; it is not something that a person collects and, in a moment of purposeful clarity, unleashes. Barad continues, "Intra-actions include the larger material arrangement [. . .] that effects an *agential cut* between 'subject' and 'object' (in contrast to the more familiar Cartesian cut which takes this distinction for granted). That is, the agential cut enacts a resolution *within* the phenomenon of the inherent ontological (and semantic) indeterminacy" (139–40). Although tempted to adopt Barad's language and refer to these posthumous duets as "intra-mundane," we retain the "inter" prefix to draw attention to the performed naturalization of the separation of living and dead mundanities, the continual production of an agential cut that assigns prime mover status to living humans while objectivizing the "dead" as inert, without futures, and non-effective.

Standard reckonings of agency are also limited by temporal orientations that privilege the present and the future, and often constrict causality to a "here and now" operation. What of distended pasts that swell up with delays, pre-echoes, calls, and incitements that spill over into multiple presents and futures? This is one of the key points of the intermundane—we can't ascribe with any certainty a direction to temporal flows; performative notions of straightforward intention and unidirectional purpose only come into being within nonlinear temporalities. The topology of causality cannot be reduced to a one-to-one relationship between action and result, for effectivity is enacted by intra-active and overlapping agencies in a manner that exceeds commonplace notions of intentionality. Effects are unpredictably durative, and can be indirect, delayed, unintended, and even unmarked. We might even say that this is the only guarantee that sound recording offers: being recorded means being enrolled in futures (and pasts) that one cannot wholly predict nor control. Crucially, having a future means having an effect. As Bruno Latour tells us, "An actor that makes no difference is not an actor at all" (2005:153).

Having a future, having an effect, making a difference. We are now drawn to the notion of effectivity, where "having" an effect is not understood in a proprietary sense, but rather as the enactment of agencies that make a difference—through making a difference, by having an effect, an agency is delineated. In a recording collaboration, what has effects? Certainly, not just living humans, all fleshy and present; sounds, machines, discourses—all manner of non-humans, material and nonmaterial—also matter. This is not to argue for or against technological determinism; it is to say that effects are generated and absorbed by all kinds of entities. Importantly, these entities are enacted *through* mutual effectivities. They do not preexist their enrollment in temporary assemblages, but are constituted, diffracted, translated, and variously deferred by other agencies in these assemblages.

Moving beyond human exceptionalism by framing agency as effectivity allows us to rebuild the idea of personhood to encompass far more than a simple body or a hunk of flesh, as if personhood could be limited to the boundaries of the epidermal wall. In our framing, personhood is not equivalent to a lone body, but is distributed among and articulated with other entities that are textual, technological, juridical, and affective (for a similar approach, see Strathern 1992 and 1988). Personhood is always collaborative, cutting across clear distinctions of materiality/discourse, technology/organicity, and bounded lifetimes/eternal deaths. We mention "bounded lifetimes/eternal deaths" because agency as effectivity is not only unpredictably durative; it is also distributed among entities that have different capabilities, resources, and "lifetimes." To say "personhood is distributed" does not mean that all entities within distributed assemblages have equal and unrestricted access to all possible forms of allocation. Translations, diffractions, and deferrals happen precisely because of unwanted intrusions and interferences, disproportionate rights, uneven abilities to wield force and shape outcomes. Personhood is distributed, but this does not mean that all modalities of distribution are ethical, a point to which we will return at the end of this essay.

Our primary focus is on how this agential cut of the intermundane is performed in the sonic practices of the recording studio, where collaboration is now understood to involve humans and nonhumans, all distributed and all effective. This perspective runs counter to the common understanding that collaboration necessarily entails face-to-face encounter, where participants can reach unanimity, supported by an equivalence of input and capacity. There is also an expectation of synergy or transcendence—the result of a collaboration will be magical and more than simply the sum of its constitutive inputs. Actual recorded collaborations, however, reveal numerous and even contradictory allegiances among emerging agencies, practices of temporal and spatial discontinuity, and asymmetrical distributions of power and ability. Intermundane collaborations are no different.

In this article, we generate a series of terms that have emerged out of our engagement with intermundane collaborations; although we discuss these terms in greater detail later in our analysis, we present them here as a kind of pre-echo: revertibility, recombinatoriality, rhizophonia, corpauralities, perforation, leakage effects, and deadness. *Revertibility* refers to a temporal process of undoing a work of recording in some way, whereby presumptive wholes can be disarticulated and taken back to a prior stage in a process of assemblage, upsetting straightforward, cumulative forms of co-labor. As we will show, there are varying degrees of revertibility in the history of sound recording and reproduction. The related concept of *recombinatoriality*, on the other hand, describes the capacity toward articulating what are taken to be discrete, non-identical parts into new arrangements. Recombinatoriality is a general tendency or imperative that emerged in technology-saturated post-World War II environments, and its specific surfacing in the context of sound recording assumes (1) that elements are defined by the breaches between them and (2) that these breaches can be sutured.

Rhizophonia describes the fundamentally fragmented yet proliferative condition of sound reproduction and recording, where sounds and bodies are constantly dislocated, relocated, and co-located in temporary aural configurations. We don't offer up rhizophonia as schizophonia's other, to use R. Murray Schafer's well-trodden term (1977). It's not the missing twin. Rather, we suggest it as a *replacement* for schizophonia, itself a problematic, tautological term that seems to describe an exception (sound severed from source) to some impossible, full presence (sound as identical with its source; see Sterne 2003:20–21). Indeed, schizophonia describes sound itself. All sounds are severed from their sources—that's what makes sound sound. Rhizophonia is our term for taking account both of sound's extensity and the impossibility of a perfect identity between sound and source.

To account for human positionings within rhizophonic structures, we offer the term *corpauralities* to describe the imbrication of sounds with fleshy bodies. Humanly made sounds are never devoid of bodies, and there is no body that isn't constituted through sonic formations. However, corpauralities are not simply traces or residues of prior sonic acts—we're more concerned with the proleptic condition of corpaural assemblages than we are with the mere persistence of a prior sounding. In our discussion of the recording studio that follows, we use the idea of the corpaural not simply to call attention to the relation between sounds and individual bodies—what might be called "sonic bodies"—but also the ways that these corpauralities infuse with and cling to others. In this sense, the corpaural helps to sonify the idea of distributed personhood that we develop here.

Of course, there are limits to distribution, and rhizophonic structures don't proliferate in any which way; the production of corpauralities is always managed and contained. Obstacles and blockages can interrupt flows, or flows can traverse obstacles through certain well-defined openings, which we call *perforations*. A perforation controls and focuses flows between two spaces, but maintains separation between them. In the recording studio, sonically sealed spaces such as the control room or the vocal isolation booth depend on perforations that channel sound from one area to the next.

But sound can and does escape its assigned channels. For example, a sound might leak from one instrument into a microphone intended for another, separate sound source. Any of the possible responses to this leakage—separating the sources further in space, partitioning them with baffles or even walls, or recording the two sounds at different times and later recombining them on tape—is what we call a *leakage effect*. More schematically, leakage effects occur when an activity in one area expands unexpectedly into another area, setting in motion a second process, project, or concern. This "setting in motion" often conditions an unforeseen act of translation or transference from one realm to another.

Taken together, these terms—revertibility, recombinatoriality, rhizophonia, corpauralities, perforation, leakage effects—come together under a broader frame that we call deadness. It's not our intent to raise (or even raze) one more binary, so we do not conceptualize deadness as the other to liveness. Rather, deadness emerges out of what is for us an unhelpful and overvalued schism between presence and absence that undergirds much literature on performance. Deadness speaks to the distended temporalities and spatialities of all performance, much the way all ontologies are really hauntologies, spurred into being through the portended traces of too many histories to name and too many futures to subsume in a stable, locatable present. As we will argue below, the topologies of deadness—those never-ending emplacements within concatenations of displacements—are patterned and re-patterned through specific arrangements of co-labor, or the interpenetrating, distributed effectivities of all entities that have effects. In our understanding, deadness describes the necessary choreographies of all productive encounter, and by exploring it here we hope to enlarge (albeit tangentially) the conversation in Marxist scholarship concerning dead and living labor. As Dipesh Chakrabarty explains, "Marx would ground resistance to capital in this apparently mysterious factor called 'life'" (2000:60). In Chakrabarty's historical analysis, the living worker always carries with him unique histories, dispositions, and habits, "ways of being human [. . .], acted out in manners that do not lend themselves to the reproduction of the logic of capital" (67). Our investigation into the intermundane suggests an extension of this important point—that not only living human workers, but also the ostensibly "dead" labor of technology and discipline, and even the "dead labor" of the human dead—contains within it the seeds of unpredictable futures that can and do retrace worlds. Although the idea of deadness arose out of our analysis of posthumous duets (and, as shall be made clearer below, out of our inquiries into the dead spaces of recording studios themselves), its usefulness extends beyond the sonic realms of musical production to all kinds of co-labor.

The six concepts introduced above are integral to deadness. The paired terms revertibility and recombinatoriality refer to the sedimented pasts and possible futures of any contingent assemblage, and call attention to the ways in which these assemblages can be dis- and reassembled. Rhizophonia describes the perpetual non-identity of sounds and their sources. Corpauralities consist of anterior corporeal states that are registered in sound and anterior sonic states that are registered in the body—put simply, every sounding body will be taken up by another. Lastly, the entwined terms perforation and leakage effects suggest that attempts to regulate passages from one state to another are thwarted, always necessitating ever-new forms of containment.

Unforgetting the Dead

It's 1961. Nat "King" Cole stands in front of a Neumann U47 microphone in Capitol's New York studio recording facility, located on the first floor of the Eaves Costume Company building at 151 West 46th Street. Nat is in the large "live room" of Studio A, joined by conductor Ralph Carmichael, who leads a small orchestra of about 25 players.[8] The musicians read from Nelson Riddle's original parts for his arrangement of "Unforgettable," the Irving Gordon tune that was the basis of Riddle and Cole's first properly credited collaboration in 1951. Producer Lee Gillete circulates between the live room and the control room, where an Ampex 300M tape machine records the action onto three separate tracks.

According to Irv Joel, an engineer who worked at the Capitol Studio between 1955 and 1969, the liveliness of the live room at Capitol New York could be modulated by adjusting reversible panels made of pegboard on one side and fiberglass covered with burlap on the other. Although the room was otherwise "open," a variety of technologies combined to segment the space during a typical recording. On the 1961 date, for example, Nat was positioned behind a small gobo to shield his vocal performance from the other sounds in the space, which were captured separately by a large number of carefully placed microphones. Routed through multiboxes, these signals could be combined and sent to the control room, where they could then be mixed, equalized, or sent back out to the facility's well-regarded echo chamber.[9] Located at the back of the main studio space, the chamber consisted of an approximately 20' × 15' × 22' room with an inclined floor, a flat back wall, and an angled front wall. The entire chamber was covered in Keene's cement and then shellacked. Reverberation was often added on the fly during live takes by sending signals through an Altec 604 loudspeaker at the front of the chamber to a pair of RCA 44BX ribbon microphones at the back. This processed signal then traveled back into the control room and on to the tape recorders.

By the early 1960s the control room at Capitol New York was restructured to take account of the major shift toward stereophonic sound that was taking place in the music industry. In short, it was divided into two control booths—one for the monitoring of mono recordings and the other for stereo. On some occasions during the early 1960s, two recording sessions took place simultaneously with parallel sets of engineers and recording equipment. We don't know if the dual control room setup was used for Nat's 1961 "Unforgettable" sessions, but these sessions certainly need to be placed within the context of this newly emergent marketplace for stereophonic recordings. Much like Victor's "revitalizations" of Caruso's early acoustic hits for the electronic era,[10] Capitol was taking advantage of changing sound-recording formats to wring a little more profit out of their superstar singer. Over the course of nine sessions in New York in spring 1961 (plus three more at Capitol's North Vine Studio in Hollywood during July 1961) they rerecorded 36 of Nat's previous mono hits, releasing the collection as the three-LP set *The Nat "King" Cole Story*. Although the Ampex 300M at the studio was not sel-sync, it *did* allow Capitol to take advantage of new technologies of reproduction. Three tracks of $1/_2$-inch tape allowed engineers to place Nat's voice alone, dead center, with the orchestra on the left and right tracks. Out in the live room with the other musicians, Nat was also dead center, encased in his gobo, his microphone close to his mouth, his sonic world immediate. But there would be leakage.

It's 1991.[11] Natalie Cole stands in front of a Neumann U67 microphone in the isolation booth of Ocean Way Studio A/B in Los Angeles. The booth, acoustically sealed off from the studio's other rooms, is still a perforated environment. Balanced cables connect her to the live room where Johnny Mandel leads a 55-piece orchestra, and to the control room where producer David Foster and engineers Al Schmitt and Rail Rogut monitor the music making of Natalie, Nat, and the orchestra. Each of the live performers wears headphones. The engineers send Nat's voice to Natalie, and a pre-recorded "human" click track to the conductor, rhythm section, and string players. Mandel conducts his own slightly altered version of Nelson Riddle's original 1951 arrangement, and Natalie sings in unison with her father.

This is neither the beginning nor the end of the process of creating the final track. In the early 1980s, Natalie had experimented with singing "Unforgettable" onstage as a duet with her father,[12] so when she moved from EMI to Elektra in the late 1980s, the idea for her to do a record of her father's music was already in place. Like Victor in 1932 and Capitol in 1961, Elektra in 1991 was seeking to recapitalize the stored star power of residual, spectral celebrity. After Natalie and Foster worked out the initial details for creating the duet, Foster used his considerable influence in the industry to have the 1961 three-track master tape exhumed from Capitol's archive at an Iron Mountain storage facility in Glendale, California. Once the master had been taken to Capitol Studio, threaded into the same type of Ampex 300M recorder that had created the original, and transferred to 24-track tape, Foster heard, to his amazement, that the original tape was in pristine condition, with Nat's voice isolated on one of the tracks.

Foster and his engineer, David Reitzas, used the tape to work up a rough sketch of the tune in Foster's home studio in Malibu. Using synth pads and keyboards, the two mapped out the song and expanded on Natalie's plan for the vocal exchanges that would occur between the singer and her father. From there, they took the tape, complete with Nat's vocal on track 3 and their synth and keyboard scratch tracks, to another studio in Hollywood.[13] There, they "bounced," or rerecorded, Nat's vocal line to track 18, muting those sections of his performance that would later be sung by Natalie. On those sections where Nat was still singing, the engineers had to address the fact that his isolation on the center track of the 1961 master was not complete— ghostly traces of the original orchestral accompaniment had seeped onto his vocal track. The engineers used analog filters "to try to strip it clean," Schmitt remembers. "We filtered out as much as we could with filters, not touching the voice. And then [. . .] we edited out the spaces in between [individual phrases]" (2007). It bears noting that this technique of revertibility is virtually identical to that undertaken in 1932 for Caruso's "Vesti la Giubba."

Yet the isolation pursued through this round of stripping was still incomplete, and Mandel's arrangement for the 1991 recording was dictated at certain moments by the need to cover up or match Riddle's. As Reitzas explains, "When Nat was singing, Johnny Mandel, the arranger, needed to stay similar with the [original] arrangement, because otherwise, you'd hear the leakage on his vocal mic, and it would sound weird. But when Natalie was singing, there was obviously no leakage, so he had more freedom to change the arrangement" (2008). The 1961 accompaniment is thus present in the 1991 version, acoustically as a (barely) audible palimpsest and formally as a framework upon which Mandel created his (barely) new arrangement.[14]

Mandel's adaptation is one of many techniques used to facilitate matching between the two recordings, an objective that continued when the engineers recorded the orchestral and rhythm tracks in February 1991 at Ocean Way Studio in Hollywood (Natalie was also on hand to sing with the orchestra and record a scratch vocal track). Matching is crucial to this discussion not simply because the marketing campaign for the album stressed its fidelity to the ethos of 1940s and '50s crooning (signaled on the album's cover through Natalie's white satin dress, an image that evokes the glamour of 1940s Hollywood as well as the elegant lining of a coffin). George Hurrell, the legendary 86-year-old Hollywood photographer, agreed to come out of retirement to shoot Natalie in the dramatically lit style of the '40s (Foster 1991). If, as we have argued, deadness is emplacement within a concatenation of displacements, then matching itself is a crucial and active technique for traversing the topologies of deadness.[15] More than mere mimesis, matching is a method for reactivating the latent capital stored in recorded performances; it is a form of managing the complex spatialities and temporalities of the intermundane. Significantly, matching is a shared process that is co-performed here by entities in 1991 *and* 1961 (and not simply a certain fidelity to an inert aesthetic past, or a pact with the commercial value of the "authentic"). In the case of the sessions at Ocean Way, we can point to four examples of matching: temporal synchronization, hand-limiting, microphone selection, and personnel decisions.

In order to synchronize the 1991 performers to Nat's pre-recorded vocal, the producers and engineers created a click track. By this time, clicks had become commonplace in popular music production, and were usually generated by mechanical means. This was not the case in 1961, however—though click tracks were ubiquitous in film production, they had not yet made the jump to projects focused purely on music recording, and the slight yet perceptible tempo fluctuations on Nat's original performance bear this out.[16] As Schmitt explains, in order to match these fluctuations, they generated a "human click": "[A] famous old drummer named Sol Gubin, who'd played a lot of Sinatra dates, put a human click on it for the orchestral musicians to work to—as the Nat Cole recording had been made without a click, the tempos obviously varied quite a bit [. . .W]e had the full orchestra play—and Natalie sing—to [. . .] Sol's human click" (in Buskin 2004). If Nat's sense of time had an effect on the 1991 performance (both technologically and musically), so too did specific engineering techniques prevalent before the development of much of the effects units available for the 1991 session. For example, in the 1950s, Schmitt had developed particular choreographies for dealing with challenges created by amplitude fluctuation in vocal performance. As he told *Sound on Sound*: "Way back, when I started in the business, we didn't have limiters to use on the vocal, so we did most of the limiting by hand. You learned the song quickly, and where the artist got big you were able to pull back the level, while you'd increase it where the artist got softer. Since I think this approach produces better results, I still work mostly that way [. . .]" (in Buskin 2004). The practice of hand-limiting, though supplemented in 1991 by what Schmitt calls "a tiny amount of Summit limiter" (which automatically manages amplitude spikes), effectively extends the "past" of recording history into the present by drawing on Schmitt's experience as an engineer in the 1950s and '60s. Schmitt also paid close attention to matching the grain of Nat and Natalie's voices. The Neumann U67 microphone they chose for her voice not only aligned with the warm sound of classic recordings, but also melded with the U47 that Nat had used 30 years prior. Finally, in addition to these processes of synchronization, hand-limiting, and microphone selection, the desire to match also manifests itself at the corporeal level through the contracting of musicians who were active during the time of the 1961 session. Some of these performers had even collaborated with Nat while he was still alive. "It was no coincidence that many of the musicians were the original players on my father's recordings," comments Natalie in her liner notes to the album.[17]

Another move, another place, another time. Soon after the Ocean Way session, Natalie entered another isolation booth, this time at Johnny Yuma Studios, where she laid down the final vocal tracks. As with any recording, the isolation was not total—other sessions, other times, and other spaces leaked into and out of this room. At this particular session, the focus of attention was on the voices of Nat and Natalie. This is where the structure of their duet was finalized. Natalie did a number of takes that were distributed across 3 different tracks (15, 17, and 23). To mix these to a "composite track" (track 16), Schmitt and Reitzas used a custom-built device specifically designed to cross-fade together different takes, folding together the best bits from each run-through (which were each punched-in composites themselves). This "comp box" facilitated another kind of matching, one of Natalie to herself. Her single performance heard on the final recording is an assemblage of many performances, and although Natalie records from a single location, multiple times are folded into the final product.

Like the comp box, the AMS DMX 15–80s Computer Controlled Stereo Digital Delay played a key role at this stage of the recording process. Schmitt and Reitzas had loaded a few phrases of Nat's performance into the machine, and used it as a sampler to digitally tune his voice to the 1991 orchestral tracks. It was only a matter of a few cents for a few phrases, Reitzas recalls, yet Schmitt still felt "a little strange" (2007) adjusting the original track (he called this process "unforgivable" [in Buskin 2004]). They also used the AMS unit to create the song's memorable third verse, in which Nat responds to his daughter phrase-by-phrase. Significantly, Natalie leads this temporally complex duet, with her father's contribution now taking the form of an echo. An echo? No, a pre-echo, sounding ahead from the past. Natalie recalls, "At one point, David [Foster] thought, 'Wouldn't it be incredible if not only she answers her father but *he answers her,* as though he was right over her shoulder?' The next morning he went into the studio with Al Schmitt, engineer extraordinaire, and figured out the technical aspect of laying Dad's voice inside the new track and moved it. As it happened, the chords worked perfectly, so he could lay Dad's voice in later. It was as though Dad had come in and redone the vocals" (Cole with Diehl 2000:246). The chords may have worked well, but the orchestral figures presented some difficulties once they had been temporally displaced. Since the decision to move Nat out of his original phrasal position in the tune was made after Mandel had written and recorded his orchestral accompaniment, they couldn't just ask him to do a new arrangement that would cover up (or re-bury) the displaced lines. Instead, as Reitzas recalled, he and Schmitt performed a second round of stripping on Nat's voice to remove as much of the 1961 ghost orchestra as possible—"Filtered it out," he explained, "then added a little more top end back on" to restore the sheen that had been worn away from the voice by excessive equalization (Reitzas 2008). The engineer's operations here demonstrate how one distinct time (the vertical relation between voice and accompaniment) can be split to occupy two temporal locations. The temptation might be to think of this move in terms of schizophonia, but the lingering traces of anterior sonic events always effect proleptic, *rhizophonic* relationships with other sonic futures.

In the interplay between Nat and Natalie that emerges in the third verse—and in their duet as a whole—their voices are im/material parts of bodies that are distributed, noncontinuous, and overlapping. To understand this intermingling in the terms of corpaurality, we must hear the voice emerging from the resonant body as the body resonates in the voice. Dislocated from the fleshy body, the voice nonetheless bears its entwined imprint; in mapping this negative presence, we encounter Avery Gordon's project of examining ghostly matters: "where finding the shape described by her absence captures perfectly the paradox of tracking through time and across all those forces that which makes its mark by being there and not being there at the same time" (1997:16). The voice's materiality is not simply a trace of a prior corporeality but is an emergent, interactive dialogic presence. As these two corpauralities draw together in the final mix, this meeting of mouths—this kiss, this touch—between father and daughter concretizes a number of articulations and absorptions. The mouth is an opening of sound and flesh,[18] and as Judith Butler observes, "the flesh is not something one has, but, rather, the web in which one lives," and touch "cannot be reducible to a unilateral action performed by a subject" (2004:181). Where does one body—one sound—begin and the other end, and in what ways do sounds gather up the world, absorb and form the bodies they meet? Nat sings of "a love that clings to me," and it is clear that the sonic is also haptic, and that haptic sonicities can cut across the mundanities of living and dead. As Natalie recalls, describing her experience singing with her father in the recording studio, "I felt as if he was more communicating with me, that he was kind of leading me in all the right things. And we were kind of holding hands" (Cole 1991b).

During the mixing process, which took place at yet another location, the Bill Schnee Studio in North Hollywood, Schmitt and Reitzas continued to facilitate vocal matching by attending to resonance—reverb and echo. Schmitt recalls:

> In terms of matching room sound, I changed the echo around a little bit—with Nat, the echo was on his voice, but I also added to it so that it matched up with Natalie's sound [. . .]. The consoles back in those days had very little; they didn't have the compressors or gates that we're now used to, so what you hear is his natural voice, and on "Unforgettable" it sounded absolutely huge. As a result, one of the problems we had was trying to get Natalie to match that, and that took a lot of work, trying to duplicate the echoes and levels and so forth. (in Buskin 2004)

Functionally, the digital effects units that Schmitt used to achieve this matching are identical to architectural echo chambers like the celebrated chambers 30 feet below the Capitol Records Tower in Hollywood (which were not used on this project). As with these celebrity crypts, digital reverb machines reanimate (or enliven) sounds that are dead (or not-yet-born) and return them to tape. Cables carry these signals and transmit them through portals, and the result is a kind of sonic "rapport," which is nothing more than carrying something back through an opening or portal.

And rapport, consonance through resonance, is the fundamental mark of the intermundane. On "Unforgettable," the rapport (or co-laboring) of dead and living engineers, musicians, and sounds is configured within a resounding network of resonant revenants. Though the collaboration between Natalie and Nat is most conspicuous, the intermundanity of the track extends to the orchestral arrangements (where scoring decisions made by Riddle in his 1951 arrangement effect a covering up by Mandel in 1991) and to the recording sensibility (which provides a sonic contact zone for engineers of both eras). We don't know the identities of the engineers on the 1961 session but traces of their labor—mic placements, hand-limiting, gear choice—surely intersect with the work of the 1991 engineers. In our interview, Reitzas asserted that he and Schmitt were the sole engineers for the vocal tracks, start to finish, but he was quick to add, "And whoever recorded Nat's vocals." During the 1991 sessions, musicians, engineers, arrangers, and producers—all essential to the making of the final product—engaged with each other across various kinds of segmentations, both spatial and temporal. This variegated form of engagement is what we call deadness.

The Responsive Co-Labors of Deadness

Deadness produces the resonances and revenances that condition all modes of sonic performance. We engage deadness not as displacement, but as emplacement in layered, rhizophonic sites of enfolded temporalities and spatialities. Within these sites, laborers are corpaural, bodies are always sonic bodies.

In the context of intermundane collaborations, liveness is enabled by the productive capacities of deadness, the distributed and noncontinuous temporalities effected by the body's translation and proliferation through recording technology.[19] What is called liveness is nothing more than a transitive effect of deadness, and deadness is nothing more than the promise of recombinatorial and revertible labor. In the particular circulation of effectivity that characterizes intermundanity, the living register the effective co-presence of the dead even as they draw and obdurate an impossible separation between mundanities. Collaboration is thus a sympathetic consonance structured in inequality, and skirmishes over rights inevitably arise.[20]

Within the economies of music production in the US, the co-laboring of the living and the dead hits its productive stride in the 1950s, when a general recombinatorial imperative achieves normative status, and sonic labor becomes ever more revertible. In the labor disputes that precede this decade, musical workers began regularly referring to themselves as "living" or "live" musicians, indicative of the lines along which they responded to the re-formation of the music industry from an entertainment model based on performance to a mass media economy based on reproduction, stockpiling, and repetitive playback (see Anderson 2006; Attali 1985; and Thornton 1995). "Living" musicians could now record "live"—indeed, in our conversations with Schmitt and Armin Steiner (who recorded many of the other tracks for the *Unforgettable* album), both of whom came of age professionally in the 1950s, liveness surfaces again and again as the preferred mode of musical co-labor: "I prefer that," Schmitt comments, "but that's just because that's the way I grew up, with everything live" (2007); while Steiner declares, "I'm a *live* person. I like to do things *live*" (2008).

But as live persons are extended and proliferated through recording technologies and practices, they constantly collaborate with the dead and the not-yet-born. Moreover, through recording itself, these live persons sign on to future networks where they will play a decidedly different role. They are the becoming dead. In these intermundane collaborations, agencies emerge from all directions in a network, and personhood is performed far beyond the epidermal wall. The living can make no special claim on effectivity, nor do they *necessarily* maintain a relationship of dominance with the dead (even though in the economies of late capitalism the particular effectivities of the living are *often* used to exploit the productive capacities of the dead). The effective agencies that we attribute to individual persons are always distributed across multiple mundanities and always involve co-labor.

As any material history of sound recording makes clear, the role played by technology cannot be overstated. Microphones, cables, tape heads, headphones, and architectures not only enable and enhance the effectivity of the living and the dead; they take on a formative role in these contingent arrangements. We are offering a model of collaboration, then, that moves beyond the interaction of human workers, whether living or dead, to register rapport among all entities that have effects. With this model, we recognize that collaboration transpires along differential axes of access, emplacement, privilege, capacity, and responsibility. Collaborations like the posthumous duets discussed in this article are built upon the restricted, yet still effective, motile emplacements of dead and living humans within mundanities teeming with all kinds of active non-humans.

The technological is not the only topology of the intermundane. The networks in which these technologies do their work are always also legal, economic, familial, affiliative, and corporate. For example, familial claims are often significant in intermundane collaborations, and inevitably lead to a cluster of questions—who has a right to make such a claim, how will the claim be administered financially, and so on. Again, the politics of access are paramount. Under US estate law, which is structured primarily around kinship ties, family members of deceased artists often have a heightened ability to secure the rights to original master recordings (intestate law makes it impossible for the dead to own property). In the case of recordings that are not controlled by the artist or the artist's family, corporate entities are typically more willing to give family members permission for access to original recordings because of the forceful place blood ties have within marketing structures dominated by celebrity. Matching thus rears its head again, this time within the realm of genetic ties and the corporate arrangements that harness these ties. In the case of "Unforgettable," family ties are crucial, if contested. Natalie's mother, Maria, has voiced reservations about the duet, admitting that she "[doesn't] like to listen to [Natalie's version]. I just feel that everything belonged to him" (*Jet* 1992:34). "Belonging" here, however, is shot through with betrayal. Less than a year before the "Unforgettable" recording session, Natalie and her four siblings learned that Nat had set up a trust fund for the children before his death, a fund that had been concealed from them for many years by their mother (Cole with Diehl 2000:290–303). Because the Cole family was earning $500,000 in royalties per year from Nat's posthumous sales, the familial and financial stakes of "Unforgettable" were high. The runaway success of the album no doubt raised them even further, and in 1995, Maria sued her five children for their portion of Nat's estate (the suit was settled out of court in 1998). Though partially incapacitated by his death in 1965, Nat acts at the center of these legal struggles, and his position indicates that flesh is not the only "web in which one lives." The story is more complex than this, but for now we should emphasize that the effectivity of singing ghosts in the techno-sonic realms of the intermundane is at least partially determined by rapidly changing laws governing the transference of wealth and property.

Family squabbles in cases like these are thus weighted with enormous financial consequences, and often lead to the denunciation of intermundane collaborations as enterprises of the living for exploiting the dead, as if only the former have agency in these exchanges.[21] Though ostensibly concerned with defending the *memory* of the dead, this objection betrays a failure to register their *agency*, their *effectivity* within a mundanity from which they seem to have been banished. Just as we can never completely predict our own effects in the world, so too can we never completely foreclose the effectivity of another entity. Nonetheless, asymmetries of power—and thus of responsibility—persist. We argue that collaborations with the dead are no different in this regard than those with the living, and we should be careful not to condemn intermundane projects out of hand. Such quick judgments can harbor the implicit assumptions that relations between the living are always ethical, or even symmetrical in terms of rights and privileges—both plainly not the case. To the extent that we have effects on other entities, these other entities also have effects on us. Being mindful of this mutual effectivity, this intra-action and co-creation of agential formations, means taking responsibility for a responsive effect. The difficult problem, the impossible question, is whether we can expect a responsive ethics, a resonant ethics, from *all* things that have effects.

This question is different than the one raised by Fred Moten: "What is your ethical responsibility to the object, what is your ethical responsibility to that insurgency of the object?" (in Cahill and Thompson 2005:51). It is far more drastic and it's not "What is the object's ethical responsibility to you?" Rather, our concern is to question what an ethics of effects might look like, one that reaches outside of the customary contact zones that are rendered along (dis)alignments of subjects and objects, and counters the stock notion that ethics is solely a human concern. The conundrum we encounter has to do with the extent to which we risk reinstating a human exceptionalism along the ethical axis that we have worked so hard to neutralize along the agentic. All entities have effects. Do all entities have ethics? What kinds of co-responsibility do the disparate yet mutually effective worlds of humans and nonhumans, material and immaterial entities, and the living, dead, and not-yet-born have for one another?

We have arrived at the idea that the worlds referenced in the term "intermundane" are co-responsive but not always co-responsible. But the "inter" in intermundane— itself suggesting, paradoxically, both reciprocal exchange and one-way entombment— betrays the complex processes of encounter that we've been speaking of here. Worlds of objects, humans, and nonhuman life do something other than simply "inter"-act and, indeed, a conception that posits mutually exclusive, ethically misaligned worlds, self-sufficient and ontologically stable, is not what we're after. These "worlds" do not preexist their enrollment in contingent assemblages; it is in and through reciprocal effectivity—collaboration—that they take shape. In the words of Donna Haraway, "The relationship is the smallest possible pattern of analysis" (2008:25–26). The term "intermundane" might better index all relationships between entities that are non-identical, but whose identities seem to be mutually instrumental. In late capitalism, deadness has emerged as a decisive patterning of intermundanity based upon ever-replenishable value, ever-resurrectable labor, ever-revertible production processes. Far from being anomalous, posthumous duets amplify and reverberate these ubiquitous acts of deadness.

Notes

1. In 2005, one marketing research company reported that advertisements featuring dead celebrities had doubled in the last 10 years (see Guthrie 2005; see also Gardner 2006).

2. The only exception to Elvis's reign at the top came in 2006, when Courtney Love sold a 25 percent stake of her holdings in Kurt Cobain's back catalog, thus netting a huge profit for the late Mr. Cobain. For the most recent *Forbes* list see Noer, Ewalt, and Hoy (2008). Michael Jackson's death in June 2009 will undoubtedly mark the emergence of a new necrophonic superstar. "This Is It," his first posthumous single, was released only four months after his death, and during an elaborately choreographed tribute at the MTV Video Music Awards (held in September 2009 in New York City), he appeared in a duet with his sister Janet, dancing to their song "Scream."

3. For "electronic deception," see Toop (1991); for "manufactured duet," see Zimmerman (1993); for "virtual duet," see Melloy (1999); for "simulated duet," see Farber (1999); for "studio-engineered duet," see Tabor (1994).

4. Twitty's part was pieced together the old fashioned way—with bits of analog tape. Soon, however, producers will be able to use software to emulate any celebrity voice (see Guernsey 2001).

5. The orchestra performed new arrangements of Sinatra's best-known tunes. Many of the Sinatra performances that feature in the show "are taken from a trial recording for a television special featuring just Sinatra and [Bill] Miller. From this it has been possible to add live musicians and dancers," writes Spencer Leigh (2006).

6. The list goes on: Ann and Paul Downing ("Are You Tired," 2004); Deborah Allen and Jim Reeves ("Don't Let Me Cross Over" and "Oh, How I Miss You Tonight," 1979); Brad Paisley and Buck Owens ("Hello Trouble," 2008); Anne Murray and Dusty Springfield ("I Just Fall in Love Again," 2008); The Bee Gees and Andy Gibb ("Immortality," 1998); Lisa Marie and Elvis Presley ("In the Ghetto," 2007); Gunther Neefs and Louis Neefs ("Laar ons een bloem," 2000); Christopher "CJ" Wallace, Jr., Faith Evans, and The Notorious B.I.G. ("One More Chance/The Legacy [Remix]," 2008); Mark Weigle and Steve Grossman ("Out," 2002); Charles Aznavour and Edith Piaf ("Plus Bleu Que Tes Yeux," 1997); Olivia Newton John and Peter Allen ("Tenterfeld Saddler," 2002); Lorrie Morgan and Keith Whitley ("'Til a Tear Becomes a Rose," 1990); Natalie and Nat King Cole ("When I Fall in Love," 1996; and "Walkin' My Baby Back Home," 2008); Katie Melua and Eva Cassidy ("What a Wonderful World," 2008); Alison Krauss and Keith Whitley ("When You Say Nothing at All," 1994). Albums of posthumous duets not mentioned above include Minnie Riperton (*Love Lives Forever*, 1980); *Elvis Presley Christmas Duets*, 2008; Clara Nunes (*ComVida*, 1995); Miles Davis (*Evolution of the Groove*, 2007); Shooter and Waylon Jennings (*Waylon Forever*, 2008). The posthumous duet phenomenon has been trenchantly satirized by *Saturday Night Live* ("Natalie Cole Sings the Songs of Dead People," 1992) and Dave Chappelle ("Tupac's New Song in the Club," 2006).

7. Al Schmitt, the engineer of the "Unforgettable" track, made clear the practical ramifications of the shift in discussing his work on Dean Martin's 2007 posthumous duet recording *Forever Cool*: "We were able to move stuff around, and it was just easier to try in things" (2007). Of course, engineers had long "eyeballed" analog recording tape and used visual markers while performing edits. Visual hegemony is not complete, however, until sounds move on screens.

8. The following narrative of the 1961 session is based on interviews with Irv Joel (2008) and Ralph Carmichael (2008); and Davis (1963:360–70). We are also indebted to Will Friedwald, and to Jordan Taylor of Bear Family Records for their help in tracking down information from this session.

9. A brief mention of the echo chamber can be found in Putnam: "In 1953, when Capitol completed their New York Studios, they built a superb reverberation room, which was always recognizable on records because of its excellent sound" (1980:9).

10. For more on record labels that revivify their dead superstars, see Eisenberg [1987] 2005:50–51.

11.   Unless otherwise noted, the following narrative of the 1991 session is drawn from Cole and Diehl (2000) and Buskin (2004); and telephone interviews with Al Schmitt (2007, 2008), David Reitzas (2008), and Rail Rogut (2008). We are grateful to Paula Salvatore at Capitol Studios for help arranging many of these interviews.

12.   Cole remembers, "In July 1986 I had sung 'Unforgettable' at the Newport Jazz Festival, and it had been very well received. I had experimented also with the song even before that— back in the early 1980s when I was still with Kevin Hunter and in Las Vegas, starting to work with an orchestra. I sang the song live with a reel-to-reel tape of Dad's voice backstage. The reel-to-reel was piped through the speakers onstage and Dad's voice would come on. Then they'd push the mute button and the orchestra would start playing. We had a little click track so that the band would start at the same time the tape did. Dad's voice would come through the house and then they'd mute his voice along with the track while the live orchestra kept playing. First Dad would sing 'Unforgettable, that's what you are,' and then I would sing 'Unforgettable, though near or far.' (It was rather crude, technologically, but it worked.) The audiences were so moved that I backed away from doing it more than a few times. Singing that song stopped the show. It completely changed the mood and left me with nowhere to go as a performer" (Cole and Diehl 2000:229).

13.   We are grateful to Al Schmitt for sharing tracksheets of these sessions with us.

14.   The similarities between Mandel's arrangement for the 1991 recording and Riddle's original arrangement was the subject of a 1994 lawsuit brought by Riddle's widow against Elektra records. Naomi Riddle claimed that "that 87 percent, or all but $8\frac{1}{2}$ of 69 bars of the 1991 version, are identical to those of the original," and that Elektra had failed to give Riddle proper recognition (and proper remuneration). Citing a trademark infringement, she sought $2 million in damages (Tabor 1994). The suit was settled for an undisclosed amount, and on subsequent pressings of the CD, Riddle was listed as "arranger," with Mandel given credit for "adaptation of original arrangement."

15.   The desire to match is not always matched by historiographic accuracy. Again and again, for example, Nat's original performance is mis-placed by writers to Capitol Studios in Los Angeles, rather than the 46th Street Studio in New York City where it actually occurred (this lapse can be found in Buskin [2004], and even in the liner notes to *Unforgettable, with Love*). There seems to be a need for temporal disjointedness to be balanced with spatial cotermineity: if there is a 30-year gap in the performances of father and daughter, there shouldn't be a 3000-mile gap separating the locations of those performances.

16.   For the 1991 project, the human-performed sync among musicians was paralleled by the machine-performed sync of SMPTE timecode, which synchronized two 24-track machines used on the project and allowed accurate transfer between them. Timecode also facilitated GML automation at the mixdown stage.

17.   Arrangers such as Ralph Burns and Bill Holman, who had fashioned charts for popular big bands during the 1940s and 1950s, were brought in to provide the project with "authentic flavor" (Buskin 2004). Engineers like Armin Steiner, who recorded many of the album tracks at Fox Sound Studios, and Schmitt, who handled mixing on the project, maintain a recording sensibility that privileges the "live," or non-overdubbed (Steiner 2008; see also Droney 2001).

18.   See Merleau-Ponty (2004): "What is again open to us, therefore, with the reversibility of the visible and the tangible, is—if not the incorporeal—at least an intercorporeal being, a presumptive domain of the visible and the tangible, which extends further than the things I touch and see at present" (259).

19.   Unlike Philip Auslander (1999), we see liveness as co-constituted with deadness not as the result of mediatization, but rather as the necessary labor arrangement of intermundanity. Media is not merely a connective technology between agencies, but is itself an effective agent.

20.   On legal skirmishes, see Laurens (2001) and Auslander (1999).

21.   See, for example, Pat Metheny's notorious criticism of Kenny G's "What a Wonderful World" collaboration with Louis Armstrong (Metheny n.d.), as well as Goodman (2000).

References

Anderson, Joel. 2004/2005. "What's Wrong with this Picture?: Dead or Alive: Protecting Actors in the Age of Virtual Reanimation." *Loyola of Los Angeles Entertainment Law Review* 25, 2:155–202.

Anderson, Tim J. 2006. *Making Easy Listening: Material Culture and Postwar American Recording*. Minneapolis: University of Minnesota Press.

Attali, Jacques. 1985. *Noise: The Political Economy of Music*. Trans. Brian Massumi. Minneapolis: University of Minnesota Press.

Auslander, Philip. 1999. *Liveness: Performance in a Mediatized Culture*. London: Routledge.

Barad, Karen. 2007. *Meeting the Universe Halfway: Quantum Physics and the Entanglement of Matter and Meaning*. Durham: Duke University Press.

Beard, Joseph J. 1993. "Casting Call at Forest Lawn: The Digital Resurrection of Deceased Entertainers—A 21st-Century Challenge for Intellectual Property Law." *Berkeley Technology Law Journal* 8, 1. www.law.berkeley.edu/journals/btlj/articles/vol8/Beard.pdf (11 October 2009).

— 2001. "Clones, Bones, and Twilight Zones: Protecting the Digital Persona of the Quick, the Dead, and the Imaginary." *Berkeley Technology Law Journal* 16, 3: 1165–1271.

Buskin, Richard. 2004. "Classic Tracks: 'Unforgettable.'" *Sound on Sound*, January. www.soundonsound.com/sos/jan04/articles/classictracks.htm (11 October 2009).

Butler, Judith. 2004. "Merleau-Ponty and the Touch of Malebranche." In *The Cambridge Companion to Merleau-Ponty*, eds. Taylor Carman and Mark B.N. Hansen, 181–205. Cambridge: Cambridge University Press.

Cahill, James Leo, and Rachel Leah Thompson. 2005. "The Insurgency of Objects: A Conversation with Fred Moten." *Octopus* 1 (Fall):45–66. http://yoda.hnet.uci.edu/fvc/vsgsa/octopus/octo_archive/vol-01-f2005/toc.html (9 October 2009).

Carmichael, Ralph. 2008. Telephone interview with authors, 29 August.

Castronovo, Russ. 2001. *Necro Citizenship: Death, Eroticism, and the Public Sphere in the Nineteenth-Century United States*. Durham: Duke University Press.

Chakrabarty, Dipesh. 2000. *Provincializing Europe: Postcolonial Thought and Historical Difference*. Princeton: Princeton University Press.

Cogan, Jim, and William Clark. 2003. *Temples of Sound: Inside the Great Recording Studios*. San Francisco: Chronicle Books.

Cole, Natalie. 1991a. "Unforgettable." On *Unforgettable with Love*. Elektra 61049–2.

— 1991b. *Unforgettable*. Steve Barron, dir. New York: Elektra Video.

Cole, Natalie, with Digby Diehl. 2000. *Angel on My Shoulder: An Autobiography*. New York: Warner Books.

Davis, John P. 1963. "A Multi-Purpose Studio Recording System." *Journal of the Audio Engineering Society* 11, 4:360–70.

Derrida, Jacques. 1994. *Specters of Marx: The State of the Debt, the Work of Mourning, and the New International*. Trans. Peggy Kamuf. New York: Routledge.

Doyle, Peter. 2005. *Echo & Reverb: Fabricating Space in Popular Music Recording, 1900–1960*. Middletown: Wesleyan University Press.

Droney, Maureen. 2001. "Armin Steiner." *Mix*, 1 May. http://mixonline.com/mag/audio_armin_steiner/ (11 October 2009).

Eisenberg, Evan. [1987] 2005. *The Recording Angel: Music, Records and Culture from Aristotle to Zappa*. New Haven: Yale University Press.

Farber, Jim. 1999. "Following in Biggie Small's Tracks." *(New York) Daily News*, 7 December.

Foster, Catherine. 1991. "Natalie Brings Smooth Sounds of Nat King Cole to a New Generation." *Christian Science Monitor*, 30 August.

Frayne, John G., A.C. Blaney, G.R. Groves, and H.F. Olson. 1976. "A Short History of Motion Picture Sound Recording in the United States." *SMPTE Journal* 85:515–28.

Fuss, Diane. 2003. "Corpse Poem." *Critical Inquiry* 30:1–30.

Galloway, Alexander R., and Eugene Thacker. 2007. *The Exploit: A Theory of Networks*. Minneapolis: University of Minnesota Press.

Gardner, Eriq. 2006. "Cult of Personalities." *IP Law and Business* 4, 1:50.

Goodman, Fred. 2000. "Duets with the Dead: Homage or Exploitation?" *New York Times*, 16 January.

Gordon, Avery F. 1997. *Ghostly Matters: Haunting and the Sociological Imagination*. Minneapolis: University of Minnesota Press.

Guernsey, Lisa. 2001. "Software Is Called Capable of Copying Any Human Voice." *New York Times*, 31 July.

Guthrie, Jonathan. 2005. "To Cut Costs and Reduce Risk Use a Dead Celebrity." *Financial Times*, 27 April.

Haraway, Donna J. 2008. *When Species Meet*. Minneapolis: University of Minnesota Press.

Hilburn, Robert. 1981. "Jim Reeves, Patsy Cline: 'Duet' Lives." *Los Angeles Times*, 14 November.

Hochheiser, Sheldon. 1992. "What Makes the Picture Talk: AT&T and the Development of Sound Motion Picture Technology." *IEEE Transactions on Education* 35:278–85.

Hoffman, Leah. 2005. "Agents of the Dead." *Forbes*, 31 October.

Jet. 1992. "Natalie Cole Gains New Fame with Father's Music Even Though her Musical Mother Disapproves." *Jet*, 24 February.

Joel, Irv. 2008. Telephone interview with authors, 10 September.

Jones, Steve, and Joli Jensen, eds. 2005. *Afterlife as Afterimage: Understanding Posthumous Fame*. New York: Peter Lang.

Kraft, John P. 1996. *Stage to Studio: Musicians and the Sound Revolution, 1890–1950*. Baltimore: Johns Hopkins University Press.

Latour, Bruno. 2005. *Reassembling the Social: An Introduction to Actor-Network-Theory*. New York: Oxford University Press.

Laurens, Rhett H. 2001. "Year of the Living Dead: California Breathes New Life into Celebrity Publicity Rights." *Hastings Communications and Entertainment Law Journal* 24:109–47.

Leigh, Spencer. 2006. "Bill Miller; Sinatra's Arranger and Accompanist." *The Independent*, 18 July.

Levinson, Nathan. 1933. "Rerecording, Dubbing or Duping." *American Cinematographer* 13, 11:6–7.

Melloy, Neil. 1999. "Celine's Family Affair." *Courier Mail* (Queensland, Australia), 13 September.

Merleau-Ponty, Maurice. 2004. "The Intertwining—The Chiasm." In *Maurice Merleau-Ponty: Basic Writings*, ed. Thomas Baldwin, trans. Alphonso Lingis, 247–71. London: Routledge.

Metheny, Pat. n.d. "Pat Metheny on Kenny G." www.jazzoasis.com/methenyonkennyg. htm (18 December 2008).

Millard, Andre J. 1995. *America on Record: A History of Recorded Sound*. Cambridge: Cambridge University Press.

Morton, David. 1995. "The History of Magnetic Recording in the United States, 1888–1978." PhD diss., Georgia Institute of Technology.

— 2000. *Off the Record: The Technology and Culture of Sound Recording in America*. New Brunswick: Rutgers University Press.

— 2004. *Sound Recording: The Life Story of a Technology*. Westport: Greenwood Press.

New York Times. 1926. "Marvels of the Vitaphone." *New York Times*, 25 July.

Noer, Michael, David M. Ewalt, and Peter Hoy, eds. 2008. "Top-Earning Dead Celebrities." *Forbes*, 27 October. www.forbes.com/2008/10/27/dead-celebrity-earning-biz-media-deadcelebs08_cx_mn_de_1027celeb_land.html (9 October 2009).

O'Brien, Charles. 2005. *Cinema's Conversion to Sound: Technology and Film Style in France and the U.S.* Bloomington: Indiana University Press.

Pakenham, Compton. 1932. "Newly Recorded Music." *New York Times*, 23 October.

Parmenter, Ross. 1941. "Records: Gypsy Music." *New York Times*, 13 July.

Pathé Pictorial. 1932. "Voice Grafting: the Latest Miracle of 'Sound' Science." *British Pathé*. www. britishpathe.com/record.php?id = 28993 (11 October 2009).

Peterson, Christopher. 2007. *Kindred Specters: Death, Mourning, and American Affinity*. Minneapolis: University of Minnesota Press.

Putnam, Milton T. 1980. "A Thirty-five Year History and Evolution of the Recording Studio." *Audio Engineering Society Preprint 1661*. www.aes.org/aeshc/pdf/putnam_history-of-recording-studios.pdf (11 October 2009).

Rayner, Alice. 2006. *Ghosts: Death's Double and the Phenomena of Theatre*. Minneapolis: University of Minnesota Press.

Reitzas, David. 2008. Telephone interview with authors, 27 August.

Rettinger, Michael. 1957. "Reverberation Chambers for Broadcasting and Recording Studios." *Journal of the Audio Engineering Society* 5, 1:18–22.

Roach, Joseph. 1996. *Cities of the Dead: Circum-Atlantic Performance*. New York: Columbia University Press.

Rogut, Rail. 2008. Telephone interview with authors, 2 September.

Schafer, R. Murray. 1977. *The Tuning of the World*. New York: Knopf.

Schmidt-Horning, Susan. 2002. "Chasing Sound: The Culture and Technology of Recording Studios in America, 1877–1977." PhD diss., Case Western Reserve University.

Schmitt, Al. 2007. Telephone interview with authors, 15 September.

— 2008. Telephone interview with authors, 1 September.

Snyder, Ross H. 2003. "Sel-Sync and the 'Octopus': How Came to be the First Recorder to Minimize Successive Copying in Overdubs." *ARSC Journal* 34, 2:209–13.

Steiner, Armin. 2008. Telephone interview with authors, 5 August.

Sterne, Jonathan. 2003. *The Audible Past: Cultural Origins of Sound Reproduction*. Durham: Duke University Press.

Strathern, Marilyn. 1988. *The Gender of the Gift: Problems with Women and Problems with Society in Melanesia*. Berkeley: University of California Press.

— 1992. *After Nature: English Kinship in the Late Twentieth Century*. Cambridge: Cambridge University Press.

Sutheim, Peter. 1989. "An Afternoon with Bill Putnam." *Journal of the Audio Engineering Society* 37, 9:723–30.

Tabor, Mary B.W. 1994. "Suit Calls an 'Unforgettable' Omission Unforgivable." *New York Times*, 14 May.

Théberge, Paul. 1997. *Any Sound You Can Imagine: Making Music/Consuming Technology*. Hanover: Wesleyan University Press.

Thompson, Emily. 2002. *The Soundscape of Modernity: Architectural Acoustics and the Culture of Listening in America, 1900–1933*. Cambridge: MIT Press.

Thornton, Sarah. 1995. *Club Cultures: Music, Media and Subcultural Capital*. Cambridge: Polity Press.

Toop, David. 1991. "Gone to Rock 'n' Roll Heaven, or Perhaps She's Stuck in Limbo." *Times* (London), 26 August.

Verdery, Katherine. 1999. *The Political Lives of Dead Bodies: Reburial and Postsocialist Change*. New York: Columbia University Press.

Weiss, Allen S. 2002. *Breathless: Sound Recording, Disembodiment, and the Transformation of Lyrical Nostalgia*. Middletown: Wesleyan University Press.

Welch, Walter L., and Leah Brodbeck Stenzel Burt. 1994. *From Tinfoil to Stereo: The Acoustic Years of the Recording Industry, 1877–1929*. Gainesville: University of Florida Press.

Zimmerman, David. 1989. "Hank Jr. Shares a 'Beer' with Dad." *USA Today*, 2 March.

— 1993. "Emmylou Harris Offers Up a Heavenly 'Prayer.'" *USA Today*, 12 October.

PART IV

Collectivities and Couplings

ANOTHER POSSIBLE ORIGIN FOR MODERN sound studies would place it in 20th-century studies of radio and broadcast. A burgeoning literature on radio in the 1930s and 1940s hailed the medium's cultural centrality and with it, new sonic cultures. Hadley Cantrill and Gordon Allport wrote that radio provided its listeners a "new mental world," and a "new type of auditory background for life" structured by new modalities of listening and interaction.[1] Audience researchers like Herda Herzog charted the range of audience responses and provided complex descriptions of radio listeners as both passive and active, participating and withdrawing, "anticipating how poststructuralism, feminism and postmodernism would inform media criticism and analysis by emphasizing people's ambivalent relationships to media content that was itself filled with contradictions."[2] Rudolf Arnheim called radio a "new experience for the artist, his audience and the theoretician."[3]

Radio still implies collectivity today, but its collectivities are of particular kinds. Paddy Scannell points out that broadcasting requires a distinctive mode of talk, a "for-anyone-as-someone" structure. Broadcast had to incorporate the form of interpersonal talk into an utterly impersonal medium. The result is that audiences could have intense affective relationships with radio personalities, even though the broadcast was strictly impersonal in orientation.[4] The problem of collectivity is one of the central issues in studies of radio. What is the relationship among concepts of audience, public, polity and nation? Frantz Fanon's classic account of radio in the Algerian revolution hinges upon Algerians hearing themselves as part of an emergent nation as they tuned in to the Voice of Algeria (or tried to). Michele Hilmes's piece in this section uses Benedict Anderson's notion of *imagined community* to describe the cultural effects of broadcasting in the United States, especially in how radio negotiated problems of immigrant and national identity.[5]

But collectivity is not just an issue for radio. Jurgen Habermas's notion of a public sphere—a complex concept that encompasses the process of democratic deliberation, the people who do it, and the space and conditions in which they come together—has a sonic dimension, from the centrality of speech to the problems of mass media, but its sonic component is rarely commented upon. All manner of publics have been constituted by audio media. Radio historians like Jason Loviglio and Alex Russo have further explored national and regional identities, but stories about recording can also be stories about publics. William Howland Kenny coined the phrase "listening alone, together," to describe the phonographic listening practices of immigrants, who listened to records alone while imagining themselves as part of a greater collectivity.[6] In her essay in this section, Ana María Ochoa shows how music, recording and folkloristic writing about that music served as the basis of an aural public sphere in Latin America, and was crucial to the establishment of Latin American modernity.

Collectivity can also work in other ways, where people check in and check out. While 20th-century cultural critics from Adorno to Debord railed against distraction, historians like Russo and David Goodman have shown the importance of distracted listening in everyday life. We might well understand distracted audition—one foot in the collective, one foot out (if you'll allow the mixed metaphor)—as a more general feature of sonic culture today. Today, public spaces in Western Europe and North America are saturated with programmed music, which carries with it another kind of ambiguous "for-anyone-as-someone" address. Anahid Kassabian's twin terms of *ubiquitous music* and *ubiquitous listening* suggest the degree to which the distracted broadcast model has moved out from broadcast media into other spheres of life, where listeners engage and disengage at a distance.[7]

If broadcast and recording were often thought in collective terms, telephony was where ideas about a different kind of collectivity got worked out.[8] Cybernetics, information theory, and transmission models of communication all in some sense descend from telephony, and they form the theoretical basis of some classic work in sound studies. One hears that paradigm in Jacques Attali's discussion of noise (in Part I), but also in Barry Truax's classic *Acoustic Communication*, which is fascinating for how it moves between theories of networked communication in engineering (the "signal processing model") and acoustic ecology to develop an account of sound in culture.[9] Of course, those ideas of networks have their own historical and theoretical legacies. Michèle Martin's essay on telephony in this section shows the degree to which women's uses of the telephone were both "unexpected" by the men who controlled the system and central to shaping the medium, even as it also helped challenge Victorian gender norms. John Durham Peters reads the phone and stories about it as reflecting anxieties about networked, mediated communication more generally. How can we really be sure of whom we are talking with on the other end? Peters's elegant readings of switchboards and Kafka echo today in the fragile connections of mobile phones and Skype calls, and in the pseudonymity of internet users.[10]

The term "user" is an interesting endpoint, for it eclipses so many other terms, like public, audience, or person, and in some sectors has covered over the many and multifarious roles we find elsewhere—from computer users, to artists and musicians, to anyone who picks up a telephone, plays an MP3 or sends a text message. Yet it is also possible to have a critique of userdom, just as we can analyze people, publics and audiences. As Gerard Goggin shows in his essay on cellular disability, assumptions about users' bodies are literally built into the devices, reinforcing other modes of social exclusion and making basic technical issues like feedback eminently political.

Notes

1   Cantril and Allport, *The Psychology of Radio*, 3, 25.
2   Douglas, *Listening In: Radio and the American Imagination from Amos 'n Andy and Edward R. Murrow to Wolfman Jack and Howard Stern*, 144–48.
3   Arnheim, *Radio*, 14.
4   Scannell, "For-anyone-as-someone structures". To be clear, Scannell does not believe this to be a unique quality of broadcast, but rather that broadcast provides insight into this quality of experience.
5   Anderson, *Imagined Communities*.
6   Habermas, *The Structural Transformation of the Public Sphere: An Inquiry into a Category of Bourgeois Society*; Loviglio, *Radio's Intimate Public: Network Broadcasting and Mass-Mediated Democracy*; Russo, *Points on the Dial: Golden Age Radio Beyond the Networks*; Kenney, *Recorded Music in American Life*.
7   Adorno, "On the Fetish Character of Music and the Regression of Listening"; Debord, *Society of the Spectacle*; Goodman, "Distracted Listening: On Not Making Sound Choices in the 1930s"; Kassabian, "Ubisub: Ubiquitous Listening and Networked Subjectivity."
8   Edwards, *The Closed World: Computers and the Politics of Discourse in Cold War America*; Mindell, *Between Human and Machine: Feedback, Control and Computing before Cybernetics*; Bowker, "How to be Universal: Some Cybernetic Strategies, 1945–70." Of course, any fuller history of networks would have to reach back not only to the electric telegraph, but to the vast range of infrastructures that have developed across different human civilizations.
9   Truax, *Acoustic Communication*.
10   See, e.g., Marvin, *When Old Technologies Were New*; Çelik, *Technology and National Identity in Turkey*.

References

Adorno, Theodor. "On the Fetish Character of Music and the Regression of Listening." In *Adorno: Essays on Music*, 288–317. Berkeley: University of California Press, 1938.

Anderson, Benedict R. *Imagined Communities: Reflections on the Origin and Spread of Nationalism*. New York: Verso, 1991.

Arnheim, Rudolf. *Radio*. London: Faber and Faber, 1936.

Bowker, Geoff. "How to be Universal: Some Cybernetic Strategies, 1945–70." *Social Studies of Science* 23, no. 1 (1993): 107–27.

Cantril, Hadley, and Gordon Allport. *The Psychology of Radio*. New York: Harper and Row, 1935.

Çelik, Burçe. *Technology and National Identity in Turkey: Mobile Communications and the Evolution of a Post-Ottoman Nation*. New York: I. B. Tauris, 2011.

Debord, Guy. *Society of the Spectacle*. Rebel Press, 1983.

Douglas, Susan. *Listening In: Radio and the American Imagination from Amos 'n Andy and Edward R. Murrow to Wolfman Jack and Howard Stern*. New York: Times Books/Random House, 1999.

Edwards, Paul. *The Closed World: Computers and the Politics of Discourse in Cold War America*. Cambridge: MIT Press, 1996.

Goodman, David. "Distracted Listening: On Not Making Sound Choices in the 1930s." In *Sound in the Age of Mechanical Reproduction*, 15–46. Philadelphia: University of Pennsylvania Press, 2009.

Habermas, Jurgen. *The Structural Transformation of the Public Sphere: An Inquiry into a Category of Bourgeois Society*. Cambridge: MIT Press, 1989.

Kassabian, Anahid. "Ubisub: Ubiquitous Listening and Networked Subjectivity." *Echo: A Music-Centered Journal* 3, no. 2 (2001). http://www.echo.ucla.edu/volume3-issue2/kassabian/index.html.

Kenney, William Howland. *Recorded Music in American Life*. New York: Oxford University Press, 2000.

Loviglio, Jason. *Radio's Intimate Public: Network Broadcasting and Mass-Mediated Democracy*. Minneapolis: University of Minnesota Press, 2005.

Marvin, Carolyn. *When Old Technologies Were New: Thinking About Electric Communication in the late Nineteenth Century*. New York: Oxford University Press, 1988.

Mindell, David. *Between Human and Machine: Feedback, Control and Computing before Cybernetics*. Baltimore: The Johns Hopkins University Press, 2002.

Russo, Alexander. *Points on the Dial: Golden Age Radio Beyond the Networks*. Durham: Duke University Press, 2010.

Scannell, Paddy. "For-anyone-as-someone structures." *Media, Culture & Society* 22, no. 1 (January 1, 2000): 5–24.

Truax, Barry. *Acoustic Communication*. Norwood: Ablex, 1984.

Chapter 27

Frantz Fanon

THIS IS THE VOICE OF ALGERIA

. . . ON THE LEVEL OF THE MASSES, which had remained relatively uninvolved in the struggle since they couldn't read the press, the necessity of having radio sets was felt. It must not be forgotten that the people's generalized illiteracy left it indifferent to things written. In the first months of the Revolution, the great majority of Algerians identified everything written in the French language as the expression of colonial domination The language in which *L'Express* and *L'Echo d' Alger* were written was the sign of the French presence.

The acquisition of a radio set in Algeria, in 1955, represented the sole means of obtaining news of the Revolution from non-French sources. This necessity assumed a compelling character when the people learned that there were Algerians in Cairo who daily drew up the balance-sheet of the liberation struggle. From Cairo, from Syria, from nearly all the Arab countries, the great pages written in the *djebels* by brothers, relatives, friends flowed back to Algeria.

Meanwhile, despite these new occurrences, the introduction of radio sets into houses and the most remote *douars* proceeded only gradually. There was no enormous rush to buy receivers. It was at the end of 1956 that the real shift occurred. At this time tracts were distributed announcing the existence of a Voice of Free Algeria. The broadcasting schedules and the wavelengths were given. This voice "that speaks from the *djebels*," not geographically limited, but bringing to all Algeria the great message of the Revolution, at once acquired an essential value. In less than twenty days the entire stock of radio sets was bought up. In the *souks*[1] trade in used receiver sets began. Algerians who had served their apprenticeship with European radio-electricians opened small shops. Moreover, the dealers had to meet new needs. The absence of electrification in immense regions in Algeria naturally created special problems for the consumer. For this reason battery-operated receivers, from 1956 on, were in great demand on Algerian territory. In a few weeks several thousand sets were sold to Algerians, who bought them as individuals, families, groups of houses, *douars*, *mechtas*.

Since 1956 the purchase of a radio in Algeria has meant, not the adoption of a modern technique for getting news, but the obtaining of access to the only means of entering into communication with the Revolution, of living with it. In the special case of the portable battery set, an improved form of the standard receiver operating on current, the specialist in technical changes in underdeveloped countries might see a sign of a radical mutation. The Algerian, in fact, gives the impression of finding short cuts and of achieving the most modern forms of news-communication without passing through the intermediary stages.[2] In reality, we have seen that this "progress" is to be explained by the absence of electric current in the Algerian *douars*.

The French authorities did not immediately realize the exceptional importance of this change in attitude of the Algerian people with regard to the radio. Traditional resistances broke down and one could see in a *douar* groups of families in which fathers, mothers, daughters, elbow to elbow, would scrutinize the radio dial waiting for the *Voice of Algeria*. Suddenly indifferent to the sterile, archaic modesty and antique social arrangements devoid of brotherhood, the Algerian family discovered itself to be immune to the off-color jokes and the libidinous references that the announcer occasionally let drop.

Almost magically—but we have seen the rapid and dialectical progression of the new national requirements—the technical instrument of the radio receiver lost its identity as an enemy object. The radio set was no longer a part of the occupier's arsenal of cultural oppression. In making of the radio a primary means of resisting the increasingly overwhelming psychological and military pressures of the occupant, Algerian society made an autonomous decision to embrace the new technique and thus tune itself in on the new signaling systems brought into being by the Revolution.

The *Voice of Fighting Algeria* was to be of capital importance in consolidating and unifying the people. We shall see that the use of the Arab, Kabyle and French languages which, as colonialism was obliged to recognize, was the expression of a non-racial conception, had the advantage of developing and of strengthening the unity of the people, of making the fighting Djurdjura area real for the Algerian patriots of Batna or of Nemours. The fragments and splinters of acts gleaned by the correspondent of a newspaper more or less attached to the colonial domination, or communicated by the opposing military authorities, lost their anarchic character and became organized into a national and Algerian political idea, assuming their place in an overall strategy of the reconquest of the people's sovereignty. The scattered acts fitted into a vast epic, and the Kabyles were no longer "the men of the mountains," but the brothers who with Ouamrane and Krim made things difficult for the enemy troops.

Having a radio meant paying one's taxes to the nation, buying the right of entry into the struggle of an assembled people.

The French authorities, however, began to realize the importance of this progress of the people in the technique of news dissemination. After a few months of hesitancy legal measures appeared. The sale of radios was now prohibited, except on presentation of a voucher issued by the military security or police services. The sale of battery sets was absolutely prohibited, and spare batteries were practically withdrawn from the market. The Algerian dealers now had the opportunity to put their patriotism to the test, and they were able to supply the people with spare batteries with exemplary regularity by resorting to various subterfuges.[3]

The Algerian who wanted to live up to the Revolution, had at last the possibility of hearing an official voice, the voice of the combatants, explain the combat to him, tell him the story of the Liberation on the march, and incorporate it into the nation's new life.

Here we come upon a phenomenon that is sufficiently unusual to retain our attention. The highly trained French services, rich with experience acquired in modern wars, past masters in the practice of "sound-wave warfare," were quick to detect the wavelengths of the broadcasting stations. The programs were then systematically jammed, and the *Voice of Fighting Algeria* soon became inaudible. A new form of struggle had come into being. Tracts were distributed telling the Algerians to keep tuned in for a period of two or three hours. In the course of a single broadcast a second station, broadcasting over a different wavelength, would relay the first jammed station. The listener, enrolled in the battle of the waves, had to figure out the tactics of the enemy, and in an almost physical way circumvent the strategy of the adversary. Very often only the operator, his ear glued to the receiver, had the unhoped-for opportunity of hearing the *Voice*. The other Algerians present in the room would receive the echo of this voice through the privileged interpreter who, at the end of the broadcast, was literally besieged. Specific questions would then be asked of this incarnated voice. Those present wanted to know about a particular battle mentioned by the French press in the last twenty-four hours, and the interpreter, embarrassed, feeling guilty, would sometimes have to admit that the *Voice* had not mentioned it.

But by common consent, after an exchange of views, it would be decided that the *Voice* had in fact spoken of these events, but that the interpreter had not caught the transmitted information. A real task of reconstruction would then begin. Everyone would participate, and the battles of yesterday and the day before would be re-fought in accordance with the deep aspirations and the unshakable faith of the group. The listener would compensate for the fragmentary nature of the news by an autonomous creation of information.

Listening to the *Voice of Fighting Algeria* was motivated not just by eagerness to hear the news, but more particularly by the inner need to be at one with the nation in its struggle, to recapture and to assume the new national formulation, to listen to and to repeat the grandeur of the epic being accomplished up there among the rocks and on the *djebels*. Every morning the Algerian would communicate the result of his hours of listening in. Every morning he would complete for the benefit of his neighbor or his comrade the things not said by the *Voice* and reply to the insidious questions asked by the enemy press. He would counter the official affirmations of the occupier, the resounding bulletins of the adversary, with official statements issued by the Revolutionary Command.

Sometimes it was the militant who would circulate the assumed point of view of the political directorate. Because of a silence on this or that fact which, if prolonged, might prove upsetting and dangerous for the people's unity, the whole nation would snatch fragments of sentences in the course of a broadcast and attach to them a decisive meaning. Imperfectly heard, obscured by an incessant jamming, forced to change wavelengths two or three times in the course of a broadcast, the *Voice of Fighting Algeria* could hardly ever be heard from beginning to end. It was a choppy, broken voice. From one village to the next, from one shack to the next, the *Voice of Algeria* would recount new things, tell of more and more glorious battles, picture vividly the collapse of the occupying power. The enemy lost its density, and at the level of the consciousness of the occupied, experienced a series of essential setbacks. Thus the *Voice of Algeria,* which for months led the life of a fugitive, which was tracked by the adversary's powerful jamming networks, and whose "word" was often inaudible, nourished the citizen's faith in the Revolution.

This *Voice* whose presence was felt, whose reality was sensed, assumed more and more weight in proportion to the number of jamming wavelengths broadcast by the specialized enemy stations. It was the power of the enemy sabotage that emphasized the reality and the intensity of the national expression. By its phantom-like character, the radio of the *Moudjahidines,* speaking in the name of Fighting Algeria, recognized as the spokesman for every Algerian, gave to the combat its maximum of reality.

Under these conditions, claiming to have heard the *Voice of Algeria* was, in a certain sense, distorting the truth, but it was above all the occasion to proclaim one's clandestine participation in the essence of the Revolution. It meant making a deliberate choice, though it was not explicit during the first months, between the enemy's congenital lie and the people's own lie, which suddenly acquired a dimension of truth.

This voice, often absent, physically inaudible, which each one felt welling up within himself, founded on an inner perception of the Fatherland, became materialized in an irrefutable way. Every Algerian, for his part, broadcast and transmitted the new language. The nature of this voice recalled in more than one way that of the Revolution: present "in the air" in isolated pieces, but not objectively.[4]

The radio receiver guaranteed this true lie. Every evening, from nine o'clock to midnight, the Algerian would listen. At the end of the evening, not hearing the *Voice,* the listener would sometimes leave the needle on a jammed wavelength or one that simply produced static, and would announce that the voice of the combatants was here. For an hour the room would be filled with the piercing, excruciating din of the jamming. Behind each modulation, each active crackling, the Algerian would imagine not only words, but concrete battles. The war of the sound waves, in the *gourbi,* re-enacts for the benefit of the citizen the armed clash of his people and colonialism. As a general rule, it is the *Voice of Algeria* that wins out. The enemy stations, once the broadcast is completed, abandon their work of sabotage. The military music of warring Algeria that concludes the broadcast can then freely fill the lungs and the heads of the faithful. These few brazen notes reward three hours of daily hope and have played a fundamental role for months in the training and strengthening of the Algerian national consciousness.

[...]

With the creation of a *Voice of Fighting Algeria,* the Algerian was vitally committed to listening to the message, to assimilating it, and soon to acting upon it. Buying a radio, getting down on one's knees with one's head against the speaker, was no longer just wanting to get the news concerning the formidable experience in progress in the country, it was *hearing* the first worlds of the nation.

Since the new Algeria on the march had decided to tell about itself and to make itself heard, the radio had become indispensable. It was the radio that enabled the *Voice* to take root in the villages and on the hills. Having a radio seriously meant *going to war.*

By means of the radio, a technique rejected before 1954, the Algerian people decided to relaunch the Revolution. Listening in on the Revolution, the Algerian existed with it, made it exist.

The memory of the "free" radios that came into being during the Second World War underlines the unique quality of the *Voice of Fighting Algeria.* The Polish, Belgian, French people, under the German occupation, were able, through the broadcasts transmitted from London, to maintain contact with a certain image of their nation. Hope, the spirit of resistance to the oppressor, were then given daily sustenance and kept alive. For example, it will be remembered that listening to the voice of *Free France* was a mode of national existence, a form of combat. The fervent and well-nigh mystical participation of the French people with the voice from London has been sufficiently commented upon to need no amplification. In France, from 1940 to 1944, listening to the voice of *Free France* was surely a vital, sought-for experience. But listening to the radio was not a new phenomenon of behavior. The voice from London had its place in the vast repertory of transmitting stations which already existed for the French before the war. From the global conflict, a pre-eminent figure emerges through the agency—that of occupied France receiving the message of hope from *Free France.* In Algeria things took on a special character. First of all, there was the stripping from the instrument its traditional burden of taboos and prohibitions. Progressively the instrument not only acquired a category of neutrality, but was endowed with a positive coefficient.

Accepting the radio technique, buying a receiver set, and participating in the life of the fighting nation, all these coincided. The frenzy with which the people exhausted the stock of radio sets gives a rather accurate idea of its desire to be involved in the dialogue that began in 1955 between the combatant and the *nation.*

In the colonial society, Radio-Alger was not just one among a number of voices. *It was the voice of the occupier.* Tuning in Radio-Alger amounted to accepting domination; it amounted to exhibiting one's desire to live on good terms with oppression. It meant giving in to the enemy. Switching on the radio meant validating the formula, "This is Algiers, the French Radio Broadcast." The acquiring of a radio handed the colonized over to the enemy's system and prepared for the banishing of hope from his heart.

The existence of the *Voice of Fighting Algeria,* on the other hand, profoundly changed the problem. Every Algerian felt himself to be called upon and wanted to become a reverberating element of the vast network of meaning born of the liberating combat. The war, daily events of military or political character, were broadly commented on in the news programs of the foreign radios. In the foreground the voice of the *djebels* stood out. We have seen that the phantom-like and quickly inaudible character of this voice in no way affected *its felt reality and its power.* Radio-Alger, Algerian Radio-Broadcasting, lost their sovereignty.

Gone were the days when mechanically switching on the radio amounted to an invitation to the enemy. For the Algerian the radio, as a technique, became transformed. The radio set was no longer directly and solely tuned in on the occupier. To the right and to the left of Radio-Alger's broadcasting band, on different and numerous wavelengths, innumerable stations could be tuned in to, among which it was possible to distinguish the friends, the enemies' accomplices, and the neutrals. Under these conditions, having a receiver was neither making oneself available to the enemy, nor giving him a voice, nor yielding on a point of principle. On the contrary, on the strict level of news, it was showing the desire to keep one's distance, to hear other voices, to take in other prospects. It was in the course of the struggle for liberation and thanks to the creation of a *Voice of Fighting Algeria* that the Algerian experienced and concretely discovered the existence of voices other than the voice of the dominator which formerly had been immeasurably amplified because of his own silence.

The old monologue of the colonial situation, already shaken by the existence of the struggle, disappeared completely by 1956. *The Voice of Fighting Algeria* and all the voices picked up by the receiver now revealed to the Algerian the tenuous, very relative character, in short, the imposture of the French voice presented until now as the only one. The occupier's voice was stripped of its authority.

The nation's *speech,* the nation's spoken *words* shape the world while at the same time renewing it.

Before 1954, native society as a whole rejected the radio, turned a deaf ear to the technical development of methods of news dissemination. There was a non-receptive attitude before this import brought in by the occupier. In the colonial situation, the radio did not satisfy any need of the Algerian people.[5] On the contrary, the radio was considered, as we have seen, a means used by the enemy to quietly carry on his work of depersonalization of the native.

The national struggle and the creation of *Free Radio Algeria* have produced a fundamental change in the people. The radio has appeared in a massive way at once and not in progressive stages. What we have witnessed is a radical transformation of the means of perception, of the very world of perception. Of Algeria it is true to say that there never was, with respect to the radio, a pattern of listening habits, of audience reaction. Insofar as mental processes are concerned, the technique had virtually to be invented. *The Voice of Algeria, created* out of nothing, brought the nation to life and endowed every citizen with a new status, *telling him so explicitly.*

After 1957, the French troops in operation formed the habit of confiscating all the radios in the course of a raid. At the same time listening in on a certain number of broadcasts was prohibited. Today things have progressed. *The Voice of Fighting Algeria* has multiplied. From Tunis, from Damascus, from Cairo, from Rabat, programs are broadcast to the people. The programs are organized by Algerians. The French services no longer try to jam these powerful and numerous broadcasts. The Algerian has the opportunity every day of listening to five or six different broadcasts in Arabic or in French, by means of which he can follow the victorious development of the Revolution step by step. As far as news is concerned, the word of the occupier has been seen to suffer a progressive devaluation. After having imposed the national voice upon that of the dominator, the radio welcomes broadcasts from all the corners of the world. The "Week of Solidarity with Algeria," organized by the Chinese people, or the resolutions of the Congress of African Peoples on the Algerian war, link the *fellah* to an immense tyranny-destroying wave.

Incorporated under these condition into the life of the nation, the radio will have an exceptional importance in the country's building phase. After the war a disparity between the people and what is intended to speak for them will no longer be possible. The revolutionary instruction on the struggle for liberation must normally be replaced by a revolutionary instruction on the building of the nation. The fruitful use that can be made of the radio can well be imagined. Algeria has enjoyed a unique experience. For several years, the radio will have been for many, one of the means of saying "no" to the occupation and of believing in the liberation. The identification of the voice of the Revolution with the fundamental truth of the nation has opened limitless horizons.

Notes

1. *souk*—market or shop. (Translator's note)
2. In the realm of military communications, the same phenomenon is to be noted. In less than fifteen months the National Army of Liberation's "liaison and telecommunications system" became equal to the best that is to be found in a modern army.
3. The arrival in Algeria by normal channels of new sets and new batteries obviously became increasingly difficult. After 1957 it was from Tunisia and Morocco, via the underground, that new supplies came. The regular introduction of these means of establishing contact with the official voice of the Revolution became as important for the people as acquiring weapons or munitions for the National Arm.
4. Along the same line should be mentioned the manner in which programs are listened to in Kabylia. In groups of scores and sometimes hundreds around a receiver, the peasants listen religiously to "the Voice of the Arabs." Few understand the literary Arabic used in these broadcasts. But the faces assume a look of gravity and the features harden when the expression *Istiqlal* (Independence) resounds in the *gourbi* (shack). An Arab voice that hammers out the word *Istiqlal* four times in an hour suffices at that level of heightened consciousness to keep alive the faith in victory.
5. In this connection may be mentioned the attitude of the French authorities in present-day Algeria. As we know, television was introduced into Algeria several years ago. Until recently, a simultaneous bilingual commentary accompanied the broadcasts. Some time ago, the Arabic commentary ceased. This fact once again confirms the aptness of the formula applied to Radio-Alger: "Frenchmen speaking to Frenchmen."

Chapter 28

Michèle Martin

GENDER AND EARLY
TELEPHONE CULTURE

IN THE 1890s, women in the wealthy classes were using a telephone system built and shaped by the economic incentives of the telephone industry and by political and ideological forces. Women's activities were not seen as being of prime importance in the business world of the telephone entrepreneurs. Nor did these entrepreneurs see the utility of this new technology for working-class housewives, or for rural populations. As Marvin pointed out, telephone-company managers thought that "women's use of men's technology would come to no good end" (1988, 23). Capitalists considered the telephone only to be a means of facilitating business activity or to link the businessman to his office when he chose to stay at home. Its initial impact on other social groups was slight.

This began to change when the telephonic network expanded to residential areas. This expansion resulted from a developmental dynamic involving several components. No general consensus among women forced telephone companies to extend the telephone system for their use. At first, women's access to the telephone on a personal basis was very much subject to their husbands' trust in the technology. Businessmen who used the telephone system generally had their offices connected to their homes. Consequently, women gained access to the telephone, at first for practices recommended by the companies, but soon for activities of their own. The early structure of telephonic networks shows that they were used primarily within friendship circles, which later expanded as new exchanges were opened. Thus, for some subscribers, the opening of an exchange was the equivalent of the "pedestrianization" of their elite telephone network. It was from within closed and approved circles that the domestic use of the telephone grew, accompanied, much later, by telephone companies' advertising of the utility of the telephone for women's practices. Only when women started to use the telephone extensively for their own activities could a (female) telephone culture emerge. Women's contribution to changing the social practices of telephone use was important, although we must be critical of contemporary male accounts of it.

Unexpected Telephone Practices

Among the new social activities developed by the telephone and practised by women, phoning friends and relatives was certainly one of the most popular. Conversing over the telephone was seen as "taking the place of visiting" (Spofford 1909). It was faster and more convenient than having to harness the horses and, sometimes, convincing the husband to make the journey. Although it is impossible to determine the percentage of residential calls made just to chat, complaints published in newspapers and magazines about women's habit of talking on the phone for "futile motives" (BCA, ncm 1919g) suggest that the telephone was regularly used for that purpose.[1] Motives for making calls included chatting, courting, discussing, gossiping, and so on. This activity came to be so popular that some newspapersmen called the telephone "our tap of communication" ("Back to the Land" 1906, 530). Since, in spite of telephone-company advertising, these calls were made at any time of the day, they multiplied contacts with friends or relatives, the more so since they did not require any preliminary preparation such as change of clothes. "Telephone service enables morning gossiping . . . afternoon visits to be paid without the necessity of dressing up or of driving on a dusty road in the hot glare of the summer's sun, or in the biting winds of a wintry day; evening visits to be returned while reclining in one's own comfortable rocking chair" (BCA, ty 9 (3) 1905, 257).

This was a significant improvement for women of the 1890s, since getting dressed was an elaborate and time-consuming process for them. According to Haller and Haller, "it was the duty of every [middle-class] woman to look as beautiful as she possibly could" (1974, 141). For the Victorian middle-class woman, "cleanliness was next to Godliness," and she was "continually advised to keep herself spotless" (Haller and Haller 1974, 145). As a consequence, she "redressed several times during the day," each time tightly bound in corset, bustle, petticoat, and extravagant dresses, in order to receive visitors, to go out to visit, or simply to "await [her] husband['s] return" (Haller and Haller 1974, 161). Telephone visiting diminished the number of "visual" contacts necessitating a change of clothes. At the same time, it permitted these women to remain in "talking" contact with each other.

The possibility of several telephonic contacts per day was said to put women "on the tenterhooks of expectation and desire": the expectation of being "called up" by someone, and the desire to call someone else up. "Thus may life be made miserable by the very attempts to make it easy and happy," said a male writer in *Chambers's Journal* ("The Telephone" 1899, 313). Use of the telephone, like that of the bicycle, was seen as a moral issue necessitating a specific set of rules. Indeed, both technologies became popular with women in the 1890s. The bicycle was considered a "curse" because, like the telephone, it provided women with "evil associations and opportunities" for contacts with strangers without the presence of a chaperone. The use of both technologies by Victorian women, then, had to be controlled by "correct etiquette" elaborated by men, who considered that, "in their weakness," women were "best protected in the privacy of the home."[2] The etiquette was intended to prevent women from using these technologies for "undesirable" and "dangerous" practices.

The "social" aspect of telephone technology had not been foreseen by the early capitalist developers of the telephone system. It is legitimate to assert that the popularity of the telephone with women was partly due to several technological characteristics specific to this means of communication. For instance, the sense of privacy created by conversations transmitted from ear to ear and involving the whole person, to borrow McLuhan's words (1964, 240), endowed telephonic communication with a kind of intimacy which women had not previously experienced. Since, in addition, telephone service was developing into a private-line system in large cities, a conversation on these lines took the form of sharing a secret. However, on party lines, which were the majority in small towns and villages and still numerous in cities, women had quite different telephonic experiences, and were attracted by other features of the means of communication.

In rural areas, the independent telephone companies that developed party lines applied much looser rules to the use of their telephones and charged much lower rates, so that in many areas almost everyone could afford a telephone. Moreover, rural communities were more closely knit socially than urban ones, although they were more sparsely distributed geographically. A letter from K.J. Dunstan, local manager in Toronto, discussing the possibility of opening an exchange in the Beaches area (which was still a rural district at the time), asserted that there was "considerable local intercourse" between the inhabitants (BCA, sb 84141b, 3146–3, 1902).[3]

All of these elements helped generate different types of telephone activities. What was considered rude and "unethical" in the set of rules specifying approved uses of the telephone became helpful behaviour within the code of unexpected practices. These represented a complete reversal of the standard uses – so much so that big-company managers were scandalized by the practices allowed on rural party lines, saying that "no company which ha[d] the best interests of itself and its subscribers at heart, [would] operate them," because they did "not embrace the highest ideals of telephony." On the other hand, some small-company managers thought that "the party line was a necessity and ha[d] come to stay" (BCA, ty 7 (6) 1904, 453). Some users eavesdropped and participated in other subscribers' conversations. The operator of the exchange of the small telephone company owned by Dr Beatty recounted that he "liked to listen in on the conversations . . . and would often feel moved to break in and give his views on the topic under discussion. This would have disconcerted town or city folks, but the doctor's subscribers . . . knew his ways and took this in their stride" (BCA, d 29909, 1967).

Actually, in the code of rural party-line activities, listening to others' conversations was not seen as eavesdropping by subscribers, but rather as participation in community life: "Every country user did [it] . . . it was the way they got the news" (BCA, d 29909, 1967). Often, in small communities, a listener entered a conversation with information which the two original callers did not have. For instance, *Telephony* reported that when a woman cut her finger while cooking dinner and phoned a friend to ask for advice, "before the friend could answer someone else piped up, 'Bind it up in salt pork.' Still another voice advised court plaster and someone else had another remedy to offer" (BCA, ty 8 (3) 1904, 211). Most of the time, though, listeners tried to go unnoticed, just as they would if they were eavesdropping on a conversation in a public place. When a man called a friend to announce his visit, he added at the end of the call, "'The rest of you on the line – Martha, Grace, Mary, Rachel – tell the men I'll buzz wood tomorrow afternoon.' The men all appeared and there was no explanation asked or offered about how they knew when to come" (BCA, qa 1936). Although this example implies a sexist tendency by presuming that women, and not men, were the listeners, it shows how party lines were used in rural communities. As one observer pointed out, "The strange part about a party line in the country is the fact that everybody listens but very, very few ever admit that they do" (BCA, qa 1936, 51). People knew that they were often overheard, but most of them did not mind. They knew that, in time, *they* would be the listeners. It was part of rural life.

One of the most important characteristics of party lines, especially in rural areas, was that they were regularly used for "meeting on the lines." For instance, when eavesdroppers decided to enter a conversation initiated by two other parties, the telephone call generated a group discussion: "It is . . . evident . . . that if one person calls up another in the far end of the town many receivers between these two points come down and sometimes more than two persons join in the conversation," the manager of an American independent company remarked (BCA, ty 8 (3) 1904, 211). Sometimes, the technological features of the telephone network were responsible for these meetings. Indeed, some small companies did not have a discriminating ringing system – the same ring applied to every house – so that when the telephone rang, all subscribers had to answer to check if the call was for them. Often, several users stayed on the line to participate in the conversation (BCA, qa 1918, 120; d 29909, 1967; d 29912, 1961). At other times, the operator was asked to connect a subscriber with several others, instigating a meeting. One operator recalled that she "would connect two or three lines and hold them open so the women could talk back and forth and arrange church meetings or other projects" (BCA, d 29909, 1967). Sometimes, a woman would keep the telephone receiver to her ear while she was working: "There sat his wife in the rocking chair. She was sewing and tied to the back of the chair was the receiver of the telephone, so adjusted that she could place her ear to it without changing her position. . . it enabled her to hear the gossip of her neighbors at the other end" (BCA, ty 6 (6) 1903, 480). Finally, party lines were also used to comfort the sick. The telephone receiver was placed on the ill person's pillow so that he or she could listen to conversations on the line and keep in contact with what was going on in the vicinity (Spofford 1909). These examples show some women's initiatives to decrease the loneliness they felt in their isolated homes. For them, the telephone was a means of staying in touch with the rest of the community. They did not need to participate directly in all activities occurring over the phone. In fact, before the advent of the radio, the telephone was the only way for these women to hear other people's voices without having to leave their homes. Most men, however, ridiculed, or altogether dismissed, these ways of using the telephone to improve women's lives.

The unexpected uses of the telephone practised by women influenced the companies' notion of its value. This technology, which had been conceived exclusively for business, seemed to have alternative uses that were worth considering. However, among these uses, only those approved by management were retained. For instance, collective calls, regularly practised by women on party lines, were gradually replaced by private lines and telephone calls between two parties.[4] However, of the practices retained by the companies, some had been created by women. One of them was the use of the telephone for sociability.

This suggests that if women had restricted their use of the telephone to that promoted by the companies, today it probably would not be such an inconspicuous technology in the household. Indeed, at the domestic level, it would still be a form of communication to be used on special occasions only. Yet, although the telephone system was adjusted to take into account some activities practised by women, it was not planned primarily for them, as their social and cultural practices were not directly taken into consideration in its expansion. Here, it is useful to use Cockburn's concept of "male tenure" over technology to explain the participation of women in the structuring of the telephone system. In her article entitled "The Relations to Technology" (1986), Cockburn suggest that men have what she calls a "tenure" over the technological sphere, which means that they "appropriate and sequester" each new area of development at the expense of women. This appropriation by men is manifested not only in development and ownership of technology but also in its uses and values, which are, according to Cockburn, mostly determined by men. She argues that "technological competence correlates strongly with masculinity and incompetence with feminity" (1986, 78). In the telephone values developed by dominant-class males, women's specific uses of a telephone system developed by and for men were clearly deemed incompetent. Women's persistence in using the system their way, and the lure of profit that these unexpected female practices represented to the telephone business, finally resulted in the development of a service that was better adapted to women. Thus, as users, women had only an indirect impact in the pattern of development of the telephone. However, their contribution was an *active* one, since some of their telephone practices forced the companies to modify their development strategy. In addition, the various uses made of the telephone engendered some social change, and a culture of the telephone was slowly developing.

The Telephone Culture

The elaborate system of telegraphy that existed before the advent of the telephone served those who later became telephone users. The telegraph, which constituted an important improvement in terms of speed over letter-writing, had been used extensively for almost fifty years. When the telephone began to be marketed, however, the telegraph came to be seen as a slow means of communication. Transactions which took days to be made by post, and hours by telegraph, could be completed instantaneously by telephone. Telephone companies' advertisements stressed the speed of the telephone in comparison to other means of communication. "The mail is quick, the telegraph is quicker, but the long-distance telephone is instantaneous and you dont [sic] have to wait for an answer," said one (BCA, d 1544, 1898). These particularities of the telephone influenced social practices. Although, as some claimed, the telephone had not "revolutionized the modes of correspondence" (BCA, d 12016, 1879b, 10), it did modify several cultural practices.

The telephone did not supplant existing means of communication. As a writer pointed out, "A letter was different from a conversation . . . In a letter, you could get down on paper exactly what you wanted to say in the best possible language, and leave out whatever didn't fit it. It was like addressing a jury without the presence of opposing

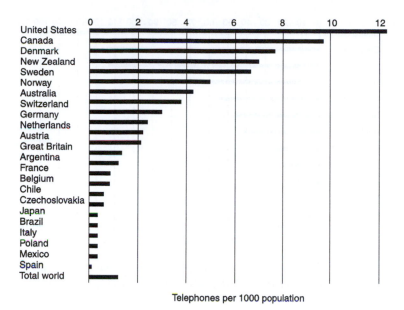

Fig. 28.1 Telephones per 100 persons in selected countries, January 1921.
(*Bell Telephone Quarterly* 1922, 1(3): 49)

counsel, in some courtroom where you had a free hand with the judge" (Langton 1987, 82). Whether for this reason or because it was less expensive, written correspondence was still extensively used. In 1905, for example, while the telephone had superseded the telegraph for short-distance communications (e.g., communications within a city), the latter was still generally used for long-distance transactions (BCA, ncm 1905a). The postal service was also regularly utilized. The rush that Bell Telephone Co. experienced in 1918, during a postal strike (BCA, nct 1918b), was evidence of massive use of the mail system at the time. Yet use of the telephone was growing rapidly all over the world (see figures 28.1 and 28.2).[5] It had evolved from being seen as a "nuisance" and an "indignity" to being a "sign of civilisation." "Failure to adopt the use of telephones," said a writer in 1905, "indicates, in general way, a backward condition, a lack of enterprise, in any modern city" (BCA, ty 7 (6) 1904, 456).

Extensive utilization of the telephone by the wealthy classes was bound to create some specific habits. Actually, use of the phone was affected by the time of the day and the weather: "The more inclement the weather, the more of people resort to their telephones. There are appointments to be cancelled or deferred and taxicabs to be summoned" (Rhodes 1929, 21). Some women would rather phone their friends than go out in the rain or the snow to visit: "We can tell what kind of weather it is from the College Exchange," said one operator, referring to residential calls (BCA, nct 1914b).[6] An observant operator divided the daily activities of "leisure class" women over the telephone as follows.

> At seven o'clock, there are scattered calls . . . for doctors . . . At eight o'clock, the nice, early-morning women come on the market with patient, affable butchers . . .

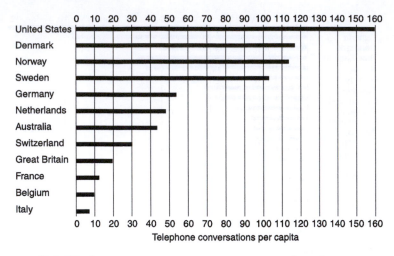

Fig. 28.2 Telephones conversations per capita in selected countries, December 1920. (*Bell Telephone Quarterly* 1922, 1(3): 50)

At ten, interminable communications between women . . . with infinite details as the clothes . . . I've known them to keep it up for three quarters of an hour.

At eleven to half past . . . nippy ladies calling up employment agencies, or stupid servant girls replying. At eleven thirty till twelve thirty there's a wild rush, everybody trying to catch everybody else for lunch.

From then till three or so there are characteristic calls of all sorts: peevish, hurried females who use the nickel 'phones in downtown drug stores . . . silly school girls mischievously calling men they don't know . . .

From three to four . . . a flurry of women trying to call up stores before they close, or in the catch of the last deliveries.

At five, wives begin to call up to know if husbands are coming home . . . 'Be sure to bring home a steak or a lobster.'

From six to seven everybody seems to be busy to call up . . . a club . . . a garage . . . towards eight, comes the nervous maiden[7] calling up her men . . .

After ten thirty come the carriage calls, garage orders, and the hotel private exchanges begin to get busy. (BCA, ncm 1907e)

Women used the telephone for various purposes. It was said that a woman "no more need[ed] to make appointments by letter with the dressmaker, or to drive to the box-office of the theater to take tickets, or to be kept waiting for forty-eight hours before she knows whether Mrs Blank can meet her or come for tea" ("Back to the Land" 1906, 530). It was faster to use the telephone, and get what she wanted without leaving her home. The fact that women were using the telephone in this manner meant that they no longer expected to meet a regular group at such locations as the market. The telephone was taking the place of the daily shopping trip, at least for some women, especially on inclement days. Housekeepers were slowly changing their daily habits, thereby modifying the characteristics of the places they used to patronize.

Technological features of telephone systems also contributed to the development of certain cultural practices. The fact that the phone allowed oral communication without visual contact created a kind of intimacy which people previously had not experienced (Barrett 1940, 129). However, these features had some drawbacks as well. Having a conversation ear to ear did not always create the desired intimacy. It was reported in some scientific journals that this mode of communication sometimes generated insecurity, especially when the person calling was unknown ("Action at a Distance" 1914, 39). Indeed, it seemed that the anonymity provided by the telephone had evil effects on the personality of some callers, so much so that the telephone was seen as having "a brutalising influence": "The sensitive-minded man who would shrink from saying a disagreeable thing in ordinary conversation, when talking through the telephone, will speak his mind . . . bluntly and argue . . . roughly . . ." (BCA, ncm 1906d). Thus, the telephone was said to encourage the use of foul language (BCA, nct 1916d) and "trespassing" by telephone. Some men importuned women over the telephone in such a persistent manner that judges deemed the offence a "breach of the peace" (BCA, ty 10 (3) 1905, 221). Thus contradictory effect created by the telephone of feeling nearby and far away at the same time seemed to embolden some people, leading to new breaches of the law to which the legal system had to adjust.

In fact, the problem of aggressiveness and "foul language" on the telephone became so serious that an amendment to the Telephone Act was passed in 1915 naming the use of "abusive language on the telephone as an offence punishable with a fine of $25 or imprisonment for 30 days" (BCA, nct 1915a).[8] Whether the telephone was entirely responsible for such behaviour is debatable. Industrialization of society was causing rapid changes in some social practices and encouraging more liberal and emancipated social behaviours. Since the instantaneous characteristic of the telephone constituted "a means of projecting personality," as stated in an advertisement (BCA, nca 1925), without the necessity of identifying oneself, it permitted some hidden features of a personality to surface. "The use of the telephone gives little room for reflection," stated a writer in the *Chambers's Journal* in 1899. "It does not improve the temper, and it engenders a feverishness in the ordinary concerns of life which does not make for domestic happiness and comfort." The telephone, by making life "so easy," represented an "immanent danger of relapsing into barbarism" ("The Telephone" 1899, 313). This notion imparted to the telephone a responsibility which should have been attributed to the social conditions created by industrial capitalism as a whole. The *only* contribution of the telephone was to *facilitate,* through the anonymity it afforded, the emergence of unpleasant characteristics which already existed.

Such evils led to the necessity to develop *telephone etiquette.* Telephone etiquette was elaborated from the standard uses prescribed by the telephone companies. People were told to use good manners on the telephone, to employ such general courteous phrases as "Please" and "Thank you," to apologize for making callers wait, to utilize "correct" language instead of familiar expressions or abridged sentences (BCA, ty 8 (2) 1904, 130). Users were also advised to answer their telephone themselves to avoid making the other party wait for them (BCA, ty 8 (4) 1904, 311), and to identify themselves when answering or calling (BCA, ty 8 (2) 1904, 130). Failure to follow telephone etiquette was seen as a matter of gender, as women were presented as the main offenders in terms of telephone manners. Operators reported that women callers "have an exasperating way of asking, 'Who is this?' when some one answers their call whose voice they do not recognize." "Girls" were accused of unduly using their employers' telephones during business hours (BCA, ncm 1915a). The ultimate abuse, however, was attributed to women who did not have a telephone at home and who used telephones in drugstores. These women were seen as the "chief patrons" in "carry[ing] on all the conversation you wish" of "the most trivial nature." They went to the nearest store and, with a "May I use a telephone, please?," they used the storekeeper's telephone and "for 20 minutes or half an hour they will carry on the most milk-and-water-conversation" (BCA, d 30114, 1965). The ultimate offence was that they left the store "without spending a cent."

Still, even when "good manners were observed," telephone calls were considered "hopelessly vulgar" for "ladies of the high society." In her book *Etiquette for Americans* (BCA, qa 1906), a "Lady of Fashion" claimed that the telephone call, due to its instantaneous character, was a "blessing in adjusting details" for a reception. However, it "should be used sparingly." Informal "invitations to bicycle or play golf [could] be transmitted in this way . . . but for most social matters, the use of the telephone [was] questionable." Moreover, there was "no excuse for telephoning an invitation when time [was] not an object, or when the person invited [was] not an intimate friend" (BCA, qa, 1906, 37). This book was written exactly thirty years after the telephone was first marketed. Old cultural practices die hard.

The only concessions made by the "Lady of Fashion" to telephone use were for intimate relationships and casual encounters. In spite of her recommendations, though, the telephone was sometimes used at first for invitations. In such cases, other means of communication were usually employed to confirm the telephone call. In Wharton's *The House of Mirth* (1905), the petty-bourgeois heroine, Miss Lily Bart, used three different means of communication for a single invitation. She first made the invitation over the telephone, the call being answered by a maid. A note written by Miss Bart and delivered by a servant was then used to confirm the telephone call. Finally, she sent a telegram to finalize the whole process. In rural areas, however, etiquette was not as binding, and telephone advertisements suggested the use of the instrument to send invitations for an "impromptu party." Instead of spending an afternoon driving from house to house to invite people, "in less than half an hour, you could ring up your friends, living miles away, and invite them to come, without trouble or fatigue" (BCA, d 21203–2, 1908). There were clear differences in accepted telephone practices between rural and urban areas.

The telephone had other cultural effects, especially in relation to letter-writing. Although people recognized the importance of letter-writing for serious matters,[9] as early as 1906 "the idea of writing a series of letters with a pen and ink, directing, sealing, and stamping the envelopes, and then waiting till the day after to-morrow for an answer simply paralyse[d]" many people ("Back to the Land"

1906, 530–31). Some writers (e.g., Lang 1906) were alarmed by the decreasing popularity of letter-writing. It "seems to be in decay," said Lang, "and no wonder, for few people have time to read a long letter . . . Indeed, talk is mainly done through the telephone . . . the art of spelling, even, may come to be lost" (1906, 508). Even the government replaced some written documents by use of the telephone. "Government by telephone!" exclaimed Casson. "This is the new idea . . . arrived at in the more efficient departments of the Federal" (1911, 899). Lang lamented that it was the end of "the excitement of reading for material in the archives." Since people telephoned instead of writing letters, it would become impossible to trace the development of political, economic, and social organizations, he said. An ex-Chancellor of the English Exchequer confessed that, during his entire career, he had not kept more than twelve letters, most of his business having been done by telephone. Lang exclaimed, "Let us rejoice that the thing was not discovered sooner! If Horace Walpole could have chatted with Horace Mason, in Florence, by telephone; or Madame de Sévigny with her daughter; or Thackeray with Mrs Brookfield; or Mr Stevenson, from Samoa, with Mr Gosse and others, our literature would be poorer" (1906, 507–8).

Undeniably, the telephone has enlarged the field of oral culture. The diary disappeared from most women's lives long ago, and communications between friends occur mostly through the telephone, at least for short-distance interactions. As a result, writing a biography of a person whose life extends past invention of the telephone with the aid of written records only is almost impossible. While the telephone is a technology of rapid and easy contact, it is also a source of transient evidence. For example, it is impossible to know exactly the number and the context of the "visits" paid by telephone during a period of its development. The only sources of information are indirect ones, such as newspaper reports, journal articles, and operators' stories, which may be biased. This means that telephone technology has hampered feminist researchers, for instance, in retracing long-distance friendships between women, which was relatively easy during the time of letter-writing. It is also impossible to trace telephone practices related to working classes. I mentioned earlier that some low-waged women working as maids used, furtively it seems, their employers' telephones. It is almost unthinkable that other members of the working classes did not use public telephones at all, in spite of their poverty. The proliferation of public telephones supports this assumption. However, since they did not have phones in their households, it is difficult to know the volume of use. The extension of oral culture due to the telephone certainly represents an inconvenience for researchers. In fact, Lang suggested that each telephone be attached to a recorder so that future generations could keep track of their ancestors! The records, he said, could be likened to letters.

Nonetheless, if there has been a loss of literature with the use of the telephone, there has also been some gain. Very early in its development, the technology was a source of stimulation for artists, and of entertainment for people. Novels were written in which the plot was based on the use of the telephone (e.g., Sayers 1921). The telephone inspired poets,[10] cartoonists (BCA, nct 1918a), and playwrights. In 1880, for example, George Bernard Shaw wrote a sketch on telephone conversations which suggested that the phone "was a tool for female's gossip" (Brooks 1977, 210).[11]

In 1923, literary works on the telephone presented its use as an "expression of female desperation" (Brooks 1977, 218). The constant was that women were rarely presented in a positive light in works about the telephone.

Other effects of the telephone on popular culture were related to its physical features. Indeed, people talked about "the telephone voice" and "the telephone ear." The telephone voice was said to be revealing of "whether gentility [was] a thin veneer or a solid substance," the "thin veneer" being proved when an unpleasant answering voice changed suddenly into "amazing mellowness" upon learning who is calling. Using the right voice over the telephone was considered a "difficult art," because the instrument deprived the voice of its nuances. As a result, only two categories of users could be identified on the basis of their voice: those who rarely used the telephone and whose timidity regarding the technology was translated into a "solemnity of the performance"; and regular users, who were relaxed and talked as if they were having an intimate conversation (BCA, tg 3 (1) 1911, 5). Several people thought that the telephone developed "a soft voice," a well-modulated, "lady-Eke voice" (BCA, tg 1 (8) 1909, 10; ty 10 (5) 1905, 360). In any case, the voice was regarded as a key element in use of the telephone, and there was general agreement among specialists that the voice itself was influenced by the new technology. The ear was also said to be affected by the telephone. The fact that the cord of the apparatus was on the left side encouraged users to hold it in the left hand and to put the receiver to their left ear. According to some researchers, this caused telephone users to become "left-eared" (BCA, ty 8 (1), 1904, 74). They discovered that those who frequently used the phone had more sensitive left ears. Left-eared and soft-voiced people were thus deemed to be a product of telephone technology.

The telephone was also said to affect physical and mental health. It was seen as a "germ collector," and doctors "urge[d] that the health department compel the telephone companies to equip their instruments with antiseptic devices which would destroy all germs as they entered the transmitter" (BCA, ncm 1906f). The number of articles written on this issue[12] shows that it was seen as a serious problem starting around 1905. Public telephones were considered unsafe because it was thought that they were packed with diphtheria, influenza, and consumption germs (BCA, ncm 1908d). It was suggested that hygienic devices be installed to lessen the risk of infection. This perception vanished as suddenly as it had appeared, without any apparent change in the telephone apparatus.

The telephone was also considered a "nerve-racking" technology because of its capacity to intrude on one's privacy at any time of the day. As one woman attested, "I have been called to the telephone three times this morning by some of my friends who just wanted to visit. Twice the bell woke the baby up and once my blackberry jam burned while I was trying to make an excuse to get away" (BCA, ty 10 (6) 1905, 429). Anxiety was increased by the fact that subscribers were instructed by the companies to answer the phone promptly.[13] Night calls were particularly aggravating, to the point that some physicians refused to have a telephone at their bedside (BCA, d 1009, 1934). It was a fact that the telephone was altering a society previously ruled by rigid, well-determined social practices.

The changes in popular practices brought about by the technology were instrumental in the creation of a telephone culture. The new form of communication created by telephone systems reproduced some social activities and modified others. One characteristic of the telephone system planned by and for the ruling classes was its speed. Casson said that the telephone had made life "more tense, alert, vivid" (1910a, 231). *Booklovers' Magazine* claimed that the telephone had "doubled pressure, condensed the world, [made] us all next-door neighbours" ("Behind the Scene at 'Central'" 1903, 390). The effect was multidimensional. The telephone was developed in response to capitalist society's requirement for faster means of communication, and it had indeed accelerated the speed of transactions. Moreover, its capacity for long-distance contact gave people the illusion that it had strengthened the nation's solidarity (Carty 1922b, 9), and eliminated class differentiation (Carty 1926a, 2). In reality, it only permitted entrenched social groups to communicate more often and more rapidly. Telephone contacts between members of the working classes and those of the ruling classes always occurred through an already existing rigid etiquette. Moreover, wealthy women on party lines often complained of the bad manners of low-wage women, and pressed the telephone companies to give them private lines.

Notes

1. See BCA, ty 1905, 10 (3), 211; ncm, 1908a; 1919a. Marvin also makes the point that men in the telephone business thought that "women failed to understand electrical messages the way their male protectors did, as scarce and expensive commodities," and that "their [women's] conversation [was] trivial and uninformative, and could [have been] easily managed face-to-face." Marvin 1988, 22–32.

2. The home, however, was itself becoming less private with the advent of the telephone. For more information on the danger of the bicycle for Victorian women, see Haller and Haller 1974, 174–87.

3. On the other hand, Fischer argues that in United States rural residents were independent and had very little intercourse with their neighbours. See Fischer 1988.

4. It is interesting to note that, a few years after Bell Telephone Co. had, with great effort, eliminated party lines in cities and built its system on the basis of private lines only, with the hope that one day it would be preeminent even in rural areas, it reintroduced, for an extra fee, a service with the advantages of the party line. The "telephone conference service," started in the early 1930s, was available for business and for "social use" (Banning 1936, 146). One difference between these services lay in the distance they covered. Party-line service was limited to local calls, whereas conference service was available for long-distance communication. Still, it was possible to adapt party-line service to long-distance service. Another important difference was that "meetings" on party lines did not involve as exclusive a group of callers as did "conference calls," since any subscriber connected to the party line could listen to or participate in conversations, whereas conference-call participants were predetermined.

5. Statistics on telephone conversations for Canada are not available. However, as figure 28.1 shows, Canada was only slightly behind the United States in terms of telephones per capita – 10 per cent of the population in Canada in comparison to 12 per cent for the United States – and Canadians had a reputation for being heavy telephone users. Consequently, the figures for telephone conversations for the United States give a good idea of what was happening here. Development of the telephone in the United States was generally comparable to that in Canada, as one might expect, since many factors were similar: the same company, with management in continual contact, same types of population, and so on. There were, however, some variations, as Fischer (1988) points out.

6.   See also Rhodes, 1927.
7.   She was probably afraid of being caught by her employer. Domestics usually were not allowed to use their employers' telephone for personal calls.
8.   The law started to be applied early in 1916. See: BCA nct 1916d; 1916e.
9.   As late as 1905, Bell managers were still writing to each other, instead of telephoning, for business matters. See: BCA, sle 1905a, b. Although they complained about the poor postal service, they continued to do business via correspondence, even to locations within telephone reach. Was the telephone too indiscreet for them—or perhaps, too expensive?
10. See BCA, d 12016, 1880e; qa 1880e, 1880d, 1914.
11. Shaw worked for a British telephone company for some years at the beginning of his writing career.
12. Here are some samples: "Telephone and Germs," *Montreal Star, 11* Sept. 1905; "New Way to Telephone," *Montreal Gazette,* 24 Jan. 1907; "The Telephone and Microbes," *Montreal Star,* 30 July 1908; "Germs in the Telephone," *Telegram,* 13 Jan. 1916; "Germ Proof Phone," *Herald,* 17 Feb. 1916.
13. As we saw earlier, the operator was instructed to ring a subscriber no more than twice.

References

Bell Canada Archives (BCA)

C. F. Sise Letters, 1880–1882 (sle)

1905a   Letters from C.F. Sise to F.P. Sise, 1 Apr., 3 May, 16 June, 20 June.
1905b   Letter form C.F. Sise to W.S. Allen, 30 June.

Documents (d)

1009	1934	No title. *Telephony,* 1 Sept.
1544	1898	Advertisement, no source.
12016		1879b "Success of the telephone." *Peterborough Review,* 19 Dec.
	1880e	"Still Single." No source.
21203–2	1908	Advertisement. *The Farmer's Advocate, 17* Dec.
29909	1967	"The life-saving line of a country doctor." E. Lunney. *Family Herald,* 2 Feb.
29912	1961	"Patient's death inspired rural telephone network." *London Free Press,* 18 Feb.
30114	1965	"The druggists 'dread'." *Montreal Gazette,* 11 Sept.

Newspaper clippings, Advertisement (nca)

1925   "The 'voice' returned." *Telephone Almanacs,* Oct.

Newspaper clippings, Montreal (ncm)

1905a   "Telephone inquiry." *Montreal Gazette,* 10 Mar.
1906d   "Brutalizing telephone." *The Graphic,* 3 Mar.
1906f   "Telephones as germ collectors." *Montreal Star,* 25 June.
1907e   "The diary of a telephone girl." *The Saturday Evening Post,* 19 Oct.

1908a   "Deplores gossip over telephone." *Montreal Herald*, 2 Apr.

1908d   "Deadly diseases locked in telephone receivers." *Herald*, 8 July.

1915a   "The etiquette of the telephone." *Evening News*, 11 Mar.

1918d   "Un ultimatum des pharmaciens à la Cie de téléphone Bell," 23 Nov., no source.

1919a   "L'abus du téléphone." *La Presse*, 10 Jan.

1919g   "Usually the public's fault." *Star,* 4 Oct.

Newspaper clippings, Toronto (nct)

1914b   "Why Central never gives wrong numbers." *Star,* 7 Mar.

1915a   "Telephone manners." *Star,* 9 Mar.

1916d   "First conviction for foul language." *Star,* 1 Feb.

1916e   "The privacy of the telephone." *News,* 25 May.

1918a   "Doings of the Duffs." *Star,* 21 Mar.

1918b   "As a result of strike." *Star,* 23 July.

Quotations and anecdotes (qa)

1880d   "Yelling through the telephone." *The Electrician,* Aug.

1906   "Shades of 1906." *Flasher and Plugs,* 20 May.

1914   "The value of the telephone." E.A. Guest, no source, 17 Nov.

1918   "The friendly phone," B.D. Fowler. *The Country Gentleman,* 30 Mar., 119–20.

1936   "The importance of a party line." *Globe and Mail,* 11 Aug.

Storage box number (sb)

84141b,3146–3   1902   Letter from K.J. Dunstan to Bell Telephone Co. management, 22 Jan.

Telephone gazette (tg)

1909   "Telephone service from an operator's standpoint," 1 (8): 10–11.

1911   "The telephone voice," 3 (1): 5.

Telephony (ty)

1903   "Rural telephone – Some amusing complications," 6 (6): 480–01.

1904   "The party line controversy," 7 (6): 452–53.

"The use of the telephone," 7 (6): 456–57.

"Is the telephone making us left-eared?" R.S. Sissoni, 8 (1): 74–75.

1904   "Bad telephone manners," 8 (2): 130.

"Heard on party line," 8 (3): 211.

1904   "Telephones and manners," 8 (4): 311.

1905   "Eliminating isolation from farm life," 9 (3): 25–28.

"Where 'Central' goes to school," 9 (3): 259–60.

"Lays telephonitis to women," 10 (3): 211.

"Telephone brakes the voice soft," 10 (5): 360.

"Troubles over the telephone," 10 (6): 429.

Other sources

"Action at a Distance." *Scientific American* 77 (1914): 39.

"Back to the Land – and the Telephone." *Spectator* 96 (1906): 530–31.

Banning, W.P. "The Growing Use of Telephone 'Conference service.'" *Bell Telephone Quarterly* 14, no. 30 (1936) 146–56.

Barrett, R.T. "The Telephone as a Social Force." *Bell Telephone Quarterly* 19 (1940): 129–38.

"Behind the Scene at 'Central.'" *Booklovers' Magazine* 2 (1903): 390–401.

Brooks, J. "The First and Only Century of Telephone Literature." In I. de S. pool, ed., *The Social Impact of the Telephone,* 208–24. Cambridge: MIT Press 1977.

Carty, J.J. "Ideals of the Telephone Service." *Bell Telephone Quarterly* 1, no. 3 (1922b): 23–37.

Casson, H.N. *The History of the Telephone.* Freeport: Books for Libraries Press 1910a.

—"The Social Value of the Telephone." *Independent* 71 (1911): 899–906.

— "Semi-Centennial of the Telephone." *Bell Telephone Quarterly* 5, no. 1 (1926a): 1–11.

Cockburn, C. "The Relations of Technology: What Implications for Theories of Sex and Class." In R. Crompton and M. Mann eds., *Gender and Stratification,* 74–85. Cambridge, UK: Polity 1986.

Fischer, C. "'Touch Someone': The Telephone Industry Discovers Sociability." *Technology and Culture* January (1988): 32–61.

Haller, J.S. and R.M. Haller. *The Physician and Sexuality in Victorian America.* New York: Norton 1974.

Lang, A. "Telephones and Letter-writing." *Critic* 48 (1906): 507–8.

Langton, J. *Natural Enemy.* New York: Penguin 1987.

Marvin, C. *When Old Technologies were New.* Cambridge: Oxford 1988.

McLuhan, M. *Understanding Media.* New York: Signet 1964.

Rhodes, F.L. "Outwitting the Weather." *Bell Telephone Quarterly* 6, no 1 (1927): 21–31.

— *Beginning of Telephony.* New York: Arno 1929.

Sayers, D.L. *The Unpleasantness at the Bellona Club.* London: NEL 1921.

Spofford, H.P. "A Rural Telephone." *Harper's Magazine* 118 (1909): 830–37.

"Telephone, The." *Chambers's Journal* 76 (1899): 310–13.

Wharton, E. *The House of Mirth.* New York: Berkley 1905.

Chapter 29

Michelle Hilmes

RADIO AND THE IMAGINED COMMUNITY

L ULLED BY THE NOTION THAT radio programming resulted from a simple and direct process of consumer choice, exercised primarily in the private sphere over trivial entertainment and leisure decisions, we lose sight of the fact that radio's public impact possessed the power to exceed by far both its makers' intentions and the momentary pleasures of the audience. Whether intentionally or not, radio really did create the voice heard round the nation; no matter what process led to the creation of its unique and oft-disparaged representations, they possessed the power to create a phenomenon greater than themselves. Perhaps the Pepsodent Company's sole intent was to sell a certain amount of toothpaste when it sponsored *Amos 'n' Andy* in 1929—and perhaps a nation tuned in solely to laugh a little and unwind after a long day—and perhaps WMAQ and NBC desired only to bring these two profitable phenomena together; nevertheless, the creation of this particular set of representations within the racial and ethnic context of the 1920s both built on and confirmed a certain set of cultural norms and values that had implications far beyond the isolated experience.

At the very least, listeners' tuning in by the tens of thousands to one specific program airing at a specific time created that shared simultaneity of experience crucial to Benedict Anderson's concept of the modern "imagined community" of nationhood. His description of the modern print-influenced citizen, the newspaper reader, even more accurately evokes the radio listener:

> [The newspaper reader] is well aware that the ceremony he performs is being replicated simultaneously by thousands (or millions) of others of whose existence he is confident, yet of whose identity he has not the slightest notion. Furthermore, this ceremony is incessantly repeated at daily or half-daily intervals throughout the calendar. What more vivid figure for the secular, historically clocked, imagined community can be envisioned? At the same time, the newspaper reader, observing exact replicas of his own paper being consumed by his subway, barbershop, or

residential neighbours, is continually reassured that the imagined world is visibly rooted in everyday life.[1]

Yet despite the rise of chains, newspapers remained a primarily local medium in the United States. Radio, more than any other agency, possessed the power not only to assert actively the unifying power of simultaneous experience but to communicate meanings about the nature of that unifying experience. Radio not only responded to the dominant social tensions of its era but, by addressing its audience's situation directly in music, comedy, and narrative drama, made those tensions the subject of its constructed symbolic universe.

Events in the last decade of the twentieth century have given us pressing new reasons to think about notions of nation and identity, and the roles that race, ethnicity, and communication play in creating them. Anderson locates the beginning of the modern sense of nation and nationality in the profit-driven spread of the medium of print—"print-capitalism, which made it possible for rapidly growing numbers of people to think about themselves, and to relate themselves to others, in profoundly new ways."[2] The spread of print, driven by commercial motives, overthrew the dominance of restrictive official languages, allowed circulation of vernaculars to a wider audience, and eventually led to the overturning of traditional authority and to a whole new concept of the relation of citizen to state, of citizen to citizen, that characterizes the modern age. This "imagined" relationship resulted from the "half fortuitous, but explosive, interaction between a system of production and productive relations (capitalism), a technology of communications (print), and the fatality of human linguistic diversity."[3] And in such an imagined relationship, based on nothing so tangible as concrete geographic boundaries, common ethnic heritage, or linguistic homogenization, but instead on assumptions, images, feelings, consciousness, it is not only the technical means of communication, but the central narratives, representations, and "memories"—and strategic forgetfulness—that they circulate that tie the nation together. "All profound changes in consciousness, by their very nature, bring with them characteristic amnesias. Out of such oblivions, in specific historical circumstances, spring narratives."[4]

The processes Anderson identifies as key resonate significantly throughout the development of radio broadcasting: a system of productive relations driven by that hallmark of twentieth-century capitalism, advertising; a technology of communications significantly different from print, yet even more capable of negotiating not only the linguistic but the ethnic and cultural diversity brought about by the transformations of the modern age; and, like film, a machine for the circulation of narratives and representations that rehearse and justify the structures of order underlying national identity.[5] We can see an awareness of these possibilities in the popular rhetoric that greeted radio from its earliest appearances.

Foremost among prevailing expectations for this new medium of "radio broadcasting" was that of unity, of connection, of "communication" in its purest sense: "Repeatedly, the achievement of cultural unity and homogeneity was held up, implicitly and explicitly, as a goal of the highest importance."[6] Radio would unite a far-flung and disparate nation, doing "more than any other agency in spreading mutual understanding to all sections of the country, to unifying our thoughts, ideals, and purposes, to making us a strong and well-knit people."[7] Echoing Anderson's description of the effects of print culture, several kinds of unity were envisioned as inherent in the spread of this new medium: physical, cultural, linguistic, and finally institutional. Radio technology, though adaptable to many uses that were not pursued, promised at the very least the same bridging of physical distance over time as other modern media of communication. This physical connection, now addressed not to individual recipients but to a vast, invisible audience at large, would most assuredly, it was felt, provide cultural unity as well. As the English language spread into every corner of the nation, "homogenization of the American mind" would follow. And even before 1926, the recognized necessity of setting up well-regulated institutional controls over this kind of power led to the formation of network broadcasting as we know it. As the nation found a voice through radio, the "imagined community" of the twentieth-century United States began to take shape.

Yet it would be a mistake to assume that it spoke univocally. The history of broadcasting is marked by struggles over appropriate use of the medium, from the amateurs and commercial interests in the early 1920s to the conflict between educational interests and networks throughout the 1930s, and this is not to mention the various internal conflicts and pressures within the institution of radio itself: between advertising agencies and networks, Chicago and New York, censors and performers, regulators and businessmen. These well-worn avenues of dispute are tied to broader areas of social controversy, and the choices made by early stations, networks, sponsors, and agencies as they invented themselves and the "business" of radio reflect the tensions of a diverse and divided society. Who would speak to whom, saying what, on whose behalf—and, conversely, who would not be allowed to speak, whose speech would be carefully limited and contained, and who would not be addressed at all—these were questions rarely asked and answered on purely economic grounds, despite broadcasting's basic commercialism. Rather, decisions on matters such as these reflected and reified structures of power and sites of resistance to the social order being created and reproduced over the invisible airwaves. We can see the first indications of these fundamental tensions in the Utopian predictions of radio's unifying power, held in tension with the dystopian possibilities that radio had to be kept from unleashing.

First of all, it seemed most obvious that the basic technical qualities of radio would unite the nation physically, across geographic space, connecting remote regions with centers of civilization and culture, tying the country together over the invisible waves of ether much as the telegraph and telephone lines had stitched America together, pole by pole, in the preceding century. Yet this new medium could also bring the public into remote private spaces, as to the housebound, the ill, and the infirm:

> The miner in his lonely mountain hut, the sailor at sea, the explorer in the frozen Arctic or Antarctic where he is completely isolated from civilization, the citizen in his home, all enjoy the best music, listen to addresses delivered by distinguished statesmen and captains of industry, reports of news events and sermons by the world's greatest preachers, no matter where they are delivered. The fact that all these forms of

information or entertainment come to him through the air is so miraculous that he never ceases to marvel at the superhuman ability of those who wrested from Nature one of her greatest secrets.[8]

Here the diminishment of physical distance and penetration into private spaces is linked explicitly to the spread of culture—and cultural hierarchies. Radio promised simultaneity of experience without direct contact, exposure to the public in the privacy of one's home. It would be twenty years before this privatized experience would begin to seem itself something of a threat; for radio's early decades, isolation was the condition that broadcasting promised to alleviate, not create, and many a paean was composed (and preserved) to celebrate this anticipated aspect of the brave new radio world.

One of the most poignant descriptions of radio's miraculous physical qualities in the popular press of the early 1920s (and there are many) comes from an account written by a mining engineer stationed in the remote Temagami Forest Reserve in Canada and appearing in *Colliers* in April 1920:

> I am in a log shack in Canada's northland. . . . Three bosom friends are here in the shack with me—my ax, my dog, and my wireless receiving set. These are vital possessions. If I lose my ax, a frozen death awaits me when the wood fire dies. If I lose my dog—well, you who love your dogs in places where human friends abound just remember where I am. If I lose my wireless set, then I am again cut off from the great outside world which I have so recently regained. . . .
>
> I reach over and touch a switch and the music of an orchestra playing at Newark, N.J., fills the room. . . . A slight turn of the magic knob and I am at Pittsburgh, Pa., listening to a man telling stories to thousands of America's listening children. With that magic knob I can command the musical programs and press news sent out from a dozen radio broadcasting stations. At will I amuse myself or garner the details of a busy world where things are happening. . . .
>
> Only yesterday to be out here was to be out of the world. But no longer. The radiophone has changed all that. Remember where I am and then you can realize how "homy" [*sic*] it is to hear a motherly voice carefully describing in detail just how to make the pie crust more flaky. No, I may be at "the back of beyond," but the whole world has marched right up to the edge of the little copper switch at my elbow.[9]

Just a few years later, RCA and AT&T were able to mobilize these expectations of physical unity to justify and promote their wired network system—despite the fact that radio's most unique and celebrated property consisted precisely of its "wireless"-ness.

However, this rhetoric of physical connection had some formidable obstacles to overcome. The erasure of distance and separation held a threat as well as a promise. In a society built on structured segmentation and social division as much as on its rhetoric of democratic equality, connectedness posed a danger to the preservation of those physical and geographic divisions supporting social distinctions, such as the separation of racial and ethnic neighborhoods, preferred leisure and cultural sites for different classes and social groups, the insulation of traditional rural society from "corrupting" city influences, and the home as private, feminine domain distinct from the masculinized public sphere.[10] Radio's "immateriality" allowed it to cross these boundaries: allowed "race" music to invade the white middle-class home, vaudeville to compete with opera in the living room, risqué city humor to raise rural eyebrows, salesmen and entertainers to find a place in the family circle. Bruce Bliven touches on this capacity and its dangers in his 1924 article, "The Legion Family and Radio":

> Ten-year-old Elizabeth is a more serious problem. Whenever she can, she gets control of the instrument, and she moves the dials until (it is usually not a difficult task) she finds a station where a jazz orchestra is playing. Then she sinks back to listen in complete contentment, nodding in rhythmic accord with the music. Her eyes seem far away, and a somewhat precocious flush comes gradually upon her cheeks. . . . Mother Legion abominates jazz.[11]

Radio's early period as a "local" medium, with stations owned and operated within a city or community, both preserved certain forms of social separation and threatened, by virtue of its diversity, pervasiveness, and escape from the usual physical mechanisms of control, many of those separations that maintained local social order. Little Elizabeth would never be allowed to go to a local jazz club, but the radio could bring the club into her living room. The creation of national networks superseded local or more random organization in a potentially invasive way, yet established a centralizing structure that could work to control the most immediately threatening aspects of local diversity and maintain local separations. Sanctioned national culture glossed over the rough edges of local or regional difference: how nice to know that Elizabeth's jazz might emanate from the respectable studios of NBC rather than that disreputable station from Chicago's South Side, playing God knows what.

Thus, radio's position in the home, while potentially importing exotic influences, could also reduce some dangers represented by exposure to the outside world. Bliven's "Legion family" acknowledged this usage too:

> Bill and Mary spend just about five times as many evenings at home as they used to; Mother Legion rejoices over this especially because of Bill, who was getting in with a rather fast crowd, which used automobiles, pocket-flasks, and road-house dance orchestras for its principal media of amusement. [Now] [t]he older children not only stay home, but they frequently bring in their friends for a radio dance.[12]

Thus, radio's space-transcending qualities, combined with its location in the family circle, held out both promise and threat. Clearly, the *what* of broadcasting would become the next pressing issue—what would come out of that miraculous set and into the living room: abominable jazz, transporting one's children away into exotic and dangerous cultural spaces? Or the strengthening of family unity through shared and culturally sanctioned experiences?

Proceeding "logically," then, from radio's physical function was its power to unify the nation culturally—for better or worse. Usually this goal was elided with the physical—as something radio would "naturally" accomplish, by the inherent character of its technology—yet this naturalizing discourse often masked implicit assumptions about exactly which aspects of the "national culture" were inherently more worthy of universal acceptance than others. Established religion (largely Christian), accepted educational offerings, official "high" culture and art—symphonic music as opposed to low jazz, "legitimate" drama, poetry readings and lectures by "experts"—this was the stuff of radio as envisioned by accounts in the press, and indeed as promoted particularly by official organs of broadcasting: the "best," the "distinguished," the "greatest." NBC announced its arrival in November 1926 by promising "quality" in broadcasting, and its definitions of exactly what this quality would consist of followed closely the myriad articles and speeches that preceded it.[13] Radio's official social role would be one of uplift, of cultural improvement, very much echoing a similar rhetoric developing out of the British Broadcasting Company at the time—yet with very different results.

For never was there a time in the development of broadcasting in the United States when commercialism, and its avenue of access to the popular, did not form a central core of the listening experience. Despite Roland Marchand's characterization of radio as "the last genteel hope," describing the initial "opposition" of networks and advertising agencies to descend to the level of hucksterism on radio that would later characterize it, in fact this reluctance existed more on the level of rhetoric than of practice.[14] Many accounts testify to the pervasiveness of commercial announcements on the air from the very earliest days, whether as plugs for the music stores that provided the records broadcast or as readings of bedtime stories for children from the newspapers that published them, or outright ownership of stations by newspapers or department stores whose chief purpose was the promotion of the parent business. Even by 1922 this was obvious to observers:

> Driblets of advertising, most of it indirect so far, to be sure, but still unmistakable, are floating through the ether every day. Concerts are seasoned here and there with a dash of advertising paprika. You can't miss it: every little classic number has a slogan all its own, if it's only the mere mention of the name—*and* the address, *and* the phone number—of the music house which arranged the programme. More of this sort of thing may be expected. And once the avalanche gets a good start, nothing short of an Act of Congress or a repetition of Noah's excitement will suffice to stop it.[15]

These broadcasters, while often paying heed to "public service" responsibilities, nevertheless had good reason to follow those tastes and desires of their publics most conducive to attracting business—as found, often, in other forms of popular entertainment—and much less reason to be concerned with public image in the eyes of official bodies than the corporate giants.

Commercialism created a popular "pull" in early radio, as it had for the penny press, vaudeville, popular music, and movies, so that alongside radio's Utopian discourse of uplift and education there existed for those concerned with cultural control a continuous dystopian fear of the popular, of those diverse and suspect cultural traditions and social groups whose access to the airwaves had begun with the amateurs and extended across the nation. Radio's commercial base gave an automatic entrée to just such elements, it was feared, and therefore the establishment of centralized institutions of control and responsibility became paramount. Occupying a central position in this set of tensions was the vast audience of women—always forming the majority of the radio and television audience—whose identification with disturbing concepts of the "mass" and vulgar popularism threatened to undermine radio's high-culture image, yet whose purchasing power provided the sine qua non of broadcasting economics.[16] Of course, commercialism retained its own objectives and exclusions, and the following chapters will trace not only the tension between official/high culture and commercial/popular pull, but also those tensions within radio's commercial discourse itself that promoted some aspects of popular culture and excluded others in the interests of advertising.

As part and parcel of this physical and cultural unification, it went almost without saying that linguistic unity would be one of broadcasting's main effects. Not only English, but proper, uninflected English, would become the national standard and norm—not a goal to be taken lightly amid the ethnic and regional diversity of the 1920s. Across many parts of the country, even among second- and third-generation immigrants, languages of the native countries continued to be spoken, at home and in church if not in school. The sudden access of the English language into the kitchens and living rooms of several-generation native but only marginally acculturated U.S. citizens would achieve a homogenizing effect rarely discussed but readily apparent.

However, if standard "announcers'" English provided a national ideal, it also worked to cast into cultural disrepute the colorful variety not only of languages, but of accents and regional dialects whose possessors now found themselves to be "different"—and not only different, but not as good.[17] It could be argued that such a standard had always existed, in the universities, boardrooms, and country clubs of the nation's cultural elite, and that radio's homogenization of accent simply made de facto norms more readily "knowable" by the public at large—an exclusive knowledge becoming more widely available—yet with expanded access came expanded expectations. Soon even widely accepted accents, such as the elite southern, became unacceptable on national network broadcasts. Speaking not only grammatically "correct" but also "nonaccented" English became a ticket into the middle class for the sons and daughters (and even great-grandsons and great-granddaughters) of immigrants; radio reinforced what local classroom education could not.

Yet radio's unprecedented verbal flood did not leave the English language unscathed by the experience. A breezy, slang-filled style of speech soon became the preferred radio mode, and networks and other bastions of "correct English" fought a losing battle to preserve the finer points of diction and pronunciation.[18] Local announcers and hosts brought regional and personal variations to the mike; indeed, many listeners spoke out strongly against attempts to install "pussy willow English" as the official dialect:

If a friend should talk to you in the stilted, unnatural sing-song of the broadcaster telling the folks where to go for somebody's soap you would end by throwing the nearest cake at him. There is a smug and utterly unsincere familiarity, a servile condescension to the listener, which must be maddening to an American public that will not endure such talking in the family or in the shop.[19]

NBC might have been presumed to have learned its lesson as early as 1925, when the popular showman "Roxy," told by WEAF management to modify his casual, vernacular delivery to a more "dignified," "formal" style consistent with station image, received a deluge of mail from fans objecting to his sudden stiffness and demanding their old friend back. Hundreds of newspapers across the country carried the story, even those much too distant to receive WEAF's signal. This clash between the high-culture aspirations of many of broadcasting's early outlets (even to the point of mandating that the unseen announcers wear formal dress) and the informal, popular tendency preferred by many in the audience would be repeated often as radio practices took shape. Not so stuffy as the highbrow written word, yet hewing to a standard well above and more unitary than the everyday, broadcast English helped to set a new popular norm across the country.

One broadcaster, later to become NBC's head of program production on the West Coast, addressing an audience of San Francisco police officers, explicitly linked radio's linguistic, cultural, and physical functions not only to Americanization but to restoration of social order:

Curiously, little is said about the problems offered by the mixture of races included in the word "American." . . . In America no . . . homogeneity exists, or can be obtained, until the entire population has been taught to speak the same language, adopt the same customs, yield to the same laws, from childhood. Now, thanks to radio, the whole country is flooded with the English language spoken by master-elocutionists. American history, American laws, American social customs are the theme of countless radio broadcasters whose words are reaching millions of our people, shaping their lives toward common understanding of American principles, American standards of living. . . . Wholesale broadcasting coupled with restricted immigration can not fail eventually to unite the entire American people into closer communion than anything yet achieved in the history of our development.[20]

Another contemporary article predicted that "those groups which still cling to alien tongues will have English forced upon them, the more they listen to broadcasting; with the result that radio proves to be an important if unconscious Americanizing influence."[21]

Yet radio's efforts toward linguistic control masked a basic transgressive quality of the medium itself, one that posed a less obvious but even more dangerous threat to social hierarchy and order: its ability to transcend the visual. In a society based on visual cues, where appearance superseded almost every other social indicator,[22] radio's ability to escape visual overdetermination had the potential to set off a virtual riot of social signifiers—indeed, this is one of radio's most fascinating attributes. Adults played the roles of children and animals, two-hundred-pound women played romantic ingenues, and ninety-pound men played superheroes; whites frequently impersonated blacks, though rarely vice versa; and one of America's most popular entertainers was a wooden dummy. Women could masquerade as men and, much more often, men as women—and further, men could enter the home to entertain the woman of the house seductively over her morning coffee; women had the potential to enter the public sphere and assume the voice of authority, evading the customary physical and social barriers. How could one be sure a person belonged to his or her purported racial or ethnic group over the radio? How could class distinction be maintained without its usual context of visual cues?

Radio responded by obsessively rehearsing these distinctions, endlessly circulating and performing structured representations of ethnicity, race, gender, and other concentrated sites of social and cultural norms—all through language, dialect, and carefully selected aural context. Early radio seemed absorbed with the portrayal of "difference," of the exotic, from the *Cliquot Club Eskimoes* and the *A&P Gypsies* to the narrative development of *Amos 'n' Andy* and *The Goldbergs*. This was frequently accomplished by the use of distinct and stereotypical dialects and accents, carried over from the realm of vaudeville and the minstrel show. The prevalence of minstrel routines, characters, and dialect on early radio is frequently overlooked, and their use points to central sites of tension within U.S. culture, as the culturally undesirable was projected onto an easily identifiable, culturally devalued minority group.

Variety programs developed elaborate frameworks for incorporating "other" characters into their regularly repeating nucleus of performers, perhaps brought to their fullest flower by Fred Allen in "Allen's Alley"—populated by the likes of Mrs. Nussbaum, Ajax Cassidy, Senator Beauregard Claghorn, and Titus Moody. The flip side of this otherness was the rehearsing of the "norm," the typical American family, in such precursors of the television domestic sitcom as *Vic and Sade, One Man's Family,* and *The Aldrich Family.* In place of traditional class attributes, radio created its own caste of celebrities, drawing as well on the visually familiar ranks of Hollywood stars. The problem of "anchoring" the slippery and potentially transgressive signification of radio's aural signifiers to the set of intended and authorized meanings of networks and producers became increasingly central to network functions, giving rise to "continuity acceptance" and later "standards and practices" departments that helped to legitimate the networks' existence and functions.[23]

Institutional unity, it soon became apparent, had to be established if radio's dystopian potential—physical, cultural, linguistic—were to be held in check so that its Utopian "nature" could be fulfilled. Until a comprehensive institutional structure could be developed, a state of experimentation and regional difference existed that allowed for competing definitions of radio's business and concerns, some of which were clearly perceived as transgressive. The importance of Chicago as a center of broadcast innovation points up the culturally homogenizing power of networks as structures stabilized in the late 1920s and early 1930s. Most of the program forms and many of the programs themselves soon to become the most popular on NBC and

CBS originated not with the official broadcasting outlets of the major radio companies, usually located in New York, but in the newspaper- and department store-owned stations of Chicago's hectic commercial environment. As these programs found national sponsorship and a national audience over the networks, they were adapted to fit "higher," more stringent network standards, and standard formats emerged on which imitations and early forms of "spin-offs" could build. However, continuing sources of organizational tension, such as the rapidly developing dominance of advertising agencies in program production—in particular over daytime serial production, throughout broadcasting's history—also resisted network control and containment.

The institution of NBC in 1926 and CBS two years later effectively provided the technical, economic, and cultural unification envisioned in Anderson's model of the imagined nation, on which future legislation would rest—and further consolidate. It could be argued that the decisive factor leading to the defeat of educational or public control of radio occurred not in 1934, after the great Communications Act debates, but in the years from 1922 to 1926, as wired interconnection of stations gradually undermined radio's local base and made advertising support nearly inevitable. Certainly by 1934, as one active participant admitted, the "rugged individualism" of commercial competition had set the structures of private dominance past the point of alteration: "What individualism really means in matters of this sort is the practice of proceeding helter-skelter without any plan until an impossible situation has developed, and all sorts of vested interests have been created, and then trying to impose a plan retrospectively in face of innumerable technical and legal obstacles."[24] This is certainly true of the "American system" of commercial network broadcasting by 1934: a de facto and never officially agreed-upon industrial and cultural standard appeared firmly in place, where it would work to centralize and unify American cultural experience and identity as no other medium had ever attempted.

Physically, culturally, in a common language and through national semipublic institutions, radio spoke to, and about, a nation. Like Gertrude Berg—and with uncanny echoes of Benedict Anderson—one 1924 writer clearly envisioned the "Social Destiny of Radio":

> Look at a map of the United States, of Canada, of any country, and try to conjure up a picture of what radio broadcasting will eventually mean to the hundreds of little towns that are set down in type so small that it can hardly be read. How unrelated they seem! Then picture the tens of thousands of homes in the cities, the valleys, along the rivers, homes not noted at all on the map. These little towns, these unmarked homes in vast countries seem disconnected. It is only an idea that holds them together,— the idea that they form part of a territory called "our country." One home in Chicago might as well be in Zanzibar so far as another in Massachusets is concerned, were it not for this binding sense of nationality. If these little towns and villages so remote from one another, so nationally related and yet physically so unrelated, could be made to acquire a sense of intimacy, if they could be brought into direct contact with each other! . . . This is exactly what radio is bringing about.[25]

Notes

1. Benedict Anderson, *Imagined Communities: Reflections on the Origin and Spread of Nationalism* (London: Verso, 1983), 35.
2. Ibid., 36.
3. Ibid., 42–43.
4. Ibid., 204.
5. For discussion of these issues in film, see Lester Friedman, ed., *Unspeakable Images: Ethnicity and the American Cinema* (Urbana: University of Illinois Press, 1991).
6. Susan Douglas, *The Invention of American Broadcasting 1899–1922* (Baltimore: John Hopkins University Press, 1987), 306–7.
7. Stanley Frost, "Radio Dreams that Can Come True," *Colliers,* June 10, 1922, 16.
8. Frank Leroy Blanchard, "Experiences of a National Advertiser with Broadcasting," April 15, 1930, station files—KDKA, BPL.
9. M. J. Caveney, "New Voices in the Wilderness," *Colliers,* April 1920, 18.
10. Lynn Spigel discusses popular fears of the invasive qualities of TV in undermining paternal authority in the family in *Make Room for TV: Television and the Family Ideal in Postwar America* (Chicago: University of Chicago Press, 1992).
11. Bruce Bliven, "The Legion Family and the Radio: What We Hear when We Tune In," *Century Magazine,* October 1924, 813.
12. Ibid., 818.
13. For the cultural precedents of this phenomenon, see Lawrence W. Levine, *Highbrow/Lowbrow: The Emergence of Cultural Hierarchy in America* (Cambridge: Harvard University Press, 1988).
14. Roland Marchand, *Advertising the American Dream: Making Way for Modernity 1920–1940* (Berkeley: University of California Press, 1985), 88–94.
15. Joseph H. Jackson, "Should Radio Be Used for Advertising?" *Radio Broadcast,* November 1922, 76.
16. At the extreme of cultural deviance, even after the standardization caused by networks and frequency regulation following the 1927 Radio Act, a few broadcasters managed to escape the disciplinary reach of official regulation by moving across the Rio Grande into Mexico. See Gene Fowler and Bill Crawford, *Border Radio* (New York: Limelight, 1990).
17. Anderson refers to "languages of power": "Certain dialects inevitably were 'closer' to each print-language and dominated their final forms. Their disadvantaged cousins, still assimilable to the emerging print-language, lost caste, above all because they were unsuccessful (or only relatively successful) in insisting on their own print-form." *Imagined Communities,* 45.
18. Kitty Parsons, "Announcers' English," *Scholastic Magazine,* January 11, 1936, 13, 27; S. H. Hawkins, "Here's the IDEAL Announcer!" *Radio Age,* April 1925, 50, 52; "The High and Mighty Place of the Announcer," *Radio Broadcast,* December 1926, 180–81.
19. "Pussy Willow English," *Saturday Review of Literature,* June 16, 1934, 752. On Roxy, see James C. Young, "New Fashions in Radio Programs," *Radio Broadcast,* May 1925, 83–89.
20. Don E. Gilman, quoted in Arthur Garbette, "Interview with Don E. Gilman," *San Francisco Police and Peace Officers' Journal,* February 1929, 28–29.
21. Charles M. Adams, "Radio and Our Spoken Language: Local Differences Are Negligible, But Radio Shows Up Personalities," *Radio News,* September 1927, 208.
22. See Robert H. Wiebe, *The Segmented Society: An Introduction to the Meaning of America* (New York: Oxford University Press, 1975), 30–33; Marchand, *Advertising the American Dream,* 208–17; Stuart Ewen, *Captains of Consciousness: Advertising and the Social Roots of Consumer Culture* (New York: McGraw-Hill, 1976).
23. See Matthew Murray, "Television Wipes Its Feet: The Commercial and Ethical Considerations behind the Adoption of the Television Code," *Journal of Popular Film and Television* 21 (Fall 1993): 128–38.

24.   William A. Orton, *America in Search of a Culture* (Boston: Little, Brown, 1933), quoted in Levering Tyson, "Where Is American Radio Heading?" in Levering Tyson and Judith Waller, *The Future of Radio and Educational Broadcasting* (Chicago: University of Chicago Press, 1934), 18.

25.   Waldemar Kaempffert, "The Social Destiny of Radio," *Forum* 71 (June 1924): 771.

Chapter 30

John Durham Peters

THE TELEPHONIC UNCANNY AND THE PROBLEM OF COMMUNICATION

Reach Out and Touch Someone: The Telephonic Uncanny

[**W**RITING IN 1909, SOCIOLOGIST CHARLES** Horton] Cooley thought that communication had made the old scale of distances obsolete. He and his contemporaries lived in a universe in which ghostly effigies of human personalities were beginning to swim everywhere. He saw nothing uncanny or suspicious in mediated communication. Subsequent developments in media culture raised the question just how much the body could remain an indifferent presence to communication. Touch, as it happens, could not be suppressed forever.

Take the telephone, for instance. The telephone, after fits and starts, has solidified its use as a means of staying in personal touch with individuals who are not immediately at hand, while wireless technologies (radio and television) have largely gone in the opposite direction of having a diffuse and general addressee. In principle, both telephone and wireless technologies can be either a central exchange for many voices (party lines or radio broadcasting) or a means of point-to-point contact (cellular phones or ham radio). The issue is not so much the inherent properties of the medium as the social constellation of speakers and hearers that became enforced as normative. Radio became the carrier of messages aimed for low-resolution address, and the telephone, of those for high-resolution.

In the dawn of telephone systems, the personal touch was omnipresent. Every call was placed with the aid of a human operator, and up to the 1880s there were no telephone *numbers:* operators simply used the names of subscribers to track the slots on the switchboard. It took the Bell system several years, in fact, to persuade all its customers to switch to numbers. Even then many local exchanges had prefixes based on a sense of local geography—Pennsylvania 6–5000, for example. Even so, the idea of confidential conversation heard only by two people was slow in coming, just as it was in the mails. One technical problem resolved early was how to get only one specific telephone in a networked system to ring, for all would ring when one was called. The telephone, like all media of multiplication (transmission and recording), was essentially a public medium. Just as Warren and Brandeis in the 1890s sought to establish a right to privacy and the anonymously posted letter arose in the 1850s, telephone managers in the 1890s and early 1900s sought to secure private channels of contact between unique addresses.[1] The task again was to domesticate the plurality of media by the singularity of "communication."

Before automated switching, the routine medium of routing telephone calls was the switchboard operator. We have met this figure before—passive, neutral or feminine gender identity, servicing an apparatus of message delivery—in the spiritualist medium and in Bartleby the scrivener. An Ontario newspaper in the 1890s reported on operators: "The girls then, are automata. . . . They looked as cold and passionless as icebergs," and an early training manual prescribed that each "operator must now be made as nearly as possible a paragon of perfection, a kind of human machine, the exponent of speed and courtesy; a creature spirited enough to move like chain lightning, and with perfect accuracy; docile enough to deny herself the privilege of the last word."[2] These descriptions have the virtue, at least, of explicitness: the operator's body—her voice, gestures and fatigue—was, like that of typists as well, a key site of psychotechnical discipline.[3] The telephone operator antedates the cyborg, a plastically gendered creature formed of electrical wiring and the organic body.[4] Like spiritualist mediums, operators inhabit a profoundly liminal space. The female body hidden at the heart of a national communications network, appearing only in impersonal voice, is an archetypal figure. In popular culture the operator was often treated as a heroine who, knowing everyone's habits, could bring people together in emergencies: the operator as matchmaker, lifeguard, or angel of mercy. She was always betwixt and between.[5]

Like Diotima's Eros, operators had the job of managing the gaps and ferrying messages back and forth across the chasm. Indeed, there was something sexy about operators, with their voices traveling across the expanses. As an American manager wrote in 1905, "There is something about the sound of the voice of a girl on the wire that sets a young man into a wooing mood."[6] The telephone itself has been sung and lamented as an agent of romantic coupling and haunting, being a classic go-between for lovers. Marriages were performed over the telephone, as over the radio, an obligatory coming-of-age event for each new medium of distance communication.[7] The arrows of Eros and of electrical circuit diagrams here converge. Note too that the couplet—public radio, private telephone—has made the notion of a radio-sex industry sound laughable, but with 900 numbers there is, alas, a thriving phone-sex business.

Once the switchboard connection was made, there were still address gaps. Without access to the bodily presence of the other, initial interaction on the telephone dramatized the likelihood that one did not know whom one was addressing. In face-to-face interaction we usually know whom we are speaking to, save in cases of imposture or more difficult philosophical questions of identity. Negotiations of identity became routine in telephone etiquette. When my second son was younger, he would call a friend's house and speak to whoever answered as if that person were his friend and knew who was calling. He hadn't yet learned to identify himself or the interlocutor, failing to recognize the need for connection management in a medium that cloaks presence. Different styles of decorum arose to manage the missing persons over the telephone. In the Netherlands, telephone speakers are expected to identify themselves at once: those answering must answer with their names, and the callers must do so as well. In the United States norms of self-identification are far more relaxed, and some callers never bother to identify themselves at all, assuming their voice is recognized. In habitual face-to-face interaction, such work at initial coupling is always implicit; thanks to the media-stimulated dream of wondrous contact, we have grown accustomed in the twentieth century to finding such problems everywhere in communication.

In early telephone culture modes of interaction were sought that dispensed with the need for cues of presence.[8] The telephone could be both a handicap (in its blindness) and a sensory extension (a hearing aid and voice amplification device). A 1915 piece states the telephone's deficiencies with remarkable economy: "Conversation by telephone is talk shorn of all the adventitious aids that spring from the fact of physical and visual proximity." The undifferentiated totality of the face-to-face setting is redescribed according to the new audiovisual order of silent cinema and pictureless telephones. "There is no flashing glance to 'register,' as the movie actors have it, wrath; no curling lip to betoken scorn; no twinkling eye to suggest whimsicality; none of the charm of personal presence that might give substance to an attenuated argument or power to a feeble retort. The voice must do it all."[9]

The telephone could be strange indeed. In it, the face-to-face setting could be redefined as a communication problem, with its "adventitious aids" of "physical and visual proximity" that had never before been distinct channels. The historian Catherine Covert argued that the telephone served cultural critics as an ordinary baseline against which to measure the weirdness of radio in the years after the Great War. In contrast to the supernatural world of radio was "the quite worldly experience of Americans with the telephone—as a direct connection between human beings."[10] In fact, the telephone evoked many of the same anxieties as radio: strange voices entering the home, forced encounters, the disappearance of one's words into an empty black hole, and absent faces of the listeners. An *Atlantic Monthly* piece from 1920, written in the voice of a neurasthenic woman, notes: "It is bad to hear myself talk on any occasion. It is worse to talk into an empty black hole, without the comfort and guide of a responsive face before me." The telephone's lack of manners also irks her. "It makes no preambles and respects no privacies," rings without regard to how occupied one may be in other tasks, and pulls one into "unexplained encounters" with strangers.[11] Our writer notes the classic features of dissemination; Socrates too was worried about odd encounters and indifference to the personal situation.

The looseness of personal identification lies at the core of the telephone's eeriness. Even today, there is nothing quite so unnerving as a caller who repeatedly calls and hangs up or who never identifies himself (it is usually a he) and simply breathes into the phone. Such violations of etiquette call forth the primal uncanniness of the medium. Taking "obscene" in the original sense of something appearing that is supposed to be concealed (off-scene), the notion of an obscene phone call is a redundancy. In ways that foreshadow recent concerns about how loosened markers of personal identity allow abusive discourse in cyberspace, such as the tirades known as "flames," commentators attributed telephone rudeness to the loss of instantaneous recognition in the face-to-face setting.[12] In the words of one 1918 writer, "There are men who, as someone has put it, take advantage of their 'low visibility' over the telephone to act as they never would if face to face with you."[13] The relative anonymity of the Internet, it is similarly argued, allows people to get away with vituperative modes of discourse they would never dare in person.

The telephone also contributed to the modern derangement of dialogue by splitting conversation into two halves that meet only in the cyberspace of the wires. Dialogue, despite its reputation for closeness and immediacy, occurs over the telephone in a no-man's-land as elusive as writing itself. The effect of such flayed discourse has been compared to schizophrenia and to crosscutting in film editing.[14] Mark Twain caught both schizoid and comic dimensions in his satire "A Telephonic Conversation":

> Then followed that queerest of all the queer things in this world—a conversation with only one end to it. You hear questions asked; you don't hear the answer. You hear invitations given; you hear no thanks in return. You have listening pauses of dead silence, followed by irrelevant or unjustifiable exclamations of glad surprise or sorrow or dismay. You can't make head or tail of the talk, because you never hear anything that the person at the other end of the wire says.

The piece then offers an account of one such "conversation," a premise for Twain to indulge in a series of droll nonsequiturs, such as:

> Pause.
>   It's forty-ninth Deuteronomy, sixty-fourth to ninety-seventh inclusive.
> I think we ought all to read it often.
>   Pause.
>   Perhaps so; I generally use a hair-pin.[15]

The subtext of the story, corroborating other comments of the period, is the contrast between masculine gruffness and abruptness on the phone and feminine talkativeness; it is the male narrator, for instance, who is asked to ring the central office for a female member of his household.

Two one-sided conversations that couple only in virtual space: this is the nature of speech on the telephone. Naturally, the question arises whether such coupling ever occurs. In Dorothy Parker's early 1930s monologue, "A Telephone Call," a woman pleads frenziedly with God to have a man friend call, but in the course of the monologue he does not; the title of the story names what never takes place. Waiting for a call that never comes exemplifies not only the loneliness of the neglected lover but the whole problem of how to know that one has made contact at all; it is not by accident that the monologue is addressed to God. Parker gives us a neat communication circuit: she places a call that seeks as its answer another call. The voice of desire seeks another voice of desire. Aldous Huxley's "Over the Telephone" from the same era reverses the gender of the supplicant: a young poet mentally rehearses his grandiloquent invitation to a woman friend to attend the opera, imaginatively taking the entire evening to its happy conclusion as the lovers kiss in his flat. When after many mishaps the operator finally makes the connection with the woman, however, he stumbles hopelessly and she declines owing to a previous engagement: "Despairingly, Walter took the receiver from his ear. The voice squeaked away impotently into the air like the ghost of a Punch and Judy show." The breach in telephonic communication, like that of the planned date, is marked as an erotic failure, squeaking impotently into the air.[16] Such an attempt at "communication" is at best a situation of hermeneutic rupture, two sides barred from each other by some deep distance.

Kafka and the Telephone

The spookiest of all explorers of the telephone, and of "communication" as two monologues that may never connect, even in imagined space, was Franz Kafka. All hermeneutics is the art of reading texts by an unintended audience; it is a mode of eavesdropping. Facing the dead, or a partner who cannot, will not, or does not respond, can leave one in a tizzy of guesswork. Mediated communication, as by the telephone, teaches us that we are always eavesdropping. How is the voice of Parker's monologue to know what the lack of a call signifies—rejection, a lost number, or nothing at all? All that separates desolation from elation is a phone call. The exploding of dialogue into two remotely linked halves makes the validity of interpretation obscure. The inability to distinguish inner projections from outer messages flourishes in conditions where interpreters have to bear the weight of the entire communication circuit. This inability, psychologically conceived, is called paranoia; socially conceived, we should call it mass communication. Those who have ears to hear will hear. Kafka is our guide to these conditions.

In a short parable called "The Neighbor," Kafka extends the idealist architecture by making the walls too thin rather than too thick.[17] The narrator, a young business-man, tells how an identical office adjacent his own is rented by another young businessman named Harras, whose business is mysterious but seems the same as his own. The two never meet, only brush past each other on the stairs. Their only relations are mediated and imagined; they never actually converse with each other. The walls are so miserably thin, however, that everything can be heard in the neighboring office. Even worse, on the common wall of the two offices, the narrator has a telephone; even if it were placed on the opposite wall, Harras could still hear everything. Ever unsure whether the neighbor is listening, the narrator adopts a roundabout style of speech in his dealings over the phone and studiously never mentions the names of customers. Yet he is sure he is still betraying secrets. "If I really wanted to exaggerate— as people often do, to make things clearer to themselves—I could say: Harras needs no telephone, he uses mine."

Harras is no wiretapper. This is a story of a doppelgänger and a telephone, both of which involve enigmatic splittings of identity and conversation. Harras (as the narrator surmises) eavesdrops on the ghosts that proliferate in the space between the two termini of the telephone conversation. Thus he is able to outsmart the narrator: by figuring out who and where the person on the other end of the line is, Harras speeds through the city and meets the customer before the narrator is even off the phone, working against him (or so fantasizes the narrator). In a new twist on telephone harassment, Harras uses the telephone not simply to breathe or threaten, but to transport his person as fleetly as electrical speech. The parable is not only a meditation on surveillance and the futility of coded speech to conceal secrets, but a fantasy on the comparative advantage of presence. Kafka catches the horror of speaking on the phone when one's double—the proxy of the voice—goes streaking through the wires to appear in the presence of the telephone partner. Anyone who has ever used a phone to discuss a sensitive matter knows how your double can arrive on the other end and work against you. The narrator's paranoia—literally, the sense of other minds—is appropriate to a system of mechanically multiplied personal tokens.

Another telephone scene occurs in the beginning of Kafka's posthumous *The Castle* (1926). "K" enters a village inn and finds himself accosted by a representative of the Castle, a vaporous entity whose identity remains permanently veiled throughout the book and thus functions as an allegory of infinity and bureaucracy. Haughtily K claims to be "the surveyor," summoned by the Castle, and the representative checks twice with the Castle by telephone. On being recognized by the Castle the second time, K reflects that this is propitious (since it gets him off the hook from the representative, who had wanted to banish him from the country) but also unpropitious (because it means the Castle is on to him and is giving him the chance to make his next move). K does not know, cannot know, whether he has been recognized or is only party to a fabrication.

This interpretive wavering before an enigmatic answer is a fundamental experience in the modern world: carrying on a fencing match either with a partner who seems to be responding but whose motives are inscrutable or with one whose responses can never be verified as responses. Modern men and women stand before bureaucracies and their representations or wait by telephones in the same way that sinners stood before the God who hides his face: anxiously sifting the chaos of events for signs and messages. The *deus absconditus* (hidden god) of theology no longer hides in the farthest corners of the universe; his successor has moved into the infernal machines of administration. Dante's vision of the place beyond the heavens was a kaleidoscopic reflection of spheres against spheres, a multifoliate rose of infinitely refracted light. K, like the rest of us, peers into a place where the reverberations are not optical but informational. (Game theory, uniquely appropriate for twentieth-century organizational culture, is the scientized form of this experience.) K does not know whether the permission to stay in the village is a mandate from the Castle itself, from some sleepy bureaucrat on the other end of the line trying to cover a possible failure to note K's arrival, or from the representative himself, fascinated by K's haughty certitudes. K must interpret the gestures from the Castle (if they indeed come from the Castle at all) with the same attentiveness with which augurs once monitored the sky above the *templum* for the flight of birds or the fall of stars. He must follow them with the falsificationist rationality of the modern scientist, carefully peeling away alternative hypotheses, checking the data for clerical errors, strenuously trying to avoid fudging the data with his own unconscious visions, wondering if the instrument was flawed or tapped the right information. To survive in the modern world, men and women must become diviners of inscrutable others, interpret the moods of secretaries, the words of department heads, the decisions of deans and

CEOs, and shake-ups in the organization of the Kremlin, White House, or Vatican as if they were the language of some hidden, murky, remote god, content to speak only in darkness and in dreams.

Walter Benjamin once said that there are two wrong ways to read Kafka: naturally and supernaturally.[18] The point is Kafka's astounding ability to hover between the two, infinitely postponing a decision. He is the greatest theorist of organizational communication of this century. As Benjamin says, "The world of offices and registries, of musty, shabby, dark rooms, is Kafka's world."[19] Kafka is the premier existential student of bureaucracy, better than Max Weber at interpreting the dark weight of official maneuvers. Kafka's world is not quite a world of conspiratorial deceptions and evil lies that might in principle be uncovered; it is a world in which the ultimate source of all messages is hidden. He knows what is at stake in deciding what is a message, what is a projection, and what is some strange undecidable charade of people in mutual collusion who do not know it or never admit it. In bureaucratic mazes, how is one to know if the memo is a disclosure or a ruse, signal or noise? K, a surveyor, one who must read the marks of ownership, never knows if such marks express a coherent design or if whatever design exists is only a paranoid projection of an overactive interpreter.

The signs are all around us; they simply refuse to tell us how to read them. We hesitate, caught between the fear of being paranoid ("everything's a message") and the fear of missing a revelation if we act as if nothing is a message. The inability to make certain whether a sign is a projection of the self or an utterance of the other, an interpretive artifact or an objective pattern in the world, confronts a variety of social types: Wizards who read tea leaves or entrails, believers who receive answers to prayers, takers of the Turing test who wager on whether the conversant is a human or a smart machine, and anyone who talks with another person on any passionate, painful, or delicate topic.

Small wonder the Kabbalah should be so intriguing a model to theorists of interpretation.[20] For Kabbalah is in part the reading of intent in things where no meaning was intended—"to read what was never written," in one of Benjamin's favorite lines. As Borges notes, it is easy to ridicule the idea that every letter of the text of the Hebrew Bible was willed, so that one may find truth in numbers, acrostics, and anagrams. According to Borges, the Kabbalist vision of Scripture was of a text in which the collaboration of chance was nil. The ridicule lies in this: We see people confusing their own prodigious interpretive powers with the mind of God, confusing the statistical regularities of Hebrew consonants with divine order. The lesson of Kabbalah is to refuse contingency. Mystical styles of reading—fate, handwriting, and so on—refuse to accept the idea that the world could be meaningless. Every dot of an *i,* fall of a leaf, flight of a bird, the pattern that a snail makes, the floating fractals of clouds—are all a secret language. In one of Borges's stories, "The God's Script" the spots on a jaguar's back hold the magical name that gives its possessor all power and the key to the universe. Such readers risk absurdity—the fate of all of Kafka's heroes, quixotic battlers against castles.

The question of who owns meaning has been raised in literary theory over the past quarter century: the reader's creativity, the author's intent, the text itself, the interpretive community, the canon, or the transaction of reader and text? Or is meaning available only for lease? This question, however, is much bigger than theory; it is a question on which life and death hang in a mediated world. The question asks: Does nature speak, does God speak, does fate speak, do bureaucracies speak, or am I just making all this up? Where do projections of my self end and where do authentic signals from the other begin? Is all meaning the spider spinning of my own fertile cogitations? Can the object itself ever break through the veil? Are all the whisperings of spirit, the designs in the entrails, the answers to prayers just so much alienated human energy? Is communication anything but overlapping monologues? Did she ask me to come to her, or am I just imagining it? Did he really say he would call?

Kafka ponders the strange communication circuit of the telephone to reveal potentials for trouble in face-to-face interaction that often are skillfully kept out of sight. He explores the twilight zones in which the signal-to-noise ratio approaches zero or infinity. In both "The Neighbor" and *The Castle,* the telephone foregrounds potentials for schizophrenia, paranoia, dissimulation, and eavesdropping that lurk in everyday speech. The common world may be habitual and sound, but breakdown allows all the primal uncanniness to return. In a blackout, or the telephone's suddenly going dead, or the static caught between the stations, we discover the gaps, not the bridges. To quote a thinker whose sensibility is often akin to Kafka's, "Pathology, with its magnification and exaggeration, can make us aware of normal phenomena which we should otherwise have missed."[21]

The historicity of Kafka's insights is beyond doubt. He dwelled in a zone where the level of message scatter was unbearable, though he died (1924) before the full splendor of radio's bazaar could be appreciated. Today most communications are voices crying in the wilderness. Turn on the radio or television and you will instantly discover a limbo of missed connections: pitch artists waxing earnest about "rock-hard abs" or engagement rings, newscasters describing the latest trauma to life and limb, songsters lamenting lost love in the musical dialects of opera and country. The paraphernalia of dead letters is no longer on display only at auctions: it is the daily stuff of public communication in our time. There are so many kinds of voices in the world, said Saint Paul. Or as Sherlock Holmes sniffed concerning the "agony columns" (personals) in turn of the century London newspapers: "'Dear me!' said he, turning over the page, 'what a chorus of groans, cries, and bleatings! What a ragbag of singular happenings! . . . Bleat, Watson—unmitigated bleat!'"[22] Unmitigated bleat mixed with the rare voice of truth crying in the wilderness: this is the formula for so much of modern communications, in spiritualism, the broadcast ether, and much of what we say to each other.

Notes

1.   See Michèle Martin, *"Hello, Central?" Gender, Technology, and Culture in the Formation of Telephone Systems* (Montreal: McGill-Queen's University Press, 1991).
2.   Martin, *"Hello, Central?"* 70, 73.
3.   See Helmut Gold and Annette Koch, eds., *Fräulein vom Amt* (Munich: Prestel, 1993), and Friedrich A. Kittler, *Grammophon, Film, Typewriter* (Berlin: Brinkmann und Bose, 1986), 273–89.

4. Donna J. Haraway, *Simians, Cyborgs, and Women: The Reinvention of Nature* (New York: Routledge, 1991), and Claudia Springer, *Electronic Eros: Bodies and Desire in the Post-industrial Age* (Austin: University of Texas Press, 1996).

5. See Herbert N. Casson, "The Social Value of the Telephone," *Independent,* 26 October 1911, 899–906; "How the Hotel Telephone Girl Sizes You Up," *American Magazine,* August 1923, 23, 70, 72; "When the 'Hello Girl' Tries Hand at Detective Work," *Literary Digest,* 5 November 1927, 52–54.

6. Martin, *"Hello, Central?"* 95. Besides the general point that distance breeds eros, Rick Altman suggests the sexiness of the female voice may owe to the suppression of high frequencies in telephone sound (designed on the model of the male voice), thus tending to make female telephone voices into sultry contraltos.

7. One example of telephone marriage is given in Mary B. Mullett, "How We Behave when We Telephone," *American Magazine,* November 1918, 44–45, 94, at 45. A 1995 *National Geographic* article pictures "first virtual reality wedding" as a physically separated couple "embracing" in virtual reality. And yet the meeting in the flesh cannot be postponed forever: "There was no question about the ending though: a real kiss after the virtual one." Joel L. Swerdlow, Louis Psihoyos, and Allen Carroll, "Information Revolution," *National Geographic Magazine* 188, 4 (1995): 35.

8. Lana Rakow, *Gender on the Line: Women, the Telephone, and Community Life* (Urbana: University of Illinois Press, 1992), 43, treats the relative ineptitude of men in the town of "Prospect" at managing telephone talk.

9. "On Conversation by Telephone," *Independent,* 10 May 1915, 229–30.

10. Catherine L. Covert, "'We May Hear Too Much': American Sensibility and the Response to Radio, 1919–24," in *Mass Media between the Wars,* 1918–41, ed. Catherine L. Covert and John D. Stevens (Syracuse: Syracuse University Press, 1984), 202.

11. "Telephone Terror," *Atlantic Monthly,* February 1920, 279–81.

12. Mark Dery, ed., *Flame Wars: The Discourse of Cyberculture* (Durham: Duke University Press, 1994).

13. Mullett, "How We Behave when We Telephone," 45.

14. Frank Kessler, "Bei Anruf Rettung!" in *Telefon und Kultur: Das Telefon im Spielfilm,* ed. B. Debatin and H. J. Wulff (Berlin: Volker Spiess, 1991), 167–73.

15. Mark Twain, "A Telephonic Conversation," in *"The $30,000 Bequest" and Other Stories* (1880; New York: Harpers, 1917), 204–8.

16. Parker, "Telephone CM," 333–39; Aldous Huxley, "Over the Telephone," in *The Smart Set Anthology,* ed. Burton Rascoe (New York: Reynal and Hitchcock, 1934), 122–28.

17. Franz Kafka, "Der Nachbar," in *Beschreibung eines Kampfes: Novellen, Skizzen, Aphorismen aus dem Nachlaß* (Frankfurt am Main: Fischer, 1989), 100–101.

18. Walter Benjamin, "Franz Kafka," in *Illuminations,* ed. Hannah Arendt (New York: Schocken, 1968), 127.

19. Benjamin, "Franz Kafka," 112.

20. See Harold Bloom, *Kabbalah and Criticism* (New York: Seabury, 1975); George Steiner, *After Babel: Aspects of Language and Translation* (New York: Oxford University Press, 1975), chap. 2; Susan A. Handelman, *The Slayers of Moses: The Emergence of Rabbinic Interpretation in Modern Literary Theory* (Albany: SUNY Press, 1982), chap. 8; Handelman, *Fragments of Redemption: Jewish Thought and Literary Theory in Benjamin, Scholem, and Levinas* (Bloomington: Indiana University Press, 1991); and Robert Alter, *Necessary Angels: Tradition and Modernity in Kafka, Benjamin, and Scholem* (Cambridge: Harvard University Press, 1991).

21. Sigmund Freud, *New Introductory Lectures on Psycho-analysis,* Great Books of the Western World, ed. Robert Maynard Hutchins, vol. 54 (1932; Chicago: Encyclopaedia Britannica, 1952), 830.

22. Arthur Conan Doyle, "The Adventure of the Red Circle," in *The Complete Sherlock Holmes* (Garden City, N.Y.: Doubleday, 1930), 2:904.

Chapter 31

Gerard Goggin

CELLULAR DISABILITY: CONSUMPTION, DESIGN AND ACCESS

OFTEN OVERLOOKED AS MEDIA USERS and cultural agents, people with disabilities number approximately half a billion people worldwide. Estimates of people with disabilities in any population vary but figures of between 15 and 20 per cent are often cited in many countries (ABS 2004; Metts 2000; on the difficulties and politics of defining and measuring the incidence of disability see Abberley 1992 and Altman 2001). While people with disabilities have had accessibility problems with many technologies, they have also as a group been avid and often pioneering users. Yet in the history of cell phone culture, disability has played a significant yet overlooked role.

In this light, this chapter looks at the consumption of cell phones by people with disabilities and the responses to this by technologists, as a neglected yet richly illustrative component of cell phone culture. To give some background, in the first section I explain contemporary social, political, and cultural approaches to understanding disability. Secondly, I discuss the incompatibility of second-generation digital cell phones for hearing-aid users and Deaf people using teletypewriters. Then I turn, thirdly, to users' cultural and social innovation, exploring Deaf people's use of short text messages (SMS). Fourthly, I contrast Deafness and cell phones with Blind people's non-use and use of SMS. Finally I conclude with reflections on disability, consumption, and cell phones.

Approaching Disability and the Cell Phone

As yet the new ways of studying disability as an integral part of humanities and social sciences are still not well understood – especially when it comes to the undertheorised area of disability and technology. In this chapter I draw upon critical disability studies (Albrecht, Seelman, and Bury 2001; Snyder, Brueggemann, and Garland-Thomson 2002). Diverse and interdisciplinary in its constitution, critical disability studies critiques the dominant understanding of disability via the medical model, where disability is believed to be located in the individual's deficient, sick, or abnormal body. It also opposes the allied, and historically anterior, charity discourse of disability, according to which the person with disability is to be pitied and controlled by benevolent institutions (Stiker 1999). As it has emerged in the United States, Canada, the United Kingdom, Europe, and Australia, critical disability studies theorists typically propose a sociopolitical approach to disability. For instance, British theorists of the social model propose a distinction between an individual's impairments (the bodily dimension) and disability which is socially produced (exemplified in the barriers society unfairly creates for the person with impairments) (Barnes and Mercer 2003). Developed with my friend and collaborator Christopher Newell, my approach seeks to go beyond classic social model accounts by acknowledging the wide range and varieties of impairment and disability; by acknowledging the interaction among gender, sex, race, class, and age in the social relations of disability; by seeking to understand the important cultural dimension of disability; and in proposing the importance of technology in the contemporary social relations of disability.

To date there has been little scholarly work at the intersection of the literatures of social study of science and technology, those of cultural and media studies, and those of critical disability studies (Goggin and Newell 2005c). This is also the case with regard to networked digital technologies now so pervasive and ubiquitous in many countries. Accessibility for people with disabilities is often now a focus of discussion yet still more often honoured in the breach (Goggin and Newell 2003). Important initiatives have been taken in the area of the World Wide Web to make the Internet accessible, yet the overlapping cluster of software, hardware, and networks associated with online communications is proving far more intractable. As the Internet merges with mobile and wireless devices, inclusive and accessible technologies for text, video, and voice communications have been overlooked or only slowly eventuated. As the National Council on Disability has noted:

> There are limitations that make cell phones either inaccessible or difficult to use (and, therefore, possibly undesirable). People who have visual impairments may have the most difficulty reading the display and accessing visual information. People who are deaf or hard of hearing may have difficulty carrying on a verbal conversation and detecting auditory alerts. People with a mobility disability may have difficulty making accurate inputs and simultaneously handling the phone and manipulating the controls. People who have cognitive disabilities may have difficulty understanding metaphors that are used and remembering how to access information.
>
> (NCD 2004: 102–3)

The topic of access generally, and accessibility for people with disabilities specifically, has been much ventilated over the past decade, not least under the not especially helpful rhetoric of the 'digital divide' (Warschauer 2003). Access is certainly important as a concept but it needs to be placed within a general account of technology, culture, and the social. In this chapter, however, my focus is squarely on disability, and indeed the politics of bodies and ability, as an integral part of cell phone culture.

Designing Disability: The Case of Digital Cell Phones

As we have seen in chapter 2 [see original publication], cellular phones were commercially introduced around the world from the late 1970s, commencing with in-car phones. When hand-held cell phones became available from the mid-1980s onwards these were very bulky. Obviously, at this stage, the cell phone was difficult for many people with disabilities to hold and use. With advances in miniaturisation, computerisation, and manufacturing, cell phones became smaller and lighter. This made them easier to use for some consumers, but more difficult for others because of the dexterity and nimbleness demanded by tiny buttons and interfaces. Many people with disabilities did use cell phones for a range of purposes, including safety, security, and mobility assistance. There is much further to say on first-generation cell phones and people with disabilities (with important perspectives in Von Tetzchner 1991 and Roe 1993), but I will now turn to second-generation digital technologies.

When second-generation cellular systems were introduced around the world from the early 1990s onwards, their new features opened up new possibilities but created new forms of exclusion also:

> The present trend of marketing mobile phones that are smaller but with an ever-increasing number of features, ranging from memory store to calculator functions, is good for many people – but not for everybody. Blind people cannot use text-based information on the screen at all [including phonebook maintenance and use], while those who are partially-sighted have great difficulty with very small displays. Voice outputs are of no use to deaf people and may be difficult for those who are simply hard of hearing. The extensive range of network based facilities like automatic answering and voicemail: functions, text messages and call progress announcements require either useful vision or useful hearing, if not both. The Internet-based applications, such as sending and receiving Emails, surfing the net and engaging in e-commerce, are all visually oriented and so exclude blind consumers. Manufacturers and service providers seem to give low priority to solving these problems, for example by offering alternative output modes.
>
> (Shipley and Gill 2000)

Here cell phones illustrate the general proposition that when technology is reshaped it is because of certain sorts of imagined users and use, with particular sorts of 'normal' (or rather normalised) bodies and abilities. Typically people with disabilities do not fit into these categories of the normal (sometimes referred to as 'normate'), and are often not seen either as fitting the ideas of public markets that such normal bodies support. New designs which might allow other uses, by people with disabilities for instance, come often by another route:

Yet some problems are being overcome: hands-free operation is now offered on some models, not in response to demand by disabled people who have difficulty in using a very small keypad, but because it is wanted by drivers who wish to use their mobile phones in a moving vehicle.

(2000)

For people with disabilities there were also significant difficulties with second-generation cell phones, overlapping other sites of conflict over the technology (such as fears that electromagnetic emission from phones or towers might cause cancer). Not long after the new digital mobile system had been developed and was starting to be introduced commercially in a number of countries in the early 1990s, it was revealed that this technology emitted a high level of electromagnetic interference. Once the existence of these cell phone emissions became widely known, there was much public agitation, indeed panic, as I examine in chapter 6 [see original publication]. While the potential for cell phones to cause damage to health and safety was much noticed, there was much less public discussion, let alone awareness, of an associated matter: such interference had the potential to cause a buzzing sound in people's hearing aids, as well as actually making the phones difficult to use for people with hearing aids (Berger 1997; Burwood and Le Strange 1993; ETSI 1993; Joyner et al. 1993; NTAD 1994; Roe 1993). Internationally, phone companies, governments, and regulators put much effort into managing the public outcry. In doing so, they appeared to be motivated by a concern that this new, expensive technology might not be adopted by consumers, despite widespread support from governments.

In effect, cell phone companies regarded hearing aids *rather* than cell phones as the principal problem needing to be addressed. Attention was directed to the need for hearing aids to cope with higher levels of electromagnetic emission, something that was seen as important given the wide range of technologies emitting such signals – not just cell phones. A European standard was introduced in 1990 requiring hearing aids to be immune to emissions from cell phones. Research was also conducted on removing the source of emission further away from the hearing aid, and eventually 'handsfree kits' were designed for hearing aid users as a solution. Even this solution did not provide assistance for many, and other tactics were required on the part of the disability movement. In Australia, for instance, the disability movement needed to invoke the human rights and anti-discrimination law framework in order for the matter to be successfully addressed: the Human Rights and Equal Opportunity Commission (HREOC) conducted a public inquiry into the matter, which resulted in a conciliation some eighteen months later (Goggin and Newell 2005b; HREOC 2000). Despite such interventions and measures such as 'hands-free kits', the problem remains – and is only partially solved in some countries with the availability of the alternative digital mobile technology, CDMA.

In early 1996 the US FCC convened a summit of the wireless industry, hearing industry, and consumers in an effort to resolve the hearing aid and cell phone compatibility matter (Berger 1997; Victorian 1998). This meeting precipitated the formation of a dedicated taskforce under the aegis of the American National Standards Institute (ANSI) to develop a standard on immunity and emissions requirements and test protocols, which devices are required to meet (Victorian 2004). This work culminated in an American standard (namely ANSI C63. 19, see ANSI 2001; also Victorian and Preves 2004). In July 2003, the FCC reopened hearings into the issue. It gave federal imprimatur to the ANSI C63.19 standard, and also ordered a rolling timetable and further accessibility improvements. Other requirements included that within two years every major handset manufacturer and service provider must offer at least two cellular telephones that reduce interference to a level defined in the standard; and that by early 2008, half of all cell phone handsets have interference down to these levels or less (FCC 2003; Victorian 2004).

A related aspect of the construction of disability in digital cellular telephony lay at the intersection of a newer technological system and an older one, with their overlapping yet distinctive cultural practices. Deaf people in a number of Western countries, especially the USA, had developed a rich repertoire of communications and cultural practices using an early form of text communications. Devised in the early to mid 1960s, this technology was variously called the Telecommunications Device for the Deaf (TDD), teletypewriter (TTY), Deaf telephones, or just text telephone (Lang 2000). TTY communication involves two keyboard devices being connected to the telecommunications network to send and receive text messages. Many Deaf people own their own text phones, and, to meet the requirements of legislation such as the 1990 *Americans with Disabilities Act,* TTY payphones may be found in public places such as airports. From its inception this form of text phone communication by Deaf people relied on the Baudot standard developed for telexes. With the advent and growing popularity of computers and online communication in the 1990s, devices and standards were developed such as V. 18 that used the ASCII standard but incorporated the Baudot standard also (Hellström 2002).

The technical breakthrough that had made the TTY possible was a coupling device that allowed sounds transmitted over the telephone to be translated into data, and eventually, alphabetic letters (Lang 2000). Like modems, this meant that TTYs functioned compatibly (within limits) over the telecommunications network. TTYs also worked satisfactorily with first-generation analogue cell phones: 'Analog systems work fairly well with teletype devices (TTYs). Some phones have built in modular jacks into which a TTY can be plugged; other phones can be used with an adapter' (NCD 2004: 103). However, the much vaunted second-generation digital system threatened this interworking or knitting together of technologies:

> Initially, digital systems did not work well with TTYs. Digital wireless transmissions inherently contain errors, but error correction techniques can reduce the problem for speech. Digital networks are less forgiving in the case of the tones generated by TTY devices, however, and the transmission errors can cause characters to be lost or changed, resulting in unintelligible messages.
>
> (NCD 2004: 103)

In his account of Deaf people and telecommunications in Australia, Harper observes that:

> When the government decided to move from an analogue to digital telecommunications system in 2000, on the premise that it would improve

the wireless network access to a wider range of the Australian people, it did nothing to find a solution for those who were losing a service – Deaf people using TTYs on an analogue mobile service.

(P. Harper 2003)

The consequences of second-generation cell phones for the Deaf community were quite significant. In Australia, for instance, as the national relay provider, Australian Communication Exchange (ACE) argued:

In the late 1990s, telecommunications access for people with a disability made a tremendous leap forward and the future looked positive . . . However, in three short years since 2000, more than half of the telecommunications network is now not accessible to people who are Deaf or have a hearing or speech impairment despite the existence of the disability discrimination and telecommunications legislation [due to shutdown of the analogue network in 2000, and complete switch to digital mobile networks].

(ACE quoted in Goggin and Newell 2004: 416)

This experience was one shared by Deaf people around the world, underscoring the 'glocal' nature of mobile telecommunications: the shaping of this eminently global technology through local arenas. Internationally, it took concerted pressure from the Deaf community and their supporters, with alliances of users, scientists and technologists, academics, and interested industry across national, regional, and international settings, and also the invocation of general disability discrimination legislation in various countries, before the cell phone manufacturers and telecommunications carriers took this problem seriously.

In the USA, for instance, the Federal Communications Commission, which played a central role in the reshaping of telecommunications and disability through the 1990s (Goggin and Newell 2003), issued a requirement in 1996 that carriers were responsible for ensuring connection of 911 (emergency) calls over digital wireless networks for callers using a TTY. Certainly this was only the beginning of the process: 'The deadline for compliance was extended repeatedly as various wireless carriers worked to provide a solution' (NCD 2004: 104). An industry group, the TTY Forum, comprising carriers, wireless handset and infrastructure manufacturers, TTY manufacturers, telecommunications relay service providers, and disability consumer organisations, worked from 1997 onwards to ensure the networks would be able to carry 911 calls via TTY by the mid-2002 deadline set by the regulator (Harkins and Barbin 2002; NCD 2004). A number of larger providers met this deadline and implemented wireless TTY compatibility, including AT&T Wireless Systems, Cingular Wireless, NexTel, Sprint PCS, T-Mobile (formerly Voicestream), and Verizon Wireless (TAP 2002). Despite this, a number of carriers still petitioned the FCC for an extension.

There were certainly some genuine difficulties faced in the endeavour of achieving compatibility of cell phone networks and handsets with TTY devices. These included redesign to accommodate the speed and tone of TTY Baudot signals and 'setting standards for the interface between TTY devices and digital wireless cell phones operating with several different digital standards' (TTY Forum 2002; NCD 2004: 10S). At the end of the process, however, there is evidence to suggest that in the USA reasonable compatibility has been reached between cell phones and TTYs in non-emergency situations, though difficulties still remain with wireless 911 TTY calls (especially related to some of the equipment used by operators or emergency services answering calls) (NCD 2004: 105). However, not all cell phones are compatible with TTYs, and consumers have been urged to test their TTY with their wireless provider (TAP 2002). Elsewhere the problems of TTY and mobile compatibility also remain.

Seeing Telephony: Deaf People and Text Messaging

We have seen how the needs and desires of hard-of-hearing and Deaf cell phone users were not initially understood or envisaged as part of the design of second-generation digital mobile networks. Also that this set of design and consumption issues has not been widely noticed and discussed. To explore these issues further I now turn to a case which has received significant publicity, Deaf people's invention of text messaging.

Deaf people have long used text communications. As we have seen, from the 1960s onwards Deaf people had established a set of communicative and cultural practices around the TTY. Coupling TTYs with cellular devices, something attempted by some users with analogue cell phones, offered new telecommunicative possibilities for Deaf people. While the introduction of digital cell phones made mobile TTY communications difficult, another unexpected possibility was gradually opened up – text messaging. While a definitive history of the Deaf adoption of SMS has yet to be written, the outlines of this episode have now become widely known :

> The deaf have taken to this technology as an answer to their prayers. As texters in countries like Australia, Britain, and Israel, where the mobile phone service providers have agreed to interconnect their networks, they can take their means of communication with them as far as they can go and reach anyone who has a mobile phone.
>
> (Power and Power 2004: 334)

But although there have been few detailed studies of Deaf people's adoption and use of text messaging (an exception being Bakken 2005), one central theme in available accounts is that users can now communicate with other Deaf and hearing people without the intermediary of a human TTY relay operator. Power and Power point out that abbreviating text has 'long been familiar to [Deaf people] because it is used in TTY conversations', and that the characteristics of the SMS genre 'suit the sometimes-limited English of Deaf people' (2004: 335). Indeed there is some evidence to suggest that the rate of use of SMS among Deaf people is higher than their hearing counterparts (P. Harper 2003; Power and Power 2004).

Certainly Deaf people's creative use of cell phones caught the attention of mainstream media:

> Over the last few years, the mobile phone has emerged as a popular device for what at first may seem an unlikely user group: the deaf and other people who are hard of hearing . . . This usage shows how a group of people can take up a technology that was not initially designed or marketed to them, and adapt it to suit their own needs and purposes.
>
> (Wurtzel 2002)

Service providers in a range of areas including emergency services, police, and education institutions began to realise the potential to reach Deaf people via SMS.

Just like the rise of text messaging in general, once mainstream cell phone companies noticed the Deaf community's avid use of text messaging, they were keen to market to Deaf consumers, and also publicise this use for wider, public consumption. In September 2001, for example, Vodafone New Zealand sponsored 2001 Deaf Awareness Week:

> Text messaging is more than just a youth craze turned mainstream – it also gives deaf people the chance to communicate via mobile phone . . . Vodafone New Zealand's GM Company Communications, Avon Adams said it was good to see text messaging providing options for the deaf community. 'Text messages are free to receive and only 20c to send to anywhere in the world. They open up a realm of possibilities to deaf and hearing impaired people who can't make use of voice-based communications,' said Ms Adams.
>
> (Vodafone NZ 2001)

Redesign of the technology in light of such use was slower in coming: 'As the technology was not developed with this community in mind, operators and manufacturers have been slow to tailor offerings for the deaf and hard of hearing' (Wurtzel 2002). One problem for Deaf people is that SMS only supports asynchronous rather than real-time interaction (P. Harper 2003) – as it is a store-and-forward technology resembling email in this respect – despite the often very fast communication it can often afford. Also text messages need be written in hearing languages such as English rather than native sign language, and the frequent text messaging required by Deaf users can be quite costly.

Despite such challenges, Deaf users have also avidly taken up devices such as text-messaging pagers and portable digital assistants – with the T-Mobile Sidekick becoming a cult object among some communities of users (Kilner 2005). Mobile devices are also being used with Internet protocol relay services, for instance with America Online and MCI's 'My IP-relay' service launched in 2004 (AOL and MCI 2004). This enables Deaf people to have their phone calls transcribed by relay operators, and sent to them over the Internet, and then to have their instant message replies read back to the hearing person by the relay operator (La Vallee 2005).

As new textual media, the cell phone and associated technologies are deeply involved in significant and hotly debated transformations in Deaf identity and community: 'These technologies have begun to alter how Deaf people contact and communicate remotely with each other' (P. Harper 2003). Like wider debates regarding cell phones that have had an important function in shaping this media culture, there are those who praise the utility, function, freedoms, intimacies, and sociability such technology brings to Deaf people and others who lament the threat to older social forms. For example, face-to-face contact and gatherings have been much prized by Deaf communities, not least as a way to communicate via the visual and tactile medium of native sign language. In this respect Deaf clubs have been an important social and cultural institution, and fears have been expressed that the mediated communications offered by SMS, instant messaging, and the Internet will lead to an attenuation of social ties and cultural norms, and the disappearance of important customs (see Kunerth 2005, and response from Laird 2005). These fears have been more generally raised regarding cell phones, and have a long history in the reception of new media (Marvin 1988; Winston 1998). I would also suggest that notions of the cell phone are being socially and culturally shaped by the innovations of these users, and their imaginings of the technology. Thus SMS takes its place in a historical ensemble of technologies and communicative and cultural practices, including TTYs, fax machines, and, more recently, electronic mail and instant messaging (Bowe 2002; Lang 2000; Power and Power 2004).

Blinded by SMS

From the celebrated Deaf use of SMS, we now move to a contrasting case where a disability culture and its desires and needs regarding a technology have not been reflected in values, design, or narratives of use. In doing so, I am mindful of the problematic, dynamic, yet intensely invested categories of 'Deaf' and 'Blind', and the entire vexed taxonomic enterprise of knowing the truth of a person via an impairment label (for a critique of this see the opening chapter of Goggin and Newell 2005a).

As with people with disabilities in general, and Deaf users in particular, a useful starting point is the thesis that for Blind users the cell phone has gone hand-in-hand with new personal and collective possibilities. As Jolley notes:

> People who are blind have enjoyed the flexibility that results from mobile communications. Using their mobile phones they can find each other more easily in public places, and they have the added security of being able to make a phone call if they are lost or feeling endangered.
>
> (Jolley 2003: 27)

Yet, to propose an antithesis, the technology has not been imagined or designed with Blind users in mind.

Jolley usefully summarises a number of taken-for-granted features of cell phones that Blind people most often cannot use:

> People who are blind have very limited access to the standard features of mobile phones. In general terms they can only make calls by manually entering the number to be called, and they can receive calls if the phone rings or vibrates. But they do not know the battery strength, the signal

strength, if the PIN has been wrongly entered, if calls are missed, if the phone is accidentally on divert, or anything else that is shown on the screen. They cannot use the menu system, the telephone directory system, or anything but the most elementary speed dialing features. And, of course, they cannot use SMS. These features have been introduced gradually, as network services have been enhanced, and as new models of mobile phones have been released.

(2003: 27)

People with low vision also face problems:

Many people with low vision find it difficult to find a mobile phone with a large enough, brightly lit screen that they can comfortably read. So if they cannot read the screen, people with low vision face the same denial of access to the features of their mobile phones as do people who are blind.

(2003: 27)

The author of a comprehensive series of articles on cell phone accessibility for Blind users for an American Federation of Blind publication (Burton 2004, 2005a; Burton and Uslan 2003, 2004a, 2004b; Burton et al. 2003) offers this account:

In the early days of cell phones, when they were used only to make and receive calls, accessibility was not a major issue. As long as visually impaired people could tactilely identify the control buttons on the cell phone, it was no problem to make and receive calls. However, they were left out of the loop when the evolution of cell phones brought display screens and other new advances, such as phone books, text messaging, and e-mail, into the mix. Although people who are visually impaired were still able to perform the basic functions of making and receiving calls, the manufacturers did not design these new phones in a way that would allow them to independently access the new, more advanced features. There was no text-to-speech functionality to accommodate cell phone users who are blind, and there were no display screens with the visual characteristics, such as large fonts or highly contrasting colors, that would accommodate users who have low vision.

(Burton 2005b)

As cell phone manufacturers and service providers did not collectively envisage and design mobile technological systems with affordances and capabilities for Blind users, it has been largely left to specialist disability technology providers to design purpose-built workarounds. This could only be done with high-end phones such as Nokia's Symbian Series 60 that allowed third parties to add software programs and applications to cell phones (Molloy 2004). The company Cingular Wireless, for example, has licensed for the US market a software application called TALKS. TALKS is able to read screen-based menus, instructions, and content, and convert these into synthetic speech, using either the phone's speaker option or plug-in earphones or headset. Another application is Mobile Speak. It is designed to work with the Symbian series 60 operating system, to be carrier independent, to access 'most of the functionality of the device', and is offered in a number of languages (to date mostly English and European languages but also Turkish, Arabic, and Chinese). As well as a number of Nokia phones, it also works with the Siemens SX1 (Mobile Speak 2005). Another product is offered by Code Factory, a Spanish developer of 'software solutions for the blind and visually impaired' (www.codefactory.es). Code Factory also offers a related product called Mobile Accessibility, 'a complete mobile phone solution for the blind and vision-impaired' (Code Factory 2005). There is much to be said about the politics of artefacts here, and the inscription of the boundaries between mainstream and specialist technology. However, one index of these matters is the prohibitive price of adaptive software.

As well as applications for or adaptions of existing phones, in 2003 Spanish technology company Owasys announced the world's first cell phone specifically designed for Blind people. (After all, producing a *national* cell phone has been an important project for some countries, so why not a *disabled* cell phone?) When the phone was exhibited in Britain a company representative explained their thinking:

> We thought there were parts of the consumer market whose demands were not very well covered by the big players . . . From our conversations with ONCE (the blind people's organisation in Spain) and RNIB here in the UK, it was clear that there was a need among blind people for a product like this.
>
> (Adams-Spink 2003)

It is not clear to what extent Owasys's dedicated product has been taken up by Blind users, or whether most are more comfortable with a screenreader or application option (at least those who can afford it, and have the skills and training to use it). One difficulty may be slow and costly progress on approvals in different countries. In addition, the Owasys phone has fewer features than a phone running a screenreader, and carries a comparable price to a high-end phone plus screen-reading software.

As the capabilities of mobile devices expand, so too do creative options emerge, extending the capabilities of the cell phone for Blind people. In mid-2005 Motorola announced a software upgrade for one of its phones, to enable text to speech reading of menus, messages, and other screen-based phone features. A technology company called vOICe, – 'See with your ears!: Wearable Bionics used by the Blind Aim: Vision through Brain Plasticity' – has developed an aural camera phone designed for Blind users (The vOICe 2005), which translates images into soundscapes which are transmitted to the user via headphones (Sandhana 2003). The company has a Utopian vision for its innovation:

> Within a decade, second-hand camera phones could become an affordable platform for use of The vOICe by blind people living in developing countries! These phones can at the same time serve many general communication, Internet access and computing needs for the sighted poor, while doubling as a digital camera.
>
> (The vOICe 2005)

There is other software now available that allows a person to use a phone camera to identify the colour of objects (via a 'talking color identifier'). These offer ingenious, if relatively untested, reinterpretations of the visual cultural and multimedia features that now ship with the majority of cell phones.

If such options are in cell phones and mobile technologies are available for disabled users, these also reconfigure technological and cultural possibilities for all users. Significant numbers of Blind people are indeed now using text messaging and other data features on cell phones, as well as portable digital assistants, wireless laptop computers, and other devices. These innovative uses of mobile and wireless technologies build on and complement other media innovations of Blind users, such as braille, radio, Internet, audio recording, podcasting, blogging, talking books, and new digital publication standards such as Daisy (www.daisy.org). Outside Blind community and cultural lists, websites, journals, and circles, there is little recognition in other audiences of innovative uses of cell phones (cf. Goggin and Noonan 2006). Not surprising, perhaps, that progress in reshaping cell phone technology for Blind users is still slow at the time of writing (HREOC 2005).

Noonan's 2001 appraisal of the situation sadly remains a valid diagnosis:

> there are only two significantly developed zones of [blindness] accessibility momentum – PC access, predominantly via Microsoft's Windows 32 operating systems; and Web accessibility, predominantly driven by the WAI [Web Accessibility Initiative] . . . This is important to consider when we note recent projections in the IT industry that more than half of the internet connections by 2002 (or 2005 in other estimates) are expected to be from non-PC devices. This means that they will be from technologies which, currently, have no means of accessibility to their visual output. This raises the important question as to how people will be able to access set-top-boxes, WAP-capable mobile phones, personal organisers, smart domestic appliances and the like, which are solely visual (and non-textual) in output.
>
> (Noonan 2000)

The implications of such an impasse in technology are far reaching. SMS is now intensively used around the world, especially by young people, and is often an important aspect of cultural participation and social membership. Such emergent norms mean that Blind people's lack of access to SMS, and neglect in the design and shaping of mobile technologies more broadly, can lead to significant social exclusion.

Cell Phones and Next-Generation Disability

As the sources cited here make clear, study and discussion of disability and the cell phone is largely to be found in the specialised technical, service provider, or advocacy literatures and fora. There is still little discussion of disability to be found in telecommunications, new media, or Internet studies literature, and there are even fewer scholarly discussions of social and cultural aspects of mobile communications technologies. In seeking to stimulate such inquiry, I have been able to sketch only briefly three different case studies in disability and the cell phone. There is a great deal of empirical work that remains to be undertaken, first to establish the histories of disability and technology touched upon here, and second to debate and theorise these. This is an important research agenda, not only as a matter of human rights and justice but also because these narratives unsettle our taken-for-granted theories of technology. From a different perspective, I would note that Internet, games, and new media studies have made much of the role of the user in appropriating, domesticating, developing and actually producing networked digital technology and its associated cultural forms and content. There is much interest among cell phone and mobile technology scholars in questions of use and consumption. People with disabilities are mostly overlooked as users, consumers, and audiences, when they could be profitably credited as everyday, do-it-yourself consumer-producers of cell phones and media.

To understand cell phones and disability adequately, indeed cell phone culture in general, one needs to confront some deeply ideological notions (or myths) of technology. The term ideology is appropriate because it marks the operation of power: the social construction, or shaping, of disability in technology has decisively to do with relations of power (Goggin and Newell 2003). It is often very puzzling to those dedicated to the pursuit of accessible technology for people with disabilities that time and time again new technology brings not the much vaunted benefits (indeed salvation), but instead insidious new forms of exclusion, regulation, and control. Why, the proponent of accessible technology asks, if accessibility and 'universal design' are such simple, fruitful, and potentially profitable principles (NCD 2004), do we nearly always find that technologies are designed without imagining that people with disabilities will be among their users? My suspicion is that stubbornly resistant aspects of achieving inclusive technologies form part of a larger project of dismantling the oppressive power relations of disability in our societies, in which, *mutatis mutandis,* people with disabilities have long been seen as *other,* indeed, all too often still, as inhuman (Goggin and Newell 2005a).

References

Abberley, P. (1992) 'Counting us out: a discussion of the OPCS surveys', *Disability, Handicap and Society*, 7: 139–55.

Adams-Spink, G. (2003) 'UK debut for "blind mobile"', *BBC News*, 21 November, http:// news.bbc. co.uk/1/hi/technology/3226314.stm (accessed 1 August 2005).

Albrecht, G.L., Seelman, K.D. and Bury, M. (eds) (2001) *Handbook of Disability Studies*, London and Thousand Oaks, CA: Sage.

Altman, B.M. (2001) 'Disability definitions, models, classification schemes, and applications', in G.L. Albrecht, K.D. Seelman and M. Bury (eds), *Handbook of Disability Studies*, Thousand Oaks, CA: Sage, pp. 97–122.

America Online (AOL) and MCI (2004) 'America Online and MCI enable deaf and hard-of-hearing individuals to receive incoming calls anywhere, anytime using their own, unique phone number', media release, 13 December, http://www.timewarner. com/ corp/newsroom/pr/0,20812,1007089,00.html (accessed 24 June 2005).

American National Standards Institute (ANSI) (2001) *Method of Measurement of Compatibility between Wireless Communication Devices and Hearing Aids, C63.19*, Washington, DC: ANSI.

Australian Bureau of Statistics (ABS) (2004) *Disability, Ageing and Carers: Summary of Findings*, Canberra: ABS.

Bakken, F. (2005) 'SMS use among deaf teens and young adults in Norway', in R. Harper, L. Palen and A. Taylor (eds), *The Inside Text: Social, Cultural and Design Perspectives on SMS*, Dordrecht: Springer, pp. 161–74.

Barnes, C. and Mercer, G. (2003) *Disability*, Cambridge: Polity Press.

Berger, M.S. (1997) 'Hearing aid compatibility with wireless communications devices', in *Proceedings of the IEEE International Symposium on Electromagnetic Compatibility*, pp. 123–28.

Bowe, F. (2002) 'Deaf and hard of hearing Americans' instant messaging and e-mail use: a national survey', *American Annals of the Deaf*, 147: 6–10.

Burton, D. (2004) 'The signal gets stronger: three cell phones with speech output', *AccessWorld*, 5.4, http://www.afb.org/afbpress/pub.asp?DocID=aw050406.

——(2005a) 'Two more approaches: a review of the LG VX 4500 cell phone from Verizon Wireless and Microsoft's Voice Command Software', *AccessWorld*, 6.3, http:// www.afb.org/afbpress/pub.asp?DocID=aw060308.

——(2005b) 'You get to choose: an overview of accessible cell phones', *AccessWorld*, 6.2, http://www.afb.org/afbpress/pub.asp?DocID=aw060206.

Burton, D. and Uslan, M. (2003) 'Answering the call: top-of-the-line cell phones, part 1', *AccessWorld*, 4.3, http://www.afb.org/afbpress/pub.asp?DocID=aw040302.

——(2004a) 'Do cell phones equal software equal access: part 1?', *AccessWorld*, 5.1, http://www.afb.org/afbpress/pub.asp?DocID=aw040606.

——(2004b) 'Do cell phones equal software equal access: part 2?' *AccessWorld*, 5.1, http://www.afb.org/afbpress/pub.asp?DocID=aw050106.

Burton, D., Uslan, M., Schnell, K. and Swisher, C. (2003) 'Answering the call: top-of-the-line cell phones, part 2', *AccessWorld*, 4.4, http://www.afb.org/afbpress/pub.asp?DocID = aw040404.

Burwood, E. and Le Strange, R. (1993) *Interference to Hearing Aids by the New Digital Mobile Telephone Systems, Global Systems for Mobile (GSM) Communications Standard*, Sydney: National Acoustic Laboratories.

Code Factory (2005) 'Mobile accessibility', http://www.codefactory.es/mobile_accessibility/maccessibility (accessed 24 June 2005).

European Telecommunications Standards Institute (ETSI) (1993) *Technical Report, GSM 05.90, GSM EMC Considerations*, Sophia-Antipolis: European Telecommunications Standards Institute.

Federal Communications Commission (FCC) (2003) 'FCC acts to promote accessibility of digital wireless phones to individuals with hearing disabilities', media release, 10 July, http://hraunfoss.fcc.gov/edocs_public/attachmatch/DOC-236430A1.pdf (accessed 30 June 2005).

Goggin, G. and Newell, C. (2003) *Digital Disability: The Social Construction of Disability in New Media*, Lanham, MD: Rowman & Littlefield.

——(2004) 'Disabled e-nation: telecommunications, disability and national policy', *Prometheus: Journal of Issues in Technological Change, Innovation, Information Economics, Communication and Science Policy*, 22: 411–22.

——(2005a) *Disability in Australia: Exposing a Social Apartheid*, Sydney: University of NSW Press.

—— (2005b) 'Foucault on the phone: disability and the mobility of government', in S. Tremain (ed.), *Foucault and the Government of Disability*, Ann Arbor: University of Michigan Press.

— (2005c) 'Technology and disability', special double-issue of *Disability Studies Quarterly*, 25.2 and 3, http://www.dsq-sds.org/_articles_html/2005/spring/.

Goggin, G. and Noonan, T. (2006) 'Blogging disability: the interface between new cultural movements and Internet technology', in A. Bruns and J. Jacobs (eds), *Uses of Blogs*, New York: Peter Lang.

Harkins, J. and Barbin, C. (2002) 'Cell phones get smart – and more accessible', *Silent News*, http://tap.gallaudet.edu/WirelessTelecom/AccessibleCell.htm (accessed 12 May 2005).

Harper, P. (2003) 'Networking the Deaf nation', *Australian Journal of Communication*, 30: 153–66.

Hellström, G. (2002) Standardization of text telephony, http://www.omnitor.se/english/standards (accessed 15 March 2002).

Human Rights and Equal Opportunity Commission (HREOC) (2000) *Inquiry on Mobile Phone Access for Hearing Aid Users*, Sydney: HREOC, http://www.hreoc.gov.au/disability_rights/inquiries/MP_index/mp_index.html (accessed 19 July 2005).

Jolley, W. (2003) *When the Tide Comes In: Towards Accessible Telecommunications for People with Disabilities in Australia*, Sydney: Human Rights and Equal Opportunity Commission, http://www.hreoc.gov.au/disability_rights/communications/tide.htm (accessed 20 June 2005).

Joyner, K.H. et al. (1993) *Interference to Hearing Aids by the New Digital Mobile Telephone System, Global System for Mobile (GSM) Communication Standard*, Sydney: National Acoustic Laboratory.

Kilner, K. (2005) 'The latest: not just trendy. T-Mobile Sidekicks are more than a fashion statement for the deaf community', *Web@devil*, 28 April, http://www.statepress.com/issues/2005/04/28/arts/693124?s (accessed 1 August 2005).

Kunerth, J. (2005) 'Deaf culture fades', *Sun-Sentinel* (South Florida), 27 January 2005; also at http://www.deafcoffee.com/ (accessed 27 June 2005).

La Vallee, A. (2005) 'For the deaf, instant messaging reaches out and touches', *Columbia News Service*, 1 March, http://jscms.jrn.columbia.edu/cns/2005-03-01/lavalleedeafmessage (accessed 1 August 2005).

Laird, G. (2005) 'Deaf culture fades – misleading?', *Grant W Laird Jr Blog*, http://grantlairdjr.com/b2evolution/index.php/all/2005/02/01/p149 (accessed 1 August 2005).

Lang, H.G. (2000) *A Phone of Our Own: The Deaf Insurrection against Ma Bell*, Washington, DC: Gallaudet University Press.

Marvin, C. (1988) *When Old Technologies Were New: Thinking about Electric Communication in the Late Nineteenth Century*, New York: Oxford University Press.

Metts, R.L. (2000) *Disability Issues, Trends and Recommendations for the World Bank*, Washington, DC: World Bank.

Mobile Speak (2005) 'The screen reader made for you', http://mobilespeak.codfact.com/ (accessed 24 June 2005).

Molloy, F. (2004) 'Scene and heard', *The Age (Melbourne)*, 30 October.

National Council on Disability (NCD) (2004) *Design for Inclusion: Creating a New Marketplace*, Washington, DC: NCD, http://www.ncd.gov/newsroom/publications/2004/publications.htm (accessed 12 May 2005).

National Telecom Agency Denmark (NTAD) (1994) *Interference with Hearing Aids Caused by GSM Digital Cellular Telephones and DECT Digital Cordless Telephones*, Conclusive report by the working group on GSM and DECT telephones and hearing aids, Copenhagen: NTAD.

Noonan, T. (2000) *Blind Citizens Australia Submission to the Human Rights and Equal Opportunity Inquiry into Electronic Commerce*, http://www.hreoc.gov.au/disability_rights/inquiries/ecom_subs/bca1.htm (accessed 12 July 2005).

Power, M. and Power, D. (2004) 'Everyone here speaks TXT: deaf people using SMS in Australia and the rest of the world', *Journal of Deaf Studies and Deaf Education*, 9: 333–43.

Roe, P. (ed.) (1993) *Telephones and Hearing Aids*, proceedings of the COST 219 seminar, The Hague, March 17 1993, XIII/61/94-EN.

Sandhana, L. (2003) 'Blind "see with sound"', *BBC News*, http://news.bbc.co.uk/2/hi/science/nature/3171226.stm (accessed 1 August 2005).

Shipley, T. and Gill, J. (2000) *Call Barred? Inclusive Design of Wireless Systems*, London: Royal National Institute of the Blind, http://www.tiresias.org/phoneability/wireless.htm (accessed 1 August 2005).

Snyder, S.L., Brueggemann, B.J. and Garland-Thomson, R. (eds) (2002) *Disability Studies: Enabling the Humanities*, New York: Modern Language Association of America.

Stiker, H.-J. (1999) *A History of Disability*, trans. W. Sayers, Ann Arbor: University of Michigan Press.

Telecommunications Access Program (TAP) (2002) 'Wireless telephones and TTYs', Washington, DC: TAP, Gallaudet University, http://tap.gallaudet.edu/WirelessPhoneTTY0902.htm (accessed 12 May 2005).

TTY Forum (2002), 'TTY Forum consensus statement for the FCC', TTY Forum, sponsored by Alliance for Telecommunications Industry Solutions, 27 June, http://www.atis.org/atis/tty/ttyforum.htm (accessed 20 June 2005).

Victorian, T. (1998) 'Update on digital cellular telephone interference and hearing aid compatibility', *Hearing Journal*, 51: 53–60.

—(2004) 'Hearing aid compatibility: technical update', *Audiology Online*, 12 June, http://www.audiologyonline.com/articles/pf_arc_disp.asp?id = 1263 (accessed 25 July 2005).

Victorian, T. and Preves, D. (2004) 'Progress achieved in setting standards for hearing aid/digital cell phone compatibility', *Hearing Journal*, 57: 25–29.

Vodafone New Zealand (2001), 'Txt messaging provides a world of mobility for the deaf', media release, http://www.vodafone.co.nz/aboutus/media_releases/12.4_20010921.jsp (accessed 31 May 2005).

The vOICe (2005) 'The vOICe MIDlet for mobile camera phones', http://www.seeingwithsound.com/ (accessed 24 June 2005).

Von Tetzchner, S. (ed.) (1991) *Issues in Telecommunication and Disability*, COST 219, CECDGXIII (EUR 13845 EN), Brussels: COST 219.

Warschauer, M. (2003) *Technology and Social Inclusion: Rethinking the Digital Divide*, Cambridge, MA: MIT Press.

Winston, B. (1998) *Media Technology and Society: A History: From the Telegraph to the Internet*, London: Routledge.

Wurtzel, J. (2002), 'Deaf go mobile phone crazy', *BBC News*, 8 February, http://news.bbc.co.uk/1/hi/sci/tech/1808872.stm (accessed 1 August 2005).

Chapter 32

Ana María Ochoa Gautier

SOCIAL TRANSCULTURATION, EPISTEMOLOGIES OF PURIFICATION AND THE AURAL PUBLIC SPHERE IN LATIN AMERICA

DURING THE PAST DECADE, graduate programs in musicology and ethnomusicology have begun to consolidate in different parts of Latin America. This coincides with an increased interest in the topic of traditional and popular musics by students coming from diverse areas of the humanities and social sciences with the concomitant consolidation of different regional professional associations dedicated to studying the topic.[1] This is undoubtedly a response to the intensification of the aural that has come about due to the technological, economic and structural transformation of the modes of circulation of sound in the past two decades. By intensification of the aural I mean the increasing importance of the sonic for a decentred modernity no longer exclusively (or even primarily) defined by the primacy of the lettered word nor by developmentalist models (Martín-Barbero, 2003) coupled with a 'sonic turn'—that is,

> the increasing significance of the acoustic as simultaneously a site for analysis, a medium for aesthetic engagement, and a model for theorization. (Drobnick, 2004, 10)

This coincides with transformations in the structure of music knowledge under global conditions which are recasting the relations among and between Latin American scholars as well as between North and South.

One of the reasons for this intensification of the aural in Latin America is the revalorization, resignification and increased circulation of what historically have been considered 'traditional' musics as well as the rise of new forms of popular music. One witnesses, for example, the sharp rise of the world music industry and the closely allied global heritage industry (Travassos, 2006); the exacerbated production of different types of music in local studios that operate beyond the circuits of the official entertainment industry enacted through different styles and politics of self production and circulation (Vianna, 2006; Ochoa, 2003); the transformation of the Latin music industry, particularly in the US and Spain in the midst of the reorganization of the economic and managerial structures of the industry between North and South (Yudice, 2003; Aparicio & Jáquez, 2003); the proliferation of new popular music genres that disrupt and redefine the mainstream popular sonic sphere; and the intensified use of what historically have been considered 'traditional' sounds in everything from electronic and *avant garde* music, to heritage revitalization movements. In this paper I wish to explore how practices of sonic recontextualization enacted by both folklorists and the music industry have been crucial to the constitution of an aural modernity. This is mediated simultaneously by the contradictory practices of epistemologies of purification—which seek to provincialize sounds in order to ascribe them a place in the modern ecumene and epistemologies of transculturation—which either enact or disrupt such practices of purification. Through this I wish to argue that the aural has been a sphere of crucial constitution of Latin America's highly unequal modernity (García Canclini, 2002), one that is significant not only in the contemporary sonic turn but that played a role in defining the very idea of a Latin American lettered modernity.

Sonic Recontextualization

As stated by Feld, the history of academic sonic typologies and modes of approaching music as a study object are deeply embedded in the politics of the global circulation of sound (Feld, 2000). Sound technology has been used since the early days of comparative musicology to assist in the enterprise of musical documentation (Sterne, 2003; Brady, 1999) thus transforming the nature of the oral/aural divide and non-Western music's archaeology. Moreover, the poetics and politics of musical recontextualization and schizophonia are essential to understanding genealogies of musical knowledge about non-Western music because one of the fundamental methodological steps in these studies is that of entextualization—that is, the act of framing the musical object to be studied through multiple modes of 'capturing' it. As such, the construction of knowledge about traditional musics shares with the recording industry the act of musical entextualization and recontextualization as fundamental practices.

One of the most challenging dimensions of the current intensification of musical recontextualization processes in Latin America has been the return of interests, discourses and practices of what historically have been considered traditional musics side by side and often in interaction with the rise of new popular music genres. In a paper entitled 'Reflection on the ideological history of Latin American ethnomusicology', Behague wrote, in 1991, that

> the basic problem [in Latin American ethnomusicology] has been and
> continues to be a lack of conceptual distinction between 'musical folklore'
> as thought and practised throughout Latin American ethnomusicology.
> (1991, p. 60)

He was echoing, perhaps, many Latin American musicians and scholars who since the 1960s had launched trenchant critiques on certain forms of folklorism that had prevailed during the first half of the twentieth century and had played a crucial role in nationalistic cultural policies. However, one of the most striking features of the current recontextualization of sounds—which involves localizing global sounds as well as globalizing local ones—has been how many of the ideas originally tied to notions of musical folklore have returned under new guises and new activist pretexts to explain modes of signification of different types of music. One particularly salient mode of such signification involves the politics of belonging in which musical genres (traditional or popular) are deployed in order to articulate a) ties to place, b) communicative and communal ideals of spontaneity and affect that have been historically associated to an aesthetics of orality, and c) an ascribed sense of deeply felt identification. This intensification of the aural has thus also yielded a revitalization and resignification of place-based musical theories that are often constituted through ideologies originally associated with musical folklore, even when they are enacted in the name of what would be considered non-folkloric musics.

Simultaneously, we have an increasing use of certain popular musics, which historically have not been tied to place-based politics, serving as a crucial sonic agenda for the constitution of musical practices that often defy notions of musical belonging, heritage or resistance. Musics that are neither 'youth music' nor 'folk', nor easily tied to either a social movement or a revolutionary aesthetic, but whose technological mediations, forms of constructing identification and regional localizations defy, at least in their initial stages of consolidation, easy musical typologies or associations—such is the case with genres such as Brazilian *technobrega*, Argentinean *cumbia villera, nacrocorridos*, Peruvian *chicha,* or Brazilian *brega* (Araujo, 1998; Cragnolini, 2005; Vianna, 2006; Simonnet, 2001). These types of music often lie outside the parameters of canonic validation—neither heritage nor youth nor revolutionary aesthetics—and are often likened to ideologies of bad taste and, by association, to that which is socially considered low class and vulgar. But simultaneously, their imbrication with either dystopian imaginations that reveal the extremes of contemporary Latin America's societal exclusions (Cragnolini, 2005), as well as with illegal transnational economies (in their symbolic celebration or economic association with narcotraffic for example), points to what Martín-Barbero calls the unease of modernity (*los malestares de la modernidad*) (2003). Thus, as discourses about belonging are reenacted in the multiple realms of the heritage industry, music itself becomes more about 'increasingly complicated pluralities and uneven experiences' (Feld, 2000, p. 146). This dispersal of the aural into different modalities signifies, in Latin America, not a postmodern fragmentation but rather a rearticulation of the plurality characteristic of decentring a long history of a modernity plagued by silencing, inequalities and disencounters (Martín-Barbero, 2003).

The recontextualization of musics from Latin America in different arenas, or the globalization of local sounds, is, of course, nothing new to the region. One could, in fact, construct a history of the signification of Latin American aurality by attending to the particularities of the multiple historical moments in which local sounds have been recontextualized and resignified.[2] This has been constitutive of what Thomas Turino has identified as a history of cosmopolitan musical nationalisms in the region since the early nineteenth century (Turino, 2003). Given that today the intensified circulation of what historically have been considered local musics everywhere is now quite commonplace and ubiquitous (Feld, 2000; Stokes, 2004), and the disaggregation of the elements of these musics into sonic features to be sampled and interspersed with, between and onto other types of music, has become increasingly *standard* in and across different genres, then the very idea of musical hybridity as an exceptional recourse becomes questionable. Rather, we need to consider a genealogy of histories of recontextualization that involves different forms of production of oral textualities (Goodman, 2002) as constitutive of aural modernity.[3] From this vantage point, the history of twentieth century aurality in Latin America can be seen (or heard) as one of constant processes of recontextualization—of differential historical schizophonic moments one could say—done through different politics and aesthetics of sonic transformation and mixing—from the *avant garde* to different forms of the popular, from the mainstream to the countercultural. Here, hybridity appears less as a symptom of high modernity (if by hybridity we mean intergeneric relations that were historically non-existent as the term tends to be used in popular music studies). Rather, we have a reiterative process of entextualization and recontextualization that was intensified at the moment of the invention of sound reproduction in the late nineteenth century, through which music became a crucial feature of twentieth century modernities (Erlmann, 1999; Turino, 2000).

What is fascinating to me, then, is precisely the opposite of the oft-mentioned late twentieth century sonic hybridities—that processes of sonic recontextualization, of musical schizophonia and sonic disaggregation and reconfiguration seem to be seen, again and again, as a profound innovation, as going against the grain, as a practice deeply based in the idea of discovering something new for the first time, each time they are enacted, even when following previously set models. Thus, what are historically considered as local types of music (and the sounds associated with it) are not only apparently dying out because of their association to folklore and/or to the ever vanishing natives (Bauman & Briggs, 2003). By that very same token they are always readily available for (re)discovery and thus for the reconstitution of musics, knowledges and existential paradigms that are based on them. But today this happens not only with musics associated to what has been historically named as folklore. It happens with all musics that in practice are used to establish links with place and history as a primary means of musical identification and belonging even when they are perceived primarily as mass mediated or transnational musics (Samuels, 2004). The practice of re-localizing and re-temporalizing music then, seems to provide an inexhaustible fountain of musical youth or newness to be discovered anew in expeditions into different forms of sonic localizations (entextualizations, recontextualizations, replications) by each generation.

These different moments and processes of musical recontextualization are always accompanied by an intense debate about the meaning of sonic localism and sonic temporality and its place in Latin American modernity, in other words, they are constitutive of an aural public sphere, or more poetically, and following Angel Rama, of Latin America as an aural region. In his book *The Lettered City*, Rama argued for the role of control over the written word as crucial to the constitution of Latin American forms of administration and power. He saw the written word, concentrated in the cities where lettered elites reside, as constitutive of a highly unequal public sphere where only a minority had access to its communicative constitution (Rama,

2002[1984]). In speaking about Latin America as an aural region, I argue that under the contemporary processes of social globalization and regionalization coupled with the transformations in the technologies of sound, the public sphere is increasingly mediated by the aural. These processes are, if not subverting, at least displacing the relation between the sonic and the lettered word. The public sphere is being redefined to include forms of participation which are not channeled by the forms of debate or participation historically recognized as such by the official polity (Martín-Barbero, 2001; Winocur, 2002). Here the technological enhancement of the aurality of the media that has occurred with digitalization plays a crucial role in recasting the very idea of participation (Winocur, 2002; Vianna, 2006). The intermediality of the sonic sphere—from face-to-face communication to radio, cinema and television, to the self-production of recordings to internet and cell phone communication—becomes an increasingly privileged site of constitution of a (contested) public sphere. I emphasize the aural as opposed to the audiovisual (highlighted by Martín-Barbero) because the aural's intense intermediality makes it constitutive also of lettered and face-to-face communications which signal different types of mediations in the multitemporal imaginaries of postcolonial modernities. Moreover, this shift from the lettered city to the aural region also involves a recognition of the role of Latin American sonic globalization as crucial to the constitution of the region's audiovisuality in a global context, a displacement of the lettered city as that which embodies the region's sign of particularity proffered in the time of the literary boom (Franco, 2002). This is not so much an issue of the sonic replacing the lettered, as a move from the gaze to listening as a locus of analysis and political struggle (Drobnick, 2004).

What the recent processes of musical recontexualization show us, then, is not so much a new historical phase of musical recontextualization or yet other modes of musical hybridization—which they are, of course—but rather a displacement in the power of signification and mediation of the aural in the constitution of Latin America's public sphere. High modernity here appears as profoundly imbued by the sonic as an increasingly conscious and manipulable sphere of communicability. The rise of the sonic is profoundly tied to the displacement of ideologies of *mestizaje* that were crucial to the nation-building phase in the early twentieth century. It is also tied to the rise of diversity as a crucial site of political constitution (Gros, 2000) as well as to the technological transformations that have highlighted the aural's intermediality—the way it transverses and constitutes multiple sites of communication, even those primarily perceived as visual such as cinema and television (Chion, 1994[1990]).

This moment of intense paradoxical recontextualization of sounds, its relation to the structuring of knowledge about music and the rise of the aural as a theoretical analytical category as crucial to high modernity, can no longer be explained by recourses tied to notions of retraditionalization (such as revivals) or, on the opposite side, to the uses of the idea of hybridity as a synonym for musical fusion. It actually necessitates a fundamental reconceptualization on the role of the temporal and spatial dimensions of the sonic and their existential and epistemological significance under the changing technological and social conditions of a globalized world. Today it has become *normative* that the circulation and marketing of musical genres historically considered under the aegis of folklore or intangible heritages occurs side by side and/or is interspersed with what historically has been considered mass music, classical music of the Western world and new forms of sonic codification and typologies (ambient, electronic, new age, new genres, etc.) through shared modes of technological processing of sounds.[4]

To comprehend this transformation it is crucial to try to understand the patterns of the structure of knowledge on traditional and popular music in Latin America throughout the twentieth century as a crucial sphere of signification of the sonic—one that mediates the lettered city and the aural region and, as such, pre-figures many of the issues that concern Latin Americans in a sonically imbued high modernity. The search for ethnomusicological studies and alternative forms of disciplinary formation has been an interest of postmodern metropolitan ethnomusicology. The question is how does one frame such epistemological outreach when it is constructed as a question formulated *from* the metropolis *to* the periphery? Within a postcolonial critique, the use of the word 'ethnomusicology' when looking at peripheral traditional and popular music studies has the potential of enacting an erasure of the diversity of origins and histories of such studies, by placing the North American (or German) lineage as an originary practice from which the others developed. In other words, it assumes disciplinary practices 'described in terms of a metropolitan matrix' (Restrepo & Escobar, 2005, p. 115) that generates an 'asymmetrical ignorance' because it tends to validate traditional and popular music studies only when they take the form of metropolitan disciplinary practice. I would like to argue, rather, that the epistemological structure of studies of traditional and popular musics in Latin America, despite clear trajectories that can be identified as ethnomusicological, cannot be understood adequately within this frame. Instead, the determining epistemological relation of studies in traditional and popular musics in the region occurs, I would propose here, between cultural policy, the multiple methodologies used to study traditional and popular musics and dispersed textualities embodied in different practices of writing about music—from journalism, to fiction, to written compositions, to formal academic forms of writing. This is why I prefer to use the term 'studies of traditional and popular music' and not the word ethnomusicology. In terms of cultural policy, two elements are crucial: the relationship between folkloristics and ethnomusicology, in other words between epistemologies of purification and traditional and popular music studies, on the one hand, and the rise of the music industry, on the other.

Folklore and the Aural Public Sphere in the Era of Nationalism

Crucial to the constitution of what I am calling the aural public sphere was the emergence of folklore studies in Latin America which arose from the 1880s/1920s and lasted to the late 1970s.[5] But the practice of folkloristics itself was a highly heterogeneous one (de Carvalho, 1979–80). Jose Jorge de Carvalho distinguishes between types of folklore studies in Latin America on the basis of

> the concrete sphere of knowledges collected by them and the type of interpretation that they search with their works and the discipline or area of intellectual work in which they are inserted, *in case that it is possible to determine that.* (p. 67, my italics)

Notice, again, the very dispersal and the impossibility to determine a typical figure that embodies the intellectual involved in traditional and popular music studies. De Carvalho groups the types of studies into descriptive studies, formalist studies (the category where formal musical analysis is most present), studies of the history of culture and sociological and anthropological studies. But despite the diversity of their writings and labour, we must ask why are these writers ascribed to the area of folkloristics, if not necessarily as a discipline, at least as a practice? That is, what do they share? De Carvalho mentions scholars such as Celso Lara, Augusto Raúl Cortázar, Luís de Cámara Cascudo, Darío Guevara, Manuel Danneman, Mario de Andrade, Oneida Olvarenga, among others. One could, of course, expand this list. But the point here is not to be exhaustive but rather to explore the significance of the types of articulations and simultaneity of practices for a general understanding of the role of epistemologies of purification in constituting the aural public sphere.

These scholars shared an interest in identifying and visibilizing local musics as part of a project of valorization of sonic localism that was crucial to nationalist postcolonial projects. In all cases this involved some sort of practice of recognizing and/or collecting sonic items. How this was done differed from one individual to another, according, on the one hand, to their training—that is, according to whether they were anthropologists, musicologists, composers, writers or simply defined themselves primarily as folklorists—or according to whether music was a central or secondary interest in their general intellectual pursuits. Sometimes these practices were articulated into broader nationalist projects but often remained only of regional significance (Vilhena, 1997). In most cases, folkloristics made part of a broader disciplinary or creative practice that gave its practitioners their main insertion into public space, even when their work as folklorists became their bread winning labour in certain periods of their lives. Mario de Andrade, Alejo Carpentier and Manuel Zapata Olivella are much better known as fiction writers; Fernando Ortiz as an anthropologist; Carlos Vega and Isabel Aretz are probably better described as ethnomusicologists or musicologists. We also find many composers who also collected folklore and were deeply embedded in its politics—Carpentier himself, Heitor Villalobos in Brazil and Carlos Chavez in Mexico to name the obvious.

Many of these intellectuals not only documented and wrote about local musics, many of them also held public posts—temporary or of longer duration—in folklore institutes, radio stations, music studios, and cultural departments in official ministries, in which positions their role was to mobilize folklore for specific political and aesthetic ends within early twentieth century processes of nationalization. For example, Alejo Carpentier worked in radio for much of his life, promoted several son groups in Cuba and abroad and was later involved as an official representative of the Castro government in Venezuela (Brennan, 2001). Mario de Andrade founded the folklore institutes of Brazil, enacted expeditions of recording that are still a model of musical documentation that produces discussion and debate (Travassos, 1997). Delia Zapata Olivella created the national folklore ballet of Colombia and, with her brother Manuel, who also made radio programs and was a fiction writer, organized some of the first tours of Colombian Caribbean folk musicians to Europe and Russia in the 1950s. Sometimes these activities did not even involve a paid job or public recognition and they were done as a practice of engagement with sonic localism for nationalistic purposes.

Theirs was a direct intervention in cultural policy or in what George Yudice has called 'the expediency of culture', namely, the usage of culture for political ends (Yudice, 2003). This 'undisciplined practice' complicated any clear politico-epistemological distinction between the intellectual as a privileged figure in the constitution of a cultural public sphere or, to the contrary, as a subaltern figure whose possibilities of articulation into broad nationalistic agendas were often fragmentary (Vilhena, 1997; Boyer & Lomnitz, 2005; de Carvalho, 1979–80). In other words, their practice of folkloristics was deeply embedded in a politics of intervention that sought to reorganize the practices and signification of the sonic but this did not necessarily imply a privileged location as an intellectual in the public sphere.

Underlying these practices was a rather fragile—perhaps even non-existent—disciplinary unity. Instead, all these individuals were part of a network of relations that included composers, musicians, writers, ethnographers, folklorists and public personnel which actually acted as their main 'cohort'. In other words, what fed into their disciplinary and creative work was not a specific 'department' or even a university, despite repeated concerted efforts of institutionalization or associative mobilization. This meant that many individuals worked in isolation, in projects that were constantly in need of being restructured due to lack of institutional emplacement and often through very lonely endeavours—friendship did not solve the economic and professional needs that would have been provided by institutionalization. The relations of mediation between and across these networks of relation were thus very different from one individual to another or even from one period of a person's life (where he or she might have a temporary post for example) to another. Whether such interventions were articulated into a broader public sphere or remained as isolated efforts then depended on a variety of factors—from institutional relations, types of mediations, personal relations to populist and nationalist politics.

Several of these scholars studying local musics were engaged in creative activities—musical composition, writing of novels or poetry, or writing a literarily imbued ethnography—which were profoundly informed by their folklore studies or their personal relations to the practitioners of these musics (Vianna, 2002[1995]; Coronil, 1995). What we have then is a dispersal of the folkloric function of recognition of local sounds and of aurality into multiple *textual* practices—that of the *avant garde* composer and his or her *oeuvre,* the anthropologist and his or her *ethnography,* or the writer and his or her *text (novel, poetry, essay),* the person engaged in the composition of popular music and his or her songs. The transformation of sound into verbal and lettered significance occurs, then, not only through the practices of codi-fication of the sonic in academic texts but also through the place of the aural in defining the significance of the lettered: epistemologies of purification are meant to inform not only folkloristics and the rise of the music industry but also vanguard aesthetic practices and thus act as a *resource,* and were thus constitutive of a lettered modernity.

Many of these individuals dealt both with the classical *avant garde* and the traditional/popular, thus eliding, in their own work, the division between musicology as the study of Western classical music and ethnomusicology as the study of traditional 'non-Western' musics.[6] However, paradoxically enough, conservatories and music departments in Latin America have only recently begun to recognize the practice of local non-Western musics as valid—all other musical practices have historically been seen as formally less sophisticated than Western art music and rejected as a conservatory study object which is one of the reasons why local music studies are dispersed into other arenas (Behague, 1991). Thus while Western art music was meant to *enact* high art, folk and popular music were meant to *expedite* the local: in folklore texts, in vanguard creativity, in cultural policy. In other words, Yudice's expediency of culture, which he identifies as a new episteme in today's art world (albeit one with historical underpinnings), has actually been a defining quality of the aurality that represents sonic locality since the inception of its identification.

We have then, a multi-layered process of practices of musical entextualization and recontextualization, what I am calling sonic transculturation. This involves the collection of sounds, the description of sounds into multiple disciplines, the cultural practices through which these sounds are embedded into politics of recontextualization and the creative textualities and entextualizations into which these sounds are embedded. By sonic transculturation I mean a 'general restructuring' (Rama, 1982, p. 39) of the practices, modes of signification and circulation of the sonic. This 'general restructuring' rearticulates the relation between the local, the national and the global through multiple practices that imbue sounds with notions of place-based originality and representativeness in an intensely transnational sphere. The aural public sphere, Latin America as an aural region, is thus constituted by the mediations and (dis) junctures between these different practices enacted by the sonic transculturators— that is, all of those involved in this reorganization whether as musicians, intellectuals, or figures that move between different capacities. This often involved the immersion of the individuals who practised this separability into *contradictory* practices of recontextualization demanded by their simultaneous investment in cultural policy, *avant garde* creativity, the media, the nationalistic agendas of folkloristics and in the different types of mediations and articulations enacted through these different investments. Thus musical nationalist cosmopolitanism is a project fraught with the contradictions of mediating between the local and the metropolis (Turino, 2000; 2003). What does this say of the political significance and inscription of the intellectuals that participated in these complex networks and of the significance of epistemologies of purification in postcolonial contexts? What does it tell us about the ways in which many of the ideas associated with local musics are being recast and resignified in today's intensified aural recontextualizations?

Sonic Transculturation and Genealogies of Aurality

Luís Rodolfo Vilhena writes that it is a loss to the social sciences that the work of folklorists in Brazil during the early twentieth century was excluded from the consolidation of social sciences and thus became a neglected disciplinary history (1997). Likewise, Isabel Aretz herself wrote that 'ethnomusicology is still not sufficiently important among us and it seems it does not fit in a general history of culture . . .' (1991, p. 7). The study of traditional and popular musics, as a discipline, seems to belong nowhere and yet the ideas tied to epistemologies of sonic purification are tremendously strong and persistent in several fields—an issue easily seen in the resignification of the parameters of folkloristics under the new terminologies of traditional popular culture and intangible heritage in the 1960s and in the 1990s respectively. As such, it is simultaneously a subaltern discipline and quite a powerful discursive formation that permeates different disciplinary fields as well as different practices that went into rendering sonic localism into an autonomous sphere. I would like to suggest that the study of traditional musics, rather than a discipline, was a dispersed epistemology of sonic purification constitutive of what Silviano Santiago calls the Latin American 'in-between' (2001) in which the politics and poetics of local sounds are differentially embedded in multiple practices and disciplines that are not easily ascribable to a single space. The in-between here refers both to Latin American sonic transculturators' relation to a metropolitan centre that provides the model for *avant garde* aesthetics and for disciplinary constructions yet one that needs to be transcended in order to achieve differentiation, as well as to the need to reconfigure the place of the local through heterogeneous practices of entextualization and recontextualization.

What becomes extremely intriguing about these intellectuals in the first half of the twentieth century is their paradoxical and contradictory relation to the local. While their creative writing or compositional practices place them squarely in the vanguardist, modernist project, establishing ruptures with previous nineteenth century modes of conceptualizing artistic vanguards and local culture in order to construct regionally specific modernisms and modernities, their descriptions of local music and its role in the nation-state often reclaim a status of perpetuation for the folkloric text in its sameness—i.e. in what has been described (or is entextualized and described by them) as its pure form (Travassos, 1997). The paradox enacted depends on a division of sonic labour: while creative transculturation is a practice that can be embodied by certain figures (*avant garde* composers, folklorists, musicians of the popular identified as valid, and writers) it depends on others whose proper place is to represent 'the local' without deviating from it. But this division is not a division between the 'traditional' sounds and 'popular' ones. For the former cohort, it is absolutely proper not only to document these groups as folklore but also to intervene in popularizing them or in using them as a resource for *avant garde* creativity. Thus, part of their effort was to make them visible in Paris, New York and at home as an iconic sign of a differential modernity, the 'fetishization of local sounds' (Stokes, 2004) upon which the national and transnational recognition of the region's aural differential modernity is still largely based. These scholars thus often established an ellipsis between the folkloric and the popular which is controversial in Latin America until today: we find a hierarchical differentiation between what are considered proper 'folkloric' sounds versus 'popular' sounds, yet, often, the same genres and musicians are used to simultaneously embody the folkloric and the popular, by the very fact of being inserted into the commercial and representational circuits that popularize them as well as lead them into folkloric canonization.

Paradoxically, many of these sonic transculturators wrote critiques against the 'commercialization' of folk music, while being active in their popularization (Brennan, 2001; Sandroni, 2004; Wade, 2000; Ochoa, 2003). These critiques, of course, changed in form and signification from one person to another and from one historical period to another, but they do identify a discursive field of sonic exclusion. They regard as improper the transformation of these sounds in such a way that they disrupt the work of purification of the local—generally by people from the music industry with no link to these nationalizing projects or by the 'folk' themselves. Commercialization here refers to the process of transforming local sounds in such a way that they neither act as a resource for the *avant garde*, nor an aesthetics for the local, nor an aesthetics of the popular that re-presents the local, but rather an aesthetics that ruptures the sonic fetishization of the local and thus links these commercialized music to 'bad taste' and to 'vulgarity'. That is, stylistic and sonic practices that defy certain notions of the aural public sphere disrupting its con-stitution as a Bourdieuan sphere of distinction and thus upsetting the project of racial, class and ethnic exclusions and hierarchies constitutive of the project of Enlightened modernity. These exclusions and hierarchies coupled with the aforementioned in-betweenness is what makes Latin American postcolonial sonic modernity a highly unequal one. Sonic transculturation, to be canonically valid, then, can only be enacted by certain figures and through certain musical procedures that assure a 'proper' aesthetics. The periphery, in this case, is defined not so much by the idealized folkloric, but by the transculturations that are considered 'vulgar'. Exclusions of race, ethnicity, gender, sexuality and class are often mediated by this term: the binary opposition that underlies these exclusions is not between the traditional and the popular but rather between transculturations epistemologically validated through practices of purification and those that are not.

Yet the simultaneity of contradictory processes of aural separability disrupt the force of this binary as the only possibility for a postcolonial sonic modernity making it a highly embattled project. The historical paradox is that these musics often get validated once their popularization is mediated by different values and mediations of canonization, including the canonization of different modes of commercialization. This is why, in Latin America, the origins of popular music are often described as initially rejected and often later embraced by cultural or entertainment mediators and elites. Tango, capoeira, son, vallenato, samba, among others—and their practitioners, of course—were all considered vulgar before their canonic validation. Once they became national symbols or valued by the entertainment industry then the politics of relation between aesthetic inclusion (of previously excluded music due to racial, class, sexual or ethnic politics) and social inclusion became more complicated. Since the intellectual figures that enacted these projects were themselves contradictorily and differentially emplaced in their possibilities of mediation and articulation of their own political agendas, it was impossible to determine these mediators solely as cultural elite figures. In some cases they clearly were, but in other cases the politics of mediation and disjuncture between fields of exclusion and participation were highly diverse from one figure to another. What we have then is a highly contested field characterized by multiple mediations in which the politics of sonic validation and/or exclusion are articulated in contradictory ways in an embattled sonic modernity. Sonic localism then appears as a highly contested sphere.

A question emerges: is the act of epistemological purification of sounds one that already contains the only political means of interpreting and recontextualizing those sounds? That is, can it only be used to construct social inequality as suggested by

Bauman and Briggs? I would suggest rather that it is the opposite: the act of purification of the sonic is actually wrought with innumerable possibilities of political articulation and interpretation often beyond and above those that entextualize the sonic object itself. The intense discussion on ideas about folklore and popular musics in the 1960s and 1970s which yielded the rise of such terminologies as traditional popular music to replace the unwanted ideological and nationalistic implications of folkloristics and the rise of the notion of intangible heritage in the 1990s to replace the exclusions of the 1960s both signify the contested political nature of these practices; yet they signify their simultaneous re-enactment under differential politics. The invisibilization produced by the politics of purification is re-enacted not only for the sake of creating social inequality but also by social movements and others whose intention it is precisely to contest those inequalities. That is why, as Steven Feld has shown us in the field of world music, this process often is wrought with divisive politics: if for some world music evokes a celebratory politics of diversity and recognizability, for others it evokes the contested politics of the musical market in a capitalist world where recognition is increasingly mediated by the politics of neoliberalism. That is why, also, as academics deconstruct the history of sonic inequalities imbued in the history of folkloristics and popular music genres in Latin America, the members of social movements often take these same representations and use them for expediting a sonic politics of recognition and mediation.[7]

But more than that, once a musical object is separated from its original context it enters a realm of symbolic interpretation that can be highly ambiguous. The work of anthropologists Ohnuki Tierney on the militarization of Japanese aesthetics during the Second World War and of David Samuels on the use of country music in the San Carlos Apache reservation in Arizona has made us aware that once decontextualized, music, as a particularly marked and heightened poetic field, is easily amenable to multiple modes of indexical and iconic interpetations that imbue it with different semantic content. Thus one and the same sound or musical genre can come to mean or be used in very different ways, not only in different contexts but often in the same contexts by different groups of people and individuals. An issue highlighted by the intense intermediality of the sonic and by music as an item easily amenable to multiple processes of separation and recontextualization.

I want to propose that what has become reified in Latin America is not so much a discipline as a type of articulation between (i) practices and discourses of recontextualization of local musics—what Bauman and Briggs named epistemologies of purification; and (ii) practices and discourses of sonic transculturation—what, following Ortiz and Rama I will call epistemologies of transculturation, that is epistemologies that validate the hybrid and are located in the in-between as a sphere of intervention. Both of these feed into each other and constitute each other in contradictory and complex ways. Thus, sonic modernity is always presented as an unfinished project because the very existence of the colonial/modern and of the traditional/modern is precisely based on the cyclical relations of these articulations (Bauman & Briggs, 2003). Hybridity in this sense is less a transformation of tradition—a statement to enter or leave modernity to use García Canclini's (1989) words—than it is a reification, through multiple practices of transculturation, of the traditional/modern in order to construct it as permanently inexhaustible. And in the contested sites of unequal modernities, such articulations tend to be complexly interwoven due to the dispersal of the mediators of these articulations into different types of labour, institutional insertion, types of intervention and modes of textual expression. Rather than a binary division between tradition and modernity, or thinking of tradition as a backdrop for modernity, what we hear here is multiple mediations enacting a constant relation between sonic transculturation and purification. And what the simultaneity of multiple forms of recontextualization does (that of the industry, that of intellectuals, that of social and artistic movements) is complicate the erasure enacted through practices of purification and their canonic validity. Furthermore, this wreaks havoc in the colonial constitution of the idea of an Enlightened modernity as the dominant version of modernity. Aurality is thus a crucial site of constitution of the disencounters of modernities (Ramos, 1989) and the struggle between Enlightened and modernities otherwise is frequently a struggle between a lettered model of modernity that provincializes the aural and an aural otherwise in which ethnic heritages, class differences, sexual and gender inequalities become contested sites of sonic intervention and interpretation. Thus, the circulation of 'traditional' sounds under new types of codification—from folklore to the traditional popular to intangible heritage—is a permanent feature of a modernity that by its very practices of invisibilization is constituted as in permanent need of reinvention.

The current recasting of the study of traditional and popular musics in the South undoubtedly takes place under the shadow of 'dominant' ethnomusicologies.[8] Paraphrasing Restrepo and Escobar, by dominant ethnomusicologies I mean

> the discursive formations and institutional practices that have been associated with the normalization of anthropology [in this case ethnomusicology] under academic modalities chiefly in

the United States, Britain and France. Dominant ethnomusicologies

> include the diverse processes of professionalization and institutionalization that accompanied the consolidation of disciplinary canons and subjectivities, and through which anthropologists [ethnomusicologists] recognize themselves and are recognized by others as such. (Restrepo & Escobar 2005, p. 103)

If the exploration of musical knowledges otherwise is to have political significance in Latin America, then it entails listening to the ways in which this genealogical history points simultaneously to possibilities of futurity and to histories of exclusion that can easily be rearticulated. Likewise, if the project of deprovincializing ethnomusicological knowledge in the North is to have any significance, then it involves less the search for an essence in other forms of similar disciplinary structures than for practices and relations in a heterogeneous epistemological field, a task that is ever more urgent as the North American academy's power to articulate itself as a centre of information, academic standardization and an axis of canonic validation becomes ever more pervasive (Richard, 2001).

Notes

1   For example, the Latin American branch of the International Association for the Studies of Traditional and Popular Music began in August 2000, and the Brazilian Association for Ethnomusicology began in 2001.

2   For example, many of the sounds being used today by young musicians in Buenos Aires, Bogotá or Rio de Janeiro, were brought to national and international attention in the processes of folklorization and popularization that began in the 1920s and lasted until the 1970s and that gave rise to such national and popular music as Brazilian samba, Argentinean tango, Cuban son, Colombian cumbia or Mexican corrido. Also, during the 1960s and 1970s, left-wing musical movements, such as the New Song Movement in Spanish speaking Latin America and Caribbean, and Tropicália and MPB in Brazil redefined the notions of folklorization that had been prevalent until then, enacting a new relation between the local and the metropolitan and between musical politics, musical knowledge and sonic commercialization. Also during that period genres such as salsa and reggae were consolidated through and by transnational and diasporic relations. And currently, different ethnic and class based social movements involved with both transnational popular music and local heritages, as well as urban and regional based musicians that creolize transnational and local music, are recasting this relation under new guises.

3   Even when a process of traditionalization is enacted—minimizing processes of hybridity to keep to an idea of inherited tradition, such a choice is consciously made (see de Carvalho, 1979–80) thus making generic ascription and heritage a discursive formation in permanent negotiation.

4   It is no accident that this comes about with a radical reorganization of 'the music industry' or the modes of circulation and marketing of sounds. This bears significance not only regarding issues of 'piracy', but rather exceeds it in the sense that unofficial and self-organized forms of circulation of sound prevail today in many regions of the world—from the selling of self produced CDs through networks of aesthetic belonging (Ochoa, 2003) to the use of instant duplication made available by digital sonic technology to circulate musical events as sonic artefacts (Vianna, 2002[1995]), to the reinterpretation of the radio as a crucial site for the formation of a diverse musical heritage (Samuels, 2004).

5   I am not implying here that folklore studies do not continue but rather that their presence in the public sphere has been transformed by the rise of social movements, NGOs and the new discourses and politics on intangible heritage adopted and/or promoted by UNESCO and the nation-states.

6   What we have here is quite a long tradition in which practices of transculturation and purification enact a different type of disciplinary boundary than the one that exists in the metropolitan regions that clearly distinguishes between musicology and ethnomusicology as separate disciplinary histories. Thus, the idea that people normally trained to privilege Western classical music, engage with 'other' musics does not come, necessarily from the break up of the canon generated by the influence of cultural studies and poststructuralism.

7   See García Canclini (2002) for a similar critique of the transformation of the meaning and usages of culture today.

8   For example, the Associação Brasileira de Etnomusicologia was created after the ICTM congress in Rio de Janeiro and the Latin American IASPM is related to the international IASPM, of British based origins. I do not mean to imply that these associations would not have emerged without this presence thus condemning the Latin American academy to a mimetic unoriginality. Rather, what I wish to point out is that the emergence of these transformations takes place at the unequal intersection of the local and the global and not as isolated gestures.

References

Aparicio, F. R., & Jáquez, C. F. (2003). Introduction. *Musical migrations.* New York: Palgrave Macmillan.

Araujo, S. (1998). Music and conflict in urban Brazil. *Latin American Music Review, 9(1,* Spring), 50–89.

Aretz, I. (1991). *Historia de la etnomusicología en América Latina.* Caracas: Fundef Conac, OEA.

Bauman, R., & Briggs, C. L. (2003). *Voices of modernity: Language ideologies and the politics of inequality.* Cambridge: Cambridge University Press.

Behague, G. (1991). Reflection on the ideological history of Latin American ethnomusicology. In B. Nettl & P. V. Bohlman (Eds.), *Comparative musicology and anthropology of music.* Chicago & London: University of Chicago Press.

Bohlman, P. V. (1991). Representation and cultural critique in the history of ethnomusicology. In B. Nettl & P. V. Bohlman (Eds.), *Comparative musicology and anthropology of music.* Chicago & London: The University of Chicago Press.

Boyer, D., & Lomnitz, C. (2005). Intellectuals and nationalism: Anthropological engagements. *Annual Review of Anthropology, 34,* 105–20.

Brady, E. (1999). *A spiral way.* Jackson: University Press of Mississippi.

Brennan, T. (2001). Introduction. In A. Carpentier, *Music in Cuba.* English ed. Minneapolis & London: University of Minnesota Press.

Chakrabarty, D. (2000). *Provincializing Europe.* Princeton & Oxford: Princeton University Press.

Chion, M. (1994[1990]). *Audio-vision. Sound on screen.* New York: Columbia University Press.

Coronil, F. (1995). Introduction: Transculturation and the politics of theory: countering the center, Cuban counterpoint. *Cuban counterpoint.* Durham: Duke University Press.

Cragnolini, A. (2005). Soportando la violencia. In M. Ulhoa & A. M. Ochoa (Eds.), *Música popular na América Latina, Pontos de Escuta.* Porto Alegre: UFRGS Editora.

De Carvalho, J. J. (1979). Folklore: ¿Ciencia o área de estudio? *Revista INIDEF, 4,* 59–71.

Drobnick, J. (2004). Listening awry. In J. Drobnick (Ed.), *Aural cultures.* Toronto: YYZ Books.

Erlmann, V. (1999). *Music, modernity and the global imagination.* New York, Oxford: Oxford University Press.

Feld, S. (2000). A sweet lullaby for world music. *Public Culture, 12(1),* 145–72.

Feld, S., & Fox, A. (1994). Music and language. *Annual Review of Anthropology, 23,* 25–53.

Franco, J. (2002). *The decline and fall of the lettered city.* Cambridge & London: Harvard University Press.

García Canclini, N. (1989). *Culturas híbridas, Estrategias para entrar y salir de la modernidad.* México: Grijalbo, Consejo nacional para la cultura y las artes.

— (2002). *Latinoamericanos buscando lugar en este siglo.* Buenos Aires, Barcelona, México: Paidós.

Goodman, J. E. (2002). Writing empire, underwriting nation: discursive histories of Kabyle Berber oral texts. *American Ethnologist, 29(1),* 86–122.

Grimson, A. (2000). Interculturalidad y comunicación. *Enciclopedia latinoamericana de sociocultura y comunicación*. A. Ford (Ed.). Buenos Aires: Norma.

Gros, C. (2000). *Políticas de la etnicidad: idetnidad, estado y modernidad*. Bogotá: Instituto Colombiano de Antropología e Historia.

Grosz, E. (2005). *Time travels. Feminism, nature, power*. Durham & London: Duke University Press.

Lee, D. S. (1993). Native American. In H. Myers (Ed.), *Ethnomusicology historical and regional studies*. New York & London: W.W. Norton and Company.

Martín-Barbero, J. (2001). *Al sur de la modernidad*. Pittsburgh: Instituto Internacional de Literatura Iberoamericana.

— (2003). Nuestros malestares en la modernidad. In H. Herlinghaus & M. Moraña (Eds.), *Fronteras de la modernidad en América Latina*. Pittsburgh: Instituto Internacional de Literatura Iberoamericana.

Mignolo, W. (1995). *The darker side of the renaissance, literacy, territoriality and colonization*. Ann Arbor: University of Michigan Press.

Miñana, C. (2000). Entre el folklore y la etnomusicología: 60 años de estudios sobre la música popular tradicional en Colombia. *A contratiempo, 11,* 36–49.

Moore, R. D. (1997). *Nationalizing blackness, Afrocubanismo and artistic revolution in Havana 1920s–1940s*. Pittsburgh: University of Pittsburgh Press.

Ochoa, A. M. (2003). *Músicas locales en tiempos de globalización*. Buenos Aires: Norma.

Ohnuki-Tierney, E. (2002). *Kamikaze, cherry blossoms and nationalism, the militarization of Japanese aesthetics*. Chicago & London: University of Chicago Press.

Rama, A. (1982). *Transculturación narrativa en América Latina*. México: Siglo XXI Editores.

— (2002[1984]). *La ciudad letrada*. Hanover: Ediciones del Norte.

Ramos, J. (1989). *Desencuentros de la modernidad en América Latina, literatura y política en el siglo XIX*. México: Fondo de Cultura Económica.

Restrepo, E., & Escobar, A. (2005). Other anthropologies and anthropology otherwise. *Critique of Anthropology, 25(2),* 99–129.

Richard, N. (2001). Globalización académica, estudios culturales y crítica latinoamericana. In D. Mato (Ed.), *Estudios latinoamericanos sobre cultura y transformaciones sociales en tiempos de globalización*. Buenos Aires: CLACSO.

Romero, R. (2001). Tragedies and celebrations: Imagining foreign and local scholarships. *Latin American Music Review, 22(1),* 48–62.

Samuels, D. (2004). *Putting a song on top of it. Expression and identity on the San Carlos Apache Reservation*. Tucson: University of Arizona Press.

Sandroni, C. (2001). *Feitiço Decente: transformações do samba no Rio de Janeiro, 1917–1933*. Rio de Janeiro, RJ: Jorge Zahar Editor: Editora UFRJ.

— (2004). Adeus a' MPB. In B. Cavalcante, H. Starling, & J. Eisenberg (Eds.), *Decantando a república*. Vol. 1, Rio de Janeiro: Editora Nova Fronteira, Editora Fundação Perseu Abramo.

Santiago, S. (2001). Latin American discourse: The space in-between. In A. L. Gazzola (Ed.), *Silviano Santiago, The space in-between, essays on Latin American culture*. Durham: Duke University Press.

Simonnet, H. (2001). *Banda, Mexican musical life across borders*. Middletown: Wesleyan University Press.

Sterne, J. (2003). *The audible past: Cultural origins of sound reproduction*. Durham: Duke University Press.

Stokes, M. (2004). Music and the global order. *Annual Review of Anthropology, 33,* 47–72.

Travassos, E. (1997). *Os mandarins milagrosos*. Rio de Janeiro: Funarte, Jorge Zahar Editor.

— (2006). Músicas de ellos y músicas nuestras. In A. M. Ochoa (Ed.), Separata músicas brasileñas contemporáneas. *Revista Número, 49,* xviii.

Turino, T. (2000). *Nationalists, cosmopolitans and popular music in Zimbabwe*. Chicago & London: University of Chicago Press.

— (2003). Nationalism and Latin American music: selected case studies and theoretical considerations. *Latin American Music Review, 24(2),* 169–209.

Vianna, H. (2002[1995]). O *mistério do samba*. Rio de Janeiro: Jorge Zahar Editor, Editora UFRJ.

— (2006). *Diario de viaje*. In A. M. Ochoa (Ed.), Separata músicas brasileñas contemporáneas, *Revista Número, 49,* iii.

Vilhena, L. R. (1997). *Projeto e missão, o movimento folclorico brasileiro 1947–1964*. Rio de Janeiro: Fundação Getulio Vargas Eds., Ministério de Cultura, Funarte.

Wade, P. (2000). *Music, race and nation, música tropical in Colombia*. Chicago & London: University of Chicago Press.

Winocur, R. (2002). *Ciudadanos mediáticos, la construcción de lo público en la radio*. Barcelona: Gedisa.

Yudice, G. (2003). *The expediency of culture*. Durham: Duke University Press.

PART V

The Sonic Arts: Aesthetics, Experience, Interpretation

E VERY SECTION OF THIS READER could no doubt be expanded into a reader of its own, but this section is particularly explosive in that regard, given the number of collections that focus on popular music, expanded musicologies, and sound art. By their measure, my collapse of such heterogeneous practices into "the sonic arts" is a little unfair. Several robust traditions of aesthetic analysis are relevant to sound students: musicology and ethnomusicology, popular music studies, sound art and art history (not to mention acoustic ecology, literary analysis, and other approaches represented elsewhere in this reader). Traditionally, this aesthetically-minded work is then organized according to longstanding divisions like the split between high culture and low culture, where "serious" music and art are often treated separately from their more "popular" forms.

These divisions come with methodological stakes. For instance, when Leonard Meyer published *Emotion and Meaning in Music* in 1957, he expanded the aesthetics of the Western concert tradition to music in general. By focusing on melody and harmonic structure, and combining that music theory with gestalt psychology, Meyer argued that music sounds like emotion feels. Yet, as Charlie Keil showed a few years later, a better theory of musical meaning would start from something like jazz, with its emphasis on rhythm and groove, which was much more like music from other parts of the world. Together with writers like Steven Feld and Christopher Small, Keil helped develop a theory of musical meaning and practice that was separate from the presuppositions of the concert tradition.[1]

Today, musicologists are more likely to write across genres of music, rather than restricting the field to the limits of Western concert traditions,[2] and writers on sound art connect it with to other relevant sonic traditions, where music school compositions, glitch productions and sound art installations can be considered side by side, and alongside sound effects in radio, television and cinema. Paul Hegarty's *Noise/Music*, for instance, places sound art up against practices in punk rock and Japanese noise music. Caleb Kelly's *Cracked Media*, combines questions from the study of sound art with those of contemporary media theory in service of developing an analysis of sound art that is both medium-specific and attentive to its character as sound. Caryl Flinn's study of film music, meanwhile, connects Hollywood conventions with romantic ideologies associated with the Western art music tradition. Mark Katz's study of "phonograph effects" uses the history of technology to explain aesthetic changes in performance, like the increasing fashion for violin vibrato.[3] In using a term like "the sonic arts," I want to think within these trans-aesthetic trends in scholarship.

Georgina Born's chapter brings the sensibility of popular music studies and anthropology to one of the most celebrated institutions of avant-garde music composition, IRCAM (Institut de Recherche et Coordination Acoustique/Musique). Rather than taking them on their own terms, Born treats high cultural aesthetics as themselves cultural forms to be studied and critiqued. In so doing, she shows how the methods and questions applied to popular music in the 1980s and 1990s helped to open up a space for sound studies.[4] If Born's chapter rethinks avant-garde music as a cultural practice, Tara Rodgers takes up Born's challenge from a different perspective. Building on the work of feminists like Donna Haraway and Susan McClary, Rodgers rethinks how histories of electronic music are told. Like McClary, who read the gendered terms of formalist musicology for their politics, and like Haraway, who read the gendered forms of science and technology for their politics, Rodgers interrogates given concepts of sound reproduction and poses an alternative historiography. She asks how thinking of women as producers of electronic music transforms our understanding of it—a point that is worth extrapolating to the sonic arts more generally.[5]

Histories of sound and art can take many different forms. Brandon Labelle's essay maps a field of sound art practice today and links it to historical precedents. Richard Leppert's essay in this section posits the concept of a *sonoric landscape* that is both heard and seen, and uses analyses of paintings to get at otherwise lost sound cultures. If Leppert reads the politics of sonic space off painting, Michael Veal listens to them. Veal connects the use of echo and reverb in dub music with the experience of the black diaspora. For him, the shattered songs and soundscapes reverberate a different kind of consciousness for both maker and listener, a fundamentally discontinuous state of being. Veal thus interprets dub as a result of and a contribution to a diasporic consciousness that reaches across the black Atlantic.[6]

Douglas Kahn's contribution thinks noise across categories, both in canonized antecedents of modern sound art, like Marinetti's art of noises, and in literature and poetry, thus elaborating a history of sound art in terms of a history of sound in the arts. His work has done much to open up the possibility of both a vigorous academic study of sound art separate from its making, and to pose sound as a problem for the more traditional humanities and social sciences.[7] Yet Kahn also gives aesthetic work its due as itself containing theoretical propositions that must be beheld, a point directly made by Kodwo Eshun, for whom "speaking for the music" defeats the point of listening to it. Pushing back against notions of blackness as internally coherent, Eshun's manifesto posits then-contemporary black musics ("post soul") as enacting a distributed, technologized subjectivity through sound and rhythm, and upending many of the pieties about authenticity in music journalism and cultural studies.

Notes

1   Meyer, *Emotion and Meaning in Music*; Keil, "Motion and Feeling Through Music";
     Feld, "Aesthetics as Iconicity of Style (uptown title) or (downtown title) 'Lift-Up-
     Over-Sounding': Getting into the Kaluli Groove"; Small, *Musicking: The Meanings
     of Performing and Listening*; Suzanne Langer offers an interesting contrast to
     Meyer——she treated music as more fully symbolic but still extrapolated from the
     Western concert tradition. See Langer, *Philosophy in a New Key; A Study in the
     Symbolism of Reason, Rite, and Art.*
2   See, e.g., Auner, "'Sing It for Me'"; Butler, *Unlocking the Groove.*
3   Hegarty, *Noise/Music: A History*; Kelly, *Cracked Media*; Flinn, *Strains of Utopia:
     Gender, Nostalgia and Hollywood Film Music*; Katz, *Capturing Sound: How
     Technology has Changed Music*; see also Hainge, "Of Glitch and Men: The Place of
     the Human in the Successful Integration of Failure and Noise in the Digital Realm."
4   See, e.g., Frith, *Performing Rites: On the Value of Popular Music*; Grossberg,
     Dancing In Spite of Myself: Essays on Popular Culture; Gracyk, *Rhythm and Noise:
     An Aesthetics of Rock*; Berland, "Radio Space and Industrial Time: Music Formats,
     Local Narrative and Technological Mediation"; Brackett, *Interpreting Popular
     Music*; Negus, *Popular Music in Theory*; Tagg, "Kojak – 50 Seconds of Television
     Music: Toward the Analysis of Affect in Popular Music"; Whitely, *Sexing the Groove:
     Popular Music and Gender*; Swiss, Sloop, and Herman, *Mapping the Beat: Popular
     Music and Contemporary Theory.*
5   Haraway, *Simians, Cyborgs and Women*; McClary, *Feminine Endings: Music, Gender,
     and Sexuality.*
6   Gilroy, *The Black Atlantic: Modernity and Double Consciousness.*
7   See, e.g., Kahn and Whitehead, *Wireless Imaginations: Sound, Radio and the Avant-
     Garde*; Kahn, "Track Organology."

References

Auner, Joseph. "'Sing It for Me': Posthuman Ventriloquism in Recent Popular Music."
     Journal of the Royal Musical Association 128, no. 1 (January 1, 2003): 98–122.
Berland, Jody. "Radio Space and Industrial Time: Music Formats, Local Narrative and
     Technological Mediation." *Popular Music* 9, no. 2 (1990): 179–92.
Brackett, David. *Interpreting Popular Music.* Berkeley: University of California Press,
     2000.
Butler, Mark Jonathan. *Unlocking the Groove: Rhythm, Meter, and Musical Design in
     Electronic Dance Music.* Indiana University Press, 2006.
Feld, Steven. "Aesthetics as Iconicity of Style (uptown title) or (downtown title) 'Lift-Up-
     Over-Sounding': Getting into the Kaluli Groove." In *Music Grooves.* Chicago:
     University of Chicago Press, 1996.
Flinn, Caryl. *Strains of Utopia: Gender, Nostalgia and Hollywood Film Music.* Princeton:
     Princeton University Press, 1992.
Frith, Simon. *Performing Rites: On the Value of Popular Music.* Cambridge, Mass.: Harvard
     University Press, 1996.
Gilroy, Paul. *The Black Atlantic: Modernity and Double Consciousness.* Cambridge:
     Harvard University Press, 1994.
Gracyk, Theodore. *Rhythm and Noise: An Aesthetics of Rock.* Durham: Duke University
     Press, 1996.

Grossberg, Lawrence. *Dancing In Spite of Myself: Essays on Popular Culture*. Durham: Duke University Press, 1997.

Hainge, Greg. "Of Glitch and Men: The Place of the Human in the Successful Integration of Failure and Noise in the Digital Realm." *Communication Theory* 17, no. 1 (2007): 26–42.

Haraway, Donna. *Simians, Cyborgs and Women*. New York: Routledge, 1991.

Hegarty, Paul. *Noise/Music: A History*. New York: Continuum, 2007.

Kahn, Douglas. "Track Organology." *October*, no. 55 (1990): 67–78.

Kahn, Douglas, and Gregory Whitehead. *Wireless Imaginations: Sound, Radio and the Avant-Garde*. Cambridge: MIT Press, 1992.

Katz, Mark. *Capturing Sound: How Technology has Changed Music*. Berkeley: University of California Press, 2004.

Keil, Charles. "Motion and Feeling Through Music." In *Music Grooves*, 53–76. Chicago: University of Chicago Press, 1994.

Kelly, Caleb. *Cracked Media: The Sound of Malfunction*. MIT Press, 2009.

Langer, Susanne K. *Philosophy in a New Key; A Study in the Symbolism of Reason, Rite, and Art*. Cambridge: Harvard University Press, 1957.

McClary, Susan. *Feminine Endings: Music, Gender, and Sexuality*. Minneapolis: University of Minnesota Press, 1991.

Meyer, Leonard B. *Emotion and Meaning in Music*. Chicago: University of Chicago Press, 1956.

Negus, Keith. *Popular Music in Theory: An Introduction*. Hanover, NH: University Press of New England, 1997.

Small, Christopher. *Musicking: The Meanings of Performing and Listening*. Hanover: Wesleyan University Press, 1998.

Swiss, Thomas, John M. Sloop, and Andrew Herman. *Mapping the Beat: Popular Music and Contemporary Theory*. Malden, MA: Blackwell Publishers, 1998.

Tagg, Philip. "Kojak – 50 Seconds of Television Music: Toward the Analysis of Affect in Popular Music". Musikvetenskapliga institutionen vid Göteborgs universitet, 1979.

Whitely, Sheila. *Sexing the Groove: Popular Music and Gender*. New York: Routledge, 1997.

Chapter 33

Richard Leppert

READING THE SONORIC LANDSCAPE

The Sonoric Landscape, Representation, and Embodiment

THE SERIOUSNESS AND INTENSITY OF DEBATE over sonoric meaning is notable in the histories of musical codification, virtually all of which focus on the different social and cultural consequences of authorized and unauthorized sounds. Indeed, so significant is the need to exert control over sonority, I would suggest, that the history of the West itself could profitably be rewritten as an account of sonoric difference: from Plato to the Parents' Music Resource Center, I doubt there is a generation that has escaped the deeply self-conscious concern for ordering the world sonorically.

The landscape, as opposed to the earth as a physical entity, is a perception, a specific and ultimately confined view of a portion of the land that seems "worth" viewing because it is somehow noteworthy. Thus landscape is the different within the same; it is what draws attention to itself. What we define, and separate out, as a landscape appears in our consciousness as something at once "itself" and a representation of itself. That is, when a portion of land is raised in our consciousness to the status of land*scape*, the physical entity is reconstituted in our minds as something in excess of the factual. This excess is experienced as a representation—and as such is discursive. By the phrase "sonoric landscape" I wish to evoke the ubiquity of sonority—a sweep of sound as broad as the land itself. But I also wish to evoke the particularity of *musical* sonority in the larger agglomeration of sounds and the particularities of different musical sonorities.

Sonoric landscapes are both heard and seen. They exist because of human experience and human consciousness. Music (the part of the larger sonoric landscape that interests me) connects to the *visible* human body, not only as the receiver of sound but also as its agent or producer. The human embodiment of music is central to any understanding of music's socio-cultural agency. The semantic content of music— its discursive "argument"—is never solely about its sound and the act of hearing. It is instead about the complex relations between sound and hearing as these are registered and as they mediate the entire experience of being. That experience is physical; intellectual, in the broad meaning of the word; and spiritual, though hardly restricted to the religious or the mystical. But it is especially to be understood as the result of mediations between the ear and the eye. The sonoric landscape is peopled and hence interactive. It is external to the human subject yet internalized by its sight and sound.

The terms *power* and *desire* in my chapter title [see original publication] foreclose the discursive particularities that can be explored in a single essay. I did not choose this pair arbitrarily. After all, to argue that musical discourse possesses agency is to raise questions about power. Yet I do not mean any and all power, but power operating at the level of social and cultural organization—power, that is, in its most obvious connection to the political, narrowly defined. Since music, especially art music, so often these days seems removed from power (one of aestheticism's more peculiar "accomplishments," though an utterly false consciousness if ever there was one), then arguably I should try to relocate it precisely in this more "difficult" space. The category "desire" provides me entry into the *embodied* relations between the private and the public, which, through music, act to shape individual human subjects as well as classes of subjects.

Sound and Social Order

In 1607 the Antwerp painter Abel Grimmer produced a small panel representing spring, one of the four seasons. The image represents a feudal hierarchy and the beneficent prosperity it presumably provided. The subject is poignant given the historical circumstances, namely, the end of a period of bloody conflict between the Spanish Netherlands and its overseers in Spain.[1] Embedded in European representations of the seasons—popular from the Middle Ages onward—are ideals of recurrence, predictability, and the banishment of chaos as well as antagonisms and anxieties about nature and culture and the roles they assigned to people. Spring located the dialectical relation between nature and culture in human desire and sexuality, expressions of hope for new life and general social fecundity. What especially interests me is the role that certain kinds of music play in the representation.

The painting frames a society that is coherent, ordered, hierarchical, static, and peaceful. Hierarchy is evident in the differences between persons, notably between the landed nobility and the peasants who work the land. Stasis, represented perhaps less obviously, is the quality most directly tied to peacefulness. This is not "Spring 1607"; it is "Every Spring" or, more accurately, the visualization of a desire for, and possibly a confidence in, perpetual recurrence.

The cycle of time encoded by definition into representations of the seasons is as integral to agricultural societies as images encapsulating the loss of a day-to-day relation to nature are to our own society—the calendar imagery of endangered species, the Public Television specials on the destruction of the Amazon rain forest, and so forth. To perceive the cycles of time does not eliminate anxiety over the powers that operate in a seasonal spiral. The cycle of all life is biologically established, but any particular life, however its experiences may be constrained by the individual's position in the social hierarchy, is nonetheless lived actively, dynamically, and consciously. Before taking these issues up in detail, I need to describe the picture.

In Grimmer's *Spring* the château of a feudal lord looms in the background, emphasizing his formal garden, probably an herb garden, with all that suggests about medicine and healing. The area under cultivation is laid out geometrically but has none of the statuary or fountains appropriate to a purely decorative garden. Workers prepare the beds, turning soil, raking the earth, seeding, planting slips, spreading fertilizer, watering. Just outside the garden enclosure two men prune a tree, and two women shear sheep. They are all either servants or peasants. Those for whom they labor disport themselves on the grass in a bower, where musicians play while the listeners drink or embrace, as well as above the bower, beneath a topiaried shrub, where several more people, sketchily painted, enjoy social intercourse. Some of them appear to make music, though it is hard to be certain of this. Nearby a couple alone embrace in a small boat on the river, within earshot of the music making. On the horizon, behind a forest, rooftops and a tower stand in for a town or city. In sum, the image's primary details are those of landscape architecture (the beds), intense horticulture (topiary), and architecture proper (not only buildings but also such details as the fencing), though the whole is not rationalized to the degree found in later bourgeois art.[2]

The painting's composition is simultaneously medieval and early modern, its form confronting the changing social constructions in the region during the early seventeenth century. Its modernity locates itself in the strong, off-center diagonals of the garden bed that direct our eyes toward the aristocrats under the bower. Its medieval character, but a conflicted one, locates itself in the activities of the foreground, where our eyes cannot rest on any one figure but wander from person to person, vignette to vignette. A medieval harmony asserts itself in the full social hierarchy represented; I have said as much already. But the stasis necessary for this hierarchy is flawed.

The first flaw, an especially dangerous one, is evident even before we sort out the picture's narrative. It locates itself in the painting's compositional vanishing point, though it is not so neatly established as it will be in later art—is it the castle tower, the town tower, or the meeting of land and sky between the two? The vanishing point is nothing if not a conception of *dynamic,* not static, space. The far horizon establishes difference; it is neither town, nor castle, nor cultivated land, and its ownership is ambiguous. Yet the horizon is made visually relevant once it is incorporated into the composition by means of the vanishing point. Its status rises; the far away means something to the near at hand. Its emptiness, which draws us, is powerful. Like something repressed, it returns; indeed it intrudes. Without the vanishing point, what matters is the world "as shown." Once our eyes are drawn to the distant by means of the vanishing point, the world "as shown" is at once "enriched"—literally and metaphorically deepened—and made more terrestrial, less philosophical. But it is also made relative, part of something else, hence inadequate and unfinished. The guarantee of stasis is undercut. The horizon is a threat whose semantic power acts within the dimension of time, guaranteeing change; it makes space a problematic category, a discursive terrain. Land is no longer a static, unproblematic category for representation; it is instead a depth, a space, a distance: a more-than-this. Land ownership becomes visually fetishized once the land one possesses (here the space close up) is differentiated from what one has not (distant, unconvincingly "claimed" space). Thus this painting incorporates and problematizes the perception of space and time central to the formation of the modern world. To perceive these elements as dynamic was at once to challenge feudalism and to mark the prerequisites for capitalism.

I ask indulgence for an apparent detour, for this history is fundamental to my discussion of music. The connection I seek to establish is this: music, like no other medium of discursive practice, acts simultaneously in space and in time. Although theater does too, it does so differently, because its predominant "text" is words, whereas music's is sonorities as such, even when words are present (worded music). Music is simultaneously more and less than the concrete: it is abstract, yet it is inevitably made and experienced as embodied. Music, unlike theater, has a mystical substance; as an "embodied abstraction" it simultaneously is and is not. It fills space but cannot be measured; and it disappears as absolutely as a shadow once light fades.

Music bears relation to the shadow: it is the *is not* of that which is; it is the account of the real that itself is both real and not real. In no other human practice does agency depend so specifically on being and not being; in this respect music relates to spirituality. This much is true of music throughout human history. What is different and additional at the moment of *Spring,* 1607, is that now and for the first time representationally, hence experientially, the dimensions of time and space in which music operates were severely problematized in Western European experience. The comparatively static and cyclical feudal world, which had been slowly dying for more than a century, was being subsumed under the dynamism of mercantilism and soon-to-be capitalism. Space and time were becoming the dimensions through which human dynamism and agency were understood to operate most fruitfully, in the process giving rise to modern conceptions of the human individual and the activities of individualism. Cycle was about to disappear in favor of vector. Music's history could be read as the prophet. But the feudal and proto-capitalist sides of this history would necessarily read the prophecy differently, each according to its own interests. The ideal audience for this image would find its visual pleasure in a reading premised on feudal continuance, even though the representation itself could not but acknowledge feudalism's decline.

In the center foreground of *Spring* a man bends to his shovel. He and a companion at the extreme left, also holding a shovel, occupy more picture space than other figures and far more than any of the nobility. Our interest in them develops not from any individuality, for they have none, but from their roles as workers and their proximity to our own space. Their faces are not shown; what matters is their strength, marshaled to a task. If we shift our focus to the other workers, men and women alike, we see that they too are mostly faceless and that those whose faces are represented betray not individuality so much as the hardness of their labors (the woman at the extreme left foreground), their contentment (the woman farthest right poking seeds into the ground), and even a kind of lumpish stupidity (the men raking and casting seeds). I say "lumpish" advisedly, for the painter consistently represents the workers as low to the ground, their bodies, shaped like swelled turnips, differentiating them from the two women of superior class looking on at the right side of the garden and giving instructions. The workers' bodies also contrast with those of their social superiors under the bower, notably the male lutenist stretched out comfortably on the ground and his servant who pours wine: long-legged, far from the ground, so to speak.

Yet the nobility themselves are little more than dashes of color; they too are essentially "faceless," so small that we can do little more than call them by their social type. But we see enough, because difference is the key, and difference is unquestionably and unambiguously established. Faces or portraits are not at issue. The scene is a bit of Flanders—as though Flanders were the whole world, excepting again the difficulty with the vanishing point. That *represented* world—I am not arguing about the "real" world of Flanders, only the pictorial one—is typecast, and only the roles matter, not who fills them. So long as the roles hold, everything else matters less and can be made to fit the general scheme. The aristocracy's certainty of position and authority is visually enhanced by its retreat into the background to pursue its pleasures. In later bourgeois images the self-image is foregrounded, openly asserted, and such retreats seldom occur; even in Grimmer's painting, however, prebourgeois anxiety about social position may be evident in both the revelers' proximity to their fortress and the river-as-moat that separates them from their work force.[3]

Contemplation and the Body

The image is structured by three related differences: work from leisure, peasant from aristocrat, and *silence from music*. I am not arguing that the painting's foreground—the nonmusical portion—strikes us as "literally" silent, for the memory traces it activates in viewers do include sound. Sheep, for example, commonly bleat when being sheared, not liking to be held for shearing and often being nicked. And workers are hardly silent in all their labors. Gardeners may hum to themselves, making their own music while engaged in light labor like scattering seeds, if not during more taxing jobs like spading earth. But for the most part the sounds their labors suggest are not musical. More to the point, the painter offers us no encouragement to "see" the laborers singing, whereas he requires us to acknowledge the music of the nobility.

Thus the painting represents two landscapes and two soundscapes. In the foreground is a formal garden, of the sort that would reach its apogee and richest discursive manifestation at Versailles roughly two centuries later. In the background, at the vanishing point to the right of the château, is a forest in an apparently primeval state. The forest is a privileged space, both legally and symbolically. (Poaching game carried severe penalties in forested lands held as private hunting preserves, where the authorized killing of game served not only to supply the princely table with exotic meats but also to signal the princely power of life and death within the domain.) The soundscapes register themselves by simultaneous presence and absence: music fills the air under the bower, opposing the putative silence of the foreground. Expressed via Saussurian semiotics, the *is* (music) defines itself by means of the *is not* (silence, or nonmusic) and vice versa. As such, music—a particular kind of music—represents itself as the sonoric simulacrum of one sort of life, private life, with *private* conflated with privilege and prestige. Private music, ironically represented "in public" so that privacy as such can be visually valorized, is the sonoric overlay that gives meaning to the entire scene, both for the revelers and for the laborers who may overhear sounds that define what they themselves are not.

The immediate function of the music under the bower is love. Those for whom that music is played are the couple with their backs to us between the men playing viol and lute, the couple in the boat, and the couple standing and embracing in dark recess. But overriding the music's amatory function is its role as an agent of social order, manifested in the contemplation of the couple listening between the two instrumentalists. That is, music's pleasure is "purposeful" and not merely something in the air, like the chirpings of birds. It invites conscious audition, of sufficient seriousness that the one couple turn their backs to us to hear. What they listen to and for—by definition—is a sonoric discourse, probably one that interpolates them less in the present, which after all is momentarily uncontested to the extent that it simply *is,* than in the future, which more than ever before is up for grabs, not only because feudalism is dying but also specifically because Flanders was experiencing upheavals at the moment of the painting's production.

The incorporation into the image of "art music" and its audition as the central "event" among the nobility establishes an opposition between contemplation (thought) and physical labor (in essence, nonthought). Such music is self-conscious, intentional, inherently and necessarily "rational." It is not spontaneous but planned, so as to sanction and articulate sonorically a meaning of the physical events transpiring not only under the bower but also in the painting's foreground. To the extent that this music is listened to, it is a passive engagement; but because passivity functions here as a sign of social division, it is a means of valorizing social difference. Not accidentally, it recapitulates the ancient Boethian precedence of the critic/auditor over the producer.

It is well known that opera houses, well into the nineteenth century, were the locus for conversation and other activities as much as for listening and that audiences commonly quieted down en masse only to hear favorite musical bits. It is also established that the gradual silencing of talk and the increasing expectation that audiences attend to musical performance in both opera theater and concert hall developed with the middle class's enshrinement of symphonic instrumental music. Attentiveness to music—what Adorno termed contemplation—may of course be explained as a laudable enhancement of high art, but it is neither that simple nor entirely benign.

The problematics of contemplation, a "mental" activity, emerge the moment mind intersects with body. The etiquette of "contemplation" is, before anything else, a controlling of the body in time, a working against the body, whether self-imposed or imposed by others (like parents who discipline their squirming children). And it is an etiquette that turns music from an inherently participatory activity into a passive one in which the listener maintains physical stasis by exerting the cultural force of will against the body's desires. The auditor may move toes in time to the beat but not hum, stomp feet, sway the torso, or bob the head: bodily reaction to music in the concert hall must be neither audible nor visible. To give oneself over to any of these reactions invites rebuke.[4]

I will not sort out here the full complexities and ramifications of this etiquette, but will instead identify just one facet that applies most directly to my concerns, namely, that the etiquette invokes, mirrors, and replicates macrocosmic mechanisms for establishing social order. The etiquette of physical passivity, simultaneously imposed and self-imposed, reflects the achievement of social hegemony in part through cultural practice. "Consent" is manufactured, gradually learned and internalized, rather than imposed by raw force, as Antonio Gramsci pointed out many years ago.[5] Further, a socially required passivity of reception becomes a simulacrum of the socially correct meaning of the performance itself. Both the sonorities heard and the act of performance itself are disciplines.[6] The music being contemplated draws attention to itself, raises the stakes of its presence, specifically as an "activity" whose valorization is organized by rendering the body static. Music in this guise acts as a sonoric surveillance on the body, holding it captive to contemplation with the social proscription of physical reaction.[7] Not incidentally, whether the auditor actually contemplates is perfectly irrelevant to the demand.

Music and Difference

In *Spring* music possesses and creates prestige by imposing its presence in relation to lived, *linear* time, this despite the typically cyclical experience of time in agricultural societies. I want to connect this matter first to erotics, then to music. One common feudal articulation of linear time occurs in the mythology of courtly love. Though the "literary practice" of courtly love predates by several centuries the period of my concern, the courtship central to it occupies the group under the bower. Courtly love, as idealized and theorized by Andreas Capellanus in the twelfth century,[8] valorized relationships whose intensity depended on the indefinite postponement of the physical. The lover's platonic suffering could be enjoyed for many years; indeed, the longer the wait, the sweeter the agony. Any reader of *The Romance of the Rose,* the best known verse account of chivalric love, is aware that delay—prolonged through tens of thousands of lines—articulated desire and was itself an object of desire worthy of intense contemplation. Delay and desire are premised on a grid of time. And that grid, on which one plays out one's life by willfully waiting, charts an excessive control over time, one that enables the lover to wait in a world where the ability to wait establishes status.

In the painting time is valorized in an equation, whose product is prestige, that depends on our witnessing simultaneous but opposing events confirming that while some must work, others must not and that if one kind of work is physical, the other is overtly and actively mental: contemplative listening. Contemplative listening is not philosophically removed from the world, as later aesthetic theory would have it; it is instead the sign of one's control and domination of the world. Music, as a phenomenon that acts through time, when heard contemplatively stops all other activities. As such, it *is* an exercise of power, a political act. It is worth noting that "contemplative" sensual desire, that odd privilege of "doing without," is explicitly opposed to the sensual archaeology of the lower social strata, as characterized in endless numbers of contemporaneous representations, where the order of the day is rampant physical groping in an uncertain, unstable time frame. For the peasantry, the sensual is formulated temporally as instantaneous, the mythology of chivalric love disappearing in the lunge of bodies striving to copulate.[9] Nonetheless, as regards the private music making represented in *Spring,* an irony has to be faced. To account for the political capital of privacy, the sonoric-visual signs of that privacy, music making and lovemaking together, have to be made visually public, have to be voyeuristically displayed. In *this* sense representation, whether visual or sonoric, is the simulacrum not of strength but of weakness, an acknowledgment that culture is process and that all process incorporates the promise of change.

Music is a possession to be paraded before Grimmer's laborers, and before viewers outside the picture frame, as the sight and sound of difference. But since music itself is "simply air," what it encodes of power is the power over time. For some, the world can be made to stop while the air is filled with music's emptiness. Music's power, according to this formulation, *is* its emptiness, which constitutes itself ironically as a sign of fullness and excess. It can be no wonder that with the advent of the bourgeois world, but with notable recourse to Plato, so much anxiety was manifested about music as a waste of time. That the emergent bourgeoisie were so consistently reproachful about musicians in their ranks, especially male musicians, is hardly surprising given both the class's hatred for the perquisites and discursive practices of the nobility and its ironic fetishization of time as money. Nor can it be surprising that the bourgeoisie themselves quickly figured out how music—to be sure, music of their "own sort"—could be engaged sonorically to represent their interests.

Representations of the seasons are visual idealizations of feudal ideology, feudal hierarchy, and feudal consciousness. They are mental projections, visually articulated, about a future that continues and perfectly realizes the present. They are less the world as it truly is than the world as it is desired, but with desire seamlessly constructed out of present circumstances. Not incidentally, therein lies the inherent anxiety of representation: "A visual image, so long as it is not being used as a mask or disguise, is always a comment on an *absence.* The depiction comments on the absence of what is being depicted. Visual images, based on appearances, always speak of *dis*appearance."[10] As for music, the representation does not, strictly speaking, address the reality of performance practices. But that is not to suggest that musical images like Grimmer's bear no relation to musical life. Grimmer's musicians and their audience must relate closely to the functions of music in the society represented; if not, their presence would be nonsensical: discursive practice disallows "empty decoration."

Grimmer, in deciding to organize his image around the full social spectrum, had to face the issue of what he would have the nobility *do.* Apart from warring and hunting, the nobility ordinarily conveyed their rank by an absence of physical activity. But in an image whose subject—spring—requires an orderly presentation of peace (no warring) and growth or new life (no hunting), the nobility nonetheless need to be shown *using* the time they supposedly controlled, over which no power is so absolute as that of appearing to do nothing while others do for you. Music is the ideal activity to make the point clear. One can make music oneself with a minimum of physicality, like the lounging lutenist, or one can pay someone else, like the violist, to make it in one's presence; the result is something at once beautiful *and* produced. It is something cultural, not natural; the manifestation of another level of power, it is nevertheless *nothing.* The power of music making is not only the power to control time through the expenditure of leisure; it is also the license to waste time. Music is visually extravagant. (The possibility that music, as a productless entity, was trivial has troubled philosophers, moralists, and politicians throughout Western history, though these concerns only reached their zenith in post-Renaissance Europe.)[11]

Music's pleasures and relevance have virtually never been denied. Indeed, music's most virulent enemies have often condemned music, or some music, precisely for the pleasures it provides and the effects of its audition on the social fabric. Even when judged a trivial pursuit, in other words, music retains its relevance, a negative one. Throughout history music has existed in conflict with what, sonorically, it is its purpose to define. Music is condemned, if not interdicted, as much as it is praised and supported. It is necessary to realize that debates about music are not about nothing. The disputes in any age between ancients and moderns concern the sonoric portion of the social order and the identity of the human subject, especially the sensual subject, therein. That is why Grimmer, ultimately responsible to the interests of his patrons—who might sit under a bower but would not wield shovels—represented the only music possible, just as music itself is very nearly the only "activity" ideologically and politically available to project ideological "correctness."

There is a complementary way of expressing this point. *Spring* is a narrative that strives visually for closure, doubly postulated as a successful ending, a non-challenge, and an account sealed off from the outside. Any narrative not only produces a world but also, by that very act, necessarily excludes as well. The activities of including and excluding are never innocent, accidental, or semantically void. They betray an interest—stakes. Moreover, the concern with closure in representation incorporates a gendered response to storytelling, a characteristic of male psycho-sexual efforts to gain and maintain control.[12]

In hierarchical societies there cannot be one undifferentiated body of music. The musics that exist must be classified, and their differences must be articulated *in words*. Unclassified sound, soundscape without the registration of difference, is the sonoric allowance of either democracy or anarchy. Valorization must occur; sound as a dimension of human activity and human agency cannot be left out of the socio-cultural equation. The Platonic metaphor conflating musical harmony and world harmony was not accidental, as Plato himself makes clear in his diatribe on listening—however abstract his conception and nonscientific his "astronomy." Musical classification for Plato is essential because sonoric control is one guarantee of the utopia he envisions.

Notes

1.   See pp. 246–47 n. 21 [see original publication].
2.   See the different, though partly complementary, accounts of what I would call rationalized landscape painting by Ann Bermingham, *Landscape and Ideology: The English Rustic Tradition, 1740–1860* (Berkeley and Los Angeles: University of California Press, 1986); and John Barrell, *The Dark Side of the Landscape: The Rural Poor in English Painting, 1730–1840* (Cambridge: Cambridge University Press, 1980).
3.   In the painting a small river separates foreground from background; it marks the division between the two types of human subject represented. But the stream's presence is obscured or disguised at the crucial point where the two groups of people come into closest

proximity. Here the division seems momentarily to disappear, as if the river itself disappeared, as if the two groups engaged in free intercourse after all. But this is merely an illusion of oneness. Indeed, the river disappears as a barrier only to have its function taken up by a hedge, and the hedge opens up, like a gate, to lead to the river bank: access is controlled. To cross the barrier one needs a boat, and the only boat in the picture is occupied by aristocratic lovers, who look, not toward the workers, but toward the château, the architectural confirmation of their identity and the guarantee that they will retain their status.

4. Cf. Laura Mulvey, *Visual and Other Pleasures* (Bloomington: Indiana University Press, 1989), p. 167: "The mind/body opposition is characteristic of other oppositions of dominance (black/white, colonized/conqueror, peasant/noble, bourgeoisie/worker) and in each case the oppressed are linked to nature (the body) and the dominant to culture (and the mind)."

5. Antonio Gramsci, *An Antonio Gramsci Reader: Selected Writings, 1916–1935,* ed. David Forgacs (New York: Schocken Books, 1988), pp. 306–7. In a later passage (p. 356), Gramsci acknowledges music in his list of "sources of linguistic conformism" through which the socially dominant articulate their interests and inculcate them in the population at large. He is primarily concerned here with the linguistic means of mass producing consent: the educational system, newspapers, theater, film, radio, and so forth. Music enters in a discussion of relations between "the more educated and less educated strata of the population" via the following lengthy parenthetical insight: "A question which is perhaps not given all the attention it deserves is that of the 'words' in verse learnt by heart in the form of songs, snatches of operas, etc. It should be noted that the people do not bother really to memorize these words, which are often strange, antiquated and baroque, but reduce them to kinds of nursery rhymes that are only helpful for remembering the tune." Gramsci does not consider how the music itself performs the role of agent via its own sonorities beyond the semantic quotient of the word text the music accompanies, which is the argument I am advancing, though he implies as much when he points out music's power to overwhelm words.

6. I am borrowing here from Michel Foucault, *Discipline and Punish: The Birth of the Prison,* trans. Alan Sheridan (New York: Vintage Books, 1979).

7. See further Christopher Small, *Music, Society, Education* (New York: Schirmer, 1977), chapter 1, "The Perfect Cadence and the Concert Hall," pp. 7–33.

8. Andreas Capellanus, *The Art of Courtly Love,* trans. John Jay Parray (New York: Norton, 1969).

9. Among the best painted examples are works by David Teniers the Younger, on which see my "David Teniers the Younger and the Image of Music," *Jaarboek, Koninklijk Museum voor Schone Kunsten* (Antwerp, 1978), pp. 63–155 passim.

10. John Berger, "Painting and Time," in *The Sense of Sight,* ed. Lloyd Spencer (New York: Pantheon Books, 1985), p. 207.

11. I have written extensively about this phenomenon in my book *Music and Image: Domesticity, Ideology, and Socio-Cultural Formation in Eighteenth-Century England* (Cambridge: Cambridge University Press, 1989).

12. See Mulvey, "Film, Feminism, and the Avant-Garde," in *Visual and Other Pleasures,* pp. 11–26.

Chapter 34

Georgina Born

MUSIC RESEARCH AND PSYCHOACOUSTICS

THE RELATED DOMAINS OF PSYCHOACOUSTICS AND MUSIC research also had a pivotal ideological position in 1984 within IRCAM, and they were propounded by the musicians' group as the way forward for musical composition. The musicians' meetings were initiated in urgent response to a massive planning document for the future of IRCAM, written by the incumbent Scientific Director at the start of '84, which hardly mentioned music or music research at all. That autumn he left IRCAM and his plans were never realized; but internal conflict between the scientific side and those who saw themselves as upholding IRCAM's musical ideals appeared to be chronic. As the musicians' meetings developed, they worked on defining two levels of future music research: the main research themes, and the social organization of research, for which they proposed new collaborative teams reminiscent of Boulez's Bauhaus model. This was a bid for more autonomy, power, and resources for music research, which the group felt to be under threat. By insisting on the centrality of IRCAM's future and long-term orientation, its musical goals and social organization, the group embodied a fundamentalist return to Boulez's original vision.

Central to the musicians' group engagement with music research and psychoacoustics in 1984 were interrelated concerns with timbre and with musical form. This must be understood in the context of historical developments arising from the impasses of musical modernism earlier in the century and their contemporary legacy.

The functional tonal music system upon which baroque, classical, and romantic music was based centered on manipulations of pitch, while timbre was a relatively neglected parameter of composition. With the gradual dissolution of functional tonality in late romanticism and early modernism, composers showed increased awareness of timbre, whether in Debussy's exploration of tone color or Varèse's extension of the range of sound materials. However, Schoenberg was the first to theorize timbre as a major musical parameter with his 1911 concept of *Klangfarbenmelodie*: a "melody" defined by successive changes of timbre rather than pitch. Webern, in his pointillist works, pursued this by experimenting with timbral contrasts as a structuring device.

As we saw in chapter 2 [see original publication], the main thrust of the postwar avant-garde under the ideology of total serialism was the scientific extension of serialism to control all musical parameters, including timbre. But attempts to control timbre in this way by electronic synthesis, such as those by Stockhausen, produced poor, monotonous results. This was not the only postwar expression of an interest in timbre. Perhaps in reaction to the rationalist excesses of total serialism, during the '60s an eclectic range of composers – from the Poles Lutoslawski and Penderecki of the *Klangfarbenschule*, to Xenakis, Berio, and indeed Stockhausen – evinced a looser, sometimes mystical concern with sound color. At the same time Schaeffer was taking further the idea of timbre as a structural dimension with his aim of constructing a *solfège* of timbres for *musique concrète*. But it was the failure of early electronic synthesis in the service of total serialism, and of the acoustic analyses informing it, that led to efforts by scientists such as Risset to gain better analyses of timbre. I noted before how important computer technology became in allowing a new kind of feedback between timbral analysis and digital synthesis, with the idea that, in theory, digital synthesis could produce any timbre, given appropriate information.

This generation of researchers came to believe that physical descriptions alone could not explain the perceptually or musically meaningful aspects of timbre, so psychoacoustical research was deemed necessary to find the most perceptually important dimensions. These analyses helped to achieve a more organic range of synthesized timbres, revealing at the same time the extraordinary complexity of timbre for both analysis and synthesis – something that we will see continues to pose problems for computer music.

Some psychoacoustic research was employed, however, in a harsher critique of total serialism. Composers and researchers hostile to serialism and concerned with the audience's bewildered incomprehension of this music turned to perception studies to explain it. They argued that serialism transgressed the perceptual limits of the listener and was too complex and fragmented to be musically meaningful. In some cases, the scientific refutation of serialism was allied to a postmodern call for a return to tonality. This research did not simply criticize serialism as music, then, but offered a scientific critique based on purported universals of human perception.

A final factor in this history concerns another major problem in twentieth-century composition: the absence of any coherent approach to musical form since the advent of modernism. This refers to the high-level organization of musical sound horizontally, through time, but also vertically, as with tonal harmony. Classical musical form had continued into late romanticism, but with the break from tonality around the turn of the century came the question of new forms to match the new musical systems of atonality and then serialism. Boulez in 1951 chided Schoenberg for the "contradiction" of retaining classical form despite his invention of serialism, and Boulez's view – that musical modernism must seek new forms to suit new sound materials – became orthodox. Yet over the century no sustained modernist approach to form emerged, so that the problem of new musical forms has remained central to debates around modernism and its limits and has been high on the compositional agenda.

More recently two important developments have occurred, both dependent on the computer. The first links issues of form with timbre and time. We have seen that throughout the century composers have considered whether timbral change can structure music in time. Computer synthesis offers ways to further this, since unlike *musique concrète* and electronic synthesis, every component of a digitally simulated timbre is built up completely from scratch so that the timbre is no longer inviolate but, in theory, infinitely malleable. The technology has therefore come to be seen as a means of taking two such simulated timbral objects and, through an analysis of their components, building a "bridge" or "transition" between them. According to this approach, timbral objects need no longer remain discrete, but may be transformed, melted into one another, thereby creating unprecedented possibilities for structural movement by timbral change. Hence, while at the micro level each partial in the timbre is rapidly evolving in time, at the macro level the transitions construct higher-level musical time — a "timbral syntax."

One possibility of timbral transition, then, is that the microtemporal processes within the timbre and the formal macroprocesses constructed by timbral syntax could be related. The composer could derive macromusical forms from microtimbral processes — generate the whole from the seed — or vice versa, and so create unity. This is a highly sophisticated version of the notion of unifying micro and macro that we saw in chapter 6 [see original publication] was a rhetoric widespread within IRCAM and that continues the organicism of the tradition of German romanticism as reinterpreted by Schoenberg. In 1984 this approach was the pinnacle to which IRCAM's musicians' group vanguard in various ways aspired: an organicism doubly consecrated through its mediation by the latest, most astute scientific analyses and by the unique musical possibilities of advanced computer technologies. Since in 1984 the Chant and Formes programs were considered by many in the group to come closest to offering tools to pursue these ideas, the destinies of the Chant/Formes group and that of the vanguard were closely entwined.

The second development around musical form has involved a different level of computer applications. The work of writers such as Meyer (1956) indicates the parallels that have been developed in the past between information theory and music analysis. In disciplines related to computer science we can trace a development from information theory through cognitive science to artificial intelligence, a kind of applied cognitive modeling with the computer both as analytic tool and means of simulation. AI is based on the analysis of forms of knowledge to extract their essential content and logic or "rules," which are then redescribed as a structure of inference and written as an "intelligent" computer program, such as an "expert system," that represents a simulation of that knowledge system. Similarly, in music there has been a development from music analysis as a purely analytic field to one that, employing the computer and in conjunction with the rise of cognitive music studies and AI, aims to provide both computer analyses of musical structure and also computerized models of "musical knowledge" or "rules" as aids to composition. The computer has therefore come to be seen as a tool for analyzing the deep structures or "cognitive rules" characteristic of certain musics, but equally for simulating these rules — and indeed for generating entirely new abstract structures as frameworks for composition.

There are two observations to be made. First, we can see in these developments, due to the mediation of the computer as both analytic tool and simulator, a subtle but profound elision between analysis and composition: the two are close to becoming as one. Thus, at IRCAM in 1984 the main psychoacoustician, HM, constantly entertained the desire to compose since he saw his cognitive analytical work as generating compositional ideas, yet other composers' use of his research disappointed him.[1]

Second, the computer's ability to produce elegant abstract models has meant that its generation of new conceptual schemes for music, in particular mathematical and cognitive structural models, has become quite autonomous from the analysis of extant musics. This lay, for example, behind the AI-influenced approach of IRCAM's Formes program, with its generalized and abstract, hierarchical ordering of objects and events in time.

Both of these developments, along with the constant conceptual foraging for scientific analogies to structure composition that I described in the last chapter [see original publication], evidence a continuity with deeper characteristics of musical modernism. They should be grasped as an extreme contemporary expression of modernist theoreticism, the tendency for theory to become prior to, prescriptive of, and constitutive of compositional practice.

In this genealogy the scientific study of cognitive universals takes a central place, both psychoacoustic study of microtimbral and temporal processes and cognitive study of musical structure. We have seen a convergence from several directions of interrelated concerns with timbre and sound material, timbre and temporality, timbre and form, and timbre and perception. All were considered to be enhanced by the computer, since in theory it enables "any imaginable sound" or musical structure to be both analyzed and simulated. Yet it is also obvious that timbre becomes a rhetorical catchall subsuming many diverse preoccupations, and that "timbre," "temporality," and "perception" become generalized discursive themes. Motivated by major problems of musical modernism – the sense of sterility attached to composition techniques such as serialism based originally on the primacy of pitch, the lack of an approach to musical form, the errors of midcentury rationalism and scientism, the conceptual weakness of *musique concrète* – research on timbre and perception has been held, at IRCAM and more widely, to offer ways forward.

Overall, it is striking that the response to the deep musical and philosophical impasses that arose around early and midcentury serialist modernism has been to amend and improve the rationalism and scientism through increasingly sophisticated scientific and technological mediation. Far from rejecting the deeper epistemological character of modernism, postserialism has refined and complexified it, for example in the elision of computerized music analysis with compositional genesis. As we will see in greater depth, the discourse within which IRCAM is situated is a scientistic refinement of the classic concerns of modernism.

This legacy, with little overt hostility to serialism, lay behind the continuous reference to perception, timbre, and form by the IRCAM vanguard, for whom the study of musical perception and cognition would lay the basis for new sound materials and new musical forms. In 1984 there were, by consensus, two main psychoacousticians at IRCAM, neither employed as such: Pedagogy director RIG and junior tutor HM, both of whom had trained in cognitive music psychology.

IRCAM's psychoacoustic research at this time examined how listening organizes the physical world by differentiation and integration. The issue of aural integration can be illustrated by pitch perception, which involves the unconscious integration of many different harmonic partials (frequencies within the harmonic series) into a single sound object. This psychoacoustical phenomenon is called "fusion," and it was a theme of HM's research.

Work on harmonic fusion has fed into study of the contrasting perception of "inharmonics": those sounds, like bells, that are not based on a single harmonic series. Research has shown that we do not hear inharmonics as fused single objects; rather, we search unconsciously within them for the patterns of the harmonic series and hear them as a set of overlapping, incomplete harmonic pitches. In fact, when we perceive a pattern of higher harmonics within an inharmonic but the fundamental harmonic frequency is physically missing, the brain projects a phantom fundamental to replace the missing one, a phenomenon known as "virtual pitch." These apparent details were major interests of IRCAM's vanguard, since digital synthesis has the unique potential to construct infinite numbers of inharmonics and to change over time their "internal" structure of frequencies (or spectrum) so as to produce interesting senses of movement "within" the the sound – another kind of timbral transition, known at IRCAM as the "evolution of spectral form." Thus research on inharmonics, virtuals, fusion, and the "internal evolution" of sounds was seen as potentially valuable for composition.

The phenomenon of aural differentiation can be illustrated by RIG's studies of timbre. It is known that listeners have the capacity to differentiate relatively between pitches, so that they hear pitch intervals as relatively the same (for example a fifth, an octave) even if at absolutely different registers. RIG's work in the 1970s examined whether subjects have a similar cognitive capacity to differentiate between timbres, which are both physically and perceptually multidimensional. He focused on the "multidimensional scaling" of timbre and the notion of perceiving "timbral analogies." Subjects were asked to judge the similarity or difference between instrumental timbres (oboe and cello, clarinet and voice) sounding the same pitch. This gave a distribution of timbres according to perceived likeness and difference, though little understanding of the parameters underlying these judgments. From this, RIG drew up graphic representations of timbral perception in terms of two-dimensional and three-dimensional spatial distributions. These were meant to provide predictive maps of how to create perceptually interesting new timbres, as well as to serve as guidelines for the simulation of perceptually valid timbral transitions. The research aimed to inform both the synthesis of new sound materials and, through timbral syntax, new compositional forms. The implicit message: "where pitch was, let there be timbre."

Composer AV's project in 1984, described in the next chapter [see original publication], was an attempt to put some of this psychoacoustical work on timbral transition into compositional practice. In the following dialogue, HM, who was involved in the project, discussed the aims as well as problems that arose. But the exchange also conveys well the strategy whereby issues of perception are brought in as a hopeful way out of what has been, essentially, an aesthetic failure. The failure was an attempt to create a musically meaningful "interpolation" between two distinct timbres by synthesizing glissandi (slides) between their component frequencies.

Rather than reconsider whether such an aim is unmusical, HM preferred to think of the aim – a key principle of the music vanguard as informed by psychoacoustics – as correct, but the method used as perceptually at "too low a level." The answer, for him, was therefore not to think of a new musical aim but to be more scientific.

> *HM:* In his first visit in '82, AV wanted to work on timbral transition – from an oboe to a soprano voice sound – and we did that using Chant on the PDP10 with MC's help. Then he wanted transitions from very complicated inharmonic sounds like a gong or tam-tam into a soprano. But the problem is: even at the level of physical modeling, there's no similarity at all between those two things. I wrote him some [software] instruments that would allow him to take any given set of frequencies and have them interpolated in some bizarre fashion with another. It was a total failure. All we got is this large glissando which was not at all satisfactory for timbral transformation. So we started to think of other ways. . . .
>
> We learned that it's not just to do with the frequency dimension. It's much more complicated. I've been playing a lot recently with this notion of the coherence of the behavior of sound objects, and what coherence means in one case is totally different from another case. So for that to be successful you'd have to be making the interpolations at a much higher level of behavior of the elements, because simply thinking at an acoustic level is not satisfactory. We did get some partially satisfactory results, based on a notion I came up with of a sort of pivot – a period of time in which things decompose and recompose into other objects. That was much better; we'd totally disintegrate one sound and then have it re-form over a specified time into the other sound.
>
> *GB:* What you seem to be saying about timbral transformation is that the idea of interpolation as a continuous process is contradicted by realizing how precise are the coherences of timbres as discrete objects? . . .
>
> *HM:* I wouldn't say it's contradicted: I think it *is* contradicted at the level we were dealing with it. But that's like trying to talk about social organization at the level of molecules – we were trying to deal with it at too low a level. It implies having a much better knowledge about what we mean by coherence in each case; so that when transformation takes place, it's at a *perceptually relevant* level, so that coherence is maintained, or incoherence if that's desired, at a level that's *believable* to the ear.
>
> *GB:* So you're still convinced of the idea that there could be a syntax of timbral transformations that could in itself be some kind of syntactic language?
>
> *HM:* Yes, I think so.

The absences in IRCAM's psychoacoustics are also significant. As well as being central to the *stage*, psychoacoustics was the subject of IRCAM's main public lecture series in 1984 called "Perception and Composition." Both courses dealt with timbre, inharmonics, and so on, but neither dealt at any length with rhythm as a musical dimension. Only the public lectures had a session called "Rhythm and

Time Perception," which looked at issues of time, memory, and duration rather than rhythmic issues of pulsation, beat, repetition – phenomena associated aesthetically with jazz and popular musics. Musical time in total serialism is conceived in terms of calculated durations that construct extremely complex and irregular rhythmic structures. RIG, who gave the lecture and who we have seen was keen on jazz, nonetheless spent all his time on a critique of this serialist approach and its lack of perceptual validity. He talked with relish, as follows.

> Boulez was a guinea pig in an experiment in complex rhythmic perception at Bell Labs. The idea was: can a composer really hear the differences if a performer of his music plays very complex rhythms right or wrong? For example, in $^6/_8$ a 7 over 6, or 19s over 13s, and so on – such as one finds often in the music of Carter or Ferneyhough. The results? Boulez and a well-known avant-garde violinist both showed great *errors,* and in opposite directions! So this shows that the ideas of rhythmic perception of someone like Carter are *wrong!* They are impossible to realize on two levels: that of production by a player and that of perception by a listener, even a highly skilled one!

RIG ended the thirty-minute talk: "I was going to talk about another level – why one jazz drummer will have 'swing' and another won't! But I guess I'll leave that for another evening." He therefore managed only the briefest reference, amounting to an evasion, of the issue of sophisticated rhythm in other musics such as jazz; and this, on the tail of an elaborate perceptual critique of serialist rhythm that signaled his ongoing ideological battle with Boulez.

This incident highlights the specificity of the musical terrain that IRCAM's psychoacoustic research addressed and upon which it erected "universal" models of human perception. In fact, during 1984 there was one research project devoted to analyzing the "rules" of jazz improvisation, which may seem to contradict my point about the aesthetic limits and the universalizing character of IRCAM's psychoacoustics. But the project was weak, its status low, and it was bugged by illegitimacy, above all because it was seen as not sufficiently generalizable by contrast with the rest of IRCAM's psychoacoustics, which was presumed to be.[2] In his lectures, HM appeared to have a sophisticated grasp of the issue of musical-cultural differences, admitting that "our cognitive abilities are experience-based, culturally specific." Yet challenged by a student who posed the extreme cultural determinist position – "But I hear no sound, nor any music, outside a certain aesthetic and historical context: it's all in these contexts!" – HM said nothing and the issue was never elaborated. Rather, on another occasion HM opted for a different perspective that evades cultural or aesthetic specificity, this time by dissolving it into an extreme individualism: the poststructuralist idea of music as a radically "open text," HM talked of "listeners [recreating] music by their own taste structure, so there are a multiplicity of different meanings or readings in a certain music." As we have seen, this rhetoric was also at times characteristic of Boulez.

Finally, it is worth noting that RIG's experiments in timbral perception involved just nine subjects: of these, all were IRCAM workers and one was Boulez. It is on the basis of these thin experiments employing very culturally specific subjects that RIG drew data to be interpreted in terms of universals of timbral perception and intended in turn to generate apparently aesthetically independent techniques of timbral syntax. This throws into relief the claims of the research to embody culturally independent perceptual or musical universals, and it emphasizes the ideological nature of the scientific claims to universality.

Notes

1.   Interestingly, this was later modified. A friend reported of HM in 1987, "He's given up on the idea of becoming a composer. He accepts that he's a good psychoacoustician, but that doesn't mean he's a good composer or can become one."

2.   The project, on computer analysis of the "rules" of jazz improvisation, involved two outsiders unpaid by IRCAM: a postgraduate who knew nothing of music and a French musicologist who had written on jazz phrasing. In May the project came before a Music Research meeting for assessment where, despite the backing of RIG, its legitimacy was continually questioned. Another director asked dubiously, "Is this *really* a music research project? How do you see it being generalized here?"

3.   For the overriding purpose of maintaining the anonymity of my informants, in this section, with permission, I have not divulged the journal's name or given full references for the short quotes taken from articles.

4.   MC meant here that the speakers in his room linked to the interconnected speaker system were always turned on, in order that he could overhear *stagiaires'* sounds and so judge their talent

5.   Lyotard argues that the self-legitimation by the quest for truth characteristic of science until the late nineteenth century has been "delegitimized": "a process of delegitimation fueled by the demand for legitimation itself . . . an internal erosion of the legitimacy principle of knowledge" (Lyotard 1984, 39). He summarizes: "The goal is no longer truth, but performativity. . . . The State and/or company must abandon the idealist and humanist narratives of legitimation. . . . Scientists, technicians, and instruments are purchased not to find truth, but to augment power" (ibid., 46).

References

Jean-François Lyotard, *The Postmodern Condition: A Report on Knowledge*. Translated by Geoff Bennington and Brian Massumi. Foreword by Fredric Jameson. Minneapolis: University of Minnesota Press, 1984.

Leonard Meyer, *Emotion and Meaning in Music*. Chicago: University of Chicago Press, 1956.

Chapter 35

Douglas Kahn

NOISES OF THE AVANT-GARDE

Bruitism

EARLIER THIS CENTURY IN EUROPE when men, mostly, got together in cafés and made noise as art, noise became very significant. One café in particular, the Cabaret Voltaire of Zurich Dada, left a legacy of artistic revolution. This noise was made significant in part by making others—primarily women and non-Europeans—insignificant in a context of war and religion. Situated in the middle of World War I both geographically (Switzerland) and chronologically (1916), Cabaret Voltaire was filled with people who were lucky enough to have escaped by stealth or wealth the horrors gripping the rest of Europe. Noise music, noise making, and even sound poetry and simultaneous poetry in Dada fell under the term *bruitism,* and although bruitism was varied and used any number of noise-making devices, its emblem at the Cabaret Voltaire was Richard Huelsenbeck banging on the big drum. As Huelsenbeck himself would have it, all of Dada itself "beats a drum, wails, sneers and lashes out."[1] Tristan Tzara described it this way in his "Zurich Chronicle": "the big drum is brought in, Huelsenbeck against 200, Trou-serfly accentuated by the very big drum and little bells on his left foot—the people protest shout smash windowpanes kill each other demolish fight here come the police interruption."[2] *Trou-serfly* refers to Huelsenbeck's bruitist poem "Plane," a mix of nonsense words and letters, "behold the way the placenta creams in the high school boys' butterfly nets/sokobauno sokobauno/the vicar closeth his trou-serfly rataplan rataplan his trou-serfly and his hair juts ou-out of his ears/the buckcatapult the buckcatapult fa-alls from the sky and the grandmother hoiks up her breasts."[3]

The Italian Futurists, who had been involved in the traffic of noise since 1913, proved to be an inspiration for Dada noise, as Huelsenbeck wrote in 1920: "[Dadaism] disseminated the BRUITIST music of the futurists (whose purely Italian concerns it has no desire to generalize)."[4] He was actually relying on reports, and not very accurate ones, about Italian Futurist noise. He credited F. T. Marinetti with inventing the *art of noises* (a common mistake), thought that Russolo's noise music was imitative, and thought that it was performed on a ragtag assortment of instruments instead of on noise-intoning instruments designed by Russolo and Ugo Piatti specifically for the purpose:

> From Marinetti we also borrowed "bruitism," or noise music, *le concert bruitiste,* which, of blessed memory, had created such a stir at the first appearance of the Futurists in Milan, where they had regaled the audience with *le reveil de la capitale.* I spoke on the significance of bruitism at a number of open Dada gatherings.
>
> "*Le bruit,*" noise with imitative effects, was introduced into art (in this connection we can hardly speak of individual arts, music or literature) by Marinetti, who used a chorus of typewriters, kettledrums, rattles and pot-covers to suggest the "awakening of the capital"; at first it was intended as nothing more than a rather violent reminder of the colourfulness of life.[5]

Huelsenbeck thought that the Italian Futurists were to be commended for being on the side of noises and other nonabstract *things:* "tables, houses, frying-pans, urinals, women, etc." Huelsenbeck's endorsement of this list was telling, for it included the things known as women in close proximity to urinals, no less. Furthermore, everything on the list was a domestic item, or when they were public, they were kept for the use of men out of sight. He went on to state that things took on an independent life of their own, left their unexceptional habitat of domestic space, to march off into the exceptional event and public province of men—war: "The highest expression of the conflict of things, as a spontaneous eruption of possibilities, as movement, as a simultaneous poem, as a symphony of cries, shots, commands, embodying an attempted solution of the problem of life in motion. . . . Every movement naturally produces noise."[6] War as the highest expression of *things,* their vitality exposed by the dynamics of combat and voiced in their movement as noise. Even though Huelsenbeck was not an advocate of war, in his acclimation of Italian Futurist noise, which as see below arose from war, he became rhetorically associated with it. The new art favored noise made from actual things; war simply did it better.

Like other aspects of the avant-garde and modernist arts, the Dadaists found a source for bruitism in primitivism. Prior to coming to Zurich, Huelsenbeck had recited some "Negro poems" at an expressionist evening in Berlin. The first evening he entered the Cabaret Voltaire, he met the owner of the building, the former seaman Jan Ephraim, and recited for him "some Negro poems that I had made up myself":[7]

> "They sound very good," he said, "but unfortunately they're not Negro poems. I spent a good part of my life among Negroes, and the songs they sing are very different from the ones you just recited." He was one of those people who take things literally, and retain them verbatim. My Negro poems all ended with the refrain "Umba, umba," which I roared and spouted over and over again into the audience.[8]

Ephraim later brought him poems ostensibly written in a "Negro language" from either Africa or the South Seas, which Huelsenbeck went on to recite in front of an audience—that is, with the addition of *umba umba,* which "no force on earth could have gotten me to leave out."[9] Perhaps this was the germ of an enduring interest for Huelsenbeck for he would set sail to Africa during the mid-1920s, similar to Tristan Tzara's own study of African languages and culture, but during the days of the Cabaret Voltaire his Negro poems were clearly part of the trivializing appropriation of other cultures that Europeans found necessary to vitalize their own.

Thus, the grinding sound of power relations are heard here in the way noises *contain* the other, in both senses of the word. Noises are informed by the sounds, languages, and social position of others. It is only because certain types of people are outside any representation of social harmony that their speech and other sounds associated with them are considered to be noise. In the process of appropriation these others are subjected to forms of containment they have already known in other less semiotic exercises. Because they were bohemian or antimilitarist, the male artists making most of the noise were themselves on the margins of society. When they sought the source of noise from others even further outside the main, it was not because they experienced any sense of camaraderie of mutual exclusion but because they still had a base in the norms of their culture from which these others signified noise. This admixture meant that when they marshaled the noise of others to transgress or attack aspects of different dominant cultures, they reinforced other aspects of domination. Avant-garde noise, in other words, both marshals and mutes the noise of the other: power is attacked at the expense of the less powerful, and society itself is both attacked and reinforced.

Polyglot was yet another tactic of linguistic noise at the Cabaret Voltaire. In speculating on the genesis of Hugo Ball's famous set of six sound poems, Rudolf Kuenzli offers the following explanation: "Ball's experiments with sound poems might even be taken as an attempt to overcome the language barrier in the Cabaret Voltaire, since the audience consisted of Russians, French, Poles, Italians, Germans, etc., who were all living in Zurich in order to escape the First World War."[10] Given the economic motivation for the Cabaret to stay open, Ball's sound poems were an attempt to break down the segregation of nights held for special language- and nation-based audiences. As Marcel Janco recounts, "We held Russian events where anyone could go up on the podium and sing popular Russian music, Romanian evenings with Romanian dancers and music, and so on."[11] Ball's move toward predominantly phonic content was therefore an attempt to generate a transcultural appeal within language, similar to the one already rehearsed within ideas of music as a universal communicator.

Kuenzli supports his claim by pointing out that the six sound poems were atypical of all of Ball's other writings and thus seemed to be pitched to the local concerns of the Cabaret Voltaire. Driven into the refuge of Swiss neutrality, Ball's *Verse ohne Worte* (poetry without words) was, additionally and perhaps more precisely, a verse without German language, with its militarist associations amid the other languages of the exile community. It could therefore serve Ball as the *vox humana* to express the disgust he had for his homeland. Neutrality meant meaninglessness. To this can be added Ball's vigorous support of the poetic codification of polyglot practice: the poem

"L'amiral cherche une maison à louer" (The Admiral is looking for a house to rent). It was simultaneously recited in German, English, and French (as well as in nonsense words, vocables, singing, and whistling), moving in and out of relations of translation, by Richard Huelsenbeck, Marcel Janco, and Tristan Tzara at the Cabaret Voltaire on 29 March 1916.[12] Again, the polyglot has lost its specific qualities to become *the voice,* in this case, at risk in a world of noise. As Ball wrote:

> All the styles of the last twenty years came together yesterday. Huelsenbeck, Tzara, and Janco took the floor with a *poème simultan*. That is a contrapuntal recitative in which three or more voices speak, sing, whistle, etc., at the same time in such a way that the elegiac, humorous, or bizarre content of the piece is brought out by these combinations. In such a simultaneous poem, the willful quality of an organic work is given powerful expression, and so is its limitation by the accompaniment. Noises (an *rrrrr* drawn out for minutes, or crashes, or sirens, etc.) are superior to the human voice in energy.
>
> The "simultaneous poem" has to do with the value of the voice. The human organ represents the soul, the individuality in its wanderings with its demonic companions. The noises represent the background— the inarticulate, the disastrous, the decisive. The poem tries to elucidate the fact that man is swallowed up in the mechanistic process. In a typically compressed way it shows the conflict of the *vox humana* with a world that threatens, ensnares, and destroys it, a world whose rhythm and noise are ineluctable.[13]

For Ball, the "mechanistic process" was part of a powerful belief in matter over the spirit that had produced the "modern necrophilia," and the machine was something that "gives a sham life to dead matter . . . death working systematically, counterfeiting life."[14] The mechanical process he loathes most is that associated with language and journalism: the printing press, the machine that in itself "tells more lies than any newspaper it prints." The repetition destroys human rhythms, just as the pacing of caged animals happens in repetitious patterns, and there is nothing more horrifying than "a walk through the noisy workroom of a modern printing shop. The animal sounds, the stinking liquids. All the senses focused on what is bestial, monstrous, and yet unreal."[15]

As Ball said in a statement given prior to reciting the sound poems themselves, "In these phonetic poems we totally renounce the language that journalism has abused and corrupted. We must return to the [Rimbaudian] alchemy of the word, we must even give up the word too, to keep for poetry its last and holiest refuge."[16] Ball's *holiest refuge* for poetry against a journalism and the noisy machines that printed it was grounded in Christianity. His *ohne Worte* was in actuality the sound of *das Wort,* a place where words are disassembled into the *voice* in order to leave the Word intact. It is true that the Cabaret Voltaire is not usually thought of as a crossroads between Bethlehem and Golgotha, but it was on such sacrosanct ground that Ball had already tested noise early in the month prior to reciting his six sound poems, with his staging of the bruitist *A Nativity Play.*[17] The onomatopoeia that had become submerged and subtle in his sound poems, "touching lightly on a hundred ideas at the same time without naming them,"[18] was much more imitative in the play, conventionally depicting the wind (*f f f f f ffffff*) and animal sounds, Joseph and Mary muttering their prayers, and less conventionally depicting The Angel (sound of a propeller), The Star (*zoke, zoke, zzzzzzzzzzzoooooke,* etc.), among others. The audience did not let the noise get in the way of their reverence for Christmas in the summertime, even the nationalities in the audience whose devotion to Jesus Christ couldn't be taken for granted watched "with real astonishment." However, Ball was "ashamed of the noise of the performance, the mixture of styles and moods."[19]

In less than three weeks he was standing in a stiff bishop's costume performing his own brand of Edenic language of the sound poems. Moreover, while reciting them,

> I noticed that my voice had no choice but to take on the ancient cadence of priestly lamentation, that style of liturgical singing that wails in all the Catholic churches of East and West. I do not know what gave me the idea of this music, but I began to chant my vowel sequences in a church style like a recitative, and tried not only to look serious but to force myself to be serious. For a moment it seemed as if there were a pale, bewildered face in my cubist mask, that half-frightened, half-curious face of a ten-year-old boy, trembling and hanging avidly on the priest's words in the requiems and high masses in his home parish. Then the lights went out, as I had ordered, and bathed in sweat, I was carried down off the stage like a magical bishop.[20]

It seems clear that the "half-frightened, half-curious face of a ten-year-old boy" Ball mentions in his description was himself, the actual boy whose kisses had worn down a spot on the wooden frame surrounding the picture of the Virgin Mary above his bed. Although his religious fervency may have gone dormant until his conversion back into Catholicism during the mid-1920s, Christianity remained Ball's touchstone throughout his Dada days. Within the sound poems themselves, along with the primitivist and onomatopoeic words, Richard Sheppard has detected the trace of some inadvertent sound poetry recited by Jesus Christ after hanging on the cross for nine hours. The nonwords "elomen elomen lefitalominai" in Ball's sound poem "Wolken" (Clouds) resembles Jesus' "ELI, ELI, LAMA SABACHTHANI?" (Matthew 27:46), which are the words "My God, my God, why hast thou forsaken me?"[21] Moreover, all the poems hearkened back to Corinthians: "For he that speaketh in an *unknown* tongue speaketh not unto men, but unto God: for no man understandeth *him;* how be it in the spirit he speaketh mysteries" (14:2). In this sense, the clatter of foreign tongues in the Cabaret Voltaire was countered with an even more foreign tongue.

Noise and Simultaneity

"One hears *shit* from every corner of the universe."

Blaise Cendrars[22]

Simultaneism in the avant-garde was closely associated with noise in two ways: as the product of an instantaneous awareness of numerous events occurring at any one time in space, whether that might be the space of a café or the entire earth, and the product of an additional collapse of time into that already collapsed space. Richard Huelsenbeck, in discussing its literary variants within Dadaism, thought that simultaneism attempted "to transform the problem of the ear into a problem of the face"[23]—in other words, the flow of time needed to understand individual speech versus the capability, when the face becomes a unified perceptual organ, to grasp a multitude of entities in an instant. Objects and events in time come to occupy the same spatial instant: "While I, for example, become successively aware that I boxed an old woman on the ear yesterday and washed my hands an hour ago, the screeching of a streetcar brake and the crash of a brick falling off the roof next door reach my ear simultaneously and my (outward or inward) eye rouses itself to seize, in the simultaneity of these events, a swift meaning of life."[24] Huelsenbeck goes on to explain how simultaneism was closely associated with the noise of bruitism. He cites music to seek a working definition of noise but not as a place where numerous tones can simultaneously exist in harmony and counterpoint: "Just as physics distinguishes between tones (which can be expressed in mathematical formulae) and noises, which are completely baffling to its symbolism and abstractionism, because they are a direct objectivization of dark vital force, here the distinction between a succession and 'simultaneity,' which defies formulation because it is a direct symbol of action. And so ultimately a simultaneous poem means nothing but 'Hurrah for life!'"[25] At another time he differentiates between bruitism and simultaneity, as the former melding the sound of a yawn with, again, screeching streetcar brakes, and the latter a melange of actions:

> *The Bruitist poem*
> represents a streetcar as it is, the essence of the streetcar with the yawning
> of Schulze the coupon clipper and the screeching of brakes

> *The Simultaneist poem*
> teaches a sense of the merry-go-round of all things; while Herr Schulze
> reads his paper, the Balkan crosses the bridge at Nish, a pig squeals in
> Butcher Nuttke's cellar.[26]

One simultaneous poem by Tristan Tzara (Zurich, April 1919) was fortuitously compounded by the audience's own *bruitism* and simultaneity; it was "performed by twenty people who did not always keep in time with each other. This was what the audience, and especially its younger members, had been waiting for. Shouts, whistles, chanting in unison, laughter . . . all of which mingled more or less antiharmoniously with the bellowing of the twenty on the platform."[27]

Huelsenbeck credited F. T. Marinetti and the Italian Futurists with the invention of literary simultaneity, but the Dada practice he referred to was limited to a coterminous utterance along the lines of *L'amiral cherche une maison à louer,* whereas Marinetti also entertained the function of wirelessness within simultaneism. Transmissional space shared the same atmosphere as acoustic simultaneity, however, whereas the cohabitation of a space by several speakers in a room could render the immediacy of speech nonsensical, the simultaneity of signals could potentially operate in a much more abstract way. For instance, Marinetti thought that all conventions of relationality, traditionally confined as they were to local and manageable structures and comparisons, would break down once they were pummeled with a global infinitude of possible relations all arriving at once with a newfound speed having "no connecting wires" and that the new disposition to this transmissional reality, the *wireless imagination,* required a radical response from among the arts.[28] Also, the polyglot of the cabaret took on other meanings when anywhere in the globe could be figuratively invoked.

Guillaume Apollinaire claimed to have originated the term *simultaneity* in 1912 in reference to the arts, against the similar claims made by Henri-Martin Barzun, who had argued for simultaneous poetry performances, some aided by a phonograph (*Voix, rhythmes et chants simultanés,* 1913). However, Apollinaire was concerned with painting and not literature and in particular the paintings of Robert Delaunay. Like Delaunay, Apollinaire's simultaneism was linked to the supremacy of sight: "Our eyes serve as the essential sensibility between *nature* and our *soul.* Our soul maintains its life in harmony. Harmony is engendered only by the *simultaneity* with which the measures and proportions of light reach the soul, the supreme sense of our eyes. This simultaneity alone is creation; everything else is merely enumeration, contemplation, study. This simultaneity is life itself."[29] Delaunay let it be known that his distaste was for things outside the service of color: "I am horrified by *music* and *noise.*"[30] Nevertheless, no matter how simultaneism could be represented in vision, light, and color, it was best experienced through transmissional and acoustical means.

The simultaneity of noise mimics that of the signal in the first part of Cendrars's major novel *Dan Yack* (1927), where Antarctica becomes the Eiffel Tower[31] of the bourgeois world traveler. One pole gives way to another—Antarctica the nonnation gathering point of all nations, the place where citizenship is gravitationally pulled down into a frigid universalism. Instead of a wireless, Dan Yack comes equipped on the ship from Tasmania to Antarctica with means to invoke the rest of the world: six phonograph machines and a cache of recordings. Although "Music bores me stiff, I don't like anything except the nasal bleating of phonographs and the loud roar of gramophones,"[32] he is nevertheless able to imagine in such nasal bleating the desirable bodies of female singers: "Dan Yack swore that it was a buxom little blonde, wiggling her hips as she sang. 'I can just see her bare legs, Captain. There are little folds above her knees.'"[33] The Captain is apparently not amused, so Dan Yack offers to play him a recording of a sea lion getting its throat cut or the clubbing and skinning of 60,000 seals. Dan Yack steps out of the bath, puts on the phonograph and begins to shave:

> In the silence one could hear the razor scraping through the hairs, then the click of the gramophone, then a deafening rumble and suddenly a frightful scream that filled the cabin. It was the sea-lion having its throat cut. Its cry rose to a crescendo. Then there was the far-off barking of a million seals, followed by a long moan. Next, the voice of a man shouting at the top of his lungs: "Kill it, John! Kill it!" A gunshot. Then no more. Then, once again, the baying, but retreating farther and farther into the distance. And finally, the hoarse sound of a ship's siren.
>
> Or perhaps it was the beast's death-cry.

> Dan Yack had stepped back into his tub. A smell of vetiver wafted through the cabin. The needle, at the end of its track, scratched and fretted.[34]

Once in Antarctica and after suffering its night, Dan Yack thinks he sees the spring sun in the play of long shadows (cinema?), but others are not convinced. To herald the sun Dan Yack sets up several phonographs and gramophones to play simultaneously. From these erupt the simulated sounds of nations all at once, as if they were flowing centripetally down along wireless longitudinal lines, the global simultaneity of silent transmissions is modeled through the ability for sounds to occupy the same space:

> He wound up all his phonographs and all his gramophones and set them up on the big table in order of size. He put a record or a cylinder on each one. Then, moving as quickly as possible from one to the other, he set them all going. They were triggered off almost simultaneously. The turntables started to spin. There was a multiple whirring noise, then a nasal voice roared: "'The Marseillaise'! . . . played by the trumpeters of the Garde Républicaine!"
>
> But before the phrase was finished, overlapping with it, two other machines struck up, a quarter of a turn later, like cannons firing a salute on a day of national celebration: *Bojé Tzara chrani*. Then the Garde Républicaine broke into the "The Marseillaise" with great fanfare of bugles and drums, while another machine burst forth with "God Save the King" played on the bagpipes!
>
> There was a racket fit to wake the dead. The gramophones tried to drown each other out.
>
> "The sun! The sun!" yelled Dan Yack.
>
> He was beaming.
>
> He started up the last phonograph and the languorous voice of Fragson joined in the tumult: *"Manon . . . voici le . . . sssolei!"*. . .
>
> The gramophones started up again, louder than ever. The room echoed to the cries of the crowd, applause, thousands of voices, trumpets, the brouhaha of processions, a million shuffling feet.
>
> At last the Tsar died on a final, dying all of *phew-phew;* then it was the King's turn to fall silent; "The Marseillaise" still rolled on, warlike and democratic; it stopped abruptly on a crash of the big bass drum.
>
> rrrrrrererererearararararararararara . . . gasped the records in their death-throes.[35]

Fragson's anthem to love then served as the denouement to this cacophony of simultaneous nationalisms and the crowds and masses associated with them. The noise in this case was understandable—that is, because each song within this agglomerate had been repeated so often, each could be listened to and ignored. It was sufficient to know that each song existed and interacted among other songs at any one moment. The lack of a need to listen invited the eradication of the specifics of any one song, just as the idea of the nation eradicates the actual differences of the people living there. Those who sing certain anthems collapse themselves into the body of the head of state from where they sing a narcissistic praise song to their own disappearance.

It might seem like Dan Yack set the anthems resounding with one another to civilize the landscape—that it is a clinical case study for colonialism or, as Franz Fanon said of Radio Algeria, that "It is one of the means of escaping the inert, passive, and sterilizing pressure of the 'native' environment. It is, according to the settler's expression, 'the only way to still feel like a civilized man.'"[36] But Dan Yack was looking for just this type of ciphering of crowds to reproduce the pomp and circumstance appropriate for a procession of the sun. The cacophony of these combined crowds would lure the sun, which would provide the warmth that these absent crowds could not, and as these crowds die out they leave only the absence of love and the individual warmth it too might provide; in the nasal bleating of the phonographic death throes of the crowd he can imagine at least one body. If these sounds were supposed to signal the powers and pleasures of colonial civilization, their international dispersion, their pathetic simulation of crowds through decrepit technology, would have a poor chance against the transformations brought about by the sun.

In Dan Yack's multiple phonograph installation, noise was also underscored by surface noise, skipping and repeating grooves, and the sound of the mechanism—its nasal bleating and the scratching and fretting needle at the end of its track. The exhaustion of materials, the fatigue of the spring, and the deterioration of the mechanism impinged on the age, health, endurance, and commitment of the human voice. What may begin as anthem may end as dirge. What captures vitality may choke it. Ord-Hume reported about the fate of many phonographic novelties when he cited the late-nineteenth-century cigarette dispenser that once asked the opener of the box, "Would you care for a cigarette?" but then wore down to "Aaahjjouaaakkmmenn?"[37] The funereal phonograph in Joyce's *Ulysses* was simply catching up with the moldering body beneath: "Kraahraark! Hellohellohello amawfullyglad kraaark awfully gladaseeragain hellohello amarawk kopthsth." Thus, on the other side of a dynamic, transgressive noise, the "trajectory of a word tossed like a screeching phonograph record,"[38] as Tzara said, we can hear the mournful lament at the decay of technological enthusiasm.

The Future of War Noises

The most important single achievement in the early history of avant-garde noise was the Italian Futurist Luigi Russolo's *art of noises*. Included under this term were his manifesto of 1913, a book of 1916, the music he developed through the design of his new noise-intoning instruments, the *intonarumori,* and a new form of notation. The art of noises seemingly came out of nowhere: there was no easily observable precedent for it within music, and it came from an unlikely person. Although Russolo belonged to a family of musicians, within Italian Futurism he belonged instead to the first group of painters. On his transition, he effectively displaced Balilla Pratella as the movement's in-house composer and became the public face for music and noise within Italian Futurism. Within the avant-garde as a whole Russolo's art of noises would become synonymous with noise itself, although often it would be wrongly attributed to the movement's impresario F. T. Marinetti or to Italian Futurism in general. Besides the connections with bruitism mentioned above, the composers who were provoked positively or negatively by Russolo's noise included Ravel, Debussy, Prokofiev, Stravinsky, Antheil, Satie, Milhaud, Honegger, Varèse, and Cowell. The imitative sounds within Jean Cocteau's libretto, if not Satie's score, for Diaghilev's production *Parade* derived from the art of noises. It had an impact on aspects of the Russian avant-garde, including the poetry of Mayakovsky and the films of Dziga Vertov, on Vorticism in England (including Ezra Pound), and on Moholy-Nagy and Mondrian. The latter addressed Russolo's ideas in two lengthy essays in an attempt to formulate his own *neoplastic* music. The influence of Russolo's noise eventually waned but was then revived in the wake of *musique concrète* in the 1950s and has become widely recognized as a precursor to a range of artistic activities as the second half of the century rolls to a close.

Russolo's art of noises appears to be an ineluctable expression of the machines and motors of modernity, yet if that were the case, an art of noises seemingly would have arisen much earlier elsewhere. Although Italy arrived late to the industrial revolution, its accelerated growth rivaled that of any spot on the continent: it was not so much modernism per se but modernism hitting the ground at full speed. The way this abruptness foreshortened the future amid Italy's agrarian past provided a local model for Italy's retrograde position among the European avant-gardes, especially from F. T. Marinetti's Parisian vantage point. Motivated by a combined nationalism and national embarrassment and buoyed by his family's wealth, Marinetti set off to shape his own avant-garde. The Italian Futurists could soon be heard berating Italy as the land where museums and ruins spread across the cultural landscape like a crop of tombstones and were leading them forward with Marinetti's revelation in *The Founding and Manifesto of Futurism* that a roaring car is more beautiful than the *Victory of Samothrace*. Russolo founded his art of noises on the same sentiment: "*We delight much more in combining in our thoughts the noises of trams, of automobile engines, of carriages and brawling crowds, than in hearing again the* Eroica *or the* Pastorale."[39] This, in itself, gave an urban and technological flavor to his modernism that distinguished it from the resident Italian Futurist composer Francesco Balilla Pratella, whose music allied itself to Futurism primarily on the program of a nationalism rooted in the peasantry. Pratella's *Manifesto of Futurist Music* (11 October 1910) did indeed state that Futurism ought to "express the musical soul of crowds, of the great industrial shipyards, the trains, the transatlantics, battle ships, cars and airplanes,"[40] but he was to say later that these were not his sentiments but those Marinetti interjected during the editing process.[41] Pratella had already composed and performed his Futurist music and penned three manifestos by the time Russolo took up his art of noise. As a gesture, Russolo's manifesto "The Art of Noises" appeared on 11 March 1913, exactly one year after Pratella's "Technical Manifesto of Futurist Music," and was published in the form of a deferential open letter:

> Dear Balilla Pratella, Great Futurist Composer,
>   In Rome, at the very crowded Teatro Costanzi, while I was listening
> to the orchestral performance of your revolutionary MUSICA

FUTURISTA with my friends Marinetti, Boccioni and Balla, I conceived a new art: The Art of Noises, the logical consequence of your marvelous innovations.[42]

The manifesto ends with equal respect: "to my dear Pratella, to your futuristic genius." The Pratella concert mentioned was in reality only a matter of days before the release of Russolo's manifesto, hardly enough time to develop ideas at the level of ambition and coherence displayed. The manifesto was apparently finished three months prior to Pratella's concert but postponed so as to not disrupt ongoing preparations and embarrass a fellow Futurist. Moreover, the opening and closing niceties are contradicted by the manifesto's central themes, which demean the conventional musical basis on which Pratella's music is founded.[43]

Pratella's music was dissonant for the time but hardly enough to inspire a radical break into noise. Yet music was not the only art using sound within Italian Futurism; there were also the onomatopoetic practices of Marinetti's *parole in libertà* (words-in-freedom, or free words). Russolo included in his manifesto a letter from Marinetti in which *parole in libertà* were used to report on the sounds of military combat at Adrianople, the ZANG-TUMB-TUUUMB of the cannons, the taratatata of the machine guns, and other sounds interspersed with musical instructions and allusions. Here is just an excerpt of the "marvelous *free words* the orchestra of a great battle"[44] that Russolo included in the manifesto:

> Far far back of the orchestra pools muddying huffing goaded oxen wagons *pluff-plaff* horse action *flic flac zing zing shaaack* laughing whinnies the *tiiinkling jiiingling* tramping 3 Bulgarian battalions marching *croooc-craaac* [slowly] Shumi Maritza or Karvavena *ZANG-TUMB-TUUUMB toc-toc-toc-toc* [fast] *croooc-craaac* [slowly] cries of officers slamming about like brass plates pan here *paak* there *BUUUM ching chaak* [very fast] *cha-cha-cha-cha-chaak* down there up there all around high up look out your head beautiful![45]

The passage ends with the image of "the orchestra of the noises of war swelling under a held note of silence in the high sky round golden balloon that observes the firing."[46] The graphic element of a surveillance balloon as a musical note, foreshortens the noises of war below into an orchestra, just as Marinetti's plane rides above battlefields had foreshortened military action into the orthographic form of *parole in libertà*.[47]

By citing Marinetti's *parole in libertà* text within his own text, Russolo achieved several things. He deferred to the authority of Marinetti as the founder and leader of Italian Futurism, an authority supported by Marinetti's ability to bankroll the movement's activities; for Russolo, Marinetti was "my dear and great friend . . . who is still vibrating from the great acoustic emotion of his experience assisting in the siege of Adrianople."[48] Within the context of the text itself, the violent fact of war acted as a rhetorical device, persuading the reader-listener of the inevitability of noise through its disciplinary role in the negotiation of lives and nations. War noises also staked a claim within the avant-garde land grab of the future because they were *the newest noises* and required new artistic means for their expression.[49] Finally, war noises were valued by Russolo because he valued war. Thus, the emphasis conferred on the fighting sounds of Marinetti's combat *parole* situates militarism at the founding of Futurist noise. The incursion of militarism into the musical project of Russolo's art of noises can thus be understood as an auditive negotiation between music and war.[50]

War was a longtime preoccupation for Marinetti. The bombast of his pre-Futurist writings, where his words were projected out over the endless ocean was but a rehearsal for a voice that could trumpet the scope if not the decibel level of massive scenes of destruction. He officially let loose the battle cry with his first manifesto in 1909: "We will glorify war—the world's only hygiene—militarism, patriotism, the destructive gesture of freedom-bringers, beautiful ideas worth dying for, and scorn for women."[51] Marinetti's report "from the trenches of Adrianopolis" was included in Russolo's manifesto under the guise of a personal correspondence, but Marinetti had actually been performing the piece publicly prior to the publication of the manifesto, and he had linked military sounds and *parole in libertà* already the year before.[52] As Marinetti recounted, "I finished that short synthesizing noise-making poem while witnessing the machine-gunning of three thousand horses ordered by the Turkish general who was the governor before the fortress fell."[53] He transmitted these sounds as he traveled from the front with its "long worms we swallowed from the necks of the bottles filled with water from puddles"[54] to aristocratic drawing rooms and bohemian haunts of Sofia, St. Petersburg, Berlin, London, Paris, Rome, Milan, and elsewhere. Velimir Khlebnikov marked Marinetti's visit to Russia with a letter addressed to "You untalented loudmouth. . . . I am convinced that we will meet one day to the sound of cannons, in a duel between the Italo-German coalition and the Slavs, on the Dalmation coast. I suggest Dubrovnik as the place for our seconds to meet."[55] Aleksei Kruchenykh, the Russian Futurist exponent of *zaum,* was likewise unimpressed for other reasons, "The Italian 'amateurish' Futurists, with their endless ra ta ta ra ta ta, are like Maeterlinck's heroines who think that 'door' repeated a hundred times opens up to revelation."[56] A visit to Berlin in 1913 left Rudolf Leonhard with the recollection that Marinetti "loved and worshipped war, because it made a noise and because he had no desire to know what else it did. With his noise for noise's sake he genuinely but unintentionally caricatured art for art's sake."[57]

Just weeks before World War I, C. R. W. Nevinson witnessed Marinetti perform in London: "Marinetti recited a poem about the siege of Adrianople with various kinds of onomatopoeic noises and crashes in free verse, while all the time the band downstairs played 'You made me love you. I didn't want to do it.'"[58] The poet Harold Monro admired Marinetti's inventiveness but thought as poetry his declamations were nothing more than "an advanced form of verbal photography."[59] Henry Nevinson, father of C. R. W. Nevinson and like Marinetti a war correspondent, explained that he himself had "heard many recitations and have tried to describe many battles. But listen to Marinetti's recitation of one of his battle scenes . . . the noise, the confusion, the surprise of death, the terror and courage, the shouting, curses, blood and agony— all were recalled by that amazing succession of words, performed or enacted by the poet with such passion and abandonment that no one could escape the spell of listening."[60] Wyndham Lewis, alluding to Erich Maria Remarque's *All Quiet on the Western Front,* remembered it this way:

It was a matter of astonishment what Marinetti could do with his unaided voice. He certainly made an extraordinary amount of noise. A day of attack upon the Western Front, with all the "heavies" hammering together, right back to the horizon, was nothing to it. My equanimity when first subjected to the sounds of mass-bombardment in Flanders was possibly due to my marinettian preparation—it seemed "all quiet" to me, in fact, by comparison.[61]

Marinetti in his manifesto "Dynamic and Synoptic Declamation" detailed a performance at the Doré Gallery (28 April 1914) in London:

> Dynamically and synoptically I declaimed several passages from my *ZANG TOMB TUUMB* (the *Siege of Adrianople*). On the table in front of me I had a telephone, some boards, and matching hammers that permitted me to imitate the Turkish general's orders and the sounds of artillery and machine-gun fire.
>
> Blackboards had been set up in three parts of the hall, to which in succession I either ran or walked, to sketch rapidly an analogy with chalk. My listeners, as they turned to follow me in all my evolutions, participated, their entire bodies inflamed with emotion, in the violet effects of the battle described by my words-in-freedom.
>
> There were two big drums in a distant room, from which the painter Nevinson, my colleague, produced the boom of cannon, when I told him to do so over the telephone.
>
> The swelling interest of the English audience became frantic enthusiasm when I achieved the greatest dynamism by alternating the Bulgarian song "Sciumi Maritza" with the dazzle of my images and the clamor of the onomatopoeic artillery.[62]

Marinetti argued for a poetics open to the forces exerted by the new technologies of transportation, communication, and information, all of which were thrown, among other purposes, into the conduct of military combat.[63] In the Italo-Turkish War he had witnessed the first use of airplanes in modern warfare, and it was the whirling propeller of an airplane that had "taught" him the destruction of syntax.[64] Another new technology of modern warfare was the observation balloon equipped with wireless telegraphy, both the vantage point of the balloon and the collapsing of distance in telegraphy having the some capacity for foreshortening and abstraction. Marinetti represented these balloons in the "round golden balloon that observes the firing" (in the *parole in libertà* quoted in Russolo's manifesto) and the orthographic poem "Captive Turkish Balloon," where one of the ephemeral lines of TSF (wireless telegraphy), which would normally report troupe movements, transmits to "Tsarigraad."[65] For Marinetti, the poet too was supposed to receive and transmit vibrationally, to become a wireless observer of the grand panorama of the battlefield, to "telegraphically transmit the analogical foundation of life with the same economical speed that a telegraph imposes on the swift accounts of reporters and war correspondents."[66]

But Marinetti, Russolo, and other Italian Futurists sought much more than poetics and rhetorical ploys within warfare, and World War I gave them all they had bargained for. Perhaps least among their worries was how the war interrupted the series of Russolo's concerts, which no doubt would have secured him wider fame. According to one report a total of about 30,000 spectators were in attendance over the course of twelve performances at the London Coliseum, and the tour was just beginning:

> From London we should have gone on to Liverpool, to Dublin, Glasgow, Edinburgh and Vienna, and then started another long tour that included Moscow, Berlin and Paris. The war caused it all to be postponed. Meanwhile in Italy, the long period of neutrality started. And there began our long struggle for intervention, which lasted until that glorious May when war was declared. Then, abandoning everything to enlist voluntarily, I left for the front, together with my futurist friends, Marinetti, Boccioni, Piatti, Sant'Elia, and Sironi. And I was lucky enough to fight in the midst of the marvelous and grand tragic symphony of modern war.[67]

Italy's reluctance to intervene caused great frustration among the Futurists. In protest, Russolo, Marinetti, Boccioni, and others staged an interventionist demonstration at the Teatro dal Verme during a performance of Puccini. The next evening they burned an Austrian flag and, after fighting with audience members, were arrested and detained for five days. Six months later, Russolo was successfully inducted, served briefly in a cyclists battalion, later became an Alpinist, and, in November 1915, engaged in combat for the possession of several ridges. Umberto Boccioni could hardly wait for the threatening sounds of battle: "Zuiii Zuiii Tan Tan. Bullets all around. Volunteers calm on the ground shoot Pan Pan. Crack shot Sergeant Massai on his feet shoots, first shrapnel explodes. We arrive hearing a shout we throw ourselves to the ground: shrapnel explodes twenty steps away and I shout: At last."[68] The war had permeated Marinetti's thinking so completely that he even argued for full-scale militarism within his "Manifesto of the Futurist Dance" (8 July 1917), outlining the "first three Futurist dances from the three mechanisms of war: shrapnel, the machine gun, and the airplane."[69] In part 1 of the *Dance of the Shrapnel* he wanted to "give the fusion of the mountain with the parabola of the shrapnel. The fusion of the carnal human song with the mechanical noise of shrapnel. To give the ideal synthesis of the war: a mountain soldier who carelessly sings beneath an uninterrupted vault of shrapnel. *Movement 1:* With the feet mark the *boom-boom* of the projectile coming from the cannon's mouth," etc.[70] The dances were to be accompanied by the *organized noises* and *special effects* of Russolo's intonarumori.

Russolo devoted an entire chapter of his book *The Art of Noises* to "The Noises of War." In it he implies that the battlefield serves as a model for modern listening and an art of noises since in combat the ear is much more privileged than it is in daily life: it can judge with "greater certainty than the eye!"[71] "From noise, the different calibers of grenades and shrapnels can be known even before they explode. Noise enables us to discern a marching patrol in deepest darkness, even to judging the number of men that compose it. From the intensity of rifle fire, the number of defenders of a given position can be determined. There is no movement or activity that is not revealed by noise."[72] The most remarkable thing about this chapter is that it concentrates almost entirely on ordnance and ignores the sounds of dying humans or animals; the closest Russolo gets to the sounds of the species endangered by war is the *katzenmusik* of shrapnel.[73] It is interesting, in this respect, to contrast Russolo's acoustic account of the battlefield with Erich Maria Remarque's *All Quiet on the Western Front,* or in the original German *Im Westen nichts Neues* (1929). On the one hand, Remarque better describes the *aesthetics,* literally the heightening of the senses (compare with anesthesia), of combat:

> The moment that the first shells whistle over and the air is rent with the explosions there is suddenly in our veins, in our hands, in our eyes a tense waiting, a watching, a heightening alertness, a strange sharpening of the senses. The body with one bound is in full readiness.
>
> It often seems to me as though it were the vibrating, shuddering air that with a noiseless leap springs upon us; or as though the front itself emitted an electric current which awakened unknown nerve centers.[74]

The experience of combat engenders a new relationship a person has with the earth, animals, other humans, as well as what Walter Benjamin called the unwitting *wooing of the cosmos* involved in modern warfare.[75] This sense of spirituality, spectacle, and attunement would be well suited to an argument for a new art form if Remarque did not also describe the absolute horror accompanying the seduction.

Like Russolo, Remarque details the prioritization given the ear in combat, whether it is for listening for troupe carriers behind the enemy lines; for the bells, gongs, and clappers to warn of that other counteraction of sight—gas; or for differentiating the sounds of artillery shells.[76] However, whereas Russolo will describe the sounds of shells using musical terms, Remarque will concentrate on matters of life and death: "[The young recruits] get killed simply because they hardly can tell shrapnel from high-explosive, they are mown down because they are listening anxiously to the roar of the big coal-boxes falling in the rear, and miss the light, piping whistle of the low spreading daisy-cutters."[77] Remarque also details the sounds of injured, dying, and dead soldiers. One wounded soldier can be heard for three days but he cannot be found; he must be lying facedown "for it is only when a man has his mouth close to the ground that it is impossible to gauge the direction of the cry. . . . He grows gradually hoarser. The voice is so strangely pitched that it seems to be everywhere."[78] The first night he calls for help, the second his cries are mixed with delirious conversation with his family back home, the third he simply weeps, and then he is silent until one last death rattle. But it does not stop there, for the dead refuse to remain silent: "Many have their bellies swollen up like balloons. They hiss, belch, and make movements. The gases in them make noises."[79]

The sounds of an enemy soldier dying, indeed, accompanies the most important turning point in *All Quiet on the Western Front.* The protagonist seeking refuge in a shell hole repeatedly stabs a soldier who stumbles in. It is the first time he has injured or killed anyone in hand-to-hand combat, without the consolation of distance, and as if to impress the immediacy of the act further, he shares the shell hole with the wounded man, who pathetically gurgles for hours on end as he dies: "It sounds to me as though he bellows, every gasping breath is like a cry, a thunder—but it is only my heart pounding."[80] The soldier is too weak to cry out, so he will not have to be stabbed in the throat. The protagonist wants to close his ears to the gurgling, but that would also render him deaf to the signals of the continuing battle; instead, he must listen as every gasp lays his heart bare. The most unbearable sound is the silence after the soldier dies. He fills the silence frantically with his own speech: "You were only an idea to me before, an abstraction that lived in my mind and called forth its appropriate response. It was that abstraction I stabbed."[81] He eventually calms down and promises the dead man, "Today you, tomorrow me. But if I come out of it, comrade, I will fight against this, that has struck us both down."[82]

Russolo wrote "The Noises of War" during a break in his service in 1916 before returning to the field, and, although sounds produced by the human voice were absent, in the *Art of Noises* manifesto of 1913 he did include as one of the "*6 families of noises* of the futurist orchestra that we will soon realize mechanically" a number of sounds that could easily have been encountered on the battlefield: "shouts, screams, shrieks, wails, hoots, howls, death rattles and sobs."[83] Within this family of noises, *howling* formed a class of intonarumori: the *ululatori*, "the most musical of the noise instruments. The howling that they produce is almost human; and while they recall the siren to some extent, they are also a little like the sounds of the string bass, the cello, and the violin."[84] Whether it was immersing oneself in the sonic surrounds of battle and fixing on the acoustical descriptions of shrapnel or of immersing oneself in the sounds of the world and extracting a music, Russolo appears to be involved at every point in the same process of abstraction that Remarque's protagonist decried, "that abstraction I stabbed."

The sounds of actual pained voices became more of a personal reality for Russolo after returning to the front where, serving as an alpinist, he suffered a serious head injury from an exploding grenade (17 December 1917). Prefigured in Marinetti's *Dance of the Shrapnel,* he also became a sad realization of a poetic prophecy made by Marinetti in "Let's Murder the Moonshine" (1909): "And we ourselves will give the example, abandoning ourselves to the raging Tailoress of battles who, when she has sewn us into handsome scarlet uniforms, gorgeous in the sun, will anoint our hair with flame and brush it smooth with projectiles."[85] Russolo required eighteen months of hospital care and harbored a partial paralysis lasting years longer. In 1921, during a concert in Paris that was disrupted by the Dadaists, Marinetti appealed to the audience on behalf of Russolo because of his war wounds:

> The Italian *bruitistes,* led by Marinetti, were giving a performance of works written for their new instruments. These works were pale, insipid and melodious in spite of Russolo's noise-music, and the Dadaists who attended did not fail to express their feelings—and very loudly. Marinetti asked indulgence for Russolo, who had been wounded in the war and had undergone a serious operation on his skull. This moved the Dadaists to demonstrate violently how little impressed they were by a reference to the war.[86]

Marinetti had also been seriously wounded in the war, and Futurist architect Sant'Elia, Russolo's close friend Umberto Boccioni, and millions of others were killed. Long afterward, the war continued to resonate among the bodies that were left. George Antheil wrote of the 1920s, "Negro music made us remember at least that we still had bodies which had not been exploded by shrapnel."[87]

The violence encouraged and the carnage suppressed within Russolo's engagement with war noises was present at the founding of the art of noises with the inclusion of Marinetti's onomatopoeic reportage. Modernism in general played a role, certainly, but it played a more specific role through the noises produced in a clash of modern warfare, of an industrial technology given over to the quick kill instead of its usual protracted grind among the cogs. Although Russolo would eventually become antifascist, during the second decade of this century he was never antiwar. Warfare as an intensification of modernism never promised a peace through accelerated cycles of technological development, as Walter Benjamin wrote: "Now and then one hears of something 'reassuring' such as the invention of a sensitive listening device that registers the whir of propellers at great distances. And a few months later a soundless airplane is invented."[88] Russolo's battlefield never invented its way into silence. Instead, his invention relied on the theater of war, where the newest speeding metals cannot help but make an impression on their listeners in accordance with the two highest attributes Marinetti prescribed for manifesto writing itself: violence and precision. The ear *will* become more attentive because "in modern warfare, mechanical and metallic, the element of sight is almost zero. The sense, the significance, and the expressiveness of noises, however, are infinite."[89] In this way Russolo's well-known words—"Let us cross a large modern capital with our ears more attentive than eyes"—sounds like marching orders, even though within discussions of twentieth-century music and the arts his gait is most often confused with the saunter of a *flâneur* or the focused mycological prowl of John Cage.[90] In the same respect, and as we shall see in the celebrations of other emphatic sounds of modernism, turning a deaf ear to the violences will not silence them.

Notes

1.   Richard Huelsenbeck, introduction to *The Dada Almanac*, ed. Richard Huelsenbeck (1920), English edition by Malcolm Green (London: Atlas Press, 1993), 10.
2.   Tristan Tzara, "Zurich Chronicle," ibid., 21.
3.   Richard Huelsenbeck, "Plane," ibid., 20.
4.   Richard Huelsenbeck, "Collective Dada Manifesto" (1920), in *The Dada Painters and Poets: An Anthology*, ed. Robert Motherwell (New York: Hall, 1981), 245.
5.   Richard Huelsenbeck, "En Avant Dada" (1920), ibid., 25.
6.   Ibid., 26.
7.   Richard Huelsenbeck, *Memoirs of a Dada Drummer* (New York: Viking Press, 1969), 8–9.
8.   Ibid.
9.   Ibid. That he would concoct poems from another language in the first place is reminiscent of the spontaneous knowledge of language claimed by the Russian Futurist Aleksei Kruchenykh in his *Explodity* (1913): "On April 27 at 3 o'clock in the afternoon I instantaneously mastered to perfection all languages. Such is the poet of the current era I am here reporting my verses in Japanese Spanish and Hebrew:

iké mina ni
sirm ksi
iamakh alik
zel
GO OSNEG KAID
M R BATUL'BA
VINU AE KSEL
VERTUM DAXH
GIZ
SHISH"

Kruchenykh's language acquisition was not performed as noise but was instead enacted, in this respect at least, under the guise of a universal language. Aleksei Kruchenykh, "From *Explodity*," in *Russian Futurism through Its Manifestoes, 1912–1928,* ed. Anna Lawton and Herbert Eagle (Ithaca: Cornell University Press, 1988), 65–66. Vladimir Markov in his standard text, *Russian Futurism: A History* (Berkeley: University of California, 1968), noted that "much of the Russian *zaum*," or the transrational verse of which Kruchenykh was the most radical practitioner, was "written to imitate the sound of foreign tongues" (20). The Italian Futurists also imitated foreign languages, including African ones that no doubt reminded them of their colonial exploits.

10.   Rudolf E. Kuenzli, "Hugo Ball: Verse without Words," *Dada/Surrealism,* no. 8 (1978): 30–35.

11.   Francis M. Naumann, "Janco/Dada: An Interview with Marcel Janco," *Arts Magazine* 57, no. 3 (November 1982): 80–86.

12.   The poem is reproduced in *Dada Performance,* ed. Mel Gordon (New York: PAJ, 1987), 38–39.

13.   Hugo Ball, *Flight out of Time: A Dada Diary* (New York: Viking Press, 1974), 57.

14.   Ibid., 4.

15.   Ibid.

16.   Ball (24 June 1916), ibid., 71. All six sound poems are reprinted in Harold B. Segel, *Turn-of-the-Century Cabaret* (New York: Columbia University Press, 1987), 337–39. For a good introduction to the performative practices of the Cabaret Voltaire, see Segel's chapter on Zurich Dada (321–65) and Annabelle Melzer, *Latest Rage the Big Drum: Dada and Surrealist Performance* (Ann Arbor: UMI Research Press, 1980).

17.   See *Dada Performance,* 40.

18.   Ball, *Flight out of Time,* 68.

19.   (3 June 1916), ibid., 65. There was a tradition of noise making in the Christian church. For the three days prior to Easter when bells were banned, rattles were used in their place to signal certain events, within processionals, and as ritual devices.

20.   (23 June 1916), ibid., 71. Ball knew he was not the first modern artist to give up the word. He was well aware of Chritian Morgenstern's *Songs of the Gallows* (1905) and, through Kandinsky, the *zaum* poetry of Aleksei Kruchenykh, Velimir Khlebnikov (although his version of it was not really comparable), and others in Russia. Ball was probably most directly influenced by Kandinsky himself, both because of their personal contact and because of the spiritual basis for Kandinsky's own artworks. About a year after the sound poems Ball gave a lecture on Kandinsky in which he said that in his *Der gelbe Klang* (The Yellow Sound) Kandinsky was "the first to discover and apply the most abstract expression of sound in language, consisting of harmonized vowels and consonants." ("Kandinsky" [7 April 1917], in *Flight out of Time,* 324.) The script for Kandinsky's *son et lumière* was printed in *Der Blaue Reiter Almanac* in 1912, the same year as the publication of *Concerning the Spiritual in Art* and the same year Ball met Kandinsky. In *Der gelbe Klang* intelligible words were kept at a bare minimum, and there were plenty of voices *ohne Worte.* Just as darkness fell on the end of Ball's recitation, at the end of scene 3, "Suddenly, one hears from behind the stage a shrill tenor voice filled with fear, shouting entirely indistinguishable words very

quickly (one hears frequently [the letter] *a*: e.g., "Kalasimunafakola!"). Pause. For a moment it becomes dark." Wassily Kandinsky, *Complete Writings on Art,* vol. 1, ed. Kenneth C. Lindsay and Peter Vergo (Boston: G. K. Hall & Co., 1982), 278.

21. Richard Sheppard, "Dada and Mysticism: Influences and Affinities," in *Dada Spectrum: The Dialectics of Revolt,* ed. Stephen C. Foster and Rudolf E. Kuenzli (Madison: Coda Press, 1979), 92–113.

22. Blaise Cendrars, "Crépitements," in *Selected Writings of Blaise Cendrars,* (New York: New Directions, 1966), 72.

23. Huelsenbeck, *En Avant Dada,* 35.

24. Ibid., 36.

25. Ibid.

26. Richard Huelsenbeck, "Collective Dada Manifesto" (1920), in *The Dada Painters and Poets,* 244. We are reminded of Satie's question, "Which do you prefer, music or pork butchery?" Christopher Schiff, "Banging on a Windowpane," in *Wireless Imagination: Sound, Radio and the Avant-garde,* ed. Douglas Kahn and Gregory Whitehead (Cambridge: MIT Press, 1992), 159.

27. Hans Richter, *Dada Art and Anti-Art* (New York: McGraw-Hill, 1965), 77.

28. F. T. Marinetti, *Stung by Salt and War: Creative Texts of the Italian Avant-Gardist F. T. Marinetti,* translated in Richard J. Pioli (New York: Lang, 1987), 48.

29. Guillaume Apollinaire, "Through the Salon des Independents," in *Apollinaire on Art,* ed. Leroy Breunig (New York: Da Capo Press, 1972), 286–93.

30. Robert Delaunay, *The New Art of Color: The Writings of Robert and Sonia Delaunay,* trans. David Shapiro and Arthur A. Cohen (New York: Viking Press, 1978), 116 (emphasis in the original).

31. For many artists the Eiffel Tower was the emblematic oracle of simultaneism, technologically gathering up and distributing France's cosmopolitanism from the reach of its wireless transmissions and receptions—"I AM THE QUEEN OF THE DAWN OF THE POLES" (Vicente Huidobro); "It was the Queen of Paris. Now it's the handmaiden of the telegraph" (Jean Cocteau); and providing the internationalism of the proletarian sort championed by Mayakovsky, "Come to Moscow! . . . It's not for you—model genius of machines—here to pine away from Apollinairic verse." Apollinaire himself rebuilt the tower in his monumental graphic poem *Lettre-Océan.* See Vicente Huidobro, "Tour Eiffel" (Geoffrey O'Brien, trans.), in *The Selected Poetry of Vicente Huidobro,* ed. David Guss (New York: New Directions, 1981), 19–21; Jean Cocteau, "Les mariés de la Tour Eiffel," (1921), in *Modern French Theatre,* ed. and trans. Michael Benedikt and George Wellwarth (New York: Dutton, 1966). See also chapters 1 and 6 in Marjorie Perloff, *The Futurist Moment: Avant-Garde, Avant-Guerre, and the Language of Rupture* (Chicago: University of Chicago Press, 1986); Vladimir Mayakovsky, "Paris" (1923), in *Mayakovsky,* trans. Herbert Marshall (New York: Hill and Wang, 1965).

32. Blaise Cendrars, *Dan Yack [Le Plan de l'aiguille]* (1927), trans. Nina Rootes (New York: Kesend, 1987), 25.

33. Ibid, 34.

34. Ibid, 36.

35. Compare with Vicente Huidobro's poem "Sale la Luna" (1918): "This afternoon I saw / The latest phonographic presses / It was a maze of screams / And songs as varied / As in foreign ports." *The Selected Poetry of Vicente Huidobro,* trans. David M. Guss (New York: New Directions, 1981), 37–43.

36. Franz Fanon, "This Is the Voice of Algeria," in *A Dying Colonialism* (1959), trans. Haakon Chevalier Chevalier (New York: Grove Press, 1965), 71. "It also gives him the feeling that colonial society is a living and palpitating reality, with its festivities, its traditions eager to establish themselves, its progress, its taking root. But especially, in the hinterland, in the so-called colonization centers, it is the only link with the cities, with Algiers, with the metropolis, with the world of the civilized."

37. Arthur W. J. G Ord-Hume, *Clockwork Music* (New York: Crown, 1973), 281–82.

38. Tristan Tzara, "Dada Manifesto 1918," in *The Dada Painters and Poets,* ed. Robert Motherwell (New York: Wittenborn, 1951), 81.

39. Luigi Russolo, "The Art of Noises Futurist Manifesto" (1913), in *The Art of Noises* (1916), trans. Barclay Brown (New York: Pendragon Press, 1986), 25 (emphasis in original).

40. Appended to Rodney Johns Payton, "The Futurist Musicians: Francesco Balilla Pratella and Luigi Russolo" (Ph.D. diss., University of Chicago, 1974), 91–96.

41. "I must say that some affirmations, of a polemic and others of a theoretical nature, which one can read in my *Manifesto* refer to a rapport between music and machines. These were neither written nor even thought by me and often are in contrast to the rest of the ideas. These inventions were added by Marinetti arbitrarily and at the last moment. I was then astonished to read them over my signature, but the act was already done." Cited ibid., 15–16.

42. Russolo, *The Art of Noises,* 23.

43. Giovanni Lista, *L'Art des bruits* (Lausanne: Editions l'Age d'Homme, 1975), 18–19.

44. Russolo, *The Art of Noises,* 26.

45. Ibid.

46. Ibid., 27.

47. See Linda Landis, "Futurists at War," in *The Futurist Imagination* (New Haven: Yale University Art Gallery, 1983), 60–75.

48. Luigi Russolo, "The Futurist Intonarumori" (22 May 1913), trans. Victoria Nes Kirby in Michael Kirby, *Futurist Performances* (New York: Dutton, 1971), 176.

49. For instance, on Marinetti's *free words,* Russolo wrote "since traditional poetry lacks suitable means for rendering the reality and the value of noises, modern war cannot be expressed lyrically without the noise instrumentation of futurist *free words.*" Russolo, "Noises of War," in *The Art of Noises,* 49.

50. Jacques Attali in his book *Noise,* trans. Brian Massumi (Minneapolis: University of Minnesota Press, 1985), understands Russolo's *art of noises* to be a premonition of World War I: "It is not by coincidence that Russolo wrote his *Art of Noises* in 1913; that noise entered music and industry entered painting just before the outbursts and wars of the twentieth century, before the rise of social noise" (10). This belongs to Attali's general assertion that social organizations of music historically prefigure political economic systems. The critique he ranges against certain social formations should not mask the fact that he grants music itself a grandiloquence not enjoyed since the music of the spheres came crashing down to earth. The problem with his specific observation regarding Russolo is that the war noise involved occurred prior to the manifesto, in the battles covered by Marinetti. Music echoed war, not vice versa. The only premonition involved might only be that regional combat prefigured the Great War, but then there would be no special powers granted music. I have found another similar formulation from André Breton, although he chose not to historiographically elevate the observation. After quoting Apollinaire's account of Alberto Savinio compositional assaults on the piano, "after each piece the blood had to be wiped off the keys," Breton notes that "two months later, the war broke out." See André Breton, "Alberto Savinio," in *Alberto Savinio: Menschengemüse zum Tachtisch* (Munich, 1980), cited in *Broken Music,* ed. Ursula Block and Michael Glasmeier (Berlin: DAAD, 1989), 220. I can think of only one legitimate instance where music preceded militarism, and that was when Bob Burns, the hillbilly comedian Spike Jones backed up on radio during the 1940s, invented an instrument out of a gas pipe and whisky funnel and called it a *bazooka,* and then the U.S. Army took the name for their new over-the-shoulder rocket launcher. Bob "Bazooka" Burns now awaits a theory of history in his image.

51. F. T. Marinetti, "The Founding and Manifesto of Futurism," trans. R. W. Flint, in *Futurist Manifestos,* ed. Umbro Apollonio (New York: Viking Press, 1973), 22.

52. Although these *parole in libertà* would not appear in publication until the 1914 collection *ZANG-TUMB-TUMB,* Marinetti had already been performing portions of them in Rome and Berlin a month before the issuance of Russolo's manifesto on 11 March 1913. In any case, the style of military onomatopoeia had already been established in 1912 with his first

example of *parole in libertà*, "Battle (Weight+Stink)." See Marinetti, *Stung by Salt and War,* 41–43. The artistic form of *parole in libertà* themselves was itself patently "born on two battlefields Tripoli and Adrianople." "From the Café Bulgaria in Sofia to the Courage of the Italians in the Balkans and the Military Spirit of Désarrois," *Marinetti: Selected Writings,* ed. R. W Flint (New York: Farrar, Straus and Giroux, 1972), 332. Marinetti reported combat action first in October 1911 during the Italo-Turkish War in Libya, which he covered as a correspondent for *L'Intransigeant* of Paris and then, about a year later, during the Balkan War at Adrianople.

53. *Marinetti: Selected Writings,* 332–33. For other sounds of horses on the battlefield, see Erich Maria Remarque, *All Quiet on the Western Front* (1929) (London: Picador Classics, 1993), 46.

54. *Marinetti: Selected Writings,* 332–33.

55. Velimir Khlebnikov, Letter to Filippo Marinetti (2 February 1914), in *Collected Works of Velimir Khlebnikov,* vol. 1, trans. Paul Schmidt (Cambridge: Harvard University Press, 1987), 87–88.

56. Kruchenykh, "New Ways of the Word (the Language of the Future, Death to Symbolism)," in *Russian Futurism through Its Manifestoes,* 76.

57. Rudolf Leonhard, "Marinetti in Berlin, 1913," in *The Era of German Expressionism,* ed. Paul Raabe (London: Calder, 1980), 115–18.

58. C. R. W Nevinson, *Paint and Prejudice* (1937), 57, cited in James Joll, *Three Intellectuals in Politics* (New York: Pantheon Books, 1960), 152.

59. Harold Monro (December 1913), cited in Alan Young, *Dada and After: Extremist Modernism and English Literature* (Manchester: Manchester University Press, 1981), 72. This was an impression gained from a previous visit to London.

60. Cited in Caroline Tisdall and Angelo Bozzolla, *Futurism* (London: Thames and Hudson, 1977), 104.

61. Wyndham Lewis, *Blasting and Bombardiering* (1937) (Berkeley: University of California Press, 1967), 33. The last sentence suggests a Parisian review of the first performance of the intonarumori at the Teatro dal Verme in Milan (21 April 1914) with its outbreak of fisticuffs: "An impressive simultaneity of bloody faces and noisy enharmonics in an infernal din. The battle of *Ernani* was a matter of insignificance beside this riot." Cited in Luigi Russolo, "Polemics, Battles, and the First Performances of the Noise Instruments," in *The Art of Noises,* 34.

62. F.T. Marinetti "Dynamic and Synoptic Declamation" (11 March 1916), in *Marinetti: Selected Writings,* 147.

63. In "Destruction of Syntax—Wireless Imagination—Words in Freedom" (*Lacerba,* 11 May and 15 June 1913), Marinetti wrote the following:

> Those who use the telephone today, the telegraph, the phonograph, the train, bicycle or automobile, the ocean liner, dirigible or airplane, the cinema or a great daily newspaper (the synthesis of a day in the whole world) do not dream that these diverse forms of communication, transportation and information exert such a decisive influence upon their psyches.
>
> Marinetti, *Stung by Salt and War,* 45.

64. See "Technical Manifesto of Futurist Literature" (May 1912), in *Marinetti: Selected Writings,* 84–89. See also Linda Landis, "Futurists at War," in *The Futurist Imagination,* 60–75.

65. A reproduction of the poem can be found in *Futurismo and Futurismi,* ed. Pontus Hulten (Milan: Bompiani, 1986), 604.

66. Marinetti, "Battle (Weight + Stink)," in *Stung by Salt and War,* 47–48.

67. Russolo, *The Art of Noises,* 36.

68. Diary entry on 19 October 1915, cited in Tisdall and Bozzolla, *Futurism,* 180.

69. F. T. Marinetti, "Manifesto of the Futurist Dance," in *Marinetti: Selected Writings,* 137–41.

70. Ibid., 139.

71. Russolo, "Noises of War," in *The Art of Noises,* 49.

72. Ibid., 50.

73. "Shrapnels do not explode on contact but are timed by a fuse that is automatically ignited at the moment of firing and continues to burn during the flight of the shell, thus setting off the explosive while the shrapnel is still some meters from the target. In these shells the whistling is violently interrupted by a furious *meow,* simultaneous with the explosion itself. No matter how short, this *meow* produces a rapid enharmonic passage, descending more than an octave. . . . I remember that soldiers remarked of the first shrapnels that there must have been a cat inside!" Ibid., 51.

74. Remarque, *All Quiet on the Western Front,* 40–41. The original German and the English translation were both 1929.

75. "Human multitudes, gases, electrical forces were hurled into the open country, high-frequency currents coursed through the landscape, new constellations rose in the sky, aerial space and ocean depths thundered with propellers, and everywhere sacrificial shafts were dug in Mother Earth." Walter Benjamin, "One-Way Street," in *Reflections,* trans. Edmund Jephcott (New York: Harcourt Brace Jovanovich, 1978), 93.

76. As Apollinaire reported in his poem "Guerre": "Contact by sound / We're firing toward noises that were heard." Guillaume Apollinarie, *Calligrammes,* trans. Anne Hyde Greet (Berkeley: University of California, 1980), 160–63. For a history of sounds within tactical communications, see chapter 8, "Signaling by Sound," of David L. Woods, *A History of Tactical Communication Techniques* (New York: Arno Press, 1974), 131–48.

77. Remarque, *All Quiet on the Western Front,* 88. Also: "We sharpen their ears to the malicious, hardly audible buzz of the smaller shells that are not easily distinguishable. They must pick them out from the general din by their insect-like hum—we explain to them that these are far more dangerous than the big ones that can be heard long beforehand" (90–91).

78. Ibid., 85.

79. Ibid., 86.

80. Ibid., 142.

81. Ibid., 147.

82. Ibid., 148.

83. Russolo, *The Art of Noises,* 28.

84. Russolo, "The Noise Instruments," in *The Art of Noises,* 78.

85. Marinetti, "Let's Murder the Moonshine," in *Marinetti: Selected Writings,* 46.

86. Georges Ribemont-Dessaignes, "History of Dada," in *The Dada Painters and Poets,* 117.

87. George Antheil, "The Negro on the Spiral," in *Negro: An Anthology* (1934), ed. Nancy Cunard (New York: Ungar, 1970), 218.

88. Walter Benjamin, "Theories of German Fascism: On the Collection of Essays *War and Warrior,* ed. Ernst Jünger," *New German Critique,* no. 17 (Spring 1979): 120–28.

89. Russolo, "The Noises of War," in *The Art of Noises,* 49.

90. Luigi Russolo, "The Art of Noises Futurist Manifesto," Ibid., 26.

Chapter 36

Kodwo Eshun

OPERATING SYSTEM FOR THE REDESIGN OF SONIC REALITY

RESPECT DUE. GOOD MUSIC SPEAKS FOR ITSELF. No Sleevenotes required. Just enjoy it. Cut the crap. Back to basics. What else is there to add?

All these troglodytic homilies are Great British cretinism masquerading as vectors into the Trad Sublime. Since the 80s, the mainstream British music press has turned to Black Music only as a rest and a refuge from the rigorous complexities of white guitar rock. Since in this laughable reversal a lyric always means more than a sound, while only guitars can embody the Zeitgeist, the Rhythmachine is locked in a retarded innocence. You can theorize words or style, but analyzing the groove is believed to kill its bodily pleasure, to drain its essence.

Allegedly at odds with the rock press, dance-press writing also turns its total inability to describe any kind of rhythm into a virtue, invoking a white Brit routine of pubs and clubs, of business as usual, the bovine sense of good blokes together. You can see that the entire British dance press – with its hagiographies and its geographies, its dj recipes, its boosterism, its personality profiles – constitutes a colossal machine for maintaining rhythm as an unwritable, ineffable mystery. And this is why Trad dance-music journalism is nothing more than lists and menus, bits and bytes: meagre, miserly, mediocre.

All today's journalism is nothing more than a giant inertia engine to put the brakes on breaks, a moronizer placing all thought on permanent pause, a *futureshock absorber,* forever shielding its readers from the future's cuts, tracks, scratches. Behind the assumed virtue of keeping rhythm mute, there is a none-too-veiled hostility towards analyzing rhythm at all. Too many ideas spoil the party. Too much speculation kills 'dance music', by 'intellectualizing' it to death.

The fuel this inertia engine runs on is fossil fuel: the live show, the proper album, the Real Song, the Real Voice, the mature, the musical, the pure, the true, the proper, the intelligent, breaking America: all notions that stink of the past, that maintain a hierarchy of the senses, that petrify music into a solid state in which everyone knows where they stand, and what real music really is.

And this is why nothing is more fun than spoiling this terminally stupid sublime, this insistence that Great Music speaks for itself.

At the Century's End, the Futurhythmachine has 2 opposing tendencies, 2 synthetic drives: the Soulful and the Postsoul. But then all music is made of both tendencies running simultaneously at all levels, so you can't merely *oppose* a humanist r&b with a posthuman Techno.

Disco remains the moment when Black Music falls from the grace of gospel tradition into the metronomic assembly line. Ignoring that disco is therefore *audibly* where the 21st C begins, 9 out of 10 cultural crits prefer their black popculture humanist, and emphatically 19th C. Like Brussels sprouts, humanism is good for you, nourishing, nurturing, soulwarming – and from Phyllis Wheatley to R. Kelly, present-day R&B is a perpetual fight for human status, a yearning for human rights, a struggle for inclusion within the human species. Allergic to cybersonic if not to sonic technology, mainstream American media – in its drive to banish alienation, and to recover a sense of the whole human being through belief systems that talk to the 'real you' – compulsively deletes any intimation of an AfroDiasporic futurism, of a 'webbed network' of computerhythms, machine mythology and conceptechnics which routes, reroutes and criss-crosses the Black Atlantic. This digital diaspora connecting the UK to the US, the Caribbean to Europe to Africa, is in Paul Gilroy's definition a 'rhizomorphic, fractal structure', a 'transcultural, international formation.'

The music of Alice Coltrane and Sun Ra, of Underground Resistance and George Russell, of Tricky and Martina, comes from the Outer Side. It alienates itself from the human; it arrives from the future. Alien Music is a synthetic recombinator, an applied art technology for amplifying the rates of becoming alien. Optimize the ratios of excentricity. Synthesize yourself.

From the outset, this Postsoul Era has been characterized by an extreme indifference towards the human. The human is a pointless and treacherous category.

And in synch with this posthuman perspective comes Black Atlantic Futurism. Whether it's the AfroFuturist *concrète* of George Russell and Roland Kirk, the Jazz Fission of Teo Macero and Miles Davis, the World 4 Electronics of Sun Ra and Herbie Hancock, the Astro Jazz of Alice Coltrane and Pharoah Sanders, the cosmophonic HipHop of Dr Octagon and Ultramagnetic MCs, the post-HipHop of The Jungle Brothers and Tricky, the Spectral Dub of Scientist and Lee Perry, the offworld Electro of Haashim and Ryuichi Sakamoto, the despotic Acid of Bam Bam and Phuture, the sinister phonoseduction of Parliament's Star Child, the hyperrhythmic psychedelia of Rob Playford and Goldie, 4 Hero and A Guy Called Gerald, Sonic Futurism always adopts a cruel, despotic, amoral attitude towards the human species.

In fact the era when the History of HipHop could exhaust Machine Music is long over. All those petitions for HipHop to be taken seriously, for the BBC to give Techno a chance, for House to receive a fair hearing: this miserable supplication should have ended years ago. For there's nothing to prove anymore: *all* these Rhythmachines are *globally* popular now.

So no more forcefeeding you Bronx fables and no more orthodox HipHop liturgies. There are more than enough of these already. Instead *More Brilliant than the Sun* will focus on the Futurhythmachines within each field, offering a close hearing of music's internal emigrants only. The Outer Thought of Tricky, the Jungle Brothers with their remedy for HipHop gone illmatic, Aerosoul art theorist Rammellzee and his mythillogical systems of Gothic Futurism and *Ikonoklast Panzerism*. No history of Techno, however compelling, but instead a zoom in on the Underground Resistance WarMachine, on the Unidentifiable Audio Object of *X-102 Discovers 'The Rings of Saturn'*. No pleas for Jungle to be accorded proper respect, but rather a magnification of certain very particular aspects of its hyperdimensionality, in 4 Hero, A Guy Called Gerald, Rob Playford and Goldie.

The history book that crams in everything only succeeds in screening out the strangeness of the Rhythmachine. In its bid for universality, such a book dispels the artificiality that all humans crave.

By contrast, *More Brilliant* goes farther in. It lingers lovingly inside a single remix, explores the psychoacoustic fictional spaces of interludes and intros, goes to extremes to extrude the illogic other studies flee. It happily deletes familiar names [so no Tupac, no NWA] and historical precedence [no lying griots, not much King Tubby, just a small side bet on the Stockhausen sweepstakes]. It avoids the nauseating American hunger for confessional biography, for 'telling your own stories in your own words'. It refuses entry to comforting origins and social context.

Everywhere, the 'street' is considered the ground and guarantee of all reality, a compulsory logic explaining all Black Music, conveniently mishearing antisocial sur-realism as social realism. Here sound is unglued from such obligations, until it eludes all social responsibility, thereby accentuating its unreality principle.

In CultStud, TechnoTheory and CyberCulture, those painfully archaic regimes, theory always comes to Music's *rescue*. The organization of sound is interpreted historically, politically, socially. Like a headmaster, theory teaches today's music a thing or 2 about life. It subdues music's ambition, reins it in, restores it to its proper place, reconciles it to its naturally belated fate.

In *More Brilliant than the Sun* the opposite happens, for once: music is encouraged in its despotic drive to crumple chronology like an empty bag of crisps, to eclipse reality in its wilful exorbitance, to put out the sun. Here music's mystifying illogicality is not chastised but systematized and intensified – into MythSciences that burst the edge of improbability, incites a proliferating series of mixillogical mathemagics at once maddening and perplexing, alarming, alluring.

MythScience is the field of knowledge invented by Sun Ra, and a term that this book uses as often as it can. A sample from Virilio defines it very simply: 'Science and technology develop the unknown, not knowledge. Science develops what is not rational.' Instead of theory saving music from itself, from its worst, which is to say its best excesses, music is heard as the pop analysis it already is. Producers are already pop theorists: Breakbeat producer Sonz of a Loop da Loop Era's term skratchadelia, instrumental HipHop producer DJ Krush's idea of turntabilization, virtualizer George Clinton's studio science of mixadelics, all these conceptechnics are used to excite theory to travel at the speed of thought, as sonic theorist Kool Keith suggested in 1987. TechnoTheory, CultStuds *et al* lose their flabby bulk, their lazy, pompous, lard-arsed, top-down dominance, becoming but a single component in a thought synthesizer which moves along several planes at once, which tracks Machine Music's lines of force.

Far from needing theory's help, music today is already *more* conceptual than at any point this century, pregnant with thoughtprobes waiting to be activated, switched on, misused.

So *More Brilliant than the Sun* draws more of its purpose from track subtitles than from TechnoTheory, or even science fiction. These *conceptechnics* are then released from the holding pens of their brackets, to migrate and mutate across the entire communication landscape. Stolen from Sleevenote Manifestos, adapted from label fictions, driven as far and as fast as possible, they misshape until they become devices to drill into the new sensory experiences, endoscopes to magnify the new mindstates Machine Music is inducing.

More Brilliant than the Sun's achievement, therefore, is to design, manufacture, fabricate, synthesize, cut, paste and edit a so-called artificial discontinuum for the Futurhythmachine.

Rejecting today's ubiquitous emphasis on black sound's necessary ethical allegiance to the street, this project opens up the new plane of Sonic Fiction, the secret life of forms, the discontinuum of AfroDiasporic Futurism, the chain reaction of PhonoFiction. It moves through the explosive forces which technology ignites in us, the temporal architecture of inner space, audiosocial space, living space, where postwar alienation breaks down into the 21st C alien.

From Sun Ra to 4 Hero, today's alien discontinuum therefore operates not through continuities, retentions, genealogies or inheritances but rather through intervals, gaps, breaks. It turns away from roots; it opposes common sense with the force of the fictional and the power of falsity.

One side effect of the alien discontinuum is the rejection of any and all notions of a compulsory black condition. Where journalism still insists on a solid state known as 'blackness', *More Brilliant* dissolves this solidarity with a corpse into a *fluidarity* maintained and exacerbated by soundmachines.

Today's cyborgs are too busy manufacturing themselves across time-space to disintensify themselves with all the Turing Tests for transatlantic, transeuropean and transafrican consciousness: affirmation, keeping it real, representing, staying true to the game, respect due, staying black. Alien Music today deliberately fails all these Tests, these putrid corpses of petrified moralism: it treats them with utter indifference; it replaces them with nothing whatsoever.

It deserts forever the nauseating and bizarre ethic of 'redemption'.

AfroDiasporic Futurism has assembled itself along inhuman routes, and it takes artificial thought to reveal this. Such relief: jaws unclench, as conviction collapses.

Where crits of CyberCult still gather, 99.9% of them will lament the disembodiment of the human by technology. But machines *don't* distance you from your emotions, in fact quite the opposite. Sound machines make you feel *more* intensely, along a broader band of emotional spectra than ever before in the 20th Century.

Sonically speaking, the posthuman era is not one of disembodiment but the exact reverse: it's a *hyperembodiment,* via the Technics SL 1200. A non-sound scientist like Richard Dawkins 'talks very happily about cultural viruses,' argues Sadie Plant, 'but doesn't think that he himself is a viral contagion.' Migrating from the lab to the studio, Sonic Science not only talks about cultural viruses, it is itself a viral contagion. It's a sensational infection by the spread of what Ishmael Reed terms antiplagues.

Machine Music doesn't call itself science because it controls technology, but because music is the artform most thoroughly undermined and recombinated and reconfigured by technics. Scientists set processes in motion which swallow them up: the scientist's brain is caught up in the net. Acid's alien frequency modulation turns on its dj-producers Phuture and Sleezy D and begins to 'stab your brain' and 'disrupt thought patterns'.

Yet in magnifying such hitherto ignored intersections of sound and science fiction – the nexus this project terms Sonic Fiction or PhonoFiction – *More Brilliant* paradoxically ends up with a portrait of music today far *more* accurate than any realistic account has managed. This is because most recent accounts of Black Music – those which form the dominant humanist strain in the commemoration of Black Music, its official histories – are more than anything wish fulfilments: scenarios in which Acid never existed, in which Electronic Jazz never arrived, in which the Era of the Rhythmachine *never happened.*

By contrast, *More Brilliant* is a mechanography, an omnidirectional exploration into mechano-informatics, the secret life of machines which opens up the vast and previously unsuspected coevolution of machines and humans in late 20th C Black Atlantic Futurism.

Alien Music is all in the breaks: the distance between Tricky and what you took to be the limits of Black Music, the gap between Underground Resistance and what you took Black Music to be, between listening to Miles & Macero's He *Loved Him Madly* and crossing all thresholds with and through it, leaving every old belief system: rock, jazz, soul, Electro, HipHop, House, Acid, Drum'n'Bass, electronics, Techno and dub – forever.

The mayday signal of Black Atlantic Futurism is unrecognizability, as either Black or Music. Sonic Futurism doesn't locate you in tradition; instead it dislocates you from origins. It uproutes you by inducing a gulf crisis, a perceptual daze rendering today's sonic discontinuum immediately audible.

The Futurist producer can *not* be trusted with music's heritage. Realizing this, UK and US dance media spring forward, to maintain these traditions the producer always abandons. Media's role is to defend an *essence,* by warding off all possible infections: journalists become missionaries on behalf of HipHop; they battle for the soul of Techno.

Which is why at Century's End you tune into sensory frequencies undetectable to the happy tinnitus of good solid journalism. You are willingly mutated by intimate machines, abducted by audio into the populations of your bodies. Sound machines throw you onto the shores of the skin you're in. The hypersensual cyborg experiences herself as a galaxy of audiotactile sensations.

You are not censors but sensors, not aesthetes but kinaesthetes. You are sensationalists. You are the newest mutants incubated in womb-speakers. Your mother, your first sound. The bedroom, the party, the dancefloor, the rave: these are the labs where the 21st C nervous systems assemble themselves, the matrices of the Futurhythmachinic Discontinuum. The future is a much better guide to the present than the past. Be prepared, be ready to trade everything you know about the history of music for a single glimpse of its future.

Chapter 37

Michael Veal

STARSHIP AFRICA

The Acoustics of Diaspora and of the Postcolony[1]

> Antillean art is this restoration of our shattered histories, our shards
> of vocabulary, our archipelago becoming a synonym for pieces broken
> off from the original continent. . . . That is the basis of the Antillean
> experience, this shipwreck of fragments, these echoes, these shards of a
> huge tribal vocabulary.
>
> —Derek Walcott, 1992

FIRST, LET US IMAGINE A TIME CAPSULE loaded with various planetary music of the twentieth century, including a sample of roots reggae music of the 1970s compiled by a Jamaican producer such as Bunny Lee or Augustus Pablo. Then, let us suppose that the producer, in error, submitted King Tubby's dub remixes instead of the vocal versions that would, at the request of the project's organizers, have ostensibly addressed some representative social/cultural/political theme of the period. How might these fragmentary texts be interpreted by unknown historians at some distant future location in space and time? Might these versions ultimately offer as vivid portrayals of their culture as would the original songs with complete lyrics? Luke Erlich (paraphrasing Lee Perry) has aptly described the dub version as a type of "x-ray" music that provides glimpses at a song's inner *musical* workings (emphasis mine),[2] but what deeper resonances be gleaned from these skeletal remains of gutted pop songs with their reverberating musical language of fragmentation and erasure?[3]

For the most part, dub mixes are remixes of pieces that originally contained lyrics. In an important sense, then, the remix decisions of engineers when remixing a song into a dub version are (as discussed in chapter 2 [see original publication]) often shaped by the original song text; consequently, the dub mix may be at least partially understood as extending the concerns of the song lyrics into (relatively) instrumental or "pure sound" territory. In this penultimate chapter, I shall draw out some of the more subtle resonances within this pure sound territory, tracing dub's reverberations by "versioning" it through the variously imagined pasts and futures animating the African diaspora (in general) and (more specifically) those animating postcolonial Jamaica.

The extensive use of reverberation/delay devices and the fragmentation of the song surface are probably the two most immediately recognizable stylistic features of dub music. As such, the idea of "echo" figures centrally in the first section of this chapter, in which I treat dub's heavy use of reverb as a sonic metaphor for the condition of diaspora. This section also explores the themes of retained Africanist aesthetics in dub, and concludes with a comparison between dub and the genre of magical realism—which I believe parallels, in literature and film, the Surrealist aspects of dub, and which I ultimately assert as an aesthetic particularly reflective of the cultural experience of (African) diaspora. The second section of the chapter builds upon ideas of musical structure introduced in chapter 2, using the formal logics of the (sound) collage to ponder a relationship between ruptures in historical narrative (the trans-Atlantic slave trade) and ruptures in musical narrative (song form). The third section of the chapter uses the trait of spatiality in the music to ponder diasporic and Afro-inflected imaginings of outer space, science fiction, and the future. In the fourth and final section of the chapter, I tie these themes together by theorizing a particular significance for dub music within the class dynamics of Jamaican society, in conjunction with the rise of the sound system DJ as a significant cultural force. Ultimately, I believe that, understood in the appropriate historical context, this strange and seemingly inscrutable music played an important role in the ongoing evolution of Jamaica's postcolonial culture.

In the opening chapter of his 1995 book *African Rhythm,* Kofi Agawu offers a richly descriptive narration of the daily soundscape in Ghana's northern Eweland.[4] In my reading, one of Agawu's goals here is to move the study of traditional African music beyond its stereotyped conceptual boundaries by demonstrating that a culture's conception of "rhythm" is not only narrowly present in their music making, but a profoundly experiential component of their total way of life. Ethnomusicologists have long spoken of the need to understand the phenomenon of music as something socially constituted; in this chapter I shall similarly discuss the characteristic treatment of song form in Jamaican dub music, not as empirical musical fact, but as something equally constituted by social and historical forces. In this light, the various stylistic processes I have referred to throughout this book are treated not merely as aspects of music, but as profoundly structural embodiments of Jamaican history and culture. And, as the final section makes clear, the musical developments also helped transform the same culture.

Reverb, Remembrance, and Reverie

The reliance on reverberation and delay devices is certainly one of the most pronounced stylistic traits of dub music, and the sensations simulated by reverb and digital delay devices—either cavernous spaces or repeated sounds, respectively—can be subsumed under the commonly used term *echo.*[5] In the sonic culture of humans, the sensation of echo is closely associated with the cognitive function of memory and the evocation of the chronological past; at the same time, it can also evoke the vastness of outer space and hence (by association), the chronological future. Most obviously, dub is about memory in the immediate sense that it is a remix, a refashioned version of an already familiar pop song; as such, it derives much of its musical and commercial power from its manipulation of the listener's prior experience of a song. In a more abstract sense, however, I am speculating that, suffusing their music with the sensation of echo during a period when the symbol of Africa was being consciously revitalized in diasporic consciousness, the creators of dub managed to evoke a cultural memory of ancestral African roots through heavy use of the reverb and echo effects and various musical strategies of African origin.

Such a "historicizing of the echo," which has also been addressed by Louis Chude-Sokei in a seminal 1997 essay, implicates dub in the diasporic tropes of exile and nostalgia shared to varying degrees by people of African descent in the New World.[6] In this interpretation, the otherworldly strain in dub music partially evokes an idealized, precolonial African utopia. It was during Michael Manley's attempt at democratic socialism in Jamaica of the 1970s, that a mood of cultural nationalism was energized by Castro's Cuba, the African American civil rights struggle, African nationalism, and the religious vision of Rastafari. All of these stimulated, in varying ways, a reevaluation of African cultural roots. Most literally, Africa was deemed by Rastas to be the site of inevitable repatriation for a people in exile—and considering the economic hardship, strife, and violence that accompanied Jamaica's attempts at social change, it was not surprising that even at the height of cultural pride, many still wished for another place to call home.

In "Reflections on Exile" (1990), Edward Said characterized exile as the "unhealable rift forced between a human being and a native place, between the self and its true home: its essential sadness can never be surmounted."[7] James Clifford, on the other hand, has observed that "diasporism" tends to oscillate in accordance with the relationship a given [sub]culture maintains with its surrounding society, with periods of antagonism tending to inspire more intense feelings of longing for an ancestral homeland.[8] Clifford also notes that the narratives of diaspora are binary in composition, drawing upon idealized images of a past in the construction of a cultural "safe space" in a hostile present.[9] Such sentiments are echoed in the words of Jamaican poet Kwame Dawes, who surmised that in Jamaica, "the Africa that is constructed is mythic and defined in terms of the current space of exile."[10] I cite these comments in order to evoke the ethos of diaspora as experienced by those of African descent during the early independence years of the 1960s and 1970s, when the idea of Africa was being revitalized throughout the African diaspora. The condition of simultaneously yearning for and being alienated from a cultural homeland that can never be fully experienced as home, and also from the very *history* of connection to that homeland, allows us to interpret dub as a cultural sound painting of a type, vividly dramatizing the experience of diasporic exile.

At what point does culture in diaspora become normalized, ceasing to be measured in relation to some originary homeland? It may seem contradictory that I discuss diaspora and exile in terms of the use of reverberation as a stylistic trait of Jamaican music, while in chapter 7 [see original publication] I spoke of a music (ragga) coming out of the same diasporic context that almost completely abandoned this stylistic trait. After all, isn't digital Jamaica still part of the African diaspora? And doesn't Africa remain an important reference point in contemporary Jamaican music? The obvious answer to both of these questions is yes. My point, however, is that the music of the roots era represented the *end* of more than four centuries in which the cultures of ancestral Africa remained largely a mystery to their descendants throughout the African diaspora. This situation is quite different today, at the turn of a new millennium. While repatriation might remain a quite remote possibility for the vast majority of Jamaicans, there is a Rastafarian settlement in Ethiopia and substantial expatriate Jamaican populations in other parts of Africa (especially Ghana). Reverberation, then, only acquires this particular significance during the historical moment concerned with exploring the ancestral past. By the mid-1980s, this moment had largely passed.

If reggae in the 1970s was in many ways a musical attempt to invoke "Africa" as a newly imagined safe space in the Caribbean present, reverberation provided the cohering agent for dub's interplay of presence/absence and of completeness/ incompleteness, evoking the intertwined experiences of exile and nostalgia, and reflecting Said's characterization of exile as "fundamentally a discontinuous state of being."[11] These fragments may also be interpreted as fragments of an African cultural memory under reconstruction, the building blocks being fragments of the post– World War II popular song form and fragmentary memories of Africa. The music's elasticity of form provided the perfect crucible for an elastic reimagining of history, a meditation crucial to the cultural consciousness of the new nation. As I shall mention later in this chapter, the invention of synthetic reverb had (via its capability for spatial simulation) granted new social classes of classical music listeners virtual access to the elite concert hall at the beginning of the twentieth century. However, it also granted those in the African diaspora virtual access to a new vision of the African past at the end of the same century.[12]

> This kind of singing, coupled with the hard reggae chop of rhythm guitar, was nothing less than a setup for secular Jamaican spirit possession, trance music of the highest order.
>
> —Stephen Davis [13]

"Africa" can also arguably be felt in much of what makes this music unique, and its effect on listeners. In his 1985 study of the relationship between music and states of altered consciousness, Gilbert Rouget distinguished between two states and their respective musical catalysts: those inducing states of *ecstatic contemplation* and those inducing states of *possession*.[14] I believe that the dub mix can, in certain respects, be seen as a catalyst for both states. By traditional definitions, reggae—notwithstanding how often and passionately it voiced Rastafarian themes—should not actually be considered a liturgical or devotional music; Rastafarians had their own Nyabinghi ceremonial music (which itself was rooted in a variety of neo-African liturgical musics such as *burru*). But, infused with the religious passion of Rastafari-influenced reggae, overtones of Euro-American psychedelia, and the political passion of the Manley years, dub nevertheless functioned in the sound system to induce states of pseudopossession and/or contemplative ecstasy in conformity with procedures ultimately rooted in traditional African music.

Possession, marked by a violent or convulsive entry to a trance state, may be the most immediately relevant interpretation.[15] Long before the advent of recording technology, the technique of disruption was frequently used in West African and diasporic traditional musics to create a sense of momentary disorientation and heightened excitement. Rouget surveys several instances in which the sudden disruption of an insistent, repeating rhythm—through its disorienting effect on the listener's nervous system—functions to induce trance or possession.[16] This retained African strategy for creating and manipulating dynamic tension acquires new dimensions in the extreme volumes of the Jamaican sound system. Having been stoked for hours with an unending stream of bass-heavy rhythms, frenzied shouts pierce the air as the sound system peaks, rhythm parts reverberate violently in and out of the mix, and the deejay's voice exclaims above it all. As Robbie Shakespeare remembers, such intensity often resulted in extreme audience responses, such as the infamous "lickshot" (firearms fired at the ceiling or into the air in response to particularly dramatic passages of music):

> When you go a dance, and you hear sound system them a play, [they have] no effects, the amplifier have just volume, bass, treble. And them used to turn off the bass, so you just get the sound through the horns; the top end a cut through, and when them put in the bass—*vroom!* People rave for that! Especially when the dub wicked, them used to go mad, man. That was one reason why a man start firing guns inna dancehall, because of dub. Ever since from way back rock steady days, when the dub part come in and them turn off the bass and then turn it back in—it sounds so *evilous* it make you fire a gun shot man! Shot used to fire in the dancehall from ever since then.[17]

With the aforementioned "inhabitability" of the dub mix in mind, the violent spatial manipulations might also be heard as functioning to liberate the body and mind from the physical rhythms of oppression by providing a convulsive glimpse of abandon; that is, "resisting the dominant disciplines of bodily reform," although not necessarily through the fits of spiritual possession that Andrew Apter suggests in his discussion of slave religion.[18] Despite the frenzied shouts that can inevitably be heard at the peak of a sound system session, the manner in which people actually dance to roots reggae is more accurately described as cool, calm, graceful, and understated. The convulsive ecstasy of possession is as often sublimated in dub into the sonic sensations of exploding and convulsing space, with its intimate psychological associations of physical movement and constraint.[19] As Lee Perry explained to Kevin Martin in 1995: "When you hear dub you fly on the music. You put your heart, your body and your spirit into the music, you gonna fly. Because if it wasn't for the music, oppression and taxes would kill you. They send taxes and oppression to hold you, a government to tell you what to do and use you like a robot. So they will torment you to death. So when you hear dub you hide from the fuckers there."[20]

That dub mixes could be described as having a "mystical" or "mysterious" feel, had as much to do with the application of reverb as it did with the Rasta-derived lyrical content. The evolution of reverberation and echo as aesthetic devices in popular music dates to the 1950s, and is largely credited to independent blues, rhythm and blues and country music recording labels such as Chess in Chicago and Sun Records in Memphis.[21] But reverb and echo had been used earlier in the recording of Western classical music, to simulate the acoustic environments of traditional performance settings such as churches and cathedrals.[22] The inevitable sonic associations that this carried—of timelessness and meditation—were equally suggested by dub mixes saturated with reverb. It was this quality that inspired Neil "Mad Professor" Fraser to launch his career as a "second wave" studio engineer creating dub music in England: "I just found that it was a music that makes you wonder and it really provides the vehicle for songs and for meditation . . . it didn't have lyrics, so there was space for incidental thought."[23] Similarly, producer Clive Chin felt that "dub music is just purely meditation,"[24] while Winston Riley considered dub "a very soothing and a relaxing music. And a meditative music too."[25] This frequent emphasis on dub as a music of meditation is significant. Rasta-influenced song texts aside for the moment, some of the more dramatic dub mixes might be considered on purely sonic terms as pseudoliturgical music of a type, invested with strong religious, magical, and psychological power deriving from the intertwined spiritual, political, and cultural tropes dominating Jamaican music during the 1970s.

When engineers slowed the tempos of their dub remixes, they eased their listeners into a sonic space conducive to more intimate and erotically charged dancing, intensified by the teasing incompleteness of the fragmented song surface and the engineer's sensuous ride across the spectrum of timbres and textures. The music became eroticized, experienced as a succession of mutating, evolving, and undulating textural/spatial sensations. But when Sasha Frere-Jones referred to Lee Perry's Black Ark music as the "Aurora borealis of reggae,"[26] he was strongly evoking the sonic subtleties and sublimities of the mix and its contemplative effect upon the listener. Such manipulations function as a sonic catalyst for a state of what Rouget terms *ecstatic contemplation,* empowering the listener through rhythm while drawing them into contemplative states through increasingly subtle manipulations of spatial and textural elements. In this way, the engineer opens a space for the remix as a mode of experiencing more subtle and/or sublime sensations within the songscape. The psychedelic strain of Euro-American pop, the Christian emphasis on otherworldly salvation, and the Rasta emphasis on Africa fused to convey a timeless, African-inflected sense of both *otherness* and *otherworldliness.* Will Montgomery, discussing the music of Lee Perry's Black Ark era, describes how "cut after cut, stretches of otherworldly matter frame despairing social commentary . . . the intensity of the urge to transform the here-and-now in the studio adds a potent and wistful militancy to these songs."[27] The "otherworldy matter" of which he speaks is sound matter, dramatizing the Afro-Caribbean-Protestant-Rastafarian longing for political liberation—recast no longer as Christian heaven, but as African Zion.

Such artistically driven transformations of reality invite comparison with a parallel regional tradition in another artistic medium. The literary genre of *magical realism* emerged during the 1960s and 1970s as a transnational phenomenon, but remains largely associated with the work of Latin America and Caribbean authors such as Gabriel García Márquez, Alejo Carpentier, Jorge Luis Borges and others.

Magical realist works characteristically rely on abrupt switches in tense and narrative mode juxtaposing realistic passages with passages of fantastic, magical, or supernatural narrative. In the words of David Mikics, these works "violat[e] the world of everyday appearances by the rich and strange world of dreams."[28] Magical realist texts have been subjected to various interpretations that tend to coalesce around two related themes. The first draws on the idea of the Caribbean as the planetary site of mixing and cultural hybridity par excellence;[29] in this interpretation, magical realism's liminal literary space between fantasy and reality functions to reconcile the diverse cultural currents flowing into the Caribbean. The reconciliation of diverse cultural histories and belief systems implies a destruction of the old in the fusion of the new; the hybrid nature of the Caribbean (especially in the context of the continued domination of Old World political, economic, and cultural structures), implies an embrace of fragmentation and juxtaposition as necessary adaptive strategies.[30]

A second interpretation of magical realism carries more political implications. Some theorists have asserted the genre as a postcolonial art form furnishing "ontological resistance" to structures of thought (including artistic forms) implicated in the colonial project. Lois Zamora and Wendy Faris have claimed that magical realism, in its subversion of colonially derived literary conventions, implicitly resists "monologic" cultural structures; as such, it is particularly useful to (and reflective of) postcolonial cultures.[31] Steven Slemon also finds magical realism "most visibly operative in cultures situated at the margins of mainstream literary traditions"[32] and considers the genre to "[have] echoes in those forms of postcolonial thought which seek to recuperate the lost voices and discarded fragments that imperialist cognitive structures push to the margins of critical consciousness. . . . [These artworks] share an interest in thematically decentering images of fixity while at the same time foregrounding the gaps and absences those fixed and monumental structures produce."[33] It was based on this particular interplay of factors that St. Lucian poet Derek Walcott could claim magical realism as "the authoritative aesthetic response to the Caribbean cultural context."[34]

What does dub share with magical realism? Its decentering of textual and musical syntax, its surreal treatment of song form, and its fragmented and/or stacked narrative voices can be thought of as a musical corollary of what Theo D'Haen describes, in magical realist literature, as the "utopian, if evanescent, promise of transfigured perception, the hypnotic reviewing of everyday existence."[35] Its reliance on practices rooted in the oral tradition—blended with the newly available technology of an emergent recording industry—strongly echoes Frederic Jameson's interpretation of magical realism (in film) as dependent on a fusion of precapitalist with nascent capitalist (especially technological) elements.[36] And, as I shall discuss toward the end of this chapter, the "gaps and absences" that populate the dub mix ultimately had a similarly political utility in Jamaica.

The Politics and Poetics of Erasure: Historical Trauma and the Jamaican Sound Collage

> What better medium than collage to express the accumulation of memories? And isn't collage the emblematic medium of the century?

Collagists . . . take bits of chaos to . . . investigate, organize and present
evidence of the activity of a culture.

—Carrie Rickey[37]

Break a vase, and the love that reassembles the fragments is stronger than
the love which took its symmetry for granted when it was whole. The
glue that fits the pieces is the sealing of its original shape. It is such a love
that reassembles our African and Asiatic fragments. . . . This gathering of
broken pieces is the care and pain of the Antilles.

—Derek Walcott

One of the historical events that continues to reverberate in cultural forms
throughout the African diaspora is the transatlantic slave trade, a historical trauma
characterized by forced erasures of cultural memory, and disruptions in linear
conceptions of history and human progress. Much of the literature on trauma has
addressed various forms of individual suffering (generally addressed through the lens
of psychoanalytic theory), as well as large-scale collective traumas such as the mass
tragedies suffered in the Holocaust, the nuclear attacks at Hiroshima and Nagasaki, or
other recent horrors (generally addressed through the lens of medical anthropology).
As Sandra Bloom (1998) has discussed, the effects of trauma seem relatively consistent
between the individual and collective spheres,[38] and integral to the trauma literature
is the concept of *testimony*—the various ways in which individuals or groups recount
traumatic experiences that have remained suppressed.[39] There have been a number of
studies tracing a connection between trauma and the formal characteristics of such
narrative "testimony," including those found in artistic production. In terms of
historical experience, James Clifford feels that "experiences of unsettlement, loss,
and recurring terror produce discrepant temporalities—broken histories that trouble
the linear, progressivist narratives."[40] Clifford is speaking in abstract terms, in relation
to the construction of broadly shared historical narratives, but Shoshana Felman, in
her study of the poetry of Holocaust survivors, concretizes this idea in terms of form
and individual artistic creation, referring to "an [historical] accident which is materially
embodied in an accidenting of the verse."[41] Might the experience of historical trauma
have echoes in dub's shattering of narrative continuity?

In general, the literature on trauma has avoided the African diaspora, and the
narratives produced within the cultural aftermath of the slave trade. One exception
is Paul Gilroy's "Living Memory and the Slave Sublime," which directly engages the
issue of historical trauma as it concerns people of African descent.[42] Another is the
work of visual artist Arthur Jafa, who has sought to understand the structural and
aesthetic implications of historical trauma on African American art making. Both
Gilroy and Jafa perceive the legacy of the slavery experience as structurally coded
within the expressive forms of the African diaspora. Gilroy finds such historical
experience reflected within what he terms "radically unfinished" expressive forms
that are "mark[ed] indelibly as the products of slavery."[43] In his interpretation, a legacy
of unresolved psychic terror gives coded voice to the "unspeakable terrors" of black
history via the narrative ruptures found in a variety of diasporic expressive forms.[44]
Jafa has referenced dub music more directly in his idea of "primal sites":

those group experiences that reconfigure who we [African Americans] are as a community. One of the critical primal sites would be the Middle Passage. If you understand the level of horror directed towards a group of people, then you start getting some sense of the magnitude, impact, and level of trauma that that had on the African American community, and how it was particularly one of the earliest group experiences that reshaped an "African psyche" into the beginning of an African American psyche. . . . Now, for example, you look at Black music and see certain structural things that really are about reclaiming this whole sense of absence, loss, not knowing. One of the things I'm thinking about is dub music . . . it ends up really speaking about common experiences because the structure of the music is about things dropping out and coming back in, really reclaiming this whole sense of loss, rupture, and repair that is very common across the experience of black people in the diaspora.[45]

In this reading, an art form such as dub comes to represent a form of the "testimony" discussed by trauma theorists such as Felman. Its deconstructed song forms recalls Gilroy's "unfinished forms," while its reduction of textual meaning to nonsensical phonemes articulates his idea of "*unspeakable* (historical) terrors." In this line of reasoning, the privileging of rupture in dub music comes to symbolize the disruptions in cultural memory and the historical shattering of existential peace, encoded into the cultural nervous system and sublimated into musical sound.

Placed in the context of Kingston in the 1970s, these observations also come to symbolize the shattering of the *contemporary* peace, enabling an interpretation of dub as a language of musical "shock," bound closely with aesthetic values of dissonance, destruction, and decay.[46] After all, violence and (later) the overt symbols of warfare were crucial to the highly competitive sound system dances from its earliest days, and this dissonance was eventually sublimated into the very structure of the dub music created for the sound systems.[47] The overdubbed sounds of screeching tires, machine-gun fire, and police sirens in some of King Tubby's dub mixes, the rough clientele that reportedly patronized his sound system,[48] and the ultimate destruction of his system itself at the hands of Kingston police—all attest to these musicians' movement within a vortex of social "counterforces" reflecting political and cultural warfare. And this warfare was both outward (against agents of foreign neocolonialism and local class domination) and inward (in the politically driven "tribal" warfare of Kingston's ghettos). It was this last dynamic that ultimately detached itself from political ideals and became self-sustaining, a type of random violence born of social frustration that eventually claimed the life of King Tubby (and many others) and drove Lee Perry, Scientist, and Philip Smart into exile. In this interpretation, dub is the sound of a society tearing itself apart at the seams, an effect given broader context by erasures, tears, and disruptions in the seam of history itself.

In light of dub music's fragmented song structures, the tortured formal fragmentation of the sound system "macroset," the violently martial ethos of the sound clash, and even the violence sometimes inherent in the music's procedures of realization, the preceding ideas provide insight into what might have caused Jamaica to evolve a style unique in the constellation of world popular musics for such an interruptive manipulation of musical pleasure. It can be argued that in most Western musical forms, pleasure is generally constructed through a dynamic of tension and release within the system of functional harmony. Dub partially subverts this dynamic, reducing harmonic activity to an episodic coloration in which moments of harmony and melody are contrasted with segments of stark low-register relief (drum & bass). On the other hand, aesthetic pleasure in African-derived systems is often constructed around repetition of interlocking rhythmic patterns. Dub partially subverts this also, with its periodic disruption of rhythmic patterns. As such, the music essentially subverts the pleasure principles of two musical systems: aesthetic pleasure here is fundamentally predicated upon the fragmented narratives of the *sound collage,* which in this case seems to conform to the emotional pendulum of post-traumatic experience that allows pleasure to be experienced only fleetingly as it swings between sensations of harmonic fullness and starkness, and between sensations of rhythmic continuity and disruption.[49]

As a form predicated upon the de- and reconstruction of aesthetic logics, collage has often been called a quintessential form of the turbulent twentieth century, a form inviting potentially endless possibilities of invention and interpretation.[50] Cubists found in its flattening of pictorial perspective a means of portraying the simultaneity of time and space. Italian Futurists used its mechanically produced print and photographic source materials to proclaim their ideals of a machine age. Russian Constructivists used its fragmented syntax as a way to portray the class struggles of their society. Dadaists and Surrealists built collage through a variety of chance procedures and asserted the form as simultaneously the most organically poetic and potentially revolutionary.[51] But several understandings of collage seem particularly relevant in the context of the danced (and sound-engineered) cultural shifts and social turbulence of Jamaica's roots era. The Dada/Surrealist artist Jean Arp used collage to evoke processes of decay in both nature and art, while historians have also read in his collages "an attempt to express in new formats regenerative powers." A similar interpretation was offered by art historian Katherine Hoffman, who saw in collage "a sense of the possibility of connectedness but at the same time . . . a sense of alienation of individuals afloat in a world turned upside down."[52] A third interpretation can be found in the writing of jazz historian Krin Gabbard who has speculated (in relation to the deconstructive aspects of modern jazz vis-à-vis the American pop song tradition) that the aestheticization of error and chance in some forms of black music arguably "shows contempt for Western art music with its smooth, 'organic' surfaces, its technical precision, and its highly-stylized set of emotional codes."[53]

In his 1996 essay "The Aesthetics of the Global Imagination," ethnomusicologist Veit Erlmann speculated that the juxtaposition of radically dissimilar or decontextualized genres in certain forms of world popular music may reflect the violent historical encounter between industrial capitalist and preindustrial societies (note how closely this echoes Jameson's aforementioned observation concerning magical realism).[54] Jamaica has been a part of the global economic order at least since the period of European colonization, but Erlmann's words are nevertheless relevant to the turbulent late–cold war dynamics of the Manley-Seaga years. Like Gilroy's "unfinished forms," dub may be one of a number of diasporic musics on which a traumatic history and turbulent present has left its structural imprint, "converting the outrage of the years into a music"[55] through an aesthetic of broken, discontinuous pleasures that may represent a synaptic adaptation to long-term historical trauma,[56] but that also fit into a broader global pattern in which collage forms join the search for new realities to define the twentieth century.

Notes

1. This chapter takes its name from *Starship Africa,* the Adrian Sherwood–produced album by Creation Rebel.
2. Erlich quote in Davis and Simon 1982:105.
3. The interpretation of West African *bocio* figurines (from Benin Republic) as "empowered cadavers" is introduced in the first chapter of Blier 1995, while the Surrealist nonsense word game of "exquisite corpses" is discussed in Lewis 1988:21. Both ideas interest me in the context of dub music through their suggestions of bringing something dead or used back to life, of reinvesting a spent object with a new power. Both ideas also resonate with specific interpretations of dub (discussed later in this chapter); some formal aspects of *bocio* figurines reflect a traumatic history of slavery and internecine warfare, while the Surrealist "exquisite corpse" wordplay was a group exercise in deconstructing the logic of language, reflecting a cynicism toward the Western heritage of logic and reason in the wake of World War I.
4. Agawu 1995.
5. I am using the term *echo* in this way here, despite my distinction between the effects produced by delay (echo) and reverb (spatial simulation) devices in chapter 2.
6. Chude-Sokei 1997.
7. Said 1990:357.
8. Clifford 1994:306.
9. Ibid.:307.
10. Dawes 2001.
11. Said 1990:360.
12. Doyle (2004) relates that reverb in early recordings of classical music provided listeners "virtual access to the acoustic regime of the concert hall" (34).
13. Davis 1985:79.
14. For example, see the section titled "Trance or Ecstasy?" (Rouget 1985:3).
15. See the first two sections of Rouget 1985: "Trance and Possession" and "Music and Possession."
16. See Rouget 1985:80–81.
17. Robbie Shakespeare, interviewed March 2002.
18. Both this and the previous quotation taken from Apter 1991:255.
19. Chude-Sokei (1997) has approached this from a slightly different angle, speculating that "individual subjectivity could be lost in the pounding volume of a sound system that was devoted to freeing the body from the oppressive imbalance of black labor and white capital" (196).
20. Perry interview in K. Martin 1995.
21. See Doyle 2004:31.
22. See Eargle 1995:283.
23. Neil Fraser, interviewed May 2000.
24. Clive Chin, interviewed July 18, 2000.
25. Winston Riley, interviewed June 5, 2000.
26. Frere-Jones 1997:67.
27. Montgomery 1997:56.
28. Mikics 1995:372.
29. For example, see the introduction to Manuel 1995.

30. David Mikics paraphrases Frederic Jameson to speculate that magical realist cinema relies on disjunctions among differing cultures and social formations that "coexist in the New World as they usually do not in Western Europe." See Mikics 1995:372, and Jameson's "On Magical Realism in Film," in Jameson 1988. See also the comments of Alondra Nelson in the introduction to Nelson 2002: "flux of identity has long been the experience of African diasporic people" (3).
31. Zamora and Faris 1995:6.
32. Slemon quote in Zamora and Faris 1995:408.
33. Ibid.:415.
34. Walcott cited in Mikics 1995:371.
35. D'Haen quote in Zamora and Faris 1995:372.
36. Jameson 1986:311.
37. Carrie Rickey [1979]. "Reviews: New York," *Artforum;* excerpted in Fine 2003.
38. Bloom states that "there is an intimate and interactive relationship between the individual and the group and our individual identity is closely tied to our 'group self' . . . in fact, our group self may be the core component of our sense of personal identity. . . . Making these assumptions allows us to tentatively apply concepts rooted in individual dynamics to the psychology of the group" (quote in Tedeschi 1998:180).
39. See Felman and Laub 1992 for a comprehensive source.
40. Clifford 1994:317.
41. Felman 1995:27.
42. Gilroy 1993:chap. 6.
43. Both quotations from Gilroy 1993:105.
44. See Gilroy 1993:chap. 6.
45. From Jafa 1994.
46. This idea of an aesthetic complex of "dissonance, destruction and decay" was inspired by Susan Blier's discussion of Beninoise *bocio* figurines (Blier 1995:28).
47. See Katz 2003:7–9, and "The Dancehall as a Site of Clashing" from Stolzoff 2000:8–12.
48. See I-Roy's comments in the notes to I-Roy CD 1997.
49. This particular characterization of the "emotional pendulum" of posttraumatic experience is taken from Erikson in Caruth 1995:184.
50. See Hoffman 1989:32.
51. See ibid.:7–13 for a discussion of collage in the context of these various artistic movements.
52. Ibid.:22.
53. Gabbard 1991:111.
54. Erlmann 1996.
55. Here I am paraphrasing the words of Jorge Luis Borges as quoted in R. F. Thompson 2005:3.
56. See Glick and Bone 1990:sec. IV ("Aesthetic and Philosophic Inquiries on the Nature of Pleasure") for a discussion of *anhedonia,* or avoidance of pleasure as a symptom of trauma. The Borges reference is taken from R. F. Thompson's 2005.

References

Books and Articles

Agawu, V. Kofi. 1995. *African Rhythm: A Northern Ewe Perspective.* New York: Cambridge University Press.

Apter, Andrew. 1991. "Herskovits's Heritage: Rethinking Syncretism in the African Diaspora." *Diaspora* 1(3):235–60.

Blier, Suzanne Preston. 1995. *African Vodun: Art, Psychology, and Power.* Chicago: University of Chicago Press.

Caruth, Cathy, ed. 1995. *Trauma: Explorations in Memory.* Baltimore: Johns Hopkins University Press.

Chude-Sokei, Louis. 1997. "The Sound of Culture: Dread Discourse and the Jamaican Sound Systems." In *Language, Rhythm, & Sound: Black Popular Cultures into the Twenty-First Century,* edited by Joseph K. Adjaye and Adrianne R. Andrews. Pittsburgh, Pa.: University of Pittsburgh Press.

Clifford, James. 1994. "Diasporas." *Cultural Anthropology* 9(3):302–38.

Davis, Stephen. 1985. *Bob Marley.* Garden City, N.Y.: Doubleday.

Davis, Stephen, and Peter Simon. 1982. *Reggae International.* New York: Rogner and Bernhard.

Dawes, Kwame. 2001. *TalkYuhTalk: Interviews with Anglophone Caribbean Poets.* Charlottesville: University Press of Virginia.

Doyle, Peter. 2004. "From 'My Blue Heaven' to 'Race With the Devil': echo, reverb and (dis)ordered space in early popular music recording." *Popular Music* 23(1):31–49.

Eargle, John M. 1995. *Music, Sound, and Technology.* New York: Van Nostrand Reinhold.

Erlmann, Veit. 1996. "The Aesthetics of the Global Imagination: Reflections on World Music in the 1990s." *Public Culture* 8(3):467–87.

Felman, Shoshana. 1995. "Education and Crisis, or the Vicissitudes of Teaching." In *Trauma: Explorations in Cultural Memory,* edited by Cathy Caruth. Baltimore: Johns Hopkins University Press.

Felman, Shoshana, and Dori Laub, M.D. 1992. *Testimony: Crises of Witnessing in Literature, Psychoanalysis, and History.* New York: Routledge.

Fine, Ruth. 2003. *The Art of Romare Bearden.* Washington, D.C.: National Gallery of Art.

Frere-Jones, Sasha. 1997. "Scratching the Surface." *Village Voice* (August 13–19):67, 74.

Gabbard, Krin. 1991. "The Quoter and His Culture." *In Jazz in Mind: Essays on the History and Meanings of Jazz,* edited by Reginald T. Buckner and Steven Weiland. Detroit, Mich.: Wayne State University Press.

Gilroy, Paul. 1993. *The Black Atlantic: Modernity and Double Consciousness.* Cambridge, Mass.: Harvard University Press.

Glick, Robert, and Stanley Bone. 1990. *Pleasure Beyond the Pleasure Principle.* New Haven, Conn.: Yale University Press.

Hoffman, Katherine, ed. 1989. *Collage: Critical Views.* Studies in the Fine Arts: Criticism, No. 31. Ann Arbor, Mich.: UMI Research Press.

Jafa, Arthur. 1994. Unpublished keynote address from Organization of Black Designers Conference, Chicago, Illinois.

Jameson, Fredric. 1986. "On Magical Realism in Film." *Critical Inquiry* 12 (Winter): 301–25.

— 1988. *The Ideologies of Theory: Essays 1971–1986.* vol. 1. Minneapolis: University of Minnesota Press.

Katz, David. 2003. *Solid Foundation: An Oral History of Reggae.* New York: Bloomsbury.

Lewis, Helena. 1988. *The Politics of Surrealism.* New York: Paragon.

Manuel, Peter, with Kenneth Bilby and Michael Largey. 1995. *Caribbean Currents.* Philadelphia: Temple University Press.

Martin, Kevin. 1995. "Echo Chamber Odysseys." *Wire* (May):29–33.

Mikics, David. 1995. "Derek Walcott and Alejo Carpentier: Nature, History, and the Caribbean Writer." In *Magical Realism: Theory, History, Community,* edited and with an introduction by Lois Parkinson Zamora and Wendy B. Faris. Durham, N.C.: Duke University Press.

Montgomery, Will. 1997. "Lee Perry: Arkology." *Wire* (May):56–57.

Nelson, Alondra, ed. 2002. *Afrofuturism. Social Text* 71, 20, no. 2 (Summer).

Rouget, Gilbert. 1985. *Music and Trance: A Theory of the Relations Between Music and Possession.* Chicago: University of Chicago Press.

Said, Edward. 1990. "Reflections on Exile." In *Out There: Marginalization and Contemporary Culture.* New York: New Museum of Contemporary Art.

Stolzoff, Norman. 2000. *Wake the Town and Tell the People: Dancehall Culture in Jamaica.* Durham, N.C.: Duke University Press.

Tedeschi, Richard G., with Crystal L. Park and Lawrence G. Calhoun, eds. 1998. *Posttraumatic Growth: Positive Changes in the Aftermath of Crisis.* Mahwah, N.J.: Erlbaum.

Thompson, Robert Farris. 2005. *Tango: The Art History of Love.* New York: Pantheon.

Walcott, Derek. 1992. *The Antilles: Fragments of Epic Memory.* New York: Farrar, Straus and Giroux.

Zamora, Lois Parkinson, and Wendy B. Faris, eds. 1995. *Magical Realism: Theory, History, Community.* Durham, N.C.: Duke University Press.

Interviews

Clive Chin. May 1998, March 1999, July 2000, Queens, New York.

Neil "Mad Professor" Fraser. May 2000, Hoboken, New Jersey; June 2002, London, England.

Winston Riley. June 2000, Kingston, Jamaica.

Robbie Shakespeare. March 2002, Kingston, Jamaica.

Chapter 38

Brandon LaBelle

AUDITORY RELATIONS

SOUND IS INTRINSICALLY AND UNIGNORABLY relational: it emanates, propagates, communicates, vibrates, and agitates; it leaves a body and enters others; it binds and unhinges, harmonizes and traumatizes; it sends the body moving, the mind dreaming, the air oscillating. It seemingly eludes definition, while having profound effect.

Sound art as a practice harnesses, describes, analyzes, performs, and interrogates the condition of sound and the processes by which it operates. It has been my intention to historically follow the developments of sound as an artistic medium while teasing out sound's relational lessons. For it teaches us that space is more than its apparent materiality, that knowledge is festive, alive as a chorus of voices, and that to produce and receive sound is to be involved in connections that make privacy intensely public, and public experience distinctly personal. In this way, this writing attempts to describe what sound is always already doing, yet as framed by the eccentric and productively rich context of art and music and their respective experimental edges.

In writing such history, I have been interested in engaging with specific artists, their specific works, and their auditory operations and intuitions so as to lend more thorough consideration onto instances of sound art at its most social, its most spatial, and within its most public moments, where it is brought self-consciously into play with the intention of performing with and through surrounding space, places, and the perceiving body, inside crowds and through acts of charged listening. To register sound in the effects on perception and the hearing subject, to mark it as spatial and architectural, and therefore integral to the built environment, to speak it so as to shatter the acoustical mirror in which the self and sound bring each other into relief. And to listen intently to all that comes back. For sound itself has drawn my attention to the stirrings of interaction, the intensities of the voice, the resonances of architectures, and the potential of cultural production to address an audience.

It is my view that sound's relational condition can be traced through modes of spatiality, for sound and space in particular have a dynamic relationship. This no doubt stands at the core of the very practice of sound art—the activation of the existing relation between sound and space. It is my intent to contribute to this understanding by supplying the very equation of sound and space with degrees of complexity, detail, and argument.

Engaging the dynamic of sound and space initially leads us to a number of observations and realizations, which may at first open up perspective on sound art. First, that sound is *always* in more than one place. If I make a sound, such as clapping my hands, we hear this sound here, between my palms at the moment of clapping, but also within the room, tucked up into the corners, and immediately reverberating back, to return to the source of sound. This acoustical event implies a dynamic situation in which sound and space converse by multiplying and expanding the point of attention, or the source of sound: the materiality of a given room shapes the contours of sound, molding it according to reflection and absorption, reverberation and diffraction. At the same time, sound makes a given space appear beyond any total viewpoint: in echoing throughout the room, my clapping describes the space from a multiplicity of perspectives and locations, for the room is here, between my palms, and there, along the trajectory of sound, appearing at multiple locations within its walls, for "the sound wave arriving at the ear is the analogue of the current state of the environment, because as the wave travels, it is charged by each interaction with the environment."[1] Thus, what we hear in this clapping is more than a single sound and its source, but rather a spatial event.

Second, sound occurs among bodies; that is, clapping my hands occurs in the presence of others, either as actual people in the room, directly in front of me, or in the other room and beyond, as eavesdroppers, intentional or not. Sound is produced and inflected not only by the materiality of space but also by the presence of others, by a body there, another there, and another over there. Thus, the acoustical event is also a social one: in multiplying and expanding space, sound necessarily generates listeners and a multiplicity of acoustical "viewpoints," adding to the acoustical event the operations of sociality. Such an observation reminds acoustics that material presence is also determined by the material intervention of social events, physical movements, and the ebb and flow of crowds. Bodies lend dynamic to any acoustical play, contributing to the modulation of sound, its reflection and reverberation, its volume and intensity, and ultimately to what it may communicate. For the presence of bodies, in determining social events, is also determined by the specific sociality of such events. Whether a concert hall or a classroom, the crowd is positioned by such context, either as a kind of subarchitecture in which one takes one's place, or as a kind of built-in respect for a given situation: the body occupies the correct location, either in the foreground or background, onstage or off, in front of or behind. Because of this, the crowd adds character to sound materially, as well as socially, according to the context of the event and its inherent positioning. Therefore, my clapping would be heard differently at a concert than in a classroom.

Third, sound is never a private affair, for if we listen to something like "my speaking voice" we tend to look toward the speaker as the source of sound, as an index of personality: all eyes watch my mouth, as if this sound remains bound to my person. Yet we can see, or hear, how my voice is also immediately beyond myself, around the room, and, importantly, inside the heads of others. In this way, sound is always already a public event, in that it moves from a single source and immediately arrives at multiple destinations. It emanates and in doing so fills space and other ears. To speak then is to live in more than one head, beyond an individual mind. Listening is thus a form of participation in the sharing of a sound event, however banal. Such occurrence implies a psychological dimension to considering sound and modes of spatiality. Whereas the acoustical brings to the fore material presence, adding and subtracting space by carrying sound beyond itself, to multiple points, involved in the social organization of people and their situational dramas, it further carries with it a psychological dynamic in which sound converses with the spatial confines of mental reverberation, as a kind of "radiophonic" broadcast arriving at unseen, unknowable locations in the head.

With this in mind, we can understand how sound as relational phenomena immediately operates through modes of spatiality, from the immediate present to the distant transmission, from inside one's thoughts and toward others, from immaterial wave to material mass, from the here and now to the there and then. For the presence of architecture, found sounds, environmental noise, and the details of given locations loom as continual input into forms of listening. That is to say, the sonorous world always presses in, adding extra ingredients by which we locate ourselves.

Sound thus *performs* with and through space: it navigates geographically, reverberates acoustically, and structures socially, for sound amplifies and silences, contorts, distorts, and pushes against architecture; it escapes rooms, vibrates walls, disrupts conversation; it expands and contracts space by accumulating reverberation, relocating place beyond itself, carrying it in its wave, and inhabiting always more than one place; it misplaces and displaces; like a car speaker blasting too much music, sound overflows borders. It is boundless on the one hand, and site-specific on the other.

Site Specificity

The understanding that art brings with it the possibility to address the world, beyond an abstract or elusive category, can be seen to gain significance throughout the latter part of the twentieth century in the form of "site-specific practice" of the late 1960s and 1970s and subsequent forms of contextual practice. Such methodologies produce artwork that, rather than separate itself from the space of its presentation, aims to incorporate it into the work, from material, such as architectural features, to informational, as in the governing curatorial premise behind an exhibition or larger social and cultural conventions. From here, art self-consciously becomes critical of its own structure, offering critique to its institutions, from the museum to the language of art history, and relying more on a move away from the fabrication of objects to the dematerialized potential of events, actions, ideas, ephemera, and the politics inherent to space.

The developments of sound art, which took its defining steps from the mid to late 1960s, coincides generally with the developments of such methods, along with Performance and Installation art. It is my view that such correspondence is not by chance, for the very move away from objects toward environments, from a single object of attention and toward a multiplicity of viewpoints, from the body toward others, describes the very relational, spatial, and temporal nature of sound itself.

Sound provides a means to activate perception, spatial boundaries, bodies and voices, and the energy waves of forms of broadcast, transmission, and other modes of radiating out. Yet, paradoxically, the historicization of sound art and the historicization of site-specific and contextual practice remain separate. While sound art is finding a current footing within cultural and academic arenas, as witnessed in the plethora of exhibitions and conferences over the last five years, its history remains separate and fixed within a specialized domain that neglects the historical context of not so much experimental music but of the visual arts and its related forms of practice of the postwar and contemporary period, particularly those actively engaged in spatial questions. It is my intent to bring these two together, inserting the history and context of sound art alongside and within the history and content of site-specificity, so as to recognize how sound art is built around the very notion of context and location.

To follow the course of such a project, I have been concerned to not so much articulate a survey of works but to pick up specific projects and artists that set in motion a critical dynamic of self and the world, through the particular use of sound, beginning in the early 1950s. From this historical point, I follow the developments of sound as an artistic medium through the 1960s and 1970s, tracing such chronology by implementing thematic threads related to architecture, place, and location, asking: how does sound embed us within local environments while connecting us to a broader horizon? What consequence do forms of sound practice have on notions of spatiality and issues surrounding public space? Can we identify questions of identity and experience in relation to listening and the resonance of space?

Since the early 1950s, sound as an aesthetic category has continually gained prominence. Initially through the experimental music of John Cage and musique concrète, divisions between music and sound stimulated adventures in electronics, field recording, the spatialization of sonic presentation, and the introduction of alternative procedures. Musical composition was to take on a broader set of terms that often left behind traditional instrumentation and the control of the composer's hand. Part 1 of this book [see original publication] addresses the work of Cage as progenitor of experimental music and its emphasis on "sound" as a specific category. Oscillating between sound as worldly phenomena to music as cultural work, Cage sets the stage for a heightened consideration of listening and the "place" of sound by developing a form of critical practice. Specific works, such as 4'33" and his Black Mountain performance, are investigated as a means to uncover the principles by which sound art developed—for Cage's work positions music in relation to a broader set of questions to do with social experience and everyday life. Musique concrète and Group Ongaku are placed alongside Cage as a way to extend the North American emphasis to that of Europe and Japan, as well as to elaborate on the general thrust of the postwar period as experimental music engaged questions of found sound and environmental material. By pushing the envelope of musicality to an extreme, found objects, audience, and social space coalesce in an unstable amalgam of input and output, technologies and their inherent ability to arrest and accentuate sonic detail, and the performing body as situated within found environment come to initiate a vocabulary by which experimental music slips into sound art.

Part 2 [see original publication] sets out historically to follow Cage's influence in the work of Happenings, Environments, and Fluxus, as well as Minimalist sculpture and music and Conceptual art. The artistic developments of the 1960s introduce questions of phenomenology and presence alongside social and political concerns, demanding that art become indistinguishable from life and that objects take on relational dialogue with people. Beginning with Happenings and Environments, initiated by Allan Kaprow, Claes Oldenburg, and various students of Cage, the performativity of the body and the larger contextual frame of audience and space are made the focus of art. Such shifts are furthered in the work of Fluxus, whose perceptual games define the art object as inextricably linked to an immediacy of the real. Event scores and performances are organized around "post-cognitive" understanding, creating work to be completed in the mind of the viewer/listener. The immediate and proximate can be said to govern throughout the 1960s, and find elaboration in the works of La Monte Young in music, Robert Morris in sculpture, and Michael Asher in spatial installation. Part 2 follows, in more detail, their respective works with a view toward elaborating questions of presence, as manifest in sound, space, and bodily perception. Each artist uses sound in diverse ways, pointing toward the potential of the medium to perform phenomenally (Young), discursively (Morris), and conceptually (Asher). The concern of presence is ultimately problematized in the work of Conceptual art in the late 1960s and early 1970s through semiotic games, dematerial strategies, and performative tensions that deconstruct, politicize, and spatialize perception inside the cultural structures of language. It is my argument that Conceptual art, while causing a break with earlier work, finds its inception in the work of John Cage and can be said to problematize his project.

Part 3 [see original publication] moves into Performance art of the early 1970s, addressing the works of Vito Acconci and, in turn, Alvin Lucier, along with the contemporary work of Christof Migone, with the intention of hearing how the voice is put to use so as to unsettle social conventions of subjectivity. Lucier's *I am sitting in a room* and Acconci's *Seedbed* and *Claim* performance installations use speech to reveal an alternative view of presence by staging the self at its most volatile. Sexualized, disembodied, excessive, and self-obsessed, speech travels through technologies of reproduction and architectural containers to inaugurate spatiality as integral to subjectivity. Their work questions the phenomenology of Minimalism by subtracting from the plenitude of presence, inserting instead a "radiophonic" body, further exemplified in Christof Migone's work. How does the voice, as a sonorous expenditure of the body, locate the self against the greater social environment? What are its limitations and how does it position the self within a contextualized and situational geography? These are some of the questions pursued in the artists' works, marking them as integral to an expanded investigation of sound's spatial and relational operations.

The spatiality of sound is furthered in Part 4 [see original publication] by addressing the development of sound installation in the works of Max Neuhaus, Bernhard Leitner, Maryanne Amacher, and Michael Brewster. Sound installation, spatialized musicality, and acoustic design all situate sound in relation to architecture. Architecture is taken on, dissected, and redrawn by positioning sound work in relation to its given acoustics. Amplifying existing sounds, fostering auditory dialogues across inside and outside, tapping into structural vibrations to expand the sonic palette of tonality, and designing listening experiences by harnessing the environmental mix of found auditory events: each of these procedures come to the fore in sound installation, blossoming more fully into the beginnings of sound art as a distinct discipline. With sound installation, and the works of Neuhaus and others, sound art finds definition, demarcating itself from the legacy of experimental music and entering into a more thorough conversation with the visual arts. Shifting back, I look at Iannis Xenakis with the intention of using his work as a further example of sound's architectural potential. For Xenakis's example is indispensable to any formulation of a history of sound art by forging a dynamic mix of musical and spatial elements. To appropriate and create architecture for renewed sense of listening, sound installation moves increasingly toward public space, situating the listener within a larger framework of sonic experience that is necessarily social, thereby leaving behind the singular object or space for an enlarged environmental potential.

Extending such concerns, Part 5 [see original publication] looks toward more overt environmental investigations as found in acoustic ecology and other "soundscape" work. Acoustic ecology parallels the developments of Land art throughout the 1970s, both of which look toward the remote, distant, and "natural" landscape as source for an enlarged artistic experience. As progenitor of greater awareness of the sonic environment, acoustic ecology brings to the fore sound as a physical presence whose understanding can lead to more sensitive built environments that reduce noise levels and infuse sociality with deep listening. In addition, acoustic ecology opens up a greater field of sound to artistic and musical practice, exemplified in the works of Hildegard Westerkamp, Annea Lockwood, and Steve Peters, all of whom work with environmental sound to map its local presence. Through their respective works, I chart the ways in which sound and modes of site-specificity overlap and form an extended dialogue. Acoustic ecology articulates an elaborated sociology of sound in which music, ecology, and "sound studies" coalesce to form a hybrid research and musical practice. Yet acoustic ecology runs the risk of shutting down auditory possibilities by registering sound within an overarching framework of value: what sound is harmful and what sound isn't? Which sounds contribute to noise pollution and which sounds don't? To stage a critical perspective against acoustic ecology, I address the practice of Yasunao Tone and Bill Fontana, along with the artist group WrK, whose works draw in questions of noise, systems of information, and their environmental organization. Tone and Fontana problematize in a productive way the often naïve procedures of environmental sound practice by agitating its seeming purity.

Moving increasingly from the location of sound to its propagation, from the concert hall, as in Cage, and to the environment, in Westerkamp, Part 6 [see original publication] follows sound's expansion into global and interpersonal network space. By looking at digital networks and interactive technologies in the works of Achim Wollscheid, Atau Tanaka, and the art collective Appo33, I arrive at present forms of sound art. Contemporary sound art fulfills Marshall McLuhan's theory of the "imploded society," for sound's current location is multiple, diverse, and expansive, streamed across the globe in networked performances, seeking the potential of interpersonal spaces, which, in turn, brings sound into every space, in every time. Such current methods operate by leaving behind the phenomenology of acoustic experience in favor of the behaviors of people. It thus seems to partially return us to John Cage by once again removing the referent in favor of materiality and the living out proposed by sound's own organizational thrust. Interactive and participatory, streamed live and Web-cast, sound has gained an intensified and dynamic place within contemporary culture. It is my argument, that its relational, spatial, and temporal nature parallels theories of electronic media, for both operate on the level of mobility, connectivity, and the immaterial.

That sound has gained momentum as a field within postmodern studies is not without its philosophical, cultural, and social backing, for the auditory provides an escape route to the representational metaphysics of modernity by offering a slippery surface upon which representation blurs and the intractable forms of codified order gain elasticity. For the acoustical could be said to function "weakly" in its elusive yet ever-present signifying chains, its vibrations between, through, and against bodies by slipping through the symbolic net of the alphabetical house and delivering up the immediate presence of the real, in all its concrete materiality. It registers in the vibratory waves of tactile experience, which, rather than being debunked by technology, is brought forth, through a McLuhanesque implosion in which the body is externalized and thus implicated in the network of electric circuitry and global nerves. In short, the acoustical may function as an appropriate model for confronting such a jumble of nerves and extensions and their subsequent ethical and social implications, as transformed through the globalizing networks of signals and intensities.

With such an enlarged acoustic mirror, sound may figure as an increasingly relevant and important category to offer the self a new set of codes by which to operate, as a medium intrinsically communicational and heterogeneous, and by which to negotiate and utilize the increasingly animate and telepresent world, for sound embeds itself in the creation of meanings, while remaining elusive to their significations.

I have been interested to listen to sound as it congeals into forms of creative assertion, identifying specific artists, composers, and works that seek architecture's echo, the city's crowd, and the audience as interlocutor, as a means to uncover facets to the development of sound art. By doing so, this book contends and converses with existing literatures across disciplines, from musicology and cinema studies to art history and architectural theory, ultimately with the intention of contributing to the emerging arena of sound studies. It puts forth sound art as a field that may engage levels of sociality through understanding not only the harmonies but also the dissonances between place, self, and their interaction.

Note

1.   Barry Truax, *Acoustic Communication* (Norwood, NJ: Ablex Publishing Corporation, 1994), p. 15.

Chapter 39

Tara Rodgers

TOWARD A FEMINIST HISTORIOGRAPHY OF ELECTRONIC MUSIC

Noise and Silencing in Electronic Music Histories

MUCH LIKE TECHNOLOGIES USED IN electronic music practice, electronic music histories have been imagined and structured according to tropes of noise and silence (see Kahn 1999; Cox and Warner 2004). Histories of electronic music often begin with a prominent origin story, the avant-garde noise of the Futurists in the early twentieth century. In the beginning, the story goes, there was Luigi Russolo's Futurist manifesto, *The Art of Noises* (1913), a bold celebration of the sounds of machines, modern industry, and war. Origin stories tend to normalize hegemonic cultural practices that follow, and in electronic music, "the beauty celebrated by aestheticians [is] often stained with such things as violence, misogyny, and racism" (McClary 1991, 4; see also Kahn 1999, 56–67). Indeed, themes in Futurist writings seem to flow naturally into the colonialist discourses articulated to electronic sounds in Cold War popular culture, the sexist imagery that has characterized many electronic music album covers and advertisements, and the militaristic language that inflects contemporary music-production terminology.

The tools for making electronic music are not innocent: true sound "mediums," they are an interface to ghosts of technoscientific projects past. In the United States, links between audio and military technologies were well established by the 1920s. Broadcast radio developed in conjunction with military investment around World War I, and subsequent amplification and recording technologies emerged directly from wartime expenditures or were funded for their potential military applications. Noises of new technologies in World War II were of such magnitude as to motivate extended research toward the development of new methods for controlling sound, to safeguard effective communication in combat. Postwar research in psychoacoustics and communications that addressed these issues shared with early electronic music many of the same historical actors, machines, and institutions (Chanan 1995, 8; Edwards 1996, 210–13, 220–21).

During the Cold War, electronic sounds became firmly lodged in the public imagination, especially in association with space age and atomic research. Space age pop music featured racially exoticized portrayals of women on album covers and used electronic sounds to signify the allure and anxieties of space exploration (Taylor 2001, 87–93). In 1962, the composer Herbert Brün recounted how stereotypes and fears of atomic warfare affected his audience's opinions of electronic music: "Throughout the population, in all social circles, people, when speaking of electronic music, use phrases like the following completely unabashedly: 'Electronic music is made of electrons. Electrons split atoms and a split atom is in some way part of the atom bomb, and one doesn't fool with such things. Above all, it shows complete lack of taste and tact, to want to make music with weapons of death'" (Brün 2004, 126). These associations persist today in the terminology of electronic music: DJs "battle"; a producer "triggers" a sample with a "controller," "executes" a programming "command," types "bang" to send a signal, and tries to prevent a "crash" (Katz 2004, 114–36; McCartney 1995; Peebles 1996, 12). The very act of making electronic music thus unfolds with reference to high-tech combat, shot through with symbols of violent confrontation and domination.

This persistent militaristic terminology and aesthetic priorities of rationalistic precision and control epitomize notions of male technical competence and "hard" mastery in electronic music production. These have produced and been constituted by their opposite: nontechnical or "soft" knowledges and practices that are coded as female (McCartney 2002; Bradby 1993, 156–57; see also Turkle 1984; Oldenziel 1999). In their interview in this collection [see original publication], Le Tigre explains how standards of male-defined technological innovation do not apply equally to women:

> *Johanna Fateman:* It really struck us that, when men make mistakes, it's fetishized as a glitch . . .
> *Kathleen Hanna:* Something beautiful.
> *Johanna:* And when women do it, it's like . . .
> *Kathleen:* . . . a hideous mistake.
> *Johanna:* Right, it's not considered an artistic innovation or a statement or an intentional thing.

Le Tigre maintains a goal of "technical innovation" for every project they do, but they define this standard on their own terms.

Much work by artists in this collection is likewise unfaithful to technoscientific priorities. Mira Calix, for example, is happy to use her new computer like a "big tape recorder" for compiling the eclectic mix of electronic, acoustic, and environmental sounds she incorporates into her compositions. She has little interest in the latest software developments and instead prefers to collect and record the sounds of unique wooden instruments. Annea Lockwood resists "fixing" recorded sounds with audio technologies, "'Cause I think they're essentially not fixable. Except that of course through media, we think, we feel we can fix them. But *sounds in their natural state . . .* are not fixable, are they?" Lockwood's recordings of rivers relay shifting movements of water and evoke transitory memories of place, defying the constraints of the recording medium on which the sounds are stored. Expressing a similar dissatisfaction with fixity, Laetitia Sonami strongly dislikes making recordings of her performances, in which she digitally transforms her voice through gestures of her hand: "The idea of commitment terrifies me—that you would have to commit a sound to a particular time . . . how do I know it should be there?" These artists cultivate technological sophistication in their work, but stake out philosophical positions that run counter to using dominant technoscientific priorities of precision and control as ends in themselves.

The question of what it means "to make music with weapons of death," while exaggerated in the Herbert Brün quote above, remains relevant given the pervasiveness of military origins and metaphors in electronic music technologies and practice. Indeed, electronic sounds might not be so compelling were it not for their associations with technologies of war—and, by extension, simulations of war in film and video games would not seem so realistic without their electronic soundtracks. Because the boundary between fiction and lived reality can be an *auditory* illusion that masks real struggles over life and death (see Haraway 1991, 149), work that challenges electronic music's technoscientific priorities is all the more crucial.

Clara Rockmore's performances on the theremin provide an alternative origin story for electronic music, one that may point toward better futures. Rockmore was the most widely recognized virtuoso of the theremin, a new electronic musical instrument in the 1920s. The theremin consists of two metal antennas that sense the position of the player's hands; by moving each hand in proximity to the antennas, the player controls an oscillator's frequency (pitch) and amplitude (volume). Rockmore's performances, including a showcase of the instrument at Town Hall in New York in 1934, helped to establish electronic and experimental music as a viable art form in the public imagination (Chadabe 1997, 8–11; Martin 2001). Her Town Hall recital "left the audience spellbound that such artistic music floated on air from a source seemingly uncontrolled by human effort" (Darter and Armbruster 1984, quoted in Montague 1991, 21). The *Washington Post* noted that the theremin "plays as if by magic . . . Toward it advances a young artist, Miss Clara Rockmore. Her right hand reaches toward, but stops short of the vertical rod. In so doing, she has penetrated the area of sound, and a beautiful tone results" ("Around the World" 1936). Rockmore was authoritative in performance; the *Post's* commentary implies that she encroached on a phallic domain of virtuosity and technical mastery—reaching for the "vertical rod," "penetrating" the area—but that these transgressions were justifiable by the novel and transportive qualities of the sound. A *Times* critic wrote: "Stunning in a crimson dress, she stood over the instrument and evoked sounds . . . By moving her hands and fingers in the air she achieved tonal agility comparable to that of a singer, and a *living* tone-quality" ("Novelty Feature" 1947, emphasis added). The spellbound audiences were presented with a performance of electronic music as embodied, affective engagement with technology, characterized by nuance and care.

Rockmore opened an "elsewhere" within electronic music discourses (de Lauretis 1987, 25): a space for mutual encounters between humans and technologies, between familiarity and otherness, that motivates wonder and a sense of possibility instead of rhetorics of combat and domination. In her work on the cultural politics of emotion, Sara Ahmed writes: "The surprise of wonder is crucial to how it moves bodies . . .

wonder involves the radicalisation of our relation to the past, which is transformed into that which lives and breathes in the present" (2004, 180). Electronic music can move bodies by way of technologically mediated or generated sounds that provoke a sense of wonder. Laetitia Sonami describes the first time she heard a Putney VCS3 synthesizer as a student in the 1970s: "I was like, Wow, what is that? I was hearing sounds that were very crude, but still there was this whole sense of magic, of electricity producing sounds in ways I could not fathom."[1] Sonami was motivated to develop an instrument that respects how technology is "a projection of our dreams, illusions, desires . . ." rather than one that reduces technology to an expression of "macho" control. So while the origin story of the Futurists infuses one's orientation toward electronic music with violent noise, Rockmore's mobilization of wonder—resonant in Sonami's and others' experiences decades later—suggests a different way to navigate the history. It calls for scrutiny of how electronic music can (or has failed to) express possibilities for more imaginative and ethical encounters with technology and difference now and in the future. It enacts a shift in emphasis from "weapons of death" to evocations of living.

Like noise, the function of silence as a privileged aesthetic category in electronic music discourses deserves critical attention. One of the most noteworthy works composed by John Cage, who is a central figure in electronic and experimental music histories, is 4'33", the "silent piece." This piece troubled notions of absolute silence and arguably helped to open Western music to a wider range of sounds (Chadabe 1997, 24–26). Cage's body of work was innovative in the context of Eurological compositional traditions, but it has been taken up by some academics and journalists to define what constitutes "experimental" music in the broadest sense. This has worked to deny the influence of comparably innovative music practices by women and people of color (Lewis 1996; see also Oliveros 1984, 47–51). Thus, despite Cage's own efforts to disrupt hegemonic silences, the centrality of his work in subsequent electronic and experimental music histories has often had the effect of silencing others.

Moreover, the process-oriented compositional strategies advanced by Cage that seek to erase or reduce the influence of a composer's intent on the resulting music can be interpreted as a negation of identity; this may not be a universally desirable aesthetic for artists of historically marginalized groups who have suffered the effects of imposed forms of silencing and erasure. Indeed, feminists have often located empowerment within acts of breaking silences, by foregrounding aspects of identity. As Adrienne Rich said, "The impulse to create begins—often terribly and fearfully—in a tunnel of silence. Every real poem is the breaking of an existing silence, and the first question we might ask any poem is, *What kind of voice is breaking silence, and what kind of silence is being broken?*" (Rich 2001, 150; emphasis in original). This is a useful question to put toward the politics of noise and silencing within electronic music histories.[2]

Just as recording engineers use the processing tool known as a *noise gate* to mute audible signals below a defined threshold of volume (like the hum of a guitar amp that would interfere with the relative purity of the guitar's sound in the mix), arbitrary thresholds have often silenced women's work in historical accounts. Some of the most important contributions to the study of electronic music and sound have positioned women as outside the scope of study (Kahn 1999, 13–14); defined DJ cultures as "distinctly masculine" with relative inattention to women's participation in these cultures (Reynolds 1998, 274–75); or used observational statistics, such as that fewer than one in ten DJs is female, to explain women's absence from the text (Fikentscher 2000, 124 n. 3). Another study that discusses women artists reached some unfortunately reductive conclusions—for example, that composer Suzanne Ciani was like "a woman in a man's world who wanted to have it all" (Pinch and Trocco 2002, 170). All the above studies are formidable works of scholarship for the accounts that they provide, but their cumulative effect gives the impression that women are rarely present in DJ, electronic music, and sound art cultures; that they have not made significant contributions to these fields to the extent that men have; or that gender categories ultimately pose restrictions on professional survival.[3]

There are other rhetorical approaches that have marginalized women's work in electronic music histories. The electroacoustic composer and scholar Andra McCartney has noted that Pauline Oliveros is often isolated as the only woman in textbooks that otherwise cover a variety of men's work in detail. Recognition of Oliveros is crucial and admirable, but her isolation has at times positioned her work as representative of an essentialized, "feminine" aesthetic (McCartney 2006, 31). Pamela Z, in her interview here [see original publication], discusses a similar problem in the context of compilation CDs that feature only one woman composer. Such tokenistic representation often means that women's compositions are not analyzed in liner notes and album reviews with the level of rigor that men's work receives. In their interview, Z and Maria Chavez also comment on the politics of stylistic comparisons, noting that journalists tend to compare their work reductively to other women artists (simply because they are women) or trace their musical aesthetics to well-known men (whose influence they would not necessarily claim). This pattern enacts a double reinforcement of electronic music's male lineage, gendering important stylistic developments as male, and grouping women together as other to this master narrative. Le Tigre likewise discusses how they would like to fit in with what is considered to be "real" electronic music, but formal technical and stylistic regimes seem to exclude their aesthetic. Pamela Z concludes that gendered and racialized representations in music media tend to reduce otherness to a palatable symbol: "like the woman on the mud flaps of the truck that's the symbol of female form."[4]

Gender and Technology in Discourses of Sound Reproduction

Beneath the surface of these oversights and reductive representations, one obstacle to thinking women as *producers* of electronic music culture may be that they are always already entwined with a logic of *reproduction*—perpetuated in discourses of sound reproduction and materialized in related technologies—that ties women to age-old notions of passivity, receptivity, and maternality.[5] Feminists have demonstrated that women provide the material foundations upon which cultural worlds are built, and male modes of thought operate by denying the debt they owe to the maternal space from which all subjects emerge (Irigaray 1993, 10–12; Grosz 1995, 121; Young 2005, 128). In founding texts of Western philosophy, reproduction was established as a process in which a mother contributed formless matter, to be given shape by the father: a mother was considered to be "a mere housing, receptacle, or nurse of being rather than a coproducer" (Grosz 1994, 5; see also Ahmed 2006, 71; Irigaray 1985; Spivak 1981, 183).

In dominant discourses and practices of sound reproduction, technological forms and processes that are culturally coded as female or maternal have been systematically devalued and controlled. Histories of technology have routinely overlooked the active functions of "container technologies"—those technological forms associated with metaphors for female organs of storage and supply, and with types of labor traditionally done by women (Sofia 2000, 185). Magnetic tape is one such container technology, coded as a receptive matter to be given form and meaning by sound (Mumford 1966, 141; quoted in Sofia 2000). It is a kind of enabling background for electronic music, a passive (feminized) inscriptive surface employed to reproduce the workings of (male) culture.[6]

Control of this medium of reproduction—and faithfulness to an "original" sound—has informed technical and aesthetic priorities in discourses of sound fidelity. These values, elaborated on in popular magazines beginning in the 1950s and implemented in common practice, positioned women as threats to the self-contained spaces of hi-fi that men sought to define in middle-class homes. Women embodied the very potential for loss of sound quality by threatening men's requisite privacy to inhabit a controlled, domestic space in which they could cultivate an aesthetic appreciation of sound (Keightley 1996, 161). "Loss" was technically defined as the degradation in quality or clarity of recorded sound as it passes through the medium. In a similar way that women represented a threat to men's control of hi-fi settings in the home, the (feminized) medium of sound reproduction constituted an interference with the purity of the signal. Hi-fi discourses advocated maximizing sound fidelity by guarding the signal against loss and making the medium as transparent as possible (Morton 2000, 13–47; Sterne 2003, 215–86). A classic, masculinist technological fantasy is at work in this example: male attempts to appropriate the maternal function with technology typically exhibit a conflicting, nostalgic investment in the figure of the mother, and an antagonism and desire to overcome it (Doane 1999, 23, 29). While the medium of sound reproduction is necessary for male subjects to certify their relationship and fidelity to an imagined origin, male claims to creation are asserted through masterful control and/or erasure of this medium.

In other discourses of audio technologies, male claims to creation have been bolstered by stories of male birth and a concealed dependence on laboring women's bodies. In the mid-twentieth century, the distinctive, prized tone of Fender electric guitars relied on the laboring hands of Hispanic women workers, who meticulously wound pickups tighter than machines could (Smith 1995, 69; see also Rylan interview). Despite the crucial role of these workers, a biographer attributes the unique tone of the guitars to Leo Fender's innovations as "an American original" inventor (Smith 1995, 283). With rhetoric that does similar work, stories of male birth have functioned throughout histories of technology to confer value upon inventions by men. Thomas Edison, Samuel Morse, and Alexander Graham Bell proudly referred to their inventions as their children, a strategy by which they claimed a full role in the creation of an artifact (Sterne 2003, 180–81). In fact, at the turn of the twentieth century, women were central to how the uses of phonographs and records were defined in social contexts, often redirecting their intended designs (Gitelman 2006, 60–62).

Electronic music historiography continues to follow this pattern. *Modulations: Cinema for the Ear,* a feature-length documentary about the evolution of electronic music in the twentieth century, was released in 1998 and screened internationally. The film presents a historical narrative of electronic music that begins with the Futurists and John Cage and moves from Robert Moog, Kraftwerk, and the "pioneers" of Detroit techno to contemporary sonic experimentalists like Squarepusher and DJ Spooky. It celebrates "the nomadic drift of the posthuman techno sound" and identifies the emergence of a "universal electronic sound."[7] The credits list nearly eighty informants, all of whom are men. Patrilineality takes on an air of inevitability: a subtitle hails Karlheinz Stockhausen as "the grandfather of electronica"; the Detroit techno producers are described as "the successors" to the German pop-electronic group Kraftwerk; and in an interview about the film, the director, Iara Lee, positions John Cage over Brian Eno as "the father of ambient" (Lee 1998; Vaziri 1998).[8]

In one of the only scenes where women appear in the film, which is framed before and after by men's testimonials about the significance of the Roland TB-303 bass synthesizer in the history of electronic music, there is a fleeting glimpse of a Roland factory in Japan where women engage in repetitive labor assembling and testing keyboard synthesizers. The wide shot of many anonymous female laborers contrasts sharply with the close-up angles and star treatment of the individual male experts in the surrounding scenes. These scenes are accompanied by upbeat electronic dance music, characterized by repetitive musical structures and the seamless flow of a club DJ's mix. The audio connects disparate economies of factory labor, studio production, and dance floor pleasure along the same continuum of a global—and supposedly universal—experience of electronic sound. Women are aligned with the reproduction of mass-produced goods, while men are positioned as cultural producers and arbiters of aesthetic innovation. Women laborers in the global economy are marshaled into a celebratory montage of cultural diversity; critical differences of gender, agency, and cultural power are lost in the mix.[9] All the above examples suggest how historical narratives and technical discourses of electronic music have relied on metaphors of the feminine and maternal, as well as on women's bodies more literally, to establish a male subjectivity in sound and reproduce priorities of a male-defined culture. A patrilineal history of electronic music production is normative, and ideologies of sound reproduction circulate unmarked for a particular politics of gender.

To think against the grain of cultural ideologies that have aligned women with normative modes of heterosexual and capitalist reproduction, and to construct electronic music histories differently, we can consider how sounds themselves are reproductive. Reproductive sounds are variously *produced* by bodies, technologies, environments, and their accompanying histories; *reproduced* in multiple reflections off reverberant surfaces or in recording media; *reproducible* within spaces of memory and storage that hold sounds for future playbacks; and *productive,* by generating multiple meanings in various contexts. To account for reproductive sounds in all their temporal depth is to challenge the patrilineal lines of descent and the universalizing male claims to creation that have thus far characterized dominant discourses in electronic music.

Alongside such moves to expand the scope of existing histories, there is still some consistency among surveys that suggest that women DJs and composers number one in ten or fewer (Fikentscher 2000, 124 n. 3; Bosma 2003, 9; McCartney and Waterman 2006; Katz 2006, 580–81). The question of who is counted in electronic music historiography is inevitably informed by the politics of social and professional networks, and by limited definitions and standards of achievement.[10] What is important to take away is that the public face of electronic music—on CD releases, magazine covers, international festivals, scholarly publications—is typically male and does a certain kind of symbolic work. As Hanna Bosma points out, these forums "tell a tale of a world of creators and experts of electroacoustic music, and this probably influences the behaviour and thoughts of listeners, students, would-be composers and experts" (2003, 7–8). Another strategy is to emphasize the substance and diversity of work that *has* been accomplished by women, and this collection is a starting point for doing just that.

Throughout the history of electronic music, women have been influential as consumers and users of audio technologies; instrument builders and assemblers; directors, teachers, and students at academic electronic music studios; composers, instrumentalists, vocalists, and sound poets; producers, audio engineers, and software developers; founders of record labels; events organizers and participants; and philosophers and critics.[11] Rather than linger on observations that women may comprise only one in ten DJs or composers, we can reframe the perspective by cueing Autumn Stanley's revised history of technology (1983): with their myriad technological innovations and sounding practices, "women hold up two-thirds of the sky."

Notes

1.   Many other women in the *Pink Noises* interviews verbalize their early encounters with electronic music as a kind of epiphanic moment: "*bang . . . this* is what I've been looking for" (Matthews); "*That's it!*" (Radigue); "*Whoa! . . .* This is it" (Chavez).

2.   Feminist work on the uneven effects of silence and its disruptions, especially across differences of race and sexuality, has much to offer for thinking the politics of noise and silence in electronic and experimental music (see Cixous 1976, 880–81; hooks 1984, 12–15; Hammonds 1997; Hedges and Fishkin 1994).

3.   In a relevant commentary on academic accounts of electronic dance music, Angela McRobbie summarizes how scholars have constructed it as "virtually a female-free zone": a domain in which recreational drug use, new technologies that dissolve human-machine boundaries, and a general sensibility of subcultural abandonment converge to offer "an escape from the whole bother of gender" (1999, 145–47). These accounts have tended to exhibit—and normalize—a lack of critical inquiry into how gender continues to inform the production and distribution of knowledge in these cultures.

4.   Z's comment was allusive, but such iconic female figures appear throughout visual cultures of electronic music (Taylor 2001, 88–89; Sherburne 2002). An event featuring Canadian women artists at an experimental music festival in 2004 displayed the infamous mud-flap woman on its promotional materials (Anna Friz, e-mail to author, April 18, 2008).

5. To be clear, in this section I am taking issue with how electronic music discourses produce gendered subjects and technological forms. The perpetuation or contestation of hegemonic cultural practices can be enacted by individual people of any gender.

6. Another example of an audio technology coded as female form is an early version of the phonograph, which required singers to direct their voice down the horn—a "curious gaping orifice"—when recording. This was apparently an unsettling experience for some men. The folklorist John Avery Lomax, who traveled across America recording music in the years 1908–10, reported: "I lost many singers because the cowboys didn't like the looks of it" (Brady 1999, 40).

7. For a more thorough analysis of the relationship between post-humanism, music technology, and Afro-diasporic cultural politics, see Weheliye 2002.

8. Such examples abound in electronic music cultures, and these proliferating lines of descent rather comically begin to tie themselves into knots. Kim Cascone (2000, 14) identifies Luigi Russolo as "the 'grandfather' of contemporary 'post-digital' music"; the composer and engineer Max Mathews (2008) has been called both "the father of computer music" and "the great-grandfather of techno"; DJ Frankie Knuckles, "the godfather of house" (Fikentscher 2000, 137).

9. For further discussion of how electronics manufacturing and toxic waste disproportionately affects the health and safety of women laborers and Third World communities, see the Rylan interview [see original publication]; Fuentes and Ehrenreich 1983; Grossman 1980; Pilar 2005.

10. For example, consumers of audio technologies typically are not considered to have invented the phonograph to the same extent as Thomas Edison; those on the dance floor are not recognized as producers of underground dance music culture to the extent that DJs are—and these roles are often gendered (Gitelman 2006, 63–64; Pini 2001).

11. On women's roles in defining the uses of phonographs, microphones, and electrification technologies in the early twentieth century, see Gitelman 2006; Goldstein 1997; Lockheart 2003. On women as modernist writers and avant-garde artists concerned with sound and aurality, see Cotter 2002; Cuddy-Keane 2000; Gammel 2003; Morris 1997; Scott 2000; Wilson 2004. See McCartney 2003 and Hinkle-Turner 2006 on women who were founders of academic electronic music studios beginning in the 1960s, developers of computer music software, and/or composers of electroacoustic music. For more information about women developing computer music and sound art software, see Chadabe 1997, 158–63, 334–36, 265–67; Gagne 1993, 297–332; Polli 2005, 2006; Rodgers 2006; Scaletti 2002; Spiegel 1998. On women who facilitated electronic music's popularization through science fiction soundtracks and music for advertising, see Chadabe 1997, 66; Epstein 1974; Hodgson 2001; Milano 1979a, 1979b; Pinch and Trocco 2002, 155–70; Sherman 1982; Wierzbicki 2005; Zvonar 2004. On women who are electronic and electroacoustic instrument builders, see Fullman 1994, 2003; Hutton 2003; Oliveros 1984, 36–46; Ptak 2008; Young 1982; Rylan and Sonami interviews in this volume [see original publication]. On women who are sound installation artists: Amacher 1994, 2004; Bodle 2006; D'Souza 2002; Gercke 2000; Grant 2004; Landi 2001; Licht 1999; Schaub 2005. For an overview of women's work in performance art, radio art, experimental vocal techniques and sound poetry, see Bosma 2003; Duckworth 1995; Hume 2006; Malloy 2003; Morris 2007; Sawchuk 1994; "Lily Greenham" 2008; Waterman 2007. For an account of women's uses of hi-fi audio components in the 1970s, see Pease 1978. On women in audio engineering professions, see Peterson 1987; Potts 1994; Sandstrom 2000. Resources about women who are vocalists, DJs, or producers of electronic dance music and hip-hop include Bradby 1993; Bridges 2005; Cooper 1995; Dove 2003; Guevara 1996; Halberstam 2007; Hebert 2008; Park 2004; Raimist 1999; Rodgers 2003; Rose 1994, 146–82; Siegler 2000a and 2000b; Snapper 2004; Walker and Pelle 2001. Female Pressure (2008), an online database of women DJs, electronic music producers, and visual artists, currently lists 970 members from fifty-one countries. Women who are philosophers and critics, as well as composers, include Amacher (2004); Oram (1972); Oliveros (1984); Spiegel (2008); and Westerkamp (2000 and 2002).

References

Ahmed, Sara. 2004. *The Cultural Politics of Emotion.* New York: Routledge.

—. 2006. *Queer Phenomenology: Orientations, Objects, Others.* Durham, N.C.: Duke University Press.

Amacher, Maryanne. 1994. "Synaptic Island: A Psybertonal Topology." *Architecture as a Translation of Music,* edited by E. Martin, 32–35. New York: Princeton Architectural Press (Pamphlet Architecture 16).

—. 2004. "Psychoacoustic Phenomena in Musical Composition: Some Features of a Perceptual Geography." *FO(A)RM* 3: 16–25.

"Around the World in News, Science." 1936. *Washington Post,* May 31, PY4.

Bodle, Carrie. 2006. "Sonification/Listening Up." *Leonardo Music Journal* 16, special section: "Sound and the Social Organization of Space," guest edited by T. Rodgers: 51–52.

Bosma, Hanna. 2003. "Bodies of Evidence, Singing Cyborgs and Other Gender Issues in Electrovocal Music." *Organised Sound* 8 (1): 5–17.

Bradby, Barbara. 1993. "Sampling Sexuality: Gender, Technology and the Body in Dance Music." *Popular Music* 12 (2): 155–76.

Brady, Erika. 1999. A *Spiral Way: How the Phonograph Changed Ethnography.* Jackson: University Press of Mississippi.

Bridges, Elizabeth. 2005. "Love Parade GmbH vs. Ladyfest: Electronic Music as a Mode of Feminist Expression in Contemporary German Culture." *Women in German Yearbook* 21: 215–40.

Brün, Herbert, with Arun Chandra, ed. 2004. *When Music Resists Meaning: The Major Writings of Herbert Brün.* Middletown, Conn.: Wesleyan University Press.

Cascone, Kim. 2000. "The Aesthetics of Failure: 'Post-Digital' Tendencies in Contemporary Computer Music." *Computer Music Journal* 24 (4): 12–18.

Chadabe, Joel. 1997. *Electric Sound: The Past and Promise of Electronic Music.* Upper Saddle River, N.J.: Prentice Hall.

Chanan, Michael. 1995. *Repeated Takes: A Short History of Recording and Its Effects on Music.* New York: Verso.

Cixous, Helene. 1976. "The Laugh of the Medusa." Translated by K. Cohen and P. Cohen. *Signs* 1 (4): 875–93.

Cooper, Carol. 1995. "Disco Knights: Hidden Heroes of the New York Dance Music Underground." *Social Text* 45 (Winter): 159–65.

Cotter, Holland. 2002. "The Mama of Dada." *New York Times Book Review,* May 19, 50.

Cox, Christoph, and Daniel Warner, eds. 2004. *Audio Culture: Readings in Modern Music.* New York: Continuum.

Cuddy-Keane, Melba. 2000. "Virginia Woolf, Sound Technologies, and the New Aurality." *Virginia Woolf in the Age of Mechanical Reproduction,* edited by P. L. Caughie, 69–113. New York: Garland.

Darter, Tom, and Greg Armbruster. 1984. *The Art of Electronic Music.* New York: William Morrow.

de Lauretis, Teresa. 1987. *Technologies of Gender: Essays on Theory, Film, and Fiction.* Bloomington: Indiana University Press.

Doane, Mary Ann. 1999. "Technophilia: Technology, Representation, and the Feminine." *Cybersexualities: A Reader on Feminist Theory, Cyborgs and Cyberspace,* edited and with an introduction by J. Wolmark, 20–33. Edinburgh: Edinburgh University Press.

Dove. 2003. "Kuttin Kandi: More Than a Woman." http://www.daveyd.com/ (visited April 29, 2008).

D'Souza, Aruna. 2002. "A World of Sound." *Art in America* (April): 110–15, 161.

Duckworth, William. 1995. *Talking Music: Conversations with John Cage, Philip Glass, Laurie Anderson, and Five Generations of American Experimental Composers.* New York: Schirmer Books.

Edwards, Paul N. 1996. *The Closed World: Computers and the Politics of Discourse in Cold War America.* Cambridge, Mass.: MIT Press.

Epstein, Helen. 1974. "'The Cello Can't Play These Chords': An Electronic Music Maker." *New York Times,* July 21, 93.

Female Pressure website. 2008. http://www.femalepressure.net/ (visited April 30, 2008).

Fikentscher, Kai. 2000. *"You Better Work!" Underground Dance Music in New York City.* Hanover, N.H.: Wesleyan University Press.

Fuentes, Annette, and Barbara Ehrenreich. 1983. *Women in the Global Factory.* Boston: South End Press.

Fullman, Ellen. 1994. "Sonic Space of the Long-Stringed Instrument." *Architecture as a Translation of Music,* edited by E. Martin, 46–49. New York: Princeton Architectural Press (Pamphlet Architecture 16).

—. 2003. "The Long String Instrument." *Musicworks* 85 (Spring): 21–28.

Gagne, Cole. 1993. *Soundpieces* 2: *Interviews with American Composers.* Metuchen, N.J.: Scarecrow Press.

Gammel, Irene. 2003. *Baroness Elsa: Gender, Dada, and Everyday Modernity—A Cultural Biography.* Cambridge, Mass.: MIT Press.

Gercke, Hans. 2000. "The Garden of Dreams: About the Work of Christina Kubisch." *Klangraumlichtzeit,* edited by C. Kubisch, 42–49. Heidelberg: Kerher Verlag.

Gitelman, Lisa. 2006. *Always Already New: Media, History, and the Data of Culture.* Cambridge, Mass.: MIT Press.

Goldstein, Carolyn M. 1997. "From Service to Sales: Home Economics in Light and Power: 1920–40." *Technology and Culture* 38 (1): 121–52.

Grant, Annette. 2004. "Art: Let 7 Million Sheets of Paper Fall." *New York Times,* April 11, AR31.

Grossman, Rachel. 1980. "Women's Place in the Integrated Circuit." *Radical America* 14 (1): 29–49.

Grosz, Elizabeth. 1994. *Volatile Bodies: Toward a Corporeal Feminism.* Bloomington: Indiana University Press.

—. 1995. "Women, Chora, Dwelling." *Space, Time, and Perversion: Essays on the Politics of Bodies.* New York: Routledge.

Guevara, Nancy. 1996. "Women Writin' Rappin' Breakin'." *Dropping Science: Critical Essays on Rap Music and Hip Hop Culture,* edited by W. E. Perkins, 49–62. Philadelphia: Temple University Press.

Halberstam, Judith. 2007. "Keeping Time with Lesbians on Ecstasy." *Women and Music* 11:51–58.

Hammonds, Evelynn. 1997. "Toward a Genealogy of Black Female Sexuality: The Problematic of Silence." *Feminist Genealogies, Colonial Legacies, Democratic Futures,* edited by M. J. Alexander and C. T. Mohanty, 170–82. New York: Routledge.

Haraway, Donna. 1991. *Simians, Cyborgs, and Women: The Reinvention of Nature.* New York: Routledge.

Hebert, James. 2008. "Deejaying Still Holds the Key to Her Heart." *San Diego Tribune,* March 16, E3.

Hedges, Elaine, and Shelley Fisher Fishkin, eds. 1994. *Listening to Silences: New Essays in Feminist Criticism.* New York: Oxford University Press.

Hinkle-Turner, Elizabeth. 2006. *Women Composers and Music Technology in the United States: Crossing the Line.* Aldershot, UK: Ashgate.

Hodgson, Brian. 2001. "Delia Derbyshire: Pioneer of Electronic Music who Produced the Distinctive Sound of Dr. Who." *Guardian,* July 7, 22.

hooks, bell. 1984. *Feminist Theory: From Margin to Center.* Boston: South End Press.

Hume, Christine. 2006. "Improvisational Insurrection: The Sound Poetry of Tracie Morris." *Contemporary Literature* 47 (3): 415–39.

Hutton, Jo. 2003. "Daphne Oram: Inventor, Writer and Composer." *Organised Sound* 8 (3): 49–56.

Irigaray, Luce. 1985. *This Sex Which Is Not One.* Translated by C. Porter with C. Burke. Ithaca, N.Y.: Cornell University Press.

—. 1993. *An Ethics of Sexual Difference.* Translated by C. Burke and G. C. Gill. Ithaca, N.Y.: Cornell University Press.

Kahn, Douglas. 1999. *Noise Water Meat: A History of Sound in the Arts.* Cambridge, Mass.: MIT Press.

Katz, Mark. 2004. *Capturing Sound: How Technology Has Changed Music.* Berkeley: University of California Press.

—. 2006. "Men, Women, and Turntables: Gender and the DJ Battle." *Musical Quarterly* 89 (4): 580–99.

Keightley, Keir. 1996. "'Turn it Down!' She Shrieked: Gender, Domestic Space, and High Fidelity, 1948–59." *Popular Music* 15 (2): 149–77.

Landi, Ann. 2001. "Sonic Boom." *ARTnews* (December): 106–7.

Lee, Iara. 1998. *Modulations: Cinema for the Ear.* USA: Caipirinha Productions. DVD, 74 min.

Lewis, George. 1996. "Improvised Music after 1950: Afrological and Eurological Perspectives." *Black Music Research* 16 (1): 91–121.

Licht, Alan. 1999. "Maryanne Amacher." *Wire* 181 (March).

"Lily Greenham: Lingual Music" (album notes and review). 2008. http://stalk.net/paradigm/pd22.html (visited April 30, 2008).

Lockheart, Paula. 2003. "A History of Early Microphone Singing, 1925–39: American Mainstream Popular Singing at the Advent of Electronic Microphone Amplification." *Popular Music and Society* 26 (3): 367–85.

MacDonald, Corina. 2007. "An Interview with Tara Rodgers." *Vague Terrain 08: Process* (November), http://www.vagueterrain.net/ (visited April 23, 2008).

Malloy, Judy, ed. 2003. *Women, Art, and Technology.* Cambridge, Mass.: MIT Press.

Maloney, Kathleen. 2000. "Recognition or Division?" *XLR8R* 39:38.

Martin, Steven M. 2001. *Theremin: An Electronic Odyssey.* USA: MGM. DVD, 82 min.

Massey, Doreen B. 2005. *For Space.* London: Sage.

McCartney, Andra. 1995. "Inventing Images: Constructing and Contesting Gender in Thinking about Electroacoustic Music." *Leonardo Music Journal* 5: 57–66.

—. 2000. "Sounding Places with Hildegard Westerkamp." PhD diss., York University.

—. 2002. "New Games in the Digital Playground: Women Composers Learning and Teaching Electroacoustic Music." *Feminism and Psychology* 12 (2): 160–67.

—. 2003. "In and Out of the Sound Studio." *Organised Sound* 8 (1): 89–96.

—. 2006. "Gender, Genre and Elecroacoustic Soundmaking Practices." *Intersections: Canadian Journal of Music* 26 (2): 20–48.

McCartney, Andra, and Ellen Waterman. 2006. "Introduction: In and Out of the Sound Studio." *Intersections: Canadian Journal of Music* 26 (2): 3–19.

McClary, Susan. 1991. *Feminine Endings: Music, Gender, and Sexuality.* Minneapolis: University of Minnesota Press.

McRobbie, Angela. 1999. "'Come Alive London!' A Dialogue with Dance Music." *In the Culture Society: Art, Fashion, and Popular Music,* 144–56. New York: Routledge.

Milano, Dominic. 1979a. "Wendy Carlos." *Contemporary Keyboard* (December): 32–35+.

—. 1979b. "Rachel Elkind." *Contemporary Keyboard* (December): 36–37.

Montague, Stephen. 1991. "Rediscovering Leon Theremin." *Tempo* 177 (June): 18–23.

Morris, Adelaide. 1997. "Sound Technologies and the Modernist Epic: H.D. on the Air." *Sound States: Innovative Poetics and Acoustical Technologies,* edited by A. Morris, 32–55. Chapel Hill: University of North Carolina Press.

Morris, Tracie. 2007. "Poetics Statement: Sound Making Notes." *American Poets in the Twenty-First Century: The New Poetics,* edited by C. Rankine and L. Sewell, 210–15. Middletown, Conn.: Wesleyan University Press.

Morton, David. 2000. *Off the Record: Technology and Culture of Sound Recording in America.* New Brunswick, N.J.: Rutgers University Press.

Mumford, Lewis. 1966. *Technics and Human Development.* New York: Harcourt Brace Jovanovich.

"Novelty Feature at the Stadium." 1947. *New York Times,* July 31, 17.

Oldenziel, Ruth. 1999. *Making Technology Masculine: Men, Women and Modern Machines in America,* 1870–1045. Amsterdam: Amsterdam University Press.

Oliveros, Pauline. 1984. *Software for People: Collected Writings* 1963–80. Baltimore, Md.: Smith Publications.

Oram, Daphne. 1972. *An Individual Note of Music, Sound and Electronics.* London: Galliard Paperbacks.

Park, Jane C. H. 2004. "Cibo Matto's *Stereotype A:* Articulating Asian American Hip Hop." *East Main Street: Asian American Popular Culture,* edited by S. Dave, L. Nishime, and T. G. Owen, 292–312. New York: New York University Press.

Pease, Cynthia. 1978. "Women and the Man's World of Audio." *High Fidelity* 28 (7): 16.

Peebles, Sarah. 1996. "High-Tech versus My-Tech: Developing Systems for Electroacoustic Improvisation and Composition." *Musicworks* 66: 4–13.

Peterson, George. 1987. "Women in Sound Reinforcement: Four Success Stories." *Mix: The Recording Industry Magazine* (June): 46–120.

Pilar, Praba. 2005. *Cyberlabia: Gendered Thoughts and Conversations on Cyberspace.* Oakland, Calif.: Tela Press.

Pinch, Trevor, and Frank Trocco. 2002. *Analog Days: The Invention and Impact of the Moog Synthesizer.* Cambridge, Mass.: Harvard University Press.

Pini, Maria. 2001. *Club Cultures and Female Subjectivity: The Move from Home to House.* New York: Palgrave.

Polli, Andrea. 2005. "*Atmospherics/Weather Works:* A Spatialized Meteorological Data Sonification Project." *Leonardo* 38 (1): 31–36.

—. 2006. "*Heat and the Heartbeat of the City:* Sonifying Data Describing Climate Change." *Leonardo Music Journal* 16: 44–45.

Potts, Sally Dorgan. 1994. "Women in Audio." *EQ* (May): 50–57.

Ptak, Carly. 2008. Here See website, http://www.heresee.com/cptak.htm (visited April 23, 2008).

Raimist, Rachel. 1999. *Nobody Knows My Name.* USA. VHS, 58 min.

Reynolds, Simon. 1998. *Generation Ecstasy: Into the World of Techno and Rave Culture.* Boston, Mass.: Little, Brown.

Rich, Adrienne. 2001. *Arts of the Possible: Essays and Conversations.* New York: W. W. Norton.

Rodgers, Tara. 2003. "On the Process and Aesthetics of Sampling in Electronic Music Production." *Organised Sound* 8 (3): 313–20.

—. 2006. "Butterfly Effects: Synthesis, Emergence, and Transduction." "Wild Nature and the Digital Life," special issue of *Leonardo Electronic Almanac* 14 (7–8). http:// leoalmanac.org/ (visited November 30, 2006).

Rose, Tricia. 1994. *Black Noise: Rap Music and Black Culture in Contemporary America.* Hanover, N.H.: Wesleyan University Press.

Russolo, Luigi. 1913. "The Art of Noises: Futuristic Manifesto." *The Art of Noises*, 23–30. Translated with an introduction by B. Brown. New York: Pendragon Press, 1986.

Sandstrom, Boden. 2000. "Women Mix Engineers and the Power of Sound." *Music and Gender: Negotiating Shifting Worlds,* edited by P. Moisala and B. Diamond, 289–305. Urbana: University of Illinois Press.

Sawchuk, Kim. 1994. "Pirate Writing: Radiophonic Strategies for Feminist Techno-Perverts." *Radio Rethink: Art, Sound and Transmission,* edited by D. Augitis and D. Lander, 201–22. Banff, Alberta: Walter Phillips Gallery.

Scaletti, Carla. 2002. "Computer Music Languages, Kyma, and the Future." *Computer Music Journal* 26 (4): 69–82.

Schaub, Mirjam. 2005. *Janet Cardiff. The Walk Book.* Cologne: Walther König.

Scott, Bonnie Kime. 2000. "The Subversive Mechanics of Woolf's Gramophone in *Between the Acts.*" *Virginia Woolf in the Age of Mechanical Reproduction,* edited by P. L. Caughie, 97–114. New York: Garland.

Sherburne, Philip. 2002. "If Electronic Music Is So Progressive, Why Is the Album Art So Sexist?" *Neumu,* April 19. http://www.neumu.net/ (visited January 18, 2007).

Sherman, Howard. 1982. "Riding the New Waves." *dB: The Sound Engineering Magazine* (July): 28–33.

Siegler, Dylan. 2000a. "Heather Heart." *XLR8R* 39:35.

—. 2000b. "Kuttin Kandi." *XLR8R* 39: 36.

Smith, Richard R. 1995. *Fender: The Sound Heard 'Round the World.* Fullerton, Calif.: Garfish.

Snapper, Juliana. 2004. "Scratching the Surface: Time and Identity in Hip-Hop Turntablism." *European Journal of Cultural Studies* 7 (1): 9–25.

Sofia, Zoë. 2000. "Container Technologies." *Hypatia* 15 (2): 181–201.

Spiegel, Laurie. 1998. "Graphical Groove: Memorium for a Visual Music System." *Organised Sound* 3 (3): 187–91.

——. 2008. "Laurie Spiegel's Retiary Ramblings." http://www.retiary.org/ls/ (visited April 30, 2008).

Spivak, Gayatri Chakravorty. 1981. "French Feminism in an International Frame." *Yale French Studies* 62, Feminist Readings: French Texts/American Contexts: 154–84.

Stanley, Autumn. 1983. "Women Hold Up Two-Thirds of the Sky: Notes for a Revised History of Technology." *Machina Ex Dea: Feminist Perspectives on Technology,* edited by J. Rothschild, 5–22. New York: Pergamon Press.

Sterne, Jonathan. 2003. *The Audible Past: Cultural Origins of Sound Reproduction.* Durham, N.C.: Duke University Press.

Taylor, Timothy D. 2001. *Strange Sounds: Music, Technology and Culture.* New York: Routledge.

Théberge, Paul. 1997. *Any Sound You Can Imagine: Making Music/Consuming Technology.* Hanover, N.H.: Wesleyan University Press.

Turkle, Sherry. 1984. *The Second Self: Computers and the Human Spirit.* New York: Simon and Schuster.

Vaziri, Aidin. 1998. "Iara Lee: Eyes of Electronica." *Res* 1 (1). Available at the *Modulations* website, http://www.caipirinha.com/ (visited March 9, 2007).

Walker, Jane, and Jackie Pelle. 2001. *Spinsters.* Canada. VHS, 48 min.

Waterman, Ellen. 2007. "Radio Bodies: Discourse, Performance, Resonance." *Radio Territories,* edited by E. G. Jensen and B. Labelle, 118–34. Los Angeles: Errant Bodies Press.

Weheliye, Alexander G. 2002. "'Feenin': Posthuman Voices in Contemporary Black Popular Music." *Social Text* 71 (20, 2): 21–47.

Westerkamp, Hildegard. 2000. "The Local and Global 'Language' of Environmental Sound." Paper presented at Sound Escape, International Conference on Acoustic Ecology, Peterborough, Ontario, Canada, June 28–July 2. Hildegard Westerkamp website, http://www.sfu.ca/~westerka/ (visited April 24, 2008).

——. 2002. "Linking Soundscape Composition and Acoustic Ecology." *Organised Sound* 7 (1): 51–56.

Wierzbicki, James. 2005. *Louis and Bebe Barron's Forbidden Planet: A Film Score Guide.* Lanham, Md.: Scarecrow Press.

Wilson, Sarah. 2004. "Gertrude Stein and the Radio." *Modernism/Modernity* 11 (2): 261–78.

Young, Gayle. 1982. "The How and Why of Instrument Design." *Musicworks* 21 (Fall).

Young, Iris Marion. 2005. *On Female Body Experience: "Throwing Like a Girl" and Other Essays.* New York: Oxford University Press.

Zvonar, Richard. 2004. "Bebe Barron: Strange Cues from the Id." *e | i* 3 (Spring): 18–23.

PART VI

Voices

FINALLY, WE REACH THE VOICE. Voices are among the most personalized and most naturalized forms of subjective self-expression; speakers and auditors routinely treat them as the stuff of consciousness. This goes back to the longstanding equivalence between voice and spirit in some Christian spiritualisms, but it is just as apparent in everyday talk and action, where people articulate themselves through their voices, and assign the voices of others deep meanings. Indeed, as Gary Tomlinson has shown, people's voices are as much an object of racialization as the sight of their bodies.[1]

Marx wrote of consciousness that it is contingent, "burdened with matter which here makes its appearance in the form of agitated layers of air, sounds, in short, of language."[2] As Mladen Dolar makes clear in his chapter, voice is much more than language. It is, in some sense, what is left over before or after language. But what to do with the power of the voice? Several traditions of thought work within a notion of the voice, and speech as presence and as a fundamental modality of social enunciation. Ferdinand de Saussure's *Course in General Linguistics,* the basis of semiotics and structuralism, contrasts spoken, living language with a "deep structure" of the language itself. Drawing from the vocabularies and epistemologies of Christian spiritualism, Marshall McLuhan and Walter Ong based an entire psychosocial theory of orality around ideas of the voice as presence. For them, orality was culture before or without writing, defined by the phenomenological characteristics of the voice. But their voice was a universal one, unraced, ungendered. A vital feminist psychoanalytic tradition has more recently considered the voice as seat of subjectivity, but only insofar as it negotiates gender as a fundamental, generative category of difference. Julia Kristeva reworked Saussure's distinction between speech and language to suggest that the voice opened out into embodied desire against the more rational field of language. In her brilliant *The Acoustic Mirror*, Kaja Silverman develops a theory of gendered subject formation built around the feminine voice, and uses it to reread the history of cinema, inaugurating a debate around the significance of the embodied female voice that extends down to the present day. Steven Connor's book *Dumbstruck* turns the mystical tradition on its head, at once using it in his analysis of the voice and historicizing it through readings of oracles, witchcraft, ecstatic religious speech, and ventriloquism (and many other forms of vocal artifice).[3] Roland Barthes's essay in this section is also a classic, for how it thinks through embodiment and the singing voice as also somehow beneath and aside the fact of language.

Another tradition builds from Jacques Derrida's critique of the "metaphysics of presence." For Derrida, the idea that a voice is simply present, or present to itself, hides the more fundamental fact of difference which constitutes the possibility of meaning. In his essay, taken from a longer critique of the philosopher Edmund Husserl, Derrida argues that hearing-oneself-speak is not a fundamental act of self-presencing, but is built on a set of differences.[4] Drawing on Nietzsche and Foucault, Wendy Brown extends this line of thought when she criticizes contemporary political discourse that equates speech with agency: "expression is cast either as that which makes us free, tells 'our' truth, and puts our truth into circulation, *or* as that which oppresses us by featuring 'their' truth." Both positions "equate freedom with voice and visibility, both assume recognition to be unproblematic when we tell our own story, and both assume that such recognition is the material of power as well as pleasure. Neither confronts the regulatory potential of speaking ourselves, its capacity to bind rather than emancipate us."[5]

The critique of the mystical tradition still leaves open many questions. In his ethnography of Texas country musicians, Aaron Fox has argued that regardless of the metaphysics, voices—and more importantly, *talk*—play constitutive roles in everyday social relations. In this, Fox gestures back through generations of linguistic anthropology that take talk as the stuff of culture, going back to Franz Boas's 1889 "On Alternating Sounds," a landmark document of cultural relativism which argues that observer (or in this case, listener) bias may be a cultural phenomenon, and that Western anthropologists might therefore misunderstand and misrecognize the languages they study, which he demonstrated for Inuit speech.[6]

We might also set material context next to cultural specificity as an irreducible frame for understanding voices. In her analysis of Juliana Snapper's underwater vocal performances, Nina Eidsheim has argued for a fundamentally material conception of voice, as voices are always tied to bodies and resound in specific media.[7] The other readings in this section aim to think through voice in the wake of—and beyond—Derrida's critique. Adriana Cavarero proposes an ontology and phenomenology of "vocal uniqueness" that considers voices, rather than *the voice* as the basis of a philosophy of subjectivity. In his consideration of heavily processed voices in contemporary R&B music, Alexander Weheliye argues that "posthuman" theories of the voice need to be both embodied and deeply attentive to race, even as they leave aside older tropes of authenticity that are so often connected to race and to the voice. Jakob Smith's contribution, meanwhile, examines attempts to use mechanized laughter to produce a range of effects from the authentic to the uncanny. Smith not only provides a still all-too-rare analysis of television sound, but also shows how even the most artificial voices can still have powerful, meaningful effects for their auditors.[8]

Notes

1   Tomlinson, *The Singing of the New World: Indigenous Voices in the Era of European Contact*.
2   Marx and Engels, *The German Ideology*, 51.
3   Saussure, *Course in General Linguistics*; Carpenter and McLuhan, "Acoustic Space"; McLuhan, *The Gutenberg Galaxy: The Making of Typographic Man*; Ong, *The Presence of the Word: Some Prolegomena for Cultural and Religious History*; Kristeva, *The Kristeva Reader*; Silverman, *The Acoustic Mirror: The Female Voice in Psychoanalysis and Cinema*; Connor, *Dumbstruck: A Cultural History of Ventriloquism*; Doane, "The Voice in Cinema"; Lawrence, *Echo and Narcissus*; see also Carter, *The Sound In-Between: Voice, Space, Performance*.
4   See also Derrida, *Of Grammatology*; Derrida, "Différance."
5   Brown, *Edgework*, 83–84.
6   Fox, *Real Country: Music and Language in Working-Class Culture*; Boas, "On Alternating Sounds."
7   Eidsheim, "Sensing Voice."
8   See also Altman, "Television/Sound."

References

Altman, Rick. "Television/Sound." In *Studies in Entertainment*, 39–54. Bloomington: Indiana University Press, 1986.

Boas, Franz. "On Alternating Sounds." *American Anthropologist* 2, no. 1 (1889): 47–54.

Brown, Wendy. *Edgework: Critical Essays on Knowledge and Politics*. Princeton University Press, 2005.

Carpenter, Edmund, and Marshall McLuhan. "Acoustic Space." In *Explorations in Communication*. Boston: Beacon Press, 1960.

Carter, Paul. *The Sound In-Between: Voice, Space, Performance*. Kensington: New South Wales University Press, 1992.

Connor, Steven. *Dumbstruck: A Cultural History of Ventriloquism*. New York: Oxford University Press, 2000.

Derrida, Jacques. "Différance." In *Margins of Philosophy*, 3–27. Chicago: University of Chicago Press, 1982.

—. *Of Grammatology*. Baltimore: The Johns Hopkins University Press, 1976.

Doane, Mary Ann. "The Voice in Cinema." In *Film Sound: Theory and Practice*, edited by Elizabeth Weis and John Belton. New York: Columbia University Press, 1985.

Eidsheim, Nina Sun. "Sensing Voice: Materiality and the Lived Body in Singing and Listening." *The Senses and Society* 6, no. 2 (2011): 133–55.

Fox, Aaron. *Real Country: Music and Language in Working-Class Culture*. Durham: Duke University Press, 2004.

Kristeva, Julia. *The Kristeva Reader*. Columbia University Press, 1986.

Lawrence, Amy. *Echo and Narcissus: Women's Voices in Classical Hollywood Cinema*. Berkeley: University of California Press, 1991.

Marx, Karl, and Friedrich Engels. *The German Ideology*. New York: International Publishers Co, 1970.

McLuhan, Marshall. *The Gutenberg Galaxy: The Making of Typographic Man*. Toronto: University of Toronto Press, 1962.

Ong, Walter J. *The Presence of the Word: Some Prolegomena for Cultural and Religious History*. New Haven: Yale University Press, 1967.

Saussure, Ferdinand de. *Course in General Linguistics.* London: Duckworth, 1983.

Silverman, Kaja. *The Acoustic Mirror: The Female Voice in Psychoanalysis and Cinema.* Bloomington: Indiana University Press, 1988.

Tomlinson, Gary. *The Singing of the New World: Indigenous Voices in the Era of European Contact.* Cambridge: Cambridge University Press, 2007.

Chapter 40

Jacques Derrida

THE VOICE THAT KEEPS SILENCE

THERE IS AN UNFAILING COMPLICITY here between idealization and speech [*voix*]. An ideal object is an object whose showing may be repeated indefinitely, whose presence to *Zeigen* is indefinitely reiterable precisely because, freed from all mundane spatiality, it is a pure noema that I can express without having, at least apparently, to pass through the world. In this sense the phenomenological voice, which seems to accomplish this operation "in time," does not break with the order of *Zeigen* but belongs to the same system and carries through its function. The passage to infinity characteristic of the idealization of objects is one with the historical advent of the *phōnē*. This does not mean that we can finally understand what the movement of idealization is on the basis of a determined "function" or "faculty," concerning which we would in turn know what it *is,* thanks to our familiarity with experience, the "phenomenology of our body," or with some objective science (phonetics, phonology, or the physiology of phonation). Quite the contrary, what makes the history of the *phōnē* fully enigmatic is the fact that it is inseparable from the history of idealization, that is, from the "history of mind," or history as such.

In order to really understand where the power of the voice lies, and how metaphysics, philosophy, and the determination of being as presence constitute the epoch of speech as *technical* mastery of objective being, to properly understand the unity of *technē and phōnē,* we must think through the objectivity of the object. The ideal object is the most objective of objects; independent of the here-and-now acts and events of the empirical subjectivity which intends it, it can be repeated infinitely while remaining the same. Since its presence to intuition, its being-before the gaze, has no essential dependence on any worldly or empirical synthesis, the re-establishment of its sense in the form of presence becomes a universal and unlimited possibility. But, being *nothing* outside the world, this ideal being must be constituted, repeated, and expressed in a medium that does not impair the presence and self-presence of the acts that aim at it, a medium which both preserves the *presence of the object* before intuition and *self-presence,* the absolute proximity of the acts to themselves. The ideality of the object, which is only its being-for a nonempirical consciousness, can only be expressed in an element whose phenomenality does not have worldly form. *The name of this element is the voice. The voice is heard.* Phonic signs ("acoustical images" in Saussure's sense, or the phenomenological voice) are heard [*entendus* = "heard" plus "understood"] by the subject who proffers them in the absolute proximity of their present. The subject does not have to pass forth beyond himself to be immediately affected by his expressive activity. My words are "alive" because they seem not to leave me: not to fall outside me outside my breath, at a visible distance; not to cease to belong to me, to be at my disposition "without further props." In any event, the phenomenon of speech, the phenomenological voice, *gives itself out* in this manner. The objection will perhaps be raised that this interiority belongs to the phenomenological and ideal aspect of every signifier. The ideal form of a written signifier, for example, is not in the world, and the distinction between the grapheme and the empirical body of the corresponding graphic sign separates an inside from an outside, phenomenological consciousness from the world. And this is true for every visual or spatial signifier. And yet every nonphonic signifier involves a spatial reference in its very "phenomenon," in the phenomenological (nonworldly) sphere of experience in which it is given. The sense of being "outside," "in the world," is an essential component of its phenomenon. Apparently there is nothing like this in the phenomenon of speech. In phenomenological interiority, hearing oneself and seeing oneself are two radically different orders of self-relation. Even before a description of this difference is sketched out, we can understand why the hypothesis of the "monologue" could have sanctioned the distinction between indication and expression only by presupposing an essential tie between expression and *phōnē*. Between the phonic element (in the phenomenological sense and not that of a real sound) and expression, taken as the logical character of a signifier that is *animated* in view of the ideal presence of a *Bedeutung* (itself related to an object), there must be a necessary bond. Husserl is unable to bracket what in glossamatics is called the "substance of expression" without menacing his whole enterprise. The appeal to this substance thus plays a major philosophical role.

Let us try, then, to question the phenomenological value of the voice, its transcendent dignity with regard to every other signifying substance. We think, and will try to show, that this transcendence is only apparent. But this "appearance" is the very essence of consciousness and its history, and it determines an epoch characterized by the philosophical idea of truth and the opposition between truth and appearance, as this opposition still functions in phenomenology. It can therefore not be called "appearance" or be named within the sphere of metaphysical conceptuality. One cannot attempt to deconstruct this transcendence without descending, across the inherited concepts, toward the unnamable.

The "apparent transcendence" of the voice thus results from the fact that the signified, which is always ideal by essence, the "expressed" *Bedeutung,* is immediately present in the act of expression. This immediate presence results from the fact that the phenomenological "body" of the signifier seems to fade away at the very moment it is produced; it seems already to belong to the element of ideality. It phenomenologically reduces itself, transforming the worldly opacity of its body into pure diaphaneity. This effacement of the sensible body and its exteriority is *for consciousness* the very form of the immediate presence of the signified.

Why is the phoneme the most "ideal" of signs? Where does this complicity between sound and ideality, or rather, between voice and ideality, come from? (Hegel was more attentive to this than any other philosopher, and, from the point of view of the history of metaphysics, this is a noteworthy fact, one we will examine elsewhere.) When I speak, it belongs to the phenomenological essence of this operation that *I hear myself* [je m'entende] *at the same time* that I speak. The signifier, animated by my breath and by the meaning-intention (in Husserl's language, the expression animated by the *Bedeutungsintention*), is in absolute proximity to me. The living act, the life-giving act, the *Lebendigkeit,* which animates the body of the signifier and transforms it into a meaningful expression, the soul of language, seems not to separate itself from itself, from its own self-presence. It does not risk death in the body of a signifier that is given over to the world and the visibility of space. It can *show* the ideal object or ideal *Bedeutung* connected to it without venturing outside ideality outside the interiority of self-present life. The system of *Zeigen*, the finger and eye movements (concerning which we earlier wondered whether they were not inseparable from phenomenality) are not absent here; but they are interiorized. The phenomenon continues to be an object for the voice; indeed, insofar as the ideality of the object seems to depend on the voice and thus becomes *absolutely accessible* in it, the system which ties phenomenality to the possibility of *Zeigen* functions better than ever in the voice. *The phoneme is given as the dominated ideality of the phenomenon.*

This self-presence of the animating act in the transparent spirituality of what it animates, this inwardness of life with itself, which has always made us say that speech [*parole*] is alive, supposes, then, that the speaking subject hears himself [*s'entende*] in the present. Such is the essence or norm of speech. It is implied in the very structure of speech that the speaker *hears himself*: both that he perceives the sensible form of the phonemes and that he understands his own expressive intention. If accidents occur which seem to contradict this teleological necessity, either they will be overcome by some supplementary operation or there will be no speech. Deaf and dumb go hand in hand. He who is deaf can engage in colloquy only by shaping his acts in the form of words, whose telos requires that they be heard by him who utters them.

Considered from a purely phenomenological point of view, within the reduction, the process of speech has the originality of presenting itself already as pure pheno-menon, as having already suspended the natural attitude and the existential thesis of the world. The operation of "hearing oneself speak" is an auto-affection of a unique kind. On the one hand, it operates within the medium of universality; what appears as signified therein must be idealities that are *idealiter* indefinitely repeatable or transmissible as the same. On the other hand, the subject can hear or speak to himself and be affected by the signifier he produces, without passing through an external detour, the world, the sphere of what is not "his own." Every other form of auto-affection must either pass through what is outside the sphere of "ownness" or forego any claim to universality. When I see myself, either because I gaze upon a limited region of my body or because it is reflected in a mirror, what is outside the sphere of "my own" has already entered the field of this auto-affection, with the result that it is no longer pure. In the experience of touching and being touched, the same thing happens. In both cases, the surface of my body, as something external, must begin by being exposed in the world. But, we could ask, are there not forms of pure auto-affection in the inwardness of one's own body which do not require the intervention of any surface displayed in the world and yet are not of the order of the voice? But then these forms remain purely empirical, for they could not belong to a medium of universal signification. Now, to account for the phenomenological power of the voice, we shall have to specify the concept of pure auto-affection more precisely and describe what, in it, makes it open to universality. As pure auto-affection, the operation of hearing oneself speak seems to reduce even the inward surface of one's own body; in its phenomenal being it seems capable of dispensing with this exteriority within interiority, this interior space in which our experience or image of our own body is spread forth. This is why hearing oneself speak [*s'entendre parler*] is experienced as an absolutely pure auto-affection, occurring in a self-proximity that would in fact be the absolute reduction of space in general. It is this purity that makes it fit for universality. Requiring the intervention of no determinate surface in the world, *being produced in the world as pure auto-affection,* it is a signifying substance absolutely at our disposition. For the voice meets no obstacle to its emission in the world precisely because it is produced *as pure auto-affection.* This auto-affection is no doubt the possibility for what is called *subjectivity* or the *for-itself,* but, without it, no world *as such* would appear. For its basis involves the unity of sound (which is in the world) and *phōnē* (in the phenomenological sense). An objective "worldly" science surely can teach us nothing about the essence of the voice. But the unity of sound and voice, which allows the voice to be produced in the world as pure auto-affection, is the sole case to escape the distinction between what is worldly and what is transcendental; by the same token, it makes that distinction possible.

It is this universality which dictates that, *de jure* and by virtue of its structure, no consciousness is possible without the voice. The voice is the being which is present to itself in the form of universality, as consciousness; the voice *is* consciousness. In colloquy, the propagation of signs does not *seem* to meet any obstacles because it brings together two *phenomenological* origins of pure auto-affection. To speak to someone is doubtless to hear oneself speak, to be heard by oneself; but, at the same time, if one is heard by another, to speak is to make him *repeat immediately* in himself the hearing-oneself-speak in the very form in which I effectuated it. This immediate repetition is a reproduction of pure auto-affection without the help of anything external. This possibility of reproduction, whose structure is absolutely unique, *gives itself out* as the phenomenon of a mastery or limitless power over the signifier, since the signifier itself has the form of what is not external. Ideally, in the teleological essence of speech, it would then be possible for the signifier to be in absolute proximity to the signified aimed at in intuition and governing the meaning. The signifier would become perfectly diaphanous due to the absolute proximity to the signified. This proximity is broken when, instead of hearing myself speak, I see myself write or gesture.

This absolute proximity of the signifier to the signified, and its effacement in immediate presence, is the condition for Husserl's being able to consider the medium of expression as "unproductive" and "reflective." Paradoxically, it is also on this condition that he will be able to reduce it without loss and assert that there exists a pre-expressive stratum of sense. It is again on this condition that Husserl will accord himself the right to reduce the totality of language, be it indicative or expressive, in order to recover sense in its primordiality.

How can we understand this reduction of language when Husserl, from the *Logical Investigations* to *The Origin of Geometry,* continually thought that scientific truth, i.e., absolutely ideal objects, can be found only in "statements" and that not only spoken language but *inscription* as well was indispensable for the constitution of ideal objects, that is, objects capable of being transmitted and repeated as the same?

First, we should recognize that the more evident aspect of the movement which, for a long time under way, terminates in *The Origin of Geometry* confirms the underlying limitation of language to a secondary stratum of experience and, in the consideration of this secondary stratum, confirms the traditional phonologism of metaphysics. If writing brings the constitution of ideal objects to completion, it does so through phonetic writing:[1] It proceeds to fix, inscribe, record, and incarnate an already prepared utterance. To reactivate writing is always to reawaken an expression in an indication, a word in the body of a letter, which, as a symbol that may always remain empty, bears the threat of crisis in itself. Already speech was playing the same role by first constituting the identity of sense in thought. For example, the "protogeometer" must produce the pure ideality of the pure geometrical object in thought by a passage to the limit, assuring its transmissibility by speech, and must finally commit it to writing. By means of this written inscription, one can always repeat the original sense, that is, the act of *pure thought* which created the ideality of sense. With the possibility of progress that such an incarnation allows, there goes the ever growing risk of "forgetting" and loss of sense. It becomes more and more difficult to reconstitute the presence of the act buried under historical sedimentations. The moment of crisis is always the moment of signs.

Moreover, despite the minute detail, the rigor, and the absolute novelty of his analyses, Husserl always describes all these movements in a metaphysical conceptual system. What governs here is the absolute difference between body and soul. Writing is a body that expresses something only if we actually pronounce the verbal expression that animates it, if its space is temporalized. The word is a body that means something only if an actual intention animates it and makes it pass from the state of inert sonority (*Körper*) to that of an animated body (*Leib*), This body proper to words expresses something only if it is animated (*sinnbelebt*) by an act of meaning (*bedeuten*) which transforms it into a spiritual flesh (*geistige Leiblichkeit*). But only the *Geistigkeit* or *Lebendigkeit* is independent and primordial.[2] As such, it needs no signifier to be present to itself. Indeed, it is as much in spite of its signifiers as thanks to them that it is awakened or maintained in life. Such is the traditional side of Husserl's language.

But if Husserl had to recognize the necessity of these "incarnations," even as beneficial threats, it is because an underlying motif was disturbing and contesting the security of these traditional distinctions from within and because the possibility of writing dwelt within speech, which was itself at work in the inwardness of thought.

And here again we find all the incidences of primordial nonpresence whose emergence we have already noted on several occasions. Even while repressing difference by assigning it to the exteriority of the signifiers, Husserl could not fail to recognize its work at the origin of sense and presence. Taking auto-affection as the exercise of the voice, auto-affection supposed that a pure difference comes to divide self-presence. In this pure difference is rooted the possibility of everything we think we can exclude from auto-affection: space, the outside, the world, the body, etc. As soon as it is admitted that auto-affection is the condition for self-presence, no pure transcendental reduction is possible. But it was necessary to pass through the transcendental reduction in order to grasp this difference in what is closest to it— which cannot mean grasping it in its identity, its purity, or its origin, for it has none. We come closest to it in the movement of differance.[3]

This movement of differance is not something that happens to a transcendental subject; it produces a subject. Auto-affection is not a modality of experience that characterizes a being that would already be itself (*autos*). It produces sameness as self-relation within self-difference; it produces sameness as the nonidentical.

Shall we say that the auto-affection we have been talking about up until now concerns only the operation of the voice? Shall we say that difference concerns only the order of the phonic "signifier" or the "secondary strata" of expression? Can we always hold out for the possibility of a pure and purely self-present identity at the level Husserl wanted to disengage as a level of pre-expressive experience, that is, the level of sense prior to *Bedeutung* and expression?

It would be easy to show that such a possibility is excluded at the very root of transcendental experience.

Why, in fact, is the concept of auto-affection incumbent on us? What constitutes the originality of speech, what distinguishes it from every other element of signification, is that its substance seems to be purely temporal. And this temporality does not unfold a sense that would itself be nontemporal; even before being expressed, sense is through and through temporal. According to Husserl, the omnitemporality of ideal objects is but a mode of temporality. And when Husserl describes a sense that seems to escape temporality, he hastens to make it clear that this is only a provisional step in analysis and that he is considering a constituted temporality. However, as soon as one takes the movement of temporalization into account, as it is already analyzed in *The Phenomenology of Internal Time-Consciousness*, the concept of pure auto-affection must be employed as well. This we know is what Heidegger does in *Kant and the Problem of Metaphysics*, precisely when he is concerned with the subject of time. The "source point" or "primordial impression," that out of which the movement of temporalization is produced, is already pure auto-affection. First it is a pure production, since temporality is never the real predicate of a being. The intuition of time itself cannot be empirical; it is a receiving that receives nothing. The absolute novelty of each now is therefore engendered by nothing; it consists in a primordial impression that engenders itself:

> This pure spontaneity is an impression; it creates nothing. The new now is not a being, it is not a produced object; and every language fails to describe this pure movement other than by metaphor, that is, by borrowing its concepts from the order of the objects of experience, an order this temporalization makes possible. Husserl continually warns us against these metaphors.[4]

The process by which the living now, produced by spontaneous generation, must, in order to be a now and to be retained in another now, affect itself without recourse to anything empirical but with a new primordial actuality in which it would become a non-now, a past now—this process is indeed a pure auto-affection in which the same is the same only in being affected by the other, only by becoming the other of the same. This auto-affection must be pure since the primordial impression is here affected by nothing other than itself, by the absolute "novelty" of another primordial impression which is another now. We speak metaphorically as soon as we introduce a determinate being into the description of this "movement"; we talk about "movement" in the very terms that movement makes possible. But we have been always already adrift in ontic metaphor; temporalization here is the root of a metaphor that can only be primordial. The word "time" itself, as it has always been understood in the history of metaphysics, is a metaphor which *at the same time* both indicates and dissimulates the "movement" of this auto-affection. All the concepts of metaphysics—in particular those of activity and passivity, will and nonwill, and therefore those of affection or auto-affection, purity and impurity, etc.—*cover up* the strange "movement" of this difference.

But this pure difference, which constitutes the self-presence of the living present, introduces into self-presence from the beginning all the impurity putatively excluded from it. The living present springs forth out of its nonidentity with itself and from the possibility of a retentional trace. It is always already a trace. This trace cannot be thought out on the basis of a simple present whose life would be within itself; the self of the living present is primordially a trace. The trace is not an attribute; we cannot say that the self of the living present "primordially is" it. Being-primordial must be thought on the basis of the trace, and not the reverse. This protowriting is at work at the origin of sense. Sense, being temporal in nature, as Husserl recognized, is never simply present; it is always already engaged in the "movement" of the trace, that is, in the order of "signification." It has always already issued forth from itself into the "expressive stratum" of lived experience. Since the trace is the intimate relation of the living present with its outside, the openness upon exteriority in general, upon the sphere of what is not "one's own," etc., *the temporalization of sense is, from the outset, a "spacing."* As soon as we admit spacing both as "interval" or difference and as openness upon the outside, there can no longer be any absolute inside, for the "outside" has insinuated itself into the movement by which the inside of the nonspatial, which is called "time," appears, is constituted, is "presented." Space is "in" time; it is time's pure leaving-itself; it is the "outside-itself" as the self-relation of time. The externality of space, externality as space, does not overtake time; rather, it opens as pure "outside" "within" the movement of temporalization. If we recall now that the pure inwardness of phonic auto-affection supposed the purely temporal nature of the "expressive" process, we see that the theme of a pure inwardness of speech, or of the "hearing oneself speak," is radically contradicted by "time" itself. The going-forth "into the world" is also primordially implied in the movement of temporalization. "Time" cannot be an "absolute subjectivity" precisely because it cannot be conceived on the basis of a present and the self-presence of a present being. Like everything thought under this heading, and like all that is excluded by the most rigorous transcendental reduction, the "world" is primordially implied in the movement of temporalization. As a relation between an inside and an outside in general, an existent and a nonexistent in general, a constituting and a constituted in general, temporalization is at once the very power and limit of phenomenological reduction. Hearing oneself speak is not the inwardness of an inside that is closed in upon itself; it is the irreducible openness in the inside; it is the eye and the world within speech. *Phenomenological reduction is a scene, a theater stage.*

Also, just as expression is not added like a "stratum"[5] to the presence of a pre-expressive sense, so, in the same way, the inside of expression does not accidentally happen to be affected by the outside of indication. Their intertwining (*Verflechtung*) is primordial; it is not a contingent association that could be undone by methodic attention and patient reduction. The analysis, necessary as it is, encounters an absolute limit at this point. If indication is not added to expression, which is not added to sense, we can nonetheless speak in regard to them, of a primordial "supplement": their *addition* comes to *make up for* a deficiency, it comes to compensate for a primordial nonself-presence. And if indication—for example, writing in the everyday sense—must necessarily be "added" to speech to complete the constitution of the ideal object, if speech must be "added" to the thought identity of the object, it is because the "presence" of sense and speech had already from the start fallen short of itself.

Notes

1. It is strange that, despite the formalist motif and fidelity to Leibniz affirmed continually in his work, Husserl never placed the problem of writing in the center of his reflection and, in *The Origin of Geometry,* did not take into account the difference between phonetic and nonphonetic writing.
2. Cf. the Introduction to *The Origin of Geometry,* French ed., translated by Jacques Derrida (Paris, 1962), pp. 83–100.
3. [Derrida introduces a neologism here; from the French "*différence*" he derives the term "*différance*." As in the Latin "*differre*," the French "*différer*" bears two quite distinct significations. One has a reference to spatiality, as the English "to differ"—to be at variance, to be unlike, apart, dissimilar, distinct in nature or quality from something. This is even more evident in its cognate form, "to differentiate." The other signification has a reference to temporality as in the English "to defer"—to put off action to a future time, to delay or postpone.

    I have thus chosen to follow Derrida's employment of *différance* by rendering it as "differance" in English. This should not be too disconcerting a translation, for it incorporates the common origin of the two relevant English verbs, "to defer" and "to differ," namely the Latin *differre*.—Translator.]

    The primal impression is the absolute beginning of this generation—the primal source, that from which all others are continuously generated. In itself, however, it is not generated; it does not come into existence as that which is generated but through *spontaneous generation.* It does not grow up (it has no seed): it is primal creation (*The Phenomenology of Internal Time-Consciousness,* Appendix I; ET, p. 131; italics added).

4. See e.g., the admirable § 36 of *The Phenomenology of Internal Time-Consciousness* which proves the absence of a proper noun for this strange "movement," which, furthermore is not a movement. "For all this," concludes Husserl, "names fail us." We would still have to radicalize Husserl's intention here in a specific direction. For it is not by chance that he still designates this unnamable as an "absolute subjectivity," that is, as a being conceived on the basis of

presence as substance, *ousia, hypokeimenon:* a self-identical being in self-presence which forms the substance of a subject. What is said to be unnamable in this paragraph is not exactly something we know to be a *present* being in the form of self-presence, a substance modified into a subject, into an absolute subject whose self-presence is pure and does not depend on any external affection, any outside. *All this is present and we can name it, the proof being that its being as absolute subjectivity is not questioned.* What is unnamable, according to Husserl are only the "absolute properties" of this subject; the subject therefore is indeed designated in terms of the classical metaphysical schema which distinguishes substance (present being) from its attributes. Another schema that keeps the incomparable depth of the analysis within the closure of the metaphysics of presence is the subject-object opposition. This being whose "absolute properties" are indescribable is present as *absolute* subjectivity, is an *absolutely* present and *absolutely* self-present being, only in its opposition to the object. The object is relative; what is absolute is the subject: "We can only say that *this flux is something which we name in conformity with what is constituted,* but it is nothing temporally 'Objective.' It is absolute subjectivity and has the absolute properties of something to be denoted metaphorically as 'flux,' as a point of actuality, primal source-point, that from which springs the 'now,' and so on. In the lived experience of actuality, we have the primal source-point and a continuity of moments of reverberation (*Nachhallmomenten*). For all this, names are lacking" (*ITC,* § 36; ET, p. 100; italics added). This determination of "absolute subjectivity" would also have to be crossed out as soon as we conceive the present on the basis of difference, and not the reverse. The concept of *subjectivity* belongs *a priori and in general* to the order of the *constituted.* This holds *a fortiori* for the analogical appresentation that constitutes intersubjectivity. Intersubjectivity is inseparable from temporalization taken as the openness of the present upon an outside of itself, upon *another* absolute present. This being outside itself proper to time is its *spacing:* it is a *protostage* [*archi-scéne*]. This stage, as the relation of one present to another present *as such,* that is, as a nonderived re-presentation (*Vergegenwärtigung* or *Repräsentation*), produces the structure of signs in general as "reference," as being-for-something *(für etwas sein),* and radically precludes their reduction. There is no constituting subjectivity. The very concept of constitution itself must be deconstructed.

5.   Moreover, in the important § § 124–27 of *Ideas I,* which we shall elsewhere follow step by step, Husserl invites us—while continually speaking of an underlying stratum of pre-expressive experience—not to "hold too hard by the metaphor of stratification (*Schichtung*); expression is not of the nature of an overlaid varnish or covering garment; it is a mental formation, which exercises new intentional influences on the intentional substratum (*Unterschicht*)" (*Ideas I,* § 124; ET, p. 349).

Chapter 41

Roland Barthes

THE GRAIN OF THE VOICE

L ANGUAGE, ACCORDING TO BENVENISTE, is the only semiotic system capable of *interpreting* another semiotic system (though undoubtedly there exist limit works in the course of which a system feigns self-interpretation – *The Art of the Fugue*). How, then, does language manage when it has to interpret music? Alas, it seems, very badly. If one looks at the normal practice of music criticism (or, which is often the same thing, of conversations 'on' music), it can readily be seen that a work (or its performance) is only ever translated into the poorest of linguistic categories: the adjective. Music, by natural bent, is that which at once receives an adjective. The adjective is inevitable: this music is *this,* this execution is *that.* No doubt the moment we turn an art into a subject (for an article, for a conversation) there is nothing left but to give it predicates; in the case of music, however, such predication unfailingly takes the most facile and trivial form, that of the epithet. Naturally, this epithet, to which we are constantly led by weakness or fascination (little parlour game: talk about a piece of music without using a single adjective), has an economic function: the predicate is always the bulwark with which the subject's imaginary protects itself from the loss which threatens it. The man who provides himself or is provided with an adjective is now hurt, now pleased, but always *constituted.* There is an imaginary in music whose function is to reassure, to constitute the subject hearing it (would it be that music is dangerous – the old Platonic idea that music is an access to *jouissance,* to loss, as numerous ethnographic and popular examples would tend to show?) and this imaginary immediately comes to language via the adjective. A historical dossier ought to be assembled here, for adjectival criticism (or predicative interpretation) has taken on over the centuries certain institutional aspects. The musical adjective becomes legal whenever an *ethos* of music is postulated, each time, that is, that music is attributed a regular – natural or magical – mode of signification. Thus with the ancient Greeks, for whom it was the musical *language* (and not the contingent work) in its denotative structure which was immediately adjectival, each mode being linked to a coded expression (rude, austere, proud, virile, solemn, majestic, warlike, educative, noble, sumptuous, doleful, modest, dissolute, voluptuous); thus with the Romantics, from Schumann to Debussy, who substitute for, or add to, the simple indication of tempo (*allegro, presto, andante*) poetic, emotive predicates which are increasingly refined and which are given in the national language so as to diminish the mark of the code and develop the 'free' character of the predication (*sehr kräftig, sehr präcis, spirituel et discret,* etc.).

Are we condemned to the adjective? Are we reduced to the dilemma of either the predicable or the ineffable? To ascertain whether there are (verbal) means for talking about music without adjectives, it would be necessary to look at more or less the whole of music criticism, something which I believe has never been done and which, nevertheless, I have neither the intention nor the means of doing here. This much, however, can be said: it is not by struggling against the adjective (diverting the adjective you find on the tip of the tongue towards some substantive or verbal periphrasis) that one stands a chance of exorcising music commentary and liberating it from the fatality of predication; [rather than trying to change directly the language on music, it would be better to change the musical object itself] as it presents itself to discourse, better to alter its level of perception or intellection, to displace the fringe of contact between music and language.

It is this displacement that I want to outline, not with regard to the whole of music but simply to a part of vocal music (*lied* or *mélodie*): the very precise space (genre) of *the encounter between a language and a voice.* I shall straightaway give a name to this signifier at the level of which, I believe, the temptation of ethos can be liquidated (and thus the adjective banished): the *grain,* the grain of the voice when the latter is in a dual posture, a dual production – of language and of music.

What I shall attempt to say of the 'grain' will, of course, be only the apparently abstract side, the impossible account of an individual thrill that I constantly experience in listening to singing. In order to disengage this 'grain' from the acknowledged values of vocal music, I shall use a twofold opposition: theoretical, between the pheno-text and the geno-text (borrowing from Julia Kristeva), and paradigmatic, between two singers, one of whom I like very much (although he is no longer heard), the other very little (although one hears no one but him), Panzera and Fischer-Dieskau (here merely ciphers: I am not deifying the first nor attacking the second).

Listen to a Russian bass (a church bass – opera is a genre in which the voice has gone over in its entirety to dramatic expressivity, a voice with a grain which little signifies): something is there, manifest and stubborn (one hears only *that*), beyond (or before) the meaning of the words, their form (the litany), the melisma, and even the style of execution: something which is directly the cantor's body, brought to your ears in one and the same movement from deep down in the cavities, the muscles, the membranes, the cartilages, and from deep down in the Slavonic language, as though a single skin lined the inner flesh of the performer and the music he sings. The voice is not personal: it expresses nothing of the cantor, of his soul; it is not original (all Russian cantors have roughly the same voice), and at the same time it is individual: it has us hear a body which has no civil identity, no 'personality', but which is nevertheless a separate body. Above all, this voice bears along *directly* the symbolic, over the intelligible, the expressive: here, thrown in front of us like a packet, is the Father, his phallic stature. The 'grain' is that: the materiality of the body speaking its mother tongue; perhaps the letter, almost certainly *signifiance*.

Thus we can see in song (pending the extension of this distinction to the whole of music) the two texts described by Julia Kristeva. The *pheno-song* (if the transposition be allowed) covers all the phenomena, all the features which belong to the structure of the language being sung, the rules of the genre, the coded form of the melisma, the composer's idiolect, the style of the interpretation: in short, everything in the performance which is in the service of communication, representation, expression, everything which it is customary to talk about, which forms the tissue of cultural values (the matter of acknowledged tastes, of fashions, of critical commentaries), which takes its bearing directly on the ideological alibis of a period ('subjectivity', 'expressivity', 'dramaticism', 'personality' of the artist). The *geno-song* is the volume of the singing and speaking voice, the space where significations germinate 'from within language and in its very materiality'; it forms a signifying play having nothing to do with communication, representation (of feelings), expression; it is that apex (or that depth) of production where the melody really works at the language – not at what it says, but the voluptuousness of its sounds-signifiers, of its letters – where melody explores how the language works and identifies with that work. It is, in a very simple word but which must be taken seriously, the *diction* of the language.

From the point of view of the pheno-song, Fischer-Dieskau is assuredly an artist beyond reproach: everything in the (semantic and lyrical) structure is respected and yet nothing seduces, nothing sways us to *jouissance*. His art is inordinately expressive (the diction is dramatic, the pauses, the checkings and releasings of breath, occur like shudders of passion) and hence never exceeds culture: here it is the soul which accompanies the song, not the body. What is difficult is for the body to accompany the musical diction not with a movement of emotion but with a 'gesture-support';[1] all the more so since the whole of musical pedagogy teaches not the culture of the 'grain' of the voice but the emotive modes of its delivery – the myth of respiration. How many singing teachers have we not heard prophesying that the art of vocal music rested entirely on the mastery, the correct discipline of breathing! The breath is the *pneuma*, the soul swelling or breaking, and any exclusive art of breathing is likely to be a secretly mystical art (a mysticism levelled down to the measure of the long-playing record). The lung, a stupid organ (lights for cats!), swells but gets no erection; it is in the throat, place where the phonic metal hardens and is segmented, in the mask that *signifiance* explodes, bringing not the soul but *jouissance*. With FD, I seem only to hear the lungs, never the tongue, the glottis, the teeth, the mucous membranes, the nose. All of Panzera's art, on the contrary, was in the letters, not in the bellows (simple technical feature: you never heard him *breathe* but only divide up the phrase). An extreme rigour of thought regulated the prosody of the enunciation and the phonic economy of the French language; prejudices (generally stemming from oratorical and ecclesiastical diction) were overthrown. With regard to the consonants, too readily thought to constitute the very armature of our language (which is not, however, a Semitic one) and always prescribed as needing to be 'articulated', detached, emphasized *in order to fulfil the clarity of meaning*, Panzera recommended that in many cases they be *patinated,* given the wear of a language that had been living, functioning, and working for ages past, that they be made simply the springboard for the admirable vowels. There lay the 'truth' of language – not its functionality (clarity, expressivity, communication) – and the range of vowels received all the *signifiance* (which is meaning in its potential voluptuousness): the opposition of *é* and *è* (so necessary in conjugation), the purity – almost *electronic,* so much was its sound tightened, raised, exposed, held – of the most French of vowels, the *ü* (a vowel not derived by French from Latin). Similarly, Panzera carried his *r*'s beyond the norms of the singer – without denying those norms. His *r* was of course rolled, as in every classic art of singing, but the roll had nothing peasant-like or Canadian about it; it was an artificial roll, the paradoxical state of a letter-sound at once totally abstract (by its metallic brevity of vibration) and totally material (by its manifest deep-rootedness in the action of the throat). This phonetics – am I alone in perceiving it? am I hearing voices within the voice? but isn't it the truth of the voice to be hallucinated? (isn't the entire space of the voice an infinite one?) which was doubtless the meaning of Saussure's work on anagrams – does not exhaust *signifiance* (which is inexhaustible) but it does at least hold in check the attempts at *expressive reduction* operated by a whole culture against the poem and its melody.

It would not be too difficult to date that culture, to define it historically. FD now reigns more or less unchallenged over the recording of vocal music; he has recorded everything. If you like Schubert but not FD, then Schubert is today *forbidden* you – an example of that positive censorship (censorship by repletion) which characterizes mass culture though it is never criticized. His art – expressive, dramatic, *sentimentally clear,* borne by a voice lacking in any 'grain', in signifying weight, fits well with the demands of an *average* culture. Such a culture, defined by the growth of the number of listeners and the disappearance of practitioners (no more amateurs), wants art, wants music, provided they be clear, that they 'translate' an emotion and represent a signified (the 'meaning' of a poem); an art that inoculates pleasure (by reducing it to a known, coded emotion) and reconciles the subject to what in music *can be said:* what is said about it, predicatively, by Institution, Criticism, Opinion. Panzera does not belong to this culture (he could not have done, having sung before the coming of the microgroove record; moreover I doubt whether, were he singing today, his art would be recognized or even simply *perceived*); his reign, very great between the wars, was that of an exclusively bourgeois art (an art, that is, in no way petit-bourgeois) nearing the end of its inner development and, by a familiar distortion, separated from History. It is perhaps, precisely and less paradoxically than it seems, because this art was *already* marginal, mandarin, that it was able to bear traces of *signifiance,* to escape the tyranny of meaning.

The 'grain' of the voice is not – or is not merely – its timbre; the *signifiance* it opens cannot better be defined, indeed, than by the very friction between the music and something else, which something else is the particular language (and nowise the message). The song must speak, must *write* – for what is produced at the level of the geno-song is finally writing. This sung writing of language is, as I see it, what the French *mélodie* sometimes tried to accomplish. I am well aware that the German *lied* was intimately bound up with the German language via the Romantic poem, that the poetical culture of Schumann was immense and that this same Schumann used to say of Schubert that had he lived into old age he would have set the whole of German literature to music, but I think nevertheless that the historical meaning of the *lied* must be sought in the music (if only because of its popular origins). By contrast, the historical meaning of the *mélodie* is a certain culture of the French language. As we know, the Romantic poetry of France is more oratorical than textual; what the poetry could not accomplish on its own, however, the *mélodie* has occasionally accomplished with it, working at the language through the poem. Such a work (in the specificity here acknowledged it) is not to be seen in the general run of the *mélodies* produced which are too accommodating towards minor poets, the model of the petit-bourgeois romance, and salon usages, but in some few pieces it is indisputable – anthologically (a little by chance) in certain songs by Fauré and Duparc, massively in the later (prosodic) Fauré and the vocal work of Debussy (even if *Pelléas* is often sung badly – dramatically). What is engaged in these works is, much more than a musical style, a practical reflection (if one may put it like that) on the language; there is a progressive movement from the language to the poem, from the poem to the song and from the song to its performance. This means that the *mélodie* has little to do with the history of music and much with the theory of the text. Here again, the signifier must be redistributed.

Compare two sung deaths, both of them famous: that of Boris and that of Mélisande. Whatever Mussorgsky's intentions, the death of Boris is *expressive* or, if preferred, *hysterical;* it is overloaded with historical, affective contents. Performances of the death cannot be but dramatic: it is the triumph of the pheno-text, the smothering of *significance* under the soul as signified. Mélisande, on the contrary, only dies *prosodically.* Two extremes are joined, woven together: the perfect intelligibility of the denotation and the pure prosodic segmentation of the enunciation; between the two a salutary gap (filled out in Boris) – the *pathos,* that is to say, according to Aristotle (why not?), passion *such as men speak and imagine it,* the accepted idea of death, *endoxical* death. Mélisande dies *without any noise* (understanding the term in its cybernetic sense): nothing occurs to interfere with the signifier and there is thus no compulsion to redundance; simply, the production of a music-language with the function of preventing the singer from being expressive. As with the Russian bass, the symbolic (the death) is thrown immediately (without mediation) before us (this to forestall the stock idea which has it that what is not expressive can only be cold and intellectual; Mélisande's death is 'moving', which means that it shifts something in the chain of the signifier).

The *mélodie* disappeared – sank to the bottom – for a good many reasons, or at least the disappearance took on a good many aspects. Doubtless it succumbed to its salon image, this being a little the ridiculous form of its class origin. Mass 'good' music (records, radio) has left it behind, preferring either the more pathetic orchestra (success of Mahler) or less bourgeois instruments than the piano (harpsichord, trumpet). Above all, however, the death of the *mélodie* goes along with a much wider historical phenomenon to a large extent unconnected to the history of music or of musical taste: the French are abandoning their language, not, assuredly, as a normative set of noble values (clarity, elegance, correctness) – or at least this does not bother me very much for these are institutional values – but as a space of pleasure, of thrill, a site where language works *for nothing,* that is, in perversion (remember here the singularity – the solitude – of *Lois* by Philippe Sollers, theatre of the return of the prosodic and metrical work of the language).

The 'grain' is the body in the voice as it sings, the hand as it writes, the limb as it performs. If I perceive the 'grain' in a piece of music and accord this 'grain' a theoretical value (the emergence of the text in the work), I inevitably set up a new scheme of evaluation which will certainly be individual – I am determined to listen to my relation with the body of the man or woman singing or playing and that relation is erotic – but in no way 'subjective' (it is not the psychological 'subject' in me who is listening; the climactic pleasure hoped for is not going to reinforce – to express – that subject but, on the contrary, to lose it). The evaluation will be made outside of any law, outplaying not only the law of culture but equally that of anticulture, developing beyond the subject all the value hidden behind 'I like' or 'I don't like'. Singers especially will be ranged in what may be called, since it is a matter of my choosing without there being any reciprocal choice of me, two prostitutional categories. Thus I shall freely extol such and such a performer, little-known, minor, forgotten, dead perhaps, and turn away from such another, an acknowledged star (let us refrain from examples, no doubt of merely biographical significance); I shall extend my choice across all the genres of vocal music including popular music, where I shall have no difficulty in rediscovering the distinction between the pheno-song and the geno-song (some popular singers have a 'grain' while others, however famous, do not). What is more, leaving aside the voice, the 'grain' – or the lack of it – persists in instrumental music; if the latter no longer has language to lay open *signifiance* in all its volume, at least there is the performer's body which again forces me to evaluation. I shall not judge a performance according to the rules of interpretation, the constraints of style (anyway highly illusory), which almost all belong to the pheno-song (I shall not wax lyrical concerning the 'rigour', the 'brilliance', the 'warmth', the 'respect for what is written', etc.), but according to the image of the body (the figure) given me. I can hear with certainty – the certainty of the body, of thrill – that the harpsichord playing of Wanda Landowska comes from her inner body and not from the petty digital scramble of so many harpsichordists (so much so that it is a different instrument). As for piano music, I know at once which part of the body is playing – if it is the arm, too often, alas, muscled like a dancer's calves, the clutch of the finger-tips (despite the sweeping flourishes of the wrists), or if on the contrary it is the only erotic part of a pianist's body, the pad of the fingers whose 'grain' is so rarely heard (it is hardly necessary to recall that today, under the pressure of the mass long-playing record, there seems to be a flattening out of technique; which is paradoxical in that the various manners of playing are all flattened out *into perfection:* nothing is left but pheno-text).

This discussion has been limited to 'classical music'. It goes without saying, however, that the simple consideration of 'grain' in music could lead to a different history of music from the one we know now (which is purely pheno-textual). Were we to succeed in refining a certain 'aesthetics' of musical pleasure, then doubtless we would attach less importance to the formidable break in tonality accomplished by modernity.

Note

1. 'This is why the best way to read me is to accompany the reading with certain appropriate bodily movements. Against non-spoken writing, against non-written speech. For the gesture-support.' Philippe Sollers, *Lois,* Paris 1972, p. 108.

Chapter 42

Alexander Weheliye

DESIRING MACHINES IN BLACK POPULAR MUSIC

TO SAY THAT COMMUNICATIONS and other technologies are leading actors on the stage of contemporary R&B would amount to an understatement of gargantuan proportions; lyrically, hardly a track exists that does not mention cellular phones, beepers, two-way pagers, answering machines, various surveillance gadgets, e-mail messages, and the Internet, stressing the interdependence of contemporary interpersonal communication and informational technologies. As a result, these technologies appear both as Brechtian "A-effects" and as sonic "cinema verité" that depict the "reality" of current technologically mediated life worlds.[1] On "Beep Me 911," for instance, Missy Elliot and 702 ask an unnamed lover to beep or call them on the cell phone if she or he still loves them, the 911 functioning here as an indicator of both urgency and monumental desire.[2] Destiny's Child admonishes an unwanted admirer, a "Bug-a-Boo," to stop beeping their pagers, leaving them telephone messages, and sending them e-mail; if this techno-informational terrorism continues, they threaten to block the caller's number, have MCI cut the phone poles, throw their pager out the window, and have AOL make their e-mail stop.[3] In a different vein, the members of Blaque describe their sexual superiority by insisting that their "love goes boom like an 808," a drum machine, used on countless hip hop, house, and techno recordings, that does not mimic "human" capacities but is celebrated for its sonic and rhythmic deepness. Blaque's sexual braggadocio transforms them into "love machines" who can only describe the velocity of their lovemaking via the machinic, thus rendering the TR-808 drum machine more "human" than the human subjects themselves.[4] The increased prominence of these technological artifacts in R&B indicates the enculturation (the ways in which technological artifacts are incorporated into the quotidian) of informational technologies in cultural practices that diverge from Hayles's restricted scientific and literary archive and Eshun's alien otherworlds.

This penchant for the machinic in R&B can also be found in the genre's use of cellular telephones both as a voice distortion mechanism and as part of the sonic tapestry. Ginuwine and Aaliyah's duet, "Final Warning," lyrically not only revolves around phone numbers and cell phones, but their staged lover's quarrel is continually interspersed by sounds of a ringing cellular telephone.[5] This ringing, rather than functioning merely as sonic similitude, forms an integral element of the rhythmic dimension of this already complexly syncopated track. The ringing of the cell phone on this recording, however, is an exception rather than the rule. Generally, cellular phones have entered R&B and hip hop—the informational technological gadget de rigueur in these genres—both as a textual topic and, perhaps more importantly, as a voice distortion device. Nowhere is this clearer than on rap supergroup the Firm's "Phone Tap."[6] Chronicling the FBI surveillance of the imaginary gangster personas the rappers adopted for this project, the track features a slow beat and a Mexican-style acoustic guitar reminiscent of western film soundtracks. The rappers deliver their lyrics through a muffled microphone approximating voices on a cell phone, which achieves a haunting effect that aestheticizes surveillance practices by incorporating them into the musical text as much as it criticizes their utter infiltration of contemporary social and political formations. Most other uses of the "cell phone effect" are more benign but still noteworthy, in that they have realigned notions of voice and soul within the contemporary black popular musical landscape. Lately, almost all mainstream R&B productions feature parts of the lead or background vocal performance sounding as if they were called in over a cell phone as opposed to produced in a state-of-the-art recording studio.[7] This use of the cell phone has become so ubiquitous that in a recent article in the Village Voice, Scott Woods feels compelled to classify all female pop R&B performers as "Cell-Phone Girls."[8]

The "cell phone effect" marks the performers' recorded voices as technologically embodied. Instead of trying to downplay the technological mediation of the recording, the cell phone effect does away with any notion of the selfsame presence of the voice, imbuing, as Simon Reynolds points out, the production of the voice in contemporary R&B with a strong sense of "anti-naturalism."[9] Reynolds's argument regards the overall treatment of the voice in R&B, but the cell phone effect holds a particular prominence in this scheme as an "index of technological audibility."[10] As Jeremy Gilbert and Ewan Pearson explain, in most popular musical genres technology is frowned upon, creating a hierarchy of what counts as technological: "Such distinctions almost always proceed by rendering the technological components utilized in their favored forms invisible as technologies—they are more 'real' or 'natural,' absorbed wholly into those that play them as expressive extensions of the performing body" (112). The cell phone effect resists such principles of the "real," choosing instead to stage voice-distortion devices as both technological *and* "expressive extensions of the performing body." More importantly, the cell phone effect fails to define technological mediation and "realism" as warring opponents; instead, R&B construes these factors as thoroughly interfaced.

The technological demarcation of the voice in contemporary R&B also appears in the revival of the vocoder. Au courant in the early 1980s, this speech-synthesizing device can also be heard on a spate of recent pop and dance music recordings.[11] First used in popular music by such artists as Kraftwerk and Herbie Hancock, it exploded in the early 1980s, particularly in the electro genre, and today is in many ways a sonic index of the early 1980s' zeitgeist. The vocoder might best be thought of as a "low technology," to use Gilbert and Pearson's phrase, which achieves analog-sounding effects via digital means (122–28).[12] The use of this sonic technology forms a part of a tendency to valorize older and obsolete machinery of musical production because they sound "warmer" and more "human," which is ironic given that vocoders make the human voice sound robotic, in a now seemingly quaint C3P0 way. Because the vocoder carries undertones of nostalgia for a more "technologically innocent" era (the 1980s), it lends an aura of increased "humanity" and "soulfulness" to the singer's voice. Current invocations of the mechanized voice in black popular music render the vocoder less technological than the cell phone effect, for instance, since it sounds like a historical relic. I would now like to analyze several specific instances of vocoder use in R&B, tracing the shift from analog to digital and its ramifications on questions of soul and virtual embodiment.

Zapp was a late-seventies and early-eighties group associated with George Clinton in its infancy but later making a name for itself by virtue of heavily mechanized funk and extensive vocoder use. In fact, Zapp "embodies" the vocoder like no other musical group, at least in black popular music, since the group's idiosyncrasy was the prominence of this device on all its recordings. Today Zapp is largely known through samples of its funk oeuvre, the group's most widely recognized tracks, "More Bounce to the Ounce" and "Dancefloor," appearing on a number of hip hop tracks. EPMD, for instance, built a career on sampling bits and pieces of Zapp bass lines, rhythms, and vocals; Zapp's leader, Roger Troutman, even lent his mechanized voice to Tupac Shakur's 1996 megahit, "California Love."[13] However, Zapp also left a mark on R&B with two luscious but now somewhat dated-sounding vocoder ballads, "Computer Love" and "I Want to Be Your Man."[14] These two ballads exert a more subtle influence than the hip hop samples redacted above but provide inspiration for the reemergence of the vocoder in R&B.

In contrast to most other tracks in the Zapp canon, "Computer Love" features not only the vocoderized voice of Roger Troutman but also the "human voices" of the Gap Band's Charlie Wilson and Zapp's longtime background singer Shelley Murdock, who enjoyed a brief solo career in the 1980s. "Computer Love" commences with a very deep vocoder vociferation of "computer love," followed by what sounds like simulated scratching and a vocoderized voice in a much higher key intoning, "computerized." Then we hear the higher machinic voice articulating the title in conjunction with Charlie Wilson, creating a dialogue between the two in which the "human" succeeds the "machinic." Once the verse commences, Wilson and Murdock's voices overlap (although Wilson dominates) until the lyrics make explicit references to informational technologies, such as "could it be your face I see on my computer screen" and "thanks to my technology," which are bolstered by the vocoder in the background, leading to a crescendo in which all three voices grow higher both in pitch and volume. The chorus consists mainly of the Troutman's vocoderized singing of: "Shoo-be-do-bop shoo-do-bop I wanna love you / shoo-be-do-bop computer love," reinforced by the "feminine" "sanging" of "I wanna love you baabeee."[15] The second verse follows the same trajectory as the first until the vocoder interrupts Wilson and Murdock to proclaim: "I want to keep you up tonight / you are such a sweet delight," which gives way to an additional female solo performance telling us that she "will cherish the memory of this night." After another chorus the song eschews "meaning" by simply repeating "computer love" or "digital love" for sonic effect rather than narrative closure; the feminine presence also evaporates from the sonic text. While the title indexes Kraftwerk's earlier cut of the same name, the two aural formulations' sonic similarity is scant. Although both share a slow tempo, Kraftwerk exploits its members' stereotypically Germanic voices to excavate the nonhuman and mechanical dimension of its "computer love," as opposed to Zapp, which wields both the vocoderized and human voices to unearth the "humanity" of machinic affections.[16] The Zapp track achieves this feat by drawing on the traditions of melismatic R&B singing and creating a three-way conversation, albeit an unequal one, between the male, female, and machinic utterances on the vocal track of the song. Overall, the lyrics of the tune fail to provide a clear picture of this computer love, which is so overbearing that it can only be expressed through the combined forces of female, male, and machinic voices. Although "a special girl" appears briefly in the words, mostly the repeated incantations of "computer love" are isolated, decoupled from merely serving as the conduit for anthropomorphic desire. If read/heard solely within the tradition of R&B love songs, "Computer Love" utilizes the vocoder to intensify the longing of the male subject, and even though this current is surely prominent here, the track also suggests desire for the machine itself by deferring a conclusive or coherent identification of its target. We might say by way of Gilles Deleuze and Felix Guattari that "Computer Love" sonically formulates the following dictum: "Desire and its object are one and the same thing: the machine as a machine of a machine. Desire is a machine, and the object of desire another machine connected to it."[17]

Where Zapp employs the vocoder as a forceful and poignant "index of technological audibility," thematizing technology conspicuously in the lyrics so that the vocoder bears an obvious mimetic relevance to the textual signification of the track, 702's "You Don't Know," emblematic of current vocoder use in R&B, fails to offer any definitive correlation between the vocoder and the textual content of the song.[18] The easy and techno-determinist explanation for this development lies in the large-scale shift from analog to digital technologies in musical (re)production during the fourteen years separating the two recordings. Such technologies enable producers to add "the vocoder effect" without the singers having to physically sing into a vocoder, transforming vocals into a portion of the many "zeroes and ones" that constitute the totality of a digitally produced sound recording.[19] "You Don't Know" comes from the female trio's eponymous 1999 album and encapsulates the sonic provenances of millennial R&B succinctly. Beginning with the obligatory "shout out" to the producers of the song, the Swedish duo Soulshock and Karlin, the mid-tempo cut deploys the cell phone effect throughout and melds musical syncopation with the rhythmic singing so popular in contemporary R&B. The vocoder effect weaves in and out of the sung verses, both in the main and background vocals, without any decisive connection to the signification of the lyrics. Some of the lyrics heard through the vocoder effect during the first half of the track include: "So why won't you tell me / Why you mean so much to me?"; "Now whata girl gotta do / To make you see"; "I want your love"; "Let me down, down (down)." A portion of these lines is repeated in different parts of the recording but not characterized by the vocoder effect, only adding to the indeterminate significance of this technique. During the final two minutes the vocoder effect rears its sonic head only once, supporting the central voice as it declares: "Just don't know." As a whole, the vocoder effect alters the function of the vocoder, even if the former shares a parasitical relationship with the latter, by dispersing the machinic across the musical text rather than giving it an integral and system-maintaining role. The vocoder effect deterritorializes the vocoder, becoming one production among many to process the "human" voice in contemporary black popular music. Ironically, the vocoder effect in black popular music amplifies the human provenances of the voice, highlighting its virtual embodiment, because it conjures a previous, and allegedly more innocent, period in popular music, bolstering the "soulfulness" of the human voice. Here, the "human" and "machinic" become mere electric effects that conjoin the human voice and (intelligent) machines.[20]

Surely desire serves as the central topos for all R&B, even if as in current formations it is desire for material objects rather than human subjects; nevertheless, it is always desire that has no "real" destiny. The vocoder and vocoder effect are literalizations of Deleuze and Guattari's "desiring-machines" in that they excavate the productive and machinic provenances of desire not chained by lack found in all R&B.[21] This productive force has no object, because the performance of desire in R&B is always one-sided, invariably a rumination by the effect of a desiring subject (the R&B singer) and not the desired subject or object. In addition, R&B desire is always already a desire of the second order: the performance of desire rather than desire as such.[22] Instead, the R&B desiring machine "does not lack anything; it does not lack its object. It is, rather, the *subject* that is missing in desire, or that desire lacks a fixed subject" (*Anti-Oedipus*, 26). In the move from the vocoder to the vocoder effect, the centrality of the human voice dissipates throughout the desiring machine that is R&B. Moreover, other clearly technological treatments of the voice, such as the cell phone effect, the presence of producers in the musical texts, and thematization of informational technologies in the lyrics aggregate to form the R&B desiring machine. The vocoderized voice highlights the machinic dimension of the R&B desiring machine by synthesizing all the other parts into a "sound machine, which molecularizes and atomizes, ionizes sound matter" (*Thousand Plateaus*, 343). Deleuze and Guattari continue this trajectory by claiming that "the synthesizer makes audible the sound process itself, the production of that process, and puts it in contact with still other elements beyond sound matter" (*Thousand Plateaus*, 343). The presence of speech-synthesizing devices in R&B intensifies the technological mediation of the recorded voice per se ("the sound process itself"), since it dodges the naturalism associated with the human voice in so many other popular music genres. In circumventing this naturalism, R&B imagines interpersonal relations and informational technologies as mutually constitutive rather than antithetical foils.

The title of this essay, "Feenin," comes from a 1993 track by the R&B group Jodeci, who were among the forerunners of today's hip hop–inspired black pop. "Feenin" deploys a vocoder to transmit only the word feenin in its chorus; the rest of the track is sung in a traditional, "human" R&B singing style. The term feenin derives from fiend, as in drug fiend, and Jodeci uses it to signify all-encompassing desire. The lyrics suggest an unequivocal link between the desire for a human love object and the feenin of a junkie, in lines like the following: "All the chronic [marijuana] in the world couldn't even mess with you/You're the ultimate high"; "Girl it's worse than drugs/ Cause I'm an addict of you"; "Surely girl, without a doubt/You know you got me strung out." Thus desire, in this scenario, refuses to signify any traditional humanist provenances, instead appearing in the guise of a self-generating addiction machine. Moreover, the shift from vocoder to vocoder effect is clearly audible on K-Ci and Jo Jo's 2001 single "Crazy" when compared with the earlier recording of these two former members of Jodeci.[23] Where "Feenin" wields the vocoder to emphasize one particular aspect of the lyrics, "Crazy" weaves the vocoder effect in and out of the musical text throughout without any particular correlation between form and content, recapitulating the difference between Zapp's and 702's mechanized enunciations. Thus the term feenin, as it is sung by a black vocoderized voice, might be more apt vis-à-vis contemporary R&B than desire, since it pushes desire to the extreme. In this extreme the human subject stands in for either a mind-altering substance—locating desire for a love object in the realm of neurochemical reactions— or desire is yoked to nonhuman objects such as cars and designer clothes—moving desire from the realm of the ideal to the crassly material. This feenin dissolves the parameters of the coherent subject in such radical ways that human—all too human— desire can be represented only in the guise of the machinic, and the human is thus inextricably intertwined with various informational technologies. Taken together, these factors recast the R&B "desiring machine" as a "feenin machine," which explosively sounds the passage from soul to hypersoul.

The virtual embodied in contemporary R&B follows neither the orbit of those that usually populate the annals of cybertheory nor Eshun's Afrofuturist ruminations; instead, R&B desiring and feenin machines reticulate the human voice with intelligent machines without assuming that "information has lost its body" or that any version of black posthumanism must take on an alien form. Because, for reasons I have outlined above, black cultural practices do not have the illusion of disembodiment, they stage the body of information and technology as opposed to the lack thereof. Where Eshun zeroes in on the antihumanist cultures of Afrofuturism, Hayles discusses the history of cybernetics and informatics as well as classical science fiction and cyberpunk narratives. Eshun provides a singular account of nonhumanist black popular music as it explosively interfaces with sound technologies, but in doing so he fails to take in the ramifications of these discourses in genres that do not explicitly announce themselves as Afrofuturist, such as R&B. Hayles's conclusions seem indicative of numerous studies of virtuality and/or cyberspace, where race is heard in a minor key, and computer-mediated communication is the sole melody of the song we know all too well: the virtual. I hope I have shown that any theory of posthumanism would benefit from making race central to its trajectory, not ancillary, as well as venturing beyond purely visual notions of subjectivity. At the very least this would diversify the purview of this newly burgeoning line of inquiry while rendering this field more interesting and less myopic. We could do far worse than turn the critical dial on our radio to those lower frequencies, where the sounds of black popular music, in the immortal vocoderized words of Zapp, are "still bubbalistic, realistic, supalistic/whatever is right for you/you can find it all on your radio."[24]

While both Hayles and Eshun seek to venture beyond the category of the human as personified by a white liberal humanist subject in order to advance versions of the posthuman, I think the historical and contemporary practices of the seemingly humanist strands of black popular music and their relation to informational technologies not only expand these two notions of the posthuman but are at the forefront of coarticulating the "human" with informational technologies. These segments of mainstream black popular music, particularly in regard to the status of recorded voices and the representations of soul and subjectivity they harbor, provide different circuits to and through the (post)human. Instead of dispensing with the humanist subject altogether, these musical formations reframe it to include the subjectivity of those who have had no simple access to its Western, post-Enlightenment formulation, suggesting subjectivities embodied and disembodied, human and posthuman. My final claim is modest, but I hope no less consequential: in proclaiming the historical moment of the posthuman, we might do well to interrogate "other humanities," and not just discard this category wholly, as Eshun does, or equate humanity with the white liberal subject, as in Hayles.[25] This way, we might actually begin to ameliorate the provinciality of "humanity" in its various Western guises as opposed to simply rehashing the same old stories ad infinitum.

Notes

1. I owe the cinema verité reference to Ira Livingston.
2. Missy Misdemeanor Elliot (featuring 702), "Beep Me 911," *Supa Dupa Fly* (Elektra, 1997).
3. Destiny's Child, "Bug-a-Boo," *The Writing's on the Wall* (Sony Music, 1999).
4. Blaque, "808" (Trackmasters/Columbia, 1999). The TR-808 is a drum machine produced by Roland. As Tricia Rose explains, "the Roland TR-808 is a rap drum machine of choice for its 'fat sonic boom,' because of the way it processes bass frequencies" (Tricia Rose, *Black Noise: Rap Music and Black Culture in Contemporary America* [Hanover, N.H.: New England University Press, 1994], 75). Rose cites several hip hop producers, who describe "the boom" of the TR-808 as its capacity for detuning and thereby distorting the bass sounds to make them more intense.
5. Ginuwine and Aaliyah, "Final Warning," *100% Ginuwine* (Blackground/Sony Music, 1999).
6. The Firm, "Phone Tap," *Nas Escobar, Foxy Brown, AZ, and Nature Present The Firm: The Album* (Aftermath/Interscope, 1997).
7. Destiny's Child, Joe, TLC, Aaliyah, Janet Jackson, 702, Jamelia, Kandi, Mya, Craig David, and Missy Elliot have all used this cell phone effect on recent recordings, as have teen pop acts N'Sync, Britney Spears, and the Backstreet Boys.
8. Scott Woods, "Will You Scrub Me Tomorrow," *Village Voice*, 13–19 December 2000 (villagevoice.com/issues/0050/woods.shtml). Woods focuses mainly on pop R&B artists; however, these technological tendencies can also be found in the more traditional strand of R&B, usually designated as "neoclassical soul," which summons the golden age of soul music. Maxwell, for instance, uses a voice distortion device on "Submerge," and at the end of D'Angelo's most recent album blips of all the preceding tracks are played backward so as to remind us that we are indeed listening to a technologically mediated recording (Maxwell, "Submerge," *Embrya* [Columbia/Sony Music, 1998] and D'Angelo, *Voodoo* [Virgin, 2000]).
9. Reynolds holds that R&B producers employ "anti-naturalistic studio techniques, . . . digitally processing vocals to make them sound even more mellifluous and diabetically ultra-sweet" (Simon Reynolds, "Feminine Pressure: 2-Step Garage [The Director's Cut, Plus Footnotes]," members.aol.com/blissout/ 2step.htm, 4). The main thrust of this article concerns the sonic permutations of the British genre known as 2-Step Garage or UK Garage, which often combines U.S.–style R&B and House with the speed and syncopation of Jungle. The vocally oriented spectrum of UK Garage pushes the uttered sensibilities of U.S. R&B to its provisional conclusion by dissecting sampled and/or sung vocal parts, radically recombining them in relation to the rhythm as opposed to the melody. Adopting a

term by Bat, Reynolds calls this messing up of the vocals "vocal science" (3). For an introduction to this particular strand of UK Garage, hear Artful Dodger's mix CD *Rewind* (London/Sire, 2001).

10.   This phrase comes from Jeremy Gilbert and Ewan Pearson. I have changed the wording somewhat—they use "index of visibility"—but only in the spirit of their ideas concerning the interdependence of music and technology (Jeremy Gilbert and Ewan Pearson, *Discographies: Dance Music, Culture, and the Politics of Sound* [New York: Routledge, 1999], 112).

11.   Cher's ubiquitous "Believe" (Warner, 1998) and Madonna's "Music" (Maverick/Sire, 2000) have made extensive use of the vocoder effect. In Cher's case, much of the success of the biggest hit of her thirty-year career was attributed to the vocoder. Janet Jackson, Kandi, 3LW, Dream, and N'Sync, among others, have all produced tracks that utilize this effect. Some electronic musicians, such as IB or Console, use voice-generating software that emulates "human" speech instead of processing "human" voices and credit these on their CDs. IB, for instance, attributes the vocals to several of the tracks on his *Pop Artificielle* album (Shadow, 2000) to the *raw*™ software.

12.   The cover of Herbie Hancock's 1978 album *Sunlight* (CBS), includes a special note on his VSM 201 Sennheiser vocoder, explaining that "the voices you hear are entirely synthesized." Kraftwerk's many uses of the vocoder can be heard on the greatest-hits CD *The Mix* (Elektra/Warner Brothers, 1991). For a general overview of electro classics, consult the compilations *Street Jams: Electric Funk*, parts 1 and 2 (Rhino, 1992). As an idea, synthesizing human voices can be traced back as far as the late eighteenth century, when Austrian phonetician Wolfgang von Kempelen constructed a device that mechanically approximated the human vocal apparatus. See James Lastra, *Sound Technology and the American Cinema: Perception, Representation, Modernity* (New York: Columbia University Press, 2000), 16–60; and "Wolfgang von Kempelen's and Subsequent Speaking Machines," www.ling.su.se/staff/hartmut/kemplne.htm. Twentieth-century speech synthesis took a big leap in 1939 when Homer Dudley, a research physicist at Bell Laboratories, developed two devices—Voder and Vocoder—that analyzed and synthesized human speech by electronic means. Later, these contraptions were further developed and linked to computer technology; however, it was not until the late sixties and seventies that they found their way into the musical productions of experimental artists such as Wendy Carlos and popular musicians like Kraftwerk. See "Homer Dudley's Speech Synthesizer," www.obsolete.com/120_years/machines/vocoder; "Multimedia Communications Research Laboratory,"www.bell-labs.com/org/1133/Heritage/Synthesis; "Vocoder," www.Riteh.hr/~markb/who/jmbg/vocoders/vocoder.htm.

13.   Commencing with EPMD's first hit, "You Got's to Chill," in 1986 this development continued through most of the duo's recorded output, wherein most albums contain one or more tracks that obviously sample Zapp.

14.   Zapp, "Computer Love," *The New Zapp IV U* (Warner Brothers, 1985) and Zapp and Roger, "I Want to Be Your Man," *Zapp and Roger: All the Greatest Hits* (1988; Reprise, 1993). Tricia Rose briefly glosses the difference between Zapp's vocoder use on these two ballads and its deployment by producer Dr. Dre on the Tupac track "California Love," which featured Roger Troutman's vocoderized presence. About "I Want to Be Your Man," she writes: "Troutman is using the vocoder on top of what some might consider to be pre-high-tech narratives of 'whole' 'unmediated' human relationships." Conversely, Dr. Dre uses "the vocoder (and sampling equipment more generally) to narrate mediated and fractured relationships" (Tricia Rose, "Sound Effects: Tricia Rose Interviews Beth Coleman," in Nelson, Tu, and Hines, *Technicolor: Race, Technology, and Everyday Life*, 142–53; 147).

15.   "Sanging," as opposed to just singing, emphasizes the highly performative and "emotional" vocal styles of black musical genres such as gospel or soul that underscore the physicality of "human" voice production. The distinction is crucial here, because the affective labor is carried out by the female voice in one of the only instances where Murdock's vocal apparatus does not merely serve to prop up the masculine and machinic voices but sounds by itself. This affective excess of the black female voice can also be heard in a crucial moment

of "I Want to Be Your Man," the other well-known Zapp vocoder ballad, where the male voice sings: "Words can never say how I feel." This crisis in linguistic meaning making is followed by a vocoderized "it's too intense," heightening the way in which desire disrupts the flow of language. Finally, we hear the female voice, in her only solo performance on this track, cooing, "oohooo ohooo oooooh," in effect eschewing linguistic meaning altogether. The female voice represents the nonlingual sonorousness needed to carry out the affective labor, which neither the male nor machinic voices can. Thus the female voice becomes the channel for the sonic representation of unmitigated desire.

16. Kraftwerk, "Computer Love," *The Mix* (Elektra/Warner Brothers, 1991).

17. Gilles Deleuze and Felix Guattari, *Anti-Oedipus: Capitalism and Schizophrenia*, trans. Robert Hurley, Mark Seem, and Helen R. Lane (Minneapolis: University of Minnesota Press, 1983), 26.

18. 702, "You Don't Know," *702* (Motown, 1999).

19. The vocoder effect, in contradistinction to the vocoder as a material entity, is indicative of the wider popular music landscape where most recordings apply this effect in similar ways.

20. See Gilles Deleuze and Felix Guattari, *A Thousand Plateaus: Capitalism and Schizophrenia*, trans. Brian Massumi (Minneapolis: University of Minnesota Press, 1987). Here is how Deleuze and Guattari imagine sonic deterritorialization: "It seems that when sound deterritorializes, it becomes more and more refined; it becomes more specialized and autonomous. . . . When sound deterritorializes, it tends to dissolve, to let itself be steered by other components" (347).

21. This is a reference to Deleuze and Guattari's anti-Freudian conception of desire that is not framed by a primary lack in the subject but functions as a productive force that brings the subject into being and fuels the social machine (*Anti-Oedipus*, 1–50).

22. Here I am not suggesting that desire can ever be formulated without being mediated by a host of material and discursive forces but that this particular machination of desire incorporates its own performativity.

23. K-Ci and Jo Jo, "Crazy" (MCA, 2001).

24. Zapp, "Radio People," *The New Zapp IV U*.

25. I am borrowing the phrase "other humanities" from the title of Lisa Lowe's talk delivered at the Humanities Institute, State University of New York, Stony Brook, March 2000.

Chapter 43

Adriana Cavarero

MULTIPLE VOICES

A voice means this: there is a living person, throat, chest, feelings, who
sends into the air this voice, different from all other voices.

—Italo Calvino, "A King Listens"

The Voice According to Calvino

IN ONE OF HIS LAST, INGENIOUS TEXTS, Italo Calvino leaves us the
extraordinary figure of a king who listens. Part of a collection dedicated to the five
senses, the king in question represents hearing. He is seated immobile on the throne,
ears pricked in order to intercept and decipher the sounds that surround him.
Besieged by the logic of his own power, the only activity of the monarch consists in an
acoustic control of the realm. In the palace, which, like "a great ear," has "pavilions,
ducts, shells, labyrinths," every sound is a sign of either fidelity or betrayal.[1] There are
many hidden spies to interpret: whispers, rumors, vibrations, crashes, oceans of
silence. Naturally, there are also human voices in the palace. But "every voice that
knows it is heard by the King acquires a cold glaze"; it becomes a courtly voice,
artificial, false—not so much for what it says, but in its very sonorous materiality. The
king who listens knows this, or better, he hears it [*lo sente*].

In keeping with a tradition that goes back to the ancient tyrant, Calvino's king is
prisoner of his own system. The logic is obsessive, violent, persecutory, and suspicious.
Because he is always threatened by his imminent overthrow, the king's power imposes
on him a vigilant insomnia. However, his vigilance is, in this case, exclusively auditory.
As if in a sonorous nightmare, the regal ear is amplified to a level of perception that is
as acute as it is impotent. The king can do nothing except listen, intercept sounds, and
try to interpret their meaning. The words, which are reduced to their sonorous
materiality as sounds among sounds, do not count for their semantic valence but only
for their phonic substance. Paying little attention to what the courtiers say, the king

spies on the vocal timbre of their voices, which is, again, artificial, false, "cold" like death. In fact, the throats of the court are no longer able to emit the true and unmistakable voice of life—namely, the voice that "involves the throat, saliva, infancy, the patina of experienced life, the mind's intentions, the pleasure of giving a personal form to sound waves."

One fine day, "when in the darkness a woman's voice is released in singing, invisible at the sill of an unlighted window," the insomniac king happens to hear her. And he is aroused; he finally remembers life and rediscovers in her voice an object for his long-lost desires. The king's new emotion certainly does not depend on the song she sings, which he had heard many times before; nor does it depend on the woman herself, whom he has never seen. Rather, Calvino explains, the king is "attracted by that voice as a voice, as it offers itself in song." What attracts him, in other words, is "the pleasure this voice puts into existing: into existing as voice; but this pleasure leads you to imagine how this person might be different from every other person, as the voice is different." In short, the king discovers the uniqueness of each human being, as it gets manifested in the uniqueness of the voice. In fact, he discovers something more: "the voice could be the equivalent of the hidden and most genuine part of the person," a sort of invisible, but immediately perceptible, nucleus of uniqueness. And this voice emerges from the world of the living that is outside the deadly logic of power. Thus, for the regal ear, it opens a horizon of perception whose existential status is totally opposed to that which confines him to the acoustic games of the palace. For it is no longer a matter of capturing and deciphering threatening sounds, but rather of enjoying the sound of the "vibration of a throat of flesh." Alive and bodily, unique and unrepeatable, overcoming with her simple sonorous truth the treacherous din of the realm, a woman sings. And the king listens, distracted from his obsessive vigilance.

Taking up the theme of the voice, Calvino's story offers a series of ideas that implicitly unsettles one of philosophy's cornerstones. Prior to the entrance of the woman who sings, we are dealing with a voice that emerges from a background of acoustic signals in which vocal emission does not occupy a special role with respect to the other sounds and noises of the palace. The identification of the king with the sense of hearing in fact reduces even the words pronounced by the human beings in the palace to pure sound. And here, precisely, Calvino's fundamentally antiphilosophical intuition springs into action. In contrast to what philosophy has done for centuries, the king-ear—motivated by the essential falsity of political discourse—concentrates on the vocal and ignores the semantic.

In the context of the palace, the vocal itself is a sign of the uncertain sounds of the palace. Not only are the words of the courtiers false, but their voices are false as well; in fact, they are concordant with the threatening noises of the entire system. As with the sound of a closing door, in these voices there is a cold and artificial sound. There is no life. Which means that the human voice—as it is perceived by the ear that lies at the center of power—becomes an acoustic sign among others, a depersonalized noise to be captured and decoded. The human source of these sonorous emissions reveals nothing that is particularly human, but rather dissolves into a general order of political acoustics that controls the realm.

In fact, the female voice that is capable of remaining such without confusing itself with noises, and that is therefore capable of revealing what is peculiarly human, comes from a place that is outside of the political. This revelation has absolutely no surprising characteristics. On the contrary, it concerns the most obvious aspect of what Hannah Arendt calls the human condition: namely, the uniqueness that makes of everyone a being that is different from all the others. "That voice certainly comes from a person, unique, inimitable like every person," observes Calvino. This uniqueness would be perceptible from the gaze as well; but, in centering the story on the sense of hearing and putting the woman who sings outside the window in the darkness, Calvino proceeds in his privileging of the acoustic sphere, pulling our attention to the voice. As long as the ear shows its natural talent for perceiving the uniqueness of a voice that is alone capable of attesting to the uniqueness of each human being, the one who emits that voice must remain invisible. Calvino's text is precise. No appearance of a face corresponds to the phonic emission. Sight does not even have the role of anticipating or confirming the uniqueness captured by the ear.

The king's ear, which is accustomed to the depersonalizing effect of the acoustic order of the realm, is obviously surprised by the message of this voice. As often happens with the ear of politics—and, for similar reasons, with the ear of philosophy— it rarely strains itself to perceive the voice of the human existent as unique. Symptomatically, what escapes it is precisely this "vibration of a throat of flesh" that repeats words with an unrepeatable voice. Put differently, what escapes it is the simple vocal self-revelation of the existence, which ignores every semantic interference. The typical freedom with which human beings combine words is never a sufficient index of the uniqueness of the one who speaks. The voice, however, is always different from all other voices, even if the words are the same, as often happens in the case of a song. This difference, as Calvino underlines, has to do with the body. "A voice means this: there is a living person, throat, chest, feelings, who sends into the air this voice, different from all other voices. . . . A voice involves the throat, saliva." When the human voice vibrates, there is someone in flesh and bone who emits it.

Uniqueness is not a characteristic of Man in general, but rather of every human being insofar as he or she lives and breathes. It is worth underscoring again that this corporal root of uniqueness is also perceptible by sight—that is, by an aspect that is immediately visible to whomever looks at the other's face. The sense of hearing that is privileged here by Calvino nonetheless transfers the perception of uniqueness from the corporal surface, from the face, to the internal body. The sense of hearing, characterized as it is by organs that are internalized by highly sensitive passageways in the head, has its natural referent in a voice that also comes from internal passageways: the mouth, the throat, the network of the lungs. The play between vocal emission and acoustic perception necessarily involves the internal organs. It implicates a correspondence with the fleshy cavity that alludes to the deep body, the most bodily part of the body. The impalpability of sonorous vibrations, which is as colorless as the air, comes out of a wet mouth and arises from the red of the flesh. This is also why, as Calvino suggests, the voice is the equivalent of what the unique person has that is most hidden and most genuine. This is not an unreachable treasure, or an ineffable essence, or still less, a sort of secret nucleus of the self; rather, it is a deep vitality of the unique being who takes pleasure in revealing herself through the emission of the voice. This revelation proceeds, precisely, from inside to outside, pushing itself in the air, with concentric circles, toward another's ear.

Importantly, even from a mere physiological point of view, this implies a relation. Taken in by the relationality of the vocal emission, which broadcasts itself to the outside, the other's ear is in fact able to perceive "the pleasure that this voice puts into existing: into existing as voice." "The pleasure of giving a personal form to sound waves," says Calvino, is part of vocal self-revelation. The emission is a kind of vital pleasure [*godimento*], an acoustically perceptible breath, where one models one's own sound revealing it to be unique.

In Calvino's story, this pleasure comes from the song of a woman. In a certain sense, this is a commonplace, or rather a stereotype full of misogynist overtones. One could easily think of the various myths that the western tradition has made of the seductive, carnal, primitive, feminine voice, which goes back at least to the Homeric Sirens, or to the misogynist interpretation of them that the tradition has passed down. The inimitable originality with which Calvino notably rereads the traditional image nevertheless opens the theme of the woman who sings onto some unforeseen perspectives. In contrast to the tradition from which it derives, in the context of Calvino's story, the feminine song does not celebrate the dissolution of the one who hears it into the primitive embrace of a harmonic orgy; rather, it reveals to the listener the vital and unrepeatable uniqueness of every human being.

On the other hand, it is clear that the voice heard by the king is a singing voice. Not only because the song exalts the voice and its potential, but above all because the exclusive attention of the king on the purely vocal, and not on the semantic, finds in the song its most natural place of expression. As Calvino's story puts it, the regal ear has heard this song too many times. And we do not learn its words, which have no importance anyway here. What attracts the king is precisely the "voice as a voice, as it offers itself in song." What is more, the king, won over by the pleasure of giving himself over to sound waves, is "infected by the pleasure of making itself heard" that this voice manifests. So he tries to engage in a duet with the feminine voice that calls him, so that his baritone voice might be with hers "together in the same intention of listening." As might be expected, of course, the unhappy king does not know how to sing. If he knew how to sing, says Calvino (speaking as narrator to the king), then "the man you are or have been or could be, the you that no one knows, would be revealed in that voice." The phonic emission exalted by the song, the voice that sends itself into the air and makes the throat vibrate, has a revelatory function. Or better, more than revealing, it communicates. What it communicates is precisely the true, vital, and perceptible uniqueness of the one who emits it. At stake here is not a closed-circuit communication between one's own voice and one's own ears, but rather a communication of one's own uniqueness that is, at the same time, a relation with another unique existent. It takes at least a duet, a calling and a responding—or, better, a reciprocal intention to listen, one that is already active in the vocal emission, and that reveals and communicates everyone to the other.

In this case, the other is a woman. She is the source, the beginning and the infectious origin of the pleasure and the desire for the song discovered by the king. Calvino thus has fun staging a rigorously heterosexual, operatic duet engaging in one of the most famous stereotypes of western culture. The misogynist aspects of such a scene are well known. Song is more suited for the woman than for the man, above all because it is up to her to represent the sphere of the body as opposed to the more important realm of the spirit. Symptomatically, the symbolic patriarchal order that identifies the masculine with reason and the feminine with the body is precisely an order that privileges the semantic with respect to the vocal. In other words, even the androcentric tradition knows that the voice comes from "the vibration of a throat of flesh" and, precisely because it knows this, it catalogs the voice with the body. This voice becomes secondary, ephemeral, and inessential—reserved for women. Feminized from the start, the vocal aspect of speech and, furthermore, of song appear together as antagonistic elements in a rational, masculine sphere that centers itself, instead, on the semantic. To put it formulaically: woman sings, man thinks.

It is thus understandable why, having reduced politics to a general acoustic order, Calvino performs a truly revolutionary gesture. The king who listens in fact occupies himself only with sounds and totally overlooks the semantic. There is no rational strategy in the power of the king who hears the polyphonic "rumble of death" emit from the realm and trembles at every noise for his own fate. Thus, while it assumes an unlikely acoustic form, politics does not lose its traditional characteristics: signs of death, traps, threats, falsities continue to innervate its logic. This very heritage nevertheless allows Calvino to carry out his revolutionary gesture and to bring it to even more interesting conclusions. Already (unusually) privileged over the semantic, the acoustic sphere doubles itself in the story. On the one hand, there is the confused, untrustworthy, lethal sound of the realm. On the other hand, there is the distinct, revelatory, and vital vocalization that comes from elsewhere, from a place that is precisely outside the political sphere. The fact that this "outside" is inhabited by a woman ends up being a kind of homage to the tradition, and yet it also poses a challenge to it. Indeed, the woman here does not represent the usual primitiveness of the extrapolitical sphere, but rather the genuine truth of a vocal that forces the political to account for itself in ways that it had not foreseen.

The tradition of interpreting sexual difference from the point of view of the semantic thus gets replaced by a perspective that reinterprets this difference from a vocal perspective. Through an obligatory homage to a tradition that wants the woman to be a corporal, singing, and apolitical creature, the revolutionary privileging of the phonic allows Calvino to signify in another way precisely these stereotypically feminine qualities. Indeed, now she appears on the scene in order to attest to the truth of the vocal, which—instead of being abstract like the truths postulated by reason—proclaims simply that every human being is a unique being, and is capable of manifesting this uniqueness with the voice, calling and infecting the other, and enjoying this reciprocal manifestation. In short, she attests to a rather quotidian, familiar truth of life—namely, the uniqueness and the relationality of human beings. In the context of Calvino's story, this truth comes into even sharper relief because it emerges against a background of sheer noise in a realm where the sounds of things and the voices of men have the same, essentially hostile, ontological status.

Indeed, the king, threatened by every sound, is quite alone. His solitude does not have the romantic tinge of the outsider who rebels against the logic of the system; on the contrary, he is at its center as its key component. It thus becomes crucial that the feminine voice of the song, in the act of revealing the uniqueness of the one who emits it, shows at the same time the relational valence of the vocal sphere. Destined for the ear of another, the voice implies a listener—or better, a reciprocity of pleasure. By breaking through the confines of his exclusively acoustic role, the king is in fact inspired to make of himself a source of sonority. Momentarily deaf to the din of the realm, he discovers a new world where human voices communicate to each other first of all their uniqueness. The scene is thus reversed: it is no longer a question of intercepting a sound and decoding or interpreting it, but rather of responding to a unique voice that signifies nothing but itself. There is nothing ulterior behind this voice that would make it into a mere sonorous vehicle, an audible sign.

Discovering that he has a body, that he has one life to live, the listening king sings. But, then, obviously he is no longer king, but rather a human being rooted in his fundamental ontological condition. The simple truth of the vocal makes the crown fall without anyone ever hearing the crash.

Preliminary Outline of the Theme of the Voice; or, Philosophy Closes Its Ears

Every voice "certainly comes from a person, unique, unrepeatable like every person," Calvino assures us. He calls our attention to what we might call a vocal phenomenology of uniqueness. This is an ontology that concerns the incarnate singularity of every existence insofar as she or he manifests her- or himself vocally. Ontology and phenomenology are, of course, just names (perhaps they are too technical, or too indulgent of a certain philosophical idiom) that indicate how the human condition of uniqueness resounds in the register of the voice. Moreover, the voice shows that this condition is essentially relational. The simple truth of the vocal, announced by voices without even the mediation of articulate speech, communicates the elementary givens of existence: uniqueness, relationality, sexual difference, and age—including the "change of voice" that, especially in men, signals the onset of puberty. There would therefore be any number of reasons for making the voice a privileged theme of a speculation on the problem of ontology. But, surprisingly, authoritative precedents for this kind of speculation are lacking.

In the literary and philosophical production of the west, strange as it may seem, Calvino's story is in fact one of the few texts that encourages an investigation into what the voice as such has to offer. This strange state of affairs is even more surprising today, not only if one considers a phenomenon that is obvious to any pair of ears, but above all if one takes into account the remarkable fortune that the theme of voice has found in contemporary discourse. The thematization of the voice that I will propose here begins by taking seriously Calvino's suggestions, while finding in the thought of late modernity a theoretical horizon that is at once promising and disappointing. On the one hand, in the twentieth century (especially in the last decades), the voice became a specific object of study for various currents of thought, which analyzed the vocal sphere from a number of interpretive perspectives. On the other hand, the simple fact of the uniqueness of voices, not to mention the relationality of the vocal sphere, gained very little attention in this wide range of studies. Today, as in the past, the tradition is reticent when it comes to that which is proper to the voice.

Anyone familiar with philosophy cannot help but be suspicious of this reticence. After all, it is a symptom of a problem that has to do with the philosophical affinity for an abstract and bodiless universality, and for the domain of a word that does not come out of any throat of flesh. Calvino helps us to identify the elementary terms of the question. The uniqueness of the voice is an incontrovertible given of experience, technologically proven by digital machines that can trace it; this is not a problem. The problem arises from the obstinate way in which philosophy not only ignores this given, but stands out among the disciplines for the force with which it renders the voice insignificant. The history of the voice's relegation to insignificance is long and complex. I will try, in the pages that follow, to reconstruct and explain this history in some detail. As a start, however, it will be useful to outline some general points.

First, there is a simple but crucial caveat. The philosophical tradition does not only ignore the uniqueness of the voice, but it also ignores uniqueness as such, in whatever mode it manifests itself. The unrepeatable singularity of each human being, the embodied uniqueness that distinguishes each one from every other is, for the universalizing tastes of philosophy, a superfluity. Uniqueness is epistemologically inappropriate. Discouraging as this may seem, this still does not by itself liquidate the thematic importance of the voice. After all, the voice is a central theme for a kind of knowledge that is inaugurated in Greece as the self-clarification of logos; and that after various (but coherent) developments throughout the millennia arrives in the twentieth century vis-à-vis the obsessive theme of language. If what is at stake in the term *logos*—a notoriously equivocal word that means, among other things, "language"—is "speech" [*parola*], then the "voice" also plays a part here. To put it formulaically, speech refers to speakers, and speakers refer to their voice. Plausible as it might seem, however, this is not the road taken by philosophy. Philosophy instead chooses a path that, through precise strategies, avoids getting caught up in the very question of the voice.

The basic strategy, which is the inaugural act of metaphysics, consists in a double gesture whereby speech is separated from speakers and finds its home in thought. Or, put differently, it finds its home in a mental signified of which speech itself, in its sonorous materiality, would be the expression—its acoustic, audible sign. The voice thus gets thematized as the voice in general, a sonorous emission that neglects the vocal uniqueness of the one who emits it. In this way, the voice in general turns into the phonetic component of language as a system of signification. In this semantic and depersonalized form, the voice becomes the specific object of a discipline that— while it takes the modern name *linguistics*—actually goes back at least as far as Plato's *Cratylus*. Over and beyond the acceleration of this trend (which is itself complicated and complex) over the course of the past century, it is in fact possible to trace the theoretical developments that bring modern linguistics to inherit from classical metaphysics a programmatic lack of attention to the uniqueness of the voice. This obviously does not diminish the legitimacy of linguistic studies, but rather testifies to the ways in which forms of knowledge dedicated to the phenomenon of speech are able to focus on the voice as such without ever dealing with the singularity of each voice. In other words, the voice—as it is studied from the perspective of language, and especially from the perspective of language as a system—becomes the general sphere of sonorous articulations where what is not heard is, paradoxically, the uniqueness of the sound. Language insofar as it is a code, whose semantic soul aspires to the universal, renders imperceptible what is proper to the voice. The plural uniqueness of voices does not form the background for the methodological filter of the linguistic ear.

In another totally different quarter, one finds the methodological filter of another modern discipline that focuses its attention explicitly on the voice. Because this discipline is articulated in many ways and mobilizes different categorical horizons—as does linguistics—I shall place it under the general rubric of studies dedicated to orality. These studies have the merit of making a certain theme clear: there is a realm of speech in which the sovereignty of language yields to that of the voice. I am talking, of course, about poetry.

Poets have always known this—and in a certain sense, no one has ever known this better than Plato—but the theorization of this phenomenon, the fact that poetry has become the object of a specific kind of research, is recent. The origins of this kind of research in the first decades of the twentieth century go back to the so-called Homeric question, and in particular to the role of epic in oral cultures that do not know writing or that use it only marginally. Indeed, the vast line of research that recuperates, for the theme of the voice, a specific horizon of inquiry gets its impetus precisely from a speculation on the difference between orality and writing—two categories that are destined to be central to twentieth-century thought. Given the importance of Homer for the genesis of this theoretical perspective, the accent falls above all on the centrality of the acoustic sphere in the bard's performance. It is the voice, with its sonorous rhythms, that organizes the words of the epic song. The semantic, not yet subservient to the congealed rules of writing, bends itself to the musicality of the vocal. Above all in epic poetry, but also in all poetry, the realm of sounds thus turns out to be the musical side of language, soliciting bodily pleasure.

This very relationship between vocal pleasure and poetry—foregrounded by studies on oral cultures—becomes a central theme of another type of theoretical approach, but one that is no less important or variegated, and one that calls on contemporary thought to explore the question of the voice. A constellation of perspectives, influenced by psychoanalysis, that valorize the pulsional and pre-semantic component of the acoustic sphere have taken their place alongside studies on orality. From these perspectives, the voice plays a subversive role with respect to the disciplining codes of language—and in fact turns out not only to organize poetic song but also the poetic text, if not the text in general and therefore writing as such. The voice appears this way, not so much as the medium of communication and oral transmissions, but as the register of an economy of drives that is bound to the rhythms of the body in a way that destabilizes the rational register on which the system of speech is built. These two perspectives—which are, of course, irreducible to two precise schools of thought—are not linked, and in many ways are quite heterogeneous. The former studies orality as it stands in opposition to writing, whereas the other privileges textuality as the realm that has its chief paradigm in writing. What they have in common, nevertheless, is a tendency to "rediscover," in a positive sense, the musical and seductive power of the voice that the metaphysical tradition—starting from Plato's famous hostility toward Homer—has constantly tried to neutralize.

The most significant part of the question lies, again, not only in the fact that these two perspectives share this "rediscovery" (at once antiplatonic and antimetaphysical), but, moreover, in the surprising fact that both perspectives are indifferent to the uniqueness of the voice. Even in those theories that focus on the corporal aspect of the voice—the hot rhythms of its emission, the pleasure of the throat and saliva—the plurality of unique voices still does not emerge as a matter worthy of note. Although it gets linked to deep drives and to the vitality of breath, and although it is seen as subverting or destabilizing the codes of language, the voice still remains a voice in general. Whether in studies on orality or in studies on the vocal nature of the text, there are still no voices that, in communicating themselves, communicate their uniqueness. Rather, there is only voice: a voice that is doubtless rooted in the fleshiness of the body, but a voice of everyone and no one. Unlike linguistics—where the voice becomes the scientific object of a cold analysis that understands it from the perspective of the semantic, in order to then incorporate the voice into a coherent system—here the voice challenges the coherence of that very system. Nevertheless, this attention to the bodily resonances does not open the ear to the vocalic revelation of singular bodies. The musicality of speech, or as Calvino would say, the pleasure of giving one's own form to the sound waves, once again fails to be tuned into the plurality of voices, each one different from the other, that make up the symphony.

The relegation to insignificance that metaphysics reserves for uniqueness therefore continues to function as the unheard background of even those theories that, in principle, seek to use the voice against a writing or a language that is seen as metaphysical. The question before us is therefore, again, even more paradoxical if one takes into account the increasing number of disciplines that take the voice as an object of study. The more that the voice turns out to be a question worthy of inquiry, the more the usual deafness with respect to singular voices appears surprising.

Even those studies that claim to be novel in this regard suffer the same fate, although this time, the specific object of research gets called the *order of the vocal*. This expression was coined by Paul Zumthor, an authoritative medievalist who has broadened the horizons opened by the early studies on orality. Zumthor does not fail to point out, among other things, that "it is strange that, among all our institutional disciplines, there does not yet exist a science of the voice."[2] Attempting to remedy this state of affairs, Zumthor proposes a distinction between orality and vocality: he defines *orality* as "the functioning of the voice as the bearer of language" and *vocality* as "the whole of the activities and values that belong to the voice as such, independently of language."[3] The original aspect of vocality, as a new object of study, therefore concerns an analysis of the voice that avoids the traditional privileging of its relationship with language. It thus opens broad, divergent horizons for understanding the phenomenon of the voice—so broad and divergent, in fact, that the list of disciplines it would comprehend includes, as a start, philosophy, cultural anthropology, the history of music, phonetics, psychology, cybernetics, and ethnology, if not studies on orality and communication.[4] It is precisely the voice as voice, in its multiple manifestations, that orients an investigation that recuperates—but also puts into crisis—the specificity of various canonical disciplines. Significantly, though, even here the uniqueness of the voice remains essentially uninvestigated. Even though this line of research is dedicated to challenging the dominion of language, the voice of vocality insists on presenting itself as a voice in general.

In addition to being extremely interesting, studies dedicated to vocality are above all important because they bring to light a fundamental theoretical bond: namely, the bond between voice and speech. The voice is sound, not speech. But speech constitutes its essential destination. What is therefore at stake in any inquiry into the ontology of the voice—where uniqueness and relationality come to the fore—is a rethinking, without metaphysical prejudices, of this destination. The fundamental prejudice concerns the tendency to totalize this destination so that, outside speech, the voice is nothing but an insignificant leftover. When the register of speech is totalized—for instance, when it is identified with a language system of which the voice would be a mere function—it is indeed inevitable that the vocal emission not headed for speech is nothing but a remainder. Rather than a mere leftover, however, what is really at stake is an originary excess. Put another way, the sphere of the voice is constitutively broader than that of speech: it exceeds it. To reduce this excess to mere meaninglessness—to whatever remains when the voice is not intentioned toward a meaning, defined as the exclusive purview of speech—is one of the chief vices of logocentrism. This vice transforms the excess of the voice into a lack. Indeed, speech becomes more than an essential destination for the voice; it becomes a divider that produces the drastic alternative between an ancillary role for the voice as vocalization of mental signifieds and the notion of the voice as an extraverbal realm of meaningless emissions that are dangerously bodily, if not seductive or quasi-animal. In other words, logocentrism radically denies to the voice a meaning of its own that is not always already destined to speech. It is thus understandable why, as Zumthor points out, the perspective that cuts out for vocality its own autonomous investigation into "the whole of the activities and values that are proper to the voice, independently of language" is crucial. And it is moreover understandable why, between the two roots of western culture—Hebrew and Greek—it is symptomatically the first that nurtures the challenge that a vocal ontology of uniqueness poses to logocentrism.

This challenge—which is essentially the aim of this book [see original publication]—is ambitious but simple. In elementary terms, it consists in thinking of the relationship between voice and speech as one of uniqueness that, although it resounds first of all in the voice that is not speech, also continues to resound in the speech to which the human voice is constitutively destined. The vocal communication of uniqueness, although it inheres exclusively in the register of sound, in fact ends up being essential to that destination. Meaning—or, better, the relationality and the uniqueness of each voice that constitutes the nucleus of this meaning—passes from the acoustic sphere to speech. Precisely because speech is sonorous, to speak to one another is to communicate oneself to others in the plurality of voices. In other words, the act of speaking is relational: what it communicates first and foremost, beyond the specific content that the words communicate, is the acoustic, empirical, material relationality of singular voices.

All that needs to be understood, obviously, is the meaning of the term *speech* [*la parola*]. Because of a complex series of events having to do with the history of metaphysics, in the modern lexicon, *speech* is indeed an ambiguous and equivocal name that often ends up indicating the general idea of the verbal sphere instead of indicating a contingent, contextual sonorous articulation that emits from the mouth of someone and that is destined for the ears of another. The result of all this is the mystification of a phenomenon that is as obvious as it is essential: there is speech because there are speakers. Philosophy's strategic deafness to the plural, reciprocal communication of voices depends precisely on the methodological decision, so to speak, to ignore the elementary materiality of this phenomenon. This method— which is metaphysical in nature, but which also informs various disciplines—consists in thematizing speech while neglecting the vocality of the speakers. The uniqueness of the voice thus goes unnoticed because, methodologically, it does not make a sound. Cut off from the throats of those who emit it, speech undergoes a primary devocalization that leaves it with only the depersonalized sound of a voice in general.

In order to contest the effects of this devocalization, it is thus necessary to adopt another method—a method that takes inspiration from Calvino's story instead of from the texts of the history of philosophy. This method is faithful to the vocal phenomenology of uniqueness, and it consists in listening to speech as it resounds in the plurality of voices who—each time and always addressing themselves to one another—speak. In a certain sense, therefore, this second method functions as a kind of reversal, if not a deconstruction, of the first. It seeks to understand speech from the perspective of the voice instead of from the perspective of language. Speech, understood as speech that emits from someone's mouth, is not simply the verbal sphere of expression; it is also the point of tension between the uniqueness of the voice and the system of language. Privileging either one over the other radically changes the interpretive axes of the theoretical frame. This might seem an easy gesture, or simply a reversal of perspective, but the broader range of contemporary studies on the voice suggests that things are not so simple. Even to thematize the voice as voice—or, if one wants, as "vocality"—does not guarantee any restitution of meaning to the phenomenon of vocal uniqueness. One must have the prudence and the patience to beat down the metaphysical filter that for millennia has blocked our listening. Rather than simply vindicating an independence of the vocal order with respect to language, it is therefore a matter of recording the strategies that allowed the "pole" of language (or, better, its totalization) to neutralize the plurality of voices that constitute the other "pole" of speech. That which is proper to the voice does not lie in pure sound but rather in the relational uniqueness of a vocal emission that, far from contradicting it, announces and brings to its destination the specifically human fact of speech.

In another quarter, there are the writings of Roland Barthes, whose reflections on vocality and textuality have exerted considerable influence on contemporary thought. According to Barthes, what is proper to the voice is what he calls its *grain*. Rather than appertain to breath, the voice concerns "the materiality of the body that springs from the throat, there where the phonic metal is forged."[5] His attention, in short, falls on the oral cavity, the quintessential erotic locus. The grain of the voice has to do above all with the way in which the voice, through the pleasure of sonorous emission, works in language. What interests Barthes is "song" as a primary place of phonic and musical texture from which language grows. Indeed, he underscores that "the voice, which is the bodily aspect of speaking, is situated in the articulation of the body and of discourse," at the point of their exchange.[6] The task of the voice is therefore to be a pathway, or better, a pivotal joint between body and speech. Symptomatically, again, Barthes does not write of a body whose singularity is foregrounded, nor of a voice whose uniqueness is given any importance. Rather, the grain refers to a body of the voice and should be understood as "the way in which the voice lies in the body—or in which the body lies in the voice."[7] But here both body and voice are still presented as general categories. Indeed, in Barthes' writing, the voice and the body are categories of a depersonalized pleasure in which the embodied uniqueness of each existent (something that Barthes never thematizes) is simply dissolved along with the general categories of the subject and the individual. In other words, Barthes encourages us to focus on a vocality that far from being a pure and simple sonority, or a mere bodily remainder, consists in a power relating to speech. And, at the same time, he discourages every perspective that would find in uniqueness and in relationality the fundamental sense of this power.

It is not enough to tune into the sonority, into bodily pleasure, into the song of the flesh, or into the rhythmic drives from which this song flows; this attunement alone will not suffice to pull speech itself from the deadly grip of logocentrism. The metaphysical machine, which methodologically negates the primacy of the voice over speech, should be dismantled by transforming this primacy into an essential destination—and by keeping in mind that the metaphysical strategy that neutralizes the power of the voice is also a strategy in which the spoken exchange of "more than one voice" [*à piu voci*], each one different from the other, remains unheard for millennia. This inability to listen has many pernicious consequences. For example, it makes it so that even those philosophies that value "dialogue" and "communication" remain imprisoned in a linguistic register that ignores the relationality already put in action by the simple reciprocal communication of voices. To thematize the primacy of the voice with respect to speech, in fact, also means opening new directions for a perspective that not only focuses on a primary and radical form of relation that is not yet captured in the order of language, but that is moreover able to specify this relation as a relation among uniquenesses. This, and only this, is the meaning that the vocalic sphere consigns to speech, inasmuch as speech is its most essential destination. And this is a meaning that, through speech, moves from ontology to politics.

Notes

1.   All citations from "A King Listens" are taken from Italo Calvino, *Under the Jaguar Sun,* trans. William Weaver (New York: Harcourt Brace, 1988), 33–64. The privileging of the acoustic sphere and the importance in the story of a woman who sings are not coincidences. In its original form, Calvino's story is in fact the reelaboration of a text explicitly adapted by Calvino for a work of musical theater by Luciano Berio, which bears the same title. The project, which was developed between 1979 and 1983, was taken forward by Berio and Calvino independently; the libretto in three acts sketched out by the writer was only used in part. *A King Listens*—musical action in the texts of Calvino, Auden, Gotter, and Berio— debuted in 1984 at the Salzburger Festspiele under the direction of Lorin Maazel.

2.   Paul Zumthor, *Oral Poetry: An Introduction,* trans. Kathryn Murphy-Judy (Minneapolis: University of Minnesota Press, 1990), 44.

3.   Paul Zumthor, preface to Corrado Bologna, *Flatus vocis: Metafisica e antropologia della voce* (Bologna: Il Mulino, 2000), vii.

4.   See Bologna, *Flatus vocis,* xiii and passim. The book, edited for the first time in 1992, is, according to Zumthor himself, who wrote the preface, an exemplary and pioneering text for the study of vocality. Although insisting on the physical and bodily nature of the voice, Bologna nevertheless means by voice something like the potentiality of signification, "a confused push towards *meaning,* towards *expression,* that is towards *existing*" (23). (This expression is taken, to the letter, from Zumthor, who writes that "the voice is in fact *vouloir-dire* and the will to exist"; *Oral Poetry,* 7.) Precisely this push to signification, or to the end of which the voice would be a potentiality, thus ends up keeping the vocal bound to the decisive category of speech. This is the criticism that Vicenzo Cuomo makes of Corrado Bologna. See Cuomo, *Le parole della voce; Lineamenti di una filosofia della phonè* (Salerno: Edisud, 1998), 52. Other works in Italian on this topic include an anthology of texts that analyze the voice from different disciplinary perspectives, generating a number of suggestions but also a certain confusion. It can be found in a collection called *Fonè: La voce e la traccia,* ed. Stefano Mecatti (Florence: La casa Husher, 1985). Finally, it is symptomatic that in order to find a text in recent Italian writings that is dedicated to the uniqueness of the voice, one must turn to a literary text: *Voci* by Dacia Mariani (Milan: Rizzoli, 1994).

5.   Roland Barthes (in collaboration with Roland Havas), "Ascolto," in *Enciclopedia Einaudi* (Turin: Einaudi, 1977), 1:247.

6.   Ibid.

7.   Ibid., 1:272.

Chapter 44

Jacob Smith

LAUGHING MACHINES

THE RECORDED LAUGH HAS SERVED as a suture between audience and mass-produced media. Similarly, the laugh track was used to locate the isolated viewer in a constructed social context via the social nature of laughter. But reactions to the laugh track often drifted from the comic to the uncanny, further revealing the nature of laughter and its role in authenticating media texts. I would now like to discuss the nature of this uncanny reaction and its relation to the "laughing machine" apparatus.

Despite flurries of interest in the popular press, the apparatus and production techniques behind the laugh track were kept an industry secret and are notable by their absence. Industry magazines like *Broadcasting* and *Television* all but ignored the issue in the 1950s, despite long tirades about it in the popular press. In a 1953 article in *Variety*, Marc Daniels, the director of *I Married Joan*, noted that "laughs can be dubbed in, using chuckle tracks, laugh tracks, yock tracks or boff tracks in various combinations. . . . Why do there have to be laughs? Well . . . that is a highly controversial subject. Let's skip it" (Daniels 1953, 37). Similarly, a TV sound engineer in a 1957 *Time* article would only discuss the laugh track anonymously, "so furtive" was "the whole industry . . . about canned laughter" ("Can the Laughter" 1957). In 1959, the *Saturday Review* followed sound engineer Maxwell Russell on his job providing the laugh track for the *Sid Caesar Show*. The article describes the secretive and isolated nature of this work:

> No one in charge gave him any instructions on how to integrate the laugh machine into the program. He followed the rehearsals, marked his script according to his own hunches on where the laughs would or should come. The director did not even acknowledge his presence. It was as if he were not there. (Shayton 1959, 44)

The mystique of the laughing machine, or "Laff Box" as it was called in the industry, remained intact well into the 1960s. A 1966 *TV Guide* article described how

> if the Laff Box should start acting strangely, the Laff Boys wheel it into the men's room, locking the door behind so that no one can peek. . . . Everybody and his brother has a theory about what's inside. But mention the name "Charley Douglas" [inventor of the Laff Box] and it's like "Cosa Nostra"—everybody starts whispering. It's the most taboo topic in TV.(Hobson 1966, 4)

Coupled with this aura of secrecy, the laugh track, although introduced to a public familiar with the idea of recorded voices, seems to have been considered eerie and uncanny from the very beginning of its existence. This was the case even with professionalTV technicians:"Fellow technicians strolled over to look at the mechanical laughter, shuddered, and said they were glad they weren't operating it" (Shayton 1959, 44). One of the main means by which people expressed their sense of the uncanny nature of the laugh track was by noting that many of the people heard laughing were now dead:

> People who once, in a moment of abandon, guffawed at Stoopnagle and Budd can, without knowing it, hear their youthful follies repeated as the background for a TV film. Fred Allen, for one, can never help thinking that much of the merriment is being made by folk long dead. ("Strictly for Laughs" 1955, 46)

TV writer Larry Gelbart stated, "It's a standing joke, of course, that most of those people on the laugh track are dead now." He went on to paint a picture of laughing souls trapped in a televisual purgatory: "They laughed those laughs years ago and they'll never be allowed to stop, never" (1984, 17). Something about the recorded laugh seems to have brought these thoughts readily to mind, even to people immersed in more than a half-century of recorded sound.

Why was the recorded laugh felt to be so powerfully disturbing? For Bergson, laughter is a social sanction against frame rigidity and mechanical behavior. When someone acts like a machine, we laugh. But, following Freud's essay on the uncanny, this same ambiguity between human and machine is an important source of our experience of the uncanny. Freud began his essay by quoting Jentsch on the uncanny's link to "doubts whether an apparently animate being is really alive; or conversely, whether a lifeless object might not in fact be animate," and referring to "the impression made by wax-work figures, artificial dolls and automatons" (1997, 132). The laugh machine could similarly blur the lines between living presence and inanimate machine. In articles criticizing the laugh track and filmed television more generally, Jack Gould described practices like lip-synching that combine live and taped as zombie-like: "phony TV with performing half-breeds— half-live and half-dead, the zombies of show business" (Gould 1956, 27). A taped laugh track along with animate (although taped) performers forces the viewer to recognize these kinds of layers of presence. Freud's inclusion of epilepsy as a source of the uncanny also suggests that the spasm-like nature of laughter is prime for the production of such an effect: "These excite in the spectator the feeling that automatic, mechanical processes are at work, concealed beneath the ordinary appearance of animation" (1997, 132). The often-stated uncanniness of the laugh track, then, reveals how the spasmodic nature of the laugh, so often read as an index for the human, can just as easily appear mechanical.

For Freud, the uncanny is particularly tied to the involuntary return to the same situation, something of particular pertinence to the experience of the laugh track because of its nature as a tape loop: we hear the same laughs again and again (1997, 144). Indeed, the laugh track apparatus is an unlikely precursor to the tape-loop performances in modern avant-garde and popular music, even a kind of proto-sampler:

> [The laugh machine is] about the size of a fat suitcase standing up. Behind thin, hardware-drawer panels, small reels of tape revolve in perpetual three- to six-and-one-half-second loops. Each reel is marked to describe this specific kind of laughter it provides. The control panel is a small wood block with ten buttons, five stop and five go. Press the go button and the machine keeps repeating the appropriate laugh cycle ad infinitum. Press stop and the laugh stops at the completion of the brief cycle. (Shayton 1959, 44)

Musical analogies occurred to writers who saw the machine in action, and they repeatedly noted its "organ-like" appearance: "The engineer plays his machine like an organ, rehearses right along with the cast, tailors the laughs snugly to the lines" ("Can the Laughter" 1957, 40).[1] Charley Douglas, the man credited with creating the machine, is portrayed as playing "an organlike mechanism with six keys that when played with the left hand, can provide small chuckles, medium chuckles, small laughs, medium laughs, medium heavy laughs, and rollin'-in-the-aisles boffs" ("Strictly for Laughs" 1955, 46). The similarity to a musical instrument is heightened in descriptions of the machine that refer to chords, and themes:

> Using chords, the player can provide some 100 variations on these six basic themes; and his right hand can control the volume. Jess Oppenheimer, producer of "I Love Lucy," has another machine, dubbed the Jay-O Laughter, which he claims can produce 100 different kinds of laughs on each of its six keys. ("Strictly for Laughs" 1955, 46)

In his 1966 article, Hobson neatly combined the uncanny and the musical:

> Picture if you will Lon Chaney Sr. in "Phantom of the Opera" flailing at the pipe organ in the darkened cathedral crypt and you have some notion of the Laff Boy at work. Hunched over the keyboard of Charley's box on the darkened dubbing stage, his fingers punching at the keys, his feet manipulating the pedals, he wrings forth his fugues and caprices. He's a veritable virtuoso of titters and snorts. (Hobson 1966, 4)

These musical comparisons also underscored the fact that laying down the laugh track was a performance that relied on skill, timing, and taste:

> When the lights come up, the Laff Boy is frequently drenched in sweat. . . .
> The trick of the Laff Boy's trade is timing. . . . To manufacture a natural-
> sounding laugh, the Laff Boy must let a few "people" in his box anticipate
> a joke. This is called "giving it a little tickle." Then he might punch in a
> "sharpie" just before the main laugh. . . . Gags frequently build, each
> capping the last, so the Laff Boy must likewise build and hold his biggest
> laugh for the pay-off. (Hobson 1966, 6)

Compare this intricate and subtle performance with the degree of manipulation of
the live studio audience discussed above, and it becomes even harder to declare one
more authentic than the other.

The keyboard design of the Laff Box reveals a morphological resemblance that
helps to place it in a historic lineage that begins with Faber's laughing Turk. Moving
forward in time, it can be placed with other contemporary machines that used tape
loops like the chamberlain and the mellotron. The keyboards of these instruments
triggered recorded loops of instruments playing the notes of the scale. The mellotron
was state-of-the-art studio technology in the 1960s, and the haunting sound of its
flute setting can be heard on Beatles recordings like "Strawberry Fields Forever."
Indeed, the Beatles' recording of "Tomorrow Never Knows," which has been heralded
for its use of swirling psychedelic tape loops, pays an unconscious tribute to the
laughing machine: the loop vaguely reminiscent of the sound of seagulls is a speeded-up
recording of Paul McCartney laughing.[2]

The debate over the laugh track didn't end in the 1960s, as the comments and
career of television writer Larry Gelbart illustrate. A vehement opponent of laugh
track, Gelbart rearticulated the belief in the individual nature of laughter: "Laughter
is a very personal act. It has to start with the individual, although it can end up a
group experience. But first, it has to work for you; then you can work in a crowd"
(Gelbart 1998, 184). Gelbart reluctantly agreed to allow the laugh track on his series
M*A*S*H, but after the success of that show, Gelbart had the clout to produce his
new program, *United States*, without it:

> [We] did away with the laugh track, rejecting outright the suggestion to
> the viewer that there were three hundred people living in the same house
> as our couple, going from room to room with them and laughing their
> heads off at their intimate and/or hilarious exchanges. (1998, 94)

His rejection of the laugh track went hand in hand with his insistence that this new
series was more personal and autobiographical than anything else he had ever done.
As has often been the case with television comedy, artistic aspiration is indexed by the
lack of the laugh track.

The Laff Box and the laugh track can be placed in the context of the practices and
discourses surrounding the recorded laugh that I have traced through various media
of the past century. The use of the laugh track to simulate social experience and so
suture the audience to the prerecorded text, the uncanny experience of the Laff Box,
and the assertion that laughter is a quintessentially individual expression all illustrate
how laughter has been regarded as a powerful index for authentic human presence in

the production and reception of mass media. Returning to the scene in Steven Spielberg's *A.I.*, described in my introduction [see original publication], one can see that the laugh continues to be used to test the boundaries between the human and the mechanical. The android David's laugh works in similar ways as the media texts I have analyzed above, slipping from the human to the mechanical, from the social to the individual, from the comic to the uncanny.

Laughter has consistently been mobilized as a barometer for the authentically human, a choice that is not without consequences. Holding up laughter as the definition of the self-motivated and individual is problematic in light of its inherently social and spasmodic nature. If laughter is so connected to instinct, spasm, and the social, then its identification as a citadel of the individual self is already compromised: the raw, living laugh and the cooked recording become harder to disentangle. The anxiety about the laugh track demonstrates the potentially disturbing nature of blurring these boundaries and the difficulty of defining both the human and the mechanical, the can and the canned, in the context of modern mass media.

Notes

1. The remarkably wide range of terms used for laughter in the 1950s suggests that stage professionals perceived it in shades of nuance of an almost musical quality. Take, for example, a *Variety* article in which Ray Bolger described the limited range of laughter on the laugh track:

   > These laugh tracks have practically put the titter and the smirk and the smile and the grin out of show business. . . . I can recall when varying shades of humor actually produced giggles and chuckles as well as guffaws. But that was before TV comedy shows were filmed. Now you hear nothing but boffs. (Bolger 1954, 98)

2. Recorded loops of laughter have sometimes been used in popular music not to smooth over the mechanical nature of recording technology but to draw attention to it. For example, a number of recordings by techno artists feature the loop of a female laugh. At first, the looped laugh seems to present an authentic human expression in the context of an extremely technological musical production. But as this laugh is played and replayed, the spasm of laughter is bled of any sense of spontaneity, becoming increasingly mechanical and uncanny. See for example, Rhythm Is Rhythm's 1987 recording "Nude Photo," a title that obliquely reestablishes the connection between the performed laugh and other mediated body genres.

References

Bolger, Ray. 1954. The last laugh track. *Variety*, July 28, 98.
Can the laughter. 1957. *Time*, February 18, 38-39.
Daniels, Marc. 1953. Approximating live TV. *Variety*, July 29, 37.
Freud, Sigmund. 1997. *Writings on art and literature*. Stanford University Press.
Gelbart, Larry. 1984. *Larry Gelbart seminars at the Museum of Broadcasting*. Museum of Broadcasting, October.

——. 1998. *Laughing matters*. New York: Random House.

Gould, Jack. 1956. Live TV vs. canned. *New York Times Magazine*, February 5, 27.

Hobson, Dick. 1966. The Hollywood Sphinx and his Laff Box. *TV Guide*, July 2, 3–6.

Shayton, Robert Lewis. 1959. Laugh, soundman, laugh. *Saturday Review*, April 18, 44.

Strictly for laughs. 1955. *Newsweek*, January 10, 46.

Chapter 45

Mladen Dolar

THE LINGUISTICS OF THE VOICE

THE VOICE APPEARS TO BE THE MOST familiar thing. When I say "voice," when I use this word without further qualification, then the most immediate thing that comes to mind is no doubt the most usual one: the omnipresent use of the voice in our everyday communication. We use our voices, and we listen to voices, at every moment; all our social life is mediated by the voice, and situations where reading and writing actually take over as the medium of our sociability are, all things considered, much less common and limited (the Internet notwithstanding), even though, in a different and less tangible sense, our social being depends very much on the letter, the letter of the law—we will come back to that. We constantly inhabit the universe of voices, we are continuously bombarded by voices, we have to make our daily way through a jungle of voices, and we have to use all kinds of machetes and compasses so as not to get lost. There are the voices of other people, the voices of music, the voices of media,[1] our own voice intermingled with the lot. All those voices are shouting, whispering, crying, caressing, threatening, imploring, seducing, commanding, pleading, praying, hypnotizing, confessing, terrorizing, declaring . . . —we can immediately see a difficulty into which any treatment of the voice runs: namely, that the vocabulary is inadequate. The vocabulary may well distinguish nuances of meaning, but words fail us when we are faced with the infinite shades of the voice, which infinitely exceed meaning. It is not that our vocabulary is scanty and its deficiency should be remedied: faced with the voice, words structurally fail.

All those voices rise over the multitude of sounds and noises, another even wilder and wider jungle: sounds of nature, sounds of machines and technology. Civilization announces its progress by a lot of noise, and the more it progresses the noisier it gets. The dividing line between the two—voice and noise as well as nature and culture—is often elusive and uncertain. We have already seen in the Introduction [see original publication] that the voice can be produced by machines, so that there opens a zone of undecidability, of a between-the-two, an intermediacy, which will be, as we shall see, one of the paramount features of the voice.

Another dividing line separates voice from silence. The absence of voices and sounds is hard to endure; complete silence is immediately uncanny, it is like death, while the voice is the first sign of life. And that division as well, the one between the voice and silence, is perhaps more elusive than it seems—not all voices are heard, and perhaps the most intrusive and compelling are the unheard voices, and the most deafening thing can be silence. In isolation, in solitude, in complete loneliness, away from the madding crowd, we are not simply free of the voice—it can be that this is when another kind of voice appears, more intrusive and compelling than the usual mumbo-jumbo: the internal voice, a voice which cannot be silenced. As if the voice were the very epitome of a society that we carry with us and cannot get away from. We are social beings by the voice and through the voice; it seems that the voice stands at the axis of our social bonds, and that voices are the very texture of the social, as well as the intimate kernel of subjectivity.

The Voice and the Signifier

Let us start by considering the voice as it appears in this most common use and in its most quotidian presence: the voice which functions as the bearer of an utterance, the support of a word, a sentence, a discourse, any kind of linguistic expression. So let us first approach our object through the linguistics of the voice—if such a thing exists.

The moment we start looking at it more closely, we can see that even this most commonplace and ordinary use is full of pitfalls and paradoxes. What singles out the voice against the vast ocean of sounds and noises, what defines the voice as special among the infinite array of acoustic phenomena, is its inner relationship with meaning. The voice is something which points toward meaning, it is as if there is an arrow in it which raises the expectation of meaning, the voice is an opening toward meaning. No doubt we can ascribe meaning to all kinds of sounds, yet they seem to be deprived of it "in themselves," independent of our ascription, while the voice has an intimate connection with meaning, it is a sound which appears to be endowed in itself with the will to "say something," with an inner intentionality. We can make various other sounds with the intention of signifying something, but there the intention is external to those sounds themselves, or they function as a stand-in, a metaphoric substitute for the voice. Only the voice implies a subjectivity which "expresses itself" and itself inhabits the means of expression.[2] But if the voice is thus the quasi-natural bearer of the production of meaning, it also proves to be strangely recalcitrant to it. If we speak in order to "make sense," to signify, to convey something, then the voice is the material support of bringing about meaning, yet it does not contribute to it itself. It is, rather, something like the vanishing mediator (to use the term made famous by Fredric Jameson for a different purpose)—it makes the utterance possible, but it disappears in it, it goes up in smoke in the meaning being produced. Even on the most banal level of daily experience, when we listen to someone speak, we may at first be very much aware of his or her voice and its particular qualities, its color and accent, but soon we accommodate to it and concentrate only on the meaning that is conveyed. The voice itself is like the Wittgensteinian ladder to be discarded when we have successfully climbed to the top—that is, when we have made our ascent to the peak of meaning. The voice is the instrument, the vehicle, the medium, and the meaning is the goal. This gives rise to a spontaneous opposition where voice appears as materiality opposed to the ideality of meaning. The ideality of meaning can emerge only through the materiality of the means, but the means does not seem to contribute to meaning.

Hence we can put forward a provisional definition of the voice (in its linguistic aspect): it is *what does not contribute to making sense*.[3] It is the material element recalcitrant to meaning, and if we speak in order to say something, then the voice is precisely that which cannot be said. It is there, in the very act of saying, but it eludes any pinning down, to the point where we could maintain that it is the non-linguistic, the extralinguistic element which enables speech phenomena, but cannot itself be discerned by linguistics.

If there is an implicit teleology of the voice, then this teleology seems to conceal the dwarf of theology in its bosom, as in Benjamin's parable. There is a rather astounding theological interpretation of this in Saint Augustine. In one of his famous sermons (no. 288), he makes the following claim: John the Baptist is the voice and Christ is the word, *logos*. Indeed, this seems to follow textually from the beginning of St. John's Gospel: in the beginning was the Word, but in order for the Word to manifest itself, there has to be a mediator, a precursor in the shape of John the Baptist, who identifies himself precisely as *vox clamantis in deserto*,[4] the voice crying in the desert, while Christ, in this paradigmatic opposition, is identified with the Word, *verbum, logos*.

> The voice precedes the Word and it makes possible its understanding. . . . What is the voice, what is the word? Examine what happens in you and form your own questions and answers. This voice which merely resonates and offers no sense, this sound which comes from the mouth of someone screaming, not speaking, we call it the voice, not the word. . . . But the word, if it is to earn its name, has to be endowed with sense and by offering the sound to the ear it offers at the same time something else to the intellect. . . . Now look closely at the meaning of this sentence: "He has to increase, I have to diminish" [John 3, 30]. How, for what reason, with what intent, why could the voice, i.e. John the Baptist, say, given the difference that we just established, "He has to increase, I have to diminish"? Why? Because the voices are being effaced as the Word grows. The voice gradually loses its function as the soul progresses to Christ. So Christ has to increase and John the Baptist has to be obliterated. (Augustine, quoted by Poizat 2001, p. 130)[5]

Thus the progression from the voice to meaning is the progression from a mere—albeit necessary—mediator to the true Word: there is only a small step from linguistics to theology. So if we are to isolate the voice as an object, an entity on its own, then we have to disentangle it from this spontaneous teleology, which goes hand in hand with a certain theology of the voice as the condition of revelation of the Word.[6] We have to make our way in the opposite direction, as it were: to make a descent from the height of meaning back to what appeared to be mere means; to catch the voice as a blind spot of making sense, or as a cast-off of sense. We have to establish another framework than that which spontaneously imposes itself with the link between a certain understanding of linguistics, teleology, and theology.

If voice is what does not contribute to meaning, a crucial antinomy follows, *a dichotomy of the voice and the signifier*. The signifier possesses a logic, it can be dissected, it can be pinned down and fixed—fixed in view of its repetition, for every signifier is a signifier by virtue of being repeatable, in view of its own iterability. The signifier is a creature that can exist only insofar as it can be cloned, but its genome cannot be fixed by any positive units, it can be fixed only by a web of differences, through differential oppositions, which enable it to produce meaning. It is a strange entity that possesses no identity of its own, for it is merely a bundle, a crossing of differences in relation to other signifiers, and *nothing else*. Its material support and its particular qualities are irrelevant—all that is needed is that it is different from other signifiers (following the famous Saussurean dictum that in language there are only differences without any positive terms, and another no less famous one that language is form and not substance).[7] The signifier is not endowed with any positivity, any quality definable on its own; its only existence is a negative one (that of being "different from other signifiers"), yet its mechanisms can be disentangled and explained in that very negativity, which produces positive effects of signification.

If we take Saussure as a provisional starting point—although this doxa of our times that "in the beginning was Saussure" (a very particular kind of Word) is rather dubious—then it is easy to see that the Saussurean turn has a lot to do with the voice. If we are to take seriously the negative nature of the linguistic sign, its purely differential and oppositive value, then the voice—as the supposedly natural soil of speech, its seemingly positive substance—has to be put into question. It has to be carefully discarded as the source of an imaginary blinding that has hitherto prevented linguistics from discovering the structural determinations which enable the tricky transubstantiation of voices into linguistic signs. The voice is the impeding element that we have to be rid of in order to initiate a new science of language. Beyond the sounds of language that traditional phonetics has painstakingly described—spending a great deal of time over the technology of their production, helplessly ensnared by their physical and physiological properties—lies a very different entity that the new linguistics has to unearth: *the phoneme*. Beyond the voice "with flesh and bones" (as Jakobson will say some decades later) lies the fleshless and boneless entity defined purely by its function—*the silent sound, the soundless voice*. The new object demands a new science: instead of traditional phonetics, high hopes are now vested in phonology. The question of how different sounds are produced is seen as obsolete; what counts are the differential oppositions of phonemes, their purely relational nature, their reduction to distinctive features. They are isolated by their ability to distinguish the units of signification, but in such a way that the specific signifying distinctions are irrelevant, their only importance being that they take place, not what they might be. Phonemes lack substance, they are completely reducible to form, and they lack any signification of their own. They are just senseless quasi-algebraic elements in a formal matrix of combinations.

It is true that Saussure's *Course* has caused some confusion, since it is not in the part explicitly dealing with phonology that his novelty is to be found. We have to look elsewhere:

> In any case, it is impossible that sound, as the material element, should in itself be part of the language. Sound is merely something ancillary, a material that language uses. . . . Linguistic signals [signifiers] are not in essence phonetic. They are not physical in any way. They are constituted solely by differences which distinguish one such sound pattern from another. . . . What characterizes [the phonemes] is not, as might be thought, the specific positive properties of each; but simply the fact that they cannot be mistaken for one another. Speech sounds are first and foremost entities which are contrastive, relative and negative. (Saussure 1972, pp. 116–17)

If we take Saussure's definition in all its stringency, it turns out that it ultimately fully applies only to phonemes (such will be Jakobson's later criticism of Saussure): they are the only stratum of language which is made entirely of purely negative quantities; their identity is "a pure alterity" (Jakobson 1963, pp. 111, 116). They are the senseless atoms that, in combination, "make sense."

Phonology, defined in such a way, was destined to take a preeminent place in structural linguistics, soon turning into its showcase, the paramount demonstration of its abilities and explanatory strength. Some decades had to elapse for it to reach its fully developed form in Troubetzkoy's *Grundzüge der Phonologie* (1939) and in Jakobson's *Fundamentals of Language* (1956). Some criticism had to be made of the Saussurean presuppositions (for example, Jakobson's critique of Saussure's dogma about the linear nature of the signifier), some respect had to be duly paid to its other predecessors (Baudouin de Courtenay, Henry Sweet, and others), but its course was secure. All the sounds of a language could be described in a purely logical way; they could be placed into a logical table based simply on the presence or absence of minimal distinctive features, ruled entirely by one elementary key, the binary code. In this way, most of the oppositions of traditional phonetics could eventually be reproduced (voiced/voiceless, nasal/oral, compact/diffuse, grave/acute, labial/dental, and so on), but all those were now re-created as functions of logical oppositions, the conceptual deduction of the empirical, not as an empirical description of sounds found. As the ultimate exhibit, one could present the phonological triangle (Jakobson 1963, p. 138) as the simple deductive matrix of all phonemes and their "elementary structures of kinship," a device that would achieve some notoriety in the heyday of structuralism. Having dismantled the sounds into mere bundles of differential oppositions, phonology could then also account for the surplus that is necessarily added to purely phonemic distinctive features—the prosody, the intonation and the accent, the melody, the redundant elements, the variations, and so forth. Bones, flesh, and blood of the voice were diluted without remainder into a web of structural traits, a checklist of presences and absences.

The inaugural gesture of phonology was thus the total reduction of the voice as the substance of language. Phonology, true to its apocryphal etymology, was after killing the voice—its name is, of course, derived from the Greek *phone*, voice, but in it one can also quite appropriately hear *phonos*, murder. Phonology stabs the voice with the signifying dagger; it does away with its living presence, with its flesh and blood. This leads us to a provisional *facit*: there is no linguistics of the voice. There is only phonology, the paradigm of the linguistics of the signifier.

The phoneme is the way in which the signifier has seized and molded the voice. To be sure, its logic is pretty tricky and itself full of pitfalls and traps, it can never quite be tamed into the simple transparent matrix of differential oppositions that Saussure (and Lévi-Strauss and many others) dreamed about—that was the paramount dream of the early structuralist generation. Yet it is a logic whose mechanisms can be explored and laid down, it is a logic with which we can make sense, or, more modestly, with which we can make do in making sense (or at least nonsense). In order to speak, one has to produce the sounds of a language in such a way as to satisfy its differential matrix; the phoneme is the voice caught in the matrix, which behaves quite a bit like the Matrix from the movie. The signifier needs the voice as its support, just as the Matrix needs the poor subjects and their fantasies, but it has no materiality in itself, it just uses the voice to constitute our common "virtual reality." But the problem is that this operation always produces a remainder which cannot be made a signifier or disappear in meaning; the remainder that doesn't make sense, a leftover, a cast-off—shall we say an excrement of the signifier? The matrix silences the voice, but not quite.

How can we pursue this dimension of the voice? Let us first look at three different modes in which, in the most common experience, we stumble on the voice which is seemingly recalcitrant to the signifier: the accent, the intonation, and the timbre. We can have some inkling of the voice if we listen to someone with an accent.[8] Accent— *ad cantum*—is something which brings the voice into the vicinity of singing, and a heavy accent suddenly makes us aware of the material support of the voice which we tend immediately to discard. It appears as a distraction, or even an obstacle, to the smooth flow of signifiers and to the hermeneutics of understanding. Still, the regional accent can easily be dealt with, it can be described and codified. After all, it is a norm which differs from the ruling norm—this is what makes it an accent, and this is what makes it obtrusive, what makes it sing—and it can be described in the same way as the ruling norm. The ruling norm is but an accent which has been declared a non-accent in a gesture which always carries heavy social and political connotations. The official language is deeply wrought by the class division; there is a constant "linguistic class struggle" which underlies its constitution, and we need only remember Shaw's *Pygmalion* for an egregious demonstration.

Intonation is another way in which we can be aware of the voice, for the particular tone of the voice, its particular melody and modulation, its cadence and inflection, can decide the meaning. Intonation can turn the meaning of a sentence upside down; it can transform it into its opposite. A slight note of irony, and a serious meaning comes tumbling down; a note of distress, and the joke will backfire. Linguistic competence crucially includes not only phonology, but also the ability to cope with intonation and its multiple uses. Still, intonation is not as elusive as it may seem; it can be linguistically described and empirically verified. Jakobson tells the following story:

A former actor of Stanislavskij's Moscow Theatre told me how at his audition he was asked by the famous director to make forty different messages from the phrase *Segodnja večerom*, "This evening," by diversifying its expressive tint. He made a list of some forty emotional situations, then emitted the given phrase in accordance with each of these situations, which his audience had to recognize only from the changes in the sound shape of the same two words. For our research work in the description and analysis of contemporary Standard Russian (under the auspices of the Rockefeller Foundation) this actor was asked to repeat Stanislavskij's test. He wrote down some fifty situations framing the same elliptic sentence and made of it fifty corresponding messages for a tape recorder. Most of the messages were correctly and circumstantially decoded by Moscovite listeners. May I add that all such emotive cues easily undergo linguistic analysis. (Jakobson 1960, pp. 354–55)

So all the shades of intonation which critically contribute to meaning, far from being an ineffable abyss, present no great problem to linguistic analysis; intonation can be submitted to the same treatment as all other linguistic phenomena. It requires some additional notation, but this is just the mark of a more complex and ramified code, an extension of phonological analysis. It can be empirically tested—with the help of Rockefeller (I love this detail)—that is to say, objectively and impartially.[9] It is no coincidence that the "subject" of this experiment was an actor, since theater is the ultimate practical laboratory of endowing the same text with the shades of intonation and thereby bringing it to life, empirically testing this every evening with the audience.

Another way to be aware of the voice is through its individuality. We can almost unfailingly identify a person by the voice, the particular individual timbre, resonance, pitch, cadence, melody, the peculiar way of pronouncing certain sounds. The voice is like a fingerprint, instantly recognizable and identifiable. This fingerprint quality of the voice is something that does not contribute to meaning, nor can it be linguistically described, for its features are as a rule not linguistically relevant, they are the slight fluctuations and variations which do not violate the norm—rather, the norm itself cannot be implemented without some "personal touch," the slight trespassing which is the mark of individuality. The impersonal voice, the mechanically produced voice (answering machines, computer voices, and so on) always has a touch of the uncanny, like the voice of the mechanical creature Olympia in Hoffmann's "The Sandman," this prototype of the uncanny, whose singing was just a bit too exact.[10] Or remember the immortal Hal 2000 meeting its death in Kubrick's *2001: A Space Odyssey*, that archetypal scene of a machine pleading for its life and regressing to childhood in a completely mechanical way. The mechanical voice reproduces the pure norm without any side-effects; therefore it seems that it actually subverts the norm by giving it raw. The voice without side-effects ceases to be a "normal" voice, it is deprived of the human touch that the voice adds to the arid machinery of the signifier, threatening that humanity itself will merge with the mechanical iterability, and thus lose its footing. But if those side-effects cannot be linguistically described, they are nevertheless susceptible to physical description: we can measure their frequency and amplitude, we can take their sonogram, while on the practical level they can easily enter the realm of recognition and identification, and become the matter of (dis) liking. Paradoxically, it is the mechanical voice which confronts us with the object voice, its disturbing and uncanny nature, whereas the human touch helps us keep it at bay. The obstacle it appears to present actually enhances the sense-making effect; the seeming distraction contributes to the better fulfillment of the goal.

But if the voice does not coincide with any material modality of its presence in speech, then we could perhaps come closer to our goal if we conceived of it as coinciding with the very process of enunciation: it epitomizes something that cannot be found anywhere in the statement, in the spoken speech and its string of signifiers, nor can it be identified with their material support. In this sense the voice as the agent of enunciation sustains the signifiers and constitutes the string, as it were, that holds them together, although it is invisible because of the beads concealing it. If signifiers form a chain, then the voice may well be what fastens them into a signifying chain. And if the process of enunciation points at the locus of subjectivity in language, then voice also sustains an intimate link with the very notion of the subject. But what is the texture of this voice, this immaterial string, and what is the nature of the subject implied in it? We will come back to that.

The Linguistics of the Non-voice

After accent, intonation, and timbre, qualities that pertain to the voice in speech, we can briefly consider, on our way to the object voice, manifestations of the voice outside speech. In a somewhat academic manner, we could classify them into "prelinguistic" and "postlinguistic" phenomena, the voices beneath and beyond the signifier (following, for example, Parret 2002, p. 28). Presignifying voices comprise the physiological manifestations such as coughing and hiccups, which appear to tie the human voice to an animal nature. Thus we can read in Aristotle:

> Voice then is the impact of the inbreathed air against the "windpipe," and the agent that produces the impact is the soul resident in these parts of the body. Not every sound, as we said, made by an animal is voice (even with the tongue we may merely make a sound which is not voice, or without the tongue as in coughing); what produces the impact must have soul in it and must be accompanied by an act of imagination, for voice is a sound with *a meaning*, and is not *merely* the result of any impact of the breath as in coughing; in voice the breath in the windpipe is used as an instrument to knock with against the walls of the windpipe. (Aristotle 2001, De anima, 420b 28–37)

If voice is a sound "of what has soul in it" (420b 6), then coughing is a soulless voice which ceases to be voice proper. Both coughing and hiccups emerge without the intention of the utterer and against his or her will, they represent a break in speech, a disruption of the ascent toward meaning, an intrusion of physiology into structure. But an intriguing reversal takes place here: those voices, somatic and unattractive as they may be, are hardly ever simply external to the structure—quite the opposite, they may well enter into its core or become its double. We can easily see that there is a whole "semiotics of coughing": one coughs while preparing to speak, one uses coughing as Jakobson's phatic communication, establishing a channel for communication proper; one can use coughing as bidding for time for reflection, or as an ironic commentary which jeopardizes the sense of the utterance; as a notification of one's presence; as an interruption of a difficult silence; as part of the pragmatics of telephone communication (see Parret 2002, p. 32). There may be no linguistic features, no binary oppositions, no distinctive traits, except for the overriding one: the non-articulate itself becomes a mode of the articulate; the presymbolic acquires its value only through opposition to the symbolic, and is thus itself laden with signification precisely by virtue of being non-signifying. Physiological and inarticulate as it may be, it cannot escape the structure. It can, by its very inarticulate nature, even become the embodiment of the highest sense.

One example will suffice as the most spectacular proof: the most famous hiccups in the history of philosophy, namely those by which Aristophanes is suddenly seized in Plato's *Symposium* at the very moment when it was his turn to deliver a speech in praise of love:

> When Pausanias finally came to a pause (I've learned this sort of fine figure from our clever rhetoreticians),[11] it was Aristophanes' turn, according to Aristodemus. But he had such a bad case of the hiccups— he'd probably stuffed himself again, although, of course, it could have been anything—that making a speech was totally out of the question. So he turned to the doctor, Eryximachus, who was next in line, and said to him: "Eryximachus, it's up to you— as well it should be. Cure me or take my turn." "As a matter of fact," Eryximachus replied, "I shall do both. I shall take your turn—you can speak in my place as soon as you feel better—and I shall also cure you. While I am giving my speech, you should hold your breath for as long as you possibly can. This may well eliminate your hiccups. If it fails, the best remedy is a thorough gargle. And if even this has no effect, then tickle your nose with a feather. A sneeze or two will cure even the most persistent case. (Plato 1997, 185c–e)

The hiccups were so persistent that Aristophanes had to employ all Eryximachus' advices, and the talented Doctor Eryximachus came into history as what his name indicates: the fighter against hiccups.

What do Aristophanes' hiccups mean? This unintentional intrusion of an uncontrolled voice, which changed the order of speakers in the highly structured dramaturgy of the dialogue? Can hiccups be a philosophical statement? What does it mean that Aristophanes' speech, the most famous of all Plato's texts, the Freudian parable of the missing halves, is shifted because of the hiccups? Interpreters have been scratching their heads for more than two thousand years; some thought it was just Plato's realistic depiction of the gastronomic-philosophical feast (an instance of Pantagruelism, as Taylor put it); some thought it was a comical intermezzo introducing the comical poet by his trademark; but mostly they surmised that it cannot be so innocent, and must possess some hidden meaning. Lacan undertook a detailed reading of *Symposium* in the course of his seminar on transference (1960/61), and at some critical point he decided to consult his philosophical mentor, Alexandre Kojève. At the end of their exchange, as he was leaving, Kojève gave him this advice for further reflection: "'You will certainly not be able to interpret *Symposium* if you don't know why Aristophanes has hiccups'" (Lacan 1991, p. 78). Kojève himself did not divulge the secret; he left Lacan rather perplexed, but he spoke in such a way that ultimately the entire interpretation depends on understanding this unintelligible voice, for which one can only propose the formula: *it means that it means*. This involuntary voice rising from the body's entrails can be read as Plato's version of mana: the condensation of a senseless sound and the elusive highest meaning, something which can ultimately decide the sense of the whole. This precultural, non-cultural voice can be seen as the zero-point of signification, the incidence of meaning, itself not meaning anything, the point around which other—meaningful—voices can be ordered, as if the hiccups stood at the very focus of the structure. The voice presents a short circuit between nature and culture, between physiology and structure; its vulgar nature is mysteriously transubstantiated into meaning *tout court*.[12]

By definition, the presymbolic use of the voice is epitomized by the infant's babbling. This term, in its technical meaning, covers all the modalities of children's experimenting with their voice before they learn to use it in the standard and codified way. This is the voice which pertains to the infant by its very name—*in-fans*, the one who can't speak. Many linguists and child psychologists (most famously Piaget) have scrutinized this at some length, since what is at stake is the linguistically most crucial step linking the voice and the signifier, and the developmentally most delicate transition between the infant and the speaking being. They have seen in it "the unintentional egocentric soliloquy of the child," "a biologically conditioned 'linguistic delirium,'" and so on (see Jakobson 1968, pp. 24 ff. for a good overview), a chaotic voice-production which gradually becomes guided by a will to communicate and a disciplinatory assumption of the code. But if we think that here we will catch the voice prior to speech in its solipsistic and quasi-biological form, then we are prey to an illusion. Lacan stops to consider it for a moment in *Seminar* XI:

> The Piagetic error—for those who might think that this is a neologism, I would stress that I am referring to Mr. Piaget—is an error that lies in the notion of what is called the *egocentric* discourse of the child, defined as the stage at which he lacks . . . reciprocity. . . . The child, in this discourse, which may be tape-recorded, does not speak for himself, as one says. No doubt, he does not address the other, if one uses here the theoretical distinction derived from the function of the I and the you. But there must be others there . . . —they don't speak to a particular person, they just speak, if you'll pardon the expression, *à la cantonade*. This egocentric discourse is a case of *hail to the good listener!* (Lacan 1979, p. 208)

Infants do not babble just like that. They do not address a definite interlocutor at hand, but their solipsism is nevertheless caught into the structure of address; they address someone behind the scenes, *à la cantonade*, as French theater lingo has it; they speak *à la cantonade*—in short, *à Lacan*, to someone who can hear them, to the good listener to whom they can send a greeting (*à bon entendeur salut*). So this voice, although it does not say anything discernible, is already captured in a discourse, it displays the structure of address—Jakobson himself talks about sound gestures (1968, p. 25), meaningless sounds as gestures of address, and of "dummy dialogue," where no information is transmitted and where children most often do not imitate adults— rather the opposite: adults imitate children, they resort to babbling in what is no doubt a more successful dialogue than most. So here again, on a different level (ontogeny, if such a thing exists), we see that the voice is already caught in the structural web, that there is no voice without the other.

If we follow this logic to the end—that is, to the beginning—then we find at its source the most salient inarticulate presymbolic manifestation of the voice, which is the scream. Is the scream, notoriously the first sign of life, a form of speech? Is the infant's first scream already a greeting to the good listener? Lacan discusses this in the context of what he calls "the transformation of the scream into an appeal."[13] There might be something like the mythical primal scream, which stirred some spirits for some time,[14] but, on this account, the moment it emerges it is immediately seized by the other. The first scream may be caused by pain, by the need for food, by frustration and anxiety, but the moment the other hears it, the moment it assumes the place of its addressee, the moment the other is provoked and interpellated by it, the moment it responds to it, scream retroactively turns into appeal, it is interpreted, endowed with meaning, it is transformed into a speech addressed to the other, it assumes the first function of speech: to address the other and elicit an answer.[15] The scream becomes an appeal to the other; it needs an interpretation and an answer, it demands satisfaction. There is a French pun that Lacan is fond of: *cri pur*, a pure scream, is turned into a *cri pour*, a scream for someone. If the elusive mythical scream was at the outset caused by a need, then it retroactively turns into a demand surpassing the need: it does not aim just at the satisfaction of a need, it is a call for attention, for a reaction, it is directed toward a point in the other which is beyond satisfaction of a need, it disentangles itself from the need, and ultimately desire is nothing but the surplus of demand over need.[16] So the voice is transformed into an appeal, a speech act, in the same moment as need is transformed into desire; it is caught in a drama of appeal, eliciting an answer, provocation, demand, love. The scream, unaffected as it is by phonological constraints, is nevertheless speech in its minimal function: an address and an enunciation. It is the bearer of an enunciation to which no discernible statement can be ascribed, it represents the pure process of enunciation before the infant is capable of any statement.

But the drama of the voice is twofold here: it is not only that the other is compelled to interpret infants' wishes and demands, it is also that the voice itself, the scream, is already an attempt at interpretation: the other can respond to the appeal or not, its answer depends on its whim, and the voice is something which tries to reach the other, provoke it, seduce it, plead with it; it makes assumptions about the other's desire, it tries to influence it, sway it, elicit its love. The voice is carried by an interpretation of the unfathomable other with which it tries to cope; it tries to present itself as an object of its desire, tame its inscrutability and whim. So there is a double movement in this initial drama, interpretation of the scream and scream as interpretation of the other, and both movements would thus find their intersection in Lacan's basic tenet that desire is the desire of the other.

The presymbolic uses of the voice have a feature in common: with physiological voices, with babbling and with the scream, it appears that we are dealing with a voice external to structure, yet this apparent exteriority hits the core of the structure: it epitomizes the signifying gesture precisely by not signifying anything in particular, it presents the speech in its minimal traits, which may later get obscured by articulation. The non-structured voice miraculously starts to represent the structure as such, the signifier in general. For the signifier in general, as such, is possible only as a non-signifier.

On the "postlinguistic" side there is the realm of the voice beyond language, the voice which requires a more sophisticated cultural conditioning than the acquisition of language. This is most spectacularly illustrated by singing, but first we must briefly consider another voice manifestation which is paradoxical: laughter. Its paradox lies in the fact that it is a physiological reaction which seems close to coughing and hiccups, or even more animal-like sounds (there is a whole array, from a mild smile to uncontrollable laughter), but on the other hand laughter is a cultural trait of which only humankind is capable. Indeed, there is an ancient proposal to define the human being as "the laughing animal" (on a par with "the speaking animal"?), to see in laughter the specificity of humankind, separating it from animality. There is again the amalgamation of the highest and the lowest, culture and physiology; the inarticulate quasi-animal sounds coincide with quintessential humanity—and, after all, can culture offer anything better than laughter? This is all the more enigmatic since laughter as a specifically cultural reaction often bursts out uncontrollably, against the will and intention of the hapless subject; it seizes him or her with an unstoppable force as a series of cramps and convulsions which irrepressibly shake the body and elicit inchoate cries which cannot be consciously contained. Laughter is different from the other phenomena considered above because it seems to exceed language in both directions at the same time, as both presymbolic and beyond symbolic; it is not merely a precultural voice seized by the structure, but at the same time a highly cultural product which looks like a regression to animality. Several philosophers have stopped to ponder on this paradox, and since I cannot deal with it any further here, I can only give two classical references: Descartes, *The Passions of the Soul*, paragraphs CXXIV–CXXVI; and Kant, *The Critique of Judgment*, paragraph 54.

Singing represents a different stage: it brings the voice energetically to the forefront, on purpose, at the expense of meaning. Indeed, singing is bad communication; it prevents a clear understanding of the text (we need supertitles at the opera, which dispel the idea of an initiated elite and put the opera on the level of the cinema). The fact that singing blurs the word and makes it difficult to understand—in polyphony to the point of incomprehensibility—has served as the basis for a philosophical distrust for this flourishing of the voice at the expense of the text: for instance, for the constant efforts to regulate sacred music, all of which tried to secure an anchorage in the word, and banish fascination with the voice. Singing takes the distraction of the voice seriously, and turns the tables on the signifier; it reverses the hierarchy—let the voice take the upper hand, let the voice be the bearer of what cannot be expressed by words. *Wovon man nicht sprechen kann darüber kann man singen*: expression versus meaning, expression beyond meaning, expression which is more than meaning, yet expression which functions only in tension with meaning—it needs a signifier as the limit to transcend and to reveal its beyond. The voice appears as the surplus-meaning. The birth of the opera was accompanied by the dilemma of *prima la musica, e poi le parole*, or the other way round; the dramatic tension between the word and the voice was put into its cradle, and their impossible and problematic relationship presented its driving force. The entire history of opera, from Monteverdi to Strauss (*Capriccio*), can be written through the spyglass of this dilemma.[17]

Singing, by its massive concentration on the voice, introduces codes and standards of its own—more elusive than the linguistic ones, but nevertheless highly structured. Expression beyond language is another highly sophisticated language; its acquisition demands a long technical training, reserved for the happy few, although it has the power to affect everyone universally. Yet singing, by focusing on the voice, actually runs the risk of losing the very thing it tries to worship and revere: it turns it into a fetish object—we could say the highest rampart, the most formidable wall against the voice. The object voice that we are after cannot be dealt with by being turned into an object of immediate intense attention and of aesthetic pleasure. To put it in a formula: "If we make music and listen to it, . . . it is in order to silence what deserves to be called the voice as the object *a*" (Miller 1989, p. 184). So the fetish object is the very opposite of the voice as object *a;* but, I should hasten to add, this gesture is always ambivalent: music evokes the object voice and obfuscates it; it fetishizes it, but also opens the gap that cannot be filled. I will come back to this.

Bringing the voice from the background to the forefront entails a reversal, or a structural illusion: the voice appears to be the locus of true expression, the place where what cannot be said can nevertheless be conveyed. The voice is endowed with profundity: by not meaning anything, it appears to mean more than mere words, it becomes the bearer of some unfathomable originary meaning which, supposedly, got lost with language. It seems still to maintain the link with nature, on the one hand— the nature of a paradise lost—and on the other hand to transcend language, the cultural and symbolic barriers, in the opposite direction, as it were: it promises an ascent to divinity, an elevation above the empirical, the mediated, the limited, worldly human concerns. This illusion of transcendence accompanied the long history of the voice as the agent of the sacred, and the highly acclaimed role of music was based on its ambiguous link with both nature and divinity. When Orpheus, the emblematic and archetypal singer, sings, it is in order to tame wild beasts and bend gods; his true audience consists not of men, but of creatures beneath and above culture. Of course this promise of a state of some primordial fusion to which the voice should bear witness is always a retroactive construction. It should be stated clearly: it is only through language, via language, by the symbolic, that there is voice, and music exists only for a speaking being (see Baas 1998, p. 196). The voice as the bearer of a deeper sense, of some profound message, is a structural illusion, the core of a fantasy that the singing voice might cure the wound inflicted by culture, restore the loss that we suffered by the assumption of the symbolic order. This deceptive promise disavows the fact that the voice owes its fascination to this wound, and that its allegedly miraculous force stems from its being situated in this gap. If the psychoanalytic name for this gap is castration, then we can remember that Freud's theory of fetishism is based precisely on the fetish materializing the disavowal of castration.[18]

If there is no linguistics of the voice, only the linguistics of the signifier, then the very notion of a linguistics of the non-voice would seem preposterous. Obviously all the non-voices, from coughing and hiccups to babbling, screaming, laughing, and singing, are not linguistic voices; they are not phonemes, yet they are not simply out-side the linguistic structure: it is as if, by their very absence of articulation (or surplus-articulation in the case of singing), they were particularly apt to embody the structure as such, the structure at its minimal; or meaning as such, beyond the discernible meaning. If they are not submitted to phonology, they nevertheless embody its zero-point: the voice aiming at meaning, although neither the one nor the other can be articulated. So the paradoxical *facit* would be that there may be no linguistics of the voice, yet the non-voice which represents the voice untamed by structure is not external to linguistics. Neither is the object voice which we are pursuing.

Notes

1. "The medium is the message"—this notorious slogan should perhaps be twisted in such a way that the message of the medium pertains to its voice.
2. The French can use a handy pun with the expression *vouloir dire*: the voice "wants to say," that is, it means, there is a *vouloir-dire* inherent in the voice. Derrida has made a great case for this in one of his earliest and best books, *La voix et le phénomène* (1967), where, to put it briefly, his analysis of Husserl pinpoints the voice as the "*vouloir-dire*" of the phenomenon.
3. See Miller: "*tout ce qui, du signifiant, ne concourt pas à l'effet de signification*" (1989, p. 180). For the present purposes, I am leaving aside the difference between meaning and sense, to which I will come later.
4. John the Baptist himself refers this qualification to another point in the Bible (Isaiah 40: 3), but the examination of that point implies that the famous saying, *vox clamantis in deserto*, looks like the result of erroneous punctuation.
5. Could we go so far as to say that John the Baptist plays the same role, in relation to Christ, as Kempelen's vocal machine does in relation to the thinking machine? That John the Baptist is the hidden theological voice-dwarf of the Word?
6. But if the voice precedes the Word, and enables its Meaning, then in the second step the point of the manifestation of the Word is that it becomes flesh. The material element which had to be obliterated spectacularly reappears as the manifestation of the Word, in the guise of the flesh of ideality itself.
7. "*In the language itself, there are only differences.* Even more important than that is the fact that, although in general a difference presupposes positive terms between which the difference holds, in a language there are only differences, and no positive terms. . . . the language includes neither ideas nor sounds existing prior to the linguistic system, but only conceptual and phonetic differences arising out of that system" (Saussure 1972, p. 118).
8. Imagine someone reading the evening news on TV with a heavy regional accent. It would sound absurd, for the state, by definition, does not have an accent. A person with an accent can appear in a talk-show, speaking in her own voice, but not in an official capacity. The official voice is the voice devoid of any accent.
9. "For what is science but the absence of prejudice backed by the presence of money?" (Henry James, *The Golden Bowl*).

10.   As opposed to the voice of the Kempelen machine, which was uncanny by being "human, all too human" in its lack of precision.

11.   *Pausaníou pausoménou*—Plato is making a pun in Greek, using the similarity of sounds, and the rhetoricians he ironically refers to are no doubt the sophists, where sophistry, much to Plato's horror, appears as the kind of thinking based not only on meaning and ideas, but on the erratic nature of homonyms, puns, wordplays, and so on—all that Lacan will sum up in his concept of *la langue*, and is very relevant to our topic of the voice. I will come back to it at some length. For the best account of it, I can only refer the reader to Barbara Cassin's remarkable book *l'effet sophistique* (Paris: Gallimard, 1995).

12.   To make a quick slide from Plato to Lubitsch: in *That Uncertain Feeling*, a film made in 1941, we have one of those brilliant Lubitsch openings. A woman comes to an analyst because she has hiccups. To start with there is just a woman and a voice-symptom, the involuntary voice which condenses all her troubles, and which she doesn't dare to call by name. It seems indecent, it doesn't become a lady, it is too trivial, so she describes her trouble as follows: "It comes and it goes. When it comes I go, and when I come it goes." "The ego and the id," one is tempted to say, where hiccups appear as "it," no doubt the id which carries away the subject and condenses her being. And you will certainly not be able to interpret Lubitsch if you don't know why Merle Oberon has hiccups.

13.   See Lacan 1966, p. 679; 1994, p. 188; for extensive elaborations on the scream, see the unpublished seminar *Problèmes cruciaux pour la psychanalyse* (1964/65); also in *Identification* (1961/62). See also Poizat 1986, pp. 144–45; 1991, pp. 204–5; and 1996, pp. 191–92.

14.   Arthur Janov's *The Primal Scream* (1970) immediately became a bestseller, soon to be followed by *The Primal Revolution* (1972), *The Primal Man* (1976), and so on, and by a movement which, in the 1970s, promised to revolutionize psychotherapy. All that was needed was allegedly to regress to the deepest layer of oneself, to find one's way to the origin of it all in the scream, thus liberating oneself from the repression of culture and the symbolic torment, and finally breathe freely, with the freedom of the infant. If psychoanalysis was from the outset "the talking cure," then Janov's last book title continues to announce: *Words Won't Do It*.

15.   See the beginning of the Rome Discourse: "all speech calls for a reply. I shall show that there is no speech without a reply, even if it is met only with silence, provided that it has an auditor: this is the heart of its function in analysis" (Lacan 1989, p. 40).

16.   "For the unconditional element of demand, desire substitutes the 'absolute' condition: this condition unties the knot of that element in the proof of love that is resistant to the satisfaction of a need. Thus desire is neither the appetite for satisfaction, nor the demand for love, but the difference that results from the subtraction of the first from the second, the phenomenon of their splitting (*Spaltung*)" (Lacan 1989, p. 287). The voice is precisely the agent of this split. We could compress this to a simple formula: desire is demand minus need. See also *Identification*: "the Other will endow the scream of need with the dimension of desire" (May 2, 1962).

17.   I think it is in bad taste to quote oneself but here I must make an exception, and cite our book on the opera (Slavoj Žižek and Mladen Dolar, *Opera's Second Death*, New York and London: Routledge 2002) where this is scrutinized at greater length.

18.   "the horror of castration has set up a memorial to itself in the creation of this substitute. . . . It remains a token of triumph over the threat of castration and a protection against it" (Freud 1973–86: Vol. 7, p. 353).

References

Aristotle (2001). *The Basic Writings of Aristotle*. New York: Modern Library.

Baas, Bernard (1998). *De la chose à l'objet*. Leuven: Peeters/Vrin.

Derrida, Jacques (1967). *La voix et le phénomène*. Paris: Presses Universitaires de France.

Freud, Sigmund (1973–86). *The Pelican Freud Library*. 15 vols. Harmondsworth: Penguin.

Jakobson, Roman (1960). "Closing Statement: Linguistics and Poetics," in Thomas A. Sebeok, *Style in Language*. Cambridge, MA: MIT Press, pp. 350–77.

—— (1963). *Essais de linguistique générale I*. Paris: Minuit.

—— (1968). *Child Language, Aphasia and Phonological Universals*. The Hague and Paris: Mouton [1941].

Lacan, Jacques (1961/62) *Identification*. Unpublished seminar.

—— (1964/65). *Problèmes cruciaux pour la psychanalyse*. Unpublished seminar.

—— (1966). *Écrits*. Paris: Seuil.

—— (1979). *The Four Fundamental Concepts of Psycho-Analysis* (Seminar XJ, ed. J.-A. Miller). Harmondsworth: Penguin [1964].

—— (1989). *Écrits: A Selection*. Ed. and trans. A. Sheridan. London: Tavistock/Routledge.

—— (1991). *Le transfert* (*Le séminaire, Livre* VIII, ed. J.-A. Miller). Paris: Seuil [1960/61].

—— (1994) *La relation d'objet* (*Le séminaire, Livre IV*, ed. J.-A. Miller). Paris: Seuil [1956/57].

Miller, Jacques-Alain (1989). "Jacques Lacan et la voix," in Ivan Fonagy étal., *La voix. Actes du colloque d'Ivry*. Paris: La lysimaque.

Parret, Herman (2002). *La voix et son temps*. Brussels: De Boeck & Larder.

Plato (1997). *Complete Works*. Ed. John M. Cooper. Indianapolis/Cambridge: Hackett.

Poizat, Michel (1986). *L'Opéra ou le cri de l'ange*. Paris: Métailié.

—— (1991). *La voix du diable*. Paris: Métailié.

—— (1996). *La voix sourde*. Paris: Métailié.

—— (2001). *Vox populi, vox Dei*. Paris: Métailié.

Saussure, Ferdinand de (1972). *Cours de linguistique générale*. Paris: Payot / (1998). *Course in General Linguistics*. Ed. and Crans. Roy Harris. London: Duckworth.

Index